The Botanic Garden: A Poem, in Two Parts ; Containing the Economy of Vegetation and the Loves of the Plants ; with Philosophical Notes

Erasmus Darwin

Nabu Public Domain Reprints:

You are holding a reproduction of an original work published before 1923 that is in the public domain in the United States of America, and possibly other countries. You may freely copy and distribute this work as no entity (individual or corporate) has a copyright on the body of the work. This book may contain prior copyright references, and library stamps (as most of these works were scanned from library copies). These have been scanned and retained as part of the historical artifact.

This book may have occasional imperfections such as missing or blurred pages, poor pictures, errant marks, etc. that were either part of the original artifact, or were introduced by the scanning process. We believe this work is culturally important, and despite the imperfections, have elected to bring it back into print as part of our continuing commitment to the preservation of printed works worldwide. We appreciate your understanding of the imperfections in the preservation process, and hope you enjoy this valuable book.

ESSEX COUNTY
COUNCIL LIBRARY

ERASMUS DARWIN, M.D. & F.R.S.

Engraved by Mr Alpin

THE BOTANIC GARDEN,

A POEM, IN TWO PARTS;

CONTAINING

THE ECONOMY OF VEGETATION

AND THE

LOVES OF THE PLANTS.

WITH

PHILOSOPHICAL NOTES.

BY ERASMUS DARWIN, M. D.

LONDON:
PUBLISHED BY JONES & COMPANY,
3, ACTON PLACE, KINGSLAND ROAD.
1825.

18421.12.6

HARVARD COLLEGE LIBRARY
GIFT OF THE
CAMBRIDGE HISTORICAL SOCIETY
Feb 15, 1938

THE BOTANIC GARDEN;

PART I.

CONTAINING

THE ECONOMY OF VEGETATION;

A POEM,

WITH PHILOSOPHICAL NOTES.

It Ver, et Venus; et Veneris prænuncius ante
Pennatus graditur Zephyrus vestigia propter;
Flora quibus mater, præspergens ante viai
Cuncta, coloribus egregiis et odoribus opplet.
                                LUCRET.

ADVERTISEMENT.

THE general design of the following sheets is to inlist Imagination under the banner of Science; and to lead her votaries from the looser analogies, which dress out the imagery of poetry, to the stricter ones, which form the ratiocination of philosophy. While their particular design is to induce the ingenious to cultivate the knowledge of Botany, by introducing them to the vestibule of that delightful science, and recommending to their attention the immortal works of the celebrated Swedish Naturalist, LINNEUS.

In the first Poem, or Economy of Vegetation, the physiology of Plants is delivered; and the operation of the Elements, as far as they may be supposed to affect the growth of Vegetables. In the second Poem, or loves of the Plants, the Sexual System of Linneus is explained, with the remarkable properties of many particular plants.

TO

THE AUTHOR

OF THE

POEM ON THE LOVES OF THE PLANTS.

BY THE REV. W. B. STEPHENS.

Oft though thy genius, Darwin! amply fraught
With native wealth, explore new worlds of mind;
Whence the bright ores of drossless wisdom brought,
Stampt by the Muse's hand, enrich mankind;

   Though willing Nature to thy curious eye,
Involved in night, her mazy depths betray;
Till at their source thy piercing search descry
The streams, that bathe with life our mortal clay;

   Though, boldly soaring in sublimer mood
Through trackless skies on metaphysic wings,

Thou darest to scan the approachless Cause of Good, [Things;
And weigh with steadfast hand the sum of

   Yet wilt thou, charm'd amid his whispering bowers,
Oft with lone step by glittering Derwent stray,
Mark his green foliage, count his musky flowers,
That blush or tremble to the rising ray;

   While Fancy, seated in her rock-roof'd dell,
Listening the secrets of the vernal grove,
Breathes sweetest strains to thy symphonious shell,
And " gives new echoes to the throne of Love."

Repton, Nov. 28, 1788.

TO DR. DARWIN.

While Sargent winds with fond and curious eyes
   Through every mazy region of " the mine—"
While, as entrancing forms around him rise,
   With magic light the mineral kingdoms shine;

Behold; amid the vegetable bloom,
   O Darwin thy ambrosial rivers flow,
And suns more pure the fragrant earth illume,
   As all the vivid plants with passion glow.

Yes;—and, where'er with life creation teems,
   I trace thy spirit through the kindling whole;
As with new radiance to the genial beams
   Of Science, isles emerge, or oceans roll,
And *Nature*, in primordial beauty, seems
   To breathe, inspired by thee, the PHILOSOPHIC
     SOUL!

            R. POLWHELE.

Kenton, near Exeter,
   April 18, 1792.

TO DR. DARWIN.

Two Poets, (poets, by report,
   Not oft so well agree)
Sweet harmonist of Flora's court!
   Conspire to honour thee.

They best can judge a Poet's worth,
   Who oft themselves have known
The pangs of a poetic birth
   By labours of their own.

We, therefore pleased, extol thy song,
   Though various yet complete,
Rich in embellishment, as strong
   And learn'd as it is sweet.

No envy mingles with our praise,
   Though could our hearts repine
At any Poet's happier lays,
   They would, they must, at thine.

But we in mutual bondage knit
   Of friendship's closest tie,
Can gaze on even Darwin's wit
   With an unjaundiced eye;

And deem the bard, whoe'er he be,
   And howsoever known,
Who would not twine a wreath for thee,
   Unworthy of his own.

            W. COWPER.

Weston Underwood, Olney, Bucks,
   June 23, 1792.

TO DR. DARWIN.

As Nature lovely Science led
   Through all her flowery maze,
The volume she before her spread
   Of Darwin's radiant lays.

Coy Science starts—so started Eve
   At beauties yet unknown:
" The figure that you there perceive
   (Said Nature) is your own.

" My own? It is:—but half so fair
   I never seem'd till now:
And here, too, with a soften'd air,
   Sweet Nature! here art thou."

" Yes—in this mirror of the Bard
   We both embellish'd shine;
And grateful will unite to guard
   An artist so divine."

Thus Nature and thus Science spake
   In Flora's friendly bower;
While Darwin's glory seem'd to wa'
   New life in every flower.

This with delight two poets heard;
   Time verifies it daily;
Trust it, dear Darwin, on the word
   Of Cowper and of Hayley!

            W. HAYLEY.

Eartham, near Chichester,
   June 27, 1792.

ADDRESS
TO
THE RIVER DARWENT,

On whose Banks the Author of the Botanic Garden resides.

BY F. N. C. MUNDY, ESQ. 1792.

DARWENT, like thee thy Poet's splendid song,
   With sweet vicissitudes of ease and force
Now with enchanting smoothness glides along,
   Now pours impetuous its resounding course;

While Science marches down thy wondering dells,
   And all the Muses round her banners crowd,
Pleased to assemble in thy sparry cells,
   And chant her lessons to thy echoes proud;

While here Philosophy and Truth display
   The shining-robes those heaven-born sisters wove,

While Fays and Graces beckoning smooth their way,
And hand in hand with Flora follows Love.

Well may such radiant state increase thy pride,
    Delighted stream! though rich in native charms,
Though inborn worth and honour still reside,
    Where thy chill banks the glow of Chatsworth warms.

Though here her new found art, as that of yore,
    The spinster goddess to thy rule assigns;

Though, where her temples crowd thy peopled shore,
    Wealth gilds thy urn, and Fame thy chaplet twines.

Ah, while thy nymphs in Derby's tower'd vale
    Lead their sad quires around Milcena's bier,
What soothing sweetness breathes along the gale,
    Comes o'er the consort's heart, and balms a brother's tear!

Her new-found art, &c. Alluding to the numerous cotton mills on and near the river Derwent.

Milcena's bier. Mrs. French, sister to Mr. Mundy. Part I. Canto III. l. 308.

PROEM.

GENTLE READER,

LO, here a CAMERA OBSCURA is presented to thy view, in which are lights and shades dancing on a whited canvass, and magnified into apparent life!—if thou art perfectly at leisure for such trivial amusement, walk in and view the wonders of my ENCHANTED GARDEN.

Whereas P. OVIDIUS NASO, a great necromancer in the famous Court of AUGUSTUS CÆSAR, did by art poetic transmute men, women, and even gods and goddesses, into trees and flowers; I have undertaken by similar art to restore some of them to their original animality, after having remained prisoners so long in their respective vegetable mansions; and have here exhibited them before thee: which thou mayest contemplate as divers little pictures suspended over the chimney of a lady's dressing room, *connected only by the slight festoon of ribbons;* and which, though thou mayest not be acquainted with the originals, may amuse thee by the beauty of their persons, their graceful attitudes, or the brilliance of their dress.

                                                                    FAREWELL.

APOLOGY.

IT may be proper here to apologize for many of the subsequent conjectures on some articles of natural philosophy, as not being supported by accurate investigation or conclusive experiments. Extravagant theories however in those parts of philosophy, where our knowledge is yet imperfect, are not without their use; as they encourage the execution of laborious experiments, or the investigation of ingenious deductions, to confirm or refute them. And since natural objects are allied to each other by many affinities, every kind of theoretic distribution of them adds to our knowledge by developing some of their anologies.

The Rosicrusian doctrine of Gnomes, Sylphs, Nymphs, and Salamanders, was thought to afford a proper machinery for a Botanic poem; as it is probable, that they were originally the names of hieroglyphic figures representing the elements.

Many of the important operations of nature were shadowed or allegorized in the heathen mythology, as the first Cupid springing from the egg of Night, the marriage of Cupid and Psyche, the rape of Proserpine, the congress of Jupiter and Juno, the death and resuscitation of Adonis, &c. many of which are ingeniously explained in the works of Bacon, Vol. V. p. 47. 4th Edit. London, 1778. The Egyptians were possessed of many discoveries in philosophy and chemistry before the invention of letters; these were then expressed in hieroglyphic paintings of men and animals; which after the discovery of the alphabet were described and animated by the poets, and became first the deities of Egypt, and afterwards of Greece and Rome. Allusions to those fables were therefore thought proper ornaments to a philosophical poem, and are occasionally introduced either as represented by the poets, or preserved on the numerous gems and medallions of antiquity.

Fertilization of Egypt.

Section of the Earth.

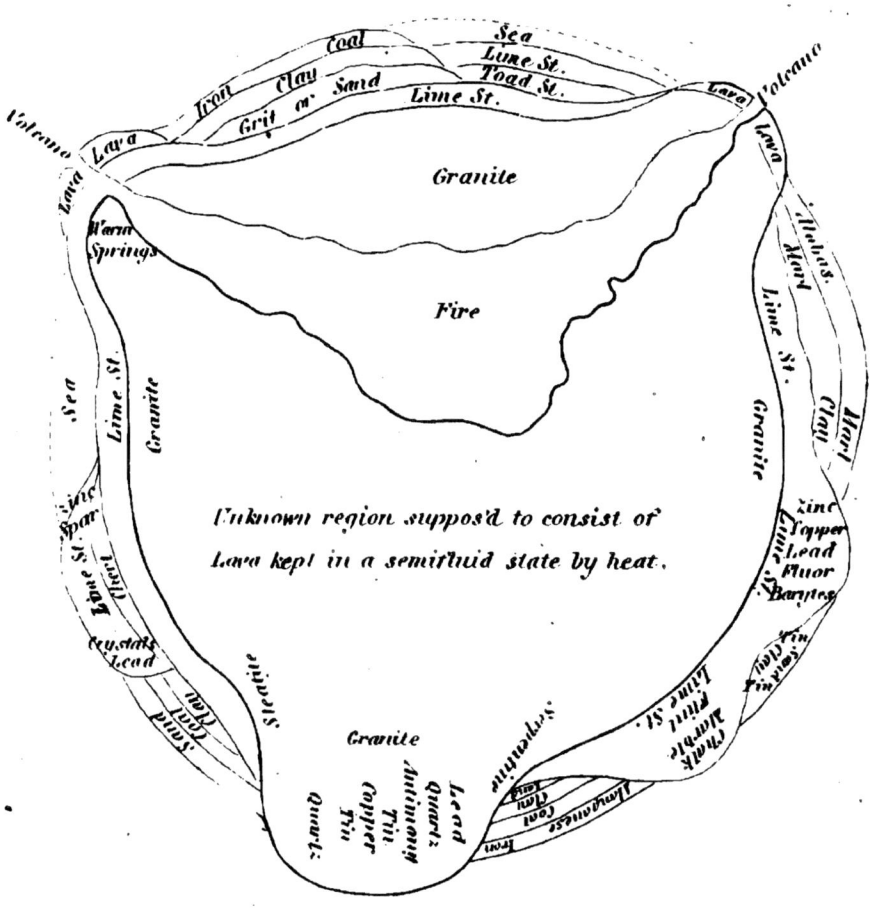

Section of the Earth.

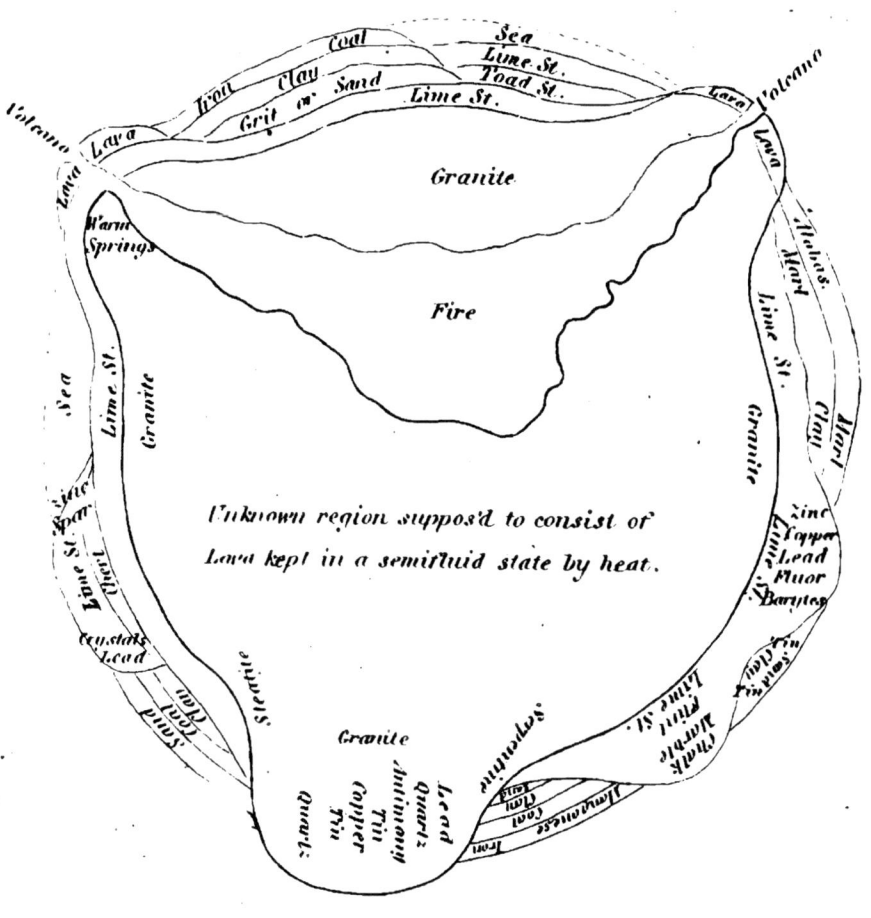

The Portland Vase.

The Tartarian Lamb.

The Portland Vase.

The Handle & Bottom of the Vase.

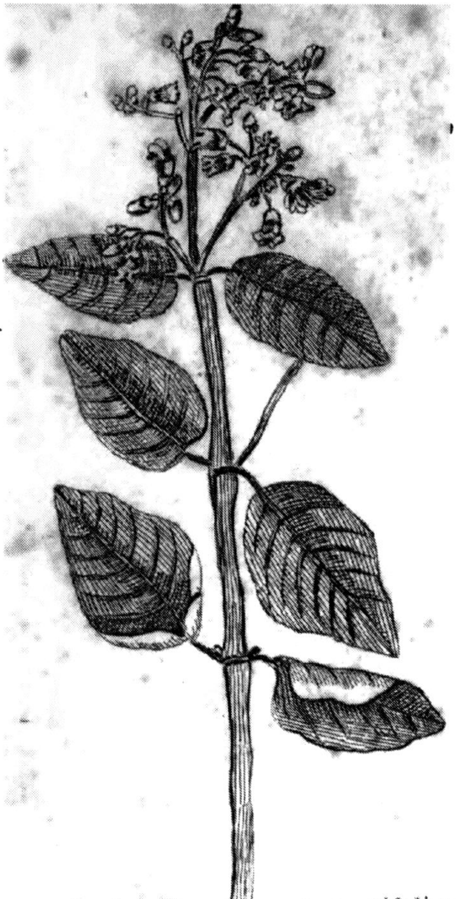

Apocynum androsæmifolium.

Dionæa Muscipula.

Gloriosa Superba.

Cypripedium.

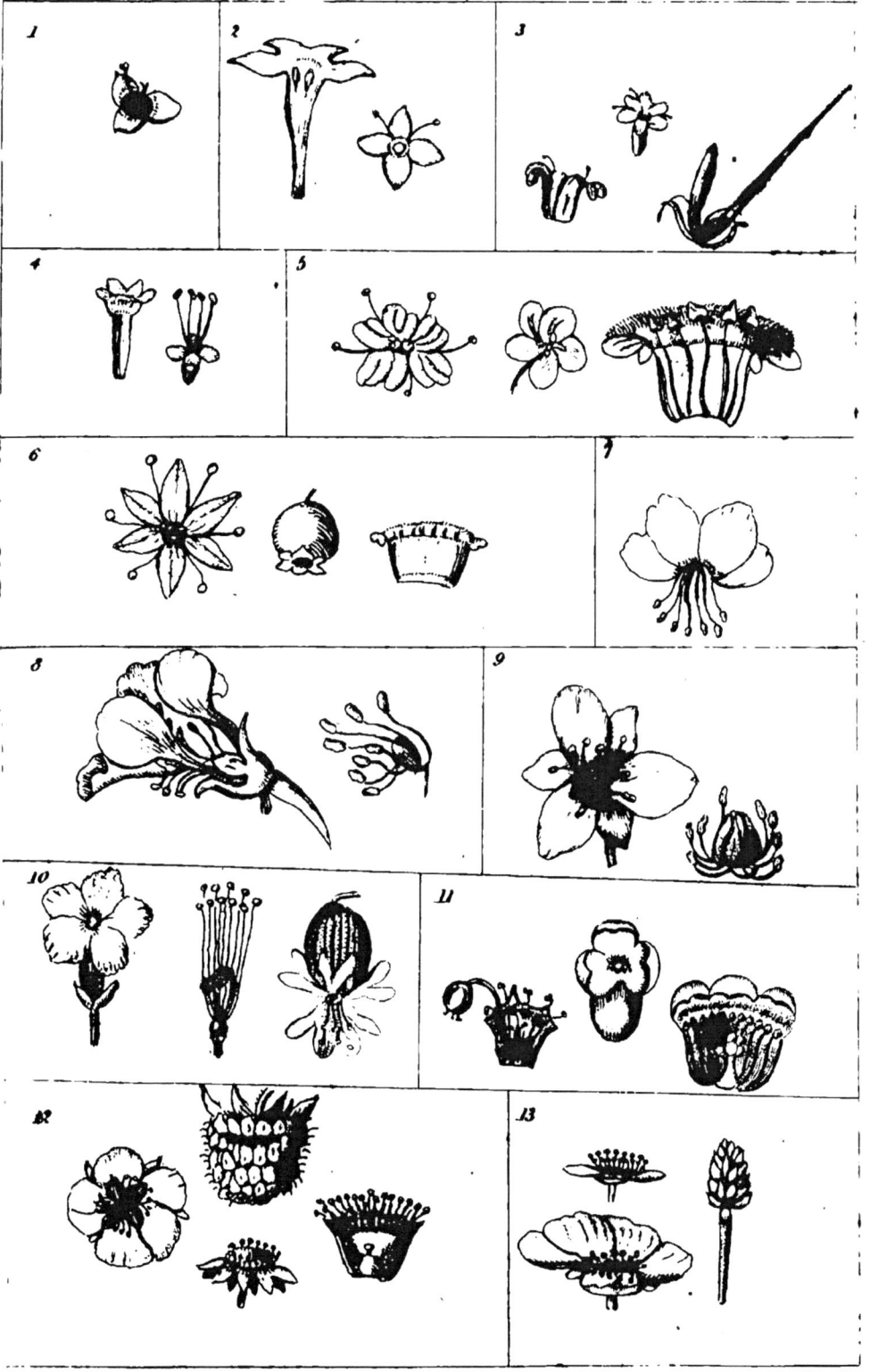

to face Page 135

Section of the Earth.

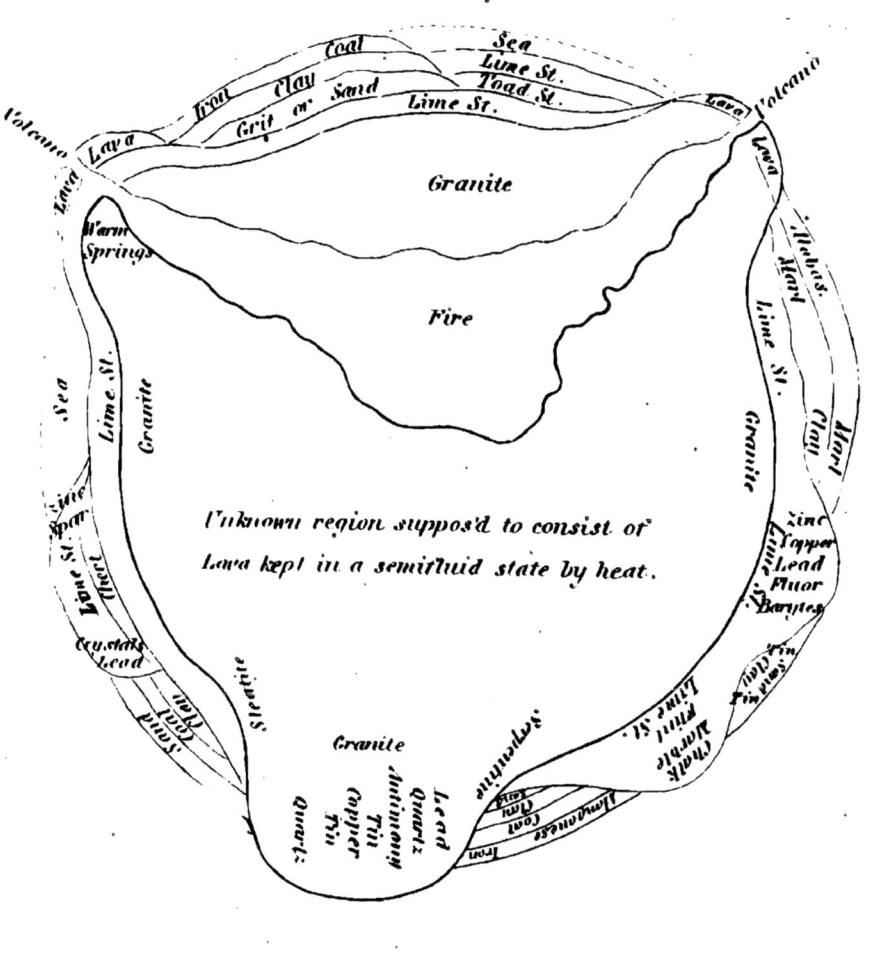

London, Published by Jones & Co. July 1 1824.

The Portland Vase.

The Tartarian Lamb.

The Portland Vase.

The Handle & Bottom of the Vase.

Apocynum androsæmifolium.

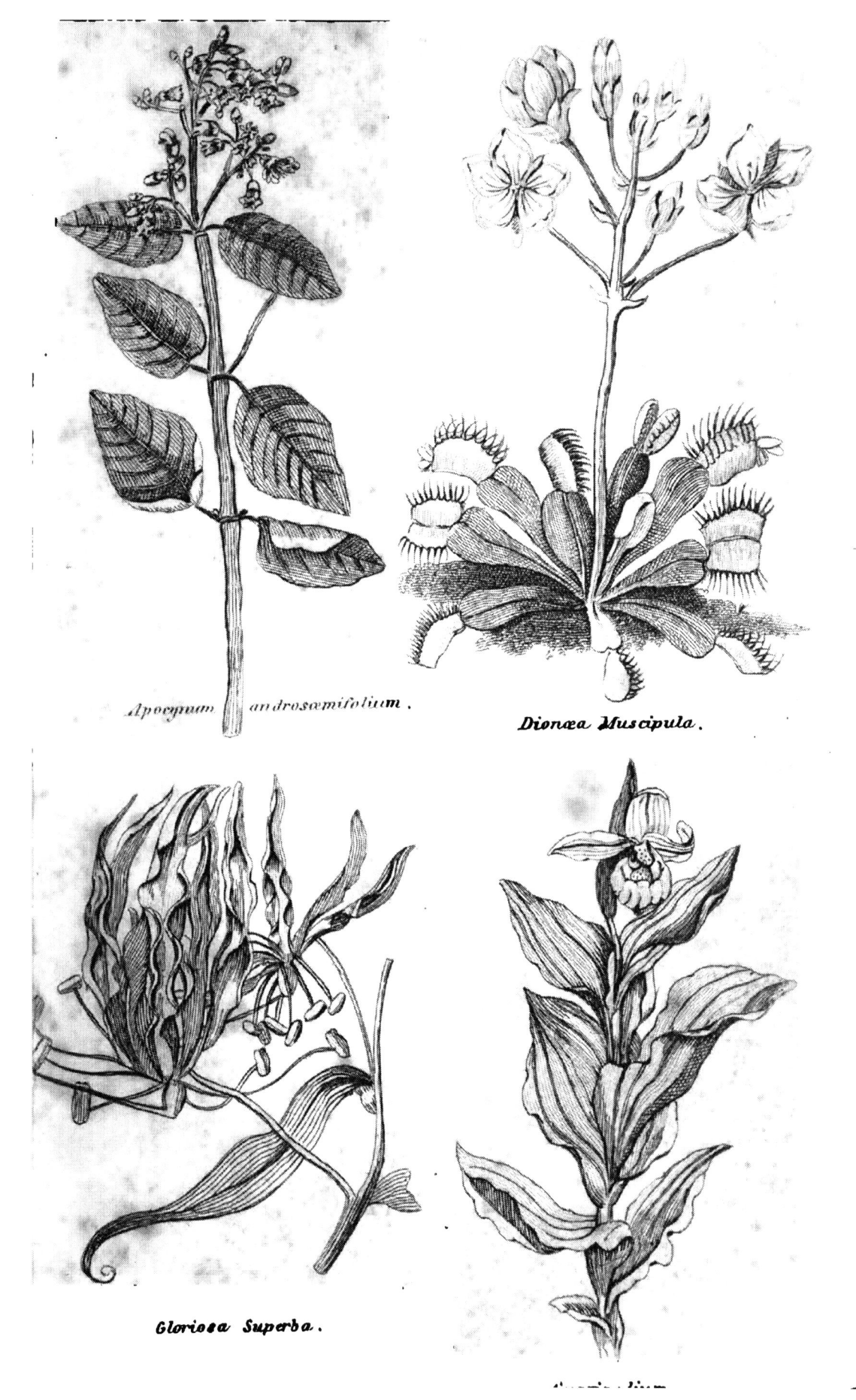

Dionæa Muscipula.

Gloriosa Superba.

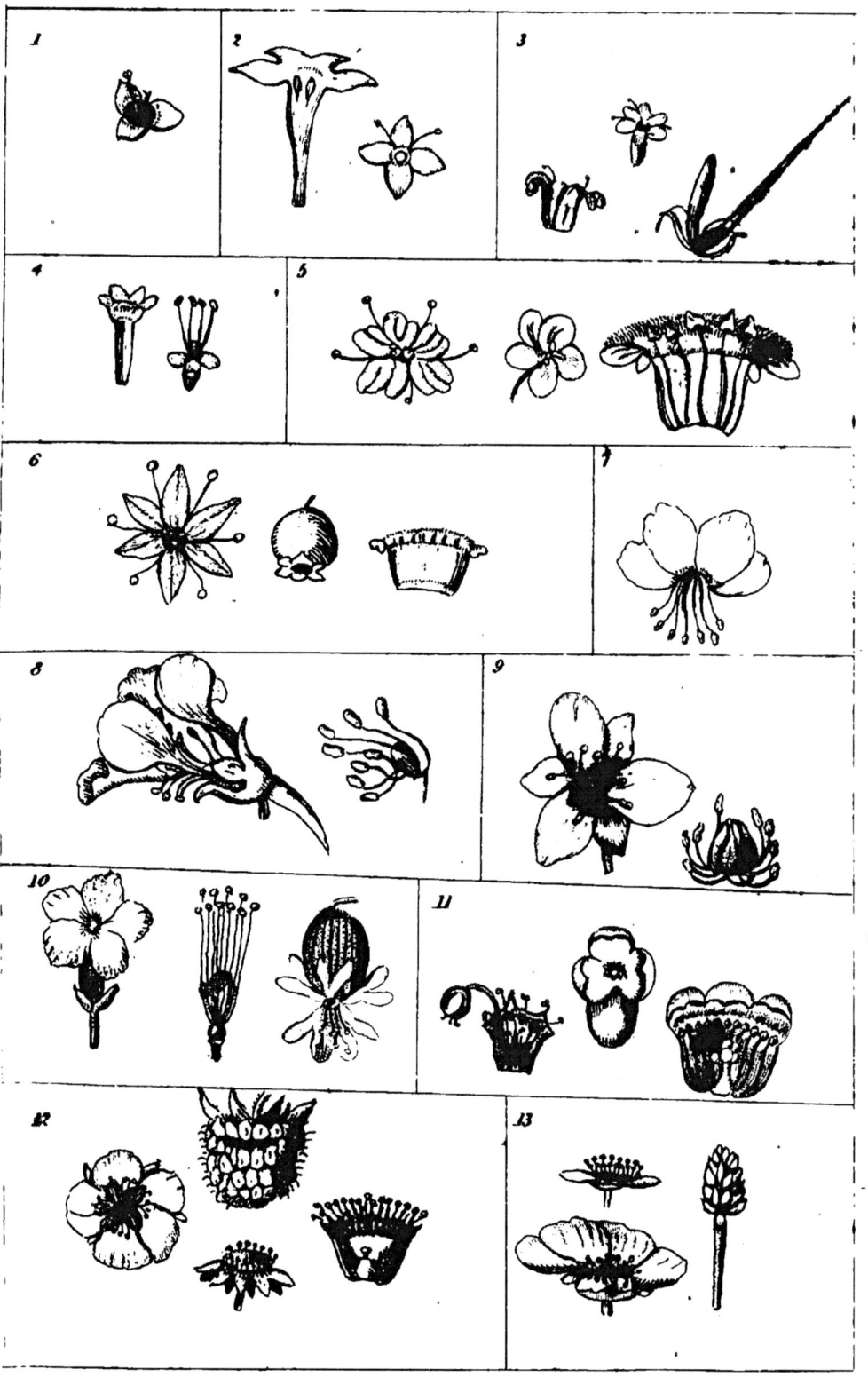

to face Page 135.

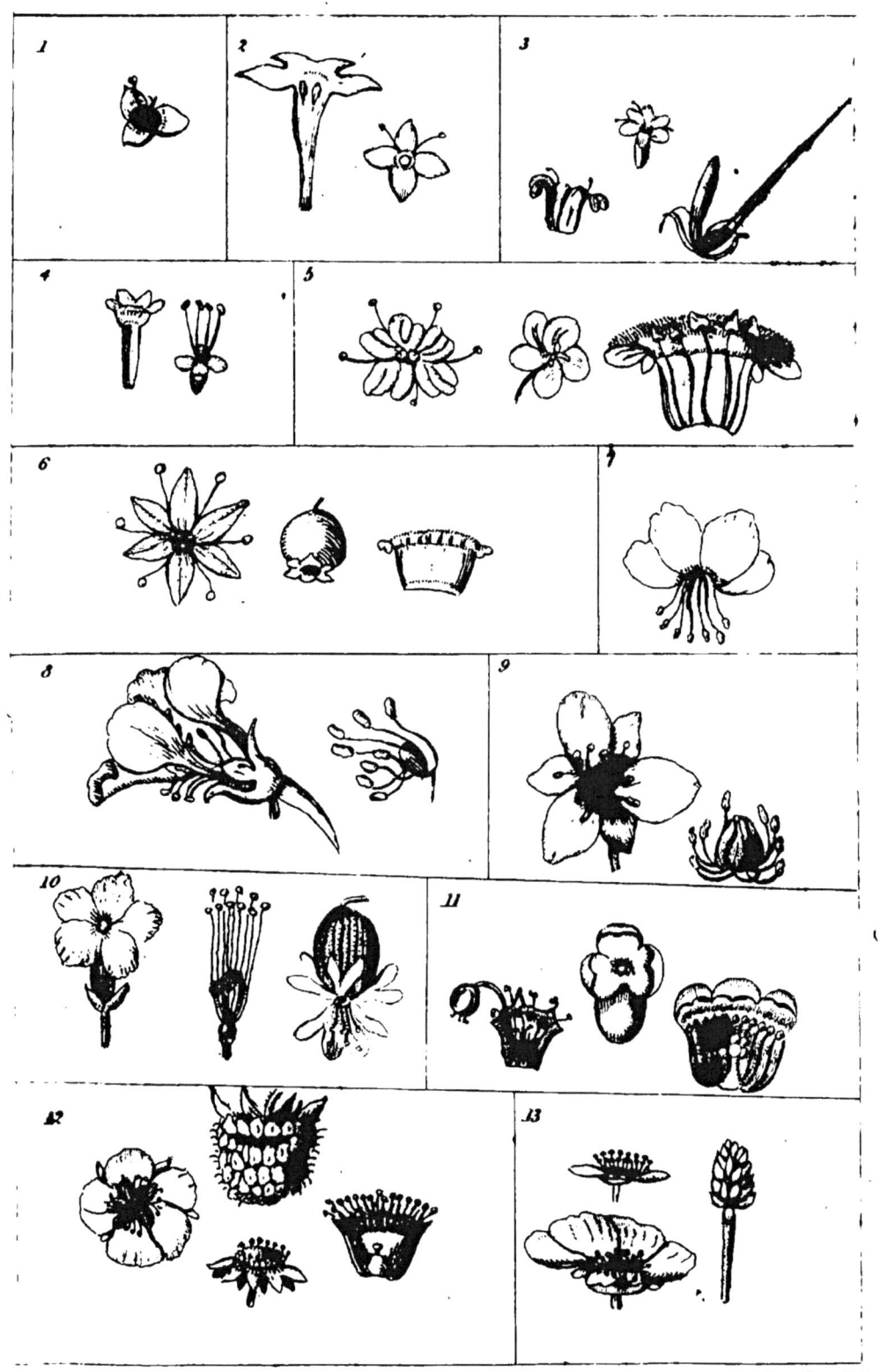

to face Page 135

Meadia.

Amaryllis formosissima.

Hedysarum gyrans.

Erythrina Corallodendron.

Meadia.

Amaryllis formosissima.

Hedysarum gyrans.

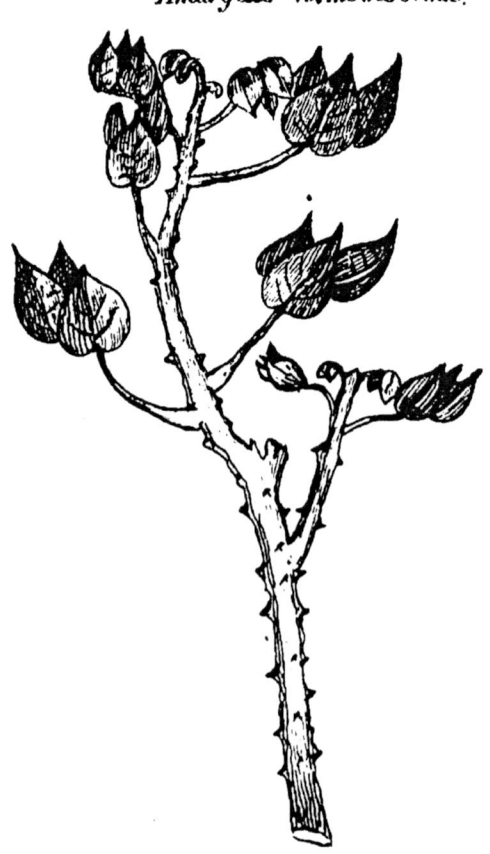

Erythrina Corallodendron.

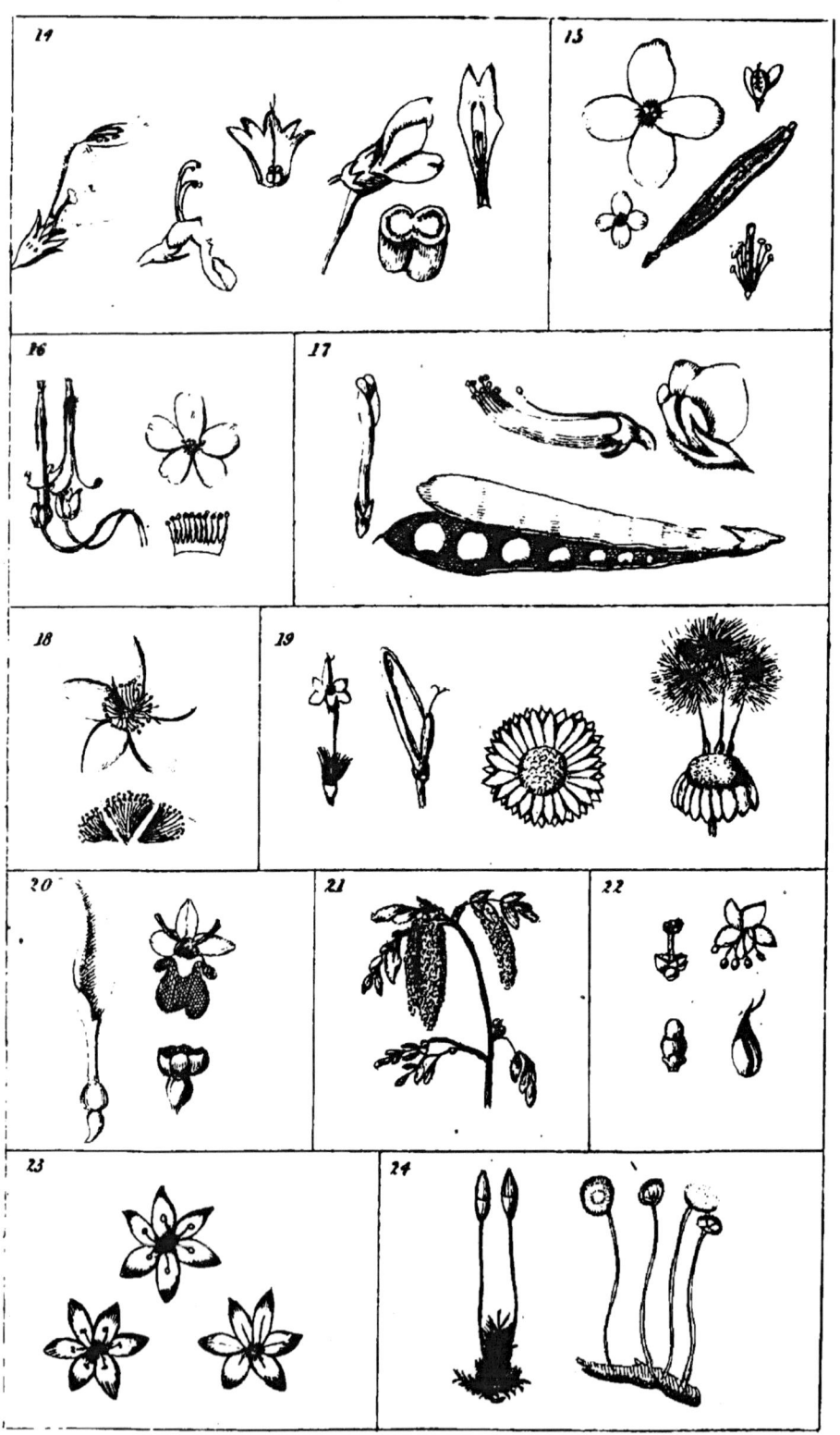

to face Page 136.

The Botanical Cupid.

Frontispiece to Loves of the Plants.

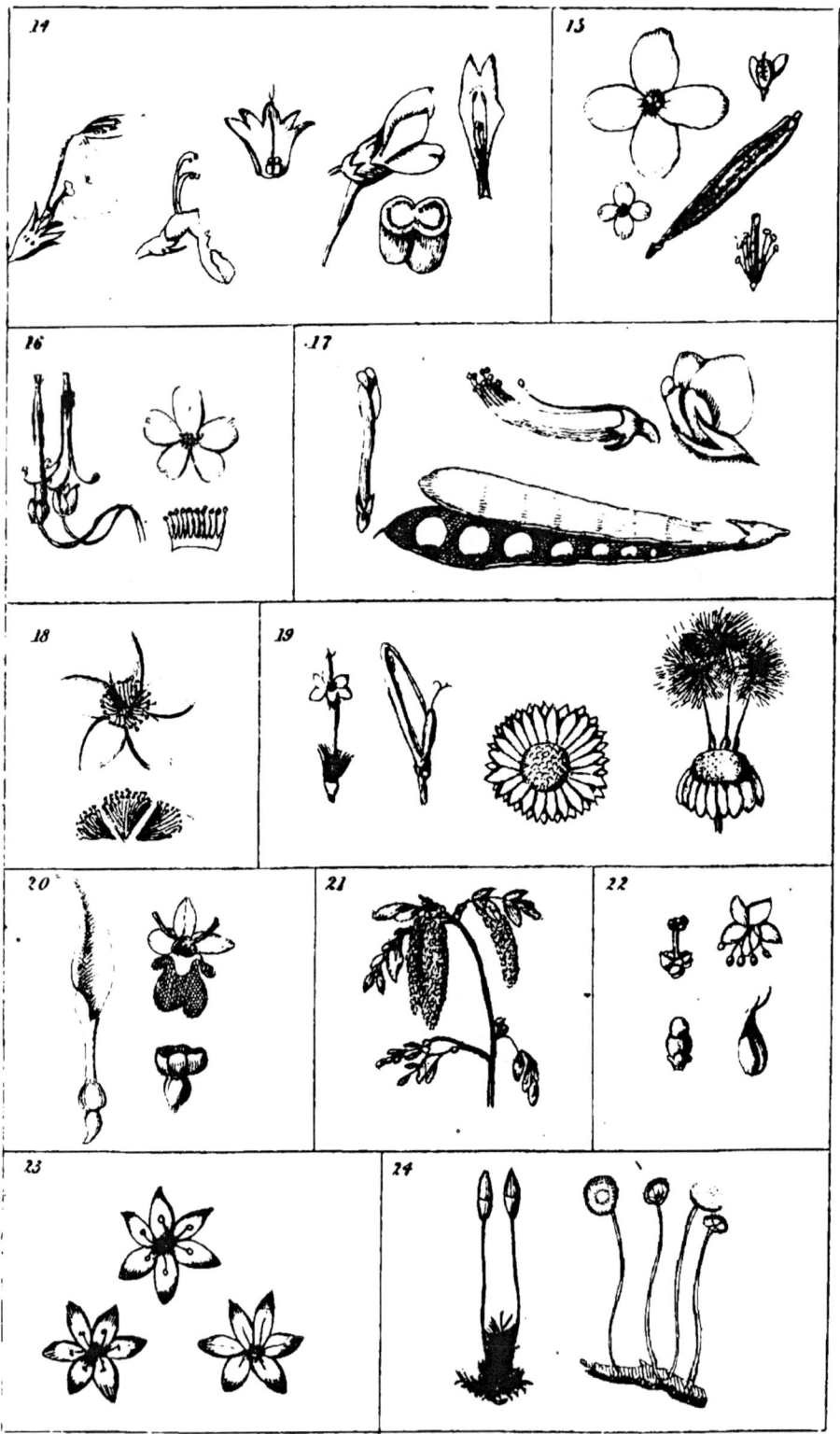

to face Page 136

The Botanical Cupid.

Frontispiece to Loves of the Plants.

THE ECONOMY OF VEGETATION.

CANTO I.

ARGUMENT.

THE *Genius of the place invites the Goddess of Botany*, 1. *She descends, is received by Spring, and the Elements*, 59. *Addresses the Nymphs of Fire. Star-light Night seen in the Camera Obscura*, 81. I. *Love created the Universe. Chaos explodes. All the Stars revolve. God*, 97. II. *Shooting Stars. Lightning. Rainbow. Colours of the Morning and Evening Skies. Exterior Atmosphere of inflammable Air. Twilight. Fire-balls. Aurora Borealis. Planets. Comets. Fixed Stars. Sun's Orb*, 115. III. 1. *Fires at the Earth's Centre. Animal Incubation*, 137. 2. *Volcanic Mountains. Venus visits the Cyclops*, 149. IV. *Heat confined on the Earth by the Air. Phosphoric lights in the Evening. Bolognian Stone. Calcined Shells. Memnon's Harp*, 173. *Ignis fatuus. Luminous Flowers. Glow-worm. Fire-fly. Luminous Sea-insects. Electric Eel. Eagle armed with Lightning*, 189. V. 1. *Discovery of Fire. Medusa*, 209. 2. *The chemical Properties of Fire. Phosphorus. Lady in Love*, 223. 3. *Gunpowder*, 237. VI. *Steam-engine applied to Pumps, Bellows, Water-engines, Corn-mills, Coining, Barges, Waggons, Flying-chariots*, 253. *Labours of Hercules. Abyla and Calpe*, 297. VII. 1. *Electric Machine. Hesperian Dragon. Electric Kiss. Halo round the heads of Saints. Electric Shock. Fairy-rings*, 335. 2. *Death of Professor Richman*, 371. 3. *Franklin draws Lightning from the Clouds. Cupid snatches the Thunderbolt from Jupiter*, 383. VIII. *Phosphoric Acid and Vital Heat produced in the Blood. The great Egg of Night*, 399. IX. *Western Wind unfettered. Naiad released. Frost assailed. Whale attacked*, 421. X. *Buds and Flowers expanded by Warmth, Electricity, and Light. Drawings with colourless sympathetic Inks; which appear when warmed by the Fire*, 457. XI. *Sirius. Jupiter and Semele. Northern Constellations. Ice-Islands navigated into the Tropic Seas. Rainy Monsoons*, 497. XII. *Points erected to procure Rain. Elijah on Mount Carmel*, 549. *Departure of the Nymphs of Fire like Sparks from artificial Fireworks*, 587.

"STAY your rude steps; whose throbbing breasts infold
The legion-fiends of Glory, or of Gold!
Stay! whose false lips seductive simpers part,
While Cunning nestles in the harlot-heart!—
For you no Dryads dress the roseate bower,
For you no Nymphs their sparkling vases pour;
Unmark'd by you, light Graces swim the green,
And hovering Cupids aim their shafts, unseen.

" But Thou! whose mind the well-attemper'd ray
Of Taste and Virtue lights with purer day; 10
Whose finer sense each soft vibration owns
With sweet responsive sympathy of tones;
So the fair flower expands its lucid form
To meet the sun, and shuts it to the storm;—
For thee my borders nurse the fragrant wreath,
My fountains murmur, and my zephyrs breathe;
Slow slides the painted snail, the gilded fly
Smooths his fine down, to charm thy curious eye;
On twinkling fins my pearly nations play,
Or win with sinuous train their trackless way;
My plumy pairs, in gay embroidery dress'd, 21
Form with ingenious bill the pensile nest,
To Love's sweet notes attune the listening dell,
And Echo sounds her soft symphonious shell.

" And, if with Thee some hapless Maid should stray
Disastrous Love companion of her way,

So the fair flower. l. 13. It seems to have been the original design of the philosophy of Epicurus to render the mind exquisitely sensible to agreeable sensations, and equally insensible to disagreeable ones.

Disastrous Love. l. 26. The scenery is taken from a botanic garden about a mile from Lichfield, where a cold bath was erected by Sir John Floyer. There is a grotto surrounded by projecting rocks, from the edges of which trickles a perpetual shower of water; and it is here represented as adapted to love-scenes, as being thence a proper residence for the modern goddess of Botany, and the easier to introduce the next poem on the Loves of the Plants according to the system of Linneus.

Oh, lead her timid steps to yonder glade,
Whose arching cliffs depending alders shade;
There, as meek Evening wakes her temperate breeze,
And moon-beams glimmer through the trembling trees;   30
The rills, that gurgle round, shall sooth her ear,
The weeping rocks shall number tear for tear;
There as sad philomel, alike forlorn,
Sings to the night from her accustomed thorn;
While at sweet intervals each falling note
Sighs in the gale, and whispers round the grot;
The sister-wo shall calm her aching breast,
And softer slumbers steal her cares to rest.—

"Winds of the north! restrain your icy gales,
Nor chill the bosom of these happy vales!   40
Hence in dark heaps, ye gathering clouds, revolve!
Disperse, ye lightnings! and, ye mists, dissolve!
—Hither, emerging from yon orient skies,
Botanic Goddess! bend thy radiant eyes;
O'er these soft scenes assume thy gentle reign,
Pomona, Ceres, Flora in thy train;
O'er the still dawn thy placid smile effuse,
And with thy silver sandals print the dews;
In noon's bright blaze thy vermil vest unfold,
And wave thy emerald banner starr'd with gold."   50

Thus spoke the Genius, as he stepp'd along,
And bade these lawns to Peace and Truth belong;
Down the steep slopes he led with modest skill;
The willing pathway, and the truant rill,
Stretch'd o'er the marshy vale yon willowy mound,
Where shines the lake amid the tufted ground,
Raised the young woodland, smooth'd the wavy green,
And gave to Beauty all the quiet scene.—

She comes!—the Goddess! through the whispering air,
Bright as the morn, descends her blushing car;
Each circling wheel a wreath of flowers entwines,   61
And gemm'd with flowers the silken harness shines;
The golden bits with flowery studs are deck'd,
And knots of flowers the crimson reins connect.—
And now on earth the silver axle rings,
And the shell sinks upon its slender springs;
Light from her airy seat the Goddess bounds,
And steps celestial press the pansied grounds.

Fair Spring advancing calls her feather'd choir,
And tunes to softer notes her laughing lyre;   70
Bids her gay hours on purple pinions move,
And arms her Zephyrs with the shafts of Love,
Pleased Gnomes, ascending from their earthy beds,
Play round her graceful footsteps, as she treads;
Gay Sylphs attendant beat the fragrant air
On winnowing wings, and waft her golden hair;   [streams,
Blue Nymphs emerging leave their sparkling
And Fiery Forms alight from orient beams;
Musk'd in the rose's lap fresh dews they shed,
Or breathe celestial lustres round her head.   80

First the fine forms her dulcet voice requires,
Which bathe or bask in elemental fires;
From each bright gem of Day's refulgent car,
From the pale sphere of every twinkling star,
From each nice pore of ocean, earth, and air,
With eye of flame the sparkling hosts repair,
Mix their gay hues, in changeful circles play,
Like motes, that tenant the meridian ray.—
So the clear Lens collects with magic power
The countless glories of the midnight hour;   90
Stars after stars with quivering lustre fall,
And twinkling glide along the whiten'd wall.—
Pleased, as they pass, she counts the glittering bands,
And stills their murmur with her waving hands;
Each listening tribe with fond expectance burns,
And now to these, and now to those, she turns.

I. "Nymphs of primeval fire! your vestal train
Hung with gold-tresses o'er the vast inane,

Pleased Gnomes. l. 73. The Rosicrucian doctrine of Gnomes, Sylphs, Nymphs, and Salamanders, affords proper machinery for a philosophic poem; as it is probable that they were originally the names of hieroglyphic figures of the Elements, or of Genii presiding over their operations. The Fairies of more modern days seem to have been derived from them, and to have inherited their powers. The Gnomes and Sylphs, as being more nearly allied to modern Fairies, are represented as either male or female, which distinguishes the latter from the Auræ of the Latin Poets, which were only female; except the winds, as Zephyrus and Auster, may be supposed to have been their husbands.

Nymphs of primeval fire. l. 97. The fluid matter of heat is perhaps the most extensive element in nature; all other bodies are immersed in it, and are preserved in their present state of solidity or fluidity by the attraction of their particles to the matter of heat. Since all known bodies are contractible into less space by depriving them of some portion of their heat, and as there is no part of nature totally deprived of heat, there is reason to believe that the particles of bodies do not touch, but are held towards each other by their self-attraction, and recede from each other by their attraction to the mass of heat which surrounds them; and thus exist in an equilibrium between these two powers. If more of the matter of heat be applied to them, they recede farther from each other, and become fluid; if still more be applied, they take an aerial form, and are termed Gasses by the modern chemists. Thus when water is heated to a certain degree, it would instantly assume the

Pierced with your silver shafts the throne of night,
And charm'd young Nature's opening eyes with light ; 100
When Love Divine, with brooding wings unfurl'd,
Call'd from the rude abyss the living world.
—' Let there be light !' proclaim'd the Almighty Lord,
Astonish'd Chaos heard the potent word ;
Through all his realms the kindling ether runs,
And the mass starts into a million suns ;

Earths round each sun with quick explosions burst,
And second planets issue from the first ;
Bend, as they journey with projectile force,
In bright ellipses their reluctant course ; 110
Orbs wheel in orbs, round centres centres roll,
And form, self-balanced, one revolving whole.
—Onward they move amid their bright abode,
Space without bound, the bosom of their God !

II. " Ethereal Powers ! you chase the shooting stars,
Or yoke the vollied lightnings to your cars,

---

form of steam, but for the pressure of the atmosphere, which prevents this change from taking place so easily ; the same is true of quicksilver, diamonds, and of perhaps all other bodies in nature ; they would first become fluid, and then æriform by appropriate degrees of heat. On the contrary, this elastic matter of heat, termed calorique in the new nomenclature of the French academicians, is liable to become consolidated itself in its combinations with some bodies, as perhaps in nitre, and probably in combustible bodies as sulphur and charcoal. See note on l. 232 of this Canto. Modern philosophers have not yet been able to decide whether light and heat be different fluids, or modifications of the same fluid, as they have many properties in common. See note on l. 468 of this Canto.

When Love Divine. l. 101. From having observed the gradual evolution of the young animal or plant from its egg or seed ; and afterwards its successive advances to its more perfect state, or maturity ; philosophers of all ages seem to have imagined, that the great world itself had likewise its infancy and its gradual progress to maturity ; this seems to have given origin to the very ancient and sublime allegory of Eros, or Divine Love, producing the world from the egg of Night, as it floated in Chaos. See l. 419 of this Canto.

The external crust of the earth, as far as it has been exposed to our view in mines or mountains, countenances this opinion ; since these have evidently for the most part had their origin from the shells of fishes, the decomposition of vegetables, and the recrements of other animal materials, and must therefore have been formed progressively from small beginnings. There are likewise some apparently useless or incomplete appendages to plants and animals, which seem to show they have gradually undergone changes from their original state ; such as the stamens without anthers, and styles without stigmas of several plants, as mentioned in the note on Curcuma, Part. II. of this work. Such as the halteres, or rudiments of wings of some two-winged insects ; and the paps of male animals ; thus swine have four toes, but two of them are imperfectly formed, and not long enough for use. The allantoide in some animals seems to have become extinct ; in others is above tenfold the size, which would seem necessary for its purpose. Buffon du Cochon. T. 6. p. 257. Perhaps all the supposed monstrous births of nature are remains of their habits of production in their former less perfect state, or attempts towards greater perfection.

Through all his realms. l. 105. Mr. Herschel has given a very sublime and curious account of the construction of the heavens with his discovery of some thousand nebulæ or clouds of stars; many of which are much larger collections of stars, than all those put together, which are visible to our naked eyes, added to those which form the galaxy, or milky zone, which surrounds us. He observes that in the vicinity of these clusters of stars there are proportionably fewer stars than in any other parts of the heavens, and hence he concludes, that they have attracted each other, on the supposition that infinite space was at first equally sprinkled with them ; as if it had at the beginning been filled with a fluid mass, which had coagulated. Mr. Herschel has further shown, that the whole sideral system is gradually moving round some centre, which may be an opake mass of matter, Philos. Trans. Vol. LXXIV. If all these Suns are moving round some great central body; they must have had a projectile force, as well as centripetal one; and may thence be supposed to have emerged or been projected from the material, where they were produced. We can have no idea of a natural power, which could project a sun out of chaos, except by comparing it to the explosions or earthquakes owing to the sudden evolution of aqueous or of other more elastic vapours ; of the power of which under immeasureable degrees of heat and compression we are yet ignorant.

It may be objected, that if the stars had been projected from a chaos by explosions, they must have returned again into it from the known laws of gravitation ; this however would not happen, if the whole chaos, like grains of gunpowder, was exploded at the same time, and dispersed through infinite space at once, or in quick succession, in every possible direction. The same objection may be stated against the possibility of the planets having been thrown from the sun by explosions ; and the secondary planets from the primary ones ; which will be spoken of more at large in the second Canto : but if the planets are supposed to have been projected from their suns, and the secondary from the primary ones, at the beginning of their course ; they might be so influenced or diverted by the attractions of the suns, or sun, in their vicinity, as to prevent their tendency to return into the body, from which they were projected.

If these innumerable and immense suns thus rising out of chaos are supposed to have thrown out their attendant planets by new explosions, as they ascended ; and those their respective satellites, filling in a moment the immensity of space with light and motion, a grander idea cannot be conceived by the mind of man.

Chase the shooting stars. l. 115. The meteors called shooting stars, the lightning, the rainbow, and the clouds, are phenomena of the

Cling round the aërial bow with prisms bright,
And pleased untwist the sevenfold threads of
    light;
Eve's silken couch with gorgeous tints adorn,
And fire the arrowy throne of rising Morn. 120
—Or, plumed with flame, in gay battalions
    spring
To brighter regions borne on broader wing;
Where lighter gases, circumfused on high,
Form the vast concave of exterior sky;
With airy lens the scatter'd rays assault,
And bend the twilight round the dusky vault;
Ride, with broad eye and scintillating hair,
The rapid fire-ball through the midnight air;

Dart from the north on pale electric streams,
Fringing Night's sable robe with transient
    beams. 130
—Or rein the planets in their swift careers,
Gilding with borrow'd light their twinkling
    spheres;
Alarm with comet-blaze the sapphire plain,
The wan stars glimmering through its silver
    train;
Gem the bright zodiac, stud the glowing pole,
Or give the sun's phlogistic orb to roll.

III. 1. "Nymphs! your fine forms with
    steps impassive mock
Earth's vaulted roofs of adamantine rock;
Round her still centre tread the burning soil,
And watch the billowy lavas, as they boil; 140
Where, in basaltic caves imprisoned deep,
Reluctant fires in dread suspension sleep;
Or sphere on sphere in widening waves expand,
And glad with genial warmth the incumbent
    land.
Thus when the mother-bird on moss-wove nest
Lulls her fond brood beneath her plumy breast;
Warmth from her tender heart diffusive springs,
And charm'd she shields them with diverging
    wings.

2. "You from deep cauldrons and unmeasur-
    ed caves 149
Blow flaming airs, or pour vitrescent waves;

---

lower regions of the atmosphere. The twilight, the meteors called fire-balls, or flying dragons, and the northern lights, inhabit the higher regions of the atmosphere. See additional notes, No. I.

Cling round the aërial bow. l. 117. See additional notes, No. II.

Eve's silken couch. l. 119. See additional Notes, No. III.

Where lighter gases. l. 123. Mr. Cavendish has shown, that the gas called inflammable air, is at least ten times lighter than common air; Mr. Lavoisier contends, that it is one of the component parts of water, and is by him called hydrogene. It is supposed to afford their principal nourishment to vegetables and thence to animals, and is perpetually rising from their decomposition; this source of it in hot climates, and in summer months, is so great as to exceed estimation. Now if this light gas passes through the atmosphere, without combining with it, it must compose another atmosphere over the aërial one; which must expand, when the pressure above it is thus taken away, to inconceivable tenuity.

If this supernatant gasseous atmosphere floats upon the aërial one, like ether upon water, what must happen? 1. it will flow from the line, where it will be produced in the greatest quantities, and become much accumulated over the poles of the earth: 2. the common air, or lower stratum of the atmosphere, will be much thinner over the poles than at the line: because if a glass globe be filled with oil and water, and whirled upon its axis, the centrifugal power will carry the heavier fluid to the circumference, and the lighter will in consequence be found round the axis. 3. There may be a place at some certain latitude between the poles and the line on each side of the equator, where the inflammable supernatant atmosphere may end, owing to the greater centrifugal force of the heavier aërial atmosphere. 4. Between the termination of the aërial and the beginning of the gasseous atmosphere, the airs will occasionally be intermixed, and thus become inflammable by the electric spark; these circumstances will assist in explaining the phenomena of fire balls, northern lights, and of some variable winds, and long-continued rains.

Since the above note was first written, Mr. Volta I am informed has applied the supposition of a supernatant atmosphere of inflammable air, to explain some phenomena in meteorology. And Mr. Lavoisier has announced his design to write on this subject. Traité de Chimie, Tom. I. I am happy to find these opinions supported by such respectable authority.

And bend the twilight. l. 126. The crepuscular atmosphere, or the region where the light of the sun ceases to be refracted to us, is estimated by philosophers to be between 40 and 50 miles high, at which time the sun is about 18 degrees below the horizon; and the rarity of the air is supposed to be from 4,000 to 10,000 times greater than at the surface of the earth. Cotes's Hydrost. p. 123. The duration of twilight differs in different seasons and in different latitudes; in England the shortest twilight is about the beginning of October and of March; in more northen latitudes, where the sun never sinks more than 18 degrees, below the horizon, the twilight continues the whole night. The time of its duration may also be occasionally affected by the varying height of the atmosphere. A number of observations on the duration of twilight in different latitudes might afford considerable information concerning the aërial strata in the higher regions of the atmosphere, and might assist in determining whether an exterior atmosphere of inflammable gas, or hydrogene, exists over the aërial one.

Alarm with comet-blaze. l. 133. See additional notes, No. IV.

The sun's phlogistic orb. l. 136. See additional notes, No. V.

Round her still centre. l. 139. Many philosophers have believed that the central parts of the earth consist of a fluid mass of burning lava, which they have called a subterraneous sun; and have supposed, that it contributes to the production of metals, and to the growth of vegetables. See additional notes, No. VI.

Or sphere on sphere. l. 143. See additional notes, No. VII.

O'er shining oceans ray volcanic light,
Or hurl innocuous embers to the night.
While with loud shouts to Etna Hecla calls,
And Andes answers from his beacon'd walls;
Sea-wilder'd crews the mountain-stars admire,
And beauty beams amid terrific fire.

"Thus when of old, as mystic bards presume,
Huge Cyclops dwelt in Etna's rocky womb,
On thundering anvils rung their loud alarms,
And leagued with Vulcan forged immortal arms;
Descending Venus sought the dark abode, 161
And sooth'd the labours of the grisly god.—
While frowning loves the threatening falchion wield,
And tittering graces peep behind the shield,
With jointed mail their fairy limbs o'erwhelm,
Or nod with pausing step the plumed helm;
With radiant eye she view'd the boiling ore,
Heard undismay'd the breathing bellows roar,
Admired their sinewy arms, and shoulders bare,
And ponderous hammers lifted high in air, 170
With smiles celestial bless'd their dazzled sight,
And beauty blazed amid infernal night.

IV. 1. "Effulgent maids! you round deciduous day,
Tress'd with soft beams, your glittering bands array;
On earth's cold bosom, as the sun retires,
Confine with folds of air the lingering fires;

O'er Eve's pale forms diffuse phosphoric light,
And deck with lambent flames the shrine of night.
So, warm'd and kindled by meridian skies,
And view'd in darkness with dilated eyes, 180
Bologna's chalks with faint ignition blaze,
Beccari's shells emit prismatic rays.

Hurl innocuous embers. l. 152. The immediate cause of volcanic eruptions is believed to be owing to the water of the sea, or from lakes, or inundations, finding itself a passage into the subterraneous fires, which may lie at great depths. This must first produce by its coldness a condensation of the vapour there existing, or a vacuum, and thus occasion parts of the earth's crust or shell to be forced down by the pressure of the incumbent atmosphere. Afterwards the water being suddenly raised into steam produces all the explosive effects of earthquakes. And by new accessions of water during the intervals of the explosions the repetition of the shocks is caused. These circumstances were hourly illustrated by the fountains of boiling water in Iceland, in which the surface of the water in the boiling wells sunk down low before every new ebullition.

Besides these eruptions occasioned by the steam of water, there seems to be a perpetual effusion of other vapours, more noxious and (as far as it is yet known) perhaps greatly more expansile than water from the Volcanos in various parts of the world. As these Volcanos are supposed to be spiracula or breathing holes to the great subterraneous fires, it is probable that the escape of elastic vapours from them is the cause, that the earthquakes of modern days are of such small extent compared to those of ancient times, of which vestiges remain in every part of the world, and on this account may be said not only to be innocuous, but useful.

Confine with folds of air. l. 176. The air, like all other bad conductors of electricity, is known to be a bad conductor of heat; and thence prevents the heat acquired from the sun's rays by the earth's surface from being so soon dissipated, in the same manner as a blanket, which may be considered as a sponge filled with air, prevents the escape of heat from the person wrapped in it. This seems to be one cause of the great degree of cold on the tops of the mountains, where the rarity of the air is greater, and it therefore becomes a better conductor both of heat and electricity. See note on Barometz, Part II. of this work.

There is however another cause to which the great coldness of mountains and of the higher regions of the atmosphere is more immediately to be ascribed, explained by Dr. Darwin in the Philos. Trans. Vol. LXXVIII. who has there proved by experiments with the air-gun and air-pump, that when any portion of the atmosphere becomes mechanically expanded, it absorbs heat from the bodies in its vicinity. And as the air which creeps along the plains, expands itself by a part of the pressure being taken off when it ascends the sides of mountains; it at the same time attracts heat from the summit of those mountains, or other bodies which happen to be immersed in it, and thus produces cold. Hence he concludes that the hot air at the bottom of the Andes becomes temperate by its own rarefaction when it ascends to the city of Quito; and by its further rarefaction becomes cooled to the freezing point when it ascends to the snowy regions on the summits of those mountains. To this also he attributes the great degree of cold experienced by the aeronauts in their balloons; and which produces hail in summer at the height of only two or three miles in the atmosphere.

Diffuse phosphoric light. l. 177. I have often been induced to believe from observation, that the twilight of the evenings is lighter than that of the mornings at the same distance from noon. Some may ascribe this to the greater height of the atmosphere in the evenings having been rarefied by the sun during the day; but as its density must at the same time be diminished, its power of refraction would continue the same. I should rather suppose that it may be owing to the phosphorescent quality (as it is called) of almost all bodies; that is, when they have been exposed to the sun, they continue to emit light for a considerable time afterwards. This is generally believed to arise either from such bodies giving out the light which they had previously absorbed; or to the continuance of a slow combustion which the light they had been previously exposed to had excited. See the next note.

Beccari's shells. l. 182. Beccari made many curious experiments on the phosphoric light, as it is called, which becomes visible on bodies brought into a dark room, after having been previously exposed to the sunshine. It appears from these experiments that almost all inflammable bodies possess this quality in a greater or less degree; white paper or linen thus examined after having been exposed to the sunshine, is luminous to an extraordinary degree; and if a person shut up in a dark room, puts one of his

So to the sacred sun in Memnon's fane,
Spontaneous concords quired the matin strain;
—Touch'd by his orient beam, responsive rings
The living lyre, and vibrates all its strings;
Accordant aisles the tender tones prolong,
And holy echoes swell the adoring song.

"You with light gas the lamps nocturnal feed,
Which dance and glimmer o'er the marshy mead;

Shine round Calendula at twilight hours,   191
And tip with silver all her saffron flowers;
Warm on her mossy couch the radiant worm,
Guard from cold dews her love-illumined form,
From leaf to leaf conduct the virgin light,
Star of the earth, and diamond of the night.
You bid in air the tropic beetle burn,
And fill with golden flame his winged urn;
Or gild the surge with insect-sparks, that swarm
Round the bright oar, the kindling prow alarm;
Or arm in waves, electric in his ire,   201
The dread Gymnotus with ethereal fire.—
Onward his course with waving tail he helms,
And mimic lightnings scare the watery realms.

---

hands out into the sun's light for a short time and then retracts it, he will be able to see that hand distinctly, and not the other. These experiments seem to countenance the idea of light being absorbed and again emitted from bodies when they are removed into darkness. But Beccari further pretended, that some calcareous compositions when exposed to red, yellow, or blue light, through coloured glasses, would on their being brought into a dark room emit coloured lights. This mistaken fact of Beccari's, Mr. Wilson decidedly refutes; and among many other curious experiments discovered, that if oyster-shells were thrown into a common fire and calcined for about half an hour, and then brought to a person who had previously been some minutes in a dark room, that many of them would exhibit beautiful irises of prismatic colours, whence probably arose Beccari's mistake. Mr. Wilson hence contends, that these kinds of phosphori do not emit the light they had previously received, but that they are set on fire by the sun's rays, and continue for some time a slow combustion after they are withdrawn from the light. Wilson's experiments on Phosphori. Dodsley, 1775.

The Bolognian stone is a selenite, or gypsum, and has been long celebrated for its phosphorescent quality after having been burnt in a sulphurous fire; and exposed when cold to the sun's light. It may be thus well imitated; calcine oyster-shells half an hour, pulverize them when cold, and add one third part of the flowers of sulphur, press them close into a small crucible, and calcine them for an hour or longer, and keep the powder in a phial close stopped. A part of this powder is to be exposed for a minute or two to the sunbeams, and then brought into a dark room. The calcined Bolognian stone becomes a calcareous hepar of sulphur; but the calcined shells, as they contain the animal acid, may also contain some of the phosphorus of Kunkel. See additional notes, No. X.

In Memnon's fane. l. 183. See additional notes, No. VIII.

The lamps nocturnal. l. 189. The ignis fatuus or Jack a lantern, so frequently alluded to by poets, is supposed to originate from the inflammable air, or hydrogene, given up from morasses; which being of a heavier kind from its impurity than that obtained from iron and water, hovers near the surface of the earth, and uniting with common air gives out light by its slow ignition. Perhaps such lights have no existence, and the reflection of a star on watery ground may have deceived the travellers, who have been said to be bewildered by them; if the fact was established it would much contribute to explain the phenomena of northern lights. I have travelled much in the night, in all seasons of the year, and over all kind of soils, but never saw one of these Will o'wisps.

Shine round Calendula. l. 191. See note on Tropæolum in Part II.

The radiant worm. l. 193. See additional notes, No. IX.

The dread Gymnotus. l. 202. The Gymnotus electricus is a native of the river Surinam in South America; those which were brought over to England about eight years ago were about three or four feet long, and gave an electric shock (as I experienced) by putting one finger on the back near its head, and another of the opposite hand into the water near its tail. In their native country they are said to exceed twenty feet in length; and kill any man who approaches them in an hostile manner. It is not only to escape its enemies that this surprizing power of the fish is used, but also to take its prey which it does by benumbing them, and then devouring them before they have time to recover, or by perfectly killing them; for the quantity of the power seemed to be determind by the will or anger of the animal; as it sometimes struck a fish twice before it was sufficiently benumbed to be easily swallowed.

The organs productive of this wonderful accumulation of electric matter have been accurately dissected and described by Mr. J. Hunter. Philos. Trans. Vol. LXV. They are so divided by membranes as to compose a very extensive surface, and are supplied with many pairs of nerves larger than any other nerves of the body; but how so large a quantity is so quickly accumulated as to produce such amazing effects in a fluid ill adapted for the purpose is not yet satisfactorily explained. The Torpedo possesses a similar power in a less degree, as was shown by Mr Walch, and another fish lately described by Mr. Paterson. Philos. Trans. Vol. LXXVI.

In the construction of the Leyden-phial, (as it is called) which is coated on both sides, it is known, that above one hundred times the quantity of positive electricity can be condensed on every square inch of the coating on one side, that could have been accumulated on the same surface if there had been no opposite coating communicating with the earth; because the negative electricity, or that part of it which caused its expansion, is now drawn off through the glass. It is also well known, that the thinner the glass is (which is thus coated on both sides so as to make a Leyden-phial,) the more electricity can be condensed on one of its surfaces, till it becomes so thin as to break, and thence discharge itself.

Now it is possible, that the quantity of electricity condensible on one side of a coated phial

So, when with bristling plumes the bird of Jove
Vindictive leaves the argent fields above,
Borne on broad wings the guilty world he awes,
And grasps the lightning in his shining claws.

V. 1. "Nymphs! your soft smiles uncultured man subdued,
And charm'd the savage from his native wood;
You, while amazed his hurrying hordes retire
From the fell havoc of devouring fire, 212
Taught the first art! with piny rods to raise
By quick attrition the domestic blaze,
Fan with soft breath, with kindling leaves provide
And list the dread destroyer on his side.
So, with bright wreath of serpent tresses crown'd,
Severe in beauty, young Medusa frown'd;
Erewhile subdued, round Wisdom's ægis roll'd
Hiss'd the dread snakes, and flamed in burnish'd gold; 220
Flash'd on her brandish'd arm the immortal shield,
And terror lighten'd o'er the dazzled field.

2. "Nymphs! you disjoin, unite, condense, expand,
And give new wonders to the chemist's hand;
On tepid clouds of rising steam aspire,
Or fix in sulphur all its solid fire;

---

may increase in some high ratio in respect to the thinness of the glass, since the power of attraction is known to decrease as the squares of the distances, to which this circumstance of electricity seems to bear some analogy. Hence if an animal membrane as thin as the silk-worm spins its silk, could be so situated as to be charged like the Leyden-bottle, without bursting, (as such thin glass would be liable to do,) it would be difficult to calculate the immense quantity of electric fluid, which might be accumulated on its surface. No land animals are yet discovered which possess this power, though the air would have been a much better medium for producing its effects; perhaps the size of the necessary apparatus would have been inconvenient to land animals.

In his shining claws. l. 208. Alluding to an antique gem in the collection of the Grand Duke of Florence. Spence.

Of devouring fire. l. 212. The first and most important discovery of mankind seems to have been that of fire. For many ages it is probable fire was esteemed a dangerous enemy, known only by its dreadful devastations; and that many lives must have been lost, and many dangerous burns and wounds must have afflicted those who first dared to subject it to the uses of life. It is said that the tall monkies of Borneo and Sumatria lie down with pleasure round any accidental fire in their woods; and are arrived to that degree of reason, that knowledge of causation, that they thrust into the remaining fire the half-burnt ends of the branches to prevent its going out. One of the nobles of the cultivated people of Otaheite, when Captain Cook treated them with tea, catched the boiling water in his hand from the cock of the tea-urn and bellowed with pain, not conceiving that water could become hot, like fire.

Tools of steel constitute another important discovery in consequence of fire; and contributed perhaps principally to give the European nations so great a superiority over the American world. By these two agents, fire and tools of steel, mankind became able to cope with the vegetable kingdom, and conquer provinces of forests, which in uncultivated countries almost exclude the growth of other vegetables, and of those animals which are necessary to our existence. Add to this, that the quantity of our food is also increased by the use of fire, for some vegetables become salutary food by means of the heat used in cookery, which are naturally either noxious or difficult of digestion; as potatoes, kidney-beans, onions, cabbages. The cassava when made into bread, is perhaps rendered mild by the heat it undergoes, more than by expressing its superfluous juice. The roots of white bryony and of arum, I am informed lose much of their acrimony by boiling.

Young Medusa frown'd. l. 218. The Egyptian Medusa is represented on ancient gems with wings on her head, snaky hair, and a beautiful countenance, which appears intensely thinking; and was supposed to represent divine wisdom. The Grecian Medusa, on Minerva's shield, as appears on other gems, has a countenance distorted with rage or pain, and is supposed to represent divine vengeance. This Medusa was one of the gorgons, at first very beautiful and terrible to her enemies; Minerva turned her hair into snakes, and Perseus having cut off her head fixed it on the shield of that goddess; the sight of which then petrified the beholders. Dannet Dict.

Or fix in sulphur. l. 226. The phenomena of chemical explosions cannot be accounted for without the supposition, that some of the bodies employed contain concentrated or solid heat combined with them, to which the French chemists have given the name of Calorique. When air is expanded in the air-pump, or water evaporated into steam, they drink up or absorb a great quantity of heat; from this analogy, when gunpowder is exploded it ought to absorb much heat, that is, in popular language, it ought to produce a great quantity of cold. When vital air is united with phlogistic matter in respiration, which seems to be a slow combustion, its volume is lessened; the carbonic acid, and perhaps phosphoric acid are produced; and heat is given out; which according to the experiments of Dr. Crawford would seem to be deposited from the vital air. But as the vital air in nitrous acid is condensed from a light elastic gas to that of a heavy fluid, it must possess less heat than before. And hence a great part of the heat, which is given out in firing gunpowder, I should suppose, must reside in the sulphur or charcoal.

Mr. Lavoisier has shown, that vital air, or oxygen, loses less of its heat when it becomes one of the component parts of nitrous acid, than in any other of its combinations; and is hence capable of giving out a great quantity of heat in the explosion of gunpowder; but as there seems to be great analogy between the matter of heat, or calorique, and the electric matter; and as the worst conductors of electricity are believed to contain the greatest quantity of that fluid,

With boundless spring elastic airs unfold,
Or fill the fine vacuities of gold;
With sudden flash vitrescent sparks reveal,
By fierce collision from the flint and steel; 230
Or mark with shining letters Kunkel's name
In the pale phosphor's self-consuming flame.
So the chaste heart of some enchanted maid
Shines with insiduous light, by love betray'd;
Round her pale bosom plays the young desire,
And slow she wastes by self-consuming fire.

3. " You taught mysterious Bacon to explore
Metallic veins, and part the dross from ore;
With sylvan coal in whirling mills combine 239
The crystal'd nitre, and the sulphurous mine;
Through wiry nets the black diffusion strain,
And close an airy ocean in a grain.—

---

there is reason to suspect that the worst conductors of heat may contain the most of that fluid; as sulphur, wax, silk, air, glass. See note on l. 176 of this Canto.
Vitrescent sparks. 1. 229. When flints are struck against other flints they have the property of giving sparks of light; but it seems to be an internal light, perhaps of electric origin, very different from the ignited sparks which are struck from flint and steel. The sparks produced by the collision of steel with flint appear to be globular particles of iron, which have been fused, and imperfectly scorified or vitrified. They are kindled by the heat produced by the collision; but their vivid light, and their fusion and vitrification are the effects of a combustion continued in these particles during their passage through the air. This opinion is confirmed by an experiment of Mr. Hawksbee, who found that these sparks could not be produced in the exhausted receiver. See Keir's Chemical Dict. art. Iron, and art. Earth, vitrifiable.
The pale phosphor. l. 232. See additional notes, No. X.
And close an airy ocean. l. 242. Gunpowder is plainly described in the works of Roger Bacon before the year 1267. He describes it in a curious manner, mentioning the sulphur and nitre, but conceals the charcoal in an anagram. The words are, Sed tamen salis petræ *lure mope can ubre*, et sulphuris, et sic faces tonitrum, et corruscationem, si scias, artificium. The words lure mope can ubre are an anagram of carbonum pulvere. Biograph. Britan. Vol. I. Bacon de Secretis Operibus, Cap. XI. He adds, that he thinks by an artifice of this kind Gideon defeated the Midianites with only three hundred men. Judges, Chap. VII. Chamb. Dict. art. Gunpowder. As Bacon does not claim this as his own invention, it is thought by many to have been of much more ancient discovery.
The permanently elastic fluid generated in the firing of gunpowder is calculated by Mr. Robins to be about 244 if the bulk of the powder be 1. And that the heat generated at the time of the explosion occasions the rarefied air thus produced to occupy about 1000 times the space of the gunpowder. This pressure may therefore be called equal to 1000 atmospheres or six tons upon a square inch. As the suddenness of this explosion must contribute much to its power, it would seem that the chamber of powder, to produce its greatest effect, should be lighted in the

Pent in dark chambers of cylindric brass,
Slumbers in grim repose the sooty mass;
Lit by the brilliant spark, from grain to grain
Runs the quick fire along the kindling train;
On the pain'd ear-drum bursts the sudden crash
Starts the red-flame, and death pursues the flash.—
Fear's feeble hand directs the fiery darts, 249
And strength and courage yield to chemic arts;
Guilt with pale brow the mimic thunder owns,
And tyrants tremble on their blood-stain'd thrones.

VI. " Nymphs! you erewhile on simmering cauldrons play'd,
And call'd delighted Savery to your aid;

---

centre of it; which I believe is not attended to in the manufacture of muskets or pistols.
From the cheapness with which a very powerful gunpowder is likely soon to be manufactured from aerated marine acid, or from a new method of forming nitrous acid by means of manganese or other calciform ores, it may probably in time be applied to move machinery, and supersede the use of steam.
There is a bitter invective in Don Quixote against the inventors of gunpowder, as it levels the strong with the weak, the knight cased in steel with the naked shepherd, those who have been trained to the sword, with those who are totally unskilful in the use of it; and throws down all the splendid distinctions of mankind. These very reasons ought to have been urged to show, that the discovery of gunpowder has been of public utility by weakening the tyranny of a few over the many.
Delighted Savery. l. 254. The invention of the steam-engine for raising water by the pressure of the air in consequence of the condensation of steam, is properly ascribed to Capt. Savery; a plate and description of this machine is given in Harris's Lexicon Technicum, art. Engine. Though the Marquis of Worcester in his Century of Inventions printed in the year 1663 had described an engine for raising water by the explosive power of steam long before Savery's. Mr. Desaguliers affirms, that Savery bought up all he could procure of the books of the Marquis of Worcester, and destroyed them, professing himself then to have discovered the power of steam by accident, which seems to have been an unfounded slander. Savery applied it to the raising of water to supply houses and gardens, but could not accomplish the draining of mines by it. Which was afterwards done by Mr. Newcomen and Mr. John Cowley at Dartmouth, in the year 1712, who added the piston.
A few years ago Mr. Watt of Glasgow much improved this machine, and with Mr. Boulton of Birmingham has applied it to a variety of purposes, such as raising water from mines, blowing bellows to fuse the ore, supplying towns with water, grinding corn, and many other purposes. There is reason to believe it may in time be applied to the rowing of barges, and the moving of carriages along the road. As the specific levity of air is too great for the support of great burdens by balloons, there seems no probable method of flying conveniently but by the power of steam, or some other explosive material, which another half century may probably discover. See additional notes, No. XI.

Bade round the youth explosive steam aspire,
In gathering clouds, and wing'd the wave with
 fire;
Bade with cold streams the quick expansion stop,
And sunk the immense of vapours to a drop.—
Press'd by the ponderous air the piston falls
Resistless, sliding through its iron walls; 260
Quick moves the balanced beam, of giant birth,
Wields his large limbs, and nodding shakes the
 earth.

" The giant-power from earth's remotest
 caves
Lifts with strong arm her dark reluctant waves;
Each cavern'd rock, and hidden den explores,
Drags her dark coals, and digs her shining
 ores.
Next, in close cells of ribbed oak confined,
Gale after gale, he crowds the struggling wind;
The imprison'd storms through brazen nostrils
 roar,
Fan the white flame, and fuse the sparkling ore.
Here high in air the rising stream he pours 271
To clay-built cisterns, or to lead-lined towers;
Fresh through a thousand pipes the wave distils,
And thirsty cities drink the exuberant rills.
There the vast mill-stone with inebriate whirl
On trembling floors his forceful fingers twirl,
Whose flinty teeth the golden harvests grind,
Feast without blood! and nourish human-kind.

" Now his hard hands on Mona's rifted crest,
Bosom'd in rock, her azure ores arrest; 280

With iron lips his rapid rollers seize
The lengthening bars, in thin expansion squeeze;
Descending screws with ponderous fly-wheels
 wound
The tawny plates, the new medallions round;
Hard dies of steel the cupreous circles cramp,
And with quick fall his massy hammers stamp.
The Harp, the Lily and the Lion join,
And George and Britain guard the sterling coin.

" Soon shall thy arm, unconquer'd Steam!
 afar
Drag the slow barge, or drive the rapid car; 290
Or on wide-waving wings expanded bear
The flying-chariot through the fields of air.
—Fair crews triumphant, leaning from above,
Shall wave their fluttering kerchiefs as they
 move;
Or warrior-bands alarm the gaping crowd,
And armies shrink beneath the shadowy cloud.

" So mighty Hercules o'er many a clime
Waved his vast mace in Virtue's cause sublime,

Feast without blood! l. 278. The benevolence of the great Author of all things is greatly manifest in the sum of his works, as Dr. Balguy has well evinced in his pamphlet on Divine Benevolence asserted, printed for Davis 1781. Yet if we may compare the parts of nature with each other, there are some circumstances of her economy which seem to contribute more to the general scale of happiness than others. Thus the nourishment of animal bodies is derived from three sources: 1. the milk given from the mother to the offspring; in this excellent contrivance the mother has pleasure in affording the sustenance to the child, and the child has pleasure in receiving it. 2. Another source of the food of animals includes seeds or eggs; in these the embryon is in a torpid or insensible state, and there is along with it laid up for its early nourishment a store of provision, as the fruit belonging to some seeds, and the oil and starch belonging to others; when these are consumed by animals the unfeeling seed or egg receives no pain, but the animal receives pleasure which consumes it. Under this article may be included the bodies of animals which die naturally. 3. But the last method of supporting animal bodies by the destruction of other living animals, as lions preying upon lambs, these upon living vegetables, and mankind upon them all, would appear to be a less perfect part of the economy of nature than those before mentioned, as contributing less to the sum of general happiness.

Mona's rifted crest. l. 279. Alluding to the very valuable copper-mines in the isle of Anglesey, the property of the Earl of Uxbridge.

With iron lips. l. 281. Mr. Boulton has lately constructed at Soho near Birmingham, a most magnificent apparatus for coining, which has cost him some thousand pounds; the whole machinery is moved by an improved steam-engine, which rolls the copper for halfpence finer than copper has before been rolled for the purpose of making money; it works the coupoirs or screw-presses for cutting out the circular pieces of copper; and coins both the faces and edges of the money at the same time, with such superior excellence and cheapness of workmanship, as well as with marks of such powerful machinery as must totally prevent clandestine imitation, and in consequence save many lives from the hand of the executioner; a circumstance worthy the attention of a great minister. If a civic crown was given in Rome for preserving the life of one citizen, Mr. Boulton should be covered with garlands of oak! By this machinery four boys of ten or twelve years old are capable of striking thirty thousand guineas in an hour, and the machine itself keeps an unerring account of the pieces struck.

So mighty Hercules. l. 297. The story of Hercules seems of great antiquity, as appears from the simplicity of his dress and armour, a lion's skin and a club; and from the nature of many of his exploits, the destruction of wild beasts and robbers. This part of the history of Hercules seems to have related to times before the invention of the bow and arrow, or of spinning flax. Other stories of Hercules are perhaps of later date, and appear to be allegorical, as his conquering the river-god Achelous, and bringing Cerberus up to day-light; the former might refer to his turning the course of a river, and draining a morass, and the latter to his exposing a part of the superstition of the times. The strangling the lion and tearing his jaws asunder, are described from a statue in the Museum Florentinum, and from an antique gem; and the grasping Anteus to death in his arms as he lifts him from the earth, is described from another ancient cameo. The famous pillars of Hercules have been variously explained. Pliny asserts that

Unmeasured strength with early art combined,
Awed, served, protected, and amazed mankind.— 300
First two dread snakes at Juno's vengeful nod
Climb'd round the cradle of the sleeping god;
Waked by the shrilling hiss, and rustling sound,
And shrieks of fair attendants trembling round,
Their gasping throats with clenching hands he holds;
And Death entwists their convoluted folds.
Next in red torrents from her sevenfold heads
Fell Hydra's blood on Lerna's lake he sheds;
Grasps Achelous with resistless force,
And drags the roaring river to his course; 310
Binds with loud bellowing and with hideous yell
The monster bull, and threefold dog of hell.

"Then, where Nemea's howling forests wave,
He drives the lion to his dusky cave;
Seized by the throat the growling fiend disarms,
And tears his gaping jaws with sinewy arms;
Lifts proud Anteus from his mother-plains,
And with strong grasp the struggling giant strains;
Back falls his fainting head, and clammy hair,
Writhe his weak limbs, and flits his life in air;—
By steps reverted o'er the blood dropp'd fen 321
He tracks huge Cacus to his murderous den;
Where, breathing flames through brazen lips, he fled,
And shakes the rock-roof'd cavern o'er his head.

"Last with wide arms the solid earth he tears,
Piles rock on rock, on mountain mountain rears;

---

the natives of Spain and of Africa believed that the mountains of Abyla and Calpè on each side of the straits of Gibraltar were the pillars of Hercules; and that they were reared by the hands of that god, and the sea admitted between them. Plin. Hist. Nat. p. 46. Edit. Manut. Venet. 1609.

If the passage between the two continents was opened by an earthquake in ancient times, as this allegorical story would seem to countenance, there must have been an immense current of water at first run into the Mediterranean from the Atlantic; since there is at present a strong stream sets always from thence into the Mediterranean. Whatever may be the cause, which now constantly operates, so as to make the surface of the Mediterranean lower than that of the Atlantic, it must have kept it very much lower before a passage for the water through the straits was opened. It is probable before such an event took place, the coasts and islands of the Mediterranean extended much further into that sea, and were then for a great extent of country destroyed by the floods occasioned by the new rise of water, and have since remained beneath the sea. Might not this give rise to the flood of Deucalion? See note on Cassia, Part II. of this work.

Heaves up huge Abyla on Afric's sand,
Crowns with high Calpè Europe's saliant strand,
Crests with opposing towers the splendid scene,
And pours from urns immense the sea between.—
—Loud o'er her whirling flood Charybdis roars,
Affrighted Scylla bellows round her shores, 332
Vesuvio groans through all his echoing caves,
And Etna thunders o'er the insurgent waves.

VII. 1. "Nymphs! your fine hands ethereal floods amass
From the warm cushion, and the whirling glass;
Beard the bright cylinder with golden wire,
And circumfuse the gravitating fire.
Cold from each point cerulean lustres gleam,
Or shoot in air the scintillating stream. 340
So, borne on brazen talons, watch'd of old
The sleepless dragon o'er his fruits of gold;
Bright beam'd his scales, his eye-balls blazed with ire,
And his wide nostrils breathed inchanted fire.

"You bid gold-leaves, in crystal lanterns held,
Approach attracted, and recede repell'd;
While paper-nymphs instinct with motion rise,
And dancing fauns the admiring sage surprize.
Or, if on wax some fearless beauty stand, 349
And touch the sparkling rod with graceful hand;

Ethereal floods amass. l. 335. The theory of the accumulation of the electric fluid by means of the glass-globe and cushion is difficult to comprehend. Dr. Franklin's idea of the pores of the glass being opened by the friction, and thence rendered capable of attracting more electric fluid, which it again parts with, as the pores contract again, seems analagous in some measure to the heat produced by the vibration, or condensation of bodies, as when a nail is hammered or filed till it becomes hot, as mentioned in additional notes, No. VII. Some philosophers have endeavoured to account for this phenomenon by supposing the existence of two electric fluids which may be called the vitreous and resinous ones, instead of the plus and minus of the same ether. But its accumulation on the rubbed glass bears great analogy to its accumulation on the surface of the Leyden bottle, and cannot perhaps be explained from any known mechanical or chemical principle. See note on Gymnotus, l. 202 of this Canto.

Cold from each point. l. 339. See additional note, No. XIII.

You bid gold-leaves. l. 345. Alluding to the very sensible electrometer improved by Mr. Bennet. It consists of two slips of gold-leaf suspended from a tin cap in a glass cylinder, which has a partial coating without, communicating with the wooden pedestal. If a stick of sealing wax be rubbed for a moment on a dry cloth, and then held in the air *at the distance of two or three feet* from the cap of this instrument, the gold leaves separate, such is its astonishing sensibility to electric influence! (See Bennet on electricity, Johnson, Lond.) The nerves of sense of animal bodies do not seem to be affected by less quantities of light or heat!

Through her fine limbs the mimic lightnings dart,
And flames innocuous eddy round her heart;
O'er her fair brow the kindling lustres glare,
Blue rays diverging from her bristling hair;
While some fond youth the kiss ethereal sips,
And soft fires issue from their meeting lips.
So round the virgin saint in silver streams
The holy halo shoots its arrowy beams.
" You crowd in coated jars the denser fire,
Pierce the thin glass, and fuse the blazing wire; 360
Or dart the red flash through the circling band
Of youths and timorous damsels, hand in hand.
—Starts the quick ether through the fibre trains
Of dancing arteries, and of tingling veins,
Goads each fine nerve, with new sensation thrill'd,
Bends the reluctant limbs with power unwill'd;
Palsy's cold hands the fierce concussion own,
And life clings trembling on her tottering throne.—

So from dark clouds the playful lightning springs, 369
Rives the firm oak, or prints the Fairy-rings.

2. " Nymphs! on that day ye shed from lucid eyes,
Celestial tears, and breathed ethereal sighs!
When Richman rear'd, by fearless haste betray'd,
The wiry rod in Nieva's fatal shade ;—
Clouds o'er the sage with fringed skirts succeed,
Flash follows flash, the warning corks recede;
Near and more near he eyed with fond amaze
The silver streams, and watch'd the sapphire blaze;
Then burst the steel, the dart electric sped, 379
And the bold sage lay number'd with the dead!
Nymphs! on that day ye shed from lucid eyes
Celestial tears, and breathed etherial sighs!

3. " You led your Franklin to your glazed retreats,
Your air-built castles, and your silken seats;

The holy halo. l. 358. I believe it is not known with certainty at what time the painters first introduced the luminous circle round the head to import a saint or holy person. It is now become a part of the symbolic language of painting, and it is much to be wished that this kind of hieroglyphic character was more frequent in that art; as it is much wanted to render historic pictures both more intelligible, and more sublime; and why should not painting as well as poetry express itself in a metaphor, or in indistinct allegory? A truly great modern painter lately endeavoured to enlarge the sphere of pictorial language, by putting a demon behind the pillow of a wicked man on his death bed. Which unfortunately for the scientific part of painting, the cold criticism of the present day has depreciated; and thus barred perhaps the only road to the farther improvement in this science.

With new sensation thrill'd. l. 365. There is probably a system of nerves in animal bodies for the purpose of perceiving heat; since the degree of this fluid is so necessary to health that we become presently injured either by its access or defect; and because almost every part of our bodies is supplied with branches from different pairs of nerves, which would not seem necessary for their motion alone. It is therefore probable, that our sensation of electricity is only of its violence in passing through our system by its suddenly distending the muscles, like any other mechanical violence; and that it is in general pain alone that we feel, and not any sensation analogous to the specific quality of the object. Nature may seem to have been niggardly to mankind in bestowing upon them so few senses; since a sense to have perceived electricity, and another to have perceived magnetism, might have been of great service to them, many ages before these fluids were discovered by accidental experiment; but it is possible an increased number of senses might have incommoded us by adding to the size of our bodies.

Palsy's cold hands. l. 367. Paralytic limbs are in general only incapable of being stimulated into action by the power of the will; since the pulse continues to beat and the fluids to be absorbed in them; and it commonly happens, when paralytic people yawn and stretch themselves, (which is not a voluntary motion,) that the affected limb moves at the same time. The temporary motion of a paralytic limb is likewise caused by passing the electric shock through it; which would seem to indicate some analogy between the electric fluid and the nervous fluid, which is separated from the blood by the brain, and thence diffused along the nerves for the purposes of motion and sensation. It probably destroys life by its sudden expansion of the nerves or fibres of the brain, in the same manner as it fuses metals and splinters wood or stone, and removes the atmosphere, when it passes from one object to another in a dense state.

Prints the fairy-rings. l. 370. See additional note, No. XIII.

When Richman rear'd. l. 373. Dr. Richman, Professor of natural philosophy at Petersburgh, about the year 1763, elevated an insulated metallic rod to collect the aërial electricity, as Dr. Franklin had previously done at Philadelphia; and as he was observing the repulsion of the balls of his electrometer approached too near the conductor, and receiving the lightning in his head with a loud explosion, was struck dead amidst his family.

You led your Franklin. l. 383. Dr. Franklin was the first that discovered that lightning consisted of electric matter; he elevated a tall rod with a wire wrapped round it, and fixing the bottom of it into a glass bottle, and preserving it from falling by means of silk-strings, he found it electrified whenever a cloud passed over it, receiving sparks by his finger from it, and charging coated phials. This great discovery taught us to defend houses and ships and temples from lightning, and also to understand, *that people are always perfectly safe in a room during a thunder storm if they keep themselves at three or four feet distance from the walls;* for the matter of lightning in passing from the clouds to the earth, or from the earth to the clouds, runs through the walls of a house, the trunk of a tree, or other elevated object; except there be some moister body, as an animal, in contact with

Bade his bold arm invade the lowering sky,
And seize the tiptoe lightnings, ere they fly;
O'er the young sage your mystic mantle spread,
And wreath'd the crown electric round his head—
Thus when on wanton wing intrepid Love
Snatch'd the raised lightning from the arm of Jove; 390
Quick o'er his knee the triple bolt he bent,
The cluster'd darts and forky arrows rent,
Snapp'd with illumined hands each flaming shaft,
His tingling fingers shook, and stamp'd and laugh'd;
Bright o'er the floor the scatter'd fragments blazed,
And gods retreating trembled as they gazed;
The immortal sire, indulgent to his child,
Bow'd his ambrosial locks, and heaven relenting smiled.

VIII. "When air's pure essence joins the vital flood,
And with phosphoric acid dyes the blood, 400
Your virgin trains the transient heat dispart,
And lead the soft combustion round the heart;
Life's holy lamp with fires successive feed,
From the crown'd forehead to the prostrate weed,
From earth's proud realms to all that swim or sweep
The yielding ether or tumultuous deep.
You swell the bulb beneath the heaving lawn,
Brood the live seed, unfold the bursting spawn;
Nurse with soft lap, and warm with fragrant breath
The embryon panting in the arms of death; 410
Youth's vivid eye with living light adorn,
And fire the rising blush of beauty's golden morn.

" Thus when the egg of night, on chaos hurl'd,
Burst, and disclosed the cradle of the world;
First from the gaping shell refulgent sprung
Immortal Love, his bow celestial strung;—
O'er the wide waste his gaudy wings unfold,
Beam his soft smiles, and wave his curls of gold;—
With silver darts he pierced the kindling frame,
And lit with torch divine the ever-living flame." 420

them, or nearly so; and in that case the lightning leaves the wall or tree, and passes through the animal; but as it can pass through metals with still greater facility, it will leave animal bodies to pass through metallic ones.

If a person in the open air be surprized by a thunder storm, he will know his danger by observing on a second watch the time which passes between the flash and the crack, and reckoning a mile for every four seconds and a half, and a little more. For sound travels at the rate of 1142 feet in a second of time, and the velocity of light through such small distances is not to be estimated. In these circumstances a person will be safer by lying down on the ground, than erect, and still safer if within a few feet of his horse; which being then a more elevated animal will receive the shock in preference as the cloud passes over. See additional notes, No. XIII.

Intrepid Love, l. 389. This allegory is uncommonly beautiful, representing Divine Justice as disarmed by Divine Love, and relenting of his purpose. It is expressed on an agate in the Great Duke's collection at Florence. Spence.

Transient heat dispart. l. 401. Dr. Crawford in his ingenious work on animal heat has endeavoured to prove, that during the combination of the pure part of the atmosphere with the phlogistic part of the blood, much of the matter of the heat is given out from the air; and that this is the great and perpetual source of the heat of animals; to which we may add that the phosphoric acid is probably produced by this combination; by which acid the colour of the blood is changed in the lungs from a deep crimson to a bright scarlet. There seems to be however another source of animal heat, though of a similar nature; and that this is from the chemical combinations produced in all the glands; since by whatever cause any glandular secretion is increased, as by friction or topical inflammation, the heat of that part becomes increased at the same time; thus after the hands have been for a time immersed in snow, on coming into a warm room, they become red and hot, without any increased pulmonary action. Besides this there would seem to be another material received from the air by respiration: which is so necessary to life, that the embryon must learn to breathe almost within a minute after its birth, or it dies. The perpetual necessity of breathing shows, that the material thus acquired is perpetually consuming or escaping, and on that account requires perpetual renovation. Perhaps the spirit of animation itself is thus acquired from the atmosphere, which if it be supposed to be finer or more subtle than the electric matter, could not long be retained in our bodies, and must therefore require perpetual renovation.

Thus when the egg of night. l. 413. There were two Cupids belonging to the ancient mythology, one much elder than the other. The elder Cupid, or Eros, or Divine Love, was the first that came out of the great egg of night, which floated in chaos, and was broken by the horns of the celestial bull, that is, was hatched by the warmth of the spring. He was winged and armed, and by his arrows and torch pierced and vivified all things, producing life and joy. Bacon, vol. V. p. 197. Quarto edit. Lond. 1778. " At this time, (says Aristophanes,) sable-winged night produced an egg, from whence sprung up like a blossom Eros, the lovely, the desirable, with his glossy golden wings." Avibus. Bryant's Mythology, vol. II. p. 350. Second edit. This interesting moment of this sublime allegory Mrs. Cosway has chosen for her very beautiful painting. She has represented Eros or Divine Love with large wings having the strength of the eagle's wings, and the splendour of the peacock's, with his hair floating in the form of flame, and with a halo of light vapour round his head; which illuminates the painting; while he is in the act of springing forwards, and with his hands separating the elements.

IX. The goddess paused, admired with con-
scious pride
The effulgent legions marshal'd by her side,
Forms sphered in fire with trembling light
array'd, [shade;
Ens without weight, and substance without
And, while tumultuous joy her bosom warms,
Waves her white hand, and calls her hosts to arms.

" Unite, illustrious nymphs ! your radiant
powers,
Call from their long repose the vernal hours.
Wake with soft touch, with rosy hands unbind
The struggling pinions of the western wind ;
Chafe his wan cheeks, his ruffled plumes repair,
And wring the rain drops from his tangled hair.
Blaze round each frosted rill, or stagnant wave,
And charm the Naiad from her silent cave ; 434
Where, shrined in ice, like Niobe she mourns,
And clasps with hoary arms her empty urns.
Call your bright myriads, trooping from afar,
With beamy helms, and glittering shafts of war ;
In phalanx firm the fiend of frost assail,
Break his white towers, and pierce his crystal
mail ; 440
To Zembla's moon-bright coasts the tyrant bear,
And chain him howling to the Northern Bear.

" So when enormous Grampus, issuing forth
From the pale regions of the icy North ;
Waves his broad tail, and opes his ribbed mouth,
And seeks on winnowing fin the breezy South ;
From towns deserted rush the breathless hosts,
Swarm round the hills, and darken all the
coasts ;
Boats follow boats along the shouting tides,
And spears and javelins pierce his blubbery
sides ; 450
Now the bold sailor, raised on pointed toe,
Whirls the wing'd harpoon on the slimy foe ;
Quick sinks the monster in his oozy bed,
The blood-stain'd surges circling o'er his head,
Steers to the frozen pole his wonted track,
And bears the iron tempest on his back.

X. " On wings of flame, ethereal virgins!
sweep
O'er earth's fair bosom, and complacent deep;
Where dwell my vegetative realms benumb'd,
In buds imprison'd, or in bulbs intomb'd, 460

Of the western wind. l. 430. The principal frosts of this country are accompanied or produced by a N. E. wind, and the thaws by a S. W. wind ; the reason of which is that the N. E. winds consist of regions of air brought from the north, which appear to acquire an easterly direction as they advance. The surface of the earth nearer the pole moves slower than it does in our latitude; whence the regions of air brought from thence, move slower, when they arrive hither, than the earth's surface with which they now become in contact; that is, they acquire an apparent easterly direction, as the earth moves from west to east faster than this new part of its atmosphere. The S. W. winds on the contrary consist of regions of air brought from the south, where the surface of the earth moves faster than in our latitude ; and have therefore a westerly direction when they arrive hither by their moving faster than the surface of the earth, with which they are in contact ; and in general the nearer to the west and the greater the velocity of these winds the warmer they should be in respect to the season of the year, since they have been brought more expeditiously from the south, than those winds which have less westerly direction, and have thence been less cooled in their passage.

Sometimes I have observed the thaw to commence immediately on the change of the wind, even within an hour, if I am not mistaken, or sooner. At other times the S. W. wind has continued a day, or even two, before the thaw has commenced ; during which time some of the frosty air, which had gone southwards, is driven back over us; and in consequence has taken a westerly direction, as well as a southern one. At other times I have observed a frost with a N. E. wind every morning, and a thaw with a S. W. wind every noon for several days together. See additional notes, No. XXXIII.

The fiend of frost. l. 439. The principal injury done to vegetation by frost is from the expansion of the water contained in the vessels of plants. Water converted into ice occupies a greater space than it did before, as appears by the bursting of bottles filled with water at the time of their freezing. Hence frost destroys those plants of our island first, which are most succulent ; and the most succulent parts first of other plants ; as their leaves and last year's shoots ; the vessels of which are distended and burst by the expansion of their freezing fluids, while the drier or more resinous plants, as pines, yews, laurels, and other ever-greens, are less liable to injury from cold. The trees in valleys are on this account more injured by the vernal frosts than those on eminences, because their early succulent shoots come out sooner. Hence fruit trees covered by a six-inch coping of a wall are less injured by the vernal frosts, because their being shielded from showers and the descending night-dews has prevented them from being moist at the time of their being frozen ; which circumstance has given occasion to a vulgar error amongst gardeners, who suppose frost to descend.

As the common heat of the earth in this climate is 48 degrees, those tender trees which will bear bending down, are easily secured from the frost by spreading them upon the ground, and covering them with straw or fern. This particularly suits fig trees, as they easily bear bending to the ground, and are furnished with an acrid juice, which secures them from the depredations of insects; but are nevertheless liable to be eaten by mice. See additional notes, No. XII.

In buds imprison'd. l. 460. The buds and bulbs of plants constitute what is termed by Linneus the Hybernaculum, or winter cradle of the embryon vegetable. The buds arise from the bark on the branches of trees, and the bulbs from the caudex of bulbous-rooted plants, or the part from which the fibres of the root are produced : they are defended from too much moisture, and from frosts, and from the depredations of insects, by various contrivances, as by scales, hairs, resinous varnishes and by acrid rinds.

The buds of trees are of two kinds, either

Pervade, pellucid forms! their cold retreat,
Ray from bright urns your viewless floods of
   heat;
From earth's deep wastes *electric* torrents pour,
Or shed from heaven the scintillating shower;

Pierce the dull root, relax its fibre-trains,
Thaw the thick blood, which lingers in its veins;
Melt with warm breath the fragrant gums, that
   bind
The expanding foliage in its scaly rind;
And as in air the laughing leaflets play,
And turn their shining bosoms to the ray,   470
Nymphs! with sweet smile each opening flower
   invite,
And on its damask eyelids pour the *light*.

"So shall my pines, Canadian wilds that
   shade,
Where no bold step has pierced the tangled glade,
High-towering palms, that part the southern
   flood
With shadowy isles and continents of wood,
Oaks, whose broad antlers crest Britannia's
   plain,
Or bear her thunders o'er the conquer'd main,
Shout, as you pass, inhale the genial skies,
And bask and brighten in your beamy eyes;   480
Bow their white heads, admire the changing
   clime,
Shake from their candied trunks the tinkling
   rime;
With bursting buds their wrinkled barks adorn,
And wed the timorous floret to her thorn;

---

flower buds or leaf buds; the former of these produce their seeds and die; the latter produce other leaf buds or flower buds and die. So that all the buds of trees may be considered as annual plants, having their embryon produced during the preceding summer. The same seems to happen with respect to bulbs; thus a tulip produces annually one flower-bearing bulb, sometimes two, and several leaf-bearing bulbs; and then the old root perishes. Next year the flower-bearing bulb produces seeds and other bulbs and perishes; while the leaf-bearing bulb, producing other bulbs only, perishes likewise; these circumstances establish a strict analogy between bulbs and buds. See additional notes, No. XIV.

Viewless floods of heat. l. 462. The fluid matter of heat, or calorique, in which all bodies are immersed, is as necessary to vegetable as to animal existence. It is not yet determinable whether heat and light be different materials, or modifications of the same materials, as they have some properties in common. They appear to be both of them equally necessary to vegetable health, since without light green vegetables become first yellow, that is, they lose the blue colour, which contributed to produce the green; and afterwards they also lose the yellow and become white; as is seen in cellery blanched or etiolated for the table by excluding the light from it.

The upper surface of leaves, which I suppose to be their organ of respiration, seems to require light as well as air; since plants which grow in windows on the inside of houses are equally solicitous to turn the upper side of their leaves to the light. Vegetables at the same time exsude or perspire a great quantity from their leaves, as animals do from their lungs; this perspirable matter as it rises from their fine vessels, (perhaps much finer than the pores of animal skins,) is divided into inconceivable tenuity; and when acted upon by the sun's light appears to be decomposed, the hydrogene becomes a part of the vegetable, composing oils or resins; and the oxygene combined with light or calorique ascends, producing the pure part of the atmosphere or vital air. Hence during the light of the day vegetables give up more pure air than their respiration injures; but not so in the night, even though equally exposed to warmth. This single fact would seem to show, that light is essentially different from heat; and it is perhaps by its combination with bodies that their combined or latent heat is set at liberty, and becomes sensible. See additional notes, No. XXXIV.

Electric torrents pour. l. 463. The influence of electricity in forwarding the germination of plants and their growth seems to be pretty well established; though Mr. Ingenhouz did not succeed in his experiments, and thence doubts the success of those of others; and though M. Rouland from his new experiments believes, that neither positive nor negative electricity increases vegetation; both which philosophers had previously been supporters of the contrary doctrine: for many other naturalists have since repeated their experiments relative to this object, and their new results have confirmed their former one. Mr. D'Ormoy and the two Roziers have found the same success in numerous experiments which they have made in the two last years; and Mr. Carmoy has shown in a convincing manner that electricity accelerates germination.

Mr. D'Ormoy not only found various seeds to vegetate sooner, and to grow taller, which were put upon his insulated table and supplied with electricity, but also that silk-worms began to spin much sooner which were kept electrified than those of the same hatch which were kept in the same place and manner, except that they were not electrified. These experiments of Mr. D'Ormoy are detailed at length in the Journal de Physique of Rozier, Tom. XXXV. p. 270.

M. Bartholon, who had before written a tract on this subject, and proposed ingenious methods for applying electricity to agriculture and gardening, has also repeated a numerous set of experiments; and shows both that natural electricity, as well as the artificial, increases the growth of plants, and the germination of seeds; and opposes Mr. Ingenhouz by very numerous and conclusive facts. Ib. Tom. XXXV. p. 401.

Since by the late discoveries or opinions of the chemists there is reason to believe that water is decomposed in the vessels of vegetables; and that the hydrogene or inflammable air, of which it in part consists, contributes to the nourishment of the plant, and to the production of its oils, resin, gums, sugar, &c. and lastly as electricity decomposes water into these two airs termed oxygene and hydrogene, there is a powerful analogy to induce us to believe that it accelerates or contributes to the growth of vegetation, and like heat may possibly enter into combination with many bodies, or form the basis of some yet unanalyzed acid.

Deep strike their roots, their lengthening tops
 revive,
And all my world of foliage wave, alive.

"Thus with hermetic art the adept combines
The royal acid with cobaltic mines;
Marks with quick pen, in lines unseen portray'd,
The blushing mead, green dell, and dusky glade;
Shades with pellucid clouds the tintless field,
And all the future group exists conceal'd; 492
Till waked by fire the dawning tablet glows,
Green springs the herb, the purple floret blows,
Hills, vales, and woods, in bright succession rise
And all the living landscape charms his eyes.

XI. "With crest of gold should sultry Sirius glare,
And with his kindling tresses scorch the air;
With points of flame the shafts of summer arm
And burn the beauties he designs to warm;—
—So erst when Jove his oath extorted mourn'd,
And clad in glory to the fair return'd; 502
While Loves at forky bolts their torches light,
And resting lightnings gild the car of night;
His blazing form the dazzled maid admired,
Met with fond lips, and in his arms expired.
Nymphs! on light pinions lead your banner'd hosts
High o'er the cliffs of Orkney's gulfy coasts;
Leave on your left the red volcanic light,
Which Hecla lifts amid the dusky night; 510
Mark on the right the Dofrine's snow-capt brow,
Where whirling Maelstrome roars and foams
 below;   [bends
Watch with unmoving eye, where Cepheus
His triple crown, his sceptred hand extends;
Where studs Cassiope with stars unknown
Her golden chair, and gems her sapphire zone;

Where with vast convolution Draco holds
The ecliptic axis in his scaly folds,
O'er half the skies his neck enormous rears, 519
And with immense meanders parts the Bears;
Onward, the kindred Bears with footstep rude
Dance round the pole, pursuing and pursued.

"There in her azure coif and starry stole,
Gray twilight sits, and rules the slumbering
 pole;   [coast,
Bends the pale moon-beams round the sparkling
And strews with livid hands eternal frost.
There, Nymphs! alight, array your dazzling
 powers,
With sudden march alarm the torpid hours;
On ice-built isles expand a thousand sails,
Hinge the strong helms, and catch the frozen
 gales. 530

Thus with hermetic art. l. 487. The sympathetic inks made by zaffre dissolved in the marine and nitrous acids have this curious property, that being brought to the fire one of them becomes green and the other red, but what is more wonderful, they again lose these colours, (unless the heat has been too great,) on their being again withdrawn from the fire. Firescreens have been thus painted, which in the cold have shown only the trunk and branches of a dead tree, and sandy hills, which on their approach to the fire have put forth green leaves and red flowers and grass upon the mountains. The process of making these inks is very easy; take zaffre, as sold by the druggists, and digest it in aqua regia, and the calx of cobalt will be dissolved; which solution must be diluted with a little common water to prevent it from making too strong an impression on the paper; the colour when the paper is heated becomes of a fine green-blue. If zaffre or regulus of cobalt be dissolved in the same manner in spirit of nitre, or aqua fortis, a reddish colour is produced on exposing the paper to heat. Chemical Dictionary by Mr. Keir, Art. Ink, Sympathetic.

With stars unknown. l. 515. Alluding to the star which appeared in the chair of Cassiopea in the year 1572, which at first surpassed Jupiter in magnitude and brightness, diminished by degrees and disappeared in 18 months; it alarmed all the astronomers of the age, and was esteemed a comet by some.

On ice built-isles. l. 529. There are many reasons to believe, from the accounts of travellers and navigators, that the islands of ice in the higher northern latitudes as well as the Glaciers on the Alps continue perpetually to increase in bulk. At certain times in the ice-mountains of Switzerland there happen cracks which have shown the great thickness of the ice, as some of these cracks have measured three or four hundred ells deep. The great islands of ice in the northern seas near Hudson's bay have been observed to have been immersed above one hundred fathoms beneath the surface of the sea, and to have risen a fifth or sixth part above the surface, and to hav measured between three and four miles in circumference. Phil. Trans. No. 465. Sect. 2.

Dr. Lister endeavoured to show that the ice of sea-water contains some salt and perhaps less air than common ice, and that it is therefore much more difficult of solution; whence he accounts for the perpetual and great increase of these floating islands of ice. Philos. Trans. No. 169.

As by a famous experiment of Mr. Boyle's it appears that ice evaporates very fast in severe frosty weather when the wind blows upon it; and as ice in a thawing state is known to contain six times more cold than water at the same degree of sensible coldness, it is easy to understand that winds blowing over islands and continents of ice perhaps much below nothing on Farenheit's scale, and coming from thence into our latitude, must bring great degrees of cold along with them. If we add to this the quantity of cold produced by the evaporation of the water as well as by the solution of the ice, we cannot doubt but that the northen ice is the principal source of the coldness of our winters, and that it is brought hither by the regions of air blowing from the north, and which take an apparent easterly direction by their coming to a part of the surface of the earth which moves faster than the latitude they come from. Hence the increase of the ice in the polar regions by increasing the cold of our climate adds at the same time to the bulk of the Glaciers of Italy and Switzerland.

The winged rocks to feverish climates guide,
Where fainting zephyrs pant upon the tide;
Pass, where to Ceuta Calpe's thunder roars,
And answering echoes shake the kindred shores;
Pass, where with palmy plumes Canary smiles,
And in her silver girdle binds her isles;
Onward, where Niger's dusky Naiad laves
A thousand kingdoms with prolific waves,
Or leads o'er golden sands her threefold train
In steamy channels to the fervid main;   540
While swarthy nations crowd the sultry coast,
Drink the fresh breeze, and hail the floating frost,
Nymphs! veil'd in mist, the melting treasures steer,
And cool with arctic snows the tropic year.
So from the burning line by monsoons driven,
Clouds sail in squadrons o'er the darken'd heaven;
Wide wastes of sand the gelid gales pervade,
And ocean cools beneath the moving shade.

If the nations who inhabit this hemisphere of the globe, instead of destroying their seamen and exhausting their wealth in unnecessary wars, could be induced to unite their labours to navigate these immense masses of ice into the more southern oceans, two great advantages would result to mankind, the tropic countries would be much cooled by their solution, and our winters in this latitude would be rendered much milder for perhaps a century or two, till the masses of ice became again enormous.

Mr. Bradley ascribes the cold winds and wet weather which sometimes happen in May and June to the solution of ice-islands accidentally floating from the north. Treatise on Husbandry and Gardening, Vol. II. p. 437. And adds, that Mr. Barham about the year 1718, in his voyage from Jamaica to England in the beginning of June, met with ice-islands coming from the north, which were surrounded with so great a fog that the ship was in danger of striking upon them, and that one of them measured sixty miles in length.

We have lately experienced an instance of ice-islands brought from the southern polar regions, on which the Guardian struck at the beginning of her passage from the Cape of Good Hope towards Botany Bay, on December 22, 1789. These islands were involved in mist, were about one hundred and fifty fathoms long, and about fifty fathoms above the surface of the water. A part from the top of one of them broke off and fell into the sea, causing an extraordinary commotion in the water and a thick smoke all around it.

Threefold train. l. 539. The river Niger after traversing an immense tract of populous country is supposed to divide itself into three other great rivers. The Rio Grande, the Gambia, and the Senegal. Gold dust is obtained from the sands of these rivers.

Wide wastes of sand. l. 547. When the sun is in the southern tropic 36 deg. distant from the zenith, the thermometer is seldom lower than 72 deg. at Gonder in Abyssinia, but it falls to 60 or 53 deg. when the sun is immediately vertical; so much does the approach of rain counteract the heat of the sun. Bruce's Travels, vol. 3, p. 670.

XII. "Should Solstice, stalking through the sickening bowers,
Suck the warm dew-drops, lap the falling showers;   550
Kneel with parch'd lip, and bending from its brink
From dripping palm the scanty river drink;
Nymphs! o'er the soil ten thousand points erect,
And high in air the electric flame collect.
Soon shall dark mists with self-attraction shroud
The blazing day, and sail in wilds of cloud;
Each silvery flower the streams aërial quaff,
Bow her sweet head, and infant harvest laugh.

"Thus when Elijah mark'd from Carmel's brow
In bright expanse the briny flood below;   560
Roll'd his red eyes amid the scorching air,
Smote his firm breast, and breathed his ardent prayer;
High in the midst a massy altar stood,
And slaughter'd offerings press'd the piles of wood;
While Israel's chiefs the sacred hill surround,
And famish'd armies crowd the dusty ground;
While proud Idolatry was leagued with dearth,
And wither'd Famine swept the desart earth.—
"Oh! mighty Lord! thy wo-worn servant hear,
Who calls thy name in agony of prayer;   570
Thy fanes dishonour'd, and thy prophets slain,
Lo! I alone survive of all thy train!—
Oh send from heaven thy sacred fire,—and pour
O'er the parch'd land the salutary shower,—
So shall thy priest thy erring flock recal,—
And speak in thunder, thou art Lord of all."

Ten thousand points erect. l. 553. The solution of water in air or in calorique, seems to acquire electric matter at the same time, as appears from an experiment of Mr. Bennet. He put some live coals into an insulated funnel of metal, and throwing on them a little water observed that the ascending stream was electrised plus, and the water which descended through the funnel was electrised minus. Hence it appears that though clouds by their change of form may sometimes become electrised minus, yet they have in general an accumulation of electricity. This accumulation of electric matter also evidently contributes to support the atmospheric vapour when it is condensed into the form of clouds, because it is seen to descend rapidly after the flashes of lightning have diminished its quantity; whence there is reason to conclude that very numerous metallic rods with fine points erected high in the air might induce it at any time to part with some of its water.

If we may trust the theory of Mr. Lavoisier concerning the composition and decomposition of water, there would seem another source of thunder showers; and that is, that the two gasses termed oxygene gas or vital air, and hydrogene gas or inflammable air, may exist in the summer atmosphere in a state of mixture but not of combination, and that the electric spark or flash of lightning may combine them and produce water instantaneously.

He cried, and kneeling on the mountain-sands,
Stretch'd high in air his supplicating hands.

Descending flames the dusky shrine illume,
Fire the wet wood, the sacred bull consume ;
Wing'd from the sea the gathering mists arise,
And floating waters darken all the skies ; 562
The king with shifted reins his chariot bends,
And wide o'er earth the airy flood descends ;
With mingling cries dispersing hosts applaud,
And shouting nations own the living God."

The goddess ceased,—the exulting tribes obey,
Start from the soil, and win their airy way ;
The vaulted skies with streams of transient rays
Shine as they pass, and earth and ocean blaze.

So from fierce wars when lawless monarchs
cease, 591
Or liberty returns with laurel'd peace ;
Bright fly the sparks, the colour'd lustres
burn,
Flash follows flash, and flame-wing'd circles
turn ;
Blue serpents sweep along the dusky air,
Imp'd by long trains of scintillating hair ;
Red rockets rise, loud cracks are heard on
high,
And showers of stars rush headlong from the
sky,
Burst, as in silver lines they hiss along,
And the quick flash unfolds the gazing
throng. 600

THE ECONOMY OF VEGETATION.

CANTO II.

ARGUMENT.

ADDRESS to the Gnomes. I. The Earth thrown from a volcano of the Sun; its atmosphere and ocean; its journey through the zodiac; vicissitude of day-light, and of seasons, 11. II. Primeval islands. Paradise, or the golden Age. Venus rising from the sea, 33. III. The first great earthquakes; continents raised from the sea; the Moon thrown from a volcano, has no atmosphere, and is frozen; the earth's diurnal motion retarded; its axis more inclined; whirls with the moon round a new centre, 67. IV. Formation of lime-stone by aqueous solution; calcareous spar; white marble; ancient statue of Hercules resting from his labours. Antinous. Apollo of Belvidere. Venus de Medici. Lady Elizabeth Foster, and Lady Melbourn by Mrs. Damer, 93. V. 1. Of morasses. Whence the product. of Salt by elutriation. Salt-mines at Cracow, 115. 2. Production of nitre. Mars and Venus caught by Vulcan, 143. 3. Production of iron. Mr. Michel's improvement of artificial magnets. Uses of Steel in agriculture, navigation, war, 183. 4. Production of Acids, whence Flint, Sea sand, Selenite, Asbestus, Fluor, Onyx, Agate, Mocho, Opal, Saphire, Ruby, Diamond. Jupiter and Europa, 215. VI. 1. New subterraneous fires from fermentation. Production of Clays; manufacture of Porcelain in China; in Italy; in England. Mr. Wedgewood's works at Etruria in Staffordshire. Cameo of a Slave in Chains; of Hope. Figures on the Portland or Barberini vase explained, 271. 2. Coal; Pyrite, Naphtha; Jet; Amber. Dr. Franklin's discovery of disarming the Tempest of its lightning. Liberty of America; of Ireland; of France, 349. VII. Ancient central subterraneous fires. Production of Tin, Copper, Zink, Lead, Mercury, Platina, Gold and Silver. Destruction of Mexico. Slavery of Africa, 395. VIII. Destruction of the armies of Cambyses, 431. IX. Gnomes like stars of an Orrery. Inroads of the Sea stopped. Rocks cultivated. Hannibal passes the Alps, 499. X. Matter circulates. Manures to Vegetables like Chyle to Animals. Plants rising from the Earth. St. Peter delivered from Prison, 537. XI. Transmigration of Matter. Death and resuscitation of Adonis. Departure of the Gnomes, 565.

AND now the goddess with attention sweet
Turns to the Gnomes, that circle round her feet;
Orb within orb approach the marshal'd trains,
And pigmy legions darken all the plains:
Thrice shout with silver tones the applauding bands,
Bow, ere she speaks, and clap their fairy hands,
So the tall grass, when noon-tide zephyr blows,
Bends its green blades in undulating rows;
Wide o'er the fields the billowy tumult spreads,
And rustling harvests bow their golden heads. 10

I. " Gnomes! your bright forms, presiding at her birth,
Clung in fond squadrons round the new-born earth;
When high in ether, with explosion dire,
From the deep craters of his realms of fire,
The whirling sun this ponderous planet hurled,
And gave the astonished void another world.
When from its vaporous air, condensed by cold,
Descending torrents into oceans roll'd;

From the deep craters. l. 14. The existence of solar volcanoes is countenanced by their analogy to terrestrial, and lunar volcanoes; and by the spots on the sun's disk, which have been shown by Dr. Wilson to be excavations through its luminous surface, and may be supposed to be the cavities from whence the planets and comets were ejected by explosions. See additional notes, No. XV. on solar volcanoes.

When from its vaporous air. l. 17. If the nucleus of the earth was thrown out from the sun by an explosion along with as large a quanity of surrounding hot vapour as its attraction would occasion to accompany it, the ponderous semi-fluid nucleus would take a spherical form from the attraction of its own parts, which would become an oblate spheroid from its diurnal revolution. As the vapour cooled, the water would be precipitated, and an ocean would surround the spherical nucleus with a superincumbent atmosphere. The nucleus of the solar lava would likewise become harder as it became cooler. To under-

And fierce attraction, with relentless force,
Bent the reluctant wanderer to its course.   20

"Where yet the Bull with diamond-eye adorns
The spring's fair forehead, and with golden
    horns;
Where yet the Lion climbs the ethereal plain,
And shakes the summer from his radiant mane;
Where Libra lifts her airy arm, and weighs,
Poised in her silver balance, nights and days;
With paler lustres where Aquarius burns,
And showers the still snow from his hoary urns;
Your ardent troops pursued the flying sphere,
Circling the starry girdle of the year;   30
While sweet vicissitudes of day and clime
Mark'd the new annals of enascent time.

II. "You trod with printless step earth's
    tender globe,
While ocean wrapp'd it in his azure robe;
Beneath his waves her hardening strata spread,
Raised her primeval islands from his bed,
Stretch'd her wide lawns, and sunk her winding
    dells,   [shells.
And deck'd her shores with corals, pearls, and

"O'er those blest isles no ice-crown'd moun-
    tains tower'd,
No lightnings darted, and no tempests lower'd;
Soft fell the vesper-drops, condensed below, 41
Or bent in air the rain-refracted bow,
Sweet breathed the zephyrs, just perceived and
    lost;
And brineless billows only kiss'd the coast;
Round the bright zodiac danced the vernal
    hours,
And Peace, the cherub, dwelt in mortal bowers!

"So young Dione, nursed beneath the waves,
And rock'd by Nereids in their coral caves,
Charm'd the blue sisterhood with playful wiles,
Lisp'd her sweet tones, and tried her tender
    smiles.   50
Then, on her beryl throne by Tritons borne,
Bright rose the goddess like the star of morn;
When with soft fires the milky dawn he leads,
And wakes to life and love the laughing meads;—
With rosy fingers, as uncurl'd they hung
Round her fair brow; her golden locks she
    wrung;
O'er the smooth surge on silver sandals stood,
And look'd enchantment on the dazzled flood.
The bright drops rolling from her lifted arms,
In slow meanders wander o'er her charms,   60

---

stand how the strata of the earth were afterwards formed from the sediments of this circumfluent ocean, the reader is referred to an ingenious Treatise on the Theory of the Earth by Mr. Whitehurst, who was many years a watchmaker and engineer at Derby, but whose ingenuity, integrity, and humanity, were rarely equalled in any station of life.

While ocean wrapp'd. l. 34. See additional notes, No. XVI. on the production of calcareous earth.

Her hardening strata spread. l. 35. The granite, or moorstone, or porphyry, constitute the oldest part of the globe, since the limestone, shells, coralloids, and other sea productions, rest upon them; and upon these sea-productions are found clay, iron, coal, salt, and siliceous sand or gritstone. Thus there seem to be three divisions of the globe distinctly marked; the first I suppose to have been the original nucleus of the earth, or lava projected from the sun; 2. over this lie the recrements of animal and vegetable matter produced in the ocean; and, 3. over these the recrements of animal and vegetable matter produced upon the land. Besides these there are bodies which owe their origin to a combination of those already mentioned, as siliceous sand, fluor, alabaster; which seem to have derived their acids originally from the vegetable kingdom, and their earthy bases from sea-productions. See additional notes, No. XVI. on calcareous earth.

Raised her primeval islands. l. 36. The nucleus of the earth, still covered with water, received perpetual increase by the immense quantities of shells and coralloids either annually produced and relinquished, or left after the death of the animals. These would gradually by their different degrees of cohesion be some of them more and others less removable by the influence of solar tides, and gentle tropical breezes, which then must have probably extended from one pole to the other; for it is supposed the moon was not yet produced, and that no storms or unequal winds had yet existence.

Hence then the primeval islands had their gradual origin, were raised but a few feet above the level of the sea, and were not exposed to the great or sudden variations of heat and cold, as is so well explained in Mr. Whitehurst's Theory of the Earth, chap. xvi. Whence the paradise of the sacred writers, and the golden age of the profane ones, seems to have had a real existence. As there can be no rainbow, when the heavens are covered with clouds, because the sun-beams are then precluded from falling upon the rain-drops opposite to the eye of the spectator, the rainbow is a mark of gentle or partial showers. Mr. Whitehurst has endeavoured to show that the primitive islands were only moistened by nocturnal dews and not by showers, as occurs at this day to the Delta of Egypt; and is thence of opinion, that the rainbow had no existence till after the production of mountains and continents. As the salt of the sea has been gradually accumulating, being washed down into it from the recrements of animal and vegetable bodies, the sea must originally have been as fresh as river water; and as it is not yet saturated with salt, must become annually more saline. See note on l. 117 of this Canto.

So young Dione. l. 47. There is an ancient gem representing Venus rising out of the ocean supported by two Tritons. From the formality of the design it would appear to be of great antiquity before the introduction of fine taste into the world. It is probable that this beautiful allegory was originally a hieroglyphic picture (before the invention of letters) descriptive of the formation of the earth from the ocean, which seems to have been an opinion of many of the most ancient philosophers.

Seek round her snowy neck their lucid track,
Pearl her white shoulders, gem her ivory back,
Round her fine waist and swelling bosom swim,
And star with glittering brine each crystal limb.
—The immortal form enamour'd nature hail'd,
And beauty blazed to heaven and earth, unvail'd.

III. "You! who then, kindling after many an age,
Saw with new fires the first volcano rage,
O'er smouldering heaps of livid sulphur swell
At earth's firm centre, and distend her shell, 70
Saw at each opening cleft the furnace glow,
And seas rush headlong on the gulfs below.—
Gnomes! how you shriek'd! when through the troubled air
Roar'd the fierce din of elemental war;
When rose the continents, and sunk the main,
And earth's huge sphere exploding burst in twain.—
Gnomes! how you gazed! when from her wounded side,
Where now the south-sea heaves its waste of tide,

Rose on swift wheels the moon's refulgent car,
Circling the solar orb, a sister-star, 80
Dimpled with vales, with shining hills emboss'd,
And roll'd round earth her airless realms of frost.

"Gnomes! how you trembled! with the dreadful force,
When earth recoiling stagger'd from her course;
When, as her line in slower circles spun,
And her shook'd axis nodded from the sun,

The first volcano. l. 68. As the earth, before the existence of earthquakes, was nearly level, and the greatest part of it covered with sea; when the first great fires began deep in the internal parts of it, those parts would become much expanded; this expansion would be gradually extended, as the heat increased, through the whole terraqueous globe of 7000 miles diameter; the crust would thence in many places open into fissures, which, by admitting the sea to flow in upon the fire, would produce not only a quantity of steam beyond calculation by its expansion, but would also by its decomposition produce inflammable air and vital air in quantities beyond conception, sufficient to effect those violent explosions, the vestiges of which all over the world excite our admiration and our study; the difficulty of understanding how subterraneous fire could exist without the presence of air has disappeared since Dr. Priestley's discovery of such great quantities of pure air which constitute all the acids, and consequently exist in all saline bodies, as sea-salt, nitre, limestone, and in all calciform ores, as manganese, calamy, ochre, and other mineral substances. See an ingenious treatise on earthquakes by Mr. Michel in the Philos. Trans.

In the first tremendous ignitions of the globe, as the continents were heaved up, the valleys, which now hold the sea, were formed by the earth subsiding into the cavities made by the rising mountains; as the steam which raised them condensed; which would thence not have any caverns of great extent remain beneath them, as some philosophers have imagined. The earthquakes of modern days are of very small extent indeed compared to those of ancient times, and are ingeniously compared by M. de Luc to the operations of a mole-hill, where from a small cavity are raised from time to time small quantities of lava or pumice stone. Monthly Review, June, 1790.

The moon's refulgent car. l. 79. See additional notes, No. XV. on solar volcanoes.

Her airless realms of frost. l. 82. If the moon had no atmosphere at the time of its elevation from the earth; or if its atmosphere was afterwards stolen from it by the earth's attraction; the water on the moon would rise quickly into vapour; and the cold produced by a certain quantity of this evaporation would congeal the remainder of it. Hence it is not probable that the moon is at present inhabited, but as it seems to have suffered and to continue to suffer much by volcanoes, a sufficient quantity of air may in process of time be generated to produce an atmosphere; which may prevent its heat from so easily escaping, and its water from so easily evaporating, and thence become fit for the production of vegetables and animals.

That the moon possesses little or no atmosphere is deduced from the undiminished lustre of the stars, at the instant when they emerge from behind her disk. That the ocean of the moon is frozen, is confirmed from there being no appearance of lunar tides; which, if they existed, would cover the part of her disk nearest the earth. See note on Canto III. l. 61.

When earth recoiling. l. 84. On supposition that the moon was thrown from the earth by the explosion of water or the generation of other vapours of greater power, the remaining part of the globe would recede from its orbit in one direction as the moon receded in another, and that in proportion to the respective momentum of each, and would afterward revolve round their common centre of gravity.

If the moon rose from any part of the earth except exactly at the line or poles, the shock would tend to turn the axis of the earth out of its previous direction. And as a mass of matter rising from deep parts of the globe would have previously acquired less diurnal velocity than the earth's surface from whence it rose, and would consequently so much retard the motion of the earth round its axis.

When the earth thus receded the shock would overturn all its buildings and forests, and the water would rush with inconceivable violence over its surface towards the new satellite, from two causes, both by its not at first acquiring the velocity with which the earth receded, and by the attraction of the new moon, as it leaves the earth; on these accounts at first there would be but one tide till the moon receded to a greater distance, and the earth moving round a common centre of gravity between them, the water on the side farthest from the moon would acquire a centrifugal force in respect to this common centre between itself and the moon.

With dreadful march the accumulated main
Swept her vast wrecks of mountain, vale, and
    plain;
And, while new tides their shouting floods unite,
And hail their queen, fair regent of the night; 90
Chain'd to one centre whirl'd the kindred
    spheres,
And mark'd with lunar cycles solar years.

IV. " Gnomes! you then bade dissolving
    shells distil
From the loose summits of each shatter'd hill,
To each fine pore and dark interstice flow,
And fill with liquid chalk the mass below.
Whence sparry forms in dusky caverns gleam
With borrow'd light, and twice refract the
    beam;
While in white beds congealing rocks beneath
Court the nice chissel, and desire to breathe. 100

" Hence wearied Hercules in marble rears
His languid limbs, and rests a thousand years;

Still, as he leans, shall young Antinous please
With careless grace, and unaffected ease;
Onward with loftier step Apollo spring,
And launch the unerring arrow from the string;
In Beauty's bashful form, the veil unfurl'd,
Ideal Venus win the gazing world.
Hence on Roubiliac's tomb shall Fame sublime
Wave her triumphant wings, and conquer
    Time; 110
Long with soft touch shall Damer's chissel
    charm,
With grace delight us, and with beauty warm;
Foster's fine form shall hearts unborn engage,
And Melbourn's smile enchant another age.

V. " Gnomes! you then taught transuding
    dews to pass
Through time-fallen woods, and root-inwove
    morass
Age after age; and with filtration fine
Dispart, from earths and sulphurs, the saline.

1. " Hence with diffusive salt old ocean
    steeps
His emerald shallows, and his sapphire deeps. 120

Dissolving shells distil. l. 93. The lime-stone rocks have had their origin from shells formed beneath the sea, the softer strata gradually dissolving and filling up the interstices of the harder ones, afterwards when these accumulations of shells were elevated above the waters the upper strata became dissolved by the actions of the air and dews, and filled up the interstices beneath, producing solid rocks of different kinds from the coarse lime-stones to the finest marbles. When those lime-stones have been in such a situation that they could form perfect crystals they are called spars, some of which possess a double refraction, as observed by Sir Isaac Newton. When these crystals are jumbled together or mixed with some colouring impurities it is termed marble, if its texture be equable and firm; if its texture be coarse and porous yet hard, it is called lime-stone; if its texture be very loose and porous it is termed chalk. In some rocks the shells remain almost unchanged and only covered, or bedded with lime-stone, which seems to have been dissolved and sunk down amongst them. In others the softer shells and bones are dissolved, and only sharks' teeth or harder echini have preserved their form inveloped in the chalk or lime-stone; in some marbles the solution has been complete and no vestiges of shell appear, as in the white kind called statuary by the workmen. See addit. notes, No. XVI.

Hence wearied Hercules. l. 101. Alluding to the celebrated Hercules of Glyco resting after his labours; and to the easy attitude of Antinous; the lofty step of the Apollo of Belvidere; and the retreating modesty of the Venus de Medici. Many of the designs by Roubiliac in Westminster Abbey are uncommonly poetical; the allegory of Time and Fame contending for the trophy of General Wade, which is here alluded to, is beautifully told; the wings of Fame are still expanded, and her hair still floating in the air; which not only shows that she has that moment arrived, but also that her force is not yet expended; at the same time, that the old figure of Time with his disordered wings is rather leaning backwards and yielding to her impulse, and must apparently in another instant be driven from his attack upon the trophy.

Foster's fine form. l. 113. Alluding to the beautiful statues of Lady Elizabeth Foster and of Lady Melbourn, executed by the honourable Mrs. Damer.

Root-inwove morass. l. 116. The great mass of matter which rests upon the lime-stone strata of the earth, or upon the granite where the lime-stone stratum has been removed by earthquakes or covered by lava, has had its origin from the recrements of vegetables and of air-breathing animals, as the lime-stone had its origin from sea animals. The whole habitable world was originally covered with woods, till mankind formed themselves into societies, and subdued them by fire and by steel. Hence woods in uncultivated countries have grown and fallen through many ages, whence morasses of immense extent; and from these as the more soluble parts were washed away first, were produced sea-salt, nitre, iron, and variety of acids, which combining with calcareous matter were productive of many fossil bodies, as flint, sea-sand, selenite, with the precious stones, and perhaps the diamond. See additional notes, No. XVII.

Hence with diffusive salt. l. 119. Salts of various kinds are produced from the recrements of animal and vegetable bodies, such as phosphoric, ammoniacal, marine salt, and others; these are washed from the earth by rains, and carried down our rivers into the sea; they seem all here to decompose each other except the marine salt, which has therefore from the beginning of the habitable world been perpetually accumulating.

There is a town in the immense salt-mines of Carcow in Poland, with a market-place, a river, a church, and a famous statue, (here supposed to be of Lot's wife) by the moist or dry appearance of which the subterranean inhabitants are said to know when the weather is fair above ground. The galleries in these mines are so numerous and so intricate, that workmen have

Oft in wide lakes, around their warmer brim
In hollow pyramids the crystals swim;
Or, fused by earth-born fires, in cubic blocks
Shoot their white forms, and harden into rocks.

" Thus cavern'd round in Cracow's mighty mines,
With crystal walls a gorgeous city shines;
Scoop'd in the briny rock long streets extend
Their hoary course, and glittering domes ascend;
Down the bright steeps, emerging into day, 129
Impetuous fountains burst their headlong way,
O'er milk-white vales in ivory channels spread,
And wondering seek their subterraneous bed.
Form'd in pellucid salt with chissel nice,
The pale lamp glimmering through the sculptured ice
With wild reverted eyes fair Lotta stands,
And spreads to heaven, in vain, her glassy hands;
Cold dews condense upon her pearly breast,
And the big tear rolls lucid down her vest.
Far gleaming o'er the town transparent fanes
Rear their white towers, and wave their golden vanes; 140
Long lines of lustres pour their trembling rays,
And the bright vault returns the mingled blaze.

2. " Hence orient nitre owes its sparkling birth,
And with prismatic crystals gems the earth,
O'er tottering domes in filmy foliage crawls,
Or frosts with branching plumes the mouldering walls.
As woos azotic gas the virgin air,
And veils in crimson clouds the yielding fair,
Indignant fire the treacherous courtship flies,
Waves his light wing, and mingles with the skies. 150

" So beauty's goddess, warm with new desire,
Left on her silver wheels, the god of fire;
Her faithless charms to fiercer Mars resign'd,
Met with fond lips, with wanton arms intwined.
—Indignant Vulcan eyed the parting fair,
And watch'd with jealous step the guilty pair;

---

frequently lost their way, their lights having been burnt out, and have perished before they could be found. Essais, &c. par M. Macquart. And though the arches of these different stories of galleries are boldly executed, yet they are not dangerous, as they are held together or supported by large masses of timber of a foot square; and these vast timbers remain perfectly sound for many centuries, while all other pillars, whether of brick, cement, or salt, soon dissolve or moulder away. Ibid. Could the timbers over water-mill wheels or cellars be thus preserved by occasionally soaking them with brine? These immense masses of rock-salt seem to have been produced by the evaporation of sea-water in the early periods of the world by subterranean fires. Dr. Hutton's Theory of the Earth. See also Théorie des Sources Salées, par M. Struve. Histoire de Sciences de Lausanne, Tom. II. This idea of Dr. Hutton's is confirmed by a fact mentioned in M. Macquart's Essais sur Mineralogie, who found a great quantity of fossil shells, principally bi-valves and madrepores, in the salt-mines of Wialiczka near Cracow. During the evaporation of the lakes of salt-water, as in artificial salt works, the salt begins to crystallize near the edge where the water is shallowest, forming hollow inverted pyramids; which, when they become of a certain size, subside by their gravity; if urged by a stronger fire the salt fuses or forms large cubes; whence the salt shaped in hollow pyramids, called flake-salt, is better tasted and preserves flesh better, than the basket or powder salt: because it is made by less heat and thence contains more of the marine acid. The sea-water about our island contains from about one twenty-eighth to one thirtieth part of sea salt, and about one eightieth of magnesian salt. See Brownrigg on Salt. See note on Ocymum, Part II. of this work.

Hence orient nitre. l. 143. Nitre is found in Bengal naturally crystallized, and is swept by brooms from earths and stones, and thence called sweepings of nitre. It has lately been found in large quantities in a natural bason of calcareous earth at Molfetta in Italy, both in thin strata between the calcareous beds, and in efflorescences of various beautiful leafy and hairy forms. An account of this nitre-bed is given by Mr. Zimmerman and abridged in Rozier's Journal de Physique, Fevrier, 1790. This acid appears to be produced in all situations where animal and vegetable matters are completely decomposed, and which are exposed to the action of the air, as on the walls of stables, and slaughter-houses; the crystals are prisms furrowed by longitudinal grooves.

Dr. Priestley discovered that nitrous air or gas, which he obtained by dissolving metals in nitrous acid, would combine rapidly with vital air, and produce with it a true nitrous acid; forming red clouds during the combination; the two airs occupy only the space before occupied by one of them, and at the same time heat is given out from the new combination. This diminution of the bulk of a mixture of nitrous gas and vital air, Dr. Priestley ingeniously used as a test of the purity of the latter; a discovery of the greatest importance in the analysis of airs.

Mr. Cavendish has since demonstrated that two parts of vital air or oxygene, and one part of phlogistic air or azote, being long exposed to electric shocks, unite and produce nitrous acid. Philos. Trans. Vols. LXXV. and LXXVIII.

Azote is one of the most abundant elements in nature, and combined with calorique or heat, it forms azotic gas or phlogistic air, and composes two thirds of the atmosphere; and is one of the principal component parts of animal bodies, and when united to vital air or oxygene produces the nitrous acid. Mr. Lavoisier found 21½ parts by weight of azote, and 43½ parts of oxygene produced 64 parts of nitrous gas, and by the further addition of 36 parts of oxygene nitrous acid was produced. Traité de Chimie. When two airs become united so as to produce an unelastic liquid much calorique or heat is of necessity expelled from the new combination, though perhaps nitrous acid and oxygenated marine acid admit more heat into their combinations than other acids.

O'er his broad neck a wiry net he flung,
Quick as he strode, the tinkling meshes rung;
Fine as the spider's flimsy thread he wove
The immortal toil to lime illicit love;   160
Steel were the knots, and steel the twisted thong,
Ring link'd in ring, indissolubly strong;
On viewless hooks along the fretted roof
He hung, unseen, the inextricable woof.—
—Quick start the springs, the webs pellucid spread,
And lock the embracing lovers on their bed;
Fierce with loud taunts vindictive Vulcan springs,
Tries all the bolts, and tightens all the strings,
Shakes with incessant shouts the bright abodes,
Claps his rude hands, and calls the festive gods.—   170
—With spreading palms the alarmed goddess tries
To veil her beauties from celestial eyes,
Writhes her fair limbs, the slender ringlets strains,
And bids her loves untie the obdurate chains;
Soft swells her panting bosom, as she turns,
And her flush'd cheek with brighter blushes burns.
Majestic grief the queen of heaven avows,
And chaste Minerva hides her helmed brows;
Attendant nymphs with bashful eyes askance
Steal of intangled Mars a transient glance;   180
Surrounding gods the circling nectar quaff,
Gaze on the fair, and envy as they laugh.

3. "Hence dusky iron sleeps in dark abodes,
And ferny foliage nestles in the nodes;

Till with wide lungs the panting bellows blow,
And waked by fire the glittering torrents flow;
—Quick whirls the wheel, the ponderous hammer falls,
Loud anvils ring amid the trembling walls,
Strokes follow strokes, the sparkling ingot shines,
Flows the red slag, the lengthening bar refines;
Cold waves, immersed, the glowing mass congeal,   191
And turn to adamant the hissing steel.

" Last Michell's hands with touch of potent charm
The polish'd rods with powers magnetic arm;

Hence dusky iron. l. 183. The production of iron from the decomposition of vegetable bodies is perpetually presented to our view; the waters oozing from all morasses are chalybeate, and deposit their ochre on being exposed to the air, the iron acquiring a calciform state from its union with oxygene or vital air. When thin morasses lie on beds of gravel the latter are generally stained by the filtration of some of the chalybeate water through them. This formation of iron from vegetable recrements is further evinced by the fern leaves and other parts of vegetables, so frequently found in the centre of the knobs or nodules of some iron ores.

In some of these nodules there is a nucleus of whiter iron-earth surrounded by many concentric strata of darker and lighter iron earth alternately. In one, which now lies before me, the nucleus is a prism of a triangular form with blunted angles, and about half an inch high, and an inch and half broad; on every side of this are concentric strata of similar iron earth alternately browner and less brown; each stratum is about a tenth of an inch in thickness, and there are ten of them in number. To what known cause can this exactly regular distribution of so many earthy strata of different colours surrounding the nucleus be ascribed? I don't know that any mineralogists have attempted an explanation of this wonderful phenomenon. I suspect it is owing to the polarity of the central nucleus. If iron-filings be regularly laid on paper by means of a small sieve, and a magnet be placed underneath, the filings will dispose themselves in concentric curves with vacant intervals between them. Now if these iron-filings are conceived to be suspended in a fluid, whose specific gravity is similar to their own, and a magnetic bar was introduced as an axis into this fluid, it is easy to foresee that the iron-filings would dispose themselves into concentric spheres, with intervals of the circumnatant fluid between them, exactly as is seen in these nodules of iron-earth. As all the lavas consist of one fourth of iron, (Kirwan's Mineral.) and almost all other known bodies, whether of animal or vegetable origin, possess more or less of this property, may not the distribution of a great portion of the globe of the earth into strata of greater or less regularity be owing to the polarity of the whole?

And turn to adamant. l. 192. The circumstances which render iron more valuable to mankind than any other metal, are, 1. Its property of being rendered hard to so great a degree, and thus constituting such excellent tools. It was the discovery of this property of iron, Mr. Locke thinks, that gave such pre-eminence to the European world over the American one. 2. Its power of being welded; that is, when two pieces are made very hot and applied together by hammering, they unite completely, unless any scale of iron intervenes; and to prevent this it is usual for smiths to dip the very hot bar in sand, a little of which fuses into fluid glass with the scale, and is squeezed out from between the uniting parts by the force of hammering. 3. Its power of acquiring magnetism.

It is however to be wished that gold or silver were discovered in as great quantity as iron, since these metals being indestructible by exposure to air, water, fire, or any common acids, would supply wholesome vessels for cookery, so much to be desired, and so difficult to obtain, and would form the most light and durable coverings for houses, as well as indestructible firegrates, ovens, and boiling vessels. See additional notes, No. XVIII. on Steel.

Last Michell's hands. l. 193. The discovery of the magnet seems to have been in very early times; it is mentioned by Plato, Lucretius, Pliny, and Galen, and is said to have taken its name of magnes from Magnesia, a sea-port of ancient Lybia.

As every piece of iron which was made magnetical by the touch of a magnet became itself a magnet, many attempts were made to improve these artificial magnets, but without much success till Servingdon Savary, Esq. made them of

With points directed to the polar stars
In one long line extend the temper'd bars;
Then thrice and thrice with steady eye he guides,
And o'er the adhesive train the magnet slides;

---

hardened steel bars, which were so powerful that one of them weighing three pounds averdupois would lift another of the same weight. Philos. Trans.

After this Dr. Knight made very successful experiments on this subject, which though he kept his method secret, seems to have excited others to turn their attention to magnetism. At this time the Rev. Mr. Michell invented an equally efficacious and more expeditious way of making strong artificial magnets, which he published in the end of the year 1750, in which he explained his method of what he called "the double touch," and which, since Dr. Knight's method has been known, appears to be somewhat different from it.

This method of rendering bars of hardened steel magnetical consists in holding vertically two or more magnetic bars nearly parallel to each other with their opposite poles very near each other, (but nevertheless separated to a small distance,) these are to be slided over a line of bars laid horizontally a few times backward and forward. See Michell on Magnetism, also a detailed account in Chambers's Dictionary.

What Mr. Michell proposed by this method was to include a very small portion of the horizontal bars, intended to be made magnetical, between the joint forces of two or more bars already magnetical, and by sliding them from end to end every part of the line of bars became successively included, and thus bars possessed of a very small degree of magnetism to begin with, would in a few times sliding backwards and forwards make the other ones much more magnetical than themselves, which are then to be taken up and used to touch the former, which are in succession to be laid down horizontally in a line.

There is still a great field remains for future discoveries in magnetism both in respect to experiment and theory; the latter consists of vague conjectures the more probable of which are perhaps those of Epinus, as they assimilate it to electricity.

One conjecture I shall add, viz. that the polarity of magnetism may be owing to the earth's rotatory motion. If heat, electricity, and magnetism are supposed to be fluids of different gravities, heat being the heaviest of them, electricity the next heavy, and magnetism the lightest, it is evident that by the quick revolution of the earth the heat will be accumulated most over the line, electricity next beneath this, and that the magnetism will be detruded to the poles and axis of the earth, like the atmosphere of common air and of inflammable gas, as explained in the note on Canto I. l. 123.

Electricity and heat will both of them displace magnetism, and this shows that they may gravitate on each other; and hence when too great a quantity of the electric fluid becomes accumulated at the poles by descending snows, or other unknown causes, it may have a tendency to rise towards the tropics by its centrifugal force, and produce the northern lights. See additional notes, No I.

The obedient steel with living instinct moves,
And veers for ever to the pole it loves.   200

" Hail, adamantine steel! magnetic lord!
King of the prow, the plowshare, and the sword!
True to the pole, by thee the pilot guides
His steady helm amid the struggling tides,
Braves with broad sail the immeasurable sea,
Cleaves the dark air, and asks no star but thee.—
By thee the plowshare rends the matted plain,
Inhumes in level rows the living grain;
Intrusive forests quit the cultured ground,   209
And Ceres laughs with golden fillets crown'd.
O'er restless realms when scowling discord flings
Her snakes, and loud the din of battle rings;
Expiring strength, and vanquish'd courage feel
Thy arm resistless, adamantine steel!

4. " Hence in fine streams diffusive acid flow,
Or wing'd with fire o'er earth's fair bosom blow;
Transmute to glittering flints her chalky lands,
Or sink on ocean's bed in countless sands.
Hence silvery selenite her crystal moulds,
And soft asbestos smooths his silky folds;   220
His cubic forms phosphoric fluor prints,
Or rays in spheres his amethystine tints.
Soft cobweb clouds transparent onyx spreads,
And playful agates weave their colour'd threads;
Gay pictured mochoes glow with landscape-dyes,
And changeful opals roll their lucid eyes;

Diffusive acids flow. l. 215. The production of marine acid from decomposing vegetable and animal matters with vital air, and of nitrous acid from azote and vital air, the former of which is united to its basis by means of the exhalations from vegetable and animal matters, constitute an analogy which induces us to believe that many other acids have either their bases or are united to vital air by means of some part of decomposing vegetable and animal matters.

The great quantities of flint sand, whether formed in mountains or in the sea, would appear to derive its acid from the new world, as it is found above the strata of lime-stone and granite which constitute the old world, and as the earthy basis of flint is probably calcareous, a great part of it seems to be produced by a conjunction of the new and old world; the recrements of air breathing animals and vegetables probably afford the acid, and the shells of marine animals the earthy basis, while another part may have derived its calcareous part also from the decomposition of vegetable and animal bodies.

The same mode of reasoning seems applicable to the siliceous stones under various names, as amethyst, onyx, agate, mochoe, opal, &c. which do not seem to have undergone any process from volcanic fires, and as these stones only differ from flint by a greater or less admixture of argillaceous and calcareous earths. The different proportions of which in each kind of stone may be seen in Mr. Kirwan's valuable Elements of Mineralogy. See additional notes, No. XIX.

Blue lambent light around the sapphire plays,
Bright rubies blush, and living diamonds blaze.

"Thus, for attractive earth, inconstant Jove
Mask'd in new shapes forsook his realms above.—
First her sweet eyes his eagle form beguiles, 231
And Hebe feeds him with ambrosial smiles;
Next the changed god a cygnet's down assumes,
And playful Leda smooths his glossy plumes;
Then glides a silver serpent, treacherous guest!
And fair Olympia folds him in her breast;
Now lows a milk-white bull on Afric's strand,
And crops with dancing head the daisy'd land.—
With rosy wreaths Europa's hand adorns
His fringed forehead, and his pearly horns; 240
Light on his back the sportive damsel bounds,
And pleased he moves along the flowery grounds;
Bears with slow step his beauteous prize aloof,
Dips in the lucid flood his ivory hoof;

Then wets his velvet knees, and wading laves
His silky sides amid the dimpling waves.
While her fond train with beckoning hands
  deplore,
Strain their blue eyes, and shriek along the shore;
Beneath her robe she draws her snowy feet,
And half-reclining on her ermine seat, 250
Round his raised neck her radiant arms she
  throws,
And rests her fair cheek on his curled brows;
Her yellow tresses wave on wanton gales,
And bent in air her azure mantle sails.
—Onward he moves, applauding Cupids guide,
And skim on shooting wing the shining tide;
Emerging Tritons leave their coral caves,
Sound their loud conchs, and smooth the circling waves,
Surround the timorous beauty, as she swims,
And gaze enamour'd on her silver limbs. 260
Now Europe's shadowy shores with loud acclaim,
Hail the fair fugitive, and shout her name;
Soft echoes warble, whispering forests nod,
And conscious nature owns the present God.
Changed from the bull, the rapturous god assumes
Immortal youth, with glow celestial blooms,
With lenient words her virgin fears disarms,
And clasps the yielding beauty in his arms;
Whence kings and heroes own illustrious birth,
Guards of mankind and demigods on earth. 270

VI. "Gnomes! as you pass'd beneath the labouring soil,
The guards and guides of nature's chemic toil,
You saw, deep-sepulchred in dusky realms,
Which earth's rock-ribbed ponderous vault o'erwhelms,
With self-born fires the mass fermenting glow,
And flame-wing'd sulphurs quit the earths below.

1. "Hence ductile clays in wide expansion spread,
Soft as the cygnet's down, their snow-white bed;
With yielding flakes successive forms reveal,
And change obedient to the whirling wheel. 280

Living diamonds blaze. l. 228. Sir Isaac Newton having observed the great power of refracting light, which the diamond possesses above all other crystallized or vitreous matter, conjectured that it was an inflammable body in some manner congealed. Insomuch that all the light is reflected which falls on any of its interior surfaces at a greater angle of incidence than 24½ degrees; whereas an artificial gem of glass does not reflect any light from its hinder surface, unless that surface is inclined in an angle of 41 deg. Hence the diamond reflects half as much more light as a factitious gem in similar circumstances; to which must be added its great transparency, and the excellent polish it is capable of. The diamond had nevertheless been placed at the head of crystals or precious stones by the mineralogists, till Bergman ranged it of late in the combustible class of bodies, because by the focus of Villette's burning mirror it was evaporated by a heat not much greater than will melt silver, and gave out light. Mr. Hoepfner however thinks the dispersion of the diamond by this great heat should be called a phosphorescent evaporation of it, rather than a combustion; and from its other analogies of crystallization, hardness, transparency, and place of its nativity, wishes again to replace it amongst the precious stones. Observ. sur la Physique, par Rozier, Tom. XXXV. p. 448. See new edition of the Translation of Cronsted, by De Costa.

Inconstant Jove. l. 229. The purer air or ether in the ancient mythology was represented by Jupiter, and the inferior air by Juno; and the conjunction of these deities was said to produce the vernal showers, and procreate all things, as is further spoken of in Canto III. l. 204. It is now discovered that pure air, or oxygene, uniting with variety of bases, forms the various kinds of acids; as the vitriolic acid from pure air and sulphur; the nitrous acid from pure air and phlogistic air, or azote; and carbonic acid, (or fixed air,) from pure air and charcoal. Some of these affinities were perhaps portrayed by the Magi of Egypt, who were probably learned in chemistry, in their hieroglyphic pictures before the invention of letters by the loves of Jupiter with terrestrial ladies. And thus physically as well as metaphysically might be said "Jovis omnia plena."

With self-born fires. l. 275. After the accumulation of plains and mountains on the calcareous rocks or granite which had been previously raised by volcanic fires, a second set of volcanic fires were produced by the fermentation of this new mass, which after the salts or acids and iron had been washed away in part by elutriation, dissipated the sulphurous parts which were insoluble in water; whence argillaceous and siliceous earths were left in some places; in others, bitumen became sublimed to the upper part of the stratum, producing coals of various degrees of purity.

Hence ductile clays. l. 277. See additional notes, No. XX.

First China's sons, with early art elate,
Form'd the gay tea-pot, and the pictured plate;
Saw with illumined brow and dazzled eyes
In the red stove vitrescent colours rise;
Speck'd her tall beakers with enamel'd stars,
Her monster-josses, and gigantic jars;
Smear'd her huge dragons with metallic hues,
With golden purples, and cobaltic blues;
Bade on wide hills her porcelain castles glare,
And glazed pagodas tremble in the air.   290

"Etruria! next beneath thy magic hands
Glides the quick wheel, the plastic clay expands,
Nerved with fine touch, thy fingers (as it turns)
Mark the nice bounds of vases, ewers, and urns;
Round each fair form in lines immortal trace
Uncopied beauty, and ideal grace.

"Gnomes! as you now dissect with hammers fine
The granite-rock, the nodul'd flint calcine;
Grind with strong arm the circling chertz betwixt,
Your pure Ka-o-lins and Pe-tun-tses mixt;   300
O'er each red saggar's burning cave preside,
The keen-eyed fire-nymphs blazing by your side; [smile,
And pleased on Wedgwood ray your partial
A new Etruria decks Britannia's isle.—

Saw with illumined brow. l. 283. No colour is distinguishable in the red-hot kiln but the red itself, till the workman introduces a small piece of dry wood, which by producing a white flame renders all the other colours visible in a moment.

With golden purples. l. 288. See additional notes, No. XXI.

Etruria! next. l. 291. Etruria may perhaps vie with China itself in the antiquity of its arts. The times of its greatest splendour were prior to the foundation of Rome, and the reign of one of its best princes, Janus, was the oldest epoch the Romans knew. The earliest historians speak of the Etruscans as being then of high antiquity, most probably a colony from Phœnicia, to which a Pelasgian colony acceded, and was united soon after Deucalion's flood. The peculiar character of their earthen vases consists in the admirable beauty, simplicity, and diversity of forms, which continue the best models of taste to the artists of the present times; and in a species of non-vitreous encaustic painting, which was reckoned, even in the time of Pliny, among the lost arts of antiquity, but which has lately been recovered by the ingenuity and industry of Mr. Wedgwood. It is supposed that the principal manufactories were about Nola, at the foot of Vesuvius; for it is in that neighbourhood that the greatest quantities of antique vases have been found; and it is said that the general taste of the inhabitants is apparently influenced by them; insomuch that strangers coming to Naples, are commonly struck with the diversity and elegance even of the most ordinary vases for common uses. See D'Huncarville's preliminary discourses to the magnificent collection of Etruscan vases, published by Sir William Hamilton.

Charm'd by your touch, the flint liquescent pours,
Through finer sieves, and falls in whiter showers;
Charm'd by your touch, the kneaded clay refines,
The biscuit hardens, the enamel shines;
Each nicer mould a softer feature drinks,   309
The bold Cameo speaks, the soft Intaglio thinks.

"To call the pearly drops from Pity's eye,
Or stay Despair's disanimating sigh,
Whether, O friend of art! the gem you mould
Rich with new taste, with ancient virtue bold;
Form the poor fetter'd slave on bended knee
From Britain's sons imploring to be free;
Or with fair Hope the brightening scenes improve,
And cheer the dreary wastes at Sydney-cove;
Or bid Mortality rejoice and mourn   319
O'er the fine forms on Portland's mystic urn.—

"*Here*, by fallen columns and disjoin'd arcades,
On mouldering stones, beneath deciduous shades,
Sits humankind in hieroglyphic state,
Serious, and pondering on their changeful state;
While with inverted torch and swimming eyes,
Sinks the fair shade of mortal life, and dies.
There the pale ghost through death's wide portal bends
His timid feet, the dusky steep descends:
With smiles assuasive Love Divine invites,
Guides on broad wing, with torch uplifted lights;   330
Immortal Life, her hand extending, courts
The lingering form, his tottering step supports;
Leads on to Pluto's realms the dreary way,
And gives him trembling to elysian day.
Beneath, in sacred robes the priestess dress'd,
The coif close-hooded, and the fluttering vest,
With pointing finger guides the initiate youth,
Unweaves the many-colour'd veil of truth,
Drives the profane from mystery's bolted door,
And silence guards the Eleusinian lore.—   340

From the poor fetter'd slave. l. 315. Alluding to two cameos of Mr. Wedgwood's manufacture; one of a slave in chains, of which he distributed many hundreds, to excite the humane to attend to and to assist in the abolition of the detestable traffic in human creatures; and the other a cameo of Hope attended by Peace, and Art, and Labour; which was made of clay from Botany Bay, to which place he sent many of them to show the inhabitants what their materials would do, and to encourage their industry. A print of this latter medallion is prefixed to Mr. Stockdale's edition of Philip's Expedition to Botany Bay, with some verses which are inserted at the end of the additional notes.

Portland's mystic urn. l. 320. See additional notes, No. XXII.

"Whether, O friend of art! your gems derive
Fine forms from Greece, and fabled gods revive;
Or bid from modern life the portrait breathe,
And bind round honour's brow the laurel wreath;
Buoyant shall sail, with fame's historic page,
Each fair medallion o'er the wrecks of age;
Nor time shall mar; nor steel, nor fire, nor rust
Touch the hard polish of the immortal bust.

"Hence sable coal his massy couch extends,
And stars of gold the sparkling pyrite blends;
Hence dull-eyed naphtha pours his pitchy streams,   351
And jet uncolour'd drinks the solar beams,
Bright amber shines on his electric throne,
And adds ethereal lustres to his own.
—Led by the phosphor-light, with daring tread
Immortal Franklin sought the fiery bed;
Where, nursed in night, incumbent tempest shrouds
His embryon thunders in circumfluent clouds,
Besieged with iron points their airy cell,
And pierced the monsters slumbering in the shell.   360

"So, borne on sounding pinions to the west,
When tyrant-power had built his eagle nest;
While from his eyry shriek'd the famish'd brood,
Clench'd their sharp claws, and champ'd their beaks for blood,

Immortal Franklin watch'd the callow crew,
And stabb'd the struggling vampires, ere they flew.
—The patriot-flame with quick contagion ran,
Hill lighted hill, and man electrised man;
Her heroes slain awhile Columbia mourn'd,
And crown'd with laurels Liberty return'd.   370

"The warrior, Liberty, with bending sails
Helm'd his bold course to fair Hibernia's vales;
—Firm as he steps along the shouting lands,
Lo! Truth and Virtue range their radiant bands;
Sad Superstition wails her empire torn,
Art plies his oar, and Commerce pours her horn.

"Long had the giant-form on Gallia's plains
Inglorious slept, unconscious of his chains;
Round his large limbs were wound a thousand strings
By the weak hands of confessors and kings;   380
O'er his closed eyes a triple veil was bound,
And steely rivets lock'd him to the ground;
While stern Bastile with iron-cage inthralls
His folded limbs, and hems in marble walls.
—Touch'd by the patriot-flame, he rent amazed
The flimsy bonds, and round and round him gazed;
Starts up from earth, above the admiring throng
Lifts his colossal form, and towers along;
High o'er his foes his hundred arms he rears,
Plowshares his swords, and pruning hooks his spears;   390
Calls to the good and brave with voice, that rolls
Like heaven's own thunder round the echoing poles;
Gives to the winds his banner broad unfurl'd,
And gathers in its shade the living world!

VII. "Gnomes! you then taught volcanic airs to force
Through bubbling lavas their resistless course,

Fine forms from Greece. l. 342. In real stones or in paste or soft coloured glass, many pieces of exquisite workmanship were produced by the ancients. Basso-relievos of various sizes were made in coarse brown earth of one colour; but of the improved kind of two or more colours, and of a true porcelain texture, none were made by the ancients, nor attempted, I believe, by the moderns, before those of Mr. Wedgwood's manufactory.

Hence sable coal. l. 349. See additional notes, No. XXIII. on coal.

Bright amber shines. l. 353. Coal has probably all been sublimed more or less from the clay, with which it was at first formed in decomposing morasses; the petroleum seems to have been separated and condensed again in superior strata, and a still finer kind of oil, as naphtha, has probably had the same origin. Some of these liquid oils have again lost their more volatile parts, and become cannel-coal, asphaltum, jet, and amber, according to the purity of the original fossil oil. Dr. Priestley has shown, that essential oils long exposed to the atmosphere absorb both the vital and phlogistic part of it; whence it is probable their becoming solid may in great measure depend, as well as by the exhalation of their more volatile parts. On distillation with volatile alcali all these fossil oils are shown to contain the acid of amber, which evinces the identity of their origin. If a piece of amber be rubbed it attracts straws and hairs, whence the discovery of electricity, and whence its name, from electron the Greek word for amber.

Immortal Franklin. l. 356. See note on Canto I. l. 383.

While stern Bastile. l. 383. "We descended with great difficulty into the dungeons, which were made too low for our standing upright; and were so dark that we were obliged at noon-day to visit them by the light of a candle. We saw the hooks of those chains, by which the prisoners were fastened by their necks to the walls of their cells; many of which being below the level of the water were in a constant state of humidity; from which issued a noxious vapour, which more than once extinguished the candles. Since the destruction of the building many subterraneous cells have been discovered under a piece of ground, which seemed only a bank of solid earth before the horrid secrets of this prison-house were disclosed. Some skeletons were found in these recesses with irons still fastened to their decayed bones." Letters from France, by H. M. Williams, p. 24.

O'er the broad walls of rifted granite climb,
And pierce the rent roof of incumbent lime,
Round sparry caves metallic lustres fling,
And bear phlogiston on their tepid wing.   400

" Hence glow, refulgent tin! thy crystal grains,
And tawny copper shoots her azure veins;
Zinc lines his fretted vault, with sable ore,
And dull galena tessellates the floor;
On vermil beds in Idria's mighty caves
The living silver rolls its ponderous waves;
With gay refractions bright platina shines,
And studs with squander'd stars his dusky mines;
Long threads of netted gold, and silvery darts,
Inlay the lazuli, and pierce the quartz;—   410
—Whence roof'd with silver beam'd Peru, of old,
And hapless Mexico was paved with gold.

" Heavens! on my sight what sanguine colours blaze!
Spain's deathless shame! the crimes of modern days!

When avarice, shrouded in religion's robe,
Sail'd to the west, and slaughter'd half the globe;
While superstition, stalking by his side,
Mock'd the loud groan, and lap'd the bloody tide;
For sacred truths announced her frenzied dreams,
And turn'd to night the sun's meridian beams.—
Hear, oh, Britannia! potent queen of isles, 421
On whom fair art, and meek religion smiles,
Now Afric's coasts thy craftier sons invade,
And theft and murder take the garb of trade!
—The slave, in chains, on supplicating knee,
Spreads his wide arms, and lifts his eyes to thee;
With hunger pale, with wounds and toil oppress'd,   rest;
' Are we not brethren?' sorrow chokes the
—Air! bear to heaven upon thy azure flood
Their innocent cries!—Earth! cover not their blood!   430

VIII. " When heaven's dread justice smites in crimes o'ergrown
The blood-nursed tyrant on his purple throne.

And pierce the rent roof. l. 398. The granite rocks and the limestone rocks have been cracked to very great depths at the time they were raised up by subterranean fires; in these cracks are found most of the metallic ores, except iron and perhaps manganese, the former of which is generally found in horizontal strata, and the latter generally near the surface of the earth.

Philosophers possessing so convenient a test for the discovery of iron by the magnet, have long since found it in all vegetable and animal matters; and of late Mr. Scheele has discovered the existence of manganese in vegetable ashes. Scheele, 56 mem. Stock. 1774. Kirwan. Min. 353. Which accounts for the production of it near the surface of the earth, and thence for its calciform appearance, or union with vital air. Bergman has likewise shown, that the limestones which become bluish or dark coloured when calcined, possess a mixture of manganese, and are thence preferable as a cement to other kinds of lime. 2 Bergman, 229. Which impregnation with manganese had probably been received from the decomposition of superincumbent vegetable matters.

These cracks or perpendicular caverns in the granite or limestone pass to unknown depths; and it is up these channels that I have endeavoured to show that the steam rises which becomes afterwards condensed, and produces the warm springs of this island and other parts of the world. (See note on Fucus, vol. II.) And up these cracks I suppose certain vapours arise, which either alone, or by meeting with something descending into them from above, have produced most of the metals; and several of the materials in which they are bedded. Thus the ponderous earth, Barytes, of Derbyshire, is found in these cracks, and is stratified frequently with lead ore, and frequently surrounds it. This ponderous earth has been found by Dr. Hoepfner in a granite in Switzerland, and may have thus been sublimed from immense depths by great heat, and have obtained its carbonic or vitriolic acid from above. Annales de Chimie. There is also reason to conclude that something from above is necessary to the formation of many of the metals: at Hawkestone in Shropshire, the seat of Sir Richard Hill, there is an elevated rock of siliceous sand which is coloured green with copper in many places high in the air; and I have in my possession a specimen of lead formed in the cavity of an iron nodule, and another of lead amid spar from a crack of a coal-stratum; all which countenance the modern production of those metals from descending materials. To which should be added, that the highest mountains of granite, which have therefore probably never been covered with marine productions on account of their early elevation, nor with vegetable or animal matters on account of their great coldness, contain no metallic ores, whilst the lower ones contain copper and tin in their cracks or veins, both in Saxony, Silesia, and Cornwall. Kirwan's Mineral. p. 374.

The transmutation of one metal into another, though hitherto undiscovered by the alchymists, does not appear impossible; such transmutations have been supposed to exist in nature, thus lapsis calaminaris may have been produced from the destruction of lead-ore, as it is generally found on the top of the veins of lead, where it has been calcined or united with air, and because masses of lead-ore are often found entirely inclosed in it. So silver is found mixed in almost all lead-ores, and sometimes in separate filaments within the cavities of lead-ore, as I am informed by Mr. Michell, and is thence probably a partial transmutation of the lead to silver, the rapid progress of modern chemistry having shown the analogy between metallic calces and acids, may lead to the power of transmuting their bases: a discovery much to be wished.

Gnomes! your bold forms unnumber'd arms
    outstretch,
And urge the vengeance o'er the guilty wretch.
Thus when Cambyses led his barbarous hosts
From Persia's rocks to Egypt's trembling coasts,
Defiled each hallow'd fane, and sacred wood,
And, drunk with fury, swell'd the Nile with
    blood;
Waved his proud banner o'er the Theban states,
And pour'd destruction through her hundred
    gates;   440
In dread divisions march'd the marshal'd bands,
And swarming armies blackened all the lands,
By Memphis these to Ethiop's sultry plains,
And those to Hammon's sand-incircled fanes.
Slow as they pass'd the indignant temples
    frown'd,
Low curses muttering from the vaulted ground;
Long ailes of cypress waved their deepen'd
    glooms,   [tombs;
And quivering spectres grinn'd amid the
Prophetic whispers breathed from Sphinx's
    tongue,   449
And Memnon's lyre with hollow murmurs rung;
Burst from each pyramid expiring groans,
And darker shadows stretch'd their lengthen'd
    cones,
Day after day their deathful rout they steer,
Lust in the van, and rapine in the rear.

" Gnomes! as they march'd, you hid the
    gather'd fruits,
The bladed grass, sweet grains, and mealy roots;
Scared the tired quails, that journey o'er their
    heads,
Retain'd the locusts in their earthy beds;
Bade on your sands no night-born dews distil,
Stay'd with vindictive hands the scanty rill. 460
Loud o'er the camp the fiend of famine shrieks,
Calls all her brood, and champs her hundred
    beaks;

O'er ten square leagues her pennons broad ex-
    pand,
And twilight swims upon the shuddering sand;
Perch'd on her crest the griffin discord clings,
And giant murder rides between her wings;
Blood from each clotted hair, and horney quill,
And showers of tears in blended streams distil;
High poised in air her spiry neck she bends, 469
Rolls her keen eye, her dragon-claws extends,
Darts from above, and tears at each fell swoop
With iron fangs the decimated troop.

" Now o'er their head the whizzing whirl-
    winds breathe,
And the live desert pants, and heaves beneath;
Tinged by the crimson sun, vast columns rise
Of eddying sands, and war amid the skies,
In red arcades the billowy plain surround,
And whirling turrets stalk along the ground.

Thus when Cambyses. l. 435. Cambyses march-
ed one army from Thebes, after having overturned the temples, ravaged the country, and
deluged it with blood, to subdue Ethiopia; this
army almost perished by famine, insomuch,
that they repeatedly slew every tenth man to
supply the remainder with food. He sent
another army to plunder the temple of Jupiter
Ammon, which perished, overwhelm'd with
sand.

Expiring groans. l. 451. Mr. Savery or Mr.
Volney, in his travels through Egypt, has given
a curious description of one of the pyramids,
with the operose method of closing them, and
immuring the body, (as they supposed,) for six
thousand years. And has endeavoured from
thence to show, that, when a monarch died,
several of his favourite courtiers were inclosed
alive with the mummy in these great masses of
stone-work; and had food and water conveyed
to them, as long as they lived, proper apertures
being left for this purpose, and for the admission
of air, and for the exclusion of any thing offensive.

And whirling turrets. l. 478. " At one o'clock
we alighted among some acacia trees at Waadi el
Halboub, having gone twenty-one miles. We
were here at once surprised and terrified by a
sight surely one of the most magnificent in the
world. In that vast expanse of desert, from
W. to N. W. of us, we saw a number of prodigious pillars of sand at different distances, at
times moving with great celerity, at others
stalking on with a majestic slowness; at intervals we thought they were coming in a very few
minutes to overwhelm us; and small quantities
of sand did actually more than once reach us.
Again they would retreat so as to be almost out
of sight, their tops reaching to the very clouds.
There the tops often separated from the bodies;
and these, once disjoined, dispersed in the air,
and did not appear more. Sometimes they were
broken in the middle, as if struck with large
canon-shot. About noon they began to advance
with considerable swiftness upon us, the wind
being very strong at north. Eleven of them
ranged along side of us about the distance of
three miles. The greatest diameter of the largest appeared to me at that distance as if it would
measure ten feet. They retired from us with a
wind at S. E. leaving an impression upon my
mind to which I can give no name, though
surely one ingredient in it was fear, with a considerable deal of wonder and astonishment. It
was in vain to think of flying; the swiftest
horse, or fastest sailing ship, could be of no use
to carry us out of this danger; and the full per-
suasion of this riveted me as if to the spot where
I stood.

" The same appearance of moving pillars of
sand presented themselves to us this day in form
and disposition like those we had seen at Waad
Halboub, only they seemed to be more in number and less in size. They came several times
in a direction close upon us, that is, I believe,
within less than two miles. They began immediately after sun rise, like a thick wood and almost darkened the sun. His rays shining
through them for near an hour, gave them an
appearance of pillars of fire. Our people now
became desperate, the Greeks shrieked and
said it was the day of judgment; Ismael pronounced it to be hell; and the Turcorories, that
the world was on fire." Bruce's Travels, Vol.
IV. p. 553—555.

—Long ranks in vain their shining blades
    extend,
To demon-gods their knees unhallow'd bend. 480
Wheel in wide circle, form in hollow square,
And now they front, and now they fly the war,
Pierce the deaf tempest with lamenting cries,
Press their parch'd lips, and close their blood-
    shot eyes.   [powers,
—Gnomes! o'er the waste you led your myriad
Climb'd on the whirls, and aim'd the flinty
    showers!
Onward resistless rolls the infuriate surge,
Clouds follow clouds, and mountains mountains
    urge;
Wave over wave the driving desert swims,
Bursts o'er their heads, inhumes their struggling
    limbs;   490
Man mounts on man, on camels camels rush,
Hosts march o'er hosts, and nations nations
    crush,—
Wheeling in air the winged islands fall,
And one great earthy ocean covers all !—
Then ceased the storm,— Night bow'd his
    Ethiop brow
To earth, and listen'd to the groans below,—
Grim horror shook,—awhile the living hill
Heaved with convulsive throes,—and all was
    still!

IX   " Gnomes! whose fine forms, impassive
    as the air,
Shrink with soft sympathy for human care; 500
Who glide unseen, on printless slippers borne,
Beneath the waving grass, and nodding corn ;
Or lay your tiny limbs, when noon-tide warms,
Where shadowy cowslips stretch their golden
    arms,—
So, mark'd on orreries in lucid signs,
Starr'd with bright points the mimic zodiac
    shines;
Borne on fine wires amid the pictured skies
With ivory orbs the planets set and rise;
Round the dwarf earth the pearly moon is roll'd,
And the sun twinkling whirls his rays of
    gold.   510
Call your bright myriads, march your mailed
    hosts,   [coasts;
With spears and helmets glittering round the
Thick as the hairs, which rear the lion's mane,
Or fringe the boar, that bays the hunter-train;
Watch, where proud surges break their treache-
    rous mounds,
And sweep resistless o'er the cultur'd grounds;
Such as ere while, impell'd o'er Belgia's plain,
Roll'd her rich ruins to the insatiate main;
With piles and piers the ruffian waves engage,
And bid indignant ocean stay his rage.   520

" Where, girt with clouds, the rifted moun-
    tain yawns,
And chills with length of shade the gelid lawns,
Climb the rude steeps, the granite-cliffs surround,
Pierce with steel points, with wooden wedges
    wound;
Break into clays the soft volcanic slags,
Or melt with acid airs the marble crags;
Crown the green summits with adventurous
    flocks,   [rocks.
And charm with novel flowers the wondering
—So when proud Rome the Afric warrior
    braved,
And high on Alps his crimson banner waved; 530
While rocks on rocks their beetling brows op-
    pose
With piny forests, and unfathom'd snows;
Onward he march'd, to Latium's velvet ground
With fires and acids burst the obdurate bound,

From this account it would appear, that the eddies of wind were owing to the long range of broken rocks, which bounded one side of the sandy desert, and bent the currents of air, which struck against their sides; and were thus like the eddies in a stream of water, which falls against oblique obstacles. This explanation is probably the true one, as these whirlwinds were not attended with rain or lightning like the tornadoes of the West Indies.

So mark'd on orreries. l. 505. The first orrery was constructed by a Mr. Rowley, a mathematician born at Litchfield; and so named from his patron the Earl of Orrery. Johnson's Dictionary.

The granite-cliffs. l. 523. On long exposure to air the granites or porphories of this country exhibit a ferruginous crust, the iron being calcined by the air first becomes visible, and is then washed away from the external surface, which becomes white or gray, and thus in time seems to decompose. The marbles seem to decompose by losing their carbonic acid, as the outside, which has been long exposed to the air, does not seem to effervesce so hastily with acids as the parts more recently broken. The immense quantity of carbonic acid, which exists in the many provinces of lime-stone, if it was extricated and decomposed, would afford charcoal enough for fuel for ages, or for the production of new vegetable or animal bodies. The volcanic slags on Mount Vesuvius are said by M. Ferber to be changed into clay by means of the sulphur-acid, and even pots made of clay and burnt or vitrified are said by him to be again reducible to ductile clay by the volcanic steams. Ferber's Travels through Italy, p. 166. See additional notes, No. XXIV.

Wooden wedges wound. l. 524. It is usual in separating large mill-stones from the siliceous sand-rocks in some parts of Derbyshire to bore horizontal holes under them in a circle, and fill these with pegs made of dry wood, which gradually swell by the moisture of the earth, and in a day or two lift up the mill-stone without breaking it.

With fires and acids. l. 534. Hannibal was said to erode his way over the Alps by fire and vinegar. The latter is supposed to allude to the vinegar and water which was the beverage of his army. In respect to the former it is not improbable, but where wood was to be had in great abundance, that fires made round lime-stone

Wide o'er the weeping vales destruction hurl'd,
And shook the rising empire of the world.

X. " Go, gentle Gnomes! resume your vernal toil,
Seek my chill tribes, which sleep beneath the soil; [lands
On gray-moss banks, green meads, or furrow'd
Spread the dark mould, white lime, and crumbling sands; 540
Each bursting bud with healthier juices feed,
Emerging scion, or awakened seed.
So, in descending streams, the silver chyle
Streaks with white clouds the golden floods of bile;
Through each nice valve the mingling currents glide,
Join their fine rills, and swell the sanguine tide;
Each countless cell, and viewless fibre seek,
Nerve the strong arm, and tinge the blushing cheek.

" Oh, watch, where bosom'd in the teeming earth, 549
Green swells the germ, impatient for its birth;
Guard from rapacious worms its tender shoots,
And drive the mining beetle from its roots;
With ceaseless efforts rend the obdurate clay,
And give my vegetable babes to day!
—Thus when an angel-form, in light array'd,
Like Howard pierced the prison's noisome shade;
Where chain'd to earth, with eyes to heaven upturn'd,
The kneeling saint in holy anguish mourn'd;—
Ray'd from his lucid vest, and halo'd brow
O'er the dark roof celestial lustres glow, 560
' Peter, arise!' with cheering voice he calls,
And sounds seraphic echo round the walls;
Locks, bolts, and chains his potent touch obey,
And pleased he leads the exulting sage to day.

XI. " You! whose fine fingers fill the organic cells,
With virgin earth, of woods and bones and shells;
Mould with retractile glue their spongy beds,
And stretch and strengthen all their fibrethreads.—

Late when the mass obeys its changeful doom,
And sinks to earth, its cradle and its tomb, 570
Gnomes! with nice eye the slow solution watch,
With fostering hand the parting atoms catch,
Join in new forms, combine with life and sense
And guide and guard the transmigrating Ens.

" So when on Lebanon's sequester'd height
The fair Adonis left the realms of light,

---

precipices would calcine them to a considerable depth, the night-dews or mountain-mists would penetrate these calcined parts and pulverize them by the force of the steam which the generated heat would produce, the winds would disperse this lime-powder, and thus by repeated fires a precipice of lime-stone might be destroyed and a passage opened. It should be added, that according to Ferber's observations, these Alps consist of lime-stone. Letters from Italy.

Mould with retractile glue. l. 567. The constituent parts of animal fibres are believed to be earth and gluten. These do not separate except by long putrefaction or by fire. The earth then effervesces with acids, and can only be converted into glass by the greatest force of fire. The gluten has continued united with the earth of the bones above 2000 years in Egyptian mummies; but by long exposure to air or moisture it dissolves and leaves only the earth. Hence bones long buried, when exposed to the air, absorb moisture and crumble into powder. Phil. Trans. No. 475. The retractibility or elasticity of the animal fibre depends on the gluten; and of these fibres are composed the membranes, muscles, and bones. Haller. Physiol. Tom. 1. p. 2.

For the chemical decomposition of animal and vegetable bodies see the ingenious work of Lavoisier, Traité de Chimie, Tom I. p. 132. who resolves all their component parts into oxygene, hydrogene, carbone, and azote, the three former of which belong principally to vegetable, and the last to animal matter.

The transmigrating Ens. l. 574. The perpetual circulation of matter in the growth and dissolution of vegetable and animal bodies seems to have given Pythagoras his idea of the metempsycosis or transmigration of spirit; which was afterwards dressed out or ridiculed in variety of amusing fables. Other philosophers have supposed, that there are two different materials or essences, which fill the universe. One of these, which has the power of commencing or producing motion, is called spirit; the other, which has the power of receiving and of communicating motion, but not of beginning it, is called matter. The former of these is supposed to be diffused through all space, filling up the interstices of the suns and planets, and constituting the gravitations of the sidereal bodies, the attractions of chemistry, with the spirit of vegetation, and of animation. The latter occupies comparatively but small space, constituting the solid parts of the suns and planets, and their atmospheres. Hence these philosophers have supposed, that both matter and spirit are equally immortal and unperishable; and that on the dissolution of vegetable or animal organization, the matter returns to the general mass of matter; and the spirit to the general mass of spirit, to enter again into new combinations, according to the original idea of Pythagoras.

The small apparent quantity of matter that exists in the universe compared to that of spirit, and the short time in which the recrements of animal or vegetable bodies become again vivified in the forms of vegetable mucor or microscopic insects, seems to have given rise to another curious fable of antiquity. That Jupiter threw down a large handful of souls upon the earth, and left them to scramble for the few bodies which were to be had.

Adonis. l. 576. The very ancient story of the beautiful Adonis passing one half of the year with Venus, and the other with Proserpine alternately, has had variety of interpretations. Some have supposed that it allegorized the summer and winter solstice; but this seems too

Bow'd his bright locks, and, fated from his birth,
To change eternal, mingled with the earth;—
With darker horror shook the conscious wood,
Groan'd the sad gales, and rivers blush'd with blood; 580
On cypress-boughs the loves their quivers hung,
Their arrows scatter'd and their bows unstrung;
And beauty's goddess, bending o'er his bier,
Breathed the soft sigh, and pour'd the tender tear.—
Admiring Proserpine through dusky glades
Led the fair phantom to Elysian shades,
Clad with new form, with finer sense combined,
And lit with purer flame the ethereal mind.
—Erewhile, emerging from infernal night,
The bright assurgent rises into light, 590
Leaves the drear chambers of the insatiate tomb,
And shines and charms with renovated bloom.—
While wondering loves the bursting grave surround,
And edge with meeting wings the yawning ground,
Stretch their fair necks, and leaning o'er the brink
View the pale regions of the dead, and shrink;
Long with broad eyes ecstatic beauty stands,
Heaves her white bosom, spreads her waxen hands;
Then with loud shriek the panting youth alarms,
' My life! my love!' and springs into his arms." 600

The goddess ceased,—the delegated throng
O'er the wide plains delighted rush along;
In dusky squadrons, and in shining groups,
Hosts follow hosts, and troops succeed to troops;
Scarce bears the bending grass the moving freight,
And nodding florets bow beneath their weight.
So when light clouds on airy pinions sail,
Flit the soft shadows o'er the waving vale;
Shade follows shade, as laughing zephyrs drive,
And all the chequer'd landscape seems alive. 610

---

obvious a fact to have needed an hieroglyphic emblem. Others have believed it to represent the corn, which was supposed to sleep in the earth during the winter months, and to rise out of it in summer. This does not accord with the climate of Egypt, where the harvest soon follows the seed-time.

It seems more probably to have been a story explaining some hieroglyphic figures representing the decomposition and resuscitation of animal matter; a sublime and interesting subject, and which seems to have given origin to the doctrine of transmigration, which had probably its birth also from the hieroglyphic treasures of Egypt. It is remarkable that the cypress groves in the ancient Greek writers, as in Theocritus, were dedicated to Venus; and afterwards became funeral emblems. Which was probably occasioned by the cypress being an accompaniment of Venus in the annual processions, in which she was supposed to lament over the funeral of Adonis; a ceremony which obtained over all the eastern world from great antiquity, and is supposed to be referred to by Ezekiel, who accuses the idolatrous woman of weeping for Thammus.

Zephyrs drive. l. 609. These lines were originally written thus,

Shade follows shade by laughing zephyrs drove,
And all the chequer'd landscape seems to move:

but were altered on account of the supposed false grammar in using the word drove for driven, according to the opinion of Dr. Lowth: at the same time it may be observed, 1. that this is in many cases only an ellipsis of the letter *n* at the end of the word; as froze, for frozen; wove, for woven; spoke, for spoken; and that then the participle accidentally becomes similar to the past tense: 2. that the language seems gradually tending to omit the letter *n* in other kind of words for the sake of euphony; as housen is become houses; eyne, eyes; thine, thy, &c. and in common conversation, the words forgot, spoke, froze, rode, are frequently used for forgotten, spoken, frozen, ridden. 3. It does not appear that any confusion would follow the indiscriminate use of the same word for the past tense and the participle passive, since the auxiliary verb *have,* or the preceding noun or pronoun always clearly distinguishes them; and lastly, rhyme-poetry must lose the use of many elegant words without this license.

THE ECONOMY OF VEGETATION.

CANTO III.

ARGUMENT.

Address to the Nymphs. I. Steam rises from the ocean, floats in clouds, descends in rain and dew, or is condensed on hills, produces springs, and rivers, and returns to the sea. So the blood circulates through the body and returns to the heart, 11. *II. 1. Tides,* 57. *2. Echinus, nautilus, pinna, cancer. Grotto of a mermaid,* 65. *3. Oil stills the waves. Coral rocks. Ship-worm, or Teredo. Maelstrome, a whirlpool on the coast of Norway,* 85. *III. Rivers from beneath the snows on the Alps. The Tiber,* 103. *IV. Overflowing of the Nile from African Monsoons,* 129. *V. 1. Giesar, a boiling fountain in Iceland, destroyed by inundation, and consequent earthquake,* 145. *2. Warm medicinal springs. Buxton. Duke and Dutchess of Devonshire,* 157. *VI. Combination of vital air and inflammable gas produces water. Which is another source of springs and rivers. Allegorical loves of Jupiter and Juno productive of vernal showers,* 201. *VII. Aquatic Taste. Distant murmur of the sea by night. Sea-horse. Nereid singing,* 261. *VIII. The Nymphs of the river Derwent lament the death of Mrs. French,* 297. *IX. Inland navigation. Monument for Mr. Brindley,* 341. *X. Pumps explained. Child sucking. Mothers exhorted to nurse their children. Cherub sleeping,* 365. *XI. Engines for extinguishing fire. Story of two lovers perishing in the flames,* 397. *XII. Charities of Miss Jones,* 447. *XIII. Marshes drained. Hercules conquers Achelous. The horn of Plenty,* 483. *XIV. Showers. Dews. Floating lands with water. Lacteal system in animals. Caravan drinking,* 529. *Departure of the Nymphs like water spiders; like northern nations skating on the ice,* 569.

AGAIN the goddess speaks!—glad echo swells
The tuneful tones along her shadowy dells,
Her wrinkling founts with soft vibration shakes,
Curls her deep wells, and rimples all her lakes,
Thrills each wide stream, Britannia's isle that laves,
Her headlong cataracts, and circumfluent waves.
—Thick as the dews, which deck the morning flowers,
Or rain-drops twinkling in the sun-bright showers,
Fair nymphs, emerging in pellucid bands,
Rise, as she turns, and whiten all the lands. 10

I. " Your buoyant troops on dimpling ocean tread,
Wafting the moist air from his oozy bed,
Aquatic nymphs!—you lead with viewless march
The winged vapours up the aerial arch,

The winged vapours. l. 14. See additional note, No. XXV. on evaporation.

On each broad cloud a thousand sails expand,
And steer the shadowy treasure o'er the land,

On each broad cloud. l. 15. The clouds consist of condensed vapour, the particles of which are too small separately to overcome the tenacity of the air, and which therefore do not descend. They are in such small spheres as to repel each other, that is, they are applied to each other by such very small surfaces, that the attraction of the particles of each drop to its own centre is greater than its attraction to the surface of the drop in its vicinity; every one has observed with what difficulty small spherules of quicksilver can be made to unite, owing to the same cause; and it is common to see on riding through shallow water on a clear day, numbers of very small spheres of water as they are thrown from the horse's feet run along the surface for many yards before they again unite with it. In many cases these spherules of water, which compose clouds, are kept from uniting by a surplus of electric fluid; and fall in violent showers as soon as that is withdrawn from them, as in thunder storms. See note on Canto I. l. 554.
If in this state a cloud becomes frozen, it is torn to pieces in its descent by the friction of the air, and falls in white flakes of snow. Or these flakes are rounded by being rubbed together by the winds, and by having their angles thawed

F

Through vernal skies the gathering drops diffuse,
Plunge in soft rains, or sink in silver dews.—
Your lucid bands condense with fingers chill
The blue mist hovering round the gelid hill ; 20

In clay-form'd beds the trickling streams collect,
Strain through white sands, through pebbly veins direct ;
Or point in rifted rocks their dubious way,
And in each bubbling fountain rise to day.

" Nymphs ! you then guide, attendant from their source,
The associate rills along their sinuous course ;
Float in bright squadrons by the willowy brink,
Or circling slow in limpid eddies sink ;
Call from her crystal cave the naiad-nymph,
Who hides her fine form in the passing lymph, 30
And, as below she braids her hyaline hair,
Eyes her soft smiles reflected in the air ;
Or sport in groups with river-boys, that lave
Their silken limbs amid the dashing wave ;
Pluck the pale primrose bending from its edge,
Or tittering dance amid the whispering sedge.—

" Onward you pass, the pine-capt hills divide,
Or feed the golden harvests on their side ;
The wide-ribb'd arch with hurrying torrents fill, [mill. 40
Shove the slow barge, or whirl the foaming mill
Or lead with beckoning hand the sparkling train
Of refluent water to its parent main,
And pleased revisit in their sea-moss vales
Blue nereid-forms array'd in shining scales,

---

off by the warmer air beneath as they descend; and part of the water produced by these angles thus dissolved is absorbed into the body of the hail-stone, as may be seen by holding a lump of snow over a candle, and there becomes frozen into ice by the quantity of cold which the hail-stone possesses beneath the freezing point, or which is produced by its quick evaporation in falling ; and thus hail-stones are often found of greater or less density according as they consist of a greater portion of snow or ice. If hail-stones consisted of the large drops of showers frozen in their descent, they would consist of pure transparent ice.

As hail is only produced in summer, and is always attended with storms, some philosophers have believed that the sudden departure of electricity from a cloud may effect something yet unknown in this phenomenon ; but it may happen in summer independent of electricity, because aqueous vapour is then raised higher in the atmosphere, whence it has further to fall, and there is warmer air below for it to fall through.

Or sink in silver dews. l. 18. During the coldness of the night the moisture before dissolved in the air is gradually precipitated, and as it subsides adheres to the bodies it falls upon. Where the attraction of the body to the particles of water is greater than the attractions of those particles to each other, it becomes spread upon their surface, or slides down them in actual contact ; as on the broad parts of the blades of moist grass : where the attraction of the surface to the water is less than the attraction of the particles of water to each other, the dew stands in drops ; as on the points and edges of grass or gorse, where the surface presented to the drop being small it attracts it so little as but just to support it without much changing its globular form : where there is no attraction between the vegetable surface and the dew drops, as on cabbage leaves, the drop does not come into contact with the leaf, but hangs over it repelled, and retains its natural form, composed of the attraction and pressure of its own parts, and thence looks like quicksilver, reflecting light from both its surfaces. Nor is this owing to any oiliness of the leaf, but simply to the polish of its surface, as a light needle may be laid on water in the same manner without touching it; for as the attractive powers of polished surfaces are greater when in actual contact, so the repulsive power is greater before contact.

The blue mist. l. 20. Mists are clouds resting on the ground ; they generally come on at the beginning of night, and either fill the moist valleys, or hang on the summits of hills, according to the degree of moisture previously dissolved, and the eduction of heat from them. The air over rivers during the warmth of the day suspends much moisture, and as the changeful surface of rivers occasions them to cool sooner than the land at the approach of evening, mists are most frequently seen to begin over rivers, and to spread themselves over moist grounds, and fill the valleys, while the mists on the tops of mountains are more properly clouds, condensed by the coldness of their situation.

On ascending up the side of a hill from a misty valley, I have observed a beautiful coloured halo round the moon when a certain thickness of mist was over me, which ceased to be visible as soon as I emerged out of it ; and well remember admiring with other spectators the shadow of the three spires of the cathedral church at Litchfield, the moon rising behind it, apparently broken off, and lying distinctly over our heads as if horizontally on the surface of the mist, which arose about as high as the roof of the church. Similar to this if on a foggy night a person turns his back to a candle and lanthorn, he will see a monstrous shadow of himself delineated on the fog, which is dense enough to reflect a part of the candle-light in the vicinity of the shadow. White's Calendar. There are some curious remarks on shadows or reflections seen on the surface of mists from high mountains in Ulloa's Voyages. The dry mist of summer 1783, was probably occasioned by volcanic eruption, as mentioned in note on Chunda, Part II. and therefore more like the atmosphere of smoke which hangs on still days over great cities.

There is a dry mist, or rather a diminished transparence of the air, which according to Mr. Saussure accompanies fair weather, while great transparence of air indicates rain. Thus when large rivers two miles broad, such as at Liverpool, appear narrow, it is said to prognosticate rain ; and when wide, fair weather. This want of transparence of the air in dry weather, may be owing to new combinations or decompositions of the vapours dissolved in it, but wants further investigation. Essais sur L'Hygrometrie, p. 357.

Round the gelid hill. ib. See additional notes, No. XXVI. on the origin of springs.

Shapes, whose broad oar the torpid wave impels, [shells.
And Tritons bellowing through their twisted

"So from the heart the sanguine stream distils
O'er beauty's radiant shrine in vermil rills,
Feeds each fine nerve, each slender hair pervades,
The skin's bright snow with living purple shades,   50
Each dimpling cheek with warmer blushes dyes,
Laughs on the lips, and lightens in the eyes.
—Erewhile absorb'd, the vagrant globules swim
From each fair feature, and proportion'd limb,
Join'd in one trunk with deeper tint return
To the warm concave of the vital urn.

II. 1. "Aquatic maids! you sway the mighty realms
Of scale and shell, which ocean overwhelms;
As night's pale queen her rising orb reveals,
And climbs the zenith with refulgent wheels,
Carr'd on the foam your glimmering legion rides,   61
Your little tridents heave the dashing tides,

Urge on the sounding shores their crystal course
Restrain their fury, or direct their force.

2. "Nymphs! you adorn, in glossy volutes roll'd,
The gaudy conch with azure, green, and gold.

Carr'd on the foam. l. 61. The phenomena of the tides have been well investigated and satisfactorily explained by Sir Isaac Newton and Dr. Halley, from the reciprocal gravitations of the earth, moon, and sun. As the earth and moon move round a centre of motion near the earth's surface, at the same time that they are proceeding in their annual orbit round the sun, it follows that the water on the side of the earth nearest this centre of motion between the earth and moon will be more attracted by the moon, and the waters on the opposite side of the earth will be less attracted by the moon, than the central parts of the earth. Add to this, that the centrifugal force of the water on the side of the earth furthest from the centre of motion, round which the earth and moon move, (which, as was said before, is near the surface of the earth) is greater than that on the opposite side of the earth. From both these causes it is easy to comprehend that the water will rise on two sides of the earth, viz. on that nearest to the moon, and its opposite side, and that it will be flattened in consequence at the quadratures, and thus produce two tides in every lunar day, which consists of about twenty-four hours and forty-eight minutes.

These tides will be also affected by the solar attraction when it coincides with the lunar one, or opposes it, as at new and full moon, and will also be much influenced by the opposing shores in every part of the earth.

Now as the moon in moving round the centre of gravity between itself and the earth describes a much larger orbit than the earth describes round the same centre, it follows that the centrifugal motion on the side of the moon opposite to the earth must be much greater than the centrifugal motion of the side of the earth opposite to the moon round the same centre. And secondly, as the attraction of the earth exerted on the moon's surface next to the earth is much greater than the attraction of the moon exerted on the earth's surface, the tides on the lunar sea, (if such there be) should be much greater than those of our ocean. Add to this, that as the same face of the moon always is turned to the earth, the lunar tides must be permanent, and if the solid parts of the moon be spherical, must always cover the phasis next to us. But as there are evidently hills and vales and volcanoes on this side of the moon, the consequence is that the moon has no ocean, or that it is frozen.

The gaudy conch. l. 66. The spiral form of many shells seems to have afforded a more frugal manner of covering the long tail of the fish with calcareous armour; since a single thin partition between the adjoining circles of the fish was sufficient to defend both surfaces, and thus much cretaceous matter is saved; and it is probable that from this spiral form they are better enabled to feel the vibrations of the element in which they exist. See note on Canto IV. l. 164. This cretaceous matter is formed by a mucous secretion from the skin of the fish, as is seen in crabfish, and others which annually cast their shells, and is at first a mucous covering, (like that of a hen's egg, when it is laid a day or two too soon,) and which gradually hardens. This may also be seen in common shell snails, if a part of their shell be broken it becomes repaired in a similar manner with mucus, which by degrees hardens into shell.

It is probable the calculi or stones found in other animals may have a similar origin, as they are formed on mucous membranes, as those of the kidney and bladder, chalk-stones in the gout, and gall-stones; and are probably owing to the inflammation of the membrane where they are produced, and vary according to the degree of inflammation of the membrane which forms them, and the kind of mucus which it naturally produces. Thus the shelly matter of different shell-fish differs from the coarser kinds which form the shells of crabs, to the finer kinds which produce the mother-pearl.

The beautiful colours of some shells originate from the thinness of the laminæ of which they consist, rather than to any colouring matter, as is seen in mother-pearl, which reflects different colours according to the obliquity of the light which falls on it. The beautiful prismatic colours seen on the Labradore stone are owing to a similar cause, viz. the thinness of the laminæ of which it consists, and has probably been formed from mother-pearl shells.

It is curious that some of the most common fossil shells are not now known in their recent state, as the cornua ammonis; and on the contrary, many shells which are very plentiful in their recent state, as limpets, sea-ears, volutes, cowries, are very rarely found fossil. Da Costa's Conchology, p. 163. Were all the ammoniæ destroyed when the continents were raised? Or do some genera of animals perish by the increasing power of their enemies? Or do they still reside at inaccessible depths in the sea? Or do some animals change their forms gradually and become new genera?

You round echinus ray his arrowy mail,
Give the keel'd nautilus his oar and sail;
Firm to his rock with silver cords suspend
The anchor'd pinna, and his cancer-friend; 70
With worm-like beard his toothless lips array,
And teach the unwieldy sturgeon to betray.—
Ambush'd in weeds, or sepulchred in sands,
In dread repose he waits the scaly bands,
Waves in red spires the living lure, and draws
The unwary plunderers to his circling jaws,
Eyes with grim joy the twinkling shoals beset,
And clasps the quick inextricable net.
You chase the warrior shark, and cumberous whale,
And guard the mermaid in her briny vale; 80
Feed the live petals of her insect-flowers,
Her shell-wrack gardens, and her sea-fan bowers;
With ores and gems adorn her coral cell,
And drop a pearl in every gaping shell.

3. " Your myriad trains o'er stagnant oceans tow,
Harness'd with gossamer, the loitering prow;
Or with fine films, suspended o'er the deep,
Or oil effusive lull the waves to sleep.

You stay the flying bark, conceal'd beneath,
Where living rocks of worm-built coral breathe;
Meet fell Teredo, as he mines the keel 91
With beaked head, and break his lips of steel;
Turn the broad helm, the fluttering canvass urge
From Maelstrome's fierce innavigable surge.
—'Mid the lorn isles of Norway's stormy main,
As sweeps o'er many a league his eddying train,
Vast watery walls in rapid circles spin,
And deep-ingulph'd the demon dwells within;
Springs o'er the fear-froze crew with harpy-claws, 99
Down his deeep den the whirling vessel draws;
Churns with his bloody mouth the dread repast,
The booming waters murmuring o'er the mast.

III. " Where with chill frown enormous Alps alarms
A thousand realms, horizon'd in his arms;
While cloudless suns meridian glories shed
From skies of silver round his hoary head,
Tall rocks of ice refract the coloured rays,
And frost sits throned amid the lambent blaze;
Nymphs! your thin forms pervade his glittering piles,
His roofs of crystal, and his glassy ailes; 110
Where in cold caves imprisoned naiads sleep,
Or chain'd on mossy couches wake and weep;
Where round dark crags indignant waters bend,
Through rifted ice, in ivory veins descend,
Seek through unfathom'd snows their devious track,
Heave the vast spars, the ribbed granites crack.

Echinus. Nautilus. l. 67, 68. See additional notes, No. XXVII.
Pinna. Cancer. l. 70. See additional notes, No. XXVII.
With worm-like beard. l. 71. See additional notes, No. XXVIII.
Feed the live petals. l. 81. There is a sea-insect described by Mr. Huges whose claws or tentacles being disposed in regular circles and tinged with variety of bright lively colours represent the petals of some most elegantly fringed and radiated flowers, as the carnation, marigold, and anemone. Philos. Trans. Abridg. Vol. IX. p. 110. The Abbe Diequemarre has further elucidated the history of the actinia; and observed their manner of taking their prey by inclosing it in these beautiful rays like a net. Phil. Trans. Vol. LXIII. and LXV. and LXVII.
And drop a pearl. l. 84. Many are the opinions both of ancient and modern writers concerning the production of pearls. Mr. Reaumur thinks they are formed like the hard concretions in many land animals, as stones of the bladder, gall-stones, and bezoar, and hence concludes them to be a disease of the fish; but there seems to be a stricter analogy between these and the calcareous productions found in crab-fish, called crab's eyes, which are formed near the stomach of the animal, and constitute a reservoir of calcareous matter against the renovation of the shell, at which time they are re-dissolved and deposited for that purpose. As the internal part of the shell of the pearl oyster or muscle consists of mother-pearl, which is a similar material to the pearl, and as the animal has annually occasion to enlarge his shell, there is reason to suspect the loose pearls are similar reservoirs of the pearly matter for that purpose.
Or with fine films. l. 87. See additional notes, No. XXIX.

Where living rocks. l. 90. The immense and dangerous rocks built by the swarms of coral insects which rise almost perpendicularly in the southern ocean like walls, are described in Cook's Voyages: a point of one of these rocks broke off and stuck in the hole which it had made in the bottom of one of his ships, which would otherwise have perished by the admission of water. The numerous lime-stone-rocks which consist of a congeries of the cells of these animals, and which constitute a great part of the solid earth, show their prodigious multiplication in all ages of the world. Specimens of these rocks are to be seen in the Limeworks at Linsel near Newport in Shropshire, in Coal-brook Dale, and in many parts of the Peak of Derbyshire. The insect has been well described by M. Peyssonnel, Ellis and others. Phil. Trans. Vol. XLVII. L. LII. and LVII.
Meet fell Teredo. l. 91. See additional notes, No. XXX.
Turn the broad helm. l. 93. See additional notes, No. XXXI.
Where round dark crags. l. 113. See additional notes, No. XXXII.
Heave the vast spars. l. 116. Water in descending down elevated situations, if the outlet for it below is not sufficient for its emission, acts with a force equal to the height of the column, as is seen in an experimental machine called the philosophical bellows, in which a few pints of water are made to raise many hundred pounds.

Rush into day, in foamy torrents shine,
And swell the imperial Danube or the Rhine.
Or feed the murmuring Tiber, as he laves   119
His realms inglorious with diminish'd waves,
Hears his lorn forum sound with eunuch-strains,
Sees dancing slaves insult his martial plains;
Parts with chill stream the dim religious bower
Time-moulder'd bastion, and dismantled tower;
By alter'd fanes and nameless villas glides,
And classic domes, that tremble on his sides;
Sighs o'er each broken urn, and yawning tomb,
And mourns the fall of liberty and Rome.

IV. "Sailing in air, when dark monsoon inshrouds
His tropic mountains in a night of clouds;   130

Or drawn by whirlwinds from the line returns,
And showers o'er Afric all his thousand urns;
High o'er his head the beams of Sirius glow,
And, dog of Nile, Anubis barks below.
Nymphs! you from cliff to cliff attendant guide
In headlong cataracts the impetuous tide;
Or lead o'er wastes of Abyssinian sands
The bright expanse to Egypt's showerless lands.
—Her long canals the sacred waters fill,
And edge with silver every peopled hill;   140
Gigantic Sphinx in circling waves admire,
And Memnon bending o'er his broken lyre;

To this cause is to be ascribed many large promontories of ice being occasionally thrown down from the Glaciers; rocks have likewise been thrown from the sides of mountains by the same cause, and large portions of earth have been removed many hundred yards from their situations at the foot of mountains. On inspecting the locomotion of about thirty acres of earth with a small house near Bilder's Bridge in Shropshire, about twenty years ago, from the foot of a mountain towards the river, I well remember it bore all the marks of having been thus lifted up, pushed away, and as it were crumpled into ridges, by a column of water contained in the mountain.

From water being thus confined in high columns between the strata of mountainous countries, it has often happened, when wells or perforations have been made into the earth, that springs have arisen much above the surface of the new well. When the new bridge was building, at Dublin, Mr. G. Semple found a spring in the bed of the river, where he meant to lay the foundation of a pier, which, by fixing iron pipes into it, he raised many feet. Treatise on Building in Water, by G. Semple.—From having observed a valley north-west of St. Alkmond's well, near Derby, at the head of which that spring of water once probably existed, and by its current formed the valley, (but which in after times found its way out in its present situation,) I suspect that St. Alkmond's well might by building round it be raised high enough to supply many streets in Derby with spring-water, which are now only supplied with river-water. See an account of an artificial spring of water, Phil. Trans. Vol. LXXV. p. 1.

In making a well at Sheerness, the water rose 300 feet above its source in the well. Phil. Trans. Vol. LXXIV.—And at Hartford, in Connecticut, there is a well which was dug seventy feet deep before water was found; then in boring an auger-hole through a rock, the water rose so fast as to make it difficult to keep it dry by pumps till they could blow the hole larger by gunpowder, which was no sooner accomplished than it filled and run over, and has been a brook for near a century. Travels through America. Lond. 1789. Lane.

Dark monsoon inshrouds. l. 129. When, from any peculiar situations of land in respect to sea, the tropic becomes more heated, when the sun is vertical over it, than the line, the periodical winds called monsoons are produced, and these are attended by rainy seasons; for as the air at the tropic is now more heated than at the line, it ascends by decrease of its specific gravity, and floods of air rush in both from the South West and North East; and these being one warmer than the other, the rain is precipitated by their mixture, as observed by Dr. Hutton. See additional notes, No. XXV. All late travellers have ascribed the rise of the Nile to the monsoons which deluge Nubia and Abyssinia with rain. The whirling of the ascending air was even seen by Mr. Bruce in Abyssinia; he says, "every morning a small cloud began to whirl round, and presently after the whole heavens became covered with clouds." By this vortex of air the N. E. winds and the S. W. winds, which flow in to supply the place of the ascending column, became mixed more rapidly, and deposited their rain in greater abundance.

Mr. Volney observes that the time of the rising of the Nile commences about the 19th of June, and that Abyssinia and the adjacent parts of Africa are deluged with rain in May, June, and July, and produce a mass of water which is three months in draining off. The Abbe La Pluche observes that as Sirius, or the dog-star, rose at the time of the commencement of the flood, its rising was watched by the astronomers, and notice given of the approach of inundation by hanging the figure of Anubis, which was that of a man with a dog's head, upon all their temples. Histoire de Ciel.

Egypt's showerless lands. l. 138. There seem to be two situations which may be conceived to be exempted from rain falling upon them, one where the constant trade-winds meet beneath the line, for here two regions of warm air are mixed together, and thence do not seem to have any cause to precipitate their vapour; and the other is, where the winds are brought from colder climates, and become warmer by their contact with the earth of a warmer one. Thus Lower Egypt is a flat country, warmed by the sun more than the higher lands on one side of it, and than the Mediterranean on the other; and hence the winds which blow over it acquire greater warmth, which ever way they come, than they possessed before, and in consequence have a tendency to acquire and not to part with their vapour like the north-east winds of this country. There is said to be a narrow spot upon the coast of Peru where rain seldom occurs; at the same time, according to Ulloa, on the mountainous regions of the Andes beyond there is almost perpetual rain. For the wind blows uniformly upon this hot part of the coast of Peru, but no cause of devaporation occurs till it begins to ascend the mountainous Andes, and then its own expansion produces cold sufficient to condense its vapour.

O'er furrow'd glebes and green savannas sweep,
And towns and temples laugh amid the deep.

V. 1. "High in the frozen north where Hecla glows,
And melts in torrents his coeval snows;
O'er isles and oceans shed a sanguine light,
Or shoots red stars amid the ebon night;
When, at his base intomb'd, with bellowing sound
Fell Giesar roar'd, and struggling shook the ground;   150
Pour'd from red nostrils, with her scalding breath,
A boiling deluge o'er the blasted heath;
And, wide in air, in misty volumes hurl'd
Contagious atoms o'er the alarmed world;
Nymphs! your bold myriads broke the infernal spell,
And crush'd the sorceress in her flinty cell.

2. "Where with soft fires in unextinguish'd urns,
Cauldron'd in rock, innocuous lava burns;
On the bright lake your gelid hands distil
In pearly showers the parsimonious rill;   160
And, as aloft the curling vapours rise
Through the cleft roof, ambitious for the skies,
In vaulted hills condense the tepid steams,
And pour to health the medicated streams.
—So in green vales amid her mountains bleak
Buxtonia smiles, the goddess-nymph of Peak;
Deep in warm waves, and pebbly baths she dwells,
And calls Hygeia to her sainted wells.

"Hither in sportive bands bright Devon leads
Graces and loves from Chatsworth's flowery meads,   170
Charm'd round the nymph, they climb the rifted rocks;
And steep in mountain-mist their golden locks;
On venturous step her sparry caves explore,
And light with radiant eyes her realms of ore;
—Oft by her bubbling founts, and shadowy domes,
In gay undress the fairy legion roams,
Their dripping palms in playful malice fill,
Or taste with ruby lip the sparkling rill;
Crowd round her baths, and, bending o'er the side,
Unclasp'd their sandals, and their zones untied,   180
Dip with gay fear the shuddering foot undress'd,
And quick retract it to the fringed vest;
Or cleave with brandish'd arms the lucid stream,
And sob, their blue eyes twinkling in the steam.
—High o'er the chequer'd vault with transient glow
Bright lustres dart, as dash the waves below;
And echo's sweet responsive voice prolongs
The dulcet tumult of their silver tongues.—
O'er their flush'd cheeks uncurling tresses flow,
And dew-drops glitter on their necks of snow;

Fell Giesar roar'd. l. 150. The boiling column of water at Giesar in Iceland was nineteen feet in diameter, and sometimes rose to the height of ninety-two feet. On cooling it deposited a siliceous matter or chalcedony forming a bason round its base. The heat of this water before it rose out of the earth could not be ascertained, as water loses all its heat above 212 (as soon as it is at liberty to expand) by the exhalation of a part, but the flinty bason which is deposited from it shows that water with great degrees of heat will dissolve siliceous matter. Van Troil's Letters on Iceland. Since the above account in the year 1780 this part of Iceland has been destroyed by an earthquake or covered with lava, which was probably effected by the force of aqueous steam, a greater quantity of water falling on the subterraneous fires than could escape by the ancient outlets and generating an increased quantity of vapour. For the dispersion of contagious vapours from volcanoes, see an account of the Harmattan in the notes on Chunda, Part II.

Buxtonia smiles. l. 166. Some arguments are mentioned in the note on Fucus, Part II. to show that the warm springs of this country do not arise from the decomposition of pyrites near the surface of the earth, but that they are produced by steam rising up the fissures of the mountains from great depths, owing to water falling on subterraneous fires, and that this steam is condensed between the strata of the incumbent mountains and collected into springs. For further proofs on this subject the reader is referred to a Letter from Dr. Darwin in Mr. Pilkington's View of Derbyshire, vol. I. p. 256.

And sob, their blue eyes. l. 184. The bath at Buxton being of 82 degrees of heat is called a warm bath, and is so compared with common spring-water which possesses but 48 degrees of heat, but is nevertheless a cold bath compared to the heat of the body which is 98. On going into this bath there is therefore always a chill perceived at the first immersion, but after having been in it a minute the chill ceases and a sensation of warmth succeeds though the body continues to be immersed in the water. The cause of this curious phenomenon is to be looked for in the laws of animal sensation and not from any properties of heat. When a person goes from clear day-light into an obscure room, for a while it appears gloomy, which gloom however in a little time ceases, and the deficiency of light becomes no longer perceived. This is not solely owing to the enlargement of the iris of the eye, since that is performed in an instant, but to this law of sensation, that when a less stimulus is applied (within certain bounds) the sensibility increases. Thus at going into a bath as much colder than the body as that of Buxton, the diminution of heat on the skin is at first perceived, but in about a minute the sensibility to heat increases, and the nerves of the skin are equally excited by the lessened stimulus. The sensation of warmth at emerging from a cold-bath, and the pain called the hot-ach, after the hands have been immersed in snow, depend on the same principle, viz. the increased sensibility of the skin after having been previously exposed to a stimulus less than usual.

Round each fair nymph her dropping mantle
  clings, 191
And Loves emerging shake their showery wings.

"Here oft her lord surveys the rude domain,
Fair arts of Greece triumphant in his train;
Lo! as he steps, the column'd pile ascends,
The blue roof closes, or the crescent bends;
New woods aspiring clothe their hills with green,
Smooth slope the lawns, the gray rock peeps between;
Relenting nature gives her hand to taste,
And health and beauty crown the laughing
  waste. 200

VI. "Nymphs! your bright squadrons watch
  with chemic eyes
The cold-elastic vapours, as they rise;
With playful force arrest them as they pass,
And to *pure air* betroth the *flaming gas*.
Round their translucent forms at once they
  fling
Their rapturous arms, with silver bosoms cling;
In fleecy clouds their fluttering wings extend,
Or from the skies in lucid showers descend;
Whence rills and rivers owe their secret birth,
And ocean's hundred arms infold the earth. 210

Here oft her lord. l. 193. Alluding to the magnificent and beautiful crescent, and superb stables, lately erected at Buxton, for the accommodation of the company, by the Duke of Devonshire; and to the plantations with which he has decorated the surrounding mountains.

And to pure air. l. 204. Until very lately water was esteemed a simple element; nor are all the most celebrated chemists of Europe yet converts to the new opinion of its decomposition. Mr. Lavoisier, and others of the French school, have most ingeniously endeavoured to show that water consists of pure air, called by them oxygene, and of inflammable air, called hydrogene, with as much of the matter of heat, or calorique, as is necessary to preserve them in the form of gas. Gas is distinguished from steam by its preserving its elasticity under the pressure of the atmosphere, and in the greatest degrees of cold yet known. The history of the progress of this great discovery is detailed in the Memoirs of the Royal Academy for 1781, and the experimental proofs of it are delivered in Lavoisier's Elements of Chemistry. The results of which are, that water consists of eighty-five parts by weight of oxygene, and fifteen parts by weight of hydrogene, with a sufficient quantity of calorique. Not only numerous chemical phænomena, but many atmospherical and vegetable facts receive clear and beautiful elucidation from this important analysis. In the atmosphere inflammable air is probably perpetually uniting with vital air, and producing moisture which descends in dews and showers, while the growth of vegetables, by the assistance of light, is perpetually again decomposing the water they imbibe from the earth, and while they retain the inflammable air for the formation of oils, wax, honey, resin, &c. they give up the vital air to replenish the atmosphere.

"So, robed by beauty's queen, with softer
  charms
Saturnia woo'd the thunderer to her arms;
O'er her fair limbs a veil of light she spread,
And bound a starry diadem on her head;
Long braids of pearl her golden tresses graced,
And the charm'd cestus sparkled round her
  waist.
—Raised o'er the woof, by beauty's hand inwrought,
Breathes a soft sigh, and glows the enamour'd
  thought;
Vows on light wings succeed, and quiver'd wiles,
Assuasive accents, and seductive smiles. 220
—Slow rolls the Cyprian car in purple pride,
And, steer'd by love, ascends admiring Ide;
Climbs the green slopes, the nodding woods pervades,
Burns round the rocks, or gleams amid the
  shades.—
Glad zephyr leads the van, and waves above
The barbed darts, and blazing torch of love;
Reverts his smiling face, and pausing flings
Soft showers of roses from aurelian wings.
Delighted fawns, in wreaths of flowers array'd,
With tiptoe wood-boys beat the chequer'd
  glade;
Alarmed Naiads, rising into air, 230
Lift o'er their silver urns their leafy hair;
Each to her oak the bashful Dryads shrink,
And azure eyes are seen at every chink.
—Love culls a flaming shaft of broadest wing,
And rests the fork upon the quivering string;
Points his arch eye aloft, with fingers strong
Draws to his curled ear the silken thong;
Loud twangs the steel, the golden arrow flies,
Trails a long line of lustre through the skies; 240
''Tis done!' he shouts, ' the mighty monarch
  feels!'
And with loud laughter shakes the silver wheels;
Bends o'er the car, and whirling, as it moves,
His loosen'd bowstring, drives the rising doves.
—Pierced on his throne the starting thunderer
  turns, [burns;
Melts with soft sighs, with kindling rapture
Clasps her fair hand, and eyes in fond amaze
The bright intruder with enamour'd gaze.
'And leaves my goddess, like a blooming bride,
The fanes of Argos for the rocks of Ide? 250
Her gorgeous palaces, and amaranth bowers,
For cliff-top'd mountains, and aërial towers?'
He said; and leading from her ivory seat
The blushing beauty to his lone retreat,

And steer'd by love. l. 222. The younger Love, or Cupid, the son of Venus, owes his existence and his attributes to much later times than the Eros, or divine Love, mentioned in Canto I. since the former is no where mentioned by Homer, though so many apt opportunities of introducing him occur in the works of that immortal bard. Bacon.

Curtain'd with night the couch imperial shrouds,
And rests the crimson cushions upon clouds.—
Earth feels the grateful influence from above,
Sighs the soft air, and ocean murmurs love;
Ethereal warmth expands his brooding wing, 259
And in still showers descends the genial spring.

VII. " Nymphs of aquatic taste! whose placid smile [isle;
Breathes sweet enchantment o'er Britannia's
Whose sportive touch in showers resplendent flings
Her lucid cataracts, and her bubbling springs;
Through peopled vales the liquid silver guides,
And swells in bright expanse her freighted tides.
You with nice ear, in tiptoe trains, pervade
Dim walks of morn or evening's silent shade;
Join the lone nightingale, her woods among,
And roll your rills symphonious to her song; 270
Through fount-full dells, and wave-worn valleys move,
And tune their echoing waterfalls to love;
Or catch, attentive to the distant roar,
The pausing murmurs of the dashing shore;
Or, as aloud she pours her liquid strain,
Pursue the nereid on the twilight main.
—Her playful sea-horse woos her soft commands,
Turns his quick ears, his webbed claws expands,
His watery way with waving volutes wins,
Or listening librates on unmoving fins. 280
The nymph emerging mounts her scaly seat,
Hangs o'er his glossy sides her silver feet,
With snow-white hands her arching veil detains,
Gives to his slimy lips the slacken'd reins,
Lifts to the star of eve her eye serene,
And chaunts the birth of beauty's radiant queen.—

O'er her fair brow her pearly comb unfurls
Her beryl locks, and parts the waving curls,
Each tangled braid with glistening teeth unbinds,
And with the floating treasure musks the winds.—
Thrill'd by the dulcet accents, as she sings, 291
The rippling wave in widening circles rings;
Night's shadowy forms along the margin gleam
With pointed ears, or dance upon the stream;
The moon transported stays her bright career,
And maddening stars shoot headlong from the sphere.

VIII. " Nymphs! whose fair eyes with vivid lustres glow
For human weal, and melt at human wo;
Late as you floated on your silver shells,
Sorrowing and slow by Derwent's willowy dells; 300
Where by tall groves his foamy flood he steers
Through ponderous arches o'er impetuous wears,
By Derby's shadowy towers reflective sweeps,
And gothic grandeur chills his dusky deeps;
You pearl'd with pity's drops his velvet sides,
Sigh'd in his gales, and murmur'd in his tides,
Waved o'er his fringed brink a deeper gloom,
And bow'd his alders o'er Milcena's tomb.

" Oft with sweet voice she led her infant-train,
Printing with graceful step his spangled plain,
Explored his twinkling swarms, that swim or fly, 311
And mark'd his florets with botanic eye.—
' Sweet bud of Spring! how frail thy transient bloom,
Fine film,' she cried, ' of nature's fairest loom!
Soon beauty fades upon its damask throne!'—
Unconscious of the worm, that mined her own!
—Pale are those lips, where soft caresses hung,
Wan the warm cheek, and mute the tender tongue,
Cold rests that feeling heart on Derwent's shore,
And those love-lighted eye-balls roll no more!

" Here her sad consort, stealing through the gloom 321
Of murmuring cloysters, gazes on her tomb;
Hangs in mute anguish o'er the scutcheon'd hearse,
Or graves with trembling style the votive verse.
' Sexton! oh, lay beneath this sacred shrine,
When time's cold hand shall close my aching eyes,
Oh, gently lay this wearied earth of mine,
Where wrapp'd in night my loved Milcena lies

And in still showers. l. 260. The allegorical interpretation of the very ancient mythology which supposes Jupiter to represent the superior part of the atmosphere or ether, and Juno the inferior air, and that the conjunction of these two produces vernal showers, as alluded to in Virgil's Georgics, is so analogous to the present important discovery of the production of water from pure air, or oxygene, and inflammable air, or hydrogene, (which from its greater levity probably resides over the former,) that one should be tempted to believe that the very ancient chemists of Egypt had discovered the composition of water, and thus represented it in their hieroglyphic figures before the invention of letters.

In the passage of Virgil Jupiter is called ether, and descends in prolific showers on the bosom of Juno, whence the spring succeeds and all nature rejoices.

Tum pater omnipotens fœcundis imbribus Æther
Conjugis in gremium lætæ descendit, et omnes
Magnus alit, magno commixtus corpore, fœtus.
      Virg. Georg. Lib. II. l. 325.

Her playful sea-horse. l. 277. Described from an antique gem.

O'er Milcena's tomb. l. 308. In memory o Mrs. French, a lady who to many other elegant accomplishments added a proficiency in botany and natural history.

'So shall with purer joy my spirit move, 329
When the last trumpet thrills the caves of death,
Catch the first whispers of my waking love,
And drink with holy kiss her kindling breath.
'The spotless fair, with blush ethereal warm,
Shall hail with sweeter smile returning day,
Rise from her marble bed a brighter form,
And win on buoyant step her airy way.
  Shall bend approved, where beckoning hosts invite,
On clouds of silver her adoring knee,
Approach with seraphim the throne of light,
—And beauty plead with angel-tongue for me!' 340

IX. "Your virgin trains on Brindley's cradle smiled,
And nursed with fairy-love the unletter'd child,
Spread round his pillow all your sacred spells,
Pierced all your springs, and open'd all your wells.—
As now on grass, with glossy folds reveal'd,
Glides the bright serpent, now in flowers conceal'd;
Far shine the scales, that gild his sinuous back,
And lucid undulations mark his track;
So with strong arm immortal Brindley leads
His long canals, and parts the velvet meads; 350
Winding in lucid lines, the watery mass
Mines the firm rock, or loads the deep morass,
With rising locks a thousand hills alarms,
Flings o'er a thousand streams its silver arms,
Feeds the long vale, the nodding woodland laves,
And plenty, arts, and commerce freight the waves.
—Nymphs! who erewhile round Brindley's early bier
On snow-white bosoms shower'd the incessant tear,
Adorn his tomb! oh, raise the marble bust,
Proclaim his honours, and protect his dust! 360
With urns inverted round the sacred shrine
Their ozier wreaths let weeping naiads twine;
While on the top mechanic genius stands,
Counts the fleet waves, and balances the lands.

X. "Nymphs! you first taught to pierce the secret caves
Of humid earth, and lift her ponderous waves;
Bade with quick stroke the sliding piston bear;
The viewless columns of incumbent air;—
Press'd by the incumbent air the floods below,
Through opening valves in foaming torrents flow, 370
Foot after foot with lessen'd impulse move,
And rising seek the vacancy above.—
So when the mother, bending o'er his charms,
Clasps her fair nurseling in delighted arms;
Throws the thin kerchief from her neck of snow,
And half unveils the pearly orbs below;
With sparkling eye the blameless plunderer owns
Her soft embraces, and endearing tones,
Seeks the salubrious fount with opening lips,
Spreads his inquiring hands, and smiles, and sips. 380

"Connubial fair! whom no fond transport warms
To lull your infant in maternal arms;
Who, bless'd in vain with tumid bosoms, hear
His tender wailings with unfeeling ear;
The soothing kiss and milky rill deny,
To the sweet pouting lip, and glistening eye!—
Ah! what avails the cradle's damask roof,
The eider bolster, and embroider'd woof!—
Oft hears the gilded couch unpity'd plains,
And many a tear the tassel'd cushion stains! 390
No voice so sweet attunes his cares to rest,
So soft no pillow, as his mother's breast!—
—Thus charm'd to sweet repose, when twilight hours
Shed their soft influence on celestial bowers,
The cherub, innocence, with smile divine
Shuts his white wings, and sleeps on beauty's shrine.

XI. "From dome to dome when flames infuriate climb,
Sweep the long street, invest the tower sublime;
Gild the tall vanes amid the astonish'd night,
And reddening heaven returns the sanguine light; 400

On Brindley's cradle smiled. l. 341. The life of Mr. Brindley, whose great abilities in the construction of canal navigation were called forth by the patronage of the Duke of Bridgewater, may be read in Dr. Kippis's Biographia Britannica, the excellence of his genius is visible in every part of this island. He died at Turnhurst, in Staffordshire, in 1772, and ought to have a monument in the cathedral church at Lichfield.

Lift her ponderous waves. l. 366. The invention of the pump is of very ancient date, being ascribed to one Ctesebes, an Athenian, whence it was called by the Latins machina Ctesebiana; but it was long before it was known that the ascent of the piston lifted the superincumbent column of the atmosphere, and that then the pressure of the surrounding air on the surface of the well below forced the water up into the vacuum, and that on that account, in the common lifting pump the water would rise only about thirty-five feet, as the weight of such a column of water was in general an equipoise to the surrounding atmosphere. The foamy appearance of water, when the pressure of the air over it is diminished, is owing to the expansion and escape of the air previously dissolved by it, or existing in its pores. When a child first sucks it only presses or champs the teat, as observed by the great Harvey, but afterwards it learns to make an incipient vacuum in its mouth, and acts by removing the pressure of the atmosphere from the nipple, like a pump.

Ah! what avails. l. 387. From an elegant little poem of Mr. Jerningham's, entitled Il Latte, exhorting ladies to nurse their own children.

While with vast strides and bristling hair aloof
Pale danger glides along the falling roof;
And giant terror howling in amaze
Moves his dark limbs across the lurid blaze.
Nymphs! you first taught the gelid wave to rise,
Hurl'd in resplendent arches to the skies;
In iron cells condensed the airy spring,
And imp'd the torrent with unfailing wing;
—On the fierce flames the shower impetuous falls,
And sudden darkness shrouds the shatter'd walls; 410
Steam, smoke, and dust, in blended volumes roll,
And night and silence repossess the pole.—

" Where were ye, Nymphs! in those, disastrous hours, [towers?
Which wrapp'd in flames Augusta's sinking
Why did ye linger in your wells and groves,
When sad Woodmason mourn'd her infant loves?
When thy fair daughters with unheeded screams,
Ill-fated Molesworth! call'd the loitering streams?—
The trembling nymph, on bloodless fingers hung
Eyes from the tottering wall the distant throng,
With ceaseless shrieks her sleeping friends alarms, 421
Drops with singed hair into her lover's arms.
The illumined mother seeks with footsteps fleet,
Where hangs the safe balcony o'er the street,
Wrap'd in her sheet her youngest hope suspends,
And panting lowers it to her tiptoe friends;

Again she hurries on affection's wings,
And now a third, and now a fourth, she brings;
Safe all her babes, she smooths her horrent brow,
And bursts through bickering flames, unscorch'd below.
So, by her son arraign'd, with feet unshod 430
O'er burning bars indignant Emma trod.

" E'en on the day when youth with beauty wed,
The flames surprised them in their nuptial bed;
Seen at the opening sash with bosom bare,
With wringing hands, and dark dishevel'd hair,
The blushing bride with wild disordered charms
Round her fond lover winds her ivory arms;
Beat, as they clasp, their throbbing hearts with fear,
And many a kiss is mixed with many a tear;
Ah me! in vain the labouring engines pour
Round their pale limbs the ineffectual shower!
—Then crash'd the floor, while shrinking crowds retire,
And love and virtue sunk amid the fire!
With piercing screams afflicted strangers mourn,
And their white ashes mingle in their urn.

XII. " Pellucid forms! whose crystal bosoms show
The shine of welfare, or the shade of woe;
Who with soft lips salute returning spring,
And hail the zephyr quivering on his wing; 450
Or watch, untired, the wintery clouds, and share
With streaming eyes my vegetable care;
Go, shove the dim mist from the mountain's brow,
Chase the white fog, which floods the vale below
Melt the thick snows, that linger on the lands,
And catch the hailstones in your little hands;
Guard the coy blossom from the pelting shower,
And dash the rimy spangles from the bower,
From each chill leaf the silvery drops repel,
And close the timorous floret's golden bell. 460

Hurl'd in resplendent arches. l. 406. The addition of an air-cell to machines for raising water to extinguish fire, was first introduced by Mr. Newsham of London, and is now applied to similar engines for washing wall-trees in gardens, and to all kinds of forcing pumps, and might be applied with advantage to lifting pumps where the water is brought from a great distance horizontally. Another kind of machine was invented by one Greyl, in which a vessel of water was every way dispersed by the explosion of gunpowder lodging in the centre of it, and lighted by an adapted match; from this idea Mr. Godfrey proposed a water-bomb of similar construction. Dr. Hales, to prevent the spreading of fire, proposed to cover the floors and stairs of the adjoining houses with earth; Mr. Hartley proposed to prevent houses from taking fire by covering the cieling with thin iron plates, and Lord Mahon by a bed of coarse mortar or plaister between the cieling and floor above it. May not this age of chemical science discover some method of injecting or soaking timber with lime-water, and afterwards with vitriolic acid, and thus fill its pores with alabaster? or of penetrating it with siliceous matter, by processes similar to those of Bergman and Achard? See Cronstedt's Mineral. 2d edit. Vol. l. p. 222.

Woodmason, Molesworth. l. 416. The histories of these unfortunate families may be seen in the Annual Register or in the Gentleman's Magazine.

Shove the dim mist. l. 458. See note on l. 20 of this Canto.
Catch the hail-stones. l. 456. See note on l. 15 of this Canto.
From each chill leaf. l. 459. The upper side of the leaf is the organ of vegetable respiration, as explained in the additional notes, No. XXXVII. hence the leaf is liable to injury from much moisture on this surface, and is destroyed by being smeared with oil, in these respects resembling the lungs of animals, or the spiracula o. insects. To prevent these injuries, some leaves repel the dew-drops from their upper surfaces, as those of cabbages; other vegetables close the upper surfaces of their leaves together in the night, or in wet weather, as the sensitive plant; others only hang their leaves downward, so as to shoot the wet from them, as kidney-beans, and many trees. See note on l. 18 of this Canto.
Golden bell. l. 460. There are muscles placed

"So should young sympathy, in female form,
Climb the tall rock, spectatress of the storm;
Life's sinking wrecks with secret sighs deplore,
And bleed for others' woes, herself on shore;
To friendless virtue, gasping on the strand,
Bare her warm heart, her virgin arms expand,
Charm with kind looks, with tender accents cheer,
And pour the sweet consolatory tear;
Grief's cureless wounds with lenient balms assuage,
Or prop with firmer staff the steps of age; 470
The lifted arm of mute despair arrest,
And snatch the dagger pointed at his breast;
Or lull to slumber envy's haggard mien,
And rob her quiver'd shafts with hand unseen.
Sound, nymphs of helicon! the trump of fame,
And teach Hibernian echoes Jones's name;
Bind round her polish'd brow the civic bay,
And drag the fair philanthropist to day.
So from secluded springs, and secret caves, 479
Her Liffy pours his bright meandering waves,
Cools the parch'd vale, the sultry mead divides,
And towns and temples star his shadowy sides.

XIII. Call your light legions, tread the swampy heath,
Pierce with sharp spades the tremulous peat beneath;
With colters bright the rushy sward bisect,
And in new veins the gushing rills direct;—
So flowers shall rise in purple light array'd,
And blossom'd orchards stretch their silver shade;
Admiring glebes their amber ears unfold,
And labour sleep amid the waving gold. 490

"Thus when young Hercules with firm disdain
Braved the soft smiles of pleasure's harlot train;
To valiant toils his forceful limbs assign'd,
And gave to virtue all his mighty mind;
Fierce Achelous rush'd from mountain-caves,
O'er sad Etolia pour'd his wasteful waves,
O'er lowing vales and bleating pastures roll'd,
Swept her red vineyards, and her glebes of gold,
Mined all her towns, uptore her rooted woods,
And famine danced upon the shining floods. 500
The youthful hero seized his curled crest,
And dash'd with lifted club the watery pest;
With waving arm the billowy tumult quell'd,
And to his course the bellowing fiend repell'd.

"Then to a snake the finny demon turn'd
His lengthen'd form, with scales of silver burn'd;
Lash'd with resistless sweep his dragon-train,
And shot meandering o'er the affrighted plain.
The hero-god, with giant fingers clasp'd
Firm round his neck, the hissing monster grasp'd; 510

---

about the footstalks of the leaves or leaflets of many plants, for the purpose of closing their upper surfaces together, or of bending them down so as to shoot off the showers or dew-drops, as mentioned in the preceding note. The claws of the petals or of the divisions of the calyx of many flowers are furnished in a similar manner with muscles, which are exerted to open or close the coral and calyx of the flower as in tragopogon, anemone. This action of opening and closing the leaves or flowers does not appear to be produced simply by *irritation* on the muscles themselves, but by the connection of those muscles with a *sensitive* sensorium, or brain, existing in each individual bud or flower. 1st. Because many flowers close from the defect of stimulus, not by the excess of it, as by darkness, which is the absence of the stimulus of light; or by cold, which is the absence of the stimulus of heat. Now the defect of heat, or the absence of food or of drink, affects our *sensations*, which had been previously accustomed to a greater quantity of them; but a muscle cannot be said to be stimulated into action by a defect of stimulus. 2d. Because the muscles around the footstalks of the subdivisions of the leaves of the sensitive plant are exerted when any injury is offered to the other extremity of the leaf, and some of the stamens of the flowers of the class Syngenesia contract themselves when others are irritated. See note on Chondrilla, Part II. of this work.

From this circumstance, the contraction of the muscles of vegetables seems to depend on a disagreeable *sensation* in some distant part, and not on the *irritation* of the muscles themselves. Thus, when a particle of dust stimulates the ball of the eye, the eye-lids are instantly closed, and when too much light pains the retina, the muscles of the iris contract its aperture, and this not by any connection or consent of the nerves of those parts, but as an effort to prevent or to remove a disagreeable sensation, which evinces that vegetables are endued with sensation, or that each bud has a common censorium, and is furnished with a brain or a central place where its nerves are connected.

Jones's name. l. 476. A young lady who devotes a great part of an ample fortune to well-chosen acts of secret charity.

Fierce Achelous. l. 495. The river Achelous deluged Etolia, by one of its branches or arms which in the ancient languages are called horns, and produced famine throughout a great tract of country; this was represented in hieroglyphic emblems by the winding course of a serpent, and the roaring of a bull with large horns. Hercules, or the emblem of strength, strangled the serpent, and tore off one horn from the bull; that is, he stopped and turned the course of one arm of the river, and restored plenty to the country. Whence the ancient emblem of the horn of plenty. Dict. par M. Danet.

With starting eyes, wide throat, and gaping teeth,
Curl his redundant folds, and writhe in death.

" And now a bull, amid the flying throng
The grisly demon foam'd, and roar'd along ;
With silver hoofs the flowery meadows spurn'd,
Roll'd his red eye, his threatening antlers turn'd
Dragg'd down to earth, the warrior's victor-hands
Press'd his deep dewlap on the imprinted sands ;
Then with quick bound his bended knee he fix'd
High on his neck, the branching horns betwixt, 520
Strain'd his strong arms, his sinewy shoulders bent,
And from his curled brow the twisted terror rent.
—Pleased fawns and nymphs with dancing step applaud,
And hang their chaplets round the resting god ;
Link their soft hands, and rear with pausing toil
The golden trophy on the furrow'd soil ;
Fill with ripe fruits, with wreathed flowers adorn,
And give to Plenty her prolific horn.

XIV. " On spring's fair lip, cerulean sisters ! pour
From airy urns the sun-illumined shower, 530
Feed with the dulcet drops my tender broods,
Mellifluous flowers, and aromatic buds ;
Hang from each bending grass and horrent thorn
The tremulous pearl, that glitters to the morn ;
Or where cold dews their secret channels lave,
And earth's dark chambers hide the stagnant wave, [lead
Oh pierce, ye nymphs ! her marble veins, and
Her gushing fountains to the thirsty mead ;
Wide o'er the shining vales, and trickling hills,
Spread the bright treasure in a thousand rills. 540

So shall my peopled realms of leaf and flower
Exult, inebriate with the genial shower ;
Dip their long tresses from the mossy brink,
With tufted roots the glassy currents drink ;
Shade your cool mansions from meridian beams,
And view their waving honours in your streams.

" Thus where the veins their confluent branches bend,
And milky eddies with the purple blend ;
The chyle's white trunk, diverging from its source,
Seeks through the vital mass its shining course ; 550
O'er each red cell, and tissued membrane spreads
In living net-work all its branching threads ;
Maze within maze its tortuous path pursues,
Winds into glands, inextricable clues ; [sips
Steals through the stomach's velvet sides, and
The silver surges with a thousand lips ;
Fills each fine pore, pervades each slender hair,
And drinks salubrious dew-drops from the air.

" Thus when to kneel in Mecca's awful gloom,
Or press with pious kiss Medina's tomb, 560
League after league, through many a lingering day,
Steer the swart caravans their sultry way ;
O'er sandy wastes on gasping camels toil,
Or print with pilgrim-steps the burning soil ;
If from lone rocks a sparkling rill descend,
O'er the green brink the kneeling nations bend,
Bathe the parch'd lip, and cool the feverish tongue,
And the clear lake reflects the mingled throng."

The goddess paused,—the listening bands awhile
Still seem to hear, and dwell upon her smile ; 570
Then with soft murmur sweep in lucid trains
Down the green slopes, and o'er the pebbly plains,
To each bright stream on silver sandals glide,
Reflective fountain, and tumultuous tide.

So shoot the spider-broods at breezy dawn,
Their glittering net-work o'er the autumnal lawn ;

Dragg'd down to earth. l. 517. Described from an antique gem.

Spread the bright treasure. l. 540. The practice of flooding lands long in use in China has been but lately introduced into this country. Besides the supplying water to the herbage in dryer seasons, it seems to defend it from frost in the early part of the year, and thus doubly advances the vegetation. The waters which rise from springs passing through marl or limestone are replete with calcareous earth, and when thrown over morasses they deposit this earth and incrust or consolidate the morass. This kind of earth is deposited in great quantity from the springs at Matlock bath, and supplies the soft porous limestone of which the houses and walls are there constructed ; and has formed the whole bank for near a mile on that side of the Derwent on which they stand.

The water of many springs contains much azotic gas, or phlogistic air, besides carbonic gas, or fixed air, as that of Buxton and Bath ; this being set at liberty may more readily contribute to the production of nitre by means of the putrescent matters which it is exposed to by being spread upon the surface of the land ; in the same manner as frequently turning over heaps of manure facilitates the nitrous process by imprisoning atmospheric air in the interstices of the putrescent materials. Water arising by land-floods brings along with it much of the most soluble parts of the manure from the higher lands to the lower ones. River-water in its clear state and those springs which are called soft are less beneficial for the purpose of watering lands, as they contain less earthy or saline matter ; and water from dissolving snow from its slow solution brings but little earth along with it, as may be seen by the comparative clearness of the water of snow-floods.

From blade to blade connect with cordage fine
The unbending grass, and live along the line;
Or bathe unwet their oily forms, and dwell
With feet repulsive on the dimpling well.   580

So when the north congeals his watery mass,
Piles high his snows, and floors his seas with
    glass;   [rays,
While many a month, unknown to warmer
Marks its slow chronicle by lunar days;

Stout youths and ruddy damsels, sportive train,
Leave the white soil, and rush upon the main;
From isle to isle the moon-bright squadrons stray,
And win in easy curves their graceful way;
On step alternate borne, with balance nice
Hang o'er the gliding steel, and hiss along the ice.   590

THE ECONOMY OF VEGETATION.

CANTO IV.

ARGUMENT.

ADDRESS *to the Sylphs.* I. *Trade-winds. Monsoons. N. E. and S. W. winds. Land and sea breezes. Irregular winds,* 9. II. *Production of vital air from oxygene and light. The marriage of Cupid and Psyche,* 25. III. 1. *Syroc. Simoom. Tornado,* 63. 2. *Fog. Contagion. Story of Thyrsis and Ægle. Love and Death,* 79. IV. 1. *Barometer. Air-pump,* 127. 2. *Air-balloon of Mongolfier. Death of Rozier. Icarus,* 143. V. *Discoveries of Dr. Priestley. Evolutions and combinations of pure air. Rape of Proserpine,* 177. VI. *Sea-balloons, or houses constructed to move under the sea. Death of Mr. Day. Of Mr. Spalding. Of Captain Pierce and his Daughters,* 207. VII. *Sylphs of music. Cecilia singing. Cupid with a lyre riding upon a lion,* 245. VIII. *Destruction of Senacherib's army by a pestilential wind. Shadow of Death,* 275. IX. 1. *Wish to possess the secret of changing the course of the winds,* 307. 2. *Monster devouring air subdued by Mr. Kirwan,* 333. X. 1. *Seeds suspended in their pods. Stars discovered by Mr. Herschel. Destruction and resuscitation of all things,* 363. 2. *Seeds within seeds, and bulbs within bulbs. Picture on the retina of the eye. Concentric strata of the earth. The great seed,* 393. 3. *The root, pith, lobes, plume, calyx, corol, sap, blood, leaves respire and absorb light. The crocodile in its egg,* 421. XI. *Opening of the flower. The petals, style, anthers, prolific dust, honey-cup. Transmutation of the silk-worm,* 453. XII. 1. *Leaf-buds changed into flower-buds by wounding the bark, or strangulating a part of the branch. Cintra,* 477. 2. *Ingrafting. Aaron's rod pullulates,* 507. XIII. 1. *Insects on tree. Humming-bird alarmed by the spider-like appearance of cyprepedia,* 521. 2. *Diseases of vegetables. Scratch on unnealed glass,* 541. XIV. 1. *Tender flowers. Amaryllis, fritillary, erythrina, mimosa, cerea,* 553. 2. *Vines. Oranges. Diana's trees. Kew garden. The royal family,* 571. XV. *Offering to Hygeia,* 617. *Departure of the Goddess,* 659.

As when at noon in Hybla's fragrant bowers
Calcalia opens all her honey'd flowers;
Contending swarms on bending branches cling,
And nations hover on aurelian wing;
So round the goddess, ere she speaks, on high
Impatient sylphs in gawdy circlets fly;
Quivering in air their painted plumes expand,
And colour'd shadows dance upon the land.

I. "Sylphs! your light troops the tropic winds confine,
And guide their streaming arrows to the line;
While in warm floods ecliptic breezes rise, 11
And sink with wings benumb'd in colder skies.
You bid monsoons on Indian seas reside,
And veer, as moves the sun, their airy tide;
While southern gales, o'er western oceans roll,
And Eurus steals his ice-winds from the pole.
Your playful trains, on sultry islands born,
Turn on fantastic toe at eve and morn;
With soft susurrant voice alternate sweep
Earth's green pavilions and encircling deep. 20
Or in itinerant cohorts, borne sublime
On tides of ether, float from clime to clime;
O'er waving autumn bend your airy ring,
Or waft the fragrant bosom of the spring.

II. "When morn, escorted by the dancing hours,
O'er the bright plains her dewy lustre showers;

Cacalia opens. l. 2. The importance of the nectarium, or honey-gland, in the vegetable economy is seen from the very complicated apparatus, which nature has formed in some flowers for the preservation of their honey from insects, as in the aconites, or monkshoods; in other plants, instead of a great apparatus, for its protection, a greater secretion of it is produced, that thence a part may be spared to the depredation of insects. The cacalia suaveolens produces so much honey, that on some days it may be smelt at a great distance from the plant. I remember once counting on one of these plants, besides bees of various kinds without number, above two hundred painted butterflies, which gave it the beautiful appearance of being covered with additional flowers.

The tropic winds. l. 9. See additional notes, No. XXXIII.

Till from her sable chariot eve serene
Drops the dark curtain o'er the brilliant scene;
You form with chemic hands the airy surge,
Mix with broad vans, with shadowy tridents urge.
Sylphs! from each sun-bright leaf, that twink-
ling shakes   31
O'er earth's green lap, or shoots amid her lakes,
Your playful bands with simpering lips invite,
And wed the enamour'd oxygene to light.—
Round their white necks with fingers interwove,
Cling the fond pair with unabating love;
Hand link'd in hand on buoyant step they rise,
And soar and glisten in unclouded skies.
Whence in bright floods the vital air expands,
And with concentric spheres involves the
lands;   40
Pervades the swarming seas, and heaving earths,
Where teeming nature broods her myriad
births;
Fills the fine lungs of all that *breathe* or *bud*,
Warms the new heart, and dyes the gushing
blood;
With life's first spark inspires the organic frame,
And, as it wastes, renews the subtile flame.

"So pure, so soft, with sweet attraction shone
Fair Psyche, kneeling at the ethereal throne;
Won with coy smiles the admiring court of
Jove,   49
And warm'd the bosom of unconquer'd love.—
Beneath a moving shade of fruits and flowers
Onward they march to Hymen's sacred bowers;
With lifted torch he lights the festive train,
Sublime, and leads them in his golden chain;
Joins the fond pair, indulgent to their vows,
And hides with mystic veil their blushing
brows.   [fling,
Round their fair forms their mingling arms they
Meet with warm lip, and clasp with rustling
wing.—
—Hence plastic nature, as oblivion whelms
Her fading forms, repeoples all her realms;   60
Soft joys disport on purple plumes unfurl'd,
And love and beauty rule the willing world.

III. 1. "Sylphs! your bold myriads on the
withering heath
Stay the fell Syroc's suffocative breath;
Arrest simoom in his realms of sand,
The poison'd javelin balanced in his hand;—

The enamour'd oxygene. l. 34. The common air of the atmosphere appears by the analysis of Dr. Priestley and other philosophers to consist of about three parts of elastic fluid unfit for respiration or combustion, called azote by the French school, and about one-fourth of pure vital air fit for the support of animal life and of combustion, called oxygene. The principal source of the azote is probably from the decomposition of all vegetable and animal matters by putrefaction and combustion; the principal source of vital air or oxygene is perhaps from the decomposition of water in the organs of vegetables by means of the sun's light. The difficulty of injecting vegetable vessels seems to show that their perspirative pores are much less than those of animals, and that the water which constitutes their perspiration is so divided at the time of its exclusion, that by means of the sun's light it becomes decomposed, the inflammable air or hydrogene, which is one of its constituent parts, being retained to form the oil, resin, wax, honey, &c. of the vegetable economy; and the other part, which united with light or heat becomes vital air or oxygene gas, rises into the atmosphere and replenishes it with the food of life.

Dr. Priestley has evinced by very ingenious experiments that the blood gives out phlogiston, and receives vital air, or oxygene gas by the lungs. And Dr. Crawford has shown that the blood acquires heat from this vital air in respiration. There is however still a something more subtile than heat, which must be obtained in respiration from the vital air, a something which life cannot exist a few minutes without, which seems necessary to the vegetable as well as to the animal world, and which, as no organized vessels can confine it, requires perpetually to be renewed. See note on Canto I. l. 401; and additional notes, No. XXXIV.

Fair Psyche. l. 48. Described from an ancient gem on a fine onyx in possession of the Duke of Marlborough, of which there is a beautiful print in Bryant's Mythol. Vol. II. p. 392. And from another ancient gem of Cupid and Psyche embracing, of which there is a print in Spence's Polymetis, p. 82.

Repeoples all her realms. l. 60.

Quæ mare navigerum et terras frugiferentes [tum
Concelebras; per te quoniam genus omne animan-
Concipitur, visitque exortum lumina solis.
LUCRET.

Arrest simoom. l. 65. "At eleven o'clock while we were with great pleasure contemplating the rugged tops of Chiggre, where we expected to solace ourselves with plenty of good water, Idris cried out with a loud voice, "Fall upon your faces, for here is the simoom!" I saw from the S. E. a haze come in colour like the purple part of a rainbow, but not so compressed or thick; it did not occupy twenty yards in breadth, and was about twelve feet high from the ground. It was a kind of a blush upon the air, and it moved very rapidly, for I scarce could turn to fall upon the ground with my head to the northward, when I felt the heat of its current plainly upon my face. We all lay flat upon the ground, as if dead, till Idris told us it was blown over. The meteor, or purple haze, which I saw was indeed passed; but the light air that still blew was of heat to threaten suffocation. For my part, I found distinctly in my breast, that I had imbibed a part of it; nor was I free of an asthmatic sensation till I had been some months in Italy." Bruce's Travels, Vol. IV. p. 557.

It is difficult to account for the narrow track of this pestilential wind, which is said not to exceed twenty yards, and for its small elevation of twelve feet. A whirlwind will pass forwards, and throw down an avenue of trees by its quick revolution as it passes; but nothing like a whirlwind is described as happening in these narrow streams of air, and whirlwinds ascend to greater heights. There seems but one known manner in which this channel of air could be effected, and that is by electricity.

The volcanic origin of these winds is men-

Fierce on blue streams he rides the tainted air,
Points his keen eye, and waves his whistling hair;
While, as he turns, the undulating soil
Rolls in red waves, and billowy deserts boil. 70

You seize tornado by his locks of mist
Burst his dense clouds, his wheeling spires untwist;
Wide o'er the west when borne on headlong gales,
Dark as meridian night, the monster sails,
Howls high in air, and shakes his curled brow,
Lashing with serpent-train the waves below,
Whirls his black arm, the forked lightnings flings,
And showers a deluge from his demon-wings.

2. " Sylphs! with light shafts you pierce the drowsy fog, 79
That lingering slumbers on the sedge-wove bog,
With webbed feet o'er midnight meadows creeps,
Or flings his hairy limbs on stagnant deeps,
You meet contagion issuing from afar,
And dash the baleful conqueror from his car;
When, guest of death! from charnal vaults he steals,
And bathes in human gore his armed wheels.

" Thus when the plague, upborne on Belgian air,
Look'd through the mist and shook his clotted hair;
O'er shrinking nations steer'd malignant clouds,
And rain'd destruction on the gasping crowds.
The beauteous Ægle felt the venom'd dart, 91
Slow roll'd her eye, and feebly throbb'd her heart;
Each fervid sigh seem'd shorter than the last,
And starting friendship shunn'd her, as she pass'd.
—With weak unsteady step the fainting maid
Seeks the cold garden's solitary shade,
Sinks on the pillowy moss her drooping head,
And prints with lifeless limbs her leafy bed.
—On wings of love her plighted swain pursues,
Shades her from winds, and shelters her from dews, 100
Extends on tapering poles the canvass roof,
Spreads o'er the straw-wove mat the flaxen woof,
Sweet buds and blossoms on her bolster strows,
And binds his kerchief round her aching brows;
Sooths with soft kiss, with tender accents charms,
And clasps the bright infection in his arms.—
With pale and languid smiles the grateful fair
Applauds his virtues, and rewards his care;
Mourns with wet cheek her fair companions fled 109
On timorous steps, or number'd with the dead;
Calls to her bosom all its scatter'd rays,
And pours on Thyrsis the collected blaze
Braves the chill night, caressing and caress'd,
And folds her hero-lover to her breast:—
Less bold, Leander at the dusky hour
Eyed, as he swam, the far love-lighted tower;
Breasted with struggling arms the tossing wave,
And sunk benighted in the watery grave.
Less bold, Tobias claim'd the nuptial bed 119
Where seven fond lovers by a fiend had bled;
And drove, instructed by his angel-guide,
The enamour'd demon from the fatal bride.—
—Sylphs! while your winnowing pinions fann'd the air,
And shed gay visions o'er the sleeping pair;

---

tioned in the note on Chunda in Part. II. of this work; it must here be added, that Professor Vairo at Naples found, that during the eruption of Vesuvius perpendicular iron bars were electric; and others have observed suffocating damps to attend these eruptions. Ferber's Travels in Italy, p. 133. And lastly, that a current of air attends the passage of electric matter, as is seen in presenting an electrized point to the flame of a candle. In Mr. Bruce's account of this simoom, it was in its course over a quite dry desert of sand, (and which was in consequence unable to conduct an electric stream into the earth beneath it,) to some moist rocks at but a few miles distance; and thence would appear to be a stream of electricity from a volcano attended with noxious air; and as the bodies of Mr. Bruce and his attendants were insulated on the sand, they would not be sensible of their increased electricity, as it passed over them; to which it may be added, that a sulphurous or suffocating sensation is said to accompany flashes of lightning, and even strong sparks of artificial electricity. In the above account of the simoom, a great redness in the air is said to be a certain sign of its approach, which may be occasioned by the eruption of flame from a distant volcano in these extensive and impenetrable deserts of sand. See Note on l. 294 of this Canto.

Tornado. l. 71. See additional notes, No. XXXIII.

On stagnant deeps. L. 82. All contagious miasmata originate either from animal bodies, as those of the small pox, or from putrid morasses; these latter produce agues in the colder climates, and malignant fevers in the warmer ones. The volcanic vapours which cause epidemic coughs, are to be ranked amongst poisons, rather than amongst the miasmata, which produce contagious diseases.

The beauteous Ægle. l. 91. When the plague raged in Holland in 1636, a young girl was seized with it, had three carbuncles, and was removed to a garden, where her lover, who was betrothed to her, attended her as a nurse, and slept with her as his wife. He remained uninfected, and she recovered, and was married to him. The story is related by Vinc. Fabricius in the Misc. Cur. Ann. II. Obs. 188.

Love round their couch effused his rosy breath,
And with his keener arrows conquer'd Death.

IV. 1. "You charm'd, indulgent Sylphs!
their learned toil,
And crown'd with fame your Torricell, and
Boyle;
Taught with sweet smiles, responsive to their
prayer,
The spring and pressure of the viewless air. 130
—How up exhausted tubes bright currents flow
Of liquid silver from the lake below,
Weigh the long column of the incumbent skies,
And with the changeful moment fall and rise.
—How, as in brazen pumps the pistons move,
The membrane-valve sustains the weight above;
Stroke follows stroke, the gelid vapour falls,
And misty dew-drops dim the crystal walls;
Rare and more rare expands the fluid thin,
And silence dwells with vacancy within.— 140
So in the mighty void with grim delight
Primeval silence reign'd with ancient night.

2. "Sylphs! your soft voices, whispering
from the skies,
Bade from low earth the bold Mongolfier rise;
Outstretch'd his buoyant ball with airy spring,
And bore the sage on levity of wing;—
Where were ye, Sylphs! when on the ethereal
main   [vain?
Young Rosiere launch'd, and call'd your aid in
Fair mounts the light balloon, by zephyr driven,
Parts the thin clouds, and sails along the
heaven;   150
Higher and yet higher the expanding bubble flies,
Lights with quick flash, and bursts amid the
skies.—
Headlong he rushes through the affrighted air
With limbs distorted, and dishevel'd hair,
Whirls round and round, the flying crowd
alarms,
And death receives him in his sable arms!—
Betrothed beauty bending o'er his bier
Breathes the loud sob, and sheds the incessant
tear;
Pursues the sad procession, as it moves   159
Through winding avenues and waving groves;
Hears the slow dirge amid the echoing aisles,
And mingles with her sighs discordant smiles.
Then with quick step advancing through the
gloom,
'I come!' she cries, and leaps into his tomb.
'Oh, stay! I follow thee to realms above!—
Oh, wait a moment for thy dying love!—
Thus, thus I clasp thee to my bursting heart!—
Close o'er us, holy earth!—We will not part!'.

"So erst with melting wax and loosen'd
strings
Sunk hapless Icarus on unfaithful wings;   170

Torricell and Boyle. l. 128. The pressure of the atmosphere was discovered by Torricelli, a disciple of Galileo, who had previously found that the air had weight. Dr. Hook and M. Du Hamel ascribe the invention of the air-pump to to Mr. Boyle, who however confesses he had some hints concerning its construction from Dr. Guerick. The vacancy at the summit of the barometer is termed the Torricellian vacuum, and the exhausted receiver of an air pump the Boylean vacuum, in honour of these two philosophers.

The mist and descending dew which appear at first exhausting the receiver of an air-pump, are explained in the Phi. Trans. Vol. LXXVIII. from the cold produced by the expansion of air. For a thermometer placed in a receiver sinks some degrees, and in a very little time, as soon as a sufficient quantity of heat can be acquired from the surrounding bodies, the dew becomes again taken up. See additional notes, No. VII. Mr. Saussure observed on placing his hygrometer in a receiver of an air-pump, that though on beginning to exhaust it the air became misty, and parted with its moisture, yet the hair of his hygrometer contracted, and the instrument pointed to greater dryness. This unexpected occurrence is explained by M. Monge, (Annales de Chymie, Tom V.), to depend on the want of the usual pressure of the atmosphere to force the aqueous particles into the pores of the hair; and M. Saussure supposes, that his vesicular vapour requires more time to be redissolved, than is necessary to dry the hair of his thermometer. Essais sur l'Hygrom. p. 226. But I suspect there is a less hypothetical way of understanding it; when a colder body is brought into warm and moist air, (as a bottle of spring-water for instance,) a steam is quickly collected on its surface; the contrary occurs when a warmer body is brought into cold and damp air, it continues free from dew so long as it continues warm; for it warms the atmosphere around it, and renders it capable of receiving instead of parting with moisture. The moment the air becomes rarefied in the receiver of the air-pump it becomes colder, as appears by the thermometer, and deposits its vapour; but the air of Mr. Saussure's hygrometer is now warmer than the air in which it is immersed, and in consequence becomes dryer than before, by warming the air which immediately surrounds it, a part of its moisture evaporating along with its heat.

Young Rosiere launch'd. l. 148. M. Pilatre du Rosiere, with a M. Romain, rose in a balloon, from Boulogne, in June 1785, and after having been about a mile high for about half an hour, the balloon took fire, and the two adventurers were dashed to pieces on their fall to the ground. Mr. Rosiere was a philosopher of great talents and activity, joined with such urbanity and elegance of manners, as conciliated the affections of his acquaintance, and rendered his misfortune universally lamented. Annual Register for 1784 and 1785, p. 329.

Betrothed beauty. l. 157. Miss Susan Dyer was engaged in a few days to marry M. Rosiere, who had promised to quit such dangerous experiments in future: she was spectatress of this sad accident, lingered some months, and died from excess of grief. The Rev. Mr. Collier, Senior Fellow of Trinity College in Cambridge was well acquainted with this amiable young lady, and suggested the introduction of her melancholy history in this place.

His scatter'd plumage danced upon the wave,
And sorrowing mermaids deck'd his watery grave;
O'er his pale corse their pearly sea-flowers shed,
And strew'd with crimson moss his marble bed;
Struck in their coral towers the pausing bell,
And wide in ocean toll'd his echoing knell.

V. " Sylphs! you, retiring to sequester'd bowers,
Where oft your Priestley woos your airy powers,
On noiseless step or quivering pinion glide,
As sits the sage with science by his side;   180
To his charm'd eye in gay undress appear,
Or pour your secrets on his raptured ear.
How nitrous gas from iron ingots driven
Drinks with red lips the purest breath of heaven;
How, while conferva from its tender hair
Gives in bright bubbles empyrean air,
The crystal floods phlogistic ores calcine,
And the pure ether marries with the mine.

" So in Sicilia's ever-blooming shade   189
When playful Proserpine from Ceres stray'd,
Led with unwary step her virgin trains
O'er Etna's steeps, and Enna's golden plains;
Pluck'd with fair hand the silver-blossom'd bower,
And purpled mead,—herself a fairer flower;
Sudden, unseen amid the twilight glade,
Rush'd gloomy Dis, and seized the trembling maid.—
Her starting damsels sprung from mossy seats,
Dropp'd from their gauzy laps the gather'd sweets,
Clung round the struggling nymph, with piercing cries   199
Pursued the chariot, and invoked the skies;—
Pleased as he grasps her in his iron arms,
Frights with soft sighs, with tender words alarms,

And wide in ocean. l. 176. Denser bodies propagate vibration or sound better than rarer ones; if two stones be struck together under the water, they may be heard a mile or two by any one whose head is immersed at that distance, according to an experiment of Dr. Franklin. If the ear be applied to one end of a long beam of timber, the stroke of a pin at the other end becomes sensible; if a poker be suspended in the middle of a garter, each end of which is pressed against the ear, the least percussions on the poker give great sounds. And I am informed by laying the ear on the ground the tread of a horse may be discerned at a great distance in the night. The organs of hearing belonging to fish are for this reason much less complicated than of quadrupeds, as the fluid they are immersed in so much better conveys its vibrations. And it is probable that some shell-fish which have twisted shells like the cochlea and semicircular canals of the ears of men and quadrupeds may have no appropriated organ for perceiving the vibrations of the element they live in, but may by their spiral form be in a manner all ear.

Where oft your Priestley. l. 178. The fame of Dr. Priestley is known in every part of the earth where science has penetrated. His various discoveries respecting the analysis of the atmosphere, and the production of variety of new airs or gasses, can only be clearly understood by reading his Experiments on Airs, (3 vols. octavo, Johnson, London.) The following are amongst his many discoveries. 1. The discovery of nitrous and dephlogisticated airs. 2. The exhibition of the acids and alkalies in the form of air. 3. Ascertaining the purity of respirable air by nitrous air. 4. The restoration of vitiated air by vegetation. 5. The influence of light to enable vegetables to yield pure air. 6. The conversion by means of light of animal and vegetable substances, that would otherwise become putrid and offensive, into nourishment of vegetables. 7. The use of respiration by the blood parting with phlogiston, and imbibing dephlogisticated air.

The experiments here alluded to are, 1. Concerning the production of nitrous gas from dissolving iron and many other metals in nitrous acid, which though first discovered by Dr. Hales (Static. Ess. Vol. I. p. 224) was fully investigated, and applied to the important purpose of distinguishing the purity of atmospheric air by Dr. Priestley. When about two measures of common air and one of nitrous gas are mixed together a red effervescence takes place, and the two airs occupy about one-fourth less space than was previously occupied by the common air alone.

2. Concerning the green substance which grows at the bottom of reservoirs of water which Dr. Priestley discovered to yield much pure air when the sun shone on it. His method of collecting this air is by placing over the green substance, which he believes to be a vegetable of the genus conferva, an inverted bell-glass previously filled with water, which subsides as the air arises; it has since been found that all vegetables give up pure air from their leaves, when the sun shines upon them, but not in the night, which may be owing to the sleep of the plant.

3. The third refers to the great quantity of pure air contained in the calces of metals. The calces were long known to weigh much more than the metallic bodies before calcination, insomuch that 100 pounds of lead will produce 112 pounds of minium; the ore of manganese, which is always found near the surface of the earth, is replete with pure air, which is now used for the purpose of bleaching. Other metals when exposed to the atmosphere attract the pure air from it, and become calces by its combination, as zinc, lead, iron; and increase in weight in proportion to the air, which they imbibe.

When playful Proserpine. l. 190. The fable of Proserpine's being seized by Pluto as she was gathering flowers, is explained by Lord Bacon to signify the combination or marriage of ethereal spirit with earthly materials. Bacon's Works, Vol. V. p. 470. edit. 4to. Lond. 1778. This allusion is still more curiously exact, from the late discovery of pure air being given up from vegetables, and that then in its unmixed state it more readily combines with metallic or inflammable bodies. From these fables, which were probably taken from ancient hieroglyphics, there is frequently reason to believe that the Egyptians possessed much chemical knowledge, which for want of alphabetical writing perished with their philosophers.

The wheels descending roll'd in smoky rings,
Infernal cupids flapp'd their demon wings;
Earth with deep yawn received the fair, amazed,
And far in night celestial beauty blazed.

VI. "Led by the sage, Lo! Britain's sons shall guide
Huge sea-balloons beneath the tossing tide;
The diving castles, roof'd with spheric glass,
Ribb'd with strong oak, and barr'd with bolts of brass, 210
Buoy'd with pure air shall endless tracks pursue,
And Priestley's hand the vital flood renew.—
Then shall Britannia rule the wealthy realms,
Which ocean's wide insatiate wave o'erwhelms;
Confine in netted bowers his scaly flocks,
Part his blue plains, and people all his rocks.
Deep, in warm waves, beneath the line that roll,
Beneath the shadowy ice-isles of the pole,
Onward, through bright meandering vales, afar,
Obedient sharks shall trail her sceptred car, 220
With harness'd necks the pearly flood disturb,
Stretch the silk rein, and champ the silver curb;
Pleased round her triumph wondering Tritons play,
And sea-maids hail her on the watery way.
—Oft shall she weep beneath the crystal waves
O'er shipwreck'd lovers weltering in their graves;
Mingling in death the brave and good behold,
With slaves to glory, and with slaves to gold;

Shrined in the deep shall Day and Spalding mourn, 229
Each in his treacherous bell, sepulchral urn!—
Oft o'er thy lovely daughters, hapless Pierce!
Her sighs shall breathe, her sorrows dew their hearse.—
With brow upturn'd to heaven, 'We will not part!'
He cried, and clasp'd them to his aching heart,
—Dash'd in dread conflict on the rocky grounds,
Crash'd the shock'd masts, the staggering wreck rebounds;
Through gaping seams the rushing deluge swims,
Chills their pale bosoms, bathes their shuddering limbs,
Climbs their white shoulders, buoys their streaming hair, 236
And the last sea-shriek bellows in the air.—
Each with loud sobs her tender sire caress'd,
And gasping strain'd him closer to her breast!
—Stretch'd on one bier they sleep beneath the brine,
And their white bones with ivory arms intwine!

VII. "Sylphs of nice ear! with beating wings you guide
The fine vibrations of the aerial tide;

Led by the sage. l. 207. Dr. Priestley's discovery of the production of pure air from such variety of substances, will probably soon be applied to the improvement of the diving-bell, as the substances which contain vital air in immense quantities are of little value, as manganese and minium. See additional notes, No. XXXIII. In every hundred weight of minium there is combined about twelve pounds of pure air: now, as sixty pounds of water are about a cubic foot, and as air is eight hundred times lighter than water, five hundred weight of minium will produce eight hundred cubic feet of air, or about six thousand gallons. Now, as this is at least thrice as pure as atmospheric air, a gallon of it may be supposed to serve for three minutes respiration for one man. At present the air cannot be set at liberty from minium by vitriolic acid without the application of some heat; this is however very likely soon to be discovered, and will then enable adventurers to journey beneath the ocean in large inverted ships or diving balloons.

Mr. Boyle relates, that Cornelius Drebelle contrived, not only a vessel to be rowed under water, but also a liquor to be carried in that vessel, which would supply the want of fresh air. The vessel was made by order of James I. and carried twelve rowers besides passengers. It was tried in the river Thames, and one of the persons who was in that submarine voyage told the particulars of the experiments to a person who related them to Mr. Boyle. Annual Register for 1774, p. 248.

Day and Spalding mourn. l. 229. Mr. Day perished in a diving bell, or diving boat, of his own construction, at Plymouth, in June 1774, in which he was to have continued for a wager twelve hours, one hundred feet deep in water, and probably perished from his not possessing all the hydrostatic knowledge that was necessary. See note on Ulva, Part II. of this work. See Annual Register for 1774, p. 245.

Mr. Spalding was professionally ingenious in the art of constructing and managing the diving bell, and had practised the business many years with success. He went down, accompanied by one of his young men, twice to view the wreck of the Imperial East-Indiaman, at the Kish bank in Ireland. On descending the third time in June, 1783, they remained about an hour under water, and had two barrels of air sent down to them, but on the signals from below not being again repeated, after a certain time, they were drawn up by their assistants, and both found dead in the bell. Annual Register for 1783, p. 206. These two unhappy events may for a time check the ardour of adventurers in traversing the bottom of the ocean, but it is probable in another half century it may be safer to travel under the ocean than over it, since Dr. Priestley's discovery or procuring pure air in such great abundance from the calces of metals.

Hapless Pierce! l. 231. The Halsewell East-Indiaman, outward bound, was wrecked off Seacomb, in the isle of Purbec, on the 6th of January, 1786; when Captain Pierce, the commander, with two young ladies, his daughters, and the greatest part of the crew and passengers, perished in the sea. Some of the officers, and about seventy seamen, escaped with great difficulty on the rocks; but Capt. Pierce finding it was impossible to save the lives of the young ladies, refused to quit the ship, and perished with them.

Join in sweet cadences the measured words,
Or stretch and modulate the trembling cords.
You strung to melody the Grecian lyre,
Breathed the rapt song, and fann'd the thought of fire, 250
Or brought in combinations, deep and clear,
Immortal harmony to Handel's ear.—
You with soft breath attune the vernal gale,
When breezy evening broods the listening vale;
Or wake the loud tumultuous sounds, that dwell
In echo's many-toned diurnal shell.
You melt in dulcet chords, when zephyr rings
The Eolian Harp, and mingle all its strings;
Or trill in air the soft symphonious chime,
When rapt Cecilia lifts her eye sublime, 260
Swell, as she breathes, her bosom's rising snow,
O'er her white teeth in tuneful accents flow,
Through her fair lips on whispering pinions move,
And form the tender sighs, that kindle love!

" So playful love on Ida's flowery sides
With ribbon-rein the indignant lion guides;
Pleased on his brinded back the lyre he rings,
And shakes delirious rapture from the strings;
Slow as the pausing monarch stalks along,
Sheaths his retractile claws, and drinks the song; 270
Soft nymphs on timid step the triumph view,
And listening fawns with beating hoofs pursue;
With pointed ears the alarmed forest starts,
And love and music soften savage hearts.

VIII. " Sylphs! your bold hosts, when Heaven with justice dread
Calls the red tempests round the guilty head,
Fierce at his nod assume vindictive forms,
And launch from airy cars the vollied storms.
From Ashur's vales when proud Senacherib trod, 279
Pour'd his swoln heart, defied the living God,
Urged with incessant shouts his glittering powers,
And Judah shook through all her massy towers;
Round her sad altars press the prostrate crowd,
Hosts beat their breasts, and suppliant chieftains bow'd;
Loud shrieks of matrons thrill'd the troubled air,
And trembling virgins rent their scatter'd hair;
High in the midst the kneeling king adored,
Spread the blaspheming scroll before the Lord,
Raised his pale hands, and breathed his pausing sighs, 289
And fixed on heaven his dim imploring eyes,—

' Oh! mighty God! amidst thy seraph-throng
Who sit'st sublime, the judge of right and wrong;
Thine the wide earth, bright sun, and starry zone, [throne;
That twinkling journey round thy golden
Thine the crystal source of life and light,
And thine the realms of death's eternal night.
Oh! bend thine ear, thy gracious eye incline,
Lo! Ashur's king blasphemes thy holy shrine,
Insults our offerings, and derides our vows,—
Oh! strike the diadem from his impious brows,
Tear from his murderous hand the bloody rod,
And teach the trembling nations, ' thou art God!' 302
—Sylphs! in what dread array with pennons broad
Onward ye floated o'er the ethereal road,
Call'd each dank steam the reeking marsh exhales,
Contagious vapours, and volcanic gales,
Gave the soft south with poisonous breath to blow,
And roll'd the dreadful whirlwind on the foe!
Hark! o'er the camp the venom'd tempest sings,
Man falls on man, on buckler buckler rings; 310
Groan answers groan, to anguish anguish yields,
And death's loud accents shake the tented fields!
—High rears the fiend his grinning jaws, and wide
Spans the pale nations with colossal stride,

Indignant lion guides. l. 266. Described from an ancient gem, expressive of the combined power of love and music, in the Museum Florent.

Volcanic gales. l. 306. The pestilential winds of the east are described by various authors under various denominations; as harmattan, samiel, samium, syrocca, kamsin, seravansum. M. de Beauchamp describes a remarkable south wind in the deserts about Bagdad, called seravansum, or poison-wind; it burns the face, impedes respiration, strips the trees of their leaves, and is said to pass on in a straight line, and often kills people in six hours. P. Cotte sur la Meteorol. Analytical Review for February, 1790. M. Volney says, the hot wind or ramsin seems to blow at the season when the sands of the deserts are the hottest; the air is then filled with an extremely subtile dust. Vol. I. p. 61. These winds blow in all directions from the deserts; in Egypt the most violent proceed from the S. S. W. at Mecca from the E. at Surat from the N. at Bassora from the N. W. at Bagdad from the W. and in Syria from the S. E.
On the south of Syria, he adds, where the Jordan flows is a country of volcanos; and it is observed that the earthquakes in Syria happen after their rainy season, which is also conformable to a similar observation made by Dr. Shaw in Barbary. Travels in Egypt, Vol. I. p. 308.
These winds seem all to be of volcanic origin, as before mentioned, with this difference, that the simoom is attended with a stream of electric matter; they seem to be in consequence of earthquakes caused by the monsoon floods, which fall on volcanic fires in Syria, at the same time that they inundate the Nile.

Waves his broad falchion with uplifted hand,
And his vast shadow darkens all the land.

IX. 1. " Ethereal cohorts! essences of air!
Make the green children of the spring your care!
Oh, Sylphs! disclose in this inquiring age
One golden secret to some favour'd sage;   320
Grant the charm'd talisman, the chain, that binds,
Or guides the changeful pinions of the winds!
—No more shall hoary Boreas, issuing forth
With Eurus, lead the tempests of the north;
Rime the pale dawn, or veil'd in flaky showers
Chill the sweet bosoms of the smiling hours.
By whispering Auster waked shall Zephyr rise,
Meet with soft kiss, and mingle in the skies,
Fan the gay floret, bend the yellow ear,
And rock the uncurtain'd cradle of the year; 330
Autumn and spring in lively union blend,
And from the skies the golden age descend.

2. " Castled on ice, beneath the circling Bear,
A vast camelion drinks and vomits air;
O'er twelve degrees his ribs gigantic bend;
And many a league his gasping jaws extend;
Half-fish, beneath, his scaly volutes spread,
And vegetable plumage crests his head;
Huge fields of air his wrinkled skin receives,
From panting gills, wide lungs, and waving leaves;
Then with dread throes subsides his bloated form,
His shriek the thunder, and his sigh the storm.
Oft high in heaven the hissing demon wins
His towering course, upborne, on winnowing fins;
Steers with expanded eye and gaping mouth,
His mass enormous to the affrighted south;
Spreads o'er the shuddering line his shadowy limbs,
And frost and famine follow as he swims.—

One golden secret. l. 320. The suddenness of the change of the wind from N. E. to S. W. seems to show that it depends on some minute chemical cause; which if it was discovered might probably, like other chemical causes, be governed by human agency; such as blowing up rocks by gunpowder, or extracting the lightning from the clouds. If this could be accomplished, it would be the most happy discovery that ever has happened to these northern latitudes, since in this country the N. E. winds bring frost, and the S. W. ones are attended with warmth and moisture; if the inferior currents of air could be kept perpetually from the S. W. supplied by new productions of air at the line, or by superior currents flowing in a contrary direction, the vegetation of this country would be doubled; as in the moist valleys of Africa, which know no frost; the number of its inhabitants would be increased, and their lives prolonged; as great abundance of the aged and infirm of mankind; as well as many birds and animals, are destroyed by severe continued frosts in this climate.

A vast camelion. l. 334. See additional notes, No. XXXIII. on the destruction and reproduction of the atmosphere.

Sylphs! round his cloud-built couch your bands array,
And mould the monster to your gentle sway; 350
Charm with soft tones, with tender touches check,
Bend to your golden yoke his willing neck,
With silver curb his yielding teeth restrain,
And give to Kirwan's hand the silken rein.
—Pleased shall the sage, the dragon-wings between,
Bend o'er discordant climes his eye serene,
With Lapland breezes cool Arabian vales,
And call to Hindostan antarctic gales,
Adorn with wreathed ears Kampschatca's brows,
And scatter roses on Zealandic snows,   360
Earth's wondering zones the genial seasons share,
And nations hail him ' Monarch of the Air.'

X. 1. " Sylphs! as you hover on ethereal wing,
Brood the green children of parturient spring!—
Where in their bursting cells my embryons rest,
I charge you, guard the vegetable nest;
Count with nice eye the myriad seeds, that swell
Each vaulted womb of husk, or pod, or shell;
Feed with sweet juices, clothe with downy hair,
Or hang, inshrined, their little orbs in air. 370

" So, late descried by Herschel's piercing sight,   [night;
Hang the bright squadrons of the twinkling

To Kirwan's hand. l. 354. Mr. Kirwan has published a valuable treatise on the temperature of climates, as a step towards investigating the theory of the winds; and has since written some ingenious papers on this subject in the Transactions of the Royal Irish Society.

The myriad seeds. l. 367. Nature would seem to have been wonderfully prodigal in her seeds of vegetables, and the spawn of fish; almost any one plant, if all its seeds should grow to maturity, would in a few years alone people the terrestrial globe. Mr. Ray asserts that 1012 seeds of tobacco weighed only one grain, and that from one tobacco plant the seeds thus calculated amounted to 360,000! The seeds of the ferns are by him supposed to exceed a million on a leaf. As the works of nature are governed by general laws, this exuberant reproduction prevents the accidental extinction of the species, at the same time that they serve for food for the higher orders of animation.

Every seed possesses a reservoir of nutriment designed for the growth of the future plant, this consists of starch, mucilage, or oil, within the coat of the seed, or of sugar and subacid pult in the fruit, which belongs to it.

For the preservation of the immature seed nature has used many ingenious methods; some are wrapped in down, as the seeds of the rose, bean, and cotton-plant; others are suspended in a large air-vessel, as those of the bladder-sena, staphylæa, and pea.

Ten thousand marshall'd stars, a silver zone,
Effuse their blended lustres round her throne;
Suns call to suns, in lucid clouds conspire,
And light exterior skies with golden fire;
Resistless rolls the illimitable sphere,
And one great circle forms the unmeasured year.
—Roll on, ye stars! exult in youthful prime,
Mark with bright curves the printless steps of time;   380
Near and more near your beamy cars approach,
And lessening orbs on lessening orbs encroach;—
Flowers of the sky! ye too to age must yield,
Frail as your silken sisters of the field!
Star after star from heaven's high arch shall rush,
Suns sink on suns, and systems systems crush,
Headlong, extinct, to one dark centre fall,
And death and night and chaos mingle all!
—Till o'er the wreck, emerging from the storm,
Immortal nature lifts her changeful form,   390
Mounts from her funeral pyre on wings of flame,
And soars and shines, another and the same.

2 'Lo! on each seed within its slender rind
Life's golden threads in endless circles wind;
Maze within maze the lucid webs are roll'd;
And, as they burst, the living flame unfold.

The pulpy acorn, ere it swells, contains
The oak's vast branches in its milky veins;
Each ravel'd bud, fine film, and fibre-line,
Traced with nice pencil on the small design.   400
The young narcissus, in its bulb compress'd,
Cradles a second nestling on its breast;
In whose fine arms a younger embryon lies,
Folds its thin leaves, and shuts its floret-eyes;
Grain within grain successive harvests dwell,
And boundless forests slumber in a shell.
—So yon gray precipice, and ivy'd towers,
Long winding meads, and intermingled bowers,
Green files of poplars, o'er the lake that bow,
And glimmering wheel, which rolls and foams below,   410
In one bright point with nice distinction lie
Plann'd on the moving tablet of the eye.
—So, fold on fold, earth's wavy plains extend,
And, sphere in sphere, its hidden strata bend;
—Incumbent spring her beamy plumes expands
O'er restless oceans, and impatient lands,
With genial lustres warms the mighty ball,
And the great seed evolves, disclosing all;
Life *buds* or *breathes* from Indus to the poles,
And the vast surface kindles, as it rolls!   420

3. "Come, ye soft sylphs! who sport on Latian land,
Come, sweet lip'd zephyr, and favonius bland!
Teach the fine seed, instinct with life, to shoot
On earth's cold bosom its descending root;

And light exterior. l. 376. I suspect this line is from Dwight's Conquest of Canaan, a poem written by a very young man, and which contains much fine versification.

Near and more near. l. 381. From the vacant spaces in some parts of the heavens, and the correspondent clusters of stars in their vicinity, Mr. Herschel concludes that the nebulæ or constellations of fixed stars are approaching each other, and must finally coalesce in one mass. Phil. Trans. Vol. LXXV.

Till o'er the wreck. l. 389. The story of the phenix rising from its own ashes with a twinkling star upon its head, seems to have been an ancient hieroglyphic emblem of the destruction and resuscitation of all things.

There is a figure of the great platonic year with a phenix on his hand on the reverse of a medal of Adrian. Spence's Polym. p. 189.

Maze within maze. l. 395. The elegant appearance on dissection of the young tulip in the bulb was first observed by Mariotte, and is mentioned in the note on tulipa in Part II. and was afterwards noticed by Du Hamel. Acad. Scien. Lewenhoeck assures us that in the bud of a currant tree he could not only discover the ligneous part but even the berries themselves, appearing like small grapes. Chamb. Dict. art. Bud. Mr. Baker says he dissected a seed of trembling grass in which a perfect plant appeared with its root sending forth two branches, from each of which several leaves or blades of grass proceeded. Microsc. Vol. I. p. 252. Mr. Bonnet saw four generations of successive plants in the bulb of a hyacinth. Bonnet Corps Organ. Vol. I. p. 103. Haller's Physiol. Vol. I. p. 91. In the terminal bud of a horse-chesnut the new flower may be seen by the naked eye covered with a mucilaginous down, and the same in the bulb of a narcissus, as I this morning observed in several of them sent me by Miss Jacson for that purpose. Sept. 16.

Mr. Ferber speaks of the pleasure he received in observing in the buds of hepatica and pedicularis hirsuta yet lying hid in the earth, and in the germs of the shrub daphne mezereon, and at the base of osmunda lunaria a perfect plant of the future year, discernible in all its parts a year before it comes forth, and in the seeds of nymphea nelumbo the leaves of the plant were seen so distinctly that the author found out by them what plant the seeds belonged to. The same of the seeds of the tulip tree or liriodendron tulipiferum. Amæn. Acad. Vol. VI.

And the great seed. l. 418. Alluding to the πρωτον ωον, or first great egg of the ancient philosophy; it had a serpent wrapped round it, emblematical of divine wisdom; an image of it was afterwards preserved and worshipped in the temple of Dioscuri, and supposed to represent the egg of Leda. See a print of it in Bryant's Mythology. It was said to have been broken by the horns of the celestial bull, that is, it was hatched by the warmth of the spring. See note on Canto I. l. 413.

And the vast surface. l. 420. L'Organization, le sentiment, le movement spontané, la vie, n'existent qu'à la surface de la terre, et dans les lieux exposés à la lumière. Traité de Chymie par M. Lavoisier, Tom. I. p. 202.

Teach the fine seed. l. 423. The seeds in their natural state fall on the surface of the earth, and having absorbed some moisture, the root shoots itself downwards into the earth, and the plume rises in air. Thus each endeavouring to seek its proper pabulum, directed by a vegetable irritability similar to that of the lacteal system, and to the lungs in animals.

With pith elastic stretch its rising stem,
Part the twin lobes, expand the throbbing gem;
Clasp in your airy arms the aspiring plume,
Fan with your balmy breath its kindling bloom,
Each widening scale and bursting film unfold,
Swell the green cup, and tint the flower with
   gold;   430
While in bright veins the silvery sap ascends,
And refluent blood in milky eddies bends;
While, spread in air, the leaves respiring play,
Or drink the golden quintessence of day.
—So from his shell on Delta's showerless isle
Bursts into life the monster of the Nile;
First in translucent lymph with cobweb-threads
The brain's fine floating tissue swells, and
   spreads;
Nerve after nerve the glistening spine descends,
The red heart dances, the aorta bends;   440
Through each new gland the purple current
   glides,
New veins meandering drink the refluent tides;

The pith seems to push up or elongate the bud by its elasticity, like the pith in the callow quills of birds. This medulla Linneus believes to consist of a bundle of fibres, which diverging breaks through the bark yet gelatinous producing the buds.

The lobes are reservoirs of prepared nutriment for the young seed, which is absorbed by its placental vessels, and converted into sugar, till it has penetrated with its roots far enough into the earth to extract sufficient moisture, and has acquired leaves to convert it into nourishment. In some plants these lobes rise from the earth and supply the place of leaves, as in kidney-beans, cucumbers, and hence seem to serve both as a placenta to the foetus and lungs to the young plant. During the process of germination the starch of the seed is converted into sugar, as is seen in the process of malting barley for the purpose of brewing. And is on this account very similar to the digestion of food in the stomachs of animals, which converts all their aliment into a chyle, which consists of mucilage, oil, and sugar; the placentation of buds will be spoken of hereafter.

The silvery sap. l. 431. See additional notes, No. XXXV.

And refluent blood. l. 432. See additional notes, No. XXXVI.

The leaves respiring play. l. 433. See additional notes, No. XXXVII.

Or drink the golden. l. 434. Linneus having observed the great influence of light on vegetation, imagined that the leaves of plants inhaled electric matter from the light with their upper surface. (System of Vegetables translated, p. 8.)

The effect of light on plants occasions the actions of the vegetable muscles of their leaf-stalks, which turn the upper side of the leaf to the light, and which open their calyxes and corols, according to the experiments of Abbe Tessier who exposed variety of plants in a cavern to different quantities of light. Hist. de L'Academie Royal. Ann. 1783. The sleep or vigilance of plants seems owing to the presence or absence of this stimulus. See note on Mimosa, Part II.

Edge over edge expands the hardening scale,
And sheaths his slimy skin in silver mail.
—Erewhile, emerging from the brooding sand,
With tyger-paw he prints the brineless strand,
High on the flood with speckled bosom swims,
Helm'd with broad tail, and oar'd with giant
   limbs;
Rolls his fierce eye-balls, clasps his iron claws,
And champs with gnashing teeth his massy
   jaws;   450
Old Nilus sighs along his cane-crown'd shores,
And swarthy Memphis trembles and adores.

XI. "Come, ye soft Sylphs! who fan the
   Paphian groves,
And bear on sportive wings the callow loves;
Call with sweet whisper, in each gale that
   blows,   [pose;
The slumbering snow-drop from her long re-
Charm the pale primrose from her clay-cold bed,
Unveil the bashful violet's tremulous head;
While from her bud the playful tulip breaks,
And young carnations peep with blushing
   cheeks;   460
Bid the closed *corol* from nocturnal cold
Curtain'd with silk the virgin *stigma* fold,
Shake into viewless air the morning dews,
And wave in light its iridescent hues.
So shall from high the bursting *anther* trust
To the mild breezes the prolific dust;
Or bow his waxen head with graceful pride,
Watch the first blushes of his waking bride,
Give to her hand the honey'd cup, or sip
Celestial nectar from her sweeter lip;   470
Hang in soft raptures o'er the yielding fair,
Love out his hour, and leave his life in air.
So in his silken sepulchre the worm,
Warm'd with new life, unfolds his larva-form;

Honey'd cup. l. 469. The nectary or honey-gland supplies food to the vegetable males and females; which like moths and butterflies live on the honey thus produced for them, till they have propagated their species, and deposited their eggs, and then die, as explained in additional note, No. XXXIX. The tops of the stamens, or anthers, are covered with wax to protect the prolific dust from the injury of showers and dews, to which it is impervious.

Love out his hour. l. 472. The vegetable passion of love is agreeably seen in the flower of the parnassia, in which the males alternately approach and recede from the female, and in the flower of nigella, or devil in the bush, in which the tall females bend down to their dwarf husbands. But I was this morning surprised to observe, among Sir Brooke Boothby's valuable collection of plants at Ashbourn, the manifest adultery of several females of the plant Collinsonia, who had bent themselves into contact with the males of other flowers of the same plant in their vicinity, neglectful of their own. Sept. 16. See additional notes, No. XXXVIII.

Unfolds his larva-form. l. 474. The flower bursts forth from its larva, the herb, naked and perfect like a butterfly from its chrysalis; winged with its corol; wing-sheathed by its

Erewhile aloft in wanton circles moves,
And woos on Hymen-wings his velvet loves.

XII. 1. " If prouder branches with exuberance rude
Point their green germs, their barren shoots
    protrude;
Wound them, ye Sylphs! with little knives, or [bind
A wiry ringlet round the swelling rind;   460
Bisect with chisel fine the root below,
Or bend to earth the inhospitable bough.
So shall each germ with new prolific power
Delay the leaf-bud, and expand the flower;
Closed in the *style* the tender pith shall end,
The lengthening wood in circling *stamens* bend;

---

calyx; consisting alone of the organs of reproduction. The males, or stamens, have their anthers replete with a prolific powder containing the vivifying fovilla; in the females, or pistils, exists the ovary, terminated by the tubular stigma. When the anthers burst and shed their bags of dust, the male fovilla is received by the prolific lymph of the stigma, and produces the seed or egg, which is nourished in the ovary. System of Vegetables translated from Linneus by the Lichfield Society, p. 10.

Wound them, ye Sylphs! l. 479. Mr. Whitmill advised to bind some of the most vigorous shoots with strong wire, and even some of the large roots; and Mr. Warner cuts, what he calls a wild worm about the body of the tree, or scores the bark quite to the wood like a screw with a sharp knife. Bradley on Gardening, Vol. II. p. 155. Mr. Fitzgerald produced flowers and fruit on wall trees by cutting off a part of the bark. Phil. Trans. Ann. 1761. M. Buffon produced the same effect by a straight bandage put round a branch, Act. Paris, Ann. 1738, and concludes that an ingrafted branch bears better from its vessels being compressed by the callus.

A complete cylinder of the bark about an inch in height was cut off from the branch of a pear tree against a wall in Mr. Howard's garden at Lichfield, about five years ago; the circumcised part is now not above half the diameter of the branch above and below it, yet this branch has been full of fruit every year since, when the other branches of the tree bore only sparingly. I lately observed that the leaves of this wounded branch were smaller and paler, and the fruit less in size, and ripened sooner than on the other parts of the tree. Another branch has the bark taken off not quite all round with much the same effect.

The theory of this curious vegetable fact has been esteemed difficult, but receives great light from the foregoing account of the individuality of buds. A flower-bud dies, when it has perfected its seed, like an annual plant, and hence requires no place on the bark for new roots to pass downwards; but on the contrary, leaf-buds, as they advance into shoots, form new buds in the axilla of every leaf, which new buds require new roots to pass down the bark, and thus thicken as well as elongate the branch; now if a wire or string be tied round the bark, many of these new roots cannot descend, and thence more of the buds will be converted into flower-buds.

It is customary to debark oak-trees in the spring, which are intended to be felled in the ensuing autumn; because the bark comes off easier at this season, and the sap-wood, or alburnum, is believed to become harder and more durable, if the tree remains till the end of summer. The trees thus stripped of their bark put forth shoots as usual with acorns on the 6th, 7th, and 8th joint, like vines; but in the branches I examined, the joints of the debarked trees were much shorter than those of other oak-trees; the acorns were more numerous; and no new buds were produced above the joints which bore acorns. From hence it appears that the branches of debarked oak-trees produce fewer leaf-buds, and more flower-buds, which last circumstance I suppose must depend on their being sooner or later debarked in the vernal months. And secondly, that the new buds of debarked oak-trees continue to obtain moisture from the alburnum after the season of the ascent of sap in other vegetables ceases; which in this unnatural state of the debarked tree may act as capillary tubes, like the alburnum of the small debarked cylinder of a pear tree abovementioned; or may continue to act as placental vessels, as happens to the animal embryon in cases of superfetation; when the fetus continues a month or two in the womb beyond its usual time, of which some instances have been recorded, the placenta continues to supply perhaps the double office both of nutrition and of respiration.

Or bend to earth. l. 482. Mr. Hitt in his treatise on fruit-trees observes that if a vigorous branch of a wall-tree be bent to the horizon, or beneath it, it loses its vigour, and becomes a bearing branch. The theory of this I suppose to depend on the difficulty with which the leaf shoots can protrude the roots necessary for their new progeny of buds upwards along the bended branch to the earth contrary to their natural habits or powers, whence more flower-shoots are produced which do not require new roots to pass along the bark of the bended branch, but which let their offspring, the seeds, fall upon the earth and seek roots for themselves.

With new prolific power. l. 483. About midsummer the new buds are formed, but it is believed by some of the Linnean school, that these buds may in their early state be either converted into flower-buds or leaf-buds according to the vigour of the vegetating branch. Thus if the upper part of a branch be cut away, the buds near the extremity of the remaining stem, having a greater proportional supply of nutriment, or possessing a greater facility of shooting their roots, or absorbent vessels, down the bark, will become leaf-buds, which might otherwise have been flower-buds, and the contrary; as explained in note on l. 479 of this canto.

Closed in the style. l. 485. " I conceive the medulla of a plant to consist of a bundle of nervous fibres, and that the propelling vital power separates their uppermost extremities. These diverging, penetrate the bark, which is now gelatinous, and become multiplied in the new gem, or leaf-bud. The ascending vessels of the bark being thus divided by the nervous fibres, which perforate it and the ascent of its fluids being thus impeded the bark is extended into a leaf. But the flower is produced, when the potrusion of the medulla is greater than the retention of the including cortical part; whence the substance of the bark is expanded in the calyx; that of the rind, (or interior bark,) in the corol; that of the wood in the stamens, that of the medulla in the pistil.

The smoother rind its soft embroidery spread
In vaulted *petals* o'er the gorgeous bed;
The wrinkled bark, in filmy mazes roll'd,
Form the green *calyx*, fold including fold; 490
Each widening *bracte* expand its foliage hard,
And hem the bright pavillion, *floral guard*.
—So the cold rill from Cintra's steepy sides,
Headlong, abrupt, in barren channels glides;
Round the rent cliffs the bark-bound Suber
    spreads,
And lazy monks recline on corky beds;
Till, led by art, the wondering water moves
Through vine hung avenues, and citron groves;
Green slopes the velvet round its silver source,
And flowers, and fruits, and foliage mark its
    course. 500
At breezy eve, along the irriguous plain
The fair Beckfordia leads her virgin train;
Seeks the cool grot, the shadowy rocks among,
And tunes the mountain-echoes to her song;
Or prints with graceful steps the margin green,
And brighter glories gild the inchanted scene.

2. " Where cruder juices swell the leafy vein,
Stint the young germ, the tender blossom stain;
On each lopp'd shoot a foster scion bind,
Pith press'd to pith, and rind applied to rind,
So shall the trunk with loftier crest ascend, 511
And wide in air its happier arms extend;
Nurse the new buds, admire the leaves un-
    known,
And blushing bend with fruitage not its own.

" Thus when in holy triumph Aaron trod,
And offer'd on the shrine his mystic rod;
First a new bark its silken tissue weaves,
New buds emerging widen into leaves;
Fair fruits protrude, enascent flowers expand,
And blush and tremble round the living wand.

XIII. 1. " Sylphs! on each oak-bud wound
    the wormy galls, 521
With pigmy spears, or crush the venom'd balls;
Fright the green locust from his foamy bed,
Unweave the caterpillar's gluey thread;
Chase the fierce earwig, scare the bloated toad,
Arrest the snail upon his slimy road;
Arm with sharp thorns the sweet-briar's
    tender wood,
And dash the cynips from her damask bud;
Steep in ambrosial dews the woodbine's bells,
And drive the night-moth from her honey'd
    cells. 530
So where the humming-bird in Chili's bowers
On murmuring pinions robs the pendent flowers;
Seeks, where fine pores their dulcet balm distil,
And sucks the treasure with proboscis-bill;
Fair cyprepedia with successful guile
Knits her smooth brow, extinguishes her smile;
A spider's bloated paunch and jointed arms
Hide her fine form, and mask her blushing
    charms;

Vegetation thus terminates in the production of new life, the ultimate medullary and cortical fibres being collected in the seeds." Linnei Systema Veget. p. 6. edit. 14.

Cintra. l. 493. A village on the side of the rock of Lisbon; around the summit are abundance of cork trees, and some excavations, which a few monks inhabit, and sleep on beds or benches of cork; near the village Mr. Beckford has an elegant seat.

Nurse the new buds. l. 513. Mr. Fairchild budded a passion-tree, whose leaves were spotted with yellow, into one which bears long fruit. The buds did not take, nevertheless in a fortnight yellow spots began to show themselves about three feet above the inoculation, and in a short time afterwards yellow spots appeared on a shoot which came out of the ground from another part of the plant. Bradley, Vol. II. p. 129. These facts are the more curious, since from experiments of ingrafting red currants on black (Ib. Vol. II.) the fruit does not acquire any change of flavour, and by many other experiments neither colour nor any other change is produced in the fruit ingrafted on other stocks.

There is an apple described in Bradley's work which is said to have one side of it a sweet fruit which boils soft, and the other side a sour fruit which boils hard, which Mr. Bradley so long ago as the year 1721 ingeniously ascribes to the farina of one of these apples impregnating the other, which would seem the more probable if we consider that each division of an apple is a separate womb, and may therefore have a separate impregnation, like puppies of different kinds in one litter. The same is said to have occurred in oranges and lemons, and grapes of different colours.

Their dulcet balm distil. l. 533. See additional notes, No. XXXIX.

Fair cyprepedia. l. 535. The cyprepedium from South America is supposed to be of larger size, and brighter colours, than that from North America, from which this print is taken; it has a large globular nectary about the size of a pigeon's egg of a fleshy colour, and an incision or depression on its upper part, much resembling the body of the large American spider; this globular nectary is attached to divergent slender petals not unlike the legs of the same animal. This spider is called by Linneus Aranea avicularia, with a convex orbicular thorax, the centre transversely excavated; he adds that it catches small birds as well as insects, and has the venomous bite of a serpent. System. Natur. Tom. I. p. 1034. M. Lonvilliers de Poincy, (Histoire Nat. des Antilles, Cap. xiv. art. III.) calls it Phalange, and describes the body to be the size of a pigeon's egg, with a hollow on its back like a navel, and mentions its catching the humming-bird in its strong nets.

The similitude of this flower to this great spider seems to be a vegetable contrivance to prevent the humming-bird from plundering its honey. About Matlock, in Derbyshire, the fly-ophris is produced, the nectary of which so much resembles the small wall-bee, perhaps the apis ichneumonea, that it may be easily mistaken for it at a small distance. It is probable that by this means it may often escape being plundered. See note on lonicera in the next poem, and on epidendrum.

A bird of our own country called a willow-wren (Motacilla) runs up the stem of the crown-

In ambush sly the mimic warrior lies 569
And on quick wing the panting plunderer flies.

2. " Shield the young harvest from devouring blight,
The smut's dark poison and the mildew white ;
Deep-rooted mould, and ergot's horn uncouth,
And break the canker's desolating tooth.
First in one point the festering wound confined
Mines unperceived beneath the shrivel'd rind ;
Then climbs the branches with increasing strength [length ;
Spreads as they spread, and lengthens with their
—Thus the slight wound ingraved on glass unneal'd
Runs in white lines along the lucid field ; 550

Imperial (Frittillaria coronalis) and sips the pendulous drops within its petals. This species of Motacilla is called by Ray Regulus non cristatus. White's Hist. of Selborne.

Shield the young harvest. l. 541. Linneus enumerates but four diseases of plants ; Erysyphe, the white mucor or mould, with sessile tawny heads, with which the leaves are sprinkled, as is frequent on the hop, humulus, maple, acer, &c.

Rubigo, the ferrugineous powder sprinkled under the leaves, frequent in lady's mantle, alchemilla, &c.

Clavus, when the seeds grow out into larger horns black without, as in rye. This is called Ergot by the French writers.

Ustulago, when the fruit, instead of seed, produces a black powder, as in barley, oats, &c. To which perhaps the honey-dew ought to have been added, and the canker, in the former of which the nourishing fluid of the plant seems to be exsuded by a retrograde motion of the cutaneous lymphatics, as in the sweating sickness of the last century. The latter is a phagedenic ulcer of the bark, very destructive to young apple-trees, and which in cherry-trees is attended with a deposition of gum-arabic, which often terminates in the death of the tree.

Ergot's horn. l. 543. There is a disease frequently affects the rye in France, and sometimes in England in moist seasons, which is called ergot, or horn-seed ; the grain becomes considerably elongated, and is either straight or crooked, containing black meal along with the white, and appears to be pierced by insects, which were probably the cause of the disease. Mr. Duhamel ascribes it to this cause, and compares it to galls on oak-leaves. By the use of this bad grain amongst the poor, diseases have been produced attended with great debility and mortification of the extremities both in France and England. Dict. Raison. art. Siegle. Phil. Transact.

On glass unneal'd. l. 549. The glass-makers occasionally make what they call *proofs*, which are cooled hastily, whereas the other glass vessels are removed from warmer ovens to cooler ones, and suffered to cool by slow degrees, which is called annealing, or nealing them. If an unnealed glass be scratched by even a grain of sand falling into it, it will seem to consider of it for some time, or even a day, and will then crack into a thousand pieces.

The same happens to a smooth-surfaced lead-ore in Derbyshire, the workmen having cleared a large face of it, scratch it with picks, and in a

Crack follows crack, to laws elastic just,
And the frail fabric shivers into dust.

XIV. 1. " Sylphs ! if with morn destructive eurus springs,
O, clasp the harebell with your velvet wings ;
Screen with thick leaves the jasmine as it blows,
And shake the white rime from the shuddering rose ;
Whilst amaryllis turns with graceful ease
Her blushing beauties, and eludes the breeze.—
Sylphs ! if at noon the fritiliary droops, 559
With drops nectareous hang her nodding cups ;
Thin clouds of gossamer in air display,
And hide the vale's chaste lily from the ray ;
Whilst erythrina o'er her tender flower
Bends all her leaves, and braves the sultry hour ;—
Shield, when cold hesper sheds his dewy light,
Mimosa's soft sensations from the night ;
Fold her thin foliage, close her timid flowers,
And with ambrosial slumbers guard her bowers ;
O'er each warm wall while Cerea flings her arms,
And wastes on night's dull eye a blaze of charms.

2. " Round her tall elm with dewy fingers twine 571
The gadding tendrils of the adventurous vine ;

---

few hours many tons of it crack to pieces, and fall, with a kind of explosion. Whitehurst's Theory of the Earth.

Glass dropped into cold water, called Prince Rupert's drops, explode when a small part of their tails are broken off, more suddenly indeed, but probably from the same cause. Are the internal particles of these elastic bodies kept so far from each other by the external crust that they are nearly in a state of repulsion into which state they are thrown by their vibrations from any violence applied ? Or, like elastic balls in certain proportions suspended in contact with each other, can motion once begun be increased by their elasticity, till the whole explodes ? And can this power be applied to any mechanical purposes?

With ambrosial slumbers. l. 568. Many vegetables during the night do not seem to respire, but to sleep like the dormant animals and insects in winter. This appears from the mimosa and many other plants closing the upper sides of their leaves together in their sleep, and thus precluding that side of them from both light and air. And from many flowers closing up the polished or interior side of their petals, which we have also endeavoured to show to be a respiratory organ.

The irritability of plants is abundantly evinced by the absorption and pulmonary circulation of their juices ; their sensibility is shown by the approaches of the males to the females, and of the females to the males in numerous instances ; and, as the essential circumstances of sleep consists in the temporary abolition of voluntary power alone, the sleep of plants evinces that they possess voluntary power ; which also indisputably appears in many of them by closing their petals or their leaves during cold, or rain, or darkness, or from mechanic violence.

From arm to arm in gay festoons suspend
Her fragrant flowers, her graceful foliage bend;
Swell with sweet juice her vermil orbs, and feed;
Shrined in transparent pulp her pearly seed;
Hang round the orange all her silver bells,
And guard her fragrance with Hesperian spells;
Bud after bud her polish'd leaves unfold,
And load her branches with successive gold. 580
So the learn'd alchemist exulting sees
Rise in his bright matrass Diana's trees;
Drop after drop, with just delay he pours
The red-fumed acid on Potosi's ores;
With sudden flash the fierce bullitions rise,
And wide in air the gas phlogistic flies;
Slow shoot, at length, in many a brilliant mass
Metallic roots across the netted glass;
Branch after branch extend their silver stems,
Bud into gold, and blossom into gems. 590

" So sits enthroned in vegetable pride
Imperial Kew by Thames's glittering side;
Obedient sails from realms unfurrow'd bring
For her the unnamed progeny of spring;
Attendant nymphs her dulcet mandates hear,
And nurse in fostering arms the tender year,
Plant the young bulb, inhume the living seed,
Prop the weak stem, the erring tendril lead;
Or fan in glass-built fanes the stranger flowers
With milder gales, and steep with warmer showers. 600

Diana's trees. l. 582. The chemists and astronomers from the earliest antiquity have used the same characters to represent the metals and the planets, which were most probably outlines or abstracts of the original hieroglyphic figures of Egypt. These afterwards acquired niches in their temples, and represented gods as well as metals and planets; whence silver is called Diana, or the moon, in the books of alchemy.
The process for making Diana's silver tree is thus described by Lemeri. Dissolve one ounce of pure silver in acid of nitre very pure and moderately strong; mix this solution with about twenty ounces of distilled water; add to this two ounces of mercury, and let it remain at rest. In about four days there will form upon the mercury a tree of silver with branches imitating vegetation.
1. As the mercury has a greater affinity than silver with the nitrous acid, the silver becomes precipitated; and, being deprived of the nitrous oxygene by the mercury, sinks down in its metallic form and lustre. 2. The attraction between silver and mercury, which causes them readily to amalgamate together, occasions the precipitated silver to adhere to the surface of the mercury in preference to any other part of the vessel. 3. The attraction of the particles of the precipitated silver to each other causes the beginning branches to thicken and elongate into trees and shrubs rooted on the mercury. For other circumstances concerning this beautiful experiment see Mr. Keir's Chemical Dictionary, art. Arbor Dianæ; a work perhaps of greater utility to mankind than the lost Alexandrian Library; the continuation of which is so eagerly expected by all, who are occupied in the arts, or attached to the sciences.

Delighted Thames through tropic umbrage glides,
And flowers antarctic, bending o'er his tides;
Drinks the new tints, the sweets unknown inhales,
And calls the sons of science to his vales.
In one bright point admiring nature eyes
The fruits and foliage of discordant skies,
Twines the gay floret with the fragrant bough,
And bends the wreath round George's royal brow.
—Sometimes retiring, from the public weal
One tranquil hour the royal partners steal; 610
Through glades exotic pass with step sublime,
Or mark the growths of Britain's happier clime;
With beauty blossom'd, and with virtue blazed,
Mark the fair scions, that themselves have raised; [pands,
Sweet blooms the rose the towering oak expands,
The grace and guard of Britain's golden lands.

XV. " Sylphs! who, round earth on purple pinions borne,
Attend the radiant chariot of the morn;
Lead the gay hours along the ethereal height,
And on each dun meridian shower the light; 620
Sylphs! who from realms of equatorial day
To climes that shudder in the polar ray,
From zone to zone pursue on shifting wing,
The bright perennial journey of the spring;
Bring my rich balms from Mecca's hallow'd glades,
Sweet flowers, that glitter in Arabia's shades;
Fruits, whose fair forms in bright succession glow
Gilding the banks of Arno, or of Po;
Each leaf, whose fragrant steam with ruby lip
Gay China's nymphs from pictured vases sip; 630
Each spicy rind, which sultry India boasts,
Scenting the night-air round her breezy coasts;
Roots, whose bold stems in bleak Siberia blow,
And gem with many a tint the eternal snow;
Barks, whose broad umbrage high in ether waves
O'er Ande's steeps, and hides his golden caves;
—And, where yon oak extends his dusky shoots
Wide o'er the rill, that bubbles from his roots;
Beneath whose arms, protected from the storm,
A turf-built altar rears its rustic form; 640
Sylphs! with religious hands fresh garlands twine,
And deck with lavish pomp Hygeia's shrine.

" Call with loud voice the sisterhood, that dwell
On floating cloud, wide wave, or bubbling well;
Stamp with charm'd foot, convoke the alarmed Gnomes
From golden beds and adamantine domes; [vite,
Each from her sphere with beckoning arm invite,
Curl'd with red flame the vestal forms of light.

Close all your spotted wings, in lucid ranks
Press with your bended knees the crowded banks, 650
Cross your meek arms, incline your wreathed brows,
And win the goddess with unwearied vows.

" Oh, wave, Hygeia ! o'er Britannia's throne
Thy serpent-wand, and mark it for thy own ;
Lead round her breezy coasts thy guardian trains,
Her nodding forests, and her waving plains ;
Shed o'er her peopled realms thy beamy smile,
And with thy airy temple crown her isle !"

The goddess ceased,—and calling from afar
The wandering zephyrs, joins them to her car ;
Mounts with light bound, and graceful, as she bends, 661
Whirls the long lash, the flexile rein extends ;
On whispering wheels the silver axle slides,
Climbs into air, and cleaves the crystal tides ;
Burst from its pearly chains, her amber hair
Streams o'er her ivory shoulders, buoy'd in air ;
Swells her white veil, with ruby clasp confined
Round her fair brow, and undulates behind ;
The lessening coursers rise in spiral rings,
Pierce the slow-sailing clouds, and stretch their shadowy wings. 670

CONTENTS

OF THE

NOTES TO PART I.

CANTO I.

	Line
ROSICRUCIAN machinery	73
All bodies are immersed in the matter of heat. Particles of bodies do not touch each other	97
Gradual progress of the formation of the earth, and of plants and animals. Monstrous births	101
Fixed stars approach towards each other; they were projected from chaos by explosion, and the planets projected from them	105
An atmosphere of inflammable air above the common atmosphere principally about the poles	123
Twilight fifty miles high. Wants further observations	126
Immediate cause of volcanoes from steam and other vapours. They prevent greater earthquakes	152
Conductors of heat. Cold on the tops of mountains	176
Phosphorescent light in the evening from all bodies	177
Phosphoric light from calcined shells. Bolognian stone. Experiments of Beccari and Wilson	182
Ignis fatuus doubtful	189
Electric Eel. Its electric organs compared to the electric Leyden phial	202
Discovery of fire. Tools of steel. Forests subdued. Quantity of food increased by cookery	212
Medusa originally an hieroglyphic of divine wisdom	218
Cause of explosions from combined heat. Heat given out from air in respiration. Oxygene loses less heat when converted into nitrous acid than in any other of its combinations	226
Sparks from the collision of flints are electric. From the collision of flint and steel are from the combustion of the steel	229
Gunpowder described by Bacon. Its power. Should be lighted in the centre. A new kind of it. Levels the weak and strong	242
Steam-engine invented by Savery. Improved by Newcomen. Perfected by Watt and Boulton	254
Divine benevolence. The parts of nature not of equal excellence	278
Mr. Boulton's steam-engine for the purpose of coining would save many lives from the executioner	281
Labours of Hercules of great antiquity. Pillars of Hercules. Surface of the Mediterranean lower than the Atlantic. Abyla and Calpe. Flood of Deucalion	297
Accumulation of electricity not from friction	335
Mr. Bennet's sensible electrometer	345
Halo of saints is pictorial language	358
We have a sense adapted to perceive heat, but not electricity	365
Paralytic limbs move by electric influence	367
Death of Professor Richman by electricity	373
Lightning drawn from the clouds. How to be safe in thunder storms	383
Animal heat from air in respiration. Perpetual necessity of respiration. Spirit of animation perpetually renewed	401
Cupid rises from the egg of night. Mrs. Cosway's painting of this subject	413
Western-winds. Their origin. Warmer than south-winds. Produce a thaw	430
Water expands in freezing. Destroys succulent plants, not resinous ones. Trees in valleys more liable to injury. Fig-trees bent to the ground in winter	439
Buds and bulbs are the winter cradle of the plant. Defended from frost and from insects. Tulip produces one flower-bulb, and several leaf-bulbs, and perishes	460

CONTENTS OF THE NOTES.

	Line
Matter of heat if different from light. Vegetables blanched by exclusion of light. Turn the upper surface of their leaves to the light. Water decomposed as it escapes from their pores. Hence vegetables purify air in the day time only	462
Electricity forwards the growth of plants. Silk-worms electrised spin sooner. Water decomposed in vegetables, and by electricity	463
Sympathetic inks which appear by heat, and disappear in the cold. Made from cobalt	487
Star in Cassiope's chair	515
Ice-islands 100 fathoms deep. Sea-ice more difficult of solution. Ice evaporates, producing great cold. Ice-islands increase. Should be navigated into southern climates. Some ice-islands have floated southwards sixty miles long. Steam attending them in warm climates	529
Monsoon cools the sands of Abyssinia	547
Ascending vapours are electrised plus, as appears from an experiment of Mr. Bennet. Electricity supports vapour in clouds. Thunder showers from combination of inflammable and vital airs	553

CANTO II.

	Line
Solar volcanoes analogous to terrestrial and lunar ones. Spots of the sun are excavations	14
Spherical form of the earth. Ocean from condensed vapour. Character of Mr. Whitehurst	17
Granite the oldest part of the earth.—Then limestone. And lastly, clay, iron, coal, sandstone. Three great concentric divisions of the globe	35
Formation of primeval islands before the production of the moon. Paradise. The Golden Age. Rainbow. Water of the sea originally fresh	36
Venus rising from the sea, an hieroglyphic emblem of the production of the earth beneath the ocean	47
First great volcanoes in the central parts of the earth. From steam, inflammable gas, and vital air. Present volcanoes like mole-hills	68
Moon has little or no atmosphere. Its ocean is frozen. Is not yet inhabited, but may be in time	82
Earth's axis changed by the ascent of the moon. Its diurnal motion retarded. One great tide	84
Limestone produced from shells. Spars with double refractions. Marble. Chalk.	93
Ancient statues of Hercules. Antinous. Apollo. Venus. Designs of Roubiliac. Monument of General Wade	101
Statues of Mrs. Damer.	113
Morasses rest on limestone. Of immense extent.	116
Salts from animal and vegetable bodies decompose each other, except marine salt. Salt mines in Poland. Timber does not decay in them. Rock-salt produced by evaporation from sea-water. Fosil shells in salt mines. Salt in hollow pyramids. In cubes. Sea-water contains about one-thirtieth of salt.	119
Nitre, native in Bengal and Italy. Nitrous gas combined with vital air produces red clouds, and the two airs occupy less space than one of them before, and give out heat. Oxygene and azote produce nitrous acid	143
Iron from decomposed vegetables. Chalybeat springs. Fern-leaves in nodules of iron. Concentric spheres of iron nodules owing to polarity, like iron-filings arranged by a magnet. Great strata of the earth owing to their polarity	183
Hardness of steel for tools. Gave superiority to the European nations. Welding of steel. Its magnetism. Uses of gold	192
Artificial magnets improved by Savery and Dr. Knight, perfected by Mr. Michel. How produced. Polarity owing to the earth's rotatory motion. The electric fluid, and the matter of heat, and magnetism, gravitate on each other. Magnetism being the lightest is found nearest the axis of the motion. Electricity produces northern lights by its centrifugal motion	193
Acids from vegetable recrements. Flint has its acid from the new world. Its base in part from the old world, and in part from the new. Precious stones	215
Diamond. Its great refraction of light. Its volatility by heat. If an inflammable body	228
Fires of the new world from fermentation. Whence sulphur and bitumen by sublimation, the clay, coal, and flint remaining	275
Colours not distinguishable in the enamel-kiln, till a bit of dry wood is introduced	283
Etrurian pottery prior to the foundation of Rome. Excelled in fine forms, and in a non-vitreous encaustic painting, which was lost till restored by Mr. Wedgwood. Still influences the taste of the inhabitants	291
Mr. Wedgwood's cameo of a slave in chains, and of Hope	315
Basso-relievos of two or more colours not made by the ancients. Invented by Mr. Wedgwood	342
Petroleum and naphtha have been sublimed. Whence jet and amber. They absorb air. Attract straws when rubbed. Electricity from electron, the Greek name for amber	353

Clefts in granite rocks in which metals are found. Iron and manganese found in all vegetables. Manganese in limestone. Warm springs from steam rising up the clefts of granite and limestone. Ponderous earth in limestone clefts and in granite. Copper, lead, iron, from descending materials. High mountains of granite contain no ores near their summits. Transmutation of metals. Of lead into calamy. Into silver	398
Armies of Cambyses destroyed by famine, and by sand-storms	435
Whirling turrets of sand described and explained	478
Granite shows iron as it decomposes. Marble decomposes. Immense quantity of charcoal exists in limestone. Volcanic flags decompose, and become clay	523
Millstones raised by wooden pegs	524
Hannibal made a passage by fire over the Alps	534
Passed tense of many words twofold, as driven or drove, spoken or spoke. A poetic licence	609

CANTO III.

Clouds consist of aqueous spheres, which do not easily unite, like globules of quicksilver, as may be seen in riding through water. Owing to electricity. Snow. Hailstones rounded by attrition and dissolution of their angles. Not from frozen drops of water	15
Dew on points and edges of grass, or hangs over cabbage-leaves. Needle floats on water	18
Mists over rivers and on mountains. Halo round the moon. Shadow of a church steeple upon a mist. Dry mist, or want of transparency of the air, a sign of fair-weather	20
Tides on both sides of the earth. Moon's tides should be much greater than the earth's tides. The ocean of the moon is frozen	61
Spiral form of shells saves calcareous matter. Serves them as an organ of hearing. Calcareous matter produced from inflamed membranes. Colours of shells, labradore-stone from mother-pearl. Fossil shells not now found recent	66
Sea-insects like flowers. Actinia	81
Production of pearls, not a disease of the fish. Crab's-eyes. Reservoirs of pearly matter	84
Rocks of coral in the south-sea. Coralloid limestone at Linsel, and Coalbrook Dale	90
Rocks thrown from mountains, ice from glaciers, and portions of earth, or morasses, removed by columns of water. Earth-motion in Shropshire. Water of wells rising above the level of the ground. St. Alkmond's well near Derby might be raised many yards, so as to serve the town. Well at Sheerness and at Hartford in Connecticut	116
Monsoons attended with rain. Overflowing of the Nile. Vortex of ascending air. Rising of the dog-star announces the floods of the Nile. Anubis hung out upon their temples	129
Situations exempt from rain. At the line in Lower Egypt. On the coast of Peru	138
Giesar, a boiling fountain in Iceland. Water with great degrees of heat dissolves siliceous matter. Earthquake from steam	150
Warm springs not from decomposed pyrites. From steam rising up fissures from great depths	166
Buxton bath possesses 82 degrees of heat. Is improperly called a warm bath. A chill at immersion, and then a sensation of warmth, like the eye in an obscure room, owing to increased sensibility of the skin	184
Water compounded of pure air and inflammable air with as much matter of heat as preserves it fluid. Perpetually decomposed by vegetables in the sun's light, and recomposed in the atmosphere	204
Mythological interpretation of Jupiter and Juno designed as an emblem of the composition of water from two airs	260
Death of Mrs. French	308
Tomb of Mr. Brindley	341
Invention of the pump. The piston lifts the atmosphere above it. The surrounding atmosphere presses up the water into the vacuum. Manner in which a child sucks	366
Air-cell in engines for extinguishing fire. Water dispersed by the explosion of Gunpowder. Houses preserved from fire by earth on the floors, by a second ceiling of iron-plates or coarse mortar. Wood impregnated with alabaster or flint	406
Muscular actions and sensations of plants	460
River Achelous. Horn of Plenty	495
Flooding lands defends them from vernal frosts. Some springs deposit calcareous earth. Some contain azotic gas, which contributes to produce nitre. Snow water less serviceable	540

CANTO IV.

Cacalia produces much honey, that a part may be taken by insects without injury	2
Analysis of common air. Source of azote. Of oxygene. Water decomposed by vegetable pores and the sun's light. Blood	

CONTENTS OF THE NOTES

	Line
gives out phlogiston and receives vital air. Acquires heat and the vivifying principle	34
Cupid and Psyche	48
Simoom, a pestilential wind. Described. Owing to volcanic electricity. Not a whirlwind	65
Contagion either animal or vegetable	82
Thyrsis escapes the plague	91
Barometer and air-pumps. Dew on exhausting the receiver though the hygrometer points to dryness. Rare air will dissolve or acquire more heat, and more moisture, and more electricity	128
Sound propagated best by dense bodies, as wood, and water, and earth. Fish in spiral shells all ear	176
Discoveries of Dr. Priestley. Green vegetable matter. Pure air contained in the calces of metals, as minium, manganese, calamy, ochre	178
Fable of Proserpine an ancient chemical emblem	190
Diving balloons supplied with pure air from minium. Account of one by Mr. Boyle	207
Mr. Day. Mr. Spalding	229
Captain Pierce and his daughters	231
Pestilential winds of volcanic origin. Jordan flows through a country of volcanoes	306
Change of wind owing to small causes. If the wind could be governed, the products of the earth would be doubled, and its number of inhabitants increased	320
Mr. Kirwan's treatise on temperature of climates	354
Seeds of plants. Spawn of fish. Nutriment lodged in seeds. Their preservation in their seed-vessels	367
Fixed stars approach each other	381
Fable of the phœnix	389
Plants visible within bulbs, and buds, and seeds	395
Great egg of night	418
Seeds shoot into the ground. Pith. Seed-lobes. Starch converted into sugar. Like animal chyle	423
Light occasions the actions of vegetable muscles. Keeps them awake	434
Vegetable love in parnassia, nigella. Vegetable adultery in collinsonia	472
Strong vegetable shoots and roots bound with wire, in part debarked, whence leaf-buds converted into flower-buds. Theory of this curious fact	479
Branches bent to the horizon bear more fruit	482
Engrafting of a spotted passion-flower produced spots upon the stock. Apple soft on one side and hard on the other	513
Cyprepedium assumes the form of a large spider to affright the humming-bird. Flyophris. Willow-wren sucks the honey of the crown-imperial	535
Diseases of plants four kinds. Honey-dew	541
Ergot a disease of rye	543
Glass unannealed. Its cracks owing to elasticity. One kind of lead-ore cracks into pieces. Prince Rupert's drops. Elastic balls	549
Sleep of plants. Their irritability, sensibility, and voluntary motions	568

ADDITIONAL NOTES.

NOTE I.—METEORS.

Ethereal Powers! you chase the shooting stars,
Or yoke the vollied lightnings to your cars.
Canto I. l. 115.

There seem to be three concentric strata of our incumbent atmosphere: in which, or between them, are produced four kinds of meteors; lightning, shooting stars, fire-balls, and northern lights. First, the lower region of air, or that which is dense enough to resist by the adhesion of its particles the descent of condensed vapour, or clouds, which may extend from one to three or four miles high. In this region the common lightning is produced from the accumulation or defect of electric matter in those floating fields of vapour either in respect to each other, or in respect to the earth beneath them, or the dissolved vapour above them, which is constantly varying both with the change of the form of the clouds, which thus evolve a greater or less surface, and also with their ever-changing degree of condensation. As the lightning is thus produced in dense air, it proceeds but a short course on account of the greater resistance which it encounters, is attended with a loud explosion, and appears with a red light.

2. The second region of the atmosphere I suppose to be that which has too little tenacity to support condensed vapour or clouds; but which yet contains invisible vapour, or water in aerial solution. This aerial solution of water differs from that dissolved in the matter of heat, as it is supported by its adhesion to the particles of air, and is not precipitated by cold. In this stratum it seems probable that the meteors called shooting stars are produced; and that they consist of electric sparks, or lightning, passing from one region to another of these invisible fields of aero-aqueous solution. The height of these shooting stars has not yet been ascertained by sufficient observation; Dr. Blagden thinks their situation is lower down in the atmosphere than that of fireballs, which he conjectures from their swift apparent motion, and ascribes their smallness to the more minute division of the electric matter of which they are supposed to consist, owing to the greater resistance of the denser medium through which they pass, than that in which the fire-balls exist. Mr. Brydone observed that the shooting stars appeared to him to be as high in the atmosphere, when he was near the summit of mount Etna, as they do when observed from the plain. Phil. Tran. Vol. LXIII.

As the stratum of air in which shooting stars are supposed to exist is much rarer than that in which lightning resides, and yet much denser than that in which fire-balls are produced, they will be attracted at a greater distance than the former, and at a less than the latter. From this rarity of the air so small a sound will be produced by their explosion, as not to reach the lower parts of the atmosphere; their quantity of light from their greater distance being small, is never seen through dense air at all, and thence does not appear red, like lightning or fire-balls. There are no apparent clouds to emit or to attract them, because the constituent parts of these aero-aqueous regions may possess an abundance or deficiency of electric matter and yet be in perfect reciprocal solution. And lastly their apparent train of light is probably owing only to a continuance of their impression on the eye; as when a fire-stick is whirled in the dark it gives the appearance of a complete circle of fire: for these white trains of shooting stars quickly vanish, and do not seem to set any thing on fire in their passage, as seems to happen in the transit of fire-balls.

3. The second region or stratum of air terminates I suppose where the twilight ceases to be refracted, that is, where the air is 3000 times rarer than at the surface of the earth; and where it seems probable that the common air ends, and is surrounded by an atmosphere of inflammable gas tenfold rarer than itself. In this region I believe fire-balls sometimes to pass, and at other times the northern lights to exist. One of these fire-balls or draco volans, was observed by Dr. Pringle and many others on Nov. 26, 1758, which was afterwards estimated to have been a mile and a half in circumference, to have been about one hundred miles high, and to have moved towards the north with a velocity of near thirty miles in a second of time. This meteor had a real tail many miles long, which threw off sparks in its course, and the whole exploded with a sound like distant thunder. Philos. Trans. Vol. LI.

Dr. Blagden has related the history of another large meteor, or fire-ball, which was seen the 18th of August, 1783, with many ingenious observations and conjectures. This was estimated to be between 60 and 70 miles high, and to travel 1000 miles at the rate of about twenty miles in a second. This fire-ball had likewise a real train of light left behind it in its passage, which varied in colour; and in some part of its course gave off sparks or explosions where it had been brightest; and a dusky red streak remained visible perhaps a minute. Philos. Trans. Vol. LXXIV.

These fire-balls differ from lightning, and from shooting stars in many remarkable circumstances; as their very great bulk, being a mile and a half in diameter; their travelling 1000 miles nearly horizontally; their throwing off sparks in their passage; and changing colours from bright blue to dusky red; and leaving a train of fire behind them, continuing about a minute. They differ from the northern lights in not being diffused, but passing from one point of the heavens to another in a defined line; and this in a region above the crepuscular atmosphere, where the air is 3000 times rarer than at the surface of the earth. There has not yet been even a conjecture which can account for these appearances!—One I shall therefore hazard; which, if it does not inform, may amuse the reader.

In the note on l. 123, it was shown that there is probably a supernatant stratum of inflammable gas or hydrogene, over the common atmosphere; and whose density at the surface where they meet, must be at least ten times less than that upon which it swims; like chemical ether floating upon water, and perhaps without any real contact. 1. In this region, where the aerial atmosphere terminates and the inflammable one begins, the quantity of tenacity or resistance must be almost inconceivable; in which a ball of electricity might pass 1000 miles with greater ease than through a thousandth part of an inch of glass. 2. Such a ball of electricity passing between inflammable and common air would set fire to them in a line as it passed along; which would differ in colour according to the greater proportionate commixture of the two airs; and from the same cause there might occur greater degrees of inflammation, or branches of fire, in some parts of its course.

As these fire-balls travel in a defined line, it is pretty evident from the known laws of electricity, that they must be attracted; and as they are a mile or more in diameter, they must be emitted from a large surface of electric matter; because large knobs give larger sparks, less diffused, and more brightly luminous, than less ones or points, and resist more forcibly the emission of the electric matter. What is there in nature can attract them at so great a distance as 1000 miles, and so forcibly as to detach an electric spark of a mile diameter? Can volcanoes at the time of their eruptions have this effect, as they are generally attended with lightning? Future observations must discover these secret operations of nature! As a stream of common air is carried along with the passage of electric aura from one body to another; it is easy to conceive, that the common air and the inflammable air between which the fire-ball is supposed to pass, will be partially intermixed by being thus agitated, and so far as it becomes intermixed it will take fire, and produce the linear flame and branching sparks above described. In this circumstance of their being attracted, and thence passing in a defined line, the fire-balls seem to differ from the coruscations of the aurora borealis, or northern lights, which probably take place in the same region of the atmosphere; where the common air exists in extreme tenuity, and is covered by a still rarer sphere of inflammable gas, ten times lighter than itself.

As the electric streams, which constitute these northern lights, seem to be repelled or radiated from an accumulation of that fluid in the north, and not attracted like the fire-balls; this accounts for the diffusion of their light, as well as the silence of their passage; while their variety of colours, and the permanency of them, and even the breadth of them, in different places, may depend on their setting on fire the mixture of inflammable and common air through which they pass; as seems to happen in the transit of fire-balls.

It was observed by Dr. Priestley that the electric shock taken through inflammable air was red, in common air it is bluish; to these circumstances perhaps some of the colours of the northern lights may bear analogy; though the density of the medium through which light is seen must principally vary its colour, as is well explained by Mr. Morgan. Phil. Trans. Vol. LXXV. Hence lightning is red when seen through a dark cloud, or near the horizon; because the more refrangible rays cannot permeate so dense a medium. But the shooting stars consist of white light, as they are generally seen on clear nights, and nearly vertical; in other situations their light is probably too faint to come to us. But as in some remarkable appearances of the northern lights, as in March, 1716, all the prismatic colours were seen quickly to succeed each other, these appear to have been owing to real combustion; as the density of the interposed medium could not be supposed to change so frequently; and therefore these colours must have been owing to different degrees of heat according to Mr. Morgan's theory of combustion. In Smith's Optics, p. 69, the prismatic colours, and optical deceptions of the northern lights are described by Mr. Cotes.

The Torricellian vacuum, if perfectly free from air, is said by Mr. Morgan and others to be a perfect non-conductor. This circumstance therefore would preclude the electric streams from rising above the atmosphere. But as Mr. Morgan did not try to pass an electric shock through a vacuum, and as air, or something containing air, surrounding the transit of electricity may be necessary to the production of light, the conclusion may perhaps still be dubious. If however the streams of the northern lights were supposed to rise above our atmosphere, they would only be visible at each extremity of their course; where they emerge from, or are again immerged into the atmosphere; but not in their journey through the vacuum; for the absence of electric light in a vacuum is sufficiently proved by the common experiment of shaking a barometer in the dark; the electricity, produced by the friction of the mercury in the glass at its top, is luminous if the barometer has a little air in it; but there is no light if the vacuum be complete.

The aurora borealis, or northern dawn, is very ingeniously accounted for by Dr. Franklin on principles of electricity. He premises the following electric phenomena: 1. That all new-fallen snow has much positive electricity standing on its surface. 2. That about twelve degrees of latitude round the poles are covered with a crust of eternal ice, which is impervious to the electric fluid. 3. That the dense part of the atmosphere rises but a few miles high; and that in the rarer parts of it the electric fluid will pass to almost any distance.

Hence he supposes there must be a great accumulation of positive electric matter on the fresh-fallen snow in the polar regions; which, not being able to pass through the crust of ice into the earth, must rise into the rare air of the upper parts of our atmosphere, which will the least resist its passage; and passing towards the equator descend again into the denser atmosphere, and thence into the earth in silent streams. And that many of the appearances attending these lights are optical deceptions, owing to the situation of the eye that beholds them; which makes all ascending parallel lines appear to converge to a point.

The idea, above explained in note on l. 128, of the existence of a sphere of inflammable gas over the aerial atmosphere would much favour this theory of Dr. Franklin; because in that case the dense aerial atmosphere would rise a much less height in the polar regions, diminishing almost to nothing at the pole itself; and thus give an easier passage to the ascent of the electric fluid. And from the great difference in the specific gravity of the two airs, and the velocity of the earth's rotation, there must be a place between the poles and the equator, where the superior atmosphere of inflammable gas would terminate; which would account for these streams of the aurora borealis not appearing near the equator; add to this that it is probable the electric fluid may be heavier than the magnetic one; and will thence by the rotation of the earth's surface ascend over the magnetic one by its centrifugal force; and may thus be induced to ride through the thin stratum of aerial atmosphere over the poles.—See note on Canto II. l. 193. I shall have no occasion again to mention this great accumulation of inflammable air over the poles; and to conjecture that these northen lights may be produced by the union of inflammable with common air, without the assistance of the electric spark to throw them into combustion.

The antiquity of the appearance of northern lights has been doubted; as none were recorded in our annals since the remarkable one on Nov. 14, 1574, till another remarkable one on March 6, 1716, and the three following nights, which was seen at the same time in Ireland, Russia, and Poland, extending near 30 degrees of longitude and from about the 50th degree of latitude over almost all the north of Europe. There is however reason to believe them of remote antiquity though inaccurately described; thus the following curious passage from the Book of Maccabees, (B. II. c. v.) is such a description of them, as might probably be given by an ignorant and alarmed people. "Through all the city, for the space of almost forty days, there were seen horsemen running in the air, in cloth of gold, and armed with lances, like a band of soldiers; and troops of horsemen in array encountering and running one against another, with shaking of shields, and multitude of pikes, and drawing of swords, and casting of darts, and glittering of golden ornaments and harness."

NOTE II.—PRIMARY COLOURS.

Cling round the aerial bow with prisms bright,
And pleased untwist the sevenfold threads of light.
CANTO I. l. 117.

The manner in which the rainbow is produced was in some measure understood before Sir Isaac Newton had discovered his theory of colours. The first person who expressly showed the rainbow to be formed by the reflection of the sunbeams from drops of falling rain was Antonio de Dominis. This was afterwards more fully and distinctly explained by Des Cartes. But what caused the diversity of its colours was not then understood; it was reserved for the immortal Newton to discover that the rays of light consisted of seven combined colours of different refrangibility, which could be separated at pleasure by a wedge of glass. Pemberton's View of Newton.

Sir Isaac Newton discovered that the prismatic spectrum was composed of seven colours, in the following proportions, violet 80, indigo 40, blue 60, green 60, yellow 48, orange 27, red 45. If all these colours be painted on a circular card in the proportion above mentioned, and the card be rapidly whirled on its centre, they produce in the eye the sensation of white. And any one of these colours may be imitated by painting a card with the two colours which are contiguous to it, in the same proportions as in the spectrum, and whirling them in the same manner.

My ingenious friend, Mr. Galton of Birmingham, ascertained in this manner by a set of experiments the following propositions; the truth of which he had preconceived from the above data:

1. Any colour in the prismatic spectrum may be imitated by a mixture of the two colours contiguous to it.
2. If any three successive colours in the prismatic spectrum are mixed, they compose only the second or middlemost colour.
3. If any four successive colours in the prismatic spectrum be mixed, a tint similar to a mixture of the second and third colours will be produced, but not precisely the same, because they are not in the same proportion.
4. If beginning with any colour in the circular spectrum, you take of the second colour a quantity equal to the first, second, and third; and add to that the fifth colour, equal in quantity to the fourth, fifth, and sixth; and with these combine the seventh colour in the proportion it exists in the spectrum, white will be produced. Because the first, second, and third, compose only the second; and the fourth, fifth, and sixth, compose only the fifth; therefore, if the seventh be added, the same effect is produced as if all the seven were employed.
5. Beginning with any colour in the circular spectrum, if you take a tint composed of a certain proportion of the second and third, (equal in quantity to the first, second, third, and fourth,) and add to this the sixth colour equal in quantity to the fifth, sixth, and seventh, white will be produced.

From these curious experiments of Mr. Galton many phenomena in the chemical changes of colours may probably become better understood; especially if, as I suppose, the same theory must apply to transmitted colours, as to reflected ones. Thus it is well known, that if the glass of manganese, which is a tint probably composed of violet and indigo, be mixed in a certain proportion with the glass of lead, which is yellow, that the mixture becomes transparent. Now, from Mr. Galton's experiments, it appears, that in reflected colours such a mixture would produce white, that is, the same as if all the colours were reflected. And therefore in transmitted colours the same circumstances must produce transparency, that is, the same as if all the colours were transmitted. For the particles which constitute the glass of manganese will transmit red, violet, indigo, and blue; and those of the glass of lead will transmit orange, yellow, and green; hence all the primary colours by a mixture of these glasses become transmitted, that is, the glass becomes transparent.

Mr. Galton has further observed that five successive prismatic colours may be combined in such proportions as to produce but one colour, a circumstance which might be of consequence in the art of painting. For if you begin at any part of the circular spectrum above described, and take the first, second, and third colours in the proportions in which they exist in the spectrum; these will compose only the second colour equal in quantity to the first, second, and third; add to these the third, fourth, and fifth, in the proportion they exist in the spectrum, and these will produce the fourth colour equal in quantity to the third, fourth, and fifth. Consequently this is precisely the same thing, as mixing the second and fourth colours only; which mixture would only produce the third colour. Therefore if you combine the first, second, fourth, and fifth in the proportions in which they exist in the spectrum, with double the quantity of the third colour, this third colour will be produced. It is probable that many of the unexpected changes in mixing colours on a painter's pallet, as well as in more fluid chemical mixtures, may depend on these principles rather than on a new arrangement or combination of their minute particles.

Mr. Galton further observes, that white may universally be produced by the combination of one prismatic colour, and a tint intermediate to two others. Which tint may be distinguished by a name compounded of the two colours, to which it is intermediate. Thus white is produced by a mixture of red with blue-green. Of orange with indigo blue. Of yellow with violet-indigo. Of green with red-violet. Of blue with orange-red. Of indigo with yellow-orange. Of violet with green-yellow. Which he further remarks exactly coincides with the theory and facts mentioned by Dr. Robert Darwin of Shrewsbury in his account of ocular spectra; who has shown that when one of these contrasted colours has been long viewed, a spectrum or appearance of the other becomes visible in the fatigued eye. Philos. Trans. Vol. LXXVI. for the year 1786.

These experiments of Mr. Galton might much assist the copper-plate printers of callicoes and papers in colours; as three colours or more might be produced by two copper-plates. Thus suppose some yellow figures were put on by the first plate, and upon some parts of these yellow figures and on the other parts of the ground blue was laid on by another copper-plate. The three colours of yellow blue and green might be produced; as green leaves with yellow and blue flowers.

NOTE III.—COLOURED CLOUDS.

Eve's silken couch with gorgeous tints adorn,
And fire the arrowy throne of rising morn.
CANTO I. l. 119.

THE rays from the rising and setting sun are refracted by our spherical atmosphere; hence the most refrangible rays, as the violet, indigo, and blue, are reflected in greater quantities from the morning and evening skies; and the least refrangible ones, as red and orange, are last seen about the setting sun. Hence Mr. Beguelin observed that the shadow of his finger on his pocket book was much bluer in the morning and evening, when the shadow was about eight times as long as the body from which it was projected. Mr. Melville observes, that the blue rays being more refrangible are bent down in the evenings by our atmosphere, while the red and orange being less refrangible continue to pass on and tinge the morning and evening clouds with their colours. See Priestley's History of Light and Colours, p. 440. But as the particles of air, like those of water, are themselves blue, a blue shadow may be seen at all times of the day, though much more beautifully in the mornings and evenings, or by means of a candle in the middle of the day. For if a shadow on a piece of white paper is produced by placing your finger between the paper and a candle in the day light, the shadow will appear very blue; the yellow light of the candle upon the other parts of the paper apparently deepens the blue by its contrast, these colours being opposite to each other, as explained in note II.

Colours are produced from clouds or mists by refraction, as well as by reflection. In riding in the night over an unequal country I observed a very beautiful coloured halo round the moon, whenever I was covered with a few feet of mist, as I ascended from the valleys; which ceased to appear when I rose above the mist. This I suppose was owing to the thinness of the stratum of mist, in which I was immersed; had it been thicker, the colours refracted by the small drops, of which a fog consists, would not have passed through it down to my eye.

There is a bright spot seen on the cornea of the eye, when we face a window, which is much attended to by portrait painters; this is the light reflected from the spherical surface of the polished cornea, and brought to a focus; if the observer is placed in this focus, he sees the image of the window; if he is placed before or behind the focus, he only sees a luminous spot, which is more luminous and of less extent, the nearer he approaches to the focus. The luminous appearance of the eyes of animals in the dusky corners of a room, or in holes in the earth, may arise in some instances from the same principle; viz. the reflection of the light from the spherical cornea; which will be coloured red or blue in some degree by the morning, evening, or meridian light; or by the objects from which that light is previously reflected. In the cavern at Colebrook Dale, where the mineral tar exsudes, the eyes of the horse, which was drawing a cart from within towards the mouth of it, appeared like two balls of phosphorous, when he was above 100 yards off, and for a long time before any other part of the animal was visible. In this case I suspect the luminous appearance to have been owing to the light, which had entered the eye, being reflected from the back surface of the vitreous humour, and thence emerging again in parallel rays from the animal's eye, as it does from the back surface of the drops of the rainbow, and from the water-drops which lie, perhaps without contact, on cabbage-leaves, and have the brilliancy of quicksilver. This accounts for this luminous appearance being best seen in those animals which have large apertures in their iris, as in cats and horses, and is the only part visible in obscure places, because this is a better reflecting surface than any other part of the animal. If any of these emergent rays from the animal's eye can be supposed to have been reflected from the choroid coat through the semi-

NOTE IV.—COMETS.

Alarm with comet-blaze the sapphire plain,
The wan stars glimmering through its silver train.
CANTO I. l. 133.

THERE have been many theories invented to account for the tails of comets. Sir Isaac Newton thinks that they consist of rare vapours raised from the nucleus of the comet, and so rarefied by the sun's heat as to have their general gravitation diminished, and that they in consequence ascend opposite to the sun, and from thence reflect the rays of light. Dr. Halley compares the light of the tails of comets to the streams of the aurora borealis, and other electric effluvia. Philos. Trans. No. 347.

Dr. Hamilton observes, that the light of small stars is seen undiminished through both the light of the tails of comets, and of the aurora borealis, and has farther illustrated their electric analogy, and adds that the tails of comets consist of a lucid self-shining substance which has not the power of refracting or reflecting the rays of light. Essays.

The tail of the comet of 1744 at one time appeared to extend above 16 degrees from its body, and must have thence been above twenty-three millions of miles long. And the comet of 1680, according to the calculations of Dr. Halley on November the 11th, was not above one semidiameter off the earth, or less than 4000 miles to the northward of the way of the earth; at which time had the earth been in that part of its orbit, what might have been the consequence! no one would probably have survived to have registered the tremendous effects.

The comet of 1531, 1607, and 1682, having returned in the year 1759, according to Dr Halley's prediction in the Philos. Trans. for 1705, there seems no reason to doubt that all the other comets will return after their proper periods. Astronomers have in general acquiesced in the conjecture of Dr. Halley, that the comets of 1532, and 1661, are one and the same comet, from the similarity of the elements of their orbits, and were therefore induced to expect its return to its perihelium in 1789. As this comet is liable to be disturbed in its ascent from the sun by the planets Jupiter and Saturn, Dr. Maskelyne expected its return to its perihelium in the beginning of the year 1789, or the latter end of the year 1788, and certainly some time before the 27th of April, 1789, which prediction has not been fulfilled. Philos. Trans. Vol. LXXVI.

As the comets are small masses of matter, and pass in their periheliun very near the sun, and become invisible to us on these accounts in a short space of time, their number has not yet been ascertained, and will probably increase with the improvement of our telescopes. M. Bode has given a table of 72 comets, whose orbits are already calculated; of these 60 pass within the earth's orbit, and only twelve without it; and most of them appear between the orbits of Venus and Mercury, or nearly midway between the sun and earth; from whence, and from the planes of their orbits, being inclined to that of the earth and other planets in all possible angles, they are believed to be less liable to interfere with, or injure each other. M. Bode afterwards inquires into the nearest approach it is possible for each of the known comets to make towards the earth's orbit. He finds that only three of them can come within a distance equal to two or three times the distance of the moon from it: and then adds the great improbability, that the earth should be in that dangerous point of its orbit, at the instant when a comet, which may have been absent some centuries, passes so rapidly past it. Historie de l'Académ. Royal. Berlin. 1792.

NOTE V.—SUN'S RAYS.

Or give the sun's phlogistic orb to roll.
CANTO I. l. 136.

THE dispute among philosophers about phlogiston is not concerning the existence of an inflammable principle, but rather whether there be one or more inflammable principles. The disciples of Stahl, which till lately included the whole chemical world, believed in the identity of phlogiston in all bodies which would flame or calcine. The disciples of Lavoisier pay homage to a plurality of phlogistons under the various names of charcoal, sulphur, metals, &c. Whatever will unite with *pure* air, and thence compose an acid, is esteemed in this ingenious theory to be a different kind of phlogistic or inflammable body. At the same time there remains a doubt whether these inflammable bodies, as metals, sulphur, charcoal, &c. may not be compounded of the same phlogiston along with some other material yet undiscovered, and thus an unity of phlogiston exist, as in the theory of Stahl, though very differently applied in the explication of chemical phenomena.

Some modern philosophers are of opinion, that the sun is the great fountain from which the earth and other planets derive all the phlogiston which they possess; and that this is formed by the combination of the solar rays with all opake bodies, but particularly with the leaves of vegetables, which they suppose to be organs adapted to absorb them. And that as animals receive their nourishment from vegetables they also obtain in a secondary manner their phlogiston from the sun. And lastly, as great masses of the mineral kingdom, which have been found in the thin crust of the earth which human labour has penetrated, have evidently been formed from the recrements of animal and vegetable bodies, these also are supposed thus to have derived their phlogiston from the sun.

Another opinion concerning the sun's rays is, that they are not luminous till they arrive at our atmosphere; and that there uniting with some part of the air they produce combustion, and light is emitted, and that an ethereal acid, yet undiscovered, is formed from this combustion.

The more probable opinion is, perhaps, that the sun is a phlogistic mass of matter, whose surface is in a state of combustion, which, like other burning bodies, emits light with immense velocity in all directions; that these rays of light act upon all opake bodies, and combining with them either displace or produce their elementary heat, and become chemically combined with the phlogostic part of them; for light is given out when phlogistic bodies unite with the oxygenous principle of the air, as in combustion, or in the reduction of metallic calxes; thus in presenting to the flame of a candle a letter-wafer, (if it be coloured with red-lead,) at the time the red-lead becomes a metallic drop, a flash of light is perceived. Dr. Alexander Wilson very ingeniously endeavours to prove that the sun is only in a state of combustion on its surface, and that the dark spots seen on the disk are excavations or caverns through the luminous crust, some of which are 4000 miles in diameter. Phil. Trans. 1774. Of this I shall have occasion to speak again.

NOTE VI.—CENTRAL FIRES.

Round her still centre tread the burning soil,
And watch the billowy lavas, as they boil.
CANTO I. L. 139.

M. DE MAIRAN, in a paper published in the Histoire de l'Académie de Sciences, 1765, has endeavoured to show that the earth receives but a small part of the heat which it possesses, from the sun's rays, but is principally heated by fires within itself. He thinks the sun is the cause of the vicissitudes of our seasons of summer and winter by a very small quantity of heat in addition to that already residing in the earth, which by emanations from the centre to the circumference renders the surface habitable, and without which, though the sun was constantly to illuminate two thirds of the globe at once, with a heat equal to that at the equator, it would soon become a mass of solid ice. His reasonings and calculations on this subject are too long and too intricate to be inserted here, but are equally curious and ingenious, and carry much conviction along with them.

The opinion that the centre of the earth consists of a large mass of burning lava, has been espoused by Boyle, Boerhave, and many other philosophers. Some of whom considering its supposed effects on vegetation and the formation of minerals have called it a second sun. There are many arguments in support of this opinion. 1. Because the power of the sun does not extend much beyond ten feet deep into the earth, all below being in winter and summer always of the same degree of heat, viz. 48, which being much warmer than the mildest frost, is supposed to be sustained by some internal distant fire. Add to this however that from experiments made some years ago by Dr. Franklin, the spring-water at Philadelphia appeared to be of 52 of heat, which seems farther to confirm this opinion, since the climates in North America are supposed to be colder than those of Europe under similar degrees of latitude. 2. M. De Luc in going 1359 feet perpendicular into the mines of Hartz on July the 5th, 1778, on a very fine day found the air at the bottom a little warmer than at the top of the shaft. Phil. Trans. Vol. LXIX. p. 488. In the mines in Hungary, which are 500 cubits deep, the heat becomes very troublesome when the miners get below 480 feet depth. *Morinus de Locis subter.* p. 131. But as some other deep mines as mentioned by Mr. Kirwan are said to possess but the common heat of the earth; and as the crust of the globe thus penetrated by human labour is so thin compared with the whole, no certain deduction can be made from these facts on either side of the question. 3. The warm-springs in many parts of the earth at great distance from any volcanoes seem to originate from the condensation of vapours arising from water which is boiled by subterraneous fires, and cooled again in their passage through a certain length of the colder soil; for the theory of chemical solution will not explain the equality of their heat at all seasons and through so many centuries. See note on Fucus in Part II. See a letter on this subject in Mr. Pilkington's View of Derbyshire from Dr. Darwin. 4. From the situations of volcanoes which are always found upon the summit of the highest mountains. For as these mountains have been lifted up and lose several of their uppermost strata as they rise, the lowest strata of the earth yet known appear at the tops of the highest hills, and the beds of the volcanoes upon these hills must in consequence belong to the lowest strata of the earth, consisting perhaps of granite or basaltes, which were produced before the existence of animal or vegetable bodies, and might constitute the original nucleus of the earth, which I have supposed to have been projected from the sun, hence the volcanoes themselves appear to be spiracula or chimneys belonging to great central fires. It is probably owing to the escape of the elastic vapours from these spiracula that the modern earthquakes are of such small extent compared with those of remote antiquity, of which the vestiges remain all over the globe. 5. The great size and height of the continents, and the great size and depth of the South-sea, Atlantic, and other oceans, evince that the first earthquakes, which produced these immense changes in the globe, must have been occasioned by central fires. 6. The very distant and expeditious communication of the shocks of some great earthquakes. The earthquake at Lisbon in 1755 was perceived in Scotland, in the Peak of Derbyshire, and in many other distant parts of Europe. The percussions of it travelled with about the velocity of sound, viz. about thirteen miles in a minute. The earthquake in 1693 extended 2600 leagues. (Goldsmith's History.) These phenomena are easily explained if the central parts of the earth consist of a fluid lava, as a percussion on one part of such a fluid mass would be felt on other parts of its confining vault, like a stroke on a fluid, contained in a bladder, which, however gentle on one side, is perceptible to the hand placed on the other; and the velocity with which such a concussion would travel would be that of sound, or thirteen miles in a minute. For further information on this part of the subject, the reader is referred to Mr. Michell's excellent Treatise on earthquakes in the Philos. Trans. Vol. LI. 7. That there is a cavity at the centre of the earth is made probable by the late experiments on the attraction of mountains by Mr. Maskelyne, who supposed from other considerations that the density of the earth near the surface should be five times less than its mean density. Phil. Trans. Vol. LXV. p. 498. But found from the attraction of the mountain Schehallien, that it is probable, the mean density of the earth is but double that of the hill. Ibid. p. 532. Hence if the first supposition be well founded there would appear to be a cavity at the centre of considerable magnitude, from whence the immense beds and mountains of lava, toadstone, basaltes, granite, &c. have been protruded. 8. The variation of the compass can only be accounted for by supposing the central parts of the earth to consist of a fluid mass, and that part of this fluid is iron, which requiring a greater degree of heat to bring it into fusion than glass or other metals, remains a solid, and the vis inertia of this fluid mass with the iron in it, occasions it to perform fewer revolutions than the crust of solid earth over it, and thus it is gradually left behind, and the place where the floating iron resides is pointed to by the direct or retrograde motions of the magnetic needle. This seems to have been nearly the opinion of Dr. Halley and Mr. Euler.

NOTE VII.—ELEMENTARY HEAT.

Or sphere on sphere in widening waves expand,
And glad with genial warmth the incumbent land.
CANTO I. l. 148.

A CERTAIN quantity of heat seems to be combined with all bodies besides the sensible quantity which gravitates like the electric fluid amongst them. This combined heat or latent heat of Dr. Black, when set at liberty by fermentation, inflammation, crystallization, freezing, or other chemical attractions, producing new *combination*, passes as a fluid element into the surrounding bodies. And by thawing, diffusion of neutral salts in water, melting, and other chemical *solutions*, a portion of heat is attracted from the bodies in the vicinity, and enters into or becomes combined with the new solutions.

Hence a *combination* of metals with acids, of essential oils and acids, of alcohol and water, of acids and water, give out heat; whilst a *solution* of snow in water or in acids, and of neutral salts in water, attract heat from the surrounding bodies. So the acid of nitre mixed with oil of cloves unites with it and produces a most violent flame; the same acid of nitre poured on snow instantly dissolves it and produces the greatest degree of cold yet known, by which at Petersburgh quicksilver was first frozen in 1760.

Water may be cooled below 32° without being frozen, if it be placed on a solid floor and secured from agitation, but when thus cooled below the freezing point the least agitation turns part of it suddenly into ice, and when this sudden freezing takes place a thermometer placed in it instantly rises as some heat is given out in the act of congelation, and the ice is thus left with the same *sensible* degree of cold as the water had possessed before it was agitated, but is nevertheless now combined with less *latent* heat.

A cubic inch of water thus cooled down to 32° mixed with an equal quantity of boiling water at 212° will cool it to the middle number between these two, or to 122. But a cubic inch of ice whose sensible cold also is but 32, mixed with an equal quantity of boiling water, will cool it six times as much as the cubic inch of cold water above mentioned, as the ice not only gains its share of the sensible or gravitating heat of the boiling water but attracts to itself also and combines with the quantity of latent heat which it had lost at the time of its congelation.

So boiling water will acquire but 212° of heat under the common pressure of the atmosphere, but the steam raised from it by its expansion or by its solution in the atmosphere combines with and carries away a prodigious quantity of heat which it again parts with on its condensation; as is seen in common distillation where the large quantity of water in the worm tub is soon heated. Hence the evaporation of ether on a thermometer soon sinks the mercury below freezing, and hence a warmth of the air in winter frequently succeeds a shower.

When the matter of heat or calorique is set at liberty from its combinations, as by inflammation, it passes into the surrounding bodies, which possess different capacities of acquiring their share of the loose or sensible heat; thus a pint measure of cold water at 48° mixed with a pint of boiling water at 212° will cool it to the degree between these two numbers, or to 154°, but it requires two pint measures of quicksilver at 58° of heat to cool one pint of water as above. These and other curious experiments are adduced by Dr. Black to evince the existence of combined or latent heat in bodies, as has been explained by some of his pupils, and well illustrated by Dr. Crawford. The world has long been in expectation of an account of his discoveries on this subject by the celebrated author himself.

As this doctrine of elementary heat in its fluid and combined state is not yet universally received, I shall here add too arguments in support of it drawn from different sources, viz. from the heat given out or absorbed by the mechanical condensation or expansion of the air, and perhaps of other bodies, and from the analogy of the various phenomena of heat with those of electricity.

I. If a thermometer be placed in the receiver of an air-pump, and the air hastily exhausted, the thermometer will sink some degrees, and the glass become steamy; the same occurs in hastily admitting a part of the air again. This I suppose to be produced by the expansion of part of the air, both during the exhaustion and re-admission of it; and that the air so expanded becomes capable of attracting from the bodies in its vicinity a part of their heat, hence the vapours contained in it and the glass receiver are for a time colder and the stream is precipitated. That the air thus parts with its moisture from the cold occasioned by its rarefaction and not simply by the rarefaction itself is evident, because in a minute or two the same rarefied air will again take up the dew deposited on the receiver; and because water will evaporate sooner in rare than in dense air.

There is a curious phenomenon similar to this observed in the fountain of Hiero constructed on a large scale at the Chemnicensian mines in Hungary. In this machine the air in a vessel is compressed by a column of water 260 feet high, a stop-cock is then opened, and as the air issues out with great vehemence, and thus becomes immediately greatly expanded, so much cold is produced that the moisture from this stream of air is precipitated in the form of snow, and ice is formed adhering to the nosel of the cock. This remarkable circumstance is described at large with a plate of the machine in Philos. Trans. Vol. LII. for 1761. p. 547.

The following experiment is related by Dr. Darwin in the Philos. Trans. Vol. LXXVIII. Having charged an air-gun as forcibly as he well could the air-cell and syringe became exceedingly hot, much more so than could be ascribed to the friction in working it; it was then left about half an hour to cool down the temperature of the air, and a thermometer having been previously fixed against a wall, the air was discharged in a continual stream on its bulb, and it sunk many degrees. From these three experiments of the steam in the exhausted receiver being deposited and re-absorbed, when a part of the air is exhausted or re-admitted, and the snow produced by the fountain of Hiero, and the extraordinary heat given out in charging, and the cold produced in discharging an air-gun, there is reason to conclude that when air is mechanically compressed the elementary fluid heat is pressed out of it, and that when it is mechanically expanded the same fluid heat is re-absorbed from the common mass.

It is probable all other bodies as well as air attract heat from their neighbours when they are mechanically expanded, and give it out when they are mechanically condensed. Thus when a vibration of the particles of hard bodies is excited by friction or by percussion, these particles mutually recede from and approach each other reciprocally; at the times of their recession from each other, the body becomes enlarged in bulk, and is then in a condition to attract heat from those in its vicinity with great and sudden power; at the times of their approach to each other this heat is again given out, but the bodies in contact having in the mean while received the heat they had thus lost, from other bodies behind them, do not so suddenly or so forcibly re-absorb the heat again from the body in vibration; hence it remains on its surface like the electric fluid on a rubbed glass globe, and for the same reason, because there is no good conductor to take it up again. Hence at every vibration more and more heat is acquired and stands loose upon the surface; as in filing metals or rubbing glass tubes; and thus a smith with a few strokes on a nail on his anvil can make it hot enough to light a brimstone match; and hence in striking flint and steel together heat enough is produced to vitrify the parts thus strucken off, the quantity of which heat is again probably increased by the new chemical combination.

II. The analogy between the phenomena of the electric fluid and of heat furnishes another argument in support of the existence of heat as a gravitating fluid. 1. They are both accumulated by friction on the excited body. 2. They are propagated easily or with difficulty along the same classes of bodies; with ease by metals, with less ease by water; and with difficulty by resins, bees-wax, silk, air, and glass. Thus glass canes or canes of sealing-wax may be melted by a blow-pipe or a candle within a quarter of an inch of the fingers which hold them, without any inconvenient heat, while a pin or other metallic substance applied to the flame of a candle so readily conducts the heat as immediately to burn the fingers. Hence clothes of silk keep the body warmer than clothes of linen of equal thickness, by confining the heat upon the body. And hence plains are so much warmer than the summits of mountains by the greater density of the air confining the acquired heat upon them. 3. They both give out light in their passage through air, perhaps not in their passage through a vacuum. 4. They both of them fuse or vitrify metals. 5. Bodies after being electrized if they are mechanically extended will receive a greater quantity of electricity, as in Dr. Franklin's experiment of the chain in the tankard; the same seems true in respect to heat as explained above. 6. Both heat and electricity contribute to suspend steam in the atmosphere by producing or increasing the repulsion of its particles. 7. They both gravitate, when they have been accumulated, till they find their equilibrium.

If we add to the above the many chemical experiments which receive an easy and elegant explanation from the supposed matter of heat, as employed in the works of Bergman and Lavoisier, I think we may reasonably allow of its existence as an element, occasionally combined with other bodies, and occasionally existing as a fluid, like the electric fluid gravitating amongst them, and that hence it may be propagated from the central fires of the earth to the whole mass, and contribute to preserve the mean heat of the earth, which in this country is about 48 degrees but variable from the greater or less effect of the sun's heat in different climates, so well explained in Mr. Kirwan's treatise on the temperature of different latitudes. 1787. Elmsly. London.

NOTE VIII.—MEMNON'S LYRE.

So to the sacred sun in Memnon's fane
Spontaneous concords quired the matin strain.
CANTO I. l. 183.

THE gigantic statue of Memnon in his temple at Thebes had a lyre in his hands, which many credible writers assure us, sounded when the rising sun shone upon it. Some philosophers have supposed that the sun's light possesses a mechanical impulse, and that the sounds above mentioned might be thence produced. Mr. Michell constructed a very tender horizontal balance, as related by Dr. Priestley in his history of light and colours, for this purpose, but some experiments with this balance which I saw made by the late Dr. Powel, who threw the focus of a large reflector on one extremity of it, were not conclusive either way, as the copper leaf of the balance approached in one experiment and receded in another.

There are however methods by which either a rotative or alternating motion may be produced by very moderate degrees of heat. If a straight glass tube, such as are used for barometers, be suspended horizontally before a fire, like a roasting spit, it will revolve by intervals; for as glass is a bad conductor of heat, the side next the fire becomes heated sooner than the opposite side, and the tube becomes bent into a bow with the external part of the curve towards the fire, this curve then falls down and produces a fourth part of a revolution of the glass tube, which thus revolves with intermediate pauses.

Another alternating motion I have seen produced by suspending a glass tube about eight inches long with bulbs at each end on a centre like a scale beam. This curious machine is filled about one third part with purest spirit of wine, the other two thirds being a vacuum, and is called a pulse glass, if it be placed in a box before the fire, so that either bulb, as it rises, may become shaded from the fire, and exposed to it when it descends, an alternate libration of it is produced. For spirit of wine in vacuo emits steam by a very small degree of heat, and this steam forces the spirit beneath it up into the upper bulb, which therefore descends. It is probable such a machine on a larger scale might be of use to open the doors or windows of hot-houses or melon-frames, when the air within them should become too much heated, or might be employed in more important mechanical purposes.

On travelling through a hot summer's day in a chaise with a box covered with leather on the fore axle-tree, I observed, as the sun shone upon the black leather, the box began to open its lid, which at noon rose above a foot, and could not without great force be pressed down; and which gradually closed again as the sun declined in the evening. This I suppose might with still greater facility be applied to the purpose of opening melon-frames or the sashes of hot-houses.

The statue of Memnon was overthrown and sawed in two by Cambyses to discover its internal structure, and is said still to exist. See Savary's Letters on Egypt. The truncated statue is said for many centuries to have saluted the rising sun with cheerful tones, and the setting sun with melancholy ones.

NOTE IX.—LUMINOUS INSECTS.

Star of the earth, and diamond of the night.
CANTO I. l. 196.

THERE are eighteen species of lampyris or glow-worm, according to Linneus, some of which are found in almost every part of the world. In many of the species the females have no wings, and are supposed to be discovered by the winged males by their shining in the night. They become much more lucid when they put themselves in motion, which would seem to indicate that their light is owing to their respiration; in which process it is probable phosphoric acid is produced by the combination of vital air with some part of the blood, and that light is given out through their transparent bodies by this slow internal combustion.

There is a fire-fly of the beetle-kind described in the Dict. Raisonné under the name of Acudia, which is said to be two inches long, and inhabits the West Indies and South America; the natives use them instead of candles, putting from one to three of them under a glass. Madam Merian says that at Surinam the light of this fly is so great, that she saw sufficiently well by one of them to paint and finish one of the figures of them in her work on insects. The largest and oldest of them are said to become four inches long, and to shine like a shooting star as they fly, and are thence called lantern-bearers. The use of this light to the insect itself seems to be that it may not fly against objects in the night; by which contrivance these insects are enabled to procure their sustenance either by night or day, as their wants may require, or their numerous enemies permit them; whereas some of our beetles have eyes adapted only to the night, and if they happen to come abroad too soon in the evening are so dazzled that they fly against every thing in their way. See note on phosphorus, No. X.

In some seas, as particularly about the coast of Malabar, as a ship floats along, it seems during the night to be surrounded with fire, and to leave a long tract of light behind it. Whenever the sea is greatly agitated, it seems converted into little stars, every drop as it breaks emits light, like bodies electrified in the dark. Mr. Bomare says, that when he was at the Port of Cettes in Languedoc, and bathing with a companion in the sea after a very hot day, they both appeared covered with fire after every immersion, and that laying his wet hand on the arm of his companion, who had not then dipped himself, the exact mark of his hand and fingers was seen in characters of fire. As numerous microscopic insects are found in this shining water, its light has been generally ascribed to them, though it seems probable that fish-slime in hot countries may become in such a state of incipient putrefaction as to give light, especially when by agitation it is more exposed to the air; otherwise it is not easy to explain why agitation should be necessary to produce this marine light. See note on phosphorus, No. X.

NOTE X.—PHOSPHORUS.

Or mark with shining letters Kunckel's name
In the pale phosphor's self-consuming flame.
CANTO I. l. 231.

KUNCKEL, a native of Hamburgh, was the first who discovered to the world the process for producing phosphorus; though Brandt and Boyle were likewise said to have previously had the art of making it. It was obtained from sal microcosmicum by evaporation in the form of an acid, but has since been found in other animal substances, as in the ashes of bones, and even in some vegetables, as in wheat flour. Keir's Chemical Dict. This phosphoric acid, is, like all other acids, united with vital air, and requires to be treated with charcoal or phlogiston to deprive it of this air; it then becomes a kind of animal sulphur, but of so inflammable a nature, that on the access of air it takes fire spontaneously, and as it burns becomes again united with vital air, and re-assumes its form of phosphoric acid.

As animal respiration seems to be a kind of slow combustion, in which it is probable that phosphoric acid is produced by the union of phosphoric with the vital air, so it is also probable that phosphoric acid is produced in the excretory or respiratory vessels of luminous insects, as the glow-worm and fire-fly, and some marine insects. From the same principle I suppose the light from putrid flesh, as from the heads of haddocks, and from putrid veal, and from rotten wood in a certain state of their putrefaction, is produced, and phosphorus thus slowly combined with air is changed into phosphoric acid. The light from the Bolognian stone, and from calcined shells, and from white paper, and linen after having been exposed for a time to the sun's light, seem to produce either the phosphoric or some other kind of acid from the sulphurous or phlogistic matter which they contain. See note on Beccari's shells, l. 182.

There is another process seems similar to this slow combustion, and that is *bleaching*. By the warmth and light of the sun the water sprinkled upon linen or cotton cloth seems to be decomposed, (if we credit the theory of M. Lavoisier,) and a part of the vital air thus set at liberty and uncombined, and not being in its elastic form, more easily dissolves the colouring or phlogistic matter of the cloth, and produces a new acid, which is itself colourless, or is washed out of the cloth by water.—The new process of bleaching confirms a part of this theory, for by uniting much vital air to marine acid by distilling it from manganese, on dipping the cloth to be bleached in water replete with this superaerated marine acid, the colouring matter disappears immediately, sooner indeed in cotton than in linen. See note XXXIV.

There is another process which I suspect bears analogy to these above mentioned, and that is the rancidity of animal fat, as of bacon; if bacon be hung up in a warm kitchen, with much salt adhering on the outside of it, the fat part of it soon becomes yellow and rancid; if it be washed with much cold water after it has imbibed the salt, and just before it is hung up, I am well informed, that it will not become rancid, or in very slight degrees. In the former case I imagine the salt on the surface of the bacon attracts water during the cold of the night, which is evaporated during the day, and that in this evaporation a part of the water becomes decomposed, as in bleaching, and its vital air uniting with greater facility in its unelastic state with the animal fat, produces an acid, perhaps of the phosphoric kind, which being of a fixed nature lies upon the bacon, giving it the yellow colour and rancid taste. It is remarkable that the superaerated marine acid does not bleach living animal substances, at least it did not whiten a part of my hand which I for some minutes exposed to it.

NOTE XI.—STEAM-ENGINE.

Quick moves the balanced beam, of giant-birth,
Wields his large limbs, and nodding shakes the earth.
CANTO I. l. 261.

THE expansive force of steam was known in some degree to the ancients; Hero of Alexandria describes an application of it to produce a rotative motion by the reaction of steam issuing from a sphere mounted upon an axis, through two small tubes bent into tangents, and issuing from the opposite sides of the equatorial diameter of the sphere, the sphere was supplied with steam by a pipe communicating with a pan of boiling water, and entering the sphere at one of its poles.

A French writer about the year 1630 describes a method of raising water to the upper part of a house by filling a chamber with steam, and suffering it to condense of itself, but it seems to have been mere theory, as his method was scarcely practicable as he describes it. In 1655 the Marquis of Worcester mentions a method of raising water by fire in his Century of Inventions, but he seems only to have availed himself of the expansive force, and not to have known the advantages arising from condensing the steam by an injection of cold water. This latter and most important improvement seems to have been made by Capt. Savery some time prior to 1698, for in that year his patent for the use of that invention was confirmed by act of parliament. This gentleman appears to have been the first who reduced the machine to practice, and exhibited it in a useful form. This method consisted only in expelling the air from a vessel by steam, and condensing the steam by an injection of cold water, which making a vacuum, the pressure of the atmosphere forced the water to ascend into the steam vessel through a pipe of 24 to 26 feet high, and by the admission of dense steam from the boiler, forcing the water in the steam-vessel to ascend to the height desired. This construction was defective because it requires very strong vessels to resist the force of the steam, and because an enormous quantity of steam was condensed by coming in contact with the cold water in the steam-vessel.

About, or soon after that time, M. Papin attempted a steam-engine on similar principles, but rather more defective in its construction.

The next improvement was made very soon afterwards by Messrs. Newcomen and Cawley of Dartmouth: it consisted in employing for the steam vessel a hollow cylinder shut at bottom and open at top, furnished with a piston sliding easily up and down in it, and made tight by oakum or hemp, and covered with water. This piston is suspended by chains from one end of a beam, moveable upon an axis in the middle of its length, to the other end of this beam are suspended the pump-rods.

The danger of bursting the vessels was avoided in this machine, as, however high the water was to be raised, it was not necessary to increase the density of the steam, but only to enlarge the diameter of the cylinder.

Another advantage was, that the cylinder not being made so cold as in Savery's method, much less steam was lost in filling it after each condensation.

The machine, however, still remained imperfect, for the cold water thrown into the cylinder acquired heat from the steam it condensed, and being in a vessel exhausted of air it produced steam itself, which in part resisted the action of the atmosphere on the piston; were this remedied by throwing in more cold water, the destruction of the steam in the next filling of the cylinder would be proportionally increased. It has therefore in practice been found advisable not to load these engines with columns of water weighing more than seven pounds for each square inch of the area of the piston. The bulk of water, when converted into steam, remained unknown until Mr. J. Watt, then of Glasgow, in 1764, determined it to be about 1800 times more rare than water. It soon occurred to Mr. Watt that a perfect engine would be that in which no steam should be condensed in filling the cylinder, and in which the steam should be so perfectly cooled as to produce nearly a perfect vacuum.

Mr. Watt having ascertained the degree of heat in which water boiled in vacuo, and under progressive degrees of pressure, and instructed by Dr. Black's discovery of latent heat, having calculated the quantity of cold water necessary to condense certain quantities of steam so far as to produce the exhaustion required, he made a communication from the cylinder to a cold vessel previously exhausted of air and water, into which the steam rushed by its elasticity, and became immediately condensed. He then adapted a cover to the cylinder, and admitted steam above the piston to press it down instead of air, and instead of applying water he used oil or grease to fill the pores of the oakum, and to lubricate the cylinder.

He next applied a pump to extract the injection water, the condensed steam, and the air, from the condensing vessel, every stroke of the engine.

To prevent the cooling of the cylinder by the contact of the external air, he surrounded it with a case containing steam, which he again protected by a covering of matters which conduct heat slowly.

This construction presented an easy means of regulating the power of the engine, for the steam being the acting power, as the pipe which admits it from the boiler is more or less opened, a greater or smaller quantity can enter during the time of a stroke, and consequently the engine can act with exactly the necessary degree of energy.

Mr. Watt gained a patent for his engine in 1768, but the further prosecution of his designs were delayed by other avocations till 1775, when in conjunction with Mr. Boulton, of Soho, near Birmingham, numerous experiments were made on a large scale by their united ingenuity, and great improvements added to the machinery, and an act of parliament obtained for the prolongation of their patent for twenty-five years; they have since that time drained many of the deep mines in Cornwall, which, but for the happy union of such genius, must immediately have ceased to work. One of these engines works a pump of eighteen inches diameter, and upwards of 100 fathom or 600 feet high, at the rate of ten to twelve strokes of seven feet long each, in a minute, and that with one fifth part of the coals which a common engine would have taken to do the same work. The power of this engine may be easier comprehended by saying that it raised a weight equal to 81,000 pounds 80 feet high in a minute, which is equal to the combined action of 200 good horses. In Newcomen's engine this would have required a cylinder of the enormous diameter of 120 inches, or ten feet; but as in this engine of Mr. Watt and Mr. Boulton the steam acts, and a vacuum is made, alternately above and below the piston, the power exerted is double to what the same cylinder would otherways produce, and is further augmented by an inequality in the length of the two ends of the lever.

These gentlemen have also, by other contrivances, applied their engines to the turning of mills for almost every purpose, of which that great pile of machinery, the Albion Mill, is a well known instance. Forges, slitting mills, and other great works, are erected, where nature has furnished no running water, and future times may boast that this grand and useful engine was invented and perfected in our own country.

Since the above article went to the press, the Albion Mill is no more; it is supposed to have been set on fire by interested or malicious incendiaries, and is burnt to the ground. Whence London has lost the credit and the advantage of possessing the most powerful machine in the world!

NOTE XII.—FROST.

In phalanx firm the fiend of frost assail.
CANTO I. l. 439.

THE cause of the expansion of water during its conversion into ice is not yet well ascertained. It was supposed to have been owing to the air being set at liberty in the act of congelation, which was before dissolved in the water, and the many air bubbles in ice were thought to countenance this opinion. But the great force with which ice expands during its congelation, so as to burst iron bombs and coehorns, according to the experiments of Major Williams at Quebec, invalidates this idea of the cause of it, and may some time be brought into use as a means of breaking rocks in mining, or projecting cannon-balls, or for other mechanical purposes, if the means of producing congelation should ever be discovered to be as easy as the means of producing combustion.

Mr. de Mairan attributes the increase of bulk of frozen water to the different arrangement of the particles of it in crystallization, as they are constantly joined at an angle of 60 degrees; and must by this disposition he thinks occupy a greater volume than if they were parallel. He found the augmentation of the water during freezing to amount to one-fourteenth, one-eighteenth, one-nineteenth, and when the water was previously purged of air to only one-twenty-second part. He adds that a piece of ice, which was at first only one-fourteenth part specifically lighter than water, on being exposed some days to the frost became one-twelfth lighter than water. Hence he thinks ice by being exposed to greater cold still increases in volume, and to this attributes the bursting of ice in ponds and on the glaciers. See Lewis's Commerce of Arts, p. 257, and the note on Muschus in the second part of this work.

This expansion of ice well accounts for the greater mischief done by vernal frosts attended with moisture, (as by hoar-frosts,) than by the dry frosts called black frosts. Mr. Lawrence in a letter to Mr. Bradley complains that the dale-mist attended with a frost on May-day had destroyed all his tender fruits; though there was a sharper frost the night before without a mist, that did him no injury; and adds, that a garden not a stone's throw from his own on a higher situation, being above the dale-mist, had received no damage. Bradley, Vol. II. p. 232.

Mr. Hunter by very curious experiments discovered that the living principle in fish, in vegetables, and even in eggs and seeds, possesses a power of resisting congelation. Phil. Trans. There can be no doubt but that the exertions of animals to avoid the pain of cold may produce in them a greater quantity of heat, at least for a time, but that vegetables, eggs, or seeds, should possess such a quality is truly wonderful. Others have imagined that animals possess a power of preventing themselves from becoming much warmer than 98 degrees of heat, when immersed in an atmosphere above that degree of heat. It is true that the increased exhalation from their bodies will in some measure cool them, as much heat is carried off by the evaporation of fluids, but this is a chemical not an animal process. The experiments made by those who continued many minutes in the air of a room heated so much above any natural atmospheric heat, do not seem conclusive, as they remained in it a less time than would have been necessary to have heated a mass of beef of the same magnitude, and the circulation of the blood in living animals, by perpetually bringing new supplies of fluid to the skin, would prevent the external surface from becoming hot much sooner than the whole mass. And thirdly, there appears no power of animal bodies to produce cold in diseases, as in scarlet fever, in which the increased action of the vessels of the skin produces heat and contributes to exhaust the animal power already too much weakened.

It has been thought by many that frosts meliorate the ground, and that they are in general salubrious to mankind. In respect to the former it is now well known that ice or snow contain no nitrous particles, and though frost, by enlarging the bulk of moist clay, leaves it softer for a time after the thaw, yet as soon as the water exhales, the clay becomes as hard as before, being pressed together by the incumbent atmosphere, and by its self-attraction, called *setting* by the potters. Add to this, that on the coasts of Africa, where frost is unknown, the fertility of the soil is almost beyond our conceptions of it. In respect to the general salubrity of frosty seasons, the bills of mortality are an evidence in the negative, as in long frosts many weakly and old people perish from debility occasioned by the cold, and many classes of birds and other wild animals are benumbed by the cold, or destroyed by the consequent scarcity of food, and many tender vegetables perish from the degree of cold.

I do not think it should be objected to this doctrine that there are moist days attended with a brisk cold wind when no visible ice appears, and which are yet more disagreeable and destructive than frosty weather. For on these days the cold moisture, which is deposited on the skin is there evaporated, and thus produces a degree of cold perhaps greater than the milder frosts. Whence even in such days both the disagreeable sensations and insalubrious effects belong to the cause above mentioned, viz. the intensity of the cold. Add to this, that in these cold moist days, as we pass along, or as the wind blows upon us, a new sheet of cold water is as it were perpetually applied to us, and hangs upon our bodies. Now as water is 800 times denser than air, and is a much better conductor of heat, we are starved with cold like those who go into a cold bath, both by the great number of particles in contact with the skin and the greater facility of receiving our heat.

It may nevertheless be true that snows of long duration in our winters may be less injurious to vegetation than great rains and shorter frosts, for two reasons. 1. Because great rains carry down many thousand pounds worth of the best part of the manure off the lands into the sea, whereas snow dissolves more gradually and thence carries away less from the land; any one may distinguish a snow flood from a rain-flood by the transparency of the water. Hence hills or fields with considerable inclination of surface should be ploughed horizontally that the furrows may stay the water from showers till it deposits its mud. 2. Snow protects vegetables from the severity of the frost, since it is always in a state of thaw where it is in contact with the earth; as the earth's heat is about 48° and the heat of thawing snow is 32° the vegetables between them are kept in a degree of heat about 40, by which many of them are preserved See note on Muschus, Part II. of this work.

NOTE XIII.—ELECTRICTY.

Cold from each point cerulean lustres gleam.
CANTO I. 1. 339.

ELECTRIC POINTS.

THERE was an idle dispute whether knobs or points were preferable on the top of conductors for the defence of houses. The design of these conductors is to permit the electric matter accumulated in the clouds to pass through them into the earth in a smaller continued stream as the cloud approaches, before it comes to what is termed striking distance; now as it is well known that accumulated electricity will pass to points at a much greater distance than it will to knobs, there can be no doubt of their preference; and it would seem that the finer the points, and the less liable to become rusty the better, as it would take off the lightning while it was still at a greater distance, and by that means preserve a greater extent of building : the very extremity of the point should be of pure silver or gold, and might be branched into a kind of brush, since one small point cannot be supposed to receive so great a quantity as a thick bar might conduct into the earth.

If an insulated metallic ball is armed with a point, like a needle, projecting from one part of it, the electric fluid will be seen in the dark to pass off from this point, so long as the ball is kept supplied with electricity. The reason of this is not difficult to comprehend, every part of the electric atmosphere which surrounds the insulated ball is attracted to that ball by a large surface of it, whereas the electric atmosphere which is near the extremity of the needle is attracted to it only by a single point ; in consequence the particles of electric matter near the surface of the ball approach towards it, and push off by their greater gravitation the particles of electric matter over the point of the needle in a continued stream.

Something like this happens in respect to the diffusion of oil on water from a pointed cork, an experiment which was many years ago shown to me by Dr. Franklin ; he cut a piece of cork about the size of a letter-wafer, and left on one edge of it a point about a sixth of an inch in length, projecting as a tangent to the circumference. This was dipped in oil and thrown on a pond of water, and continued to revolve as the oil left the point for a great many minutes. The oil descends from the floating cork upon the water being diffused upon it without friction and perhaps without contact ; but its going off at the point so forcibly as to make that cork revolve in a contrary direction seems analogous to the departure of the electric fluid from points.

Can any thing similar to either of these happen in respect to the earth's atmosphere, and give occasion to the breezes on the tops of mountains, which may be considered as points on the earth's circumference ?

FAIRY-RINGS.

There is a phenomenon supposed to be electric which is yet unaccounted for, I mean the fairy-rings, as they are called, so often seen on the grass. The numerous flashes of lightning which occur every summer are, I believe, generally discharged on the earth, and but seldom (if ever) from one cloud to another. Moist trees are the most frequent conductors of these flashes of lightning, and I am informed by purchasers of wood that innumerable trees are thus cracked and injured. At other times larger parts or prominences of clouds gradually sinking as they move along, are discharged on the moister parts of grassy plains. Now this knob or corner of a cloud in being attracted by the earth will become nearly cylindrical, as loose wool would do when drawn out into a thread, and will strike the earth with a stream of electricity perhaps two or ten yards in diameter. Now, as a stream of electricity displaces the air it passes through, it is plain no part of the grass can be burnt by it, but just the external ring of this cylinder where the grass can have access to the air, since without air nothing can be calcined. This earth, after having been so calcined, becomes a richer soil, and either funguses or a bluer grass for many years mark the place. That lightning displaces the air in its passage is evinced by the loud crack that succeeds it, which is owing to the sides of the aerial vacuum clapping together when the lightning is withdrawn. That nothing will calcine without air is now well understood from the acids produced in the burning of phlogistic substances, and may be agreeably seen by suspending a paper on an iron prong, and putting it into the centre of the blaze of an iron furnace ; it may be held there some seconds, and may be again withdrawn without its being burnt, if it be passed quickly into the flame, and out again through the external part of it which is in contact with the air. I know some circles of many yards diameter of this kind near Foremark, in Derbyshire, which annually produce large white funguses and stronger grass, and have done so, I am informed, above thirty years. This increased fertility of the ground by calcination or charring, and its continuing to operate so many years, is well worth the attention of the farmer, and shows the use of paring and burning new turf in agriculture, which produces its effect not so much by the ashes of the vegetable fibres as by charring the soil which adheres to them.

These situations, whether from eminence or from moisture, which were proper once to attract and discharge a thunder-cloud, are more liable again to experience the same. Hence many fairy-rings are often seen near each other, either without intersecting each other, as I saw this summer in a garden in Nottinghamshire, or intersecting each other as described on Arthur's seat near Edinburgh, in the Edinb. Trans. Vol. II. p. 3.

NOTE XIV.—BUDS AND BULBS.

Where dwell my vegetative realms benumb'd
In buds imprison'd, or in bulbs intomb'd.
CANTO I. l. 459.

A TREE is properly speaking a family or swarm of buds, each bud being an individual plant, for if one of these buds be torn or cut out and planted in the earth with a glass cup inverted over it to prevent its exhalation from being at first greater than its power of absorption, it will produce a tree similar to its parent; each bud has a leaf which is its lungs, appropriated to it, and the bark of the tree is a congeries of the roots of these individual buds, whence old hollow trees are often seen to have some branches flourish with vigour after the internal wood is almost entirely decayed and vanished. According to this idea Linneus has observed that trees and shrubs are roots above ground, for if a tree be inverted leaves will grow from the root-part and roots from the trunk-part. Phil. Bot. p. 39. Hence it appears that vegetables have two methods of propagating themselves, the oviparous as by seeds, and the viviparous as by their buds and bulbs, and that the individual plants, whether from seeds or buds or bulbs, are all annual productions like many kinds of insects as the silk-worm, the parent perishing in the autumn after having produced an embryon, which lies in a torpid state during the winter, and is matured in the succeeding summer. Hence Linneus names buds and bulbs the winter cradles of the plant or hybernacula, and might have given the same term to seeds, In warm climates few plants produce buds, as the vegetable life can be completed in one summer, and hence the hybernacle is not wanted; in cold climates also some plants do not produce buds, as philadelphus, frangula, viburnum, ivy, heath, wood-nightshade, rue, geranium.

The bulbs of plants are another kind of winter-cradle, or hybernacle, adhering to the descending trunk, and are found in the perennial herbaceous plants which are too tender to bear the cold of the winter. The production of these subteŕraneous winter lodges, is not yet perhaps clearly understood, they have been distributed by Linneus according to their forms into scaly, solid, coated, and jointed bulbs, which however does not elucidate their manner of production. As the buds of trees may be truly esteemed individual annual plants, their roots constituting the bark of the trees, it follows that these roots (viz. of each individual bud) spread themselves over the last year's bark, making a new bark over the old one, and thence descending cover with a new bark the old roots also in the same manner. A similar circumstance I suppose to happen in some herbaceous plants, that is, a new bark is annually produced over the old root, and thus for some years at least the old root or caudex increases in size, and puts up new stems. As these roots increase in size the central part I suppose changes like the internal wood of a tree and does not possess any vegetable life, and therefore gives out no fibres or rootlets, and hence appears bitten off, as in valerian, plantain, and devil's-bit. And this decay of the central part of the root I suppose has given occasion to the belief of the root-fibres drawing down the bulb so much insisted on by Mr. Milne in his Botanical Dictionary, Art. Bulb.

From the observations and drawings of various kinds of bulbous roots at different times of their growth, sent me by a young lady of nice observation, it appears probable that all bulbous roots properly so called perish annually in this climate: Bradley, Miller, and the author of Spectacle de la Nature, observe that the tulip annually renews its bulb, for the stalk of the old flower is found under the old dry coat but on the outside of the new bulb. This large new bulb is the flowering bulb, but besides this there are other small new bulbs produced between the coats of this large one but from the same caudex, (or circle from which the root-fibres spring;) these small bulbs are leaf-bearing bulbs, and renew themselves annually with increasing size till they bear flowers.

Miss ———— favoured me with the following curious experiment: She took a small tulip-root out of the earth when the green leaves were sufficiently high to show the flower, and placed it in a glass of water; the leaves and flower soon withered and the bulb became wrinkled and soft, but put out one small side bulb and three bulbs beneath descending an inch into the water by processes from the caudex, the old bulb in some weeks entirely decayed; on dissecting this monster, the middle descending bulb was found by its process to adhere to the caudex and to the old flower-stem, and the side ones were separated from the flower-stem by a few shrivelled coats but adhered to the caudex. Whence she concludes that these last were off-sets or leaf-bulbs which should have been seen between the coats of the new flower-bulb if it had been left to grow in the earth, and that the middle one would have been the new flower-bulb. In some years (perhaps in wet seasons) the florists are said to lose many of their tulip-roots by a similar process, the new leaf-bulbs being produced beneath the old ones by an elongation of the caudex without any new flower-bulbs.

By repeated dissections she observes that the leaf-bulbs or off-sets of tulip, crocus, gladiolus, fritillary, are renewed in the same manner as the flowering-bulbs, contrary to the opinion of many writers; this new leaf-bulb is formed on the inside of the coats from whence the leaves grow, and is more or less advanced in size as the outer coats and leaves are more or less shrivelled. In examining tulip, iris, hyacinth, harebell, the new bulb was invariably found *between* the flower-stem and the base of the innermost leaf of those roots which had flowered, and *inclosed by* the base of the innermost leaf in those roots which had not flowered, in both cases adhering to the caudex or fleshy circle from which the root-fibres spring.

Hence it is probable that the bulbs of hyacinths are renewed annually, but that this is performed from the caudex within the old bulb, the outer coat of which does not so shrivel as in crocus and fritillary, and hence this change is not so apparent. But I believe as soon as the flower is advanced the new bulbs may be seen on dissection, nor does the annual increase of the size of the root of cyclamen and of aletris capensis militate against this annual renewal of them, since the leaf-bulbs or off-sets, as described above, are increased in size as they are annually renewed. See note on orchis, and on anthoxanthum, in Part II. of this work.

NOTE XV.—SOLAR VOLCANOES.

From the deep craters of his realms of fire
The whirling sun this ponderous planet hurl'd.
CANTO II. L 14.

DR. ALEXANDER WILSON, Professor of Astronomy at Glasgow, published a paper in the Philosophical Transactions for 1774, demonstrating that the spots in the sun's disk are real cavities, excavations through the luminous material, which covers the other parts of the sun's surface. One of these cavities he found to be about four thousand miles deep and many times as wide. Some objections were made to this doctrine by M. De la Lande in the Memoirs of the French Academy for the year 1776, which however have been ably answered by Professor Wilson in reply to the Philos. Trans. for 1783. Keil observes, in his Astronomical Lectures, p. 44. "We frequently see spots in the sun which are larger and broader not only than Europe or Africa, but which even equal, if they do not exceed, the surface of the whole terraqueous globe." Now that these cavities are made in the sun's body by a process of nature similar to our earthquakes does not seem improbable on several accounts. 1. Because from this discovery of Dr. Wilson it appears that the internal parts of the sun are not in a state of inflammation or of ejecting light, like the external part or luminous ocean which covers it; and hence that a greater degree of heat or inflammation and consequent expansion or explosion may occasionally be produced in its internal or dark nucleus. 2. Because the solar spots or cavities are frequently increased or diminished in size. 3. New ones are often produced. 4. And old ones vanish. 5. Because there are brighter or more luminous parts of the sun's disk, called faculæ by Scheiner and Hevelius, which would seem to be volcanoes in the sun, or, as Dr. Wilson calls them, "eructations of matter more luminous than that which covers the sun's surface." 6. To which may be added that all the planets added together with their satellites do not amount to more than one six hundred and fiftieth part of the mass of the sun according to Sir Isaac Newton.

Now if it could be supposed that the planets were originally thrown out of the sun by larger sun-quakes than those frequent ones which occasion these spots or excavations above mentioned, what would happen? 1. According to the observations and opinion of Mr. Herschel the sun itself and all its planets are moving forwards round some other centre with an unknown velocity, which may be of opake matter corresponding with the very ancient and general idea of a chaos. Whence if a ponderous planet, as Saturn, could be supposed to be projected from the sun by an explosion, the motion of the sun itself might be at the same time disturbed in such a manner as to prevent the planet from falling again into it. 2. As the sun revolves round its own axis its form must be that of an oblate spheroid like the earth, and therefore a body projected from its surface perpendicularly upwards from that surface would not rise perpendicularly from the sun's centre, unless it happened to be projected exactly from either of its poles or from its equator. Whence it may not be necessary that a planet if thus projected from the sun by explosion should again fall into the sun. 3. They would part from the sun's surface with the velocity with which that surface was moving, and with the velocity acquired by the explosion, and would therefore move round the sun in the same direction in which the sun rotates on its axis, and perform elliptic orbits. 4. All the planets would move the same way round the sun, from this first motion acquired at leaving its surface, but their orbits would be inclined to each other according to the distance of the part, where they were thrown out, from the sun's equator. Hence those which were ejected near the sun's equator would have orbits but little inclined to each other, as the primary planets; the plain of all whose orbits are inclined but seven degrees and a half from each other. Others which were ejected near the sun's poles would have much more eccentric orbits, as they would partake so much less of the sun's rotatory motion at the time they parted from his surface, and would therefore be carried further from the sun by the velocity they had gained by the explosion which ejected them, and become comets. 5. They would all obey the same laws of motion in their revolutions round the sun; this had been determined by astronomers, who have demonstrated that they move through equal areas in equal times. 6. As their annual periods would depend on the height they rose by the explosion, these would differ in them all. 7. As their diurnal revolutions would depend on one side of the exploded matter adhering more than the other at the time it was torn off by the explosion these would also differ in the different planets, and not bear any proportion to their annual periods. Now as all these circumstances coincide with the known laws of the planetary system, they serve to strengthen this conjecture.

This coincidence of such a variety of circumstances induced M. de Buffon to suppose that the planets were all struck off from the sun's surface by the impact of a large comet, such as approached so near the sun's disk, and with such amazing velocity in the year 1680, and is expected to return in 2255. But Mr. Buffon did not recollect that these comets themselves are only planets with more eccentric orbits, and that therefore it must be asked, what had previously struck off these comets from the sun's body? 2. That if all these planets were struck off from the sun at the same time, they must have been so near as to have attracted each other, and have formed one mass. 3. That we shall want new causes for separating the secondary planets from the primary ones, and must therefore look out for some other agent, as it does not appear how the impulse of a comet could have made one planet roll round another at the time they both of them were driven off from the surface of the sun.

If it should be asked, why new planets are not frequently ejected from the sun? it may be answered, that after many large earthquakes many vents are left for the elastic vapours to escape, and hence, by the present appearance of the surface of our earth, earthquakes prodigiously larger than any recorded in history have existed, the same circumstances may have affected the sun, on whose surface there are appearances of volcanoes, as described above. Add to this, that some of the comets, and even the georgium sidus, may, for ought we know to the contrary, have been emitted from the sun in more modern days, and have been diverted from their course, and thus prevented from returning into the sun, by their approach to some of the older planets, which is somewhat countenanced by the opinion several philosophers have maintained, that the quantity of matter of the sun has decreased. Dr. Halley observed, that by comparing the proportion which the periodical time of the moon bore to that of the sun in former times, with the proportion between them at present, the moon is found to be somewhat accelerated in respect to the sun. Pemberton's View of Sir Isaac Newton, p. 247. And so large is the body of this mighty luminary, that all the planets thus thrown out of it would make scarce any perceptible diminution of it, as mentioned above. The cavity mentioned above, as measured by Dr. Wilson of 4000 miles in depth, not penetrating an hundredth part of the sun's semi-diameter; and yet, as its width was many times greater than its depth, was large enough to contain a greater body than our terrestrial world.

I do not mean to conceal, that from the laws of gravity unfolded by Sir Isaac Newton, supposing the sun to be a sphere, and to have no progressive motion, and not liable itself to be disturbed by the supposed projection of the planets from it, that such planets must return into the sun. The late Rev. William Ludlam, of Leicester, whose genius never met with reward equal to its merits, in a letter to me, dated Jan. 1787, after having shown, as mentioned above, that planets so projected from the sun would return to it, adds, " That a body as large as the moon so projected, would disturb the motion of the earth in its orbit, is certain; but the calculation of such disturbing forces is difficult. The body in some circumstances might become a satellite, and both move round their common centre of gravity, and that centre be carried in an annual orbit round the sun."

There are other circumstances which might have concurred at the time of such supposed explosions, which would render this idea not impossible. 1. The planets might be thrown out of the sun at the time the sun itself was rising from chaos, and be attracted by other suns in their vicinity rising at the same time out of chaos, which would prevent them from returning into the sun. 2. The new planet in its course or ascent from the sun, might explode and eject a satellite, or perhaps more than one, and thus by its course being affected might not return into the sun. 3. If more planets were ejected at the same time from the sun, they might attract and disturb each other's course at the time they left the body of the sun, or very soon afterwards, when they would be so much nearer each other.

NOTE XVI.—CALCAREOUS EARTH.

While ocean wrapp'd it in his azure robe.
CANTO II. l. 34.

FROM having observed that many of the highest mountains of the world consist of lime-stone replete with shells, and that these mountains bear the marks of having been lifted up by subterranean fires from the interior parts of the globe; and as lime-stone replete with shells is found at the bottom of many of our deepest mines, some philosophers have concluded that the nucleus of the earth was for many ages covered with water which was peopled with its adapted animals; that the shells and bones of these animals in a long series of time produced solid strata in the ocean surrounding the original nucleus.

These strata consist of the accumulated exuviæ of shell-fish, the animals perished age after age, but their shells remained, and in progression of time produced the amazing quantities of lime-stone which almost cover the earth. Other marine animals called coralloids raised walls and even mountains by the congeries of their calcareous habitations; these perpendicular coralline rocks make some parts of the Southern Ocean highly dangerous, as appears in the journals of Capt. Cook. From contemplating the immense strata of lime-stone, both in respect to their extent and thickness, formed from these shells of animals, philosophers have been led to conclude, that much of the water of the sea has been converted into calcareous earth by passing through their organs of digestion. The formation of calcareous earth seems more particularly to be an animal process as the formation of clay belongs to the vegetable economy; thus the shells of crabs and other testaceous fish are annually reproduced from the mucous membrane beneath them; the shells of eggs are first a mucous membrane, and the calculi of the kidneys and those found in all other parts of our system which sometimes contain calcareous earth, seem to originate from inflamed membranes; the bones themselves consist of calcareous earth united with the phosphoric or animal acid, which may be separated by dissolving the ashes of calcined bones in the nitrous acid; the various secretions of animals, as their saliva and urine, abound likewise with calcareous earth, as appears by the incrustations about the teeth and the sediments of urine. It is probable that animal mucus is a previous process towards the formation of calcareous earth; and that all the calcareous earth in the world which is seen in lime-stones, marbles, spars, alabasters, marls, (which make up the greatest part of the earth's crust, as far as it has yet been penetrated,) have been formed originally by animal and vegetable bodies from the mass of water, and that by these means the solid part of the terraqueous globe has perpetually been in an increasing state, and the water perpetually in a decreasing one.

After the mountains of shells and other recrements of aquatic animals were elevated above the water the upper heaps of them were gradually dissolved by rains and dews, and oozing through were either perfectly crystallized in smaller cavities and formed calcareous spar, or were imperfectly crystallized on the roofs of larger cavities and produced stalactites or mixing with other undissolved shells beneath them formed marbles, which were more or less crystallized and more or less pure; or lastly, after being dissolved, the water was exhaled from them in such a manner that the external parts became solid, and forming an arch prevented the internal parts from approaching each other so near as to become solid, and thus chalk was produced. I have specimens of chalk formed at the root of several stalactites, and in their central parts: and of other stalactites which are hollow like quills from a similar cause, viz. from the external part of the stalactite hardening first by its evaporation, and thus either attracting the internal dissolved particles to the crust, or preventing them from approaching each other so as to form a solid body. Of these I saw many hanging from the arched roof of a cellar under the high street in Edinburgh.

If this dissolved lime-stone met with vitriolic acid it was converted into alabaster, parting at the same time with its fixable air. If it met with the fluor acid it became fluor; if with the siliceous acid, flint; and when mixed with clay and sand, or either of them, acquires the name of marl. And under one or other of these forms composes a great part of the solid globe of the earth.

Another mode in which lime-stone appears is in the form of round granulated particles, but slightly cohering together; of this kind a bed extends over Lincoln heath, perhaps twenty miles long by ten wide. The form of this calcareous sand, its angles having been rubbed off, and the flatness of its bed, evince that that part of the country was so formed under water, the particles of sand having thus been rounded, like all other rounded pebbles. This round form of calcareous sand and of other larger pebbles is produced under water, partly by their being more or less soluble in water, and hence the angular parts become dissolved, first, by their exposing a larger surface to the action of the menstruum, and secondly, from their attrition against each other by the streams or tides, for a great length of time, successively as they were collected, and perhaps when some of them had not acquired their hardest state.

This calcareous sand has generally been called ketton-stone and believed to resemble the spawn of fish, it has acquired a form so much rounder than siliceous sand from its being of so much softer a texture and also much more soluble in water. There are other soft calcareous stones called tupha which are deposited from water on mosses, as at Matlock, from which moss it is probable the water may receive something which induces it the readier to part with its earth.

In some lime-stones the living animals seem to have been buried as well as their shells during some great convulsion of nature, these shells contain a black coaly substance within them, in others some phlogiston or volatile alkali from the bodies of the dead animals remains mixed with the stone, which is then called liver-stone as it emits a sulphurous smell on being struck, and there is a stratum about six inches thick extends a considerable way over the iron ore at Wingerworth near Chesterfield in Derbyshire, which seems evidently to have been formed from the shells of fresh-water muscles.

There is however another source of calcareous earth besides the aquatic one above described, and that is from the recrements of land animals and vegetables as found in marls, which consist of various mixtures of calcareous earth, sand, and clay, all of them perhaps principally from vegetable origin.

Dr. Hutton is of opinion that the rocks of marble have been softened by fire into a fluid mass, which he thinks under immense pressure might be done without the escape of their carbonic acid or fixed air. Edinb. Transact. Vol. I. If this ingenious idea be allowed it might account for the purity of some white marbles, as during their fluid state there might be time for their partial impurities, whether from the bodies of the animals which produced the shells, or from other extraneous matter, either to sublime to the uppermost part of the stratum or to subside to the lowermost part of it. As a confirmation of this theory of Dr. Hutton's it may be added that some calcareous stones are found mixed with lime, and have thence lost a part of their fixed air or carbonic gas, as the bath-stone, and on that account hardens on being exposed to the air, and mixed with sulphur produces calcareous liver of sulphur. Falconer on Bath-water, Vol. I. p. 156, 257. Mr. Monnet found lime in powder in the mountains of Auvergne, and suspected it of volcanic origin. Kirwan s Min. p. 22.

NOTE XVII.—MORASSES.

*Gnomes! you then taught transuding dews to pass
Through time-fall'n woods, and root-inwove morass.*
CANTO II. l. 115.

WHERE woods have repeatedly grown and perished morasses are in process of time produced, and by their long roots fill up the interstices till the whole becomes for many yards deep a mass of vegetation. This fact is curiously verified by an account given many years ago by the Earl of Cromartie, of which the following is a short abstract.

In the year 1651 the Earl of Cromartie being then nineteen years of age saw a plain in the parish of Lockburn covered over with a firm standing wood, which was so old that not only the trees had no green leaves upon them but the bark was totally thrown off, which he was there informed by the old countrymen was the universal manner in which fir-woods terminated, and that in twenty or thirty years the trees would cast themselves up by the roots. About fifteen years after he had occasion to travel the same way and observed that there was not a tree nor the appearance of a root of any of them; but in their place the whole plain where the wood stood was covered with a flat green moss or morass, and on asking the country people what was become of the wood, he was informed that no one had been at the trouble to carry it away, but that it had all been overturned by the wind, that the trees lay thick over each other, and that the moss or bog had overgrown the whole timber, which they added was occasioned by the moisture which came down from the high hills above it and stagnated upon the plain, and that nobody could yet pass over it, which however his Lordship was so incautious as to attempt and slipt up to the arm-pits. Before the year 1699 that whole piece of ground was become a solid moss wherein the peasants then dug turf or peat, which however was not yet of the best sort. Philos. Trans. No. 330. Abridg. Vol. V. p. 272.

Morasses in great length of time undergo variety of changes, first by elutriation, and afterwards by fermentation, and the consequent heat. 1. By water perpetually oozing through them the most soluble parts are first washed away, as the essential salts, these together with the salts from animal recrements are carried down the rivers into the sea, where all of them seem to decompose each other except the marine salt. Hence the ashes of peat contain little or no vegetable alkali, and are not used in the countries, where peat constitutes the fuel of the lower people, for the purpose of washing linen. The second thing which is always seen oozing from morasses is iron in solution, which produces chalybeate springs, from whence depositions of ochre and variety of iron ores. The third elutriation seems to consist of vegetable acid, which by means unknown appears to be converted into all other acids. 1. Into marine and nitrous acids as mentioned above. 2. Into vitriolic acid which is found in some morasses so plentifully as to preserve the bodies of animals from putrefaction which have been buried in them, and this acid carried away by rain and dews, and meeting with calcareous earth produces gypsum or alabaster, with clay it produces alum, and deprived of its vital air produces sulphur. 3. Fluor acid which being washed away and meeting with calcareous earth produces fluor or cubic spar. 4. The siliceous acid which seems to have been disseminated in great quantity either by solution in water or by solution in air, and appears to have produced the sand in the sea uniting with calcareous earth previously dissolved in that element, from which were afterwards formed some of the grit-stone rocks by means of a siliceous or calcareous cement. By its union with the calcareous earth of the morass other strata of siliceous sand have been produced; and by the mixture of this with clay and lime arose the beds of marl.

In other circumstances, probably where less moisture has prevailed, morasses seem to have undergone a fermentation, as other vegetable matter, new hay for instance, is liable to do from the great quantity of sugar it contains. From the great heat thus produced in the lower parts of immense beds of morass the phlogistic part, or oil, or asphaltum, becomes distilled, and rising into higher strata becomes again condensed forming coal beds of greater or less purity according to their greater or less quantity of inflammable matter; at the same time the clay beds become purer or less so, as the phlogistic part is more or less completely exhaled from them. Though coal and clay are frequently produced in this manner, yet I have no doubt but that they are likewise often produced by elutriation; in situations on declivities the clay is washed away down into the valleys, and the phlogistic part or coal left behind; this circumstance is seen in many valleys near the beds of rivers, which are covered recently by a whitish impure clay, called water-clay. See note XIX. XX. and XXIII.

Lord Cromartie has furnished another curious observation on morasses in the paper above referred to. In a moss near the town of Elgin in Murray, though there is no river or water which communicates with the moss, yet for three or four feet of depth in the moss there are little shell-fish resembling oysters with living fish in them in great quantities, though no such fish are found in the adjacent rivers, nor even in the water pits in the moss, but only in the solid substance of the moss. This curious fact not only accounts for the shells sometimes found on the surface of coals, and in the clay above them, but also for a thin stratum of shells which sometimes exists over iron-ore.

NOTE XVIII.—IRON.

Cold waves, immerged, the glowing mass congeal,
And turn to adamant the hissing steel.
CANTO II. l. 191.

As iron is formed near the surface of the earth, it becomes exposed to streams of water and of air more than most other metallic bodies, and thence becomes combined with oxygene, or vital air, and appears very frequently in its calciform state, as in variety of ochres. Manganese, and zinc, and sometimes lead, are also found near the surface of the earth, and on that account become combined with vital air, and are exhibited in their calciform state.

The avidity with which iron unites with oxygene, or vital air, in which process much heat is given out from the combining materials, is shown by a curious experiment of M. Ingenhouz. A fine iron wire twisted spirally is fixed to a cork, on the point of the spire is fixed a match made of agaric dipped in solution of nitre; the match is then ignited, and the wire with the cork put immediately into a bottle full of vital air, the match first burns vividly, and the iron soon takes fire and consumes with brilliant sparks till it is reduced to small brittle globules, gaining an addition of about one third of its weight by its union with vital air. Annales de Chymie. Traité de Chymie, par Lavoisier, c. iii.

STEEL.

It is probably owing to a total deprivation of vital air which it holds with so great avidity, that iron on being kept many hours or days in ignited charcoal becomes converted into steel, and thence acquires the faculty of being welded when red hot long before it melts, and also the power of becoming hard when immersed in cold water; both which I suppose depend on the same cause, that is, on its being a worse conductor of heat than other metals; and hence the surface both acquires heat much sooner, and loses it much sooner, than the internal parts of it, in this circumstance resembling glass.

When steel is made very hot, and suddenly immerged in very cold water, and moved about in it, the surface of the steel becomes cooled first, and thus producing a kind of case or arch over the internal part, prevents that internal part from contracting quite so much as it otherwise would do, whence it becomes brittler and harder, like the glass-drops called Prince Rupert's drops, which are made by dropping melted glass into cold water. This idea is countenanced by the circumstance that hardened steel is specifically lighter than steel which is more gradually cooled. (Nicholson's Chemistry, p. 313.) Why the brittleness and hardness of steel or glass should keep pace or be companions to each other may be difficult to conceive.

When a steel spring is forcibly bent till it break, it requires less power to bend it through the first inch than the second, and less through the second than the third; the same I suppose to happen if a wire be distended till it break by hanging weights to it; this shows that the particles may be forced from each other to a small distance by less power, than is necessary to make them recede to a greater distance; in this circumstance perhaps the attraction of cohesion differs from that of gravitation, which exerts its power inversely as the squares of the distance. Hence it appears, that if the innermost particles of a steel bar, by cooling the external surface first, are kept from approaching each other so nearly as they otherwise would do, that they become in the situation of the particles on the convex side of a bent spring, and cannot be forced farther from each other except by a greater power than would have been necessary to have made them recede thus far. And secondly, that if they be forced a little farther from each other they separate; this may be exemplified by laying two magnetic needles parallel to each other, the contrary poles together, then drawing them longitudinally from each other, they will slide with small force till they begin to separate, and will then require a stronger force to really separate them. Hence it appears, that hardness and brittleness depend on the same circumstance, that the particles are removed to a greater distance from each other, and thus resist any power more forcibly which is applied to displace them farther, this constitutes hardness. And secondly, if they are displaced by such applied force they immediately separate, and this constitutes brittleness.

Steel may be thus rendered too brittle for many purposes, on which account artists have means of softening it again, by exposing it to certain degrees of heat, for the construction of different kinds of tools, which is called tempering it. Some artists plunge large tools in very cold water as soon as they are completely ignited, and moving them about, take them out as soon as they cease to be luminous beneath the water; they are then rubbed quickly with a file or on sand to clean the surface, the heat which the metal still retains soon begins to produce a succession of colours; if a hard temper be required, the piece is dipped again and stirred about in cold water as soon as the yellow tinge appears, if it be cooled when the purple tinge appears it becomes fit for gravers' tools used in working upon metals; if cooled while blue it is proper for springs. Nicholson's Chemistry, p. 313. Keir's Chemical Dictionary.

MODERN PRODUCTION OF IRON.

The recent production of iron is evinced from the chalybeate waters which flow from morasses which lie upon gravel-beds, and which must therefore have produced iron after those gravel-beds were raised out of the sea. On the south side of the road between Cheadle and Okeymoor in Staffordshire, yellow stains of iron are seen to penetrate the gravel from a thin morass on its surface. There is a fissure eight or ten feet wide, in a gravel-bed on the eastern side of the hollow road ascending the hill about a mile from Trentham in Staffordshire, leading toward Drayton in Shropshire, which fissure is filled up with nodules of iron ore. A bank of sods is now raised against this fissure to prevent the loose iron nodules from falling into the turnpike road, and thus this natural curiosity is at present concealed from travellers. A similar fissure in a bed of marl, and filled up with iron nodules and with some large pieces of flint, is seen on the eastern side of the hollow road ascending the hill from the turnpike house about a mile from Derby in the road towards Burton. And another such fissure filled with iron nodes, appears about half a mile from Newton-Solney in Derbyshire, in the road to Burton, near the summit of the hill. These collections of iron and of flint must have been produced posterior to the elevation of all those hills, and were thence evidently of vegetable or animal origin. To which should be added, that iron is found in general in beds either near the surface of the earth, or stratified with clay, coals, or argillaceous grit, which are themselves productions of the modern world, that is, from the recrements of vegetables and air-breathing animals.

Not only iron but manganese, calamy, and even copper and lead, appear in some instances to have been of recent production. Iron and manganese are detected in all vegetable productions, and it is probable other metallic bodies might be found to exist in vegetable or animal matters, if we had tests to detect them in very minute quantities. Manganese and calamy are found in beds like iron near the surface of the earth, and in a calciform state, which countenances their modern production. The recent production of calamy, one of the ores of zinc, appears from its frequently incrusting calcareous spar in its descent from the surface of the earth into the uppermost fissures of the limestone mountains of Derbyshire. That the calamy has been carried by its solution or diffusion in water into these cavities, and not by its ascent from below in form of steam, is evinced from its not only forming a crust over the dogtooth spar, but by its afterwards dissolving or destroying the sparry crystal. I have specimens of calamy in the form of dogtooth spar, two inches high, which are hollow, and stand half an inch above the diminished sparry crystal on which they were formed, like a sheath a great deal too big for it; this seems to show, that this process was carried on in water, otherwise after the calamy had incrusted its spar, and dissolved its surface, so as to form a hollow cavern over it, it could not act further upon it except by the interposition of some medium. As these spars and calamy are formed in the fissures of mountains they must both have been formed after the elevations of those mountains.

In respect to the recent production of copper, it was before observed in note on Canto II. l. 398, that the summit of the grit-stone mountain at Hawkstone in Shropshire, is tinged with copper, which from the appearance of the blue stains seems to have descended to the parts of the rock beneath. I have a calciform ore of copper consisting of the hollow crusts of cubic cells, which has evidently been formed on crystals of fluor, which it has eroded in the same manner as the calamy erodes the calcareous crystals, from whence may be deduced in the same manner, the aqueous solution or diffusion, as well as the recent production of this calciform ore of copper.

Lead in small quantities is sometimes found in the fissures of coal beds, which fissures are previously covered with spar; and sometimes in nodules of iron-ore. Of the former I have a specimen from near Caulk in Derbyshire, and of the latter from Colebrook Dale in Shropshire. Though all these facts show that some metallic bodies are formed from vegetable or animal recrements, as iron, and perhaps manganese and calamy, all which are found near the surface of the earth; yet as the other metals are found only in fissures of rocks, which penetrate to unknown depths, they may be wholly or in part produced by ascending steams from subterraneous fires, as mentioned in note on Canto II. l. 398.

SEPTARIA OF IRON-STONE.

Over some lime works at Walsall in Staffordshire, I observed some years ago a stratum of iron earth about six inches thick, full of very large cavities; these cavities were evidently produced when the material passed from a semifluid state into a solid one; as the frit of the potters, or a mixture of clay and water is liable to crack in drying; which is owing to the further contraction of the internal part, after the crust has become hard. These hollows are liable to receive extraneous matter, as I believe gypsum, and sometimes spar, and even lead; a curious specimen of the last was presented to me by Mr. Darby of Colebrook Dale, which contains in its cavity some ounces of lead-ore. But there are other septaria of iron-stone which seem to have had a very different origin, their cavities having been formed in cooling or congealing from an ignited state, as is ingeniously deduced by Dr. Hutton from their internal structure. Edinb. Transact. Vol. I. p. 246. The volcanic origin of these curious septaria appears to me to be further evinced from their form and the places where they are found. They consist of oblate spheroids, and are found in many parts of the earth totally detached from the beds in which they lie, as at East-Lothian in Scotland. Two of these, which now lie before me, were found with many others immersed in argillaceous shale or shiver, surrounded by broken lime-stone mountains at Bradbourn near Ashbourn, in Derbyshire, and were presented to me by Mr. Buxton, a gentleman of that town. One of these is about fifteen inches in its equatorial diameter, and about six inches in its polar one, and contains beautiful star-like septaria incrusted, and in part filled with calcareous spar. The other is about eight inches in its equatorial diameter, and about four inches in its polar diameter, and is quite solid, but shows on its internal surface marks of different colours, as if a beginning separation had taken place. Now as these septaria contain fifty per cent. of iron, according to Dr. Hutton, they would soften or melt into a semi-fluid globule by subterraneous fire by less heat than the lime-stone in their vicinity; and if they were ejected through a hole or fissure would gain a circular motion along with their progressive one by their greater friction or adhesion to one side of the hole. This whirling motion would produce the oblate spheroidical form which they possess, and which as far as I know can not in any other way be accounted for. They would then harden in the air as they rose into the colder parts of the atmosphere, and as they descended into so soft a material as shale or shiver, their forms would not be injured in their fall; and their presence in materials so different from themselves becomes accounted for.

About the tropics of the large septarium above mentioned, are circular eminent lines, such as might have been left if it had been coarsely turned in a lath. These lines seem to consist of fluid matter, which seems to have exsuded in circular zones, as their edges appear blunted or retracted; and the septarium seems to have split easier in such sections parallel to its equator. Now as the crust would first begin to harden and cool after its ejection in a semifluid state, and the equatorial diameter would become gradually enlarged as it rose in the air; the internal parts being softer would slide beneath the polar crust, which might crack and permit part of the semifluid to exsude, and it is probable the adhesion would thus become less in sections parallel to the equator. Which further confirms this idea of the production of these curious septaria. A new-cast cannon ball red-hot with its crust only solid, if it were shot into the air would probably burst in its passage; as it would consist of a more fluid material than these septaria; and thus by discharging a shower of liquid iron would produce more dreadful combustion, if used in war, than could be effected by a ball, which had been cooled and was heated again: since in the latter case the ball could not have its internal parts made hotter than the crust of it, without first losing its form.

NOTE XIX.—FLINT.

Transmute to glittering flints her chalky lands,
Or sink on ocean's bed in countless sands.
CANTO II. l. 217.

1. SILICEOUS ROCKS.

THE great masses of siliceous sands which lie in rocks upon the beds of lime-stone, or which are stratified with clay, coal, and iron-ore, are evidently produced in the decomposition of vegetable or animal matters, as explained in the note on morasses. Hence the impressions of vegetable roots, and even whole trees are often found in sand-stone, as well as in coals and iron-ore. In these sand-rocks both the siliceous acid and the calcareous base seem to be produced from the materials of the morass; for though the presence of a siliceous acid and of a calcareous base have not yet been separately exhibited from flints, yet from the analogy of flint to fluor, and gypsum, and marble, and from the conversion of the latter into flint, there can be little doubt of their existence.

These siliceous sand-rocks are either held together by a siliceous cement, or have a greater or less portion of clay in them, which in some acts as a cement to the siliceous crystals, but in others is in such great abundance that in burning them they become an imperfect porcelain, and are then used to repair the roads, as at Chesterfield in Derbyshire; these are called argillaceous grit by Mr. Kirwan. In other places a calcareous matter cements the crystals together; and in other places the siliceous crystals lie in loose strata under the marl in the form of white sand: as at Normington about a mile from Derby.

The lowest beds of siliceous sand-stone produced from morasses seem to obtain their acid from the morass, and their calcareous base from the lime-stone on which it rests. These beds possess a siliceous cement, and from their greater purity and hardness are used for coarse grinding-stones and scythe-stones, and are situated on the edges of lime-stone countries, having lost the other strata of coals, or clay, or iron, which were originally produced above them. Such are the sand-rocks incumbent on lime-stone near Matlock, in Derbyshire. As these siliceous sand-rocks contain no marine productions scattered amongst them, they appear to have been elevated, torn to pieces. and many fragments of them scattered over the adjacent country by explosions, from fires within the morass from which they have been formed; and which dissipated every thing inflammable above and beneath them, except some stains of iron, with which they are in some places spotted. If these sand rocks had been accumulated beneath the sea, and elevated along with the beds of limestone on which they rest, some vestiges of marine shells either in their siliceous or calcareous state must have been discerned amongst them.

2. SILICEOUS TREES.

In many of these sand rocks are found the impressions of vegetable roots, which seem to have been the most unchangeable parts of the plant, as shells and shark's teeth are found in chalk-beds from their being the most unchangeable parts of the animal. In other instances the wood itself is penetrated, and whole trees converted into flint; specimens of which I have by me, from near Coventry, and from a gravel-pit in Shropshire near Child's Archald into the road to Drayton. Other polished specimens of vegetable flints abound in the cabinets of the curious, which evidently show the concentric circles of woody fibres, and their interstices filled with whiter siliceous matter, with the branching off of the knots when cut horizontally, and the parallel lines of wood when cut longitudinally, with uncommon beauty and variety. Of these I possess some beautiful specimens, which were presented to me by the Earl of Uxbridge.

The colours of these siliceous vegetables are generally brown, from the iron, I suppose, or manganese, which induced them to crystallize or to fuse more easily. Some of the cracks of the wood in drying are filled with white flint or calcedony, and others of them remain hollow, lined with innumerable small crystals tinged with iron, which I suppose had a share in converting their calcareous matter into siliceous crystals, because the crystals called Peak-diamonds are always found bedded in an ochreous earth; and those called Bristol-stones are situated on limestone coloured with iron. Mr. F. French presented me with a congeries of siliceous crystals, which he gathered on the crater (as he supposes) of an extinguished volcano at Cromach Water in Cumberland. The crystals are about an inch high in the shape of dogtooth or calcareous spar, covered with a dark ferruginous matter. The bed on which they rest is about an inch in thickness, and is stained with iron on its under-surface. This curious fossil shows the transmutation of calcareous earth into siliceous, as much as the siliceous shells which abound in the cabinets of the curious. There may some time be discovered in this age of science, a method of thus impregnating wood with liquid flint, which would produce pillars for the support, and tiles for the covering of houses, which would be uninflammable and endure as long as the earth beneath them.

That some siliceous productions have been in a fluid state without much heat at the time of their formation appears from the vegetable flints above described not having quite lost their organized appearance; from shells, and coralloids, and entrochi being converted into flint without losing their form; from the bason of calcedony Giesar in Iceland; and from the experiment of Mr. Bergman, who obtained thirteen regular formed crystals by suffering the powder of quartz to remain in a vessel with fluor acid for two years; these crystals were about the size of small peas, and were not so hard as quartz. Opusc. de Terra Silicea, p. 33. Mr. Achard procured both calcareous and siliceous crystals, one from calcareous earth, and the other from the earth of alum, both dissolved in water impregnated with fixed air; the water filtrating very slowly through a porous bottom of baked clay. See Journal de Physique, for January, 1778.

3. AGATES, ONYXES, SCOTS-PEBBLES.

In small cavities of these sand-rocks, I am informed, the beautiful siliceous nodules are found which are called Scots-pebbles; and which on being cut in different directions take the names of agates, onyxes, sardonyxes, &c. according to the colours of the lines or strata which they exhibit. Some of the nodules are hollow and filled with crystals, others have a nucleus of less compact siliceous matter which is generally white, surrounded with many concentric strata coloured with iron, and other alternate strata of white agate or calcedony, sometimes to the number of thirty.

I think these nodules bear evident marks of their having been in perfect fusion by either heat alone, or by water and heat, under great pressure, according to the ingenious theory of Dr. Hutton; but I do not imagine, that they were injected into cavities from materials from without, but that some vegetables or parts of vegetables containing more iron or manganese than others, facilitated the complete fusion, thus destroying the vestiges of vegetable organization, which were conspicuous in the siliceous trees above mentioned. Some of these nodules being hollow and lined with crystals, and others containing a nucleus of white siliceous matter of a looser texture, show they were composed of the materials then existing in the cavity; which consisting before of loose sand, must take up less space when fused into a solid mass.

These siliceous nodules resemble the nodules of iron-stone mentioned in note on Canto II. l. 183, in respect to their possessing a great number of concentric spheres coloured generally with iron, but they differ in this circumstance, that the concentric spheres generally obey the form of the external crust, and in their not possessing a chalybeate nucleus. The stalactites formed on the roofs of caverns are often coloured in concentric strata, by their coats being spread over each other at different times; and some of them, as the cupreous ones, possess great beauty from this formation; but as these are necessarily more or less of a cylindrical or conic form, the nodules or globular flints above described cannot have been constructed in this manner. To what law of nature then is to be referred the production of such numerous concentric spheres? I suspect to the law of congelation.

When salt and water are exposed to severe frosty air, the salt is said to be precipitated as the water freezes; that is, as the heat in which it was dissolved, is withdrawn; where the experiment is tried in a bowl or bason, this may be true, as the surface freezes first, and the salt is found at the bottom. But in a fluid exposed in a thin phial, I found by experiment, that the extraneous matter previously dissolved by the heat in the mixture was not simply set at liberty to subside, but was detruded or pushed backward as the ice was produced. The experiment was this: about two ounces of a solution of blue vitriol were accidentally frozen in a thin phial, the glass was cracked and fallen to pieces, the ice was dissolved, and I found a pillar of blue vitriol standing erect on the bottom of the broken bottle. Nor is this power of congelation more extraordinary, than that by its powerful and sudden expansion it should burst iron shells and cohorns, or throw out the plugs with which the water was secured in them above one hundred and thirty yards, according to the experiments at Quebec by Major Williams. Edin. Transact. Vol. II. p. 23.

In some siliceous nodules which now lie before me, the external crust for about the tenth of an inch consists of white agate, in others it is much thinner, and in some much thicker; corresponding with this crust there are from twenty to thirty superincumbent strata, of alternately darker and lighter colour; whence it appears, that the external crust as it cooled or froze, propelled from it the iron or manganese which was dissolved in it; this receded till it had formed an arch or vault strong enough to resist its further protrusion; then the next inner sphere or stratum as it cooled or froze, propelled forwards its colouring matter in the same manner, till another arch or sphere produced sufficient resistance to this frigorescent expulsion. Some of them have detruded their colouring matter quite to the centre, the rings continuing to become darker as they are nearer it; in others the chalybeate arch seems to have stopped half an inch from the centre, and become thicker by having attracted to itself the irony matter from the white nucleus, owing probably to its cooling less precipitately in the central parts than at the surface of the pebble.

A similar detrusion of a marly matter in circular arches or vaults obtains in the salt mines in Cheshire; from whence Dr. Hutton very ingeniously concludes, that the salt must have been liquified by heat; which would seem to be much confirmed by the above theory. Edinb. Transact. Vol. I. p. 244.

I cannot conclude this account of Scots-pebbles without observing that some of them on being sawed longitudinally asunder, seem still to possess some vestiges of the cylindrical organization of vegetables; others possess a nucleus of white agate much resembling some bulbous roots with their concentric coats, or the knots in elm-roots or crab-trees; some of these I suppose were formed in the manner above explained, during the congelation of masses of melted flint and iron; others may have been formed from a vegetable nucleus, and retain some vestiges of the organization of the plant.

4. SAND OF THE SEA.

The great abundance of siliceous sand at the bottom of the ocean may in part be washed down from the siliceous rocks above described, but in general I suppose it derives its acid only from the vegetable and animal matter of morasses, which is carried down by floods, or by the atmosphere, and becomes united in the sea with its calcareous base from shells and coralloids, and thus assumes its crystalline form at the bottom of the ocean, and is there intermixed with gravel or other matters washed from the mountains in its vicinity.

5. CHERT, OR PETROSILEX.

The rocks of marble are often alternately intermixed with strata of chert, or coarse flint, and this in beds from one to three feet thick, as at Ilam and Matlock, or of less than the tenth of an inch in thickness, as a mile or two from Bakewell in the road to Buxton. It is difficult to conceive in what manner ten or twenty strata of either lime-stone or flint, of different shades of white and black, could be laid quite regularly over each other from sediments or precipitations from the sea; it appears to me much easier to comprehend, by supposing with Dr. Hutton, that both the solid rocks of marble and the flint had been fused by great heat, (or by heat and water,) under immense pressure; by its cooling or congealing the colouring matter might be detruded, and form parallel or curvilinear strata, as above explained.

The colouring matter both of lime-stone and flint was probably owing to the flesh of peculiar animals, as well as the siliceous acid, which converted some of the lime-stone into flint; or to some strata of shell-fish having been overwhelmed when alive with new materials, while others dying in their natural situations would lose their fleshy part, either by its putrid solution in the water or by its being eaten by other sea-insects. I have some calcareous fossil shells which contain a black coaly matter in them, which was evidently the body of the animal, and others of the same kind filled with spar instead of it. The Labradore stone has I suppose its colours from the nacre or mother-pearl shells, from which it was probably produced. And there is a stratum of calcareous matter about six or eight inches thick at Wingerworth in Derbyshire over the iron-beds, which is replete with shells of fresh-water muscles, and evidently obtains its dark colour from them, as mentioned in note XVI. Many nodules of flint resemble in colour as well as in form the shells of the echinus or sea-urchin; others resemble some coralloids both in form and colour; and M. Arduini found in the Monte de Pancrasio, red flint, branching like corals, from whence they seem to have obtained both their form and their colour. Ferber's Travels in Italy, p. 42.

6. NODULES OF FLINT IN CHALK-BEDS.

As the nodules of flint found in chalk-beds possess no marks of having been rounded by attrition or solution, I conclude that they have gained their form as well as their dark colour from the flesh of the shell-fish from which they had their origin; but which have been so completely fused by heat, or heat and water, as to obliterate all vestiges of the shell, in the same manner as the nodules of agate and onyx were produced from parts of vegetables, but which had been so completely fused as to obliterate all marks of their organization, or as many iron-nodules have obtained their form and origin from peculiar vegetables.

Some nodules in chalk-beds consist of shells of echini filled up with chalk, the animal having been dissolved away by putrescence in water, or eaten by other sea-insects; other shells of echini, in which I suppose the animal's body remained, are converted into flint but still retain the form of the shell. Others, I suppose as above, being more completely fused, have become flint coloured by the animal flesh, but without the exact form either of the flesh or shell of the animal. Many of these are hollow within and lined with crystals, like the Scots-pebbles above described; but as the colouring matter of animal bodies differs but little from each other compared with those of vegetables, these flints vary less in their colours than those above mentioned. At the same time as they cooled in concentric spheres like the Scots-pebbles, they often possess faint rings of colours, and always break in conchoide forms like them.

This idea of the productions of nodules of flint in chalk-beds is countenanced from the iron which generally appears as these flints become decomposed by the air; which by uniting with the iron in their composition reduces it from a vitrescent state to that of calx, and thus renders it visible. And secondly, by there being no appearance in chalk-beds, of a string or pipe of siliceous matter connecting one nodule with another, which must have happened if the siliceous matter, or its acid, had been injected from without according to the idea of Dr. Hutton. And thirdly, because many of them have very large cavities at their centres, which should not have happened had they been formed by the injection of a material from without.

When shells or chalk are thus converted from calcareous to siliceous matter by the flesh of the animal, the new flint being heavier than the shell or chalk occupies less space than the materials it was produced from; this is the cause of frequent cavities within them, where the whole mass has not been completely fused and pressed together. In Derbyshire there are masses of coralloid and other shells which have become siliceous, and are thus left with large vacuities sometimes within and sometimes on the outside of the remaining form of the shell, like the French millstones, and I suppose might serve the same purpose; the gravel of the Derwent is full of specimens of this kind.

Since writing the above I have received a very ingenious account of chalk-beds from Dr. Menish of Chelmsford. He distinguishes chalk-beds into three kinds; such as have been raised from the sea with little disturbance of their strata, as the cliffs of Dover and Margate, which he terms *intire* chalk. Another state of chalk is where it has suffered much derangement, as the banks of the Thames at Gravesend and Dartford. And a third state where fragments of chalk have been rounded by water, which he terms *alluvial* chalk. In the first of these situations of chalk he observes, that the flint lies in strata horizontally, and generally in distinct nodules, but that he has observed two instances of solid plates or strata of flint, from an inch to two inches in thickness, interposed, between the chalk beds; one of these is in a chalk-bank by the road side at Berkhamstead, the other in a bank on the road from Chatham leading to Canterbury. Dr. Menish has further observed that many of the echini are crushed in their form, and yet filled with flint, which has taken the form of the crushed shell, and that though many flint nodules are hollow, yet that in some echini the siliceum seems to have enlarged, as it passed from a fluid to a solid state, as it swells out in a protuberance at the mouth and anus of the shell, and that though these shells are so filled with flint yet that in many places the shell itself remains calcareous. These strata of nodules and plates of flint seem to countenance their origin from the flesh of a stratum of animals which perished by some natural violence, and were buried in their shells.

7. ANGLES OF SILICEOUS SAND.

In many rocks of siliceous sand the particles retain their angular form, and in some beds of loose sand, of which there is one of considerable purity a few yards beneath the marl at Normington about a mile south of Derby. Other siliceous sands have had their angles rounded off, like the pebbles in gravel-beds. These seem to owe their globular form to two causes; one to their attrition against each other, when they may for centuries have lain at the bottom of the sea, or of rivers; where they may have been progressively accumulated, and thus progressively at the same time rubbed upon each other by the dashing of the water, and where they would be more easily rolled over each other by their gravity being so much less than in air. This is evidently now going on in the river Derwent, for though there are no lime-stone rocks for ten or fifteen miles above Derby, yet a great part of the river gravel at Derby consists of lime-stone nodules, whose angles are quite worn off in their descent down the stream.

There is however another cause which must have contributed to round the angles both of calcareous and siliceous fragments; and that is, their solubility in water; calcareous earth is perpetually found suspended in the waters which pass over it; and the earth of flints was observed by Bergman to be contained in water in the proportion of one grain to a gallon. Kirwan's Mineralogy, p. 107. In boiling water, however, it is soluble in much greater proportion, as appears from the siliceous earth sublimed in the distillation of fluor acid in glass vessels; and from the basons of calcedony which surrounded the jets of hot water near mount Hecla in Iceland. Troil on Iceland. It is probable most siliceous sands or pebbles have at some ages of the world been long exposed to aqueous steams raised by subterranean fires. And if fragments of stone were long immersed in a fluid menstruum, their angular parts would be first dissolved, on account of their greater surface.

Many beds of siliceous gravel are cemented together by a siliceous cement, and are called breccia; as the plumb-pudding stones of Hartfordshire, and the walls of a subterraneous temple excavated by Mr. Curzon, at Hagley, near Rugely, in Staffordshire; these may have been exposed to great heat, as they were immersed in water; which water under great pressure of superincumbent materials may have been rendered red-hot, as in Papin's digester; and have thus possessed powers of solution with which we are unacquainted.

8. BASALTES AND GRANITES.

Another source of siliceous stones is from the granite, or basaltes, or porphyries, which are of different hardnesses according to the materials of their composition, or to the fire they have undergone; such are the stones of Arthur's hill, near Edinburgh, of the Giant's Causeway in Ireland, and of Charnwood Forest in Leicestershire; the uppermost stratum of which last seems to have been cracked, either by its elevation, or by its hastily cooling after ignition by the contact of dews or snows, and thus breaks into angular fragments, such as the streets of London are paved with; or have had their angles rounded by attrition or by partial solution; and have thus formed the common paving stones or bowlers; as well as the gravel, which is often rolled into strata amid the siliceous sand-beds, which are either formed or collected in the sea.

In what manner such a mass of crystallized matter as the Giant's Causeway and similar columns of basaltes, could have been raised without other volcanic appearances, may be a matter not easy to comprehend; but there is another power in nature besides that of expansile vapour which may have raised some materials which have previously been in igneous or aqueous solution; and that is the act of congelation. When the water in the experiments above related of Major Williams had by congelation thrown out the plugs from the bomb-shells, a column of ice rose from the hole of the bomb six or eight inches high. Other bodies I suspect increase in bulk which crystallize in cooling, as iron and type-metal. I remember pouring eight or ten pounds of melted brimstone into a pot to cool and was surprised to see after a little time a part of the fluid beneath break a hole in the congealed crust above it, and gradually rise into a promontory several inches high; the basaltes has many marks of fusion, and of crystallization, and may thence, as well as many other kinds of rock, as of spar, marble, petrosilex, jasper, &c. have been raised by the power of congelation, a power whose quantity has not yet been ascertained, and perhaps greater and more universal than that of vapours expanded by heat. These basaltic columns rise sometimes out of mountains of granite itself, as mentioned by Dr. Beddoes, (Phil. Transact. Vol. LXXX.) and as they seem to consist of similar materials more completely fused, there is still greater reason to believe them to have been elevated in the cooling or crystallization of the mass. See note XXIV.

NOTE XX.—CLAY.

Hence ductile clays in wide expansion spread,
Soft as the cygnet's down, their snow-white bed.
CANTO II. l. 277.

THE philosophers, who have attended to the formation of the earth, have acknowledged two great agents in producing the various changes which the terraqueous globe has undergone, and these are water and fire. Some of them have perhaps ascribed too much to one of these great agents of nature, and some to the other. They have generally agreed that the stratification of materials could only be produced from sediments or precipitations, which were previously mixed or dissolved in the sea; and that whatever effects were produced by fire were performed afterwards.

There is however great difficulty in accounting for the universal stratification of the solid globe of the earth in this manner, since many of the materials, which appear in strata, could not have been suspended in water; as the nodules of flint in chalk-beds, the extensive beds of shells, and lastly the strata of coal, clay, sand, and iron-ore, which in most coal countries lie from five to seven times alternately stratified over each other, and none of them are soluble in water. Add to this, if a solution of them or a mixture of them in water could be supposed, the cause of that solution must cease before a precipitation could commence.

1. The great masses of lava, under the various names of granite, porphyry, toadstone, moor-stone, rag, and slate, which constitute the old world, may have acquired the old stratification, which some of them appear to possess, by their having been formed by successive eruptions of a fluid mass, which at different periods of ancient time arose from volcanic shafts and covered each other, the surface of the interior mass of lava would cool and become solid before the superincumbent stratum was poured over it. to the same cause may be ascribed their different compositions and textures, which are scarcely the same in any two parts of the world.

2. The stratifications of the great masses of lime-stone, which were produced from sea-shells, seem to have been formed by the different times at which the innumerable shells were produced and deposited. A colony of echini, or madrepores, or cornua ammonis, lived and perished in one period of time; in another a new colony of either similar or different shells lived and died over the former ones, producing a stratum of more recent shells over a stratum of others which had begun to petrify or to become marble; and thus from unknown depths to what are now the summits of mountains the lime-stone is disposed in strata of varying solidity and colour. These have afterwards undergone variety of changes by their solution and deposition from the water in which they were immersed, or from having been exposed to great heat under great pressure, according to the ingenious theory of Dr. Hutton. Edinb. Transact. Vol. I. See note XVI.

3. In most of the coal-countries of this island there are from five to seven beds of coal stratified with an equal number of beds, though of much greater thickness, of clay and sand-stone, and occasionally of iron-ores. In what manner to account for the stratification of these materials seems to be a problem of great difficulty. Philosophers have generally supposed that they have been arranged by the currents of the sea; but considering their insolubility in water, and their almost similar specific gravity, an accumulation of them in such distinct beds from this cause is altogether inconceivable, though some coal-countries bear marks of having been at some time immersed beneath the waves and raised again by subterranean fires.

The higher and lower parts of morasses were necessarily produced at different periods of time, see Note XVII. and would thus originally be formed in strata of different ages. For when an old wood perished, and produced a morass, many centuries would elapse before another wood could grow and perish again upon the same ground, which would thus produce a new stratum of morass over the other, differing indeed principally in its age, and perhaps as the timber might be different, in the proportions of its component parts.

Now if we suppose the lowermost stratum of a morass become ignited, like fermenting hay, (after whatever could be carried away by solution in water was gone,) what would happen? Certainly the inflammable part, the oil, sulphur, or bitumen, would burn away, and be evaporated in air; and the fixed parts would be left, as clay, lime, and iron; while some of the calcareous earth would join with the siliceous acid, and produce sand, or with the argillaceous earth, and produce marl. Thence after many centuries another bed would take fire, but with less degree of ignition, and with a greater body of morass over it, what then would happen? The bitumen and sulphur would rise and might become condensed under an impervious stratum, which might not be ignited, and there form coal of different purities according to its degree of fluidity, which would permit some of the clay to subside through it into the place from which it was sublimed.

Some centuries afterwards another similar process might take place, and either thicken the coal-bed, or produce a new clay-bed, or marl, or sand, or deposit iron upon it, according to the concomitant circumstances above mentioned.

I do not mean to contend that a few masses of some materials may not have been rolled together by currents, when the mountains were much more elevated than at present, and in consequence the rivers broader and more rapid, and the storms of rain and wind greater both in quantity and force. Some gravel-beds may have been thus washed from the mountains; and some white clay washed from morasses into valleys beneath them; and some ochres of iron dissolved and again deposited by water; and some calcareous depositions from water, (as the bank for instance on which stand the houses at Matlock-bath;) but these are all of small extent or consequence compared to the primitive rocks of granite or porphyry which form the nucleus of the earth, or to the immense strata of limestone which crust over the greatest part of this granite or porphyry; or lastly to the very extensive beds of clay, marl, sand-stone, coal, and iron, which were probably for many millions of years the only parts of our continents and islands, which were then elevated above the level of the sea, and which on that account became covered with vegetation, and thence acquired their later or superincumbent strata, which constitute, what some have termed, the new world.

There is another source of clay, and that of the finest kind, from decomposed granite; this is of a snowy white, and mixed with shining particles of mica; of this kind is an earth from the country of the Cherokees. Other kinds are from less pure lavas; Mr. Ferber asserts that the sulphurous steams from Mount Vesuvius convert the lava into clay.

"The lavas of the ancient Solfatara volcano have been undoubtedly of a vitreous nature, and these appear at present argillaceous. Some fragments of this lava are but half or at one side changed into clay, which either is viscid or ductile, or hard and stony. Clays by fire are deprived of their coherent quality, which cannot be restored to them by pulverization, nor by humectation. But the sulphureous Solfatara steams restore it, as may be easily observed on the broken pots wherein they gather the sal ammoniac; though very well baked and burnt at Naples they are mollified again by the acid steams into a viscid clay which keeps the former fire-burnt colour." Travels in Italy, p. 156.

NOTE XXI.—ENAMELS.

Smear'd her huge dragons with metallic hues,
With golden purples, and cobaltic blues.
CANTO II. 1. 287.

THE fine bright purples or rose colours which we see on China cups are not producible with any other material except gold, manganese indeed gives a purple but of a very different kind.

In Europe the application of gold to these purposes appears to be of modern invention. Cassius's discovery of the precipitate of gold by tin, and the use of that precipitate for colouring glass and enamels, are now generally known, but though the precipitate with tin be more successful in producing the ruby glass, or the colourless glass which becomes red by subsequent ignition, the tin probably contributing to prevent the gold from separating, which it is very liable to do during the fusion; yet, for enamels, the precipitates made by alcaline salts answer equally well, and give a finer red, the colour produced by the tin precipitate being a bluish purple, but with the others a rose red. I am informed that some of our best artists prefer aurum fulminans, mixing it, before it has become dry, with the white composition or enamel flux: when once it is divided by the other matter, it is ground with great safety, and without the least danger of explosion, whether moist or dry. The colour is remarkably improved and brought forth by long grinding, which accordingly makes an essential circumstance in the process.

The precipitates of gold, and the colcothar or other red preparations of iron, are called *tender* colours. The heat must be no greater than is just sufficient to make the enamel run upon the piece, for if greater, the colours will be destroyed or changed to a different kind. When the vitreous matter has just become fluid it seems as if the coloured metallic calx remained barely *intermixed* with it, like a coloured powder of exquisite tenuity suspended in water: but by stronger fire the calx is *dissolved*, and metallic colours are altered by *solution* in glass as well as in acids or alkalies.

The Saxon mines have till very lately almost exclusively supplied the rest of Europe with cobalt, or rather with its preparations, zaffre and smalt, for the exportation of the ore itself is there a capital crime. Hungary, Spain, Sweden, and some other parts of the continent, are now said to afford cobalts equal to the Saxon, and specimens have been discovered in our own island, both in Cornwall and in Scotland; but hitherto in no great quantity.

Calces of cobalt and of copper differ very materially from those above mentioned in their application for colouring enamels. In those the calx has previously acquired the intended colour, a colour which bears a red heat without injury, and all that remains is to fix it on the piece by a vitreous flux. But the blue colour of cobalt, and the green or bluish green of copper, are *produced* by vitrification, that is, by *solution* in the glass, and a strong fire is necessary for their perfection. These calces, therefore, when mixed with the enamel flux, are melted in crucibles, once or oftener, and the deep coloured opake glass, thence resulting, is ground into impalpable powder, and used for enamel. One part of either of these calces is put to ten, sixteen, or twenty parts of the flux, according to the depth of colour required. The heat of the enamel kiln is only a full red, such as is marked on Mr. Wedgwood's thermometer six degrees. It is therefore necessary that the flux be so adjusted as to melt in that low heat. The usual materials are flint, or flint-glass, with a due proportion of red-lead, or borax; or both, and sometimes a little tin calx to give opacity.

Ka-o-lin is the name given by the Chinese to their porcelain clay, and *pe-tun-tse* to the other ingredient in their China ware. Specimens of both these have been brought into England, and found to agree in quality with some of our own materials. Kaolin is the very same as a clay found in Cornwall, and the petuntse is a granite similar to the Cornish moorstone. There are differences, both in the Chinese petuntses, and the English moorstones; all of them contain micaceous and quartzy particles, in greater or less quantity, along with feltspar, which last is the essential ingredient for the porcelain manufactory. The only injurious material commonly found in them is iron, which discolours the ware in proportion to its quantity, and which our moorstones are perhaps more frequently tainted with than the Chinese. Very fine porcelain has been made from English materials, but the nature of the manufacture renders the process precarious and the profit hazardous; for the semivitrification, which constitutes porcelain, is necessarily accompanied with a degree of softness or semifusion, so that the vessels are liable to have their forms altered in the kiln, or to run together with any accidental augmentations of the fire.

NOTE XXII.—PORTLAND VASE.

Or bid mortality rejoice and mourn
O'er the fine forms of Portland's mystic urn.
CANTO II. l. 319.

THE celebrated funeral vase, long in possession of the Barberini family, and lately purchased by the Duke of Portland for a thousand guineas, is about ten inches high and six in diameter in the broadest part. The figures are of most exquisite workmanship in bas relief of white opake glass, raised on a ground of deep blue glass, which appears black except when held against the light. Mr. Wedgwood is of opinion from many circumstances that the figures have been made by cutting away the external crust of white opake glass, in the manner the finest cameos have been produced, and that it must thence have been the labour of a great many years. Some antiquarians have placed the time of its production many centuries before the Christian æra; as sculpture was said to have been declining in respect to its excellence in the time of Alexander the Great. See an account of the Barberini or Portland vase by M. D'Hancarville, and by Mr. Wedgwood.

Many opinions and conjectures have been published concerning the figures on this celebrated vase. Having carefully examined one of Mr Wedgwood's beautiful copies of this wonderful production of art, I shall add one more conjecture to the number.

Mr. Wedgwood has well observed that it does not seem probable that the Portland vase was purposely made for the ashes of any particular person deceased, because many years must have been necessary for its production. Hence it may be concluded, that the subject of its embellishments is not private history but of a general nature. This subject appears to me to be well chosen, and the story to be finely told; and that it represents what in ancient times engaged the attention of philosophers, poets, and heroes, I mean a part of the Eleusinian mysteries.

These mysteries were invented in Egypt, and afterwards transferred to Greece, and flourished more particularly at Athens, which was at the same time the seat of the fine arts. They consisted of scenical exhibitions representing and inculcating the expectation of a future life after death, and on this account were encouraged by the government, insomuch that the Athenian laws punished a discovery of their secrets with death. Dr. Warburton has with great learning and ingenuity shown that the descent of Æneas into Hell, described in the Sixth Book of Virgil, is a poetical account of the representations of the future state in the Eleusian mysteries. Divine Legation, Vol. I. p. 210.

And though some writers have differed in opinion from Dr. Warburton on this subject, because Virgil has introduced some of his own heroes into the Elysian fields, as Diephobus, Palinurus, and Dido, in the same manner as Homer had done before him, yet it is agreed that the received notions about a future state were exhibited in these mysteries, and as these poets described those received notions, they may be said, as far as these religious doctrines were concerned, to have described the mysteries.

Now as these were emblematic exhibitions they must have been as well adapted to the purposes of sculpture as of poetry, which indeed does not seem to have been uncommon, since one compartment of figures in the shield of Æneas represented the regions of Tartarus. Æn. Lib. X. The procession of torches, which according to M. De St. Croix was exhibited in these mysteries, is still to be seen in basso relievo, discovered by Spon and Wheeler. Memoires sur les Mysteres par De St. Croix, 1784. And it is very probable that the beautiful gem representing the marriage of Cupid and Psyche, as described by Apuleius, was originally descriptive of another part of the exhibitions in these mysteries, though afterwards it became a common subject of ancient art. See Divine Legat. Vol. I. p. 323. What subject could have been imagined so sublime for the ornaments of a funeral urn as the mortality of all things and their resuscitation? Where could the designer be supplied with emblems for this purpose, before the Christian æra, but from the Eleusinian mysteries?

1. The exhibitions of the mysteries were of two kinds, those which the people were permitted to see, and those which were only shown to the initiated. Concerning the latter, Aristides calls them " the most shocking and most ravishing representations." And Stobæus asserts that the initiation into the grand mysteries exactly resembles death. Divine Legat. Vol. I. p. 280, and p. 272. And Virgil in his entrance to the shades below, amongst other things of terrible form, mentions death. Æn. VI. This part of the exhibition seems to be represented in one of the compartments of the Portland vase.

Three figures of exquisite workmanship are placed by the side of a ruined column whose capital is fallen off, and lies at their feet with other disjointed stones, they sit on loose piles of stone beneath a tree, which has not the leaves of any evergreen of this climate, but may be supposed to be an elm, which Virgil places near the entrance of the infernal regions, and adds, that a dream was believed to dwell under every leaf of it. Æn. VI. l. 281. In the midst of this group reclines a female figure in a dying attitude, in which extreme languor is beautifully represented, in her hand is an inverted torch, an ancient emblem of extinguished life, the elbow of the same arm resting on a stone supports her as she sinks, while the other hand is raised and thrown over her drooping head, in some measure sustaining it, and gives with great art the idea of fainting lassitude. On the right of her sits a man, and on the left a woman, both supporting themselves on their arms, as people are liable to do when they are thinking intensely. They have their backs towards the dying figure, yet with their faces turned towards her, as if seriously contemplating her situation, but without stretching out their hands to assist her.

This central figure then appears to me to be an hieroglyphic or Eleusinian emblem of *mortal life*, that is, the lethum, or death, mentioned by Virgil amongst the terrible things exhibited at the beginning of the mysteries. The inverted torch shows the figure to be emblematic, if it had been designed to represent a real person in the act of dying there had been no necessity for the expiring torch, as the dying figure alone would have been sufficiently intelligible;—it would have been as absurd as to have put an inverted torch into the hand of a real person at the time of his expiring. Besides if this figure had represented a real dying person would not the other figures, or one of them at least, have stretched out a hand to support her, to have eased her fall among loose stones, or to have smoothed her pillow? These circumstances evince that the figure is an emblem, and therefore could not be a representation of the private history of any particular family or event.

The man and woman on each side of the dying figure must be considered as emblems, both from their similarity of situation and dress to the middle figure, and their being grouped along with it. These I think are hieroglyphic or Eleusinian emblems of *humankind*, with the backs towards the dying figure of *mortal life*, unwilling to associate with her, yet turning back their serious and attentive countenances, curious indeed to behold, yet sorry to contemplate their latter end. These figures bring strongly to one's mind the Adam and Eve of sacred writ, whom some have supposed to have been allegorical or hieroglyphic persons of Egyptian origin, but of more ancient date, amongst whom I think is Dr. Warburton. According to this opinion Adam and Eve were the names of two hieroglyphic figures representing the early state of mankind; Abel was the name of an hieroglyphic figure representing the age of pasturage, and Cain the name of another hieroglyphic symbol representing the age of agriculture, at which time the uses of iron were discovered. And as people who cultivated the earth and built houses would increase in numbers much faster by their greater production of food they would readily conquer or destroy the people who were sustained by pasturage, which was typified by Cain slaying Abel.

2. On the other compartment of this celebrated vase is exhibited an emblem of immortality, the representation of which was well known to constitute a very principal part of the shows at the Eleusinian mysteries, as Dr. Warburton has proved by variety of authority. The habitation of spirits or ghosts after death was supposed by the ancients to be placed beneath the earth, where Pluto reigned, and dispensed rewards or punishments. Hence the first figure in this group is of the *manes* or *ghost*, who having passed through an open portal is descending into a dusky region, pointing his toe with timid and unsteady step, feeling as it were his way in the gloom. This portal Æneas enters, which is described by Virgil,—*patet atri janua Ditis*, Æn. VI. l. 126; as well as the easy descent,—*facilis descensus Averni*. Ib. The darkness at the entrance to the shades is humorously described by Lucian. Div. Legat. Vol. I. p. 241. And the horror of the gates of hell was in the time of Homer become a proverb; Achilles says to Ulysses, " I hate a liar worse than the gates of hell;" the same expression is used in Isaiah, ch. xxxviii. v. 10. The *manes* or *ghost* appears lingering and fearful, and wishes to drag after him a part of his mortal garment, which however adheres to the side of the portal through which he has passed. The beauty of this allegory would have been expressed by Mr. Pope, by " We feel the ruling passion strong in death."

A little lower down in the group the manes or ghost is received by a beautiful female, a symbol of *immortal life*. This is evinced by her fondling between her knees a large and playful serpent, which from its annually renewing its external skin has from great antiquity, even as early as the fable of Prometheus, been esteemed an emblem of renovated youth. The story of the serpent acquiring immortal life from the ass of Prometheus, who carried it on his back, is told in Bacon's Works, Vol. V. p. 462. Quarto edit. Lond. 1778. For a similar purpose a serpent was wrapped round the large hieroglyphic egg in the temple of Dioscuri, as an emblem of the renewal of life from a state of death. Bryant's Mythology, Vol. II. p. 359, sec. edit. On this account also the serpent was an attendant on Æsculapius, which seems to have been the name of the hieroglyphic figure of medicine. This serpent shows this figure to be an emblem, as the torch showed the central figure of the other compartment to be an emblem, hence they agreeably correspond, and explain each other, one representing *mortal life*, and the other *immortal life*.

This emblematic figure of immortal life sits down with her feet towards the figure of Pluto, but, turning back her face towards the timid ghost, she stretches forth her hand, and taking hold of his elbow, supports his tottering steps, as well as encourages him to advance, both which circumstances are thus with wonderful ingenuity brought to the eye. At the same time the spirit loosely lays his hand upon her arm, as one walking in the dark would naturally do for the greater certainty of following his conductress, while the general part of the symbol of *immortal life*, being turned toward the figure of Pluto, shows that she is leading the phantom to his realms.

In the Pamphili gardens at Rome, Perseus in assisting Andromeda to descend from the rock takes hold of her elbow to steady or support her step, and she lays her hand loosely on his arm as in this figure. Admir. Roman. Antiq.

The figure of Pluto cannot be mistaken, as is agreed by most of the writers who have mentioned this vase; his grisly beard, and his having one foot buried in the earth, denotes the infernal monarch. He is placed at the lowest part of the group, and resting his chin on his hand, and his arm upon his knee, receives the stranger-spirit with inquisitive attention; it was before observed that when people think attentively they naturally rest their bodies in some easy attitude, that more animal power may be employed on the thinking faculty. In this group of figures there is great art shown in giving an idea of a descending plain, *viz.* from earth to Elysium, and yet all the figures are in reality on a horizontal one. This wonderful deception is produced first by the descending step of the manes or ghost; secondly, by the arm of the sitting figure of immortal life being raised up to receive him as he descends; and lastly, by Pluto having one foot sunk into the earth.

There is yet another figure which is concerned in conducting the manes or ghost to the realms of Pluto, and this is *love*. He precedes the descending spirit on expanded wings, lights him with his torch, and turning back his beautiful countenance beckons him to advance. The ancient god of love was of much higher dignity than the modern Cupid. He was the first that came out of the great egg of night, (Hesiod Theog. V. CXX. Bryant's Mythol. Vol. II. p. 348.) and is said to possess the keys of the sky, sea, and earth. As he therefore led the way into this life, he seems to constitute a proper emblem for leading the way to a future life. See Bacon's Works, Vol. I. p. 568. and Vol. III. p. 582. Quarto edit.

The introduction of love into this part of the mysteries requires a little further explanation. The Psyche of the Egyptians was one of their most favourite emblems, and represented the soul, or a future life; it was originally no other than the aurelia, or butterfly, but in after times was represented by a lovely female child with the beautiful wings of that insect. The aurelia, after its first stage as an eruca or caterpillar, lies for a season in a manner dead, and is enclosed in a sort of coffin; in this state of darkness it remains all the winter, but at the return of spring it bursts its bonds and comes out with new life, and in the most beautiful attire. The Egyptians thought this a very proper picture of the soul of man, and of the immortality to which it aspired. But as this was all owing to divine love, of which Eros was an emblem, we find this person frequently introduced as a concomitant of the soul in general or Psyche. (Bryant's Mythol. Vol. II. p. 366.) Eros, or divine love, is for the same reason a proper attendant on the manes or soul after death, and much contributes to tell the story, that is, to show that a soul or manes is designed by the descending figure. From this figure of love M. D'Hancarville imagines that Orpheus and Eurydice are typified under the figure of the manes and immortal life as above described. It may be sufficient to answer, first, that Orpheus is always represented with a lyre, of which there are prints of four different gems in Spence's Polymetis, and Virgil so describes him, Æn. VI. *cythara fretus* And secondly, that it is absurd to suppose that Eurydice was fondling and playing with a serpent that had slain her. Add to this that love seems to have been an inhabitant of the infernal regions, as exhibited in the mysteries, for Claudian, who treats more openly of the Eleusinian mysteries, when they were held in less veneration, invokes the deities to disclose to him their secrets, and amongst other things by what torch Love softens Pluto.

Dii, quibus in numerum, &c.
Vos mihi sacrarum penetralia pandite rerum,
Et vestri secreta poli, qua lampade Ditem
Flexit Amor.

In this compartment there are two trees, whose branches spread over the figures, one of them has smoother leaves like some evergreens, and might thence be supposed to have some allusion to immortality, but they may perhaps have been designed only as ornaments, or to relieve the figures, or because it was in groves, where these mysteries were originally celebrated. Thus Homer speaks of the woods of Proserpine, and mentions many trees in Tartarus, as presenting their fruits to Tantalus; Virgil speaks of the pleasant groves of Elysium; and in Spence's Polymetis there are prints of two ancient gems, one of Orpheus charming Cerberus with his lyre, and the other of Hercules binding him in a cord, each of them standing by a tree. Polymet. p. 284. As however these trees have all different foliage so clearly marked by the artist, they may have had specific meanings in the exhibitions of the mysteries, which have not reached posterity; of this kind seem to have been the tree of knowledge of good and evil, and the tree of life, in sacred writ, both which must have been emblematic or allegorical. The masks, hanging to the handles of the vase, seem to indicate that there is a concealed meaning in the figures besides their general appearance. And the priestess at the bottom, which I come now to describe, seems to show this concealed meaning to be of the sacred or Eleusinian kind.

3. The figure on the bottom of the vase is on a larger scale than the others, and less finely finished, and less elevated; and as this bottom part was afterwards cemented to the upper part, it might be executed by another artist for the sake of expedition, but there seems no reason to suppose that it was not originally designed for the upper part of it as some have conjectured. As the mysteries of Ceres were celebrated by female priests, for Porphyrius says the ancients called the priestesses of Ceres, Melissai, or bees, which were emblems of chastity, Div. Leg. Vol. I. p. 235; and, as in his Satire against the sex, Juvenal says, that few women are worthy to be priestesses of Ceres, Sat. VI. the figure at the bottom of the vase would seem to represent a priestess or hierophant, whose office it was to introduce the initiated, and point out to them and explain the exhibitions in the mysteries, and to exclude the uninitiated, calling out to them, "Far, far retire, ye profane!" and to guard the secrets of the temple. Thus the introductory hymn sung by the hierophant, according to Eusebius, begins, "I will declare a secret to the initiated, but let the doors be shut against the profane." Div. Leg. Vol. I. p. 177. The priestess or hierophant appears in this figure with a close hood, and dressed in linen, which sits close about her; except a light cloak, which flutters in the wind. Wool, as taken from slaughtered animals, was esteemed profane by the priests of Egypt, who were always dressed in linen. Apuleius, p. 64. Div. Leg. Vol. I. p. 318. Thus Eli made for Samuel a linen ephod. Sam. i. 3.

Secrecy was the foundation on which all mysteries rested; when publicly known they ceased to be mysteries; hence a discovery of them was not only punished with death by the Athenian law, but in other countries a disgrace attended the breach of a solemn oath. The priestess in the figure before us has her finger pointing to her lips as an emblem of silence. There is a figure of Harpocrates, who was of Egyptian origin, the same as Orus, with the lotus on his head, and with his finger pointing to his lips not pressed upon them, in Bryant's Mythol. Vol. II. p. 398, and another female figure standing on a lotus, as if just risen from the Nile, with her finger in the same attitude; these seem to have been representations or emblems of male and female priests of the secret mysteries. As these sorts of emblems were frequently changed by artists for their more elegant exhibition, it is possible the foliage over the head of this figure may bear some analogy to the lotus above mentioned.

This figure of secrecy seems to be here placed, with great ingenuity, as a caution to the initiated, who might understand the meaning of the emblems round the vase, not to divulge it. And this circumstance seems to account for there being no written explanation extant, and no tradition concerning these beautiful figures handed down to us along with them.

Another explanation of this figure at the bottom of the vase would seem to confirm the idea that the basso-relievos round its sides are representations of a part of the mysteries, I mean that it is the head of Atis. Lucian says that Atis was a young man of Phrygia, of uncommon beauty, that he dedicated a temple in Syria to Rhea, or Cybele, and first taught her mysteries to the Lydians, Phrygians, and Samothracians, which mysteries he brought from India. He was afterwards made an eunuch by Rhea, and lived like a woman, and assumed a feminine habit, and in that garb went over the world teaching her ceremonies and mysteries. Dict. par M. Danet, art. Atis. As this figure is covered with clothes, while those on the sides of the vase are naked, and has a Phrygian cap on the head, and as the form and features are so soft, that it is difficult to say whether it be a male or female figure, there is reason to conclude, 1. that it has reference to some particular person of some particular country; 2. that this person is Atis, the first great hierophant, or teacher of mysteries, to whom M. De la Chausse says the figure itself bears a resemblance. Museo. Capitol. Tom. IV. p. 402.

In the Museum Etruscum, Vol. I. plate 96, there is the head of Atis with feminine features, clothed with a Phrygian cap, and rising from very broad foliage, placed on a kind of term supported by the paw of a lion. Goreus in his explanation of the figure says that it is placed on a lion's foot because that animal was sacred to Cybele, and that it rises from very broad leaves, because after he became an eunuch he determined to dwell in the groves. Thus the foliage, as well as the cap and feminine features, confirm the idea of this figure at the bottom of the vase representing the head of Atis the first great hierophant, and that the figures on the sides of the vase are emblems from the ancient mysteries.

I beg leave to add that it does not appear to have been uncommon amongst the ancients to put allegorical figures on funeral vases. In the Pamphili palace at Rome there is an elaborate representation of life and death, on an ancient sarcophagus. In the first Prometheus is represented making man, and Minerva is placing a butterfly, or the soul, upon his head. In the other compartment Love extinguishes his torch in the bosom of the dying figure, and is receiving the butterfly, or Psyche, from him, with a great number of complicated emblematic figures grouped in very bad taste. Admir. Roman. Antiq.

NOTE XXIII.—COAL.

Hence sable coal his massy couch extends,
And stars of gold the sparkling pyrite blends.
                              CANTO II. l. 349.

To elucidate the formation of coal-beds I shall here describe a fountain of fossil tar, or petroleum, discovered lately near Colebrook Dale in Shropshire, the particulars of which were sent me by Dr. Robert Darwin, of Shrewsbury.

About a mile and a half below the celebrated iron bridge, constructed by the late Mr. Darby, near Colebrook Dale, on the east of the river Severn, as the workmen in October 1786 were making a subterranean canal into the mountain for the more easy acquisition and conveyance of the coals which lie under it, they found an oozing of liquid bitumen, or petroleum; and as they proceeded further cut through small cavities of different sizes from which the bitumen issued. From ten to fifteen barrels of this fossil tar, each barrel containing thirty-two gallons, were at first collected in a day, which has since however gradually diminished in quantity, so that at present the product is about seven barrels in fourteen days.

The mountain, into which this canal enters, consists of silicious sand, in which however a few marine productions, apparently in their recent state, have been found, and are now in the possession of Mr. William Reynolds, of Ketly Bank. About three hundred yards from the entrance into the mountain and about twenty-eight yards below the surface of it, the tar is found oozing from the sand-rock above into the top and sides of the canal.

Beneath the level of this canal a shaft has been sunk through a gray argillaceous substance, called in this country clunch, which is said to be a pretty certain indication of coal; beneath this lies a stratum of coal about two or three inches thick, of an inferior kind, yielding little flame in burning, and leaving much ashes; below this is a rock of a harder texture, and beneath this are found coals of an excellent quality; for the purpose of procuring which with greater facility the canal, or horizontal aperture, is now making into the mountain. July, 1788.

Beneath these coals in some places is found salt water, in other parts of the adjacent country there are beds of iron-stone, which also contain some bitumen in a less fluid state, and which are about on a level with the new canal, into which the fossil tar oozes, as above described.

There are many interesting circumstances attending the situation and accompaniments of this fountain of fossil tar, tending to develop the manner of its production. 1. As the canal passing into the mountain runs over the beds of coals, and under the reservoir of petroleum, it appears that a *natural distillation* of this fossil in the bowels of the earth must have taken place at some early period of the world, similar to the artificial distillation of coal, which has many years been carried on in this place on a smaller scale above ground. When this reservoir of petroleum was cut into, the slowness of its exsudation into the canal was not only owing to its viscidity, but to the pressure of the atmosphere, or to the necessity there was that air should at the same time insinuate itself into the small cavities from which the petroleum descended. The existence of such a distillation at some ancient time is confirmed by the thin stratum of coal beneath the canal (which covers the hard rock) having been deprived of its fossil oil, so as to burn without flame, and thus to have become a natural coak, or fossil charcoal, while the petroleum distilled from it is found in the cavities of the rock above it.

There are appearances in other places, which favour this idea of the natural distillation of petroleum; thus at Matlock, in Derbyshire, a hard bitumen is found adhering to the spar in the clefts of the lime-rocks in the form of round drops about the size of peas; which could perhaps only be deposited there in that form by sublimation.

2. The second deduction, which offers itself, is, that these beds of coal have been *exposed to a considerable degree of heat*, since the petroleum above could not be separated, as far as we know, by any other means, and that the good quality of the coals beneath the hard rock was owing to the impermeability of this rock to the bituminous vapour, and to its pressure being too great to permit its being removed by the elasticity of that vapour. Thus from the degree of heat, the degree of pressure, and the permeability of the superincumbent strata, many of the phenomena attending coal beds receive an easy explanation, which much accords with the ingenious theory of the earth by Dr. Hutton, Trans. of Edinb. Vol. I.

In some coal works the fusion of the strata of coal has been so light, that there remains the appearance of ligneous fibres, and the impression of leaves, as at Bovey near Exeter, and even seeds of vegetables, of which I have had specimens from the collieries near Polesworth in Warwickshire. In some, where the heat was not very intense and the incumbent stratum not permeable to vapour, the fossil oil has only risen to the upper part of the coal-bed, and has rendered that much more inflammable than the lower parts of it, as in the collieries near Beaudesert, the seat of the Earl of Uxbridge in Staffordshire, where the upper stratum is a perfect cannel, or candle-coal, and the lower one of an inferior quality. Over the coal-beds near Sir H. Harpur's house in Derbyshire a thin lamina of asphaltum is found in some places near the surface of the earth, which would seem to be from a distillation of petroleum from the coals below, the more fluid part of which had in process of time exhaled, or been consolidated by its absorption of air. In other coal works the upper part of the stratum is of a worse kind than the lower one, as at Alfreton and Denbigh, in Derbyshire, owing to the superincumbent stratum having permitted the exhalation of a great part of the petroleum; whilst at Widdrington in Northumberland there is first a seam of coal about six inches thick of no value, which lies under about four fathom of clay, beneath this is a white free-stone, then a hard stone, which the workmen there call a whin, then two fathom of clay, then another white stone, and under that a vein of coal three feet nine inches thick, of a similar nature to the Newcastle coal. Phil. Trans. Abridg. Vol. VI. plate II. p. 192. The similitude between the circumstances of this colliery, and of the coal beneath the fountain of tar above described, renders it highly probable that this upper thin seam of coal has suffered a similar distillation, and that the inflammable part of it had either been received into the clay above in the form of sulphur, which when burnt in the open air would produce alum; or had been dissipated for want of a receiver, where it could be condensed. The former opinion is perhaps in this case more probable, as in some other coal beds, of which I have procured accounts, the surface of the coal beneath clunch or clay is of an inferior quality, as at West Hallum in Nottinghamshire. The clunch probably from hence acquires its inflammable part, which on calcination becomes vitriolic acid. I gathered pieces of clunch converted partially into alum at a colliery near Bilston, where the ground was still on fire a few years ago.

The heat, which has thus pervaded the beds of morass, seems to have been the effect of the fermentation of their vegetable materials; as new hay sometimes takes fire even in such very small masses from the sugar it contains, and seems hence not to have been attended with any expulsion of lava, like the deeper craters of volcanoes situated in the beds of granite.

3. The marine shells found in the loose sand-rock above this reservoir of petroleum, and the coal beds beneath it, together with the existence of sea-salt beneath these coals, prove that these coal beds have been *at the bottom of the sea*, during some remote period of time, and were afterwards raised into their present situation by subterraneous expansions of vapour. This doctrine is further supported by the marks of violence, which some coal beds received at the time they were raised out of the sea, as in the collieries at Mendip in Somersetshire. In these there are seven strata of coals, equitant upon each other, with beds of clay and stone intervening; amongst which clay are found shells and fern branches. In one part of this hill the strata are disjoined, and a quantity of heterogeneous substances fill up the chasm which disjoins them, on one side of this chasm the seven strata of coal are seen corresponding in respect to their reciprocal thickness and goodness with the seven strata on the other side of the cavity, except that they have been elevated several yards higher. Phil. Trans. No. 360. abridg. Vol. V. p. 237.

The cracks in the coal bed near Ticknall in Derbyshire, and in the sand-stone rock over it, in both of which specimens of lead-ore and spar are found, confirm this opinion of their having been forcibly raised up by subterraneous fires. Over the colliery at Brown-hills near Litchfield, there is a stratum of gravel on the surface of the ground; which may be adduced as another proof to show that those coals had some time been beneath the sea, or the bed of a river. Nevertheless, these arguments only apply to the collieries above mentioned, which are few compared with those which bear no marks of having been immersed in the sea.

On the other hand the production of coals from morasses, as described in note XX. is evinced from the vegetable matters frequently found in them, and in the strata over them; as fern-leaves in nodules of iron ore, and from the bog-shells or fresh water muscles sometimes found over them, of both which I have what I believe to be specimens; and is further proved from some parts of these beds being only in part transformed to coal; and the other part still retaining not only the form, but some of the properties of wood; specimens of which are not unfrequent in the cabinets of the curious, procured from Loch Neagh in Ireland, from Bovey near Exeter, and other places; and from a famous cavern called the Temple of the Devil, near the town of Altorf in Franconia, at the foot of a mountain covered with pine and savine, in which are found large coals resembling trees of ebony; which are so far mineralized as to be heavy and compact; and so to effloresce with pyrites in some parts as to crumble to pieces; yet from other parts white ashes are produced on calcination from which *fixed alkali* is procured; which evinces their vegetable origin. (Dict. Raisonné, art. Charbon.) To these may be added another argument from the oil which is distilled from coals, and which is analogous to vegetable oil, and does not exist in any bodies truly mineral. Keir's Chemical Dictionary, art. Bitumen.

Whence it would appear, that though most collieries with their attendant strata of clay, sand-stone, and iron, were formed on the places where the vegetables grew, from which they had their origin; yet that other collections of vegetable matter were washed down from eminences by currents of water into the beds of rivers, or the neighbouring seas, and were there accumulated at different periods of time, and underwent a great degree of heat from their fermentation, in the same manner as those beds of morass which had continued on the plains where they were produced. And that by this fermentation many of them had been raised from the ocean with sand and sea-shells over them; and others from the beds of rivers with accumulations of gravel upon them.

4. For the purpose of bringing this history of the products of morasses more distinctly to the eye of the reader, I shall here subjoin two or three accounts of sinking or boring for coals, out of above twenty which I have procured from various places, though the terms are not very intelligible, being the language of the overseers of coal-works.

1. *Whitfield-mine* near the pottery in Staffordshire. Soil 1 foot, brick-clay 3 feet, shale 4. metal which is hard brown and falls in the weather 42. coal 3. warrant clay 6. brown gritstone 36. coal 3½. warrant clay 3½. bass and metal 53½. hardstone 4. shaly bass 1½. coal 4. warrant clay, depth unknown: in all about 55 yards.

2. *Coal-mine at Alfreton* in Derbyshire. Soil and clay 7 feet. fragments of stone 9. bind 13. stone 6. bind 34. stone 5. bind 2. stone 2. bind 10. coal 1½. bind 1½. stone 37. bind 7. soft coal 3. bind 3. stone 20. bind 16. coal 7½. in all about 61 yards.

3. *A basset coal-mine at Woolarton* in Nottinghamshire. Sand and gravel 6 feet. bind 21. stone 10. smut or effete coal 1. clunch 4. bind 21. stone 18. bind 18. stonebind 15. soft coal 2. clunch and bind 21. coal 7. in all about 48 yards.

4. *Coal-mine at West-Hallam* in Nottinghamshire Soil and clay 7 feet. bind 48. smut 1½. clunch 4. bind 3. stone 2. bind 1. stone 1. bind 3. stone 1. bind 16. shale 2. bind 12. shale 3. clunch, stone, and a bed of cauk 54. soft coal 4. clay and dun 1. soft coal 4½. clunch and bind 21. coal 1. broad bind 26. hard coal 6. in all about 74 yards.

As these strata generally lie inclined, I suppose parallel with the limestone on which they rest, the upper edges of them all come out to day, which is termed basseting; when the whole mass was ignited by its fermentation, it is probable that the inflammable part of some strata might thus more easily escape than of others in the form of vapour; as dews are known to slide between such strata in the production of springs; which accounts for some coal-beds being so much worse than others. See note XX.

From this account of the production of coals from morasses, it would appear that coal-beds are not to be expected beneath masses of limestone. Nevertheless I have been lately informed by my friend Mr. Michell of Thornhill, who I hope will soon favour the public with his geological investigations, that the beds of chalk are the uppermost of all the lime-stones; and that they rest on the granulated limestone, called ketton-stone; which I suppose is similar to that which covers the whole country from Leadenham to Sleaford, and from Sleaford to Lincoln; and that, thirdly, coal-delphs are frequently found beneath these two uppermost beds of limestone.

Now as these beds of chalk and of granulated lime-stone may have been formed by alluviation, on or beneath the shores of the sea, or in valleys of the land, it would seem that some coal countries, which in the great commotions of the earth had been sunk beneath the water, were thus covered with alluvial lime-stone, as well as others with alluvial basaltes, or common gravel-beds. Very extensive plains, which now consist of alluvial materials, were in the early times covered with water, which has since diminished, as the solid parts of the earth have increased. For the solid parts of the earth consisting chiefly of animal and vegetable recrements must have originally been formed or produced from the water by animal and vegetable processes; and as the solid parts of the earth may be supposed to be thrice as heavy as water, it follows that thrice the quantity of water must have vanished, compared with the quantity of earth thus produced. This may account for many immense beds of alluvial materials, as gravel, rounded sand, granulated lime-stone, and chalk, covering such extensive plains as Lincoln-heath, having become dry without the supposition of their having been again elevated from the ocean. At the same time we acquire the knowledge of one of the uses or final causes of the organized world, not indeed very flattering to our vanity, that it converts water into earth, forming islands and continents by its recrements or exuviæ.

The annexed section of a coal-mine was sent me by a member of the ingenious philosophical society at Newcastle upon Tyne, and cannot but much gratify every inquirer into the strata of coal-countries.

NOTE XXIV.—GRANITE.

Climb the rude steeps, the granite-cliffs surround.
CANTO II. l. 523.

THE lowest stratum of the earth which human labour has arrrived to, is granite; and of this likewise consist the highest mountains of the world. It is known under variety of names according to some difference in its appearance or composition, but is now generally considered by philosophers as a species of lava; if it contains quartz, felt spat, and mica in distinct crystals, it is called granite; which is found in Cornwall in rocks; and in loose stones in the gravel near Drayton in Shropshire, in the road towards Newcastle. If these parts of the composition be less distinct, or if only two of them be visible to the eye, it is termed porphyry, trap, whinstone, moorstone, slate. And if it appears in a regular angular form, it is called basaltes. The affinity of these bodies has lately been further well established by Dr. Beddoes in the Phil. Trans. Vol. LXXX.

These are all esteemed to have been volcanic productions that have undergone different degrees of heat; it is well known that in Papin's digester water may be made red hot by confinement, and will then dissolve many bodies which otherwise are little or not at all acted upon by it. From hence it may be conceived, that under immense pressure of superincumbent materials, and by great heat, these masses of lava may have undergone a kind of aqueous solution without any tendency to vitrifaction, and might thence have a power of crystallization, whence all the varieties above mentioned from the different proportion of the materials, or the different degrees of heat they may have undergone in this aqueous solution. And that the uniformity of the mixture of the original earths, as of lime, argil, silex, magnesia, and barytes, which they contain, was owing to their boiling together longer or shorter time before their elevation into mountains. See note XIX. art 8.

The seat of volcanoes seems to be principally, if not entirely, in these strata of granite; as many of them are situated on granite mountains, and throw up from time to time sheets of lava which run down over the preceding strata from the same origin; and in this they seem to differ from the heat which has separated the clay, coal, and sand in morasses, which would appear to have risen from a kind of fermentation, and thus to have pervaded the whole mass without any expuition of lava.

All the lavas from Vesuvius contain one fourth part of iron, (Kirwan's Min.) and all the five primitive earths, viz. calcareous, argillaceous, siliceous, barytic, and magnesian earths, which are also evidently produced now daily from the recrements of animal and vegetable bodies. What is to be thence concluded? Has the granite stratum in very ancient times been produced like the present calcareous and siliceous masses, according to the ingenious theory of Dr. Hutton, who says new continents are now forming at the bottom of the sea to rise in their turn, and thus the terraqueous globe has been, and will be, eternal? Or shall we suppose that this internal heated mass of granite, which forms the nucleus of the earth, was a part of the body of the sun before it was separated by an explosion? Or was the sun originally a planet, inhabited like ours, and a satellite to some other greater sun, which has long been extinguished by diffusion of its light, and around which the present sun continues to revolve, according to a conjecture of the celebrated Mr. Herschell, and which conveys to the mind a most sublime idea of the progressive and increasing excellence of the works of the Creator of all things?

For the more easy comprehension of the facts and conjectures, concerning the situation and production of the various strata of the earth, I shall here subjoin a supposed section of the globe, but without any attempt to give the proportions of the parts, or the number of them, but only their respective situation over each other, and a geological recapitulation.

GEOLOGICAL RECAPITULATION.

1. The earth was projected along with the other primary planets from the sun, which is supposed to be on fire only on its surface, emitting light without much internal heat like a ball of burning camphor.

2. The rotation of the earth round its axis was occasioned by its greater friction or adhesion to one side of the cavity from which it was ejected; and from this rotation it acquired its spheroidical form. As it cooled in its ascent from the sun its nucleus became harder; and its attendant vapours were condensed, forming the ocean.

3. The masses or mountains of granite, porphyry, basalt, and stones of similar structure, were a part of the original nucleus of the earth or consist of volcanic productions since formed.

4. On this nucleus of granite and basaltes, thus covered by the ocean, were formed the calcareous beds of lime-stone, marble, chalk, spar, from the exuviae of marine animals; with the flints, or chertz, which accompany them. And were stratified by their having been formed at different and very distant periods of time.

5. The whole terraqueous globe was burst by central fires; islands and continents were raised, consisting of granite or lava in some parts, and of lime-stone in others; and great valleys were sunk, into which the ocean retired.

6. During these central earthquakes the moon was ejected from the earth, causing new tides; and the earth's axis suffered some change in its inclination, and its rotatory motion was retarded.

7. On some parts of these islands and continents of granite or lime-stone were gradually produced extensive morasses, from the recrements of vegetables and of land animals, and from these morasses, heated by fermentation, were produced clay, marle, sand-stone, coal, iron, (with the bases of variety of acids) all which were stratified by their having been formed at different, and very distant periods of time.

8. In the elevation of the mountains very numerous and deep fissures necessarily were produced. In these fissures many of the metals are formed, partly from descending materials, and partly from ascending ones raised in vapour by subterraneous fires. In the fissures of granite or porphyry quartz is formed; in the fissures of lime-stone calcareous spar is produced.

9. During these first great volcanic fires it is probable the atmosphere was either produced, or much increased; a process which is perhaps now going on in the moon; Mr. Herschell having discovered a volcanic crater three miles broad burning on her disk.

10. The summits of the new mountains were cracked into innumerable lozenges by the cold dews or snows falling upon them when red hot. From these summits, which were then twice as high as at present, cubes and lozenges of granite and basalt, and quartz in some countries, and of marble and flints in others, descended gradually into the valleys, and were rolled together in the beds of rivers, (which were then so large as to occupy the whole valleys, which they now only intersect;) and produced the great beds of gravel, of which many valleys consist.

11. In several parts of the earth's surface subsequent earthquakes, from the fermentation of morasses, have at different periods of time deranged the position of the matters above described. Hence the gravel, which was before in the beds of rivers has in some places been raised into mountains, along with clay and coal strata which were formed from morasses and washed down from eminences into the beds of rivers or the neighbouring seas, and in part raised again with gravel or marine shells over them; but this has only obtained in few places compared with the general distribution of such materials. Hence there seem to have existed two sources of earthquakes, which have occurred at great distance of time from each other; one from the granite beds in the central parts of the earth, and the other from the morasses on its surface. All the subsequent earthquakes and volcanoes of modern days compared with these are of small extent and insignificant effect.

12. Besides the argillaceous sand-stone produced from morasses, which is stratified with clay, and coal, and iron, other great beds of siliceous sand have been formed in the sea by the combination of an unknown acid from morasses, and the calcareous matters of the ocean.

13. The warm waters which are found in

many countries, are owing to steam arising from great depths through the fissures of lime-stone or lava, elevated by subterranean fires, and condensed between the strata of the hills over them; and not from any decomposition of pyrites or manganese near the surface of the earth.

14. The columns of basaltes have been raised by the congelation or expansion of granite beds in the act of cooling from their semi-vitreous fusion.

NOTE XXV.—EVAPORATION.

Aquatic nymphs! you lead with viewless march
The winged vapours up the aerial arch.
Canto III. l. 13.

I. The atmosphere will dissolve a certain quantity of moisture as a chemical menstruum, even when it is much below the freezing point, as appears from the diminution of ice suspended in frosty air, but a much greater quantity of water is evaporated and suspended in the air by means of heat, which is perhaps the universal cause of fluidity, for water is known to boil with less heat in vacuo, which is a proof that it will evaporate faster in vacuo, and that the air therefore rather hinders than promotes its evaporation in higher degrees of heat. The quick evaporation occasioned in vacuo by a small degree of heat is agreeably seen in what is termed a pulse-glass, which consists of an exhausted tube of glass with a bulb at each end of it, and with about two-thirds of the cavity filled with alcohol, in which the spirit is instantly seen to boil by the heat of the finger-end applied on a bubble of steam in the lower bulb, and is condensed again in the upper bulb by the least conceivable comparative coldness.

2. Another circumstance evincing that heat is the principal cause of evaporation is that at the time of water being converted into steam, a great quantity of heat is taken away from the neighbouring bodies. If a thermometer be repeatedly dipped in ether, or in rectified spirit of wine, and exposed to a blast of air, to expedite the evaporation by perpetually removing the saturated air from it, the thermometer will presently sink below freezing. This warmth, taken from the ambient bodies at the time of evaporation by the steam, is again given out when the steam is condensed into water. Hence the water in a worm-tub during distillation so soon becomes hot; and hence the warmth accompanying the descent of rain in cold weather.

3. The third circumstance, showing that heat is the principal cause of evaporation, is that some of the steam becomes again condensed when any part of the heat is withdrawn. Thus when warmer south-west winds replete with moisture succeed the colder north-east winds all bodies that are dense and substantial, as stone walls, brick floors, &c. absorb some of the heat from the passing air, and its moisture becomes precipitated on them, while the north-east winds become warmer on their arrival in this latitude, and are thence disposed to take up more moisture, and are termed drying winds.

4. Heat seems to be the principal cause of the solution of many other bodies, as common salt, or blue vitriol dissolved in water, which when exposed to severe cold are precipitated, or carried, to the part of the water last frozen; this I observed in a phial filled with a solution of blue vitriol which was frozen; the phial was burst, the ice thawed, and a blue column of cupreous vitriol was left standing upright on the bottom of the broken glass, as described in Note XIX. Art. 3.

II. Hence water may either be dissolved in air, and may then be called an aerial solution or water; or it may be dissolved in the fluid matter of heat, according to the theory of M. Lavoisier, and may then be called steam. In the former case it is probable there are many other vapours which may precipitate it, as marine acid gas, or fluor acid gas. So alkaline gas and acid gas dissolved in air precipitate each other, nitrous gas precipitates vital air from its azote, and inflammable gas mixed with vital air ignited by an electric spark either produces or precipitates the water in both of them. Are there any subtle exhalations occasionally diffused in the atmosphere which may thus cause rain?

1. But as water is perhaps many hundred times more soluble in the fluid matter of heat than in air, I suppose the eduction of this heat, by whatever means it is occasioned, is the principal cause of devaporation. Thus if a region of air is brought from a warmer climate, as the S. W. winds, it becomes cooled by its contact with the earth in this latitude, and parts with so much of its moisture as was dissolved in the quantity of calorique, or heat, which it now loses, but retains that part which was suspended by its attraction to the particles of air, or by aerial solution, even in the most severe frosts.

2. A second immediate cause of rain is a stream of N. E. wind descending from a superior current of air, and mixing with the warmer S. W. wind below; or the reverse of this, viz. a superior current of S. W. wind mixing with an inferior one of N. E. wind; in both these cases the whole heaven becomes instantly clouded, and the moisture contained in the S. W. current is precipitated. This cause of devaporation has been ingeniously explained by Dr. Hutton in the Transact. of Edinburgh, Vol. I. and seems to arise from this circumstance; the particles of air of the N. E. wind educe part of the heat from the S. W. wind, and therefore the water which was dissolved by that quantity of *heat* is precipitated; all the other part of the water, which was suspended by its attraction to the particles of air, or dissolved in the remainder of the heat, continues unprecipitated.

3. A third method by which a region of air becomes cooled, and in consequence deposits much of its moisture, is from the mechanical expansion of air, when part of the pressure is taken off. In this case the expanded air becomes capable of receiving or attracting more of the matter of heat into its interstices, and the vapour, which was previously dissolved in this heat, is deposited, as is seen in the receiver of an air-pump, which becomes dewy, as the air within becomes expanded by the eduction of part of it. See Note VII. Hence when the mercury in the barometer sinks without a change of the wind the air generally becomes colder. See Note VII. on elementary heat. And it is probably from the varying pressure of the incumbent air, that in summer days small black clouds are often thus suddenly produced, and again soon vanish. See a paper in Philos. Trans. Vol. LXXVIII. intitled Frigorific Experiments on the Mechanical Expansion of Air.

4. Another portion of atmospheric water may possibly be held in solution by the electric fluid, since in thunder storms a precipitation of the water seems to be either the cause or the conse-

quence of the eduction of the electricity. But it appears more probable that the water is condensed into clouds by the eduction of its heat, and that then the surplus of electricity prevents their coalescence into larger drops, which immediately succeeds the departure of the lightning.

5. The immediate cause why the barometer sinks before rain is, first, because a region of warm air, brought to us in the place of the cold air which it had displaced, must weigh lighter, both specifically and absolutely, if the height of the warm atmosphere be supposed to be equal to that of the preceding cold one. And secondly, after the drops of rain begin to fall in any column of air, that column becomes lighter, the falling drops only adding to the pressure of the air in proportion to the resistance which they meet with in passing through that fluid.

If we could suppose water to be dissolved in air without heat, or in very low degrees of heat, I suppose the air would become heavier, as happens in many chemical solutions, but if water dissolved in the matter of heat, or calorique, be mixed with an aerial solution of water, there can be no doubt but an atmosphere consisting of such a mixture must become lighter in proportion to the quantity of calorique. On the same circumstance depends the visible vapour produced from the breath of animals in cold weather, or from a boiling kettle; the particles of cold air, with which it is mixed, steal a part of its heat, and become themselves raised in temperature, whence part of the water is precipitated in visible vapour, which, if in great quantity, sinks to the ground; if in small quantity, and the surrounding air is not previously saturated, it spreads itself till it becomes again dissolved.

NOTE XXVI.—SPRINGS.

Your lucid bands condense, with fingers chill,
The blue mist hovering round the gelid hill.
CANTO III. 1. 19.

THE surface of the earth consists of strata, many of which were formed originally beneath the sea, the mountains were afterwards forced up by subterraneous fires, as appears from the fissures in the rocks of which they consist, the quantity of volcanic productions all over the world, and the numerous remains of craters of volcanoes in mountainous countries. Hence the strata which compose the sides of mountains lie slanting downwards, and one or two or more of the external strata not reaching to the summit when the mountain was raised up, the second or third stratum or a more inferior one is there exposed to day; this may be well represented by forcibly thrusting a blunt instrument through several sheets of paper, a bur will stand up with the lowermost sheet standing highest in the centre of it. On this uppermost stratum, which is colder as it is more elevated, the dews are condensed in large quantities; and sliding down pass under the first or second or third stratum which compose the sides of the hill; and either form a morass below, or a weeping rock, by oozing out in numerous places, or many of these less currents meeting together burst out in a more copious rill.

The summits of mountains are much colder than the plains in their vicinity, owing to several causes; 1. Their being in a manner insulated or cut off from the common heat of the earth, which is always of 48 degrees, and perpetually counteracts the effects of external cold beneath that degree. 2. From their surfaces being larger in proportion to their solid contents, and hence their heat more expeditiously carried away by the ever-moving atmosphere. 3. The increasing rarity of the air as the mountain rises. All those bodies which conduct electricity well or ill, conduct the matter of heat likewise well or ill. See note VII. Atmospheric air is a bad conductor of electricity, and thence confines it on the body where it is accumulated, but when it is made very rare, as in the exhausted receiver, the electric aura passes away immediately to any distance. The same circumstance probably happens in respect to heat, which is thus kept by the denser air on the plains from escaping, but is dissipated on the hills where the air is thinner. 4. As the currents of air rise up the sides of mountains they become mechanically rarefied, the pressure of the incumbent column lessening as they ascend. Hence the expanding air absorbs heat from the mountain as it ascends, as explained in note VII. 5. There is another, and perhaps more powerful cause, I suspect, which may occasion the great cold on mountains, and in the higher parts of the atmosphere, and which has not yet been attended to; I mean that the fluid matter of heat may probably gravitate round the earth, and form an atmosphere on its surface, mixed with the aerial atmosphere, which may diminish or become rarer, as it recedes from the earth's surface, in a greater proportion than the air diminishes.

6. The great condensation of moisture on the summits of hills has another cause, which is the dashing of moving clouds against them; in misty days this is often seen to have great effect on plains, where an eminent tree by obstructing the mist as it moves along shall have a much greater quantity of moisture drop from its leaves than falls at the same time on the ground in its vicinity. Mr. White, in his history of Selborne, gives an account of a large tree so situated, from which a stream flowed during a moving mist so as to fill the cart ruts in a lane otherwise not very moist; and ingeniously adds, that trees planted about ponds of stagnant water contribute much by these means to supply the reservoir. The spherules which constitute a mist or cloud are kept from uniting by so small a power that a little agitation against the leaves of a tree, or the greater attraction of a flat moist surface, condenses or precipitates them.

If a leaf has its surface moistened, and particles of water separate from each other as in a mist be brought near the moistened surface of a leaf, each particle will be attracted more by that plain surface of water on the leaf than it can be by the surrounding particles of the mist, because globules only attract each other in one point, whereas a plain attracts a globule by a greater extent of its surface.

The common cold springs are thus formed on elevated grounds by the condensed vapours, and hence are stronger when the nights are cold after hot days in spring, than even in the wet days of winter. For the warm atmosphere during the day has dissolved much more water than it can support in solution during the cold of the night, which is thus deposited in large quantities on the hills, and yet so gradually as to soak in between the strata of them, rather than to slide off over their surfaces like showers of rain. The common heat of the internal parts of the earth is ascertained by springs which arise from strata of earth too deep to be affected by the heat of summer or the frosts of winter. Those in this country are of 48 degrees of heat, those about Philadelphia were said by Dr. Franklin to be 52; whether this variation is to be accounted for by the difference of the sun's heat in that country, according to the ingenious theory of Mr. Kirwan, or to the vicinity of subterranean fires, is not yet, I think, decided. There are, however, subterraneous streams of water not exactly produced in this manner, as streams issuing from fissures in the earth, communicating with the craters of old volcanoes; in the Peak of Derbyshire are many hollows, called swallows, where the land floods sink into the earth, and come out at some miles distant, as at Ilam near Ashborne. See note on Fica, Part II.

Other streams of cold water arise from beneath the snow on the Alps and Andes, and other high mountains, which is perpetually thawing at its under surface by the common heat of the earth, and gives rise to large rivers. For the origin of warm springs see note on Fucus, Part II.

NOTE XXVII.—SHELL FISH.

You round echinus ray his arrowy mail,
Give the keel'd nautilus his oar and sail;
Firm to his rock with silver cords suspend
The anchor'd pinna, and his cancer-friend.
CANTO III. 1. 67.

THE armour of the echinus, or sea hedge-hog, consists generally of moveable spines; (*Linnei System. Nat.* Vol. I. p. 1102.) and in that respect resembles the armour of the land animal of the same name. The irregular protuberances on other sea-shells, as on some species of the purpura, and murex, serve them as a fortification against the attacks of their enemies.

It is said that this animal foresees tempestuous weathers, and sinking to the bottom of the sea, adheres firmly to sea plants, or other bodies, by means of a substance which resembles the horns of snails. Above twelve hundred of these fillets have been counted by which this animal fixes itself; and when afloat, it contracts these fillets between the bases of its points, the number of which often amounts to two thousand. Dict. raisonné, art. Oursin de mer.

There is a kind of nautilus, called by Linneus, argonauta, whose shell has but one cell; of this animal Pliny affirms, that having exonerated its shell by throwing out the water, it swims upon the surface, extending a web of wonderful tenuity, and bending back two of its arms, and rowing with the rest, makes a sail, and at length receiving the water dives again. Plin. IX. 29. Linneus adds to his description of this animal, that like the crab Diogenes or Bernhard, it occupies a house not its own, as it is not connected to its shell, and is therefore foreign to it; who could have given credit to this if it had not been attested by so many who have with their own eyes seen this argonaut in the act of sailing? Syst. Nat. p. 1161.

The nautilus, properly so named by Linneus, has a shell consisting of many chambers, of which cups are made in the East with beautiful painting and carving on the mother-pearl. The animal is said to inhabit only the uppermost or open chamber, which is larger than the rest; and that the rest remain empty, except that the pipe, or siphunculus, which communicates from one to the other of them, is filled with an appendage of the animal like a gut or string. Mr. Hook, in his Philos. Exper. p. 306. imagines this to be a dilatable or compressible tube, like the air bladders of fish, and that by contracting or permitting it to expand, it renders its shell buoyant or the contrary. See note on Ulva, Part II.

The pinna, or sea-wing, is contained in a two-valve shell, weighing sometimes fifteen pounds, and emits a beard of fine long glossy silk-like fibres, by which it is suspended to the rocks twenty or thirty feet beneath the surface of the sea. In this situation it is so successfully attacked by the eight-footed polypus, that the species perhaps could not exist but for the exertions of the cancer pinnotheris, who lives in the same shell as a guard and companion. Amœn. Acad. Vol. II. p. 48, Lin. Syst. Nat. Vol. I. p. 1159, and p. 1040.

The pinnotheris, or pinnophylax, is a small crab naked like Bernard the Hermit, but is furnished with good eyes, and lives in the same shell with the pinna; when they want food the pinna opens its shell, and sends its faithful ally to forage; but if the cancer sees the polypus, he returns suddenly to the arms of his blind hostess, who by closing the shell avoids the fury of her enemy; otherwise, when it has procured a booty, it brings it to the opening of the shell, where it is admitted, and they divide the prey. This was observed by Haslequist in his voyage to Palestine.

The byssus of the ancients, according to Aristotle, was the beard of the pinna above mentioned, but seems to have been used by other writers indiscriminately for any spun material, which was esteemed finer or more valuable than wool. Reaumur says the threads of this byssus are not less fine or less beautiful than the silk, as it is spun by the silk-worm; the pinna on the coasts of Italy and Provence (where it is fished up by iron-hooks fixed on long poles) is called the silk-worm of the sea. The stockings and gloves manufactured from it, are of exquisite fineness, but too warm for common wear, and are thence esteemed useful in rheumatism and gout. Dict. raisonné, art. Pinne-marine. The warmth of the byssus, like that of silk, is probably owing to their being bad conductors of heat, as well as of electricity. When these fibres are broken by violence, this animal, as well as the muscle, has the power to re-produce them like the common spiders, as was observed by M. Adanson. As raw silk, and raw cobwebs, when swallowed, are liable to produce great sickness, (as I am informed,) it is probable the part of muscles, which sometimes disagrees with the people who eat them, may be this silky web, by which they attach themselves to stones. The large kind of pinna contains some mother-pearl of a reddish tinge, according to M. d'Argenville. The substance sold under the name of Indian weed, and used at the bottom of fish-lines, is probably a production of this kind; which however is scarcely to be distinguished by the eye from the tendons of a rat's tail, after they have been separated by putrefaction in water, and well cleaned and rubbed; a production, which I was once shown as a great curiosity; it had the uppermost bone of the tail adhering to it, and was said to have been used as an ornament in a lady's hair.

NOTE XXVIII.—STURGEON.

With worm-like beard his toothless lips array,
And teach the unwieldy sturgeon to betray.
                              CANTO III. l. 71.

THE Sturgeon, *Acipenser, Strurio.* Lin. Syst. Nat. Vol. I. p. 408. is a fish of great curiosity as well as of great importance; his mouth is placed under the head, without teeth, like the opening of a purse, which he has the power to push suddenly out or retract. Before this mouth under the beak or nose hang four tendrills some inches long, and which so resemble earth-worms that at first sight they may be mistaken for them. This clumsy toothless fish is supposed by this contrivance to keep himself in good condition, the solidity of his flesh evidently showing him to be a fish of prey. He is said to hide his large body amongst the weeds near the sea-coast or at the mouth of large rivers, only exposing his cirrhi or tendrils, which small fish or sea-insects mistaking for real worms approach for plunder, and are sucked into the jaws of their enemy. He has been supposed by some to root into the soil at the bottom of the sea or rivers; but the cirrhi or tendrils above mentioned, which hang from his snout over his mouth, must themselves be very inconvenient for this purpose; and as it has no jaws it evidently lives by suction, and during its residence in the sea a quantity of sea-insects are found in its stomach.

The flesh was so valued at the time of the Emperor Severus, that it was brought to table by servants with coronets on their heads, and preceded by music, which might give rise to its being in our country presented by the Lord Mayor to the King. At present it is caught in the Danube, and the Wolga, the Don, and other large rivers, for various purposes. The skin makes the best covering for carriages; isinglass is prepared from parts of the skin; cavear from the spawn; and the flesh is pickled or salted, and sent all over Europe.

NOTE XXIX.—OIL ON WATER.

Or with fine films, suspended o'er the deep,
Of oil effusive lull the waves to sleep.
                              CANTO III. l. 87.

THERE is reason to believe that when oil is poured upon water, the two surfaces do not touch each other, but that the oil is suspended over the water by their mutual repulsion. This seems to be rendered probable by the following experiment; if one drop of oil be dropped on a bason of water, it will immediately diffuse itself over the whole, for there being no friction between the two surfaces, there is nothing to prevent its spreading itself by the gravity of the upper part of it, except its own tenacity, into a pellicle of the greatest tenuity. But if a second drop of oil be put upon the former, it does not spread itself, but remains in the form of a drop, as the other already occupied the whole surface of the bason, and there is friction in oil passing over oil, though none in oil passing over water.

Hence when oil is diffused on the surface of water gentle breezes have no influence in raising waves upon it; for a small quantity of oil will cover a very great surface of water, (I suppose a spoonful will diffuse itself over some acres) and the wind blowing upon this carries it gradually forwards; and there being no friction between the two surfaces the water is not affected. On which account oil has no effect in stilling the agitation of the water after the wind ceases, as was found by the experiments of Dr. Franklin.

This circumstance, lately brought into notice by Dr. Franklin, had been mentioned by Pliny, and is said to be in use by the divers for pearls, who in windy weather take down with them a little oil in their mouths, which they occasionally give out when the inequality of the supernatant waves prevents them from seeing sufficiently distinctly for their purpose.

The wonderful tenuity with which oil can be spread upon water is evinced by a few drops projected from a bridge, where the eye is properly placed over it, passing through all the prismatic colours as it diffuses itself. And also from another curious experiment of Dr. Franklin's: he cut a piece of cork to about the size of a letter wafer, leaving a point standing off like a tangent at one edge of the circle. This piece of cork was then dipped in oil and thrown into a large pond of water, and as the oil flowed off at the point, the cork-wafer continued to revolve in a contrary direction for several minutes; the oil flowing off all that time at the pointed tangent in coloured streams. In a small pond of water this experiment does not so well succeed, as the circulation of the cork stops as soon as the water becomes covered with the pellicle of oil. See Additional Note, No. XIII. and Note on Fucus, Part II.

The ease with which oil and water slide over each other is agreeably seen if a phial be about half filled with equal parts of oil and water, and made to oscillate suspended by a string, the upper surface of the oil and the lower one of the water will always keep smooth; but the agitation of the surfaces where the oil and water meet, is curious; for their specific gravities being not very different, and their friction on each other nothing, the highest side of the water, as the phial descends in its oscillation, having acquired a greater momentum than the lowest side (from its having descended further) would rise the highest on the ascending side of the oscillation, and thence pushes the then uppermost part of the water amongst the oil.

NOTE XXX.—SHIP-WORM.

Meet fell teredo, as he mines the keel
With beaked head, and break his lips of steel.
                              CANTO III. l. 91.

THE teredo, or ship-worm, has two calcareous jaws, hemispherical, flat before, and angular behind. The shell is taper, winding, penetrating ships and submarine wood, and was brought from India into Europe. Linnei System. Nat. p. 1267. The tarieres, or sea-worms, attack and erode ships with such fury, and in such numbers, as often greatly to endanger them. It is said that our vessels have not known this new enemy above fifty years, that they were brought from the sea about the Antilles to our parts of the ocean, where they have increased prodigiously. They bore their passage in the direction of the fibres of the wood, which is their nourishment, and cannot return or pass obliquely, and thence when they come to a knot in the wood, or when two of them meet together with their stony mouths, they perish for want of food.

In the year 1731 and 1732 the United Provinces were under a dreadful alarm concerning these insects, which had made great depredation on the piles which support the banks of Zealand; but it was happily discovered a few years afterwards that these insects had totally abandoned that island, (Dict. Raisonné, art. Vers Rongeurs,) which might have been occasioned by their not being able to live in that latitude when the winter was rather severer than usual.

NOTE XXXI.—MAELSTROM.

Turn the broad helm, the flattering canvas urge
From Maelstrom's fierce innavigable surge.
CANTO III. l. 93.

ON the coast of Norway there is an extensive vortex, or eddy, which lies between the islands of Moskoe and Moskenas, and is called Moskoestrom, or Maelstrom; it occupies some leagues in circumference, and is said to be very dangerous and often destructive to vessels navigating these seas. It is not easy to understand the existence of a constant descending stream without supposing it must pass through a subterranean cavity to some other part of the earth or ocean which may lie beneath its level; as the Mediterranean seems to lie beneath the level of the Atlantic ocean, which therefore constantly flows into it through the Straits; and the waters of the Gulph of Mexico lie much above the level of the sea about the Floridas and farther northward, which gives rise to the Gulph-stream, as described in note on Cassia in Part II.

The Maelstrom is said to be still twice in about twenty-four hours when the tide is up, and most violent at the opposite times of the day. This is not difficult to account for, since when so much water is brought over the subterraneous passage, if such exists, as completely to fill it and stand many feet above it, less disturbance must appear on the surface. The Maelstrom is described in the Memoirs of the Swedish Academy of Sciences, and Pontopiddon's Hist. of Norway, and in the Universal Museum for 1763, p. 131.

The reason why eddies of water become hollow in the middle is because the water immediately over the centre of the well, or cavity, falls faster, having less friction to oppose its descent, than the water over the circumference or edges of the well. The circular motion or gyration of eddies depends on the obliquity of the course of the stream, or to the friction or opposition to it being greater on the one side of the well than the other; I have observed in water passing through a hole in the bottom of a trough, which was always kept full, the gyration of the stream might be turned either way by increasing the opposition of one side of the eddy with one's finger, or by turning the spout, through which the water was introduced, a little more obliquely to the hole on one side or on the other. Lighter bodies are liable to be retained long in eddies of water, while those rather heavier than water are soon thrown out beyond the circumference by their acquired momentum becoming greater than that of the water. Thus if equal portions of oil and water be put into a phial, and by means of a string be whirled in a circle round the hand, the water will always keep at a greater distance from the centre, whence in the eddies formed in rivers during a flood a person who endeavours to keep above water or to swim is liable to be detained in them, but on suffering himself to sink or dive he is said readily to escape. This circulation of water in descending through a hole in a vessel Dr. Franklin has ingeniously applied to the explanation of hurricanes or eddies of air.

NOTE XXXII.—GLACIERS.

Where round dark crags indignant waters bend
Through rifted ice, in ivory veins descend.
CANTO III. l. 113.

THE common heat of the interior parts of the earth being always 48 degrees, both in winter and summer, the snow which lies in contact with it is always in a thawing state; hence in ice-houses the external parts of the collection of ice is perpetually thawing and thus preserves the internal part of it; so that it is necessary to lay up many tons for the preservation of one ton. Hence in Italy considerable rivers have their source from beneath the eternal glaciers, or mountains of snow and ice.

In our country when the air in the course of a frost continues a day or two at very near 32 degrees, the common heat of the earth thaws the ice on its surface, while the thermometer remains at the freezing point. This circumstance is often observable in the rimy mornings of spring; the thermometer shall continue at the freezing point, yet all the rime will vanish except that which happens to lie on a bridge, a board, or on a cake of cow-dung, which being thus as it were insulated or cut off from so free a communication with the common heat of the earth by means of the air under the bridge, or wood, or dung, which are bad conductors of heat, continues some time longer unthawed. Hence when the ground is covered thick with snow, though the frost continues, and the sun does not shine, yet the snow is observed to decrease very sensibly. For the common heat of the earth melts the under surface of it, and the upper one evaporates by its solution in the air. The great evaporation of ice was observed by Mr. Boyle, which experiment I repeated some time ago. Having suspended a piece of ice by a wire and weighed it with care without touching it with my hand, I hung it out the whole of a clear frosty night, and found in the morning it had lost nearly a fifth of its weight. Mr. N. Wallerius has since observed that ice at the time of its congelation evaporates faster than water in its fluid form; which may be accounted for from the heat given out at the instant of freezing; (Saussure's Essais sur Hygromet. p. 249.) but this effect is only momentary.

Thus the vegetables that are covered with snow are seldom injured; since, as they lie between the thawing snow, which has 32 degrees of heat, and the covered earth which has 48, they are preserved in a degree of heat between these, viz. in 40 degrees of heat. Whence the moss on which the rein-deer feed in the northern latitudes vegetates beneath the snow; (See note on Muschus Part II.) and hence many Lapland

and Alpine plants perished through cold in the botanic garden at Upsal, for in their native situations, though the cold is much more intense, yet at its very commencement they are covered deep with snow, which remains till late in the spring. For this fact see Amænit. Academ. Vol. I. No. 48. In our climate such plants do well covered with dried fern, under which they will grow, and even flower, till the severe vernal frosts cease. For the increase of glaciers see Note on Canto I. l. 529.

NOTE XXXIII—WINDS.

While southern gales o'er western oceans roll,
And Eurus steals his ice-winds from the pole.
CANTO IV. L 15.

THE theory of the winds is yet very imperfect, in part perhaps owing to the want of observations sufficiently numerous of the exact times and places where they begin and cease to blow, but chiefly to our yet imperfect knowledge of the means by which great regions of air are either suddenly produced or suddenly destroyed.

The air is perpetually subject to increase or diminution from its combination with other bodies, or its evolution from them. The vital part of the air, called oxygene, is continually produced in this climate from the perspiration of vegetables in the sunshine, and probably from the action of light on clouds or on water in the tropical climates, where the sun has greater power, and may exert some yet unknown laws of luminous combination. Another part of the atmosphere, which is called azote, is perpetually set at liberty from animal and vegetable bodies by putrefaction or combustion, from many springs of water, from volatile alkali, and probably from fixed alkali, of which there is an exhaustless source in the water of the ocean. Both these component parts of the air are perpetually again diminished by their contact with the soil, which covers the surface of the earth, producing nitre. The oxygene is diminished in the production of all acids, of which the carbonic and muriatic exist in great abundance. The azote is diminished in the growth of animal bodies, of which it constitutes an important part, and in its combinations with many other natural productions.

They are both probably diminished in immense quantities by uniting with the inflammable air, which arises from the mud of rivers and lakes at some seasons, when the atmosphere is light: the oxygene of the air producing water, and the azote producing volatile alkali by their combinations with this inflammable air. At other seasons of the year these principles may again change their combinations, and the atmospheric air be reproduced.

Mr. Lavoisier found that one pound of charcoal in burning consumed two pounds nine ounces of vital air, or oxygene. The consumption of vital air in the process of making red lead may readily be reduced to calculation; a small barrel contains about twelve hundred weight of this commodity, 1200 pounds of lead by calcination absorb about 144 pounds of vital air; now as a cubic foot of water weighs 1000 avoirdupois ounces, and as vital air is above 800 times lighter than water, it follows that every barrel of red lead contains nearly 2000 cubic feet of vital air. If this can be performed in miniature in a small oven, what may not be done in the immense elaboratories of nature!

These great elaboratories of nature include almost all her fossil as well as her animal and vegetable productions. Dr. Priestley obtained air of greater or less purity, both vital and azotic, from almost all the fossil substances he subjected to experiment. Four ounce weight of lava from Iceland heated in an earthen retort yielded twenty ounce measures of air.

oz. wt. of		gave	oz. meas. of air
4	lava	20	
7	basaltes	104	
2	toad stone	40	
1½	granite	20	
1	elvan	3)	
7	gypsum	230	
4	blue slate	230	
4	clay	20	
4	lime-stone spar	830	
5	lime stone	1160	
3	chalk	630	
3½	white iron ore	560	
4	dark iron ore	410	
½	molybdena	25	
½	stream tin	20	
2	steatites	40	
2	barytes	26	
2	black wad	80	
4	sand-stone	75	
3	coal	00	

In this account the fixed air was previously extracted from the lime-stones by acids, and the heat applied was much less than was necessary to extract all the air from the bodies employed. Add to this the known quantities of air which are combined with the calciform ores, as the ochres of iron, manganese, calamy, gray ore of lead, and some idea may be formed of the great production of air in volcanic eruptions, as mentioned in note on Chunda, Part II. and of the perpetual absorptions and evolutions of whole oceans of air from every part of the earth.

But there would seem to be an officina aeris, a shop where air is both manufactured and destroyed in the greatest abundance within the polar circles, as will hereafter be spoken of. Can this be effected by some yet unknown law of the congelation of aqueous or saline fluids, which may set at liberty their combined heat, and convert a part both of the acid and alkali of sea-water into their component airs; or on the contrary, can the electricity of the northern lights convert inflammable air and oxygene into water, whilst the great degree of cold at the poles unites the azote with some other base? Another officina aeris, or manufacture of air, would seem to exist within the tropics, or at the line, though in a much less quantity than at the poles, owing perhaps to the action of the sun's light on the moisture suspended in the air, as will also be spoken of hereafter; but in all other parts of the earth these absorptions and evolutions of air in a greater or less degree are perpetually going on in inconceivable abundance; increased probably, and diminished at different seasons of the year by the approach or retrocession of the sun's light; future discoveries must elucidate this part of the subject. To this should be added, that as heat and electricity, and perhaps magnetism, are known to displace air, that it is not impossible but that the increased or diminished quantities of these fluids diffused in the atmosphere may increase its weight as well as its bulk; since their specific attractions or affinities to matter are very strong, they probably also possess general gravitation to the earth; a subject which wants further investigation. See Note XXVI.

SOUTH-WEST WINDS.

The velocity of the surface of the earth in moving round its axis diminishes from the equator to the poles. Whence if a region of air in this country should be suddenly removed a few degrees towards the north it must constitute a western wind, because from the velocity it had previously acquired in this climate by its friction with the earth it would for a time move quicker than the surface of the country it was removed to; the contrary must ensue when a region of air is transported from this country a few degrees southward, because the velocity it had acquired in this climate would be less than that of the earth's surface where it was removed to, whence it would appear to constitute a wind from the east, while in reality the eminent parts of the earth would be carried against the too slow air. But if this transportation of air from south to north be performed gradually, the motion of the wind will blow in the diagonal between south and west. And on the contrary, if a region of air be gradually removed from north to south it would also blow diagonally between the north and east, from whence we may safely conclude that all our winds in this country which blow from the north or east, or any point between them, consist of regions of air brought from the north; and that all our winds blowing from the south or west, or from any point between them, are regions of air brought from the south.

It frequently happens during the vernal months that after a north-east wind has passed over us for several weeks, during which time the barometer has stood at above 30½ inches, it becomes suddenly succeeded by a south-west wind, which also continues several weeks, and the barometer sinks to nearly 28½ inches. Now as two inches of the mercury in the barometer balance one-fifteenth part of the whole atmosphere, an important question here presents itself, *what is become of all this air?*

1. This great quantity of air cannot be carried in a superior current towards the line, while the inferior current flows towards the poles, because then it would equally affect the barometer, which should not therefore subside from 30½ inches to 28½ for six weeks together.

2. It cannot be owing to the air having lost all the moisture which was previously dissolved in it, because these warm south-west winds are replete with moisture, and the cold north-east winds, which weigh up the mercury in the barometer to 31 inches, consist of dry air.

3. It cannot be carried over the polar regions and be accumulated on the meridian opposite to us in its passage towards the line, as such an accumulation would equal one-fifteenth of the whole atmosphere, and cannot be supposed to remain in that situation for six weeks together.

4. It cannot depend on the existence of tides in the atmosphere, since it must then correspond to lunar periods. Nor on accumulations of air from the specific levity of the upper regions of the atmosphere, since its degree of fluidity must correspond with its tenuity, and consequently such great mountains of air cannot be supposed to exist for so many weeks together as the south-west winds sometimes continue.

5. It remains therefore that there must be at this time a great and sudden absorption of air in the polar circle by some unknown operation of nature, and that the south wind runs in to supply the deficiency. Now as this south wind consists of air brought from a part of the earth's surface which moves faster than it does in this climate it must have at the same time a direction from the west by retaining part of the velocity it had previously acquired. These south-west winds coming from a warmer country, and becoming colder by their contact with the earth of this climate, and by their expansion, (so great a part of the superincumbent atmosphere having vanished,) precipitate their moisture; and as they continue for several weeks to be absorbed in the polar circle would seem to receive a perpetual supply from the tropical regions, especially over the line, as will hereafter be spoken of.

It may sometimes happen that a north-east wind having passed over us may be bent down and driven back before it has acquired any heat from the climate, and may thus for a few hours or a day have a south-west direction, and from its descending from a higher region of the atmosphere may possess a greater degree of cold than an inferior north-east current of air.

The extreme cold of Jan. 13, 1709, at Paris, came on with a gentle south wind, and was diminished when the wind changed to the north, which is accounted for by Mr. Homberg from a reflux of air which had been flowing for some time from the north. Chemical Essays by R. Watson, Vol. V. p. 182.

It may happen that a north-east current may for a day or two pass over us and produce incessant rain by mixing with the inferior south-west current; but this as well as the former is of short duration, as its friction will soon carry the inferior current along with it, and dry or frosty weather will then succeed.

NORTH-EAST WINDS.

The north-east winds of this country consist of regions of air from the north, travelling sometimes at the rate of about a mile in two minutes during the vernal months for several weeks together from the polar regions toward the south, the mercury in the barometer standing above 30. These winds consist of air greatly cooled by the evaporation of the ice and snow over which it passes, and as they become warmer by their contact with the earth of this climate are capable of dissolving more moisture as they pass along, and are thence attended with frosts in winter and with dry hot weather in summer.

1. This great quantity of air cannot be supplied by superior currents passing in a contrary direction from south to north, because such currents must as they arise into the atmosphere a mile or two high become exposed to so great cold as to occasion them to deposit their moisture, which would fall through the inferior current upon the earth in some part of their passage.

2. The whole atmosphere must have increased in quantity, because it appears by the barometer that there exists one-fifteenth part more air over us for many weeks together, which could not be thus accumulated by difference of temperature in respect to heat, or by any aerostatic laws at present known, or by any lunar influence.

From whence it would appear that immense masses of air were set at liberty from their combinations with solid bodies, along with a sufficient quantity of combined heat, within the polar circle, or in some region to the north of us; and that they thus perpetually increase the quantity of the atmosphere; and that this is again at certain times re-absorbed, or enters into new combinations at the line or tropical regions. By which wonderful contrivance the atmosphere is perpetually renewed and rendered fit for the support of animal and vegetable life.

SOUTH-EAST WINDS.

The south-east winds of this country consist of air from the north which had passed by us, or over us, and before it had obtained the velocity of the earth's surface in this climate had been driven back, owing to a deficiency of air now commencing at the polar regions. Hence these are generally dry or freezing winds, and if they succeed north-east winds should prognosticate a change of wind from north-east to south-west; the barometer is generally about 30. They are sometimes attended with cloudy weather, or rain, owing to their having acquired an increased degree of warmth and moisture before they became retrograde; or to their being mixed with air from the south.

2. Sometimes these south-east winds consist of a vertical eddy of north-east air, without any mixture of south-west air; in that case the barometer continues above 30, and the weather is dry or frosty for four or five days together.

It should here be observed, that air being an elastic fluid must be more liable to eddies than water, and that these eddies must extend into cylinders or vortexes of greater diameter, and that if a vertical eddy of north-east air be of small diameter or has passed but a little way to the south of us before its return, it will not have gained the velocity of the earth's surface to the south of us, and will in consequence become a south-east wind.—But if the vertical eddy be of large diameter, or has passed much to the south of us, it will have acquired velocity from its friction with the earth's surface to the south of us, and will in consequence of its return become a south-west wind, producing great cold.

NORTH-WEST WINDS.

There seem to be three sources of the north-west winds of this hemisphere of the earth.

1. When a portion of southern air, which was passing over us, is driven back by accumulation of new air in the polar regions. In this case I suppose they are generally moist or rainy winds, with the barometer under 30, and if the wind had previously been in the south-west, it would seem to prognosticate a change to the north-east.

2. If a current of north wind is passing over us but a few miles high, without any easterly direction; and is bent down upon us, it must immediately possess a westerly direction, because it will now move faster than the surface of the earth where it arrives; and thus becomes changed from the north-east to a north-west wind. The descent of a north-east current of air producing a north-west wind may continue some days with clear or freezing weather, as it may be simply owing to a vertical eddy of north-east air, as will be spoken of below. It may otherwise be forced down by a current of south-west wind passing over it, and in this case it will be attended with rain for a few days by the mixture of the two airs of different degrees of heat; and will prognosticate a change of wind from north-east to south-west if the wind was previously in the north-east quarter.

3. On the eastern coast of North America the north-west winds bring frost, as the north-east winds do in this country, as appears from variety of testimony. This seems to happen from a vertical spiral eddy made in the atmosphere between the shore and the ridge of mountains which form the spine or back-bone of that continent. If a current of water runs along the hypothenuse of a triangle an eddy will be made in the included angle, which will turn round like a water-wheel as the stream passes in contact with one edge of it. The same must happen when a sheet of air flowing along from the north-east rises from the shore in a straight line to the summit of the Apalachian mountains, a part of the stream of north-east air will flow over the mountains, another part will revert and circulate spirally between the summit of the country and the eastern shore, continuing to move toward the south; and thus be changed from a north-east to a north-west wind.

This vertical spiral eddy having been in contact with the cold summits of these mountains, and descending from higher parts of the atmosphere will lose part of its heat, and thus constitute one cause of the greater coldness of the eastern sides of North America than of the European shores opposite to them, which is said to be equal to twelve degrees of north latitude, which is a wonderful fact, nor otherwise easy to be explained, since the heat of the springs at Philadelphia is said to be 52, which is greater than the medium heat of the earth in this country.

The existence of vertical eddies, or great cylinders of air rolling on the surface of the earth, is agreeable to the observations of the constructors of windmills; who on this idea place the area of the sails leaning backwards, inclined to the horizon; and believe that then they have greater power than when they are placed quite perpendicularly. The same kind of rolling cylinders of water obtain in rivers owing to the friction of the water against the earth at their bottoms; as is known by bodies having been observed to float upon their surfaces quicker than when immersed to a certain depth. These vertical eddies of air probably exist all over the earth's surface, but particularly at the bottom or sides of mountains; and more so probably in the course of the south-west than of the north-east winds; because the former fall from an eminence as it were, on a part of the earth where there is a deficiency of the quantity of air; as is shown by the sinking of the barometer: whereas the latter are pushed or squeezed forward by an addition to the atmosphere behind them, as appears by the rising of the barometer.

TRADE-WINDS.

A column of heated air becomes lighter than before, and will therefore ascend, by the pressure of the cold air which surrounds it, like a cork in water, or like heated smoke in a chimney.

Now as the sun passes twice over the equator for once over either tropic, the equator has not time to become cool; and on this account it is in general hotter at the line than at the tropics; and therefore the air over the line, except in some few instances hereafter to be mentioned, continues to ascend at all seasons of the year, pressed upwards by regions of air brought from the tropics.

This air thus brought from the tropics to the equator, would constitute a north wind on one side of the equator, and a south wind on the other; but as the surface of the earth at the equator moves quicker than the surface of the earth at the tropics, it is evident that a region of air brought from either tropic to the equator, and which had previously only acquired the velocity of the earth's surface at the tropics, will now move too slow for the earth's surface at the equator, and will thence appear to move in a direction contrary to the motion of the earth. Hence the trade-winds, though they consist of regions of air brought from the north on one side of the line, and from the south on the other, will appear to have the diagonal direction of north-east and south-east winds.

Now it is commonly believed that there are superior currents of air passing over these north-east and south-east currents in a contrary direction, and which descending near the tropics produce vertical whirlpools of air. An important question here again presents itself—*What becomes of the moisture which this heated air ought to deposit, as it cools in the upper regions of the atmosphere in its journey to the tropics?* It has been shown by Dr. Priestley and Mr. Ingenhouz that the green matter at the bottom of cisterns, and the fresh leaves of plants immersed in water, give out considerable quantities of vital air in the sun-shine; that is, the perspirable matter of plants (which is water much divided in its egress from their minute pores) becomes decomposed by the sun's light, and converted into two kinds of air, the vital and inflammable airs. The moisture contained or dissolved in the ascending heated air at the line must exist in great tenuity; and by being exposed to the great light of the sun in that climate, the water may be decomposed, and the new airs spread on the atmosphere from the line to the poles.

1. From there being no constant deposition of rains in the usual course of the trade-winds, it would appear that the water rising at the line is decomposed in its ascent.

2. From the observations of M. Bouguer on the mountain Pinchinca, one of the Cordeliers immediately under the line, there appears to be no condensible vapour above three or four miles high. Now though the atmosphere at that height may be cold to a very considerable degree; yet its total deprivation of condensible vapour would seem to show, that its water was decomposed; as there are no experiments to evince that any degree of cold hitherto known has been able to deprive air of its moisture; and great abundance of snow is deposited from the air that flows to the polar regions, though it is exposed to no greater degrees of cold in its journey thither than probably exists at four miles height in the atmosphere at the line.

3. The hygrometer of Mr. Saussure also pointed to dryness as he ascended into rarer air; the single hair of which it was constructed, contracting from deficiency of moisture. Essais sur l'Hygromet. p. 143.

From these observations it appears either that rare and cold air requires more moisture to saturate it than dense air; or that the moisture becomes decomposed and converted into air, as it ascends into these cold and rare regions of the atmosphere.

4. There seems some analogy between the circumstance of air being produced or generated in the cold parts of the atmosphere both at the line and at the poles.

MONSOONS AND TORNADOES.

1. In the Arabian and Indian seas are winds which blow six months one way, and six months the other, and are called monsoons; by the accidental dispositions of land and sea it happens, that in some places the air near the tropic is supposed to become warmer when the sun is vertical over it, than at the line. The air in these places consequently ascends pressed upon one side by the north-east regions of air, and on the other side by the south-west regions of air. For as the air brought from the south has previously obtained the velocity of the earth's surface at the line, it moves faster than the earth's surface, near the tropic where it now arrives, and becomes a south-west wind, while the air from the north becomes a north-east wind as before explained. These two winds do not so quietly join and ascend as the north-east and south-east winds, which meet at the line with equal warmth and velocity and form the trade-winds; but as they meet in contrary directions before they ascend, and cannot be supposed accurately to balance each other, a rotatory motion will be produced as they ascend like water falling through a hole, and a horizontal or spiral eddy is the consequence; these eddies are more or less rapid, and are called tornadoes in their most violent state, raising water from the ocean in the west, or sand from the deserts of the east, in less violent degrees they only mix together the two currents of north-east and south-west air, and produce by this means incessant rains; as the air of the north-east acquires some of the heat from the south-west wind, as explained in Note XXV. This circumstance of the eddies produced by the monsoon-winds was seen by Mr. Bruce in Abyssinia; he relates that for many successive mornings at the commencement of the rainy monsoon, he observed a cloud of apparently small dimension whirling round with great rapidity, and in a few minutes the heavens became covered with dark clouds and with consequent great rains. See Note on Canto III. l. 129.

2. But it is not only at the place where the air ascends at the northern extremity of the rainy monsoon, and where it forms tornadoes, as observed above by Mr. Bruce, but over a great tract of country several degrees in length in certain parts as in the Arabian sea, a perpetual rain for several months descends, similar to what happens for weeks together in our own climate in a less degree during the south-west winds. Another important question presents itself here—*If the climate to which this south-west wind arrives, is not colder than that it comes from, why should it deposit its moisture during its whole journey? if it be a colder climate, why does it come thither?* The tornadoes of air above described can extend but a little way, and it is not easy to conceive that a superior cold current of air can mix with an inferior one, and thus produce showers over ten degrees of country, since at about three miles high there is perpetual frost; and what can induce these narrow and shallow currents to flow over each other so many hundred miles?

Though the earth at the northern extremity of this monsoon may be more heated by certain circumstances of situation than at the line, yet it seems probable that the intermediate country between that and the line, may continue colder than the line, (as in other parts of the earth) and hence that the air coming from the line to supply this ascent or destruction of air at the northern extremity of the monsoon will be cooled all the way in its approach, and in consequence deposit its water. It seems probable that at the northern extremity of this monsoon, where the tornadoes or hurricanes exist, that the air not only ascends but is in part converted into water, or otherwise diminished in quantity, as no account is given of the existence of any superior currents of it.

As the south-west winds are always attended with a light atmosphere, an incipient vacancy or a great diminution of air must have taken place to the northward of them in all parts of the earth wherever they exist, and a deposition of their moisture succeeds their being cooled by the climate they arrive at, and not by a contrary current of cold air over them, since in that case the barometer would not sink. They may thus in our own country be termed monsoons without very regular periods.

3. Another cause of tornadoes independent of the monsoons is ingeniously explained by Dr. Franklin, when in the tropical countries a stratum of inferior air becomes so heated by its contact with the warm earth, that its expansion is increased more than is equivalent to the pressure of the stratum of air over it; or when the superior stratum becomes more condensed by cold than the inferior one by pressure, the upper region will descend and the lower one ascend. In this situation if one part of the atmosphere be hotter from some fortuitous circumstances, or has less pressure over it, the lower stratum will begin to ascend at this part, and resemble water falling through a hole as mentioned above. If the lower region of air was going forwards with considerable velocity, it will gain an eddy by rising up this hole in the incumbent heavy air, so that the whirlpool or tornado has not only its progressive velocity, but its circular one also, which thus lifts up or overturns every thing within its spiral whirl. By the weaker whirlwinds in this country the trees are sometimes thrown down in a line of only twenty or forty yards in breadth, making a kind of avenue through a country. In the West Indies the sea rises like a cone in the whirl, and is met by black clouds produced by the cold upper air and the warm lower air being rapidly mixed; whence are produced the great and sudden rains called water spouts; while the upper and lower airs exchange their plus or minus electricity in perpetual lightnings.

LAND AND SEA-BREEZES.

The sea being a transparent mass is less heated at its surface by the sun's rays than the land, and its continual change of surface contributes to preserve a greater uniformity in the heat of the air which hangs over it. Hence the surface of the tropical islands is more heated during the day than the sea that surrounds them, and cools more in the night by its greater elevation; whence in the afternoon, when the lands of the tropical islands have been much heated by the sun, the air over them ascends pressed upwards by the cooler air of the encircling ocean; in the morning again the land becoming cooled more than the sea, the air over it descends by its increased gravity, and blows over the ocean near its shores.

CONCLUSION.

1. There are various irregular winds besides those above described, which consist of horizontal or vertical eddies of air, owing to the inequality of the earth's surface, or the juxtaposition of the sea. Other irregular winds have their origin from increased evaporation of water, or its sudden devaporation and descent in showers; others from the partial expansion and condensation of air by heat and cold; by the accumulation or defect of electric fluid, or to the air's new production or absorption occasioned by local causes not yet discovered. See Notes VII. and XXV.

2. There seem to exist only two original winds: one consisting of air brought from the north, and the other of air brought from the south. The former of these winds has also generally an apparent direction from the east, and the latter from the west, arising from the different velocities of the earth's surface. All the other winds above described are deflections or retrogressions of some parts of these currents of air from the north or south.

3. One-fifteenth part of the atmosphere is occasionally destroyed, and occasionally re-produced by unknown causes. These causes are brought into immediate activity over a great part of the surface of the earth at nearly the same time, but always more powerful to the northward than to the southward of any given place; and would hence seem to have their principal effect in the polar circles, existing nevertheless, though with less power, toward the tropics or at the line.

For when the north-east wind blows the barometer rises, sometimes from 28½ inches to 30½, which shows a great new generation of air in the north; and when the south-west wind blows the barometer sinks as much, which shows a great destruction of air in the north. But as the north-east winds sometimes continue for five or six weeks, the newly-generated air must be destroyed at those times in the warmer climates to the south of us, or circulate in superior currents, which has been shown to be improbable from its not depositing its water. And as the south-west winds sometimes continue for some weeks, there must be a generation of air to the south at those times, or superior currents, which last has been shown to be improbable.

4. The north-east winds being generated about the poles are pushed forwards towards the tropics or line, by the pressure from behind, and hence they become warmer, as explained in Note VII. as well as by their coming into contact with a warmer part of the earth, which contributes to make these winds greedily absorb moisture in their passage. On the contrary, the south-west winds, as the atmosphere is suddenly diminished in the polar regions, are drawn as it were into an incipient vacancy, and become therefore expanded in their passage, and thus generate cold, as explained in Note VII. and are thus induced to part with their moisture, as well as by their contact with a colder part of the earth's surface. Add to this, that the difference in the sound of the north-east and south-west winds may depend on the former being pushed forwards by a pressure behind, and the latter falling as it were into a partial or incipient vacancy before; whence the former becomes more condensed, and the latter more rarefied as it passes. There is a whistle, termed a lark-call, which consists of a hollow cylinder of tin-plate, closed at each end, about half an inch in diameter, and a quarter of an inch high, with opposite holes about the size of a goose-quill through the centre of each end; if this lark-whistle be held between the lips the sound of it is manifestly different when the breath is forcibly blown through it from within outwards, and when it

is sucked from without inwards. Perhaps this might be worthy the attention of organ-builders.

5. A stop is put to this new generation of air, when about a fifteenth of the whole is produced, by its increasing pressure; and a similar boundary is fixed to its absorption or destruction by the decrease of atmospheric pressure. As water requires more heat to convert it into vapour under a heavy atmosphere than under a light one, so in letting off the water from muddy fish-ponds great quantities of air-bubbles are seen to ascend from the bottom, which were previously confined there by the pressure of the water. Similar bubbles of inflammable air are seen to arise from lakes in many seasons of the year, when the atmosphere suddenly becomes light.

6. The increased absorption and evolutions of air must, like its simple expansions, depend much on the presence or absence of heat and light, and will hence, in respect to the times and places of its production and destruction, be governed by the approach or retrocession of the sun, and on the temperature, in regard to heat, of various latitudes, and parts of the same latitude, so well explained by Mr. Kirwan.

7. Though the immediate cause of the destruction or reproduction of great masses of air at certain times, when the wind changes from north to south, or from south to north, cannot yet be ascertained; yet as there appears greater difficulty in accounting for this change of wind from any other known causes, we may still suspect that there exists in the arctic and antarctic circles a bear or dragon yet unknown to philosophers, which at times suddenly drinks up, and as suddenly at other times vomits out one-fifteenth part of the atmosphere: and hope that this or some future age will learn how to govern and domesticate a monster which might be rendered of such important service to mankind.

INSTRUMENTS.

If along with the usual registers of the weather observations were made on the winds in many parts of the earth with the three following instruments, which might be constructed at no great expense, some useful information might be acquired.

1. To mark the hour when the wind changes from north-east to south-west, and the contrary. This might be managed by making a communication from the vane of a weathercock to a clock; in such a manner, that if the vane should revolve quite round, a tooth of its revolving axis should stop the clock, or put back a small bolt on the edge of a wheel revolving once in twenty-four hours.

2. To discover whether in a year more air passed from north to south, or the contrary. This might be effected by placing a wind-mill sail of copper about nine inches diameter in a hollow cylinder about six inches long, open at both ends, and fixed on an eminent situation exactly north and south. Thence only a part of the north-east and south-west currents would affect the sail so as to turn it; and if its revolutions were counted by an adopted machinery, as the sail would turn one way with the north currents of air, and the contrary one with the south currents, the advance of the counting finger either way would show which wind had prevailed most at the end of the year.

3. To discover the rolling cylinders of air, the vane of a weathercock might be so suspended as to dip or rise vertically, as well as to have its horizontal rotation.

RECAPITULATION.

NORTH-EAST WINDS consist of air flowing from the north, where it seems to be occasionally produced: has an apparent direction from the east, owing to its not having acquired in its journey the increasing velocity of the earth's surface; these winds are analogous to the trade-winds between the tropics, and frequently continue in the vernal months for four and six weeks together, with a high barometer, and fair or frosty weather. 2. They sometimes consist of south-west air, which had passed by us or over us, driven back by a new accumulation of air in the north. These continue but a day or two, and are attended with rain. See Note XXV.

SOUTH-WEST WINDS consist of air flowing from the south, and seeming occasionally absorbed at its arrival to the more northern latitudes. It has a real direction from the west owing to its not having lost in its journey the greater velocity it had acquired from the earth's surface from whence it came. These winds are analogous to the monsoons between the tropics, and frequently continue for four or six weeks together, with a low barometer and rainy weather. 2. They sometimes consist of north-east air, which had passed by us or over us, which becomes retrograde by a commencing deficiency of air in the north. These winds continue but a day or two, attended with severer frost with a sinking barometer; their cold being increased by their expansion, as they return, into an incipient vacancy.

NORTH-WEST WINDS consist, first, of south-west winds, which have passed over us, bent down and driven back towards the south by newly generated northern air. They continue but a day or two, and are attended with rain or clouds. 2. They consist of north-east winds bent down from the higher parts of the atmosphere, and having there acquired a greater velocity than the earth's surface are frosty or fair. 3. They consist of north-east winds formed into a vertical spiral eddy, as on the eastern coasts of North America, and bring severe frost.

SOUTH-EAST WINDS consist, first, of north-east winds become retrograde, continued for a day or two, frosty or fair, sinking barometer. 2. They consist of north-east winds formed into a vertical eddy, not a spiral one, frost or fair.

NORTH WINDS consist, first, of air flowing slowly from the north, so that they acquire the velocity of the earth's surface as they approach, are fair or frosty, seldom occur. 2. They consist of retrograde south-winds; these continue but a day or two, are preceded by south-west winds; and are generally succeeded by north-east winds, cloudy or rainy, barometer rising.

SOUTH WINDS consist, first, of air flowing slowly from the south, losing their previous westerly velocity by the friction of the earth's surface as they approach, moist, seldom occur. 2. They consist of retrograde north winds; these continue but a day or two, are preceded by north-east winds, and generally succeeded by south-west winds, colder, barometer sinking.

EAST WINDS consist of air brought hastily from the north, and not impelled farther southward, owing to a sudden beginning absorption of air in the northern regions, very cold, barometer high, generally succeeded by south-west wind.

WEST WINDS consist of air brought hastily from the south, and checked from proceeding further to the north by a beginning production of air in the northern regions, warm and moist, generally succeeded by north-east wind. 2. They consist of air bent down from the higher regions of the atmosphere; if this air be from the south, and brought hastily, it becomes a wind of great velocity, moving perhaps 60 miles in an hour, is warm and rainy; if it consists of northern air bent down it is of less velocity and colder.

Application of the preceding Theory to some Extracts from a Journal of the Weather.

Dec. 1, 1790. The barometer sunk suddenly, and the wind, which had been some days north-east with frost, changed to south-east with an incessant though moderate fall of snow. A part of the northern air, which had passed by us I suppose, now became retrograde before it had acquired the velocity of the earth's surface to the south of us, and being attended by some of the southern air in its journey, the moisture of the latter became condensed and frozen by its mixture with the former.

Dec. 2, 3. The wind changed to north-west and thawed the snow. A part of the southern air, which had passed by us or over us, with the retrograde northern air above described, was now in its turn driven back, before it had lost the velocity of the surface of the earth to the south of us, and consequently became a north-west wind; and not having lost the warmth it brought from the south produced a thaw.

Dec. 4, 5. Wind changed to north-east with frost and a rising barometer. The air from the north continuing to blow, after it had driven back the southern air as above described, became a north-east wind, having less velocity than the surface of the earth in this climate, and produced frost from its coldness.

Dec. 6, 7. Wind now changed to the south-west with incessant rain and a sinking barometer. From unknown causes I suppose the quantity of air to be diminished in the polar regions, and the southern air cooled by the earth's surface, which was previously frozen, deposits its moisture for a day or two; afterwards the wind continued south-west without rain, as the surface of the earth became warmer.

March 18, 1785. There has been a long frost; a few days ago the barometer sunk to 29¼, and the frost became more severe. Because the air being expanded by a part of the pressure being taken off became colder. This day the mercury rose to 30, and the frost ceased, the wind continuing as before between north and east. *March* 19. Mercury above 30, weather still milder, no frost, wind north-east. *March* 20. The same, for the mercury rising shows that the air becomes more compressed by the weight above and in consequence gives out warmth.

April 4, 5. Frost, wind north-east, the wind changed in the middle of the day to the north-west without rain, and has done so for three or four days, becoming again north-east at night. For the sun now giving greater degree of heat, the air ascends as the sun passes the zenith, and is supplied below by the air on the western side as well as on the eastern side of the zenith during the hot part of the day; whence for a few hours, on the approach of the hot part of the day, the air acquires a westerly direction in this longitude. If the north-west wind had been caused by a retrograde motion of some southern air, which had passed over us, it would have been attended with rain or clouds.

April 10. It rained all day yesterday, the wind north-west, this morning there was a sharp frost. The evaporation of the moisture, (which fell yesterday) occasioned by the continuance of the wind, produced so much cold as to freeze the dew.

May 12. Frequent showers with a current of colder wind preceding every shower. The sinking of the rain or cloud pressed away the air from beneath it in its descent, which having been for a time shaded from the sun by the floating cloud, became cooled in some degree.

June 20. The barometer sunk, the wind became south-west, and the whole heaven was instantly covered with clouds. A part of the incumbent atmosphere having vanished, as appeared by the sinking of the barometer, the remainder became expanded by its elasticity, and thence attracted some of the matter of heat from the vapour intermixed with it, and thus in a few minutes a total devaporation took place, as in exhausting the receiver of an air-pump. See note XXV. At the place where the air is destroyed, currents both from the north and south flow in to supply the deficiency, (for it has been shown that there are no other proper winds but these two) and the mixture of these winds produces so sudden condensation of the moisture, both by the coldness of the northern air and the expansion of both of them, that lightning is given out, and an incipient tornado takes place; whence thunder is said frequently to approach against the wind.

August 28, 1732. Barometer was at 31, and *Dec.* 30, in the same year, it was at 28 2-tenths. Medical Essays, Edinburgh, Vol. II. p. 7. It appears from these journals that the mercury at Edinburgh varies sometimes nearly three inches, or one-tenth of the whole atmosphere. From the journals kept by the Royal Society at London it appears seldom to vary more than two inches, or one-fifteenth of the whole atmosphere. The quantity of the variation is said still to decrease nearer the line, and to increase in the more northern latitudes; which much confirms the idea that there exists at certain times a great destruction or production of air within the polar circle.

July 2, 1732. The westerly winds in the journal in the Medical Essays, Vol. II. above referred to, are frequently marked with the number three to show their greater velocity, whereas the easterly winds seldom approach to the number two. The greater velocity of the westerly winds than the easterly ones is well known I believe in every climate of the world; which may be thus explained from the theory above delivered. 1. When the air is still, the higher parts of the atmosphere move quicker than those parts which touch the earth, because they are at a greater distance from the axis of motion. 2. The part of the atmosphere where the north or south wind comes from is higher than the part of it where it comes to, hence the more elevated parts of the atmosphere continue to descend towards the earth as either of those winds approach. 3. When southern air is brought to us it possesses a westerly direction also, owing to the velocity it has previously acquired from the earth's surface; and if it consists of air from the higher parts of the atmosphere descending nearer the earth, this westerly velocity becomes increased. But when northern air is brought to us, it possesses an apparent easterly direction also, owing to the velocity which it has previously acquired from the earth's surface being less than that of the earth's surface in this latitude; now if the north-east wind consists of air descending from higher parts of the atmosphere, this deficiency of velocity will be less, in consequence of the same cause, *viz.* the higher parts of the atmosphere descending, as the wind approaches, increases the real velocity of the western winds, and decreases the apparent velocity of the eastern ones.

October 22. Wind changed from south-east to south-west. There is a popular prognostication that if the wind changes from the north towards the south passing through the east, it is more likely to continue in the south, than if it passes through the west, which may be thus accounted for. If the north-east wind changes to a north-west wind, it shows either that a part of the northern air descends upon us in a spiral eddy, or that a superior current of southern air is driven back; but if a north-east wind be changed into a south-east wind it shows that the northern air is become retrograde, and that in a day or two, as soon as that part of it has passed, which has not gained the velocity of the earth's surface in this latitude, it will become a south wind for a few hours, and then a south-west wind.

The writer of this imperfect sketch of anemology wishes it may incite some person of greater leisure and ability to attend to this subject, and by comparing the various meteorological journals and observations already published, to construct a more accurate and methodical treatise on this interesting branch of philosophy.

NOTE XXXIV.

VEGETABLE PERSPIRATION.

And wed the enamoured oxygene to light.
                                    CANTO IV. l. 34.

WHEN points of hairs are put into spring-water, as in the experiments of Sir B. Thompson, (Philos. Trans. LXXVII.) and exposed to the light of the sun, much air, which loosely adhered to the water, rises in bubbles, as explained in the note on Fucus, Part II. A still greater quantity of air, and of a purer kind, is emitted by Dr. Priestley's green matter, and by vegetable leaves growing in water in sun-shine, according to Mr. Ingenhouz's experiments; both which I suspect to be owing to a decomposition of the water perspired by the plant, for the edge of a capillary tube of great tenuity may be considered as a circle of points, and as the oxygene, or principle of vital air, may be expanded into a gas by the sun's light, the hydrogene or inflammable air may be detained in the pores of the vegetable.

Hence plants growing in the shade are white, and become green by being exposed to the sun's light; for their natural colour being blue, the addition of hydrogene adds yellow to this blue, and *tans* them green. I suppose a similar circumstance takes place in animal bodies; their perspirable matter as it escapes in the sun-shine becomes decomposed by the edges of their pores as in vegetables, though in less quantity, as their perspiration is less, and the greatest part of it, which exhales from the lungs, not being exposed to the sunshine, and thus by the hydrogene being retained the skin becomes *tanned* yellow. In proof of this it must be observed that both vegetable and animal substances become bleached white by the sun-beams when they are dead, as cabbage-stalks, bones, ivory, tallow, bees-wax, linen and cotton cloth; and hence I suppose the copper-coloured natives of sunny countries might become etiolated or blanched by being kept from their infancy in the dark, or removed for a few generations to more northerly climates.

It is probable that on a sunny morning much pure air becomes separated from the dew by means of the points of vegetables on which it adheres, and much inflammable air imbibed by the vegetable, or combined with it; and by the sun's light thus decomposing water the effects of it in bleaching linen seems to depend (as described in Note X.): the water is decomposed by the light at the ends or points of the cotton or thread, and the vital air unites with the phlogistic or colouring matters of the cloth, and produces a new acid, which is either itself colourless or washes out, at the same time the inflammable part of the water escapes. Hence there seems a reason why cotton bleaches so much sooner than linen, *viz.* because its fibres are three or four times shorter, and therefore protrude so many more points, which seem to facilitate the liberation of the vital air from the inflammable part of the water.

Bees' wax becomes bleached by exposure to the sun and dews in a similar manner as metals become calcined or rusty, *viz.* by the water on their surface being decomposed; and hence the inflammable material which caused the colour becomes united with vital air forming a new acid, and is washed away.

Oil close stopped in a phial not full, and exposed long to the sun's light, becomes bleached, as I suppose, by the decomposition of the water it contains; the inflammable air rising above the surface, and the vital air uniting with the colouring matter of the oil. For it is remarkable, that by shutting up a phial of bleached oil in a dark drawer, it in a little time becomes coloured again.

The following experiment shows the power of light in separating vital air from another basis, *viz.* from azote. Mr. Scheele inverted a glass vessel filled with colourless nitrous acid into another glass containing the same acid, and on exposing them to the sun's light, the inverted glass became partly filled with pure air, and the acid at the same time became coloured. Scheele in Crell's Annal. 1786. But if the vessel of colourless nitrous acid be quite full and stopped, so that no space is left for the air produced to expand itself into, no change of colour takes place. Priestley's Exp. VI. p. 344. See Keir's very excellent Chemical Dictionary, p. 99. new edition.

A sun-flower three feet and a half high, according to the experiment of Dr. Hales, perspired two pints in one day (Vegetable Statics,) which is many times as much in proportion to its surface, as is perspired from the surface and lungs of animal bodies; it follows that the vital air liberated from the surfaces of plants by the sunshine must much exceed the quantity of it absorbed by their respiration, and that hence they improve the air in which they live during the light part of the day, and thus blanched vegetables will sooner become *tanned into green* by the sun's light, than etiolated animal bodies will become *tanned yellow* by the same means.

It is hence evident, that the curious discovery of Dr. Priestley, that his green vegetable matter and other aquatic plants gave out vital air when the sun shone upon them, and the leaves of other plants did the same when immersed in water, as observed by Mr. Ingenhouz, refer to the perspiration of vegetables not to their respiration. Because Dr. Priestley observed the pure air to come from both sides of the leaves, and even from the stalks of a water-flag, whereas one side of the leaf only serves the office of lungs, and certainly not the stalks. Exper. on Air, Vol. III. And thus in respect to the circumstance in which plants and animals seemed the farthest removed from each other, I mean in their supposed mode of respiration, by which one was believed to purify the air which the other had injured, they seem to differ only in degree, and the analogy between them remains unbroken.

Plants are said by many writers to grow much faster in the night than in the day; as is particularly observable in seedlings at their rising out of the ground. This probably is a consequence of their sleep rather than of the absence of light; and in this I suppose they also resemble animal bodies.

NOTE XXXV.

VEGETABLE PLACENTATION.

While in bright veins the silvery sap ascends.
CANTO IV. l. 431.

As buds are the viviparous offspring of vegetables, it becomes necessary that they should be furnished with placental vessels for their nourishment, till they acquire lungs or leaves for the purpose of elaborating the common juices of the earth into nutriment. These vessels exist in bulbs and in seeds, and supply the young plant with a sweet juice till it acquires leaves, as is seen in converting barley into malt, and appears from the sweet taste of onions and potatoes, when they begin to grow.

The placental vessels belonging to the buds of trees are placed about the roots of most, as the vine; so many roots are furnished with sweet or mealy matter as fern-root, bryony, carrot, turnip, potato, or in the alburnum or sap-wood as in those trees which produce manna, which is deposited about the month of August, or in the joints of sugar-cane, and grasses; early in the spring the absorbent mouths of these vessels drink up moisture from the earth, with a saccharine matter lodged for that purpose during the preceding autumn, and push this nutritive fluid up the vessels of the alburnum to every individual bud, as is evinced by the experiments of Dr. Hales, and of Mr. Walker in the Edinburgh Philosophical Transact. The former observed that the sap from the stump of a vine, which he had cut off in the beginning of April, arose twenty-one feet high in tubes affixed to it for that purpose, but in a few weeks it ceased to bleed at all, and Dr. Walker marked the progress of the ascending sap, and found likewise that as soon as the leaves became expanded the sap ceased to rise; the ascending juice of some trees is so copious and so sweet during the sap-season that it is used to make wine, as the birch, betula, and sycamore, acer pseudo-platanus, and particularly the palm, and maple, acer.

During this ascent of the sap-juice each individual leaf-bud expands its new leaves, and shoots down new roots, covering by their intertexture the old bark with a new one; and as soon as these new roots (or bark) are capable of absorbing sufficient juices from the earth for the support of each bud, and the new leaves are capable of performing their office of exposing these juices to the influence of the air; the placental vessels cease to act, coalesce, and are transformed from sap-wood, or alburnum, into inert wood; serving only for the support of the new tree, which grows over them.

Thus from the pith of the new bud of the horse-chesnut five vessels pass out through the circle of the placental vessels above described and carry with them a minuter circle of those vessels; these five bundles of vessels unite after their exit, and form the foot-stalk or petiole of the new five-fingered leaf, to be spoken of hereafter. This structure is well seen by cutting off a leaf, of the horse-chesnut (Æsculus Hippocastanum) in September before it falls, as the buds of this tree are so large that the flower may be seen in them with the naked eye.

After a time, perhaps about midsummer, another bundle of vessels passes from the pith through the alburnum or sap-vessels in the bosom of each leaf, and unites by the new bark with the leaf, which becomes either a flower-bud or a leaf-bud to be expanded in the ensuing spring, for which purpose an apparatus of placental vessels are produced with proper nutriment during the progress of the summer and autumn, and thus the vegetable becomes annually increased, ten thousand buds often existing on one tree, according to the estimate of Linneus. Phil. Bot.

The vascular connexion of vegetable buds with the leaves in whose bosoms they are formed is confirmed by the following experiment, (Oct. 20, 1781.) On the extremity of a young bud of the Mimosa (sensitive plant) a small drop of acid of vitriol was put by means of a pen, and, after a few seconds, the leaf, in whose axilla it dwelt, closed and opened no more, though the drop of vitriolic acid was so small as apparently only to injure the summit of the bud. Does not this seem to show that the leaf and its bud have connecting vessels, though they arise at different times and from different parts of the medulla or pith? And, as it exists previously to it, that the leaf is the parent of the bud? or did the acid destroy both the parent bud and its foetus?

This placentation of vegetable buds is clearly evinced from the sweetness of the rising sap, and from its ceasing to rise as soon as the leaves are expanded, and thus completes the analogy between buds and bulbs. Nor need we wonder at the length of the umbilical cords of buds, since that must correspond with their situation on the tree, in the same manner as their lymphatics and arteries are proportionally elongated.

Since the above was first printed, I have thought that these sap-vessels, which bleed so much on being wounded in the vernal months, ought rather to be called umbilical than placental vessels. As they supply the young bud with nutrition; whereas the placenta of the animal foetus is a respiratory organ, as shown in Zoonomia, Vol. I. Sect. 38.

NOTE XXXVI.

VEGETABLE CIRCULATION.

And refluent blood in milky eddies bends.
CANTO IV. l. 482.

THE individuality of vegetable buds was

spoken of before, and is confirmed by the method of raising all kinds of trees by Mr. Barnes. (Method of propagating Fruit Trees, 1759. Lond. Baldwin.) He cut a branch into as many pieces as there were buds or leaves upon it, and wiping the two wounded ends dry he quickly applied to each a cement, previously warmed a little, which consisted principally of pitch, and planted them in the earth. The use of this cement I suppose to consist in its preventing the bud from bleeding to death, though the author ascribes it to its antiseptic quality.

These buds of plants, which are thus each an individual vegetable, in many circumstances resemble individual animals, but as animal bodies are detached from the earth, and move from place to place in search of food, and take that food at considerable intervals of time, and prepare it for their nourshment within their own bodies after it is taken, it is evident they must require many organs and powers which are not necessary to a stationary bud. As vegetables are immoveably fixed to the soil from whence they draw their nourishment ready prepared, and this uniformly not at returning intervals, it follows that in examining their anatome we are not to look for muscles of locomotion, as arms and legs; nor for organs to receive and prepare their nourishment, as a stomach and bowels; nor for a reservoir for it after it is prepared, as a general system of veins, which in locomotive animals contains and returns the superfluous blood which is left after the various organs of secretion have been supplied, by which contrivance they are enabled to live a long time without new supplies of food.

The parts which we may expect to find in the anatome of vegetables correspondent to those in the animal economy are, 1. A system of absorbent vessels to imbibe the moisture of the earth similar to the lacteal vessels, as in the roots of plants; and another system of absorbents similar to the lymphatics of animal bodies, opening its mouths on the internal cells and external surfaces of vegetables; and a third system of absorbent vessels correspondent with those of the placentation of the animal fœtus. 2. A pulmonary system correspondent to the lungs or gills of quadrupeds and fish, by which the fluid absorbed by the lacteals and lymphatics may be exposed to the influence of the air, this is done by the green leaves of plants, those in the air resembling lungs, and those in the water resembling gills; and by the petals of flowers. 3. Arterial systems to convey the fluid thus elaborated to the various glands of the vegetable for the purposes of its growth, nutrition, and various secretions. 4. The various glands which separate from the vegetable blood the honey, wax, gum, resin, starch, sugar, essential oil, &c. 5. The organs adapted for their propagation or reproduction. 6. Muscles to perform several motions of their parts.

I. The existence of that branch of the absorbent vessels of vegetables which resembles the lacteals of animal bodies, and imbibes their nutriment from the moist earth, is evinced by their growth so long as moisture is applied to their roots, and their quickly withering when it is withdrawn.

Besides these absorbents in the roots of plants there are others which open their mouths on the external surfaces of the bark and leaves, and on the internal surfaces of all the cells, and between the bark and the alburnum or sapwood the existence of these is shown, because a leaf plucked off and laid with its under side on water will not wither so soon as if left in the dry air, —the same if the bark alone of a branch which is separated from a tree be kept moist with water,—and lastly, by moistening the alburnum or sap-wood alone of a branch detached from a tree it will not so soon wither as if left in the dry air. By the following experiment these vessels were agreeably visible by a common magnifying glass: I placed in the summer of 1781 the footstalks of some large fig-leaves, about an inch deep in a decoction of madder, (rubia tinctorum,) and others in a decoction of logwood, (hæmatoxylum campechense,) along with some sprigs cut off from a plant of picris, these plants were chosen because their blood is white, after some hours, and on the next day, on taking out either of these and cutting off from its bottom about a quarter of an inch of the stalk an internal circle of red points appeared, which were the ends of absorbent vessels coloured red with the decoction, while an external ring of arteries was seen to bleed out hastily a milky juice, and at once evince both the absorbent and arterial system. These absorbent vessels have been called by Grew, and Malpighi, and some other philosophers, bronchi, and erroneously supposed to be air vessels. It is probable that these vessels, when cut through, may effuse their fluids and receive air, their sides being too stiff to collapse: since dry wood emits air-bubbles in the exhausted receiver in the same manner as moist wood.

The structure of these vegetable absorbents consists of a spiral line, and not of a vessel interrupted with valves like the animal lymphatics, since on breaking almost any tender leaf and drawing out some of the fibres which adhere longest this spiral structure becomes visible even to the naked eye, and distinctly so by the use of a common lens. See Grew, Plate 51.

In such a structure it is easy to conceive how a vermicular or peristaltic motion of the vessel beginning at the lowest part of it, each spiral ring successively contracting itself till it fills up the tube, must forcibly push forwards its contents, as from the roots of vines in the bleeding season: and if this vermicular motion should begin at the upper end of the vessel it is as easy to see how it must carry its contained fluid in a contrary direction. The retrograde motion of the vegetable absorbent vessels is shown by cutting a forked branch from a tree, and immersing a part of one of the forks in water, which will for many days prevent the other from withering; or it is shown by planting a willow branch with the wrong end upwards. This structure in some degree obtains in the œsophagus or throat of cows, who by similar means convey their food first downwards and afterward upwards by a retrograde motion of the annular muscles or cartilages, for the purpose of a second mastication of it.

II. The fluids thus drank up by the vegetable absorbent vessels from the earth, or from the atmosphere, or from their own cells and interstices, are carried to the foot-stalk of every leaf, where the absorbents belonging to each leaf unite into branches, forming so many pulmonary arteries, and are thence dispersed to the extremities of the leaf, as may be seen in cutting away a slice after slice the foot-stalk of a horse-chesnut in September before the leaf falls. There is then a complete circulation in the leaf, a pulmonary vein receiving the blood from the extremities of each artery on the upper side of the leaf, and joining again in the foot-stalk of the leaf these veins produce so many arteries, or aortas, which disperse the new blood over the new bark, elongating its vessels, or producing its secretions: but as a reservoir of blood could not be wanted by a vegetable bud which takes in its nutriment at all times, I imagine there is no venous system, no veins properly so called, which receive the blood which was to spare, and return it into the pulmonary or arterial system.

The want of a system of veins was countenanced by the following experiment: I cut off several stems of tall spurge, (Euphorbia heliocopia) in autumn, about the centre of the plant, and observed tenfold the quantity of milky juice ooze from the upper than from the lower extremity, which could hardly have happened if there had been a venous system of vessels to return the blood from the roots to the leaves.

Thus the vegetable circulation, complete in the lungs, but probably in the other part of the system deficient in respect to a system of returning veins, is carried forwards without a heart, like circulation through the livers of animals, where the blood brought from the intestines and mesentery by one vein is dispersed through the liver by the vena portarum, which assumes the office of an artery. See note XXXVII.

At the same time so minute are the vessels in the intertexture of the barks of plants, which belong to each individual bud, that a general circulation may possibly exist, though we have not yet been able to discover the venous part of it.

Since the above opinion was first published, I have again attended to this subject, and now think that the greater discharge of the milky blood from the upper part of the plant, than from the lower part, might be rationally ascribed to the descending arteries of the stem bleeding more rapidly and more copiously than the ascending veins. And yesterday, September 28, 1798, a cupful of decoction of madder, rubia tinctorum, was carried into the garden, and placed near a plant of tragopogon latifolium, or scorzonera, which was then in flower; a large stem of the plant was then cut asunder, and the growing end was bent down and immersed an inch or two into the coloured decoction, along with the lower end of the top, or part cut off. After about a minute they were taken out and inspected by a common lens, when an internal circle of red points was visible in both of them, with an external circle of vessels, which continued to effuse white blood; though this effusion was slower from the root-end than from the summit-end, from whence I concluded, that the arteries of the root-end had ceased to act, and that the returning veins continued to bleed; and on the contrary, that the veins of the summit part had ceased to act, and that the descending arteries continued to bleed. And lastly, that the circle of red points in both of them were the mouths of the absorbent system, which continued to act in both directions. And I was thus induced to believe the existence of a venous system corresponding to the arterial one in the barks or roots of plants, as well as in their leaves and petals.

There is however another part of the circulation of vegetable juices visible to the naked eye, and that is in the corol or petals of flowers, in which a part of the blood of the plant is exposed to the influence of the air and light in the same manner as in the foliage, as will be mentioned more at large in Notes XXXVII. and XXXIX.

These circulations of their respective fluids seem to be carried on in the vessels of plants precisely as in animal bodies, by their irritability to the stimulus of their adapted fluids, and not by any mechanical or chemical attraction, for their absorbent vessels propel the juice upwards, which they drink up from the earth, with great violence; I suppose with much greater than is exerted by the lacteals of animals, probably owing to the greater minuteness of these vessels in vegetables, and the greater rigidity of their coats. Dr Hales in the spring season cut off a vine near the ground, and by fixing tubes on the remaining stump of it, found the sap to rise twenty-one feet in the tube by the propulsive power of these absorbents of the roots of it. Veget. Stat. p. 102. Such a power cannot be produced by capillary attraction, as that could only raise a fluid nearly to the upper edge of the attracting cylinder, but not enable it to flow over that edge, and much less to rise 21 feet above it. What then can this power be owing to? Doubtless to the living activity of the absorbent vessels, and to their increased vivacity from the influence of the warmth of the spring succeeding the winter's cold, and their thence greater susceptibility to irritation from the juices which they absorb, resembling in all circumstances the action of the living vessels of animals.

NOTE XXXVII.

VEGETABLE RESPIRATION.

While spread in air the leaves respiring play.
    CANTO IV. L. 433.

I. THERE have been various opinions concerning the use of the leaves of plants in the vegetable economy. Some have contended that they are perspiratory organs; this does not seem probable from an experiment of Dr. Hales, Veg. Stat. p. 30. He found by cutting off branches of trees with apples on them, and taking off the leaves, that an apple exhaled about as much as two leaves, the surfaces of which were nearly equal to the apple; whence it would appear that apples have as good a claim to be termed perspiratory organs as leaves. Others have believed them excretory organs of excrementitious juices; but as the vapour exhaled from vegetables has no taste, this idea is no more probable than the other; add to this that in moist weather, they do not appear to perspire or exhale at all.

The internal surface of the lungs or air-vessels in men, is said to be equal to the external surface of the whole body, or about fifteen square feet; on this surface the blood is exposed to the influence of the respired air through the medium however of a thin pellicle; by this exposure to the air it has its colour changed from deep red to bright scarlet, and acquires something so necessary to the existence of life, that we can live scarcely a minute without this wonderful process.

The analogy between the leaves of plants and the lungs or gills of animals seems to embrace so many circumstances, that we can scarcely withhold our assent to their performing similar offices.

1. The great surface of the leaves compared to that of the trunk and branches of trees is such, that it would seem to be an organ well adapted for the purpose of exposing the vegetable juices

to the influence of the air; this however we shall see afterwards is probably performed only by their upper surfaces, yet even in this case the surface of the leaves in general bear a greater proportion to the surface of the tree, than the lungs of animals to their external surfaces.

2. In the lungs of animals, the blood after having been exposed to the air in the extremities of the pulmonary artery, is changed in colour from deep red to bright scarlet, and certainly in some of its essential properties; it is then collected by the pulmonary vein and returned to the heart. To show a similarity of circumstances in the leaves of plants the following experiment was made, June 24, 1781. A stalk with leaves and seed-vessels of large spurge (Euphorbia helioscopia) had been several days placed in a decoction of madder (Rubia tinctorum) so that the lower part of the stem, and two of the undermost leaves were immersed in it. After having washed the immersed leaves in clear water, I could readily discern the colour of the madder passing along the middle rib of each leaf. This red artery was beautifully visible both on the under and the upper surface of the leaf; but on the upper side many red branches were seen going from it to the extremities of the leaf, which on the other side were not visible except by looking through it against the light. On this under side a system of branching vessels carrying a pale milky fluid were seen coming from the extremities of the leaf, and covering the whole underside of it, and joining into two large veins, one on each side of the red artery in the middle rib of the leaf, and along with it descending to the footstalk or petiole. On slitting one of these leaves with scissars, and having a common magnifying lens ready, the milky blood was seen oozing out of the returning veins on each side of the red artery in the middle rib, but none of the red fluid from the artery.

All these appearances were more easily seen in a leaf of picris treated in the same manner; for in this milky plant the stems and middle rib of the leaves are sometimes naturally coloured reddish, and hence the colour of the madder seemed to pass further into the ramifications of their leaf arteries, and was there beautifully visible with the returning branches of milky veins on each side.

3. From these experiments the upper surface of the leaf appeared to be the immediate organ of respiration, because the coloured fluid was carried to the extremities of the leaf by vessels most conspicuous on the upper surface, and there changed into a milky fluid, which is the blood of the plant, and then returned by concomitant veins on the under surface, which were seen to ooze when divided with scissars, and which, in picris particularly, render the under surface of the leaves greatly whiter than the upper one.

4. As the upper surface of leaves constitutes the organ of respiration, on which the sap is exposed in the terminations of arteries beneath a thin pellicle to the action of the atmosphere, these surfaces in many plants strongly repel moisture, as cabbage-leaves, whence the particles of rain lying over their surfaces without touching them, as observed by Mr. Melville (Essays Literary and Philosoph. Edinburgh) have the appearance of globules of quick-silver. And hence leaves laid with the upper surfaces on water, wither as soon as in the dry air, but continue green many days, if placed with the under surfaces on water, as appears in the experiments of Mon. Bonnet (Usage des Feuilles.) Hence some aquatic plants, as the water-lily (Nymphœa) have the lower sides of their leaves floating on the water, while the upper surfaces remain dry in the air.

5. As those insects, which have many spiracula, or breathing apertures, as wasps and flies, are immediately suffocated by pouring oil upon them, I carefully covered with oil the surfaces of several leaves of Phlomis, of Portugal laurel, and balsams, and though it would not regularly adhere, I found them all die in a day or two.

Of aquatic leaves, see Note on Trapa and on Fucus, in Part II. to which must be added that many leaves are furnished with muscles about their footstalks, to turn their upper surfaces to the air or light, as Mimosa and Hedysarum gyrans. From all these analogies I think there can be no doubt but that leaves of trees are their lungs, giving out a phlogistic material to the atmosphere, and absorbing oxygene or vital air.

6. The great use of light to vegetation would appear from this theory to be by disengaging vital air from the water which they perspire, and thence to facilitate its union with their blood exposed beneath the thin surface of their leaves; since when pure air is thus applied, it is probable, that it can be more readily absorbed. Hence in the curious experiments of Dr. Priestley and Mr. Ingenhouz, some plants purified air less than others, that is, they perspired less in the sunshine; and Mr. Scheele found that by putting pease into water, which about half covered them, they converted the vital air into fixed air, or carbonic acid gas, in the same manner as in animal respiration. See Note XXXIV.

7. The circulation in the lungs or leaves of plants is very similar to that of fish. In fish the blood after having passed through their gills does not return to the heart as from the lungs of air-breathing animals, but the pulmonary vein taking the structure of an artery after having received the blood from the gills, which there gains a more florid colour, distributes it to the other parts of their bodies. The same structure occurs in the livers of fish, whence we see in those animals two circulations independent of the power of the heart, viz. that beginning at the termination of the veins of the gills, and branching through the muscles, and that which passes through the liver; both which are carried on by the action of those respective arteries and veins. Monro's Physiology of Fish, p. 19.

The course of the fluids in the roots, leaves, and buds of vegetables seems to be performed in a manner similar to both these. First, the absorbent vessels of the roots and surfaces unite at the footstalk of the leaf; and then, like the Vena Portarum, an artery commences without the intervention of a heart, and spreads the sap in its numerous ramifications on the upper surface of the leaf; here it changes its colour and properties, and becomes vegetable blood; and is again collected by a pulmonary vein on the under surface of the leaf. This vein, like that which receives the blood from the gills of fish, assumes the office and name of an artery, and branching again disperses the blood upward to the bud from the footstalk of the leaf, and downward to the roots; where it is all expended in the various secretions, the nourishment and growth of the plant, as fast as it is prepared.

II. The organ of respiration already spoken of belongs particularly to the shoots or buds, but there is another pulmonary system, perhaps totally independent of the green foliage, which belongs to the fructification only, I mean the corol or petals. In this there is an artery belonging to each petal, which conveys the vegetable blood to its extremities, exposing it to the light and air under a delicate membrane covering the internal surface of the petal, where it often changes its colour, as is beautifully seen in some party-coloured poppies; though it is probable some of the iridescent colours of flowers may be owing to the different degrees of tenuity of the exterior membrane of the leaf refracting the light like soap-bubbles, the vegetable blood is then returned by correspondent vegetable veins, exactly as in the green foliage; for the purposes of the important secretions of honey, wax, the finer essential oil, and the prolific dust of the anthers.

1. The vascular structure of the corol as above described, and which is visible to the naked eye, and its exposing the vegetable juices to the air and light during the day, evince that it is a pulmonary organ.

2. As the glands which produce the prolific dust of the anthers, the honey, wax, and frequently some odoriferous essential oil, are generally attached to the corol, and always fall off and perish with it, it is evident that the blood is elaborated or oxygenated in this pulmonary system for the purpose of these important secretions.

3. Many flowers, as the colchicum, and hamamelis, arise naked in autumn, no green leaves appearing till the ensuing spring; and many others put forth their flowers and complete their impregnation early in the spring before the green foliage appears, as mezereon, cherries, pears, which shows that these corols are the lungs belonging to the fructification.

4. This organ does not seem to have been necessary for the defence of the stamens and pistils, since the calyx of many flowers, as tragopogon, performs this office; and in many flowers these petals themselves are so tender as to require being shut up in the calyx during the night, for what other use then can such an apparatus of vessels be designed?

5. In the helleborus niger, Christmas-rose, after the seeds are grown to a certain size, the nectaries and stamens drop off, and the beautiful large white petals change their colour to a deep green, and gradually thus become a calyx inclosing and defending the ripening seeds, hence it would seem that the white vessels of the corol served the office of exposing the blood to the action of the air, for the purposes of separating or producing the honey, wax, and prolific dust, and when these were no longer wanted, that these vessels coalesced like the placental vessels of animals after their birth, and thus ceased to perform that office, and lost at the same time their white colour. Why should they lose their white colour, unless they at the same time lost some other property besides that of defending the seed-vessel, which they still continue to defend?

6. From these observations I am led to doubt whether green leaves be absolutely necessary to the progress of the fruit-bud after the last year's leaves are fallen off. The green leaves serve as lungs to the shoots, and foster the new buds in their bosoms, whether these buds be leaf-buds or fruit-buds; but in the early spring the fruit-buds expand their corols, which are their lungs, and seem no longer to require green-leaves; hence the vine bears fruit at one joint without leaves, and puts out a leaf-bud at another joint without fruit. And I suppose the green leaves which rise out of the earth in the spring from the colchicum are for the purpose of producing the new bulb, and its placenta, and not for the giving maturity to the seed. When currant or gooseberry trees lose their leaves by the depredation of insects, the fruit continues to be formed, though less sweet and less in size.

7. From these facts it appears that the flower-bud after the corol falls off, (which is its lungs,) and the stamens and nectary along with it, becomes simply an uterus for the purpose of supplying the growing embryon with nourishment, together with a system of absorbent vessels which bring the juices of the earth to the footstalk of the fruit, and which there changes into an artery, for the purpose of distributing the sap for the secretion of the saccharine or farinaceous, or acescent materials for the use of the embryon. At the same time as all the vessels of the different buds of trees inosculate or communicate with each other, the fruit becomes sweeter and larger when the green leaves continue on the tree, but the mature flowers themselves, (the succeeding fruit not considered) perhaps suffer little injury from the green leaves being taken off, as some florists have observed.

8. That the vessels of different vegetable buds inosculate in various parts of their circulation, is rendered probable by the increased growth of one bud, when others in its vicinity are cut away; as it thus seems to receive the nourishment which was before divided amongst many.

NOTE XXXVIII.

VEGETABLE IMPREGNATION.

Love out his hour and leave his life in air.
                              CANTO IV. L. 472.

FROM the accurate experiments and observations of Spallanzani it appears that in the spartium junceum, rush-broom, the very minute seeds were discerned in the pod at least twenty days before the flower is in full bloom, that is twenty days before fecundation. At this time also the powder of the anthers was visible, but glued fast to their summits. The seeds however at this time, and for ten days after the blossom had fallen off, appeared to consist of a gelatinous substance. On the eleventh day after the falling of the blossom the seeds became heart shaped with the basis attached by an appendage to the pod, and a white point at the apex; this white point was on pressure found to be a cavity including a drop of liquor.

On the 25th day the cavity which at first appeared at the apex was much enlarged and still full of liquor, it also contained a very small semi-transparent body, of a yellowish colour, gelatinous, and fixed by its two opposite ends to the sides of the cavity.

In a month the seed was much enlarged and its shape changed from a heart to a kidney, the little body contained in the cavity was increased in bulk and was less transparent, and gelatinous, but there yet appeared no organization.

On the 40th day the cavity now grown larger was quite filled with the body, which was covered with a thin membrane; after this membrane was removed the body appeared of a bright green, and was easily divided by the point of a needle into two portions, which manifestly formed the two lobes, and within these attached to the lower part the exceedingly small plantule was easily perceived.

The foregoing observations evince, 1. That the seeds exist in the ovarium many days before fecundation. 2. That they remain for some time solid, and then a cavity containing a liquid is formed in them. 3. That after fecundation a body begins to appear within the cavity fixed by two points to the sides, which in process of time proves to be two lobes containing a plantule. 4. That the ripe seed consists of two lobes adhering to a plantule, and surrounded by a thin membrane which is itself covered with a husk or cuticle. Spallanzani's Dissertations, Vol. II. p. 253.

The analogy between seeds and eggs has long been observed, and is confirmed by the mode of their production. The egg is known to be formed within the hen long before its impregnation; C. F. Wolf asserts that the yolk of the egg is nourished by the vessels of the mother, and that it has from those its arterial and venous branches, but that after impregnation these vessels gradually become impervious and obliterated, and that new ones are produced from the fœtus and dispersed into the yolk. Haller's Physiolog. Tom. VIII. p. 94. The young seed after fecundation, I suppose, is nourished in a similar manner from the gelatinous liquor, which is previously deposited for that purpose; the uterus of the plant producing or secreting it into a reservoir or amnios in which the embryon is lodged, and the young embryon is furnished with vessels to absorb a part of it, as in the very early embryon in the animal uterus.

The spawn of frogs and of fish is delivered from the female before its impregnation. M. Bonnet says that the male salamander darts his semen into the water, where it forms a little whitish cloud which is afterwards received by the swoln anus of the female, and she is fecundated.—He adds that marine plants approach near to these animals, as the male does not project a fine powder but a liquor which in like manner forms a little cloud in the water.—And further adds, who knows but the powder of the stamina of certain plants may make some impression on certain germs belonging to the animal kingdom! Letter XLIII. to Spallanzani, Oeuvres Philos.

Spallanzani found that the seminal fluid of frogs and dogs even when diluted with much water retained its prolific quality. Whether this quality be simply a stimulus exciting the egg into animal action, which may be called a vivifying principle, or whether part of it be actually conjoined with the egg, is not yet determined, though the latter seems more probable from the frequent resemblance of the fœtus to the male parent. A conjunction however of both the male and female influence seems necessary for the purpose of reproduction throughout all organized nature, as well in hermaphrodite insects, microscopic animals, and polypi, and exists as well in the formation of the buds of vegetables as in the production of their seeds, which is ingeniously conceived and explained by Linneus. After having compared the flower to the larva of a butterfly, consisting of petals instead of wings, calyxes instead of wingsheaths, with the organs of re-production, and having shown the use of the farina in fecundating the egg or seed, he proceeds to explain the production of the bud. The calyx of a flower, he says, is an expansion of the outer bark, the petals proceed from the inner bark or rind, the stamens from the alburnum or woody circle, and the style from the pith. In the production and impregnation of the seed a commixture of the secretions of the stamens and style are necessary; and for the production of a bud he thinks the medulla or pith bursts its integuments and mixes with the woody part or alburnum, and these forcing their passage through the rind and bark constitute the bud or viviparous progeny of the vegetable. System of Vegetables translated from Linneus, p. 8.

It has been supposed that the embryon vegetable after fecundation, by its living activity or stimulus exerted on the vessels of the parent plant, may produce the fruit or seed-lobes, as the animal fœtus produces its placenta, and as vegetable buds may be supposed to produce their umbilical vessels or roots down the bark of the tree. This in respect to the production of the fruit surrounding the seeds of trees has been assimilated to the gall-nuts on oak leaves, and to the bedeguar on briars, but there is a powerful objection to this doctrine, viz. that the fruit of figs, all which are female in this country, grow nearly as large without fecundation, and therefore the embryon has in them no self-living principle.

NOTE XXXIX.

VEGETABLE GLANDULATION.

Seeks, where fine pores their dulcet balm distil.
CANTO IV. l. 533.

THE glands of vegetables which separate from their blood the mucilage, starch, or sugar for the placentation or support of their seeds, bulbs, and buds; or those which deposit their bitter, acrid, or narcotic juices for their defence from depredations of insects or larger animals; or those which secrete resins or wax for their protection from moisture or frosts, consist of vessels too fine for the injection or absorption of coloured fluids, and have not therefore yet been exhibited to the inspection even of our glasses, and can therefore only be known by their effects, but one of the most curious and important of all vegetable secretions, that of honey, is apparent to our naked eyes, though before the discoveries of Linneus the nectary or honey-gland had not even acquired a name.

The odoriferous essential oils of several flowers seem to have been designed for their defence against the depredations of insects, while their beautiful colours were a necessary consequence of the size of the particles of their blood, or of the tenuity of the exterior membrane of the petal. The use of the prolific dust is now well ascertained, the wax which covers the anthers prevents this dust from receiving moisture, which would make it burst prematurely and thence prevent its application to the stigma, as sometimes happens in moist years and is the cause of deficient fecundation both of our fields and orchards.

The universality of the production of honey in the vegetable world, and the very complicated apparatus which nature has constructed in many flowers, as well as the acrid or deleterious juices she has furnished those flowers with (as in the Aconite) to protect this honey from rain and from the depredations of insects, seem to imply that this fluid is of very great importance in the vegetable economy; and also that it was necessary to expose it to the open air previous to its reabsorption into the vegetable vessels.

In the animal system the lachrymal gland separates its fluid into the open air for the purpose of moistening the eye; of this fluid the part which does not exhale is absorbed by the puncta lachrymalia and carried into the nostrils; but as this is not a nutritive fluid the analogy goes no further than its secretion into the open air and its reabsorption into the system; every other secreted fluid in the animal body is in part absorbed again into the system, even those which are esteemed excrementitious, as the urine and perspirable matter, of which the latter is secreted, like the honey, into the external air. That the honey is a nutritious fluid, perhaps the most so of any vegetable production, appears from its great similarity to sugar, and from its affording sustenance to such numbers of insects, which live upon it solely during summer, and lay it up for their winter provision. These proofs of its nutritive nature evince the necessity of its reabsorption into the vegetable system for some useful purpose.

This purpose however has as yet escaped the researches of philosophical botanists. M. Pontedera believes it designed to lubricate the vegetable uterus, and compares the horn-like nectaries of some flowers to the appendicle of the cæcum Intestinum of animals. (Antholog. p. 49.) Others have supposed that the honey, when reabsorbed, might serve the purpose of the liquor amnii, or white of the egg, as a nutriment for the young embryon or fecundated seed in its early state of existence. But as the nectary is found equally general in male flowers as in female ones; and as the young embryon or seed grows before the petals and nectary are expanded, and after they fall off; and thirdly, as the nectary so soon falls off after the fecundation of the pistillum; these seem to be insurmountable objections to both the above-mentioned opinions.

In this state of uncertainty conjectures may be of use so far as they lead to further experiment and investigation. In many tribes of insects, as the silk-worm, and perhaps in all the moths and butterflies, the male and female parents die as soon as the eggs are impregnated and excluded; the eggs remaining to be perfected and hatched at some future time. The same thing happens in regard to the male and female parts of flowers; the anthers and filaments, which constitute the male part of the flower, and the stigma and style, which constitute the sensitive or amatorial organ of the female part of the flower, fall off and die as soon as the seeds are impregnated, and along with these the petals and nectary. Now the moths and butterflies above mentioned, as soon as they acquire the passion and the apparatus for the reproduction of their species, lose the power of feeding upon leaves as they did before, and become nourished by what?—by honey alone.

Hence we acquire a strong analogy for the use of the nectary or secretion of honey in the vegetable economy, which is, that the male parts of flowers, and the female parts, as soon as they leave their fetus-state, expanding their petals, (which constitute their lungs,) become sensible to the passion, and gain the apparatus for the reproduction of their species, and are fed and nourished with honey like the insects above described; and that hence the nectary begins its office of producing honey, and dies or ceases to produce honey at the same time with the birth and death of the stamens and the pistils; which, whether existing in the same or in different flowers, are separate and distinct animated beings.

Previous to this time the anthers with their filaments, and the stigmas with their styles, are in their fetus-state sustained by their placental vessels, like the unexpanded leaf-bud, with the seeds existing in the vegetable womb yet unimpregnated, and the dust yet unripe in the cells of the anthers. After this period they expand their petals, which have been shown above to constitute the lungs of the flower; the placental vessels, which before nourished the anthers and the stigmas, coalesce or cease to nourish them; and they now acquire blood more oxygenated by the air, obtain the passion and power of reproduction, are sensible to heat, and cold, and moisture, and to mechanic stimulus, and become in reality insects fed with honey, similar in every respect, except their being attached to the tree on which they were produced.

Some experiments I have made this summer by cutting out the nectaries of several flowers of the aconites before the petals were open, or had become much coloured; some of these flowers near the summit of the plants produced no seeds, others lower down produced seeds; but they were not sufficiently guarded from the farina of the flowers in their vicinity; nor have I had opportunity to try if these seeds would vegetate.

I am acquainted with a philosopher, who contemplating this subject, thinks it not impossible that the first insects were the anthers or stigmas of flowers; which had by some means loosed themselves from their parent plant, like the male flowers of Vallisneria; and that many other insects have gradually in long process of time been formed from these; some acquiring wings, others fins, and others claws, from their ceaseless efforts to procure their food, or to secure themselves from injury. He contends, that none of these changes are more incomprehensible than the transformation of tadpoles into frogs, and caterpillars into butterflies.

There are parts of animal bodies, which do not require oxygenated blood for the purpose of their secretions, as the liver; which for the production of bile takes its blood from the mesenteric veins, after it must have lost the whole or a great part of its oxygenation, which it had acquired in its passage through the lungs. In like manner the pericarpium, or womb of the flower, continues to secrete its proper juices for the present nourishment of the newly animated embryon-seed; and the saccharine, acescent, or starchy matter of the fruit or seed-lobes for its future growth; in the same manner as these things went on before fecundation; that is, without any circulation of juices in the petals, or production of honey in the nectary; these having perished and fallen off with the male and female apparatus for impregnation.

It is probable that the depredations of insects on this nutritious fluid must be injurious to the products of vegetation, and would be much more so, but that the plants have either acquired means to defend their honey in part, or have learned to make more than is absolutely necessary for their own economy. In the same manner the honey-dew on trees is very injurious to them; in which disease the nutritive fluid, the vegetable-sap juice, seems to be exuded by a retrograde motion of the cutaneous lymphatics, as in the sweating sickness of the last century. To prevent the depredation of insects on honey a wealthy man in Italy is said to have poisoned his neighbour's bees, perhaps by mixing arsenic with honey, against which there is a most flowery declamation in Quintilian, No. XIII. As the use of the wax is to preserve the dust of the anthers from moisture, which would prematurely burst them, the bees which collect this for the construction of the combs or cells, must on this account also injure the vegetation of a country where they too much abound.

It is not easy to conjecture why it was necessary that this secretion of honey should be exposed to the open air in the nectary or honey-cup, for which purpose so great an apparatus for its defence from insects and from showers became necessary. This difficulty increases when we recollect that the sugar in the joints of grass, in the sugar cane, and in the roots of beets, and in ripe fruits is produced without exposure to the air.—On supposition of its serving for nutriment to the anthers and stigmas it may thus acquire greater oxygenation for the purpose of producing greater powers of sensibility, according to a doctrine lately advanced by a French philosopher, who has endeavoured to show that the oxygene, or base of vital air, is the constituent principle of our power of sensibility.

So caterpillars are fed upon the common juices of vegetables found in their leaves, till they acquire the organs of reproduction, and then they feed on honey, all I believe except the silkworm, which in this country takes no nourishment after it becomes a butterfly. Thus also the maggot of the bee, according to the observations of Mr. Hunter, is fed with raw vegetable matter, called bee-bread, which is collected from the anthers of flowers, and laid up in cells for that purpose, till the maggot becomes a winged bee, acquires greater sensibility, and is fed with honey. Phil. Trans. 1792. See Zoonomia, Sect. XIII. on vegetable animation.

From this provision of honey for the male and female parts of flowers, and from the provision of sugar, starch, oil, and mucilage, in the fruits, seed-cotyledons, roots, and buds of plants laid up for the nutriment of the expanding fœtus, not only a very numerous class of insects, but a great part of the larger animals procure their food; and thus enjoy life and pleasure without producing pain to others, for these seeds or eggs with the nutriment laid up in them are not yet endued with sensitive life.

The secretions from various vegetable glands hardened in the air produce gums, resins, and various kinds of saccharine, saponaceous, and wax-like substances, as the gum of cherry or plum-trees, gum tragacanth from the astragalus tragacantha, camphor from the laurus camphora, elemi from amyris elemifera, aneme from hymenœa courbaril, turpentine from pistacia terebinthus, balsam of Mecca from the buds of amyris opobalsamum, branches of which are placed in the temples of the East on account of their fragrance, the wood is called xylobalsamum, and the fruit carpobalsamum; aloe from a plant of the same name; myrrh from a plant not yet described; the remarkably elastic resin is brought into Europe principally in the form of flasks, which look like black leather, and are wonderfully elastic, and not penetrable by water, rectified ether dissolves it; its flexibility is increased by warmth and destroyed by cold; the tree which yields this juice is the jatropha elastica, it grows in Guaiana and the neighbouring tracts of America; its juice is said to resemble wax in becoming soft by heat, but that it acquires no elasticity till that property is communicated to it by a secret art, after which it is poured into moulds, and well dried, and can no longer be rendered fluid by heat.—Mr. de la Borde physician at Cayenne has given this account. Manna is obtained at Naples from the fraxinus ornus, or manna-ash, it partly issues spontaneously, which is preferred, and partly exudes from wounds made purposely in the month of August, many other plants yield manna more sparingly; sugar is properly made from the saccharum officinale, or sugar-cane, but is found in the roots of beet and many other plants; American wax is obtained from the myrica cerifera, candle-berry myrtle, the berries are boiled in water, and a green wax separates, with lukewarm water the wax is yellow: the seeds of croton sebiferum are lodged in tallow; there are many other vegetable exsudations used in the various arts of dyeing, varnishing, tanning, lacquering, and which supply the shop of the druggist with medicines and with poisons.

There is another analogy, which would seem to associate plants with animals, and which perhaps belongs to this note on Glandulation; I mean the similarity of their digestive powers. In the roots of growing vegetables, as in the process of making malt, the farinaceous part of the seed is converted into sugar by the vegetable power of digestion in the same manner as the farinaceous matter of seeds is converted into sweet chyle by the animal digestion. The sap-juice which rises in the vernal months from the roots of trees through the alburnum or sap-wood, owes its sweetness I suppose to a similar digestive power of the absorbent system of the young buds. This exists in many vegetables in great abundance, as in vines, sycamore, birch, and most abundantly in the palm tree, (Isert's Voyage to Guinea,) and seems to be a similar fluid in all plants, as chyle is similar in all animals.

Hence as the digested food of vegetables consists principally of sugar, and from that is produced again their mucilage, starch, and oil, and since animals are sustained by these vegetable productions, it would seem that the sugar-making process carried on in vegetable vessels was the great source of life to all organized beings. And that if our improved chemistry should ever discover the art of making sugar from fossile or aerial matter without the assistance of vegetation, food for animals would then become as plentiful as water, and mankind might live upon the earth as thick as blades of grass, with no restraint to their numbers but the want of local room.

It would seem that roots fixed in the earth and leaves innumerable waving in the air were necessary for the decomposition of water, and the conversion of it into saccharine matter, which would have been not only cumbrous but totally incompatable with the locomotion of animal bodies. For how could a man or quadruped have carried on his head or back a forest of leaves, or have had long branching lacteal or absorbent vessels terminating in the earth? Animals therefore subsist on vegetables; that is, they take the matter so far prepared, and have organs to prepare it further for the purposes of higher animation, and greater sensibility. In the same manner the apparatus of green leaves and long roots were found inconvenient for the more animated and sensitive parts of vegetable-flowers, I mean the anthers and stigmas, which are therefore separated beings, endued with the passion and power of reproduction, with lungs of their own, and fed with honey, a food ready prepared by the long roots and green leaves of the plant, and presented to their absorbent mouths.

From this outline a philosopher may catch a glimpse of the general economy of nature; and like the mariner cast upon an unknown shore who rejoiced when he saw the print of a human foot upon the sand, he may cry out with rapture "A God dwells here."

VISIT OF HOPE

TO

SIDNEY COVE, NEAR BOTANY BAY.

REFERRED TO IN CANTO II. l. 317.

WHERE Sydney Cove her lucid bosom swells,
And with wide arms the indignant storm repels;
High on a rock amid the troubled air
HOPE stood sublime, and waved her golden hair;
Calm'd with her rosy smile the tossing deep,
And with sweet accents charm'd the winds to sleep;
To each wild plain she stretch'd her snowy band,
High-waving wood, and sea-encircled strand.
"Hear me," she cried, "ye rising realms! record
Time's opening scenes, and Truth's prophetic word.—
There shall broad streets their stately walls extend,
The circus widen, and the crescent bend;
There, ray'd from cities o'er the cultured land,
Shall bright canals, and solid roads expand.—
There the proud arch, colossus-like, bestride
Yon glittering streams, and bound the chafing tide;
Embellish'd villas crown the landscape-scene,
Farms wave with gold, and orchards blush between.—
There shall tall spires, and dome-capt towers ascend,
And piers and quays their massy structures blend;
While with each breeze approaching vessels glide,
And northern treasures dance on every tide!"—
Then ceased the nymph—tumultuous echoes roar,
And Joy's loud voice was heard from shore to shore—
Her graceful steps descending press'd the plain,
And Peace, and Art, and Labour, join'd her train.

Mr. Wedgwood, having been favoured by Sir Joseph Banks with a specimen of clay from Sydney Cove, has made a few medallions of it, representing Hope encouraging Art and Labour, under the influence of Peace, to pursue the employments necessary for rendering an infant colony secure and happy. The above verses were written by the author of The Botanic Garden, to accompany these medallions.

CONTENTS

OF THE

ADDITIONAL NOTES.

Note I.—Meteors.

There are four strata of the atmosphere, and four kinds of meteors. 1. Lightning is electric, exists in visible clouds, its short course, and red light. 2. Shooting stars exist in visible vapour, without sound, white light, have no luminous trains. 3. Twilight—fire-balls move thirty miles in a second, and are about sixty miles high, have luminous trains, occasioned by an electric spark passing between the aerial and inflammable strata of the atmosphere, and mixing them, and setting them on fire in its passage; attracted by volcanic eruptions; one thousand miles through such a medium resists less than a tenth of an inch of glass. 4. Northern lights not attracted to a point but diffused—their colours—passage of electric fire in vacuo dubious—Dr. Franklin's theory of northern lights countenanced in part by the supposition of a superior atmosphere of inflammable air—antiquity of their appearance—described in Maccabees.

Note II.—Primary Colours.

The rainbow was in part understood before Sir Isaac Newton—the seven colours were discovered by him—Mr. Galton's experiments on colours—manganese and lead produce colourless glass.

Note III.—Coloured Clouds.

The rays refracted by the convexity of the atmosphere—the particles of air and of water are blue—shadow by means of a candle in the day—halo round the moon in a fog—bright spot in the corneo of the eye—light from cat's eyes in the dark, from a horse's eyes in a cavern, coloured by the choroid coat within the eye.

Note IV.—Comets.

Tails of comets from rarefied vapour, like northern lights, from electricity—twenty millions of miles long—expected comet—72 comets already described.

Note V.—Sun's Rays.

Dispute about phlogiston—the sun the fountain from whence all phlogiston is derived—its rays not luminous till they arrive at our atmosphere—light owing to their combustion with air, whence an unknown acid—the sun is on fire only on its surface—the dark spots on it are excavations through its luminous crust.

Note VI.—Central Fires.

Sun's heat much less than that from the fire at the earth's centre—sun's heat penetrates but a few feet in summer—some mines are warm—warm springs owing to subterraneous fire—situations of volcanoes on high mountains—original nucleus of the earth—deep valleys of the ocean—distant perception of earthquakes—great attraction of mountains—variation of the compass—countenance the existence of a cavity or fluid lava within the earth.

Note VII.—Elementary Heat.

Combined and sensible heat—chemical combinations attract heat, solutions reject heat—ice cools boiling water six times as much as cold water cools it—cold produced by evaporation—heat by devaporation—capacities of bodies in respect to heat, 1. Existence of the matter of heat shown from the mechanical condensation and rarefaction of air, from the steam produced in exhausting a receiver, snow from rarefied air, cold from discharging an air-gun, heat from vibration or friction—2. Matter of heat analogous to the electric fluid in many circumstances, explains many chemical phenomena.

Note VIII.—Memnon's Lyre.

Mechanical impulse of light dubious—a glass tube laid horizontally before a fire revolves—pulse-glass suspended on a centre—black leather contracts in the sunshine—Memnon's statue broken by Cambyses.

Note IX.—Luminous Insects.

Eighteen species of glow-worm, their light owing to their respiration in transparent lungs—Acudia of Surinam gives light enough to read and draw by, use of its light to the insect—luminous sea insects adhere to the skin of those who bathe in the ports of Languedoc, the light may arise from putrescent slime.

Note X.—Phosphorus.

Discovered by Kunkel, Brandt, and Boyle—produced in respiration, and by luminous insects, decayed wood, and calcined shells—bleaching a slow combustion in which the water is decomposed—rancidity of animal'fat owing to the decomposition of water on its surface—aerated marine acid does not whiten or bleach the hand.

Note XI.—Steam-Engine.

Hero of Alexandria first applied steam to machinery, next a French writer in 1630, the Marquis of Worcester in 1655, Capt. Savery in 1689, Newcomen and Cawley added the piston—the improvements of Watt and Boulton—power of one of their large engines equal to two hundred horses.

Note XII.—Frost.

Expansion of water in freezing—injury done by vernal frosts—fish, eggs, seeds, resist congelation—animals do not resist the increase of heat—frosts do not meliorate the ground, nor are in general salubrious—damp air produces cold on the skin by evaporation—snow less pernicious to agriculture than heavy rains for two reasons.

Note XIII.—Electricity.

1. *Points* preferable to knobs for defence of buildings—why points emit the electric fluid—diffusion of oil on water—mountains are points on the earth's globe—do they produce ascending currents of air? 2. *Fairy-rings* explained—advantage of paring and burning ground.

Note XIV.—Buds and Bulbs.

A tree is a swarm of individual plants—vegetables are either oviparous or viviparous—are all annual productions like many kinds of insects?—hybernacula—a new bark annually produced over the old one in trees and in some herbaceous plants, whence their roots seem end-bitten—all bulbous roots perish annually—experiment on a tulip-root—both the leaf-bulbs and the flower-bulbs are annually renewed.

Note XV.—Solar Volcanoes.

The spots in the sun are cavities, some of them four thousand miles deep, and many times as broad—internal parts of the sun are not in a state of combustion—volcanoes visible in the sun—all the planets together are less than one six hundred and fiftieth part of the sun—planets were ejected from the sun by volcanoes—many reasons showing the probability of this hypothesis—Mr. Buffon's hypothesis that planets were struck off from the sun by comets—why no new planets are ejected from the sun—some comets and the georgium sidus may be of later date—sun's matter decreased——Mr. Ludlam's opinion, that it is possible the moon might be projected from the earth.

Note XVI.—Calcareous Earth.

High mountains and deep mines replete with shells—the earth's nucleus covered with limestone—animals convert water into limestone—all the calcareous earth in the world formed in animal and vegetable bodies—solid parts of the earth increase—the water decreases—tops of calcareous mountains dissolved—whence spar, marbles, chalk, stalactites—whence alabaster, fluor, flint, granulated limestone, from solution of their angles, and by attrition—tupha deposited on moss—limestones from shells with animals in them—liver-stone from fresh-water muscles—calcareous earth from land-animals and vegetables, as marl—beds of marble softened by fire—whence Bath-stone contains lime as well as limestone.

Note XVII.—Morasses.

The production of morasses from fallen woods—account by the Earl Cromartie of a new morass—morasses lose their salts by solution in water—then their iron—their vegetable acid is converted into marine, nitrous and vitriolic acids—whence gypsum, alum, sulphur—into fluor-acid, whence fluor—into silicious acid, whence flint, the sand of the sea, and other strata of siliceous sand and marl—some morasses ferment like new hay, and, subliming their phlogistic part, form coal-beds above and clay below, which are also produced by elutriation—shell fish in some morasses, hence shells sometimes found on coals and over iron-stone.

Note XVIII.—Iron.

Calciform ores—combustion of iron in vital air—steel from deprivation of vital air—welding—hardness—brittleness like Rupert's drops—specific levity—hardness and brittleness compared—steel tempered by its colours—modern production of iron, manganese, calamy—septaria of iron-stone ejected from volcanoes—red hot cannon balls.

Note XIX.—Flint.

1. *Siliceous rocks* from morasses—their cements. 2. *Siliceous trees*—coloured by iron or manganese—Peak-diamonds—Bristol-stones—flint in form of calcareous spar—has been fluid without much heat—obtained from powdered quartz and fluor-acid by Bergman and by Achard. 3. *Agates and onyxes* found in sand-rocks—of vegetable origin—have been in complete fusion—their concentric coloured circles not from superinduction but from congelation—experiment of freezing a solution of the blue vitriol—iron and manganese repelled in spheres as the nodule of flint cooled—circular stains of marl in salt-mines—some flint nodules resemble knots of wood or roots. 4. *Sand of the sea*—its acid from morasses—its base from shells. 5. *Chert or petrosilex* stratified in cooling—their colour and their acid from sea-animals—labradore-stone from mother-pearl. 6. *Flints in chalk-beds*—their form, colour, and acid, from the flesh of sea-animals—some are hollow and lined with crystals—contain iron—not produced by injection from without—coralloids converted to flint—French millstones—flints sometimes found in solid strata. 7. *Angles*

of sand destroyed by attrition and solution in steam—siliceous breccia cemented by solution in red hot water. 8. *Basaltes and granites* are ancient lavas—basaltes raised by its congelation not by subterraneous fire.

NOTE XX.—CLAY.

FIRE and water two great agents—stratification from precipitation—many stratified materials not soluble in water. 1. Stratification of lava from successive accumulation. 2. Stratifications of limestone from the different periods of time in which the shells were deposited. 3. Stratifications of coal, and clay, and sand-stone, and iron ores, not from currents of water, but from the production of morass-beds at different periods of time—morass-beds become ignited—their bitumen and sulphur is sublimed—the clay, lime, and iron remain: whence sand, marl, coal, white clay in valleys, and gravel beds, and some ochres, and some calcareous depositions owing to alluviation—clay from decomposed granite—from the lava of Vesuvius—from vitreous lavas.

XXI.—ENAMELS.

ROSE-COLOUR and purple from gold—precipitates of gold by alkaline salt preferable to those by tin—aurum fulminans long ground—tender colours from gold or iron not dissolved but suspended in the glass—cobalts—calces of cobalt and copper require a strong fire—Ka-o-lin and Pe-tun-tse the same as our own materials.

NOTE XXII.—PORTLAND VASE.

ITS figures do not allude to private history—they represent a part of the Eleusinian mysteries—marriage of Cupid and Psyche—procession of torches—the figures in one compartment represent Mortal Life in the act of expiring, and Humankind attending to her with concern—Adam and Eve hieroglyphic figures—Abel and Cain other hieroglyphic figures—on the other compartment is represented Immortal Life, the Manes or Ghost descending into Elysium is led on by Divine Love, and received by Immortal Life, and conducted to Pluto—Trees of Life and Knowledge are emblematical—the figure at the bottom is of Atis, the first great Hierophant, or teacher of mysteries.

NOTE XXIII.—COAL.

1. A FOUNTAIN of fossile tar in Shropshire—has been distilled from the coal-beds beneath, and condensed in the cavities of a sand rock—the coal beneath is deprived of its bitumen in part—bitumen sublimed at Matlock into cavities lined with spar. 2. Coal has been exposed to heat—woody fibres and vegetable seeds in coal at Bovey and Polesworth—upper part of coal-beds more bituminous at Beaudesert—thin stratum of as phaltum near Caulk—upper part of coal-bed worse at Alfreton—upper stratum of no value at Widdrington—alum at West-Hallum—at Bilston. 3. Coal at Coalbrooke-Dale has been immersed in the sea, shown by sea-shells—marks of violence in the colliery at Mendip and at Ticknal—Lead ore and spar in coal-beds—gravel over coal near Litchfield—Coal produced from morasses shown by fern-leaves, and bog-shells, and muscle-shells—by some parts of coal being still woody—from Loch Neah and Bovey, and the temple of the devil—fixed alkali—oil.

NOTE XXIV.—GRANITE.

GRANITE the lowest stratum of the earth yet known—porphyry, trap, moor-stone, whin-stone, slate, basaltes, all volcanic productions dissolved in red-hot water—volcanoes in granite strata—differ from the heat of morasses from fermentation—the nucleus of the earth ejected from the sun—was the sun originally a planet?—supposed section of the globe.

NOTE XXV.—EVAPORATION.

1. SOLUTION of water in air—in the matter of heat—pulse-glass. 2. Heat is the principal cause of evaporation—thermometer cooled by evaporation of ether—heat given from steam to the worm-tub—warmth accompanying rain. 3. Steam condensed on the eduction of heat—moisture on cold walls—south-west and north-east winds. 4. Solution of salt and of blue vitriol in the matter of heat. II. Other vapours may precipitate steam and form rain. 1. Cold the principal cause of devaporation—hence the steam dissolved in heat is precipitated, but that dissolved in air remains even in frosts—south-west wind. 2. North-east winds mixing with south-west winds produce rain—because the cold particles of air from the north-east acquire some of the matter of heat from the south-west winds. 3. Devaporation from mechanical expansion of air, as in the receiver of an air-pump—summer clouds appear and vanish—when the barometer sinks without change of wind the weather becomes colder. 4. Solution of water in electric fluid dubious. 5. Barometer sinks from the lessened gravity of the air, and from the rain having less pressure as it falls—a mixture of a solution of water in calorique with an aerial solution of water is lighter than dry air—breath of animals in cold weather why condensed into visible vapour and dissolved again.

NOTE XXVI.—SPRINGS.

LOWEST strata of the earth appear on the highest hills—springs from dews sliding between them—mountains are colder than plains—1. from their being insulated in the air—2. from their enlarged surface—3. from the rarety of the air it becomes a better conductor of heat—4. by the air on mountains being mechanically rarefied as it ascends—5. gravitation of the matter of heat—6. the dashing of clouds against hills—of fogs against trees—springs stronger in hot days with cold nights—streams from subterranean caverns—from beneath the snow on the Alps.

NOTE XXVII.—SHELL-FISH.

THE armour of the echinus moveable—holds itself in storms to stones by 1200 or 2000 strings—nautilus rows and sails—renders its shell buoyant—pinna and cancer—byssus of the ancients was the beard of the pinna—as fine as the silk is spun by the silk-worm—gloves made of it—the beard of muscles produces sickness—Indian weed—tendons of rat's tails.

NOTE XXVIII.—STURGEON.

STURGEON'S mouth like a purse—without teeth—tendrils like worms hang before his lips, which entice small fish and sea insects mistaking them for worms—his skin used for covering carriages—isinglass made from it—caviare from the spawn.

Note XXIX.—Oil on Water.

Oil and water do not touch—a second drop of oil will not diffuse itself on the preceding one—hence it stills the waves—divers for pearl carry oil in their mouths—oil on water produces prismatic colours—oiled cork circulates on water—a phial of oil and water made to oscillate.

Note XXX.—Ship-Worm.

The teredo has calcareous jaws—a new enemy—they perish when they meet together in their ligneous canals—United Provinces alarmed for the piles of the banks of Zealand—were destroyed by a severe winter.

Note XXXI.—Maelstrom.

A whirlpool on the coast of Norway—passes through a subterraneous cavity—less violent when the tide is up—eddies become hollow in the middle—heavy bodies are thrown out by eddies—light ones retained—oil and water whirled in a phial—hurricanes explained.

Note XXXII.—Glaciers.

Snow in contact with the earth is in a state of thaw—ice-houses—rivers from beneath the snow—rime in spring vanishes by its contact with the earth—and snow by its evaporation and contact with the earth—moss vegetates beneath the snow—and Alpine plants perish at Upsal for want of snow.

Note XXXIII.—Winds.

Air is perpetually subject to increase and to diminution—oxygene is perpetually produced from vegetables in the sunshine, and from clouds in the light, and from water—azote is perpetually produced from animal and vegetable putrefaction, or combustion—from springs of water—volatile alkali—fixed alkali—sea-water—they are both perpetually diminished by their contact with the soil, producing nitre—oxygene is diminished in the production of all acids—azote by the growth of animal bodies—charcoal in burning consumes double its weight of pure air—every barrel of red-lead absorbs 2000 cubic feet of vital air—air obtained from variety of substances by Dr. Priestley—officina aeris in the polar circle, and at the Line. *South-west winds*—their westerly direction from the less velocity of the earth's surface—the contrary in respect to north-east winds—South-west winds consist of regions of air from the south—and North-east winds of regions of air from the north—when the south-west prevails for weeks, and the barometer sinks to 28, what becomes of above one-fifteenth part of the atmosphere? 1. It is not carried back by superior currents—2. Not from its loss of moisture—3. Not carried over the pole 4. Not owing to atmospheric tides or mountains 5. It is absorbed at the polar circle—hence south-west winds and rain—south-west sometimes cold. *North-east winds* consist of air from the north—cold by the evaporation of ice—are dry winds—1. Not supplied by superior currents—2. The whole atmosphere increased in quantity by air set at liberty from its combinations in the polar circles. *South-east winds* consist of north winds driven back. *North-west winds* consist of south-west winds driven back—north-west winds of America bring frost—owing to a vertical spiral eddy of air between the eastern coast and the Apalachian mountains—hence the greater cold of North America. *Trade-winds*—air over the line always hotter than at the tropics—trade-winds gain their easterly direction from the greater velocity of the earth's surface at the line—not supplied by superior currents—supplied by decomposed water in the sun's great light—1. Because there are no constant rains in the track of the trade-winds—because there is no condensible vapour above three or four miles high at the Line. *Monsoons and tornadoes*—some places at the tropic become warmer when the sun is vertical than at the line, hence the air ascends, supplied on one side by the north-east winds, and on the other by the south-west—whence an ascending eddy or tornado, raising water from the sea, or sand from the desert, and incessant rains—air diminished to the northward produces south-west winds—tornadoes from heavier air above sinking through lighter air below, which rises through a perforation—hence trees are thrown down in a narrow line of twenty or forty yards broad, the sea rises like a cone, with great rain and lightning. *Land and sea breezes*—sea less heated than land—tropical islands more heated in the day than the sea, and are cooled more in the night. *Conclusion*—irregular winds from other causes—only two original winds north and south—different sounds of north-east and south-west winds—A bear or dragon in the arctic circle that swallows at times and disembogues again above one-fifteenth part of the atmosphere—wind instruments—recapitulation.

Note XXXIV.—Vegetable Perspiration.

Pure air from Dr. Priestley's vegetable matter, and from vegetable leaves, owing to decomposition of water—the hydrogene retained by the vegetables—plants in the shade are *tanned* green by the sun's light—animal skins are *tanned* yellow by the retention of hydrogene—much pure air from dew on a sunny morning—bleaching why sooner performed on cotton than linen—bees' wax bleached—metals calcined by decomposition of water—oil bleached in the light becomes yellow again in the dark—nitrous acid coloured by being exposed to the sun—vegetables perspire more than animals, hence in the sunshine they purify air more by their perspiration than they injure it by their respiration—they grow fastest in their sleep.

Note XXXV.—Vegetable Placentation.

Buds the viviparous offspring of vegetables—placentation in bulbs and seeds—placentation of buds in the roots, hence the rising of sap in the spring, as in vines, birch, which ceases as soon as the leaves expand—production of the leaf of horse-chesnut, and of its new bud—oil of vitriol on the bud of mimosa killed the leaf also—placentation shown from the sweetness of the sap—no umbilical artery in vegetables.

Note XXXVI.—Vegetable Circulation.

Buds set in the ground will grow if prevented from bleeding to death by a cement—vegetables require no muscles of locomotion, no stomach or bowels, no general system of veins—they have, 1. Three systems of absorbent vessels—2. Two pulmonary systems—3. Arterial systems—4. Glands—5. Organs of reproduction—6. Muscles. I. Absorbent system evinced by experiments by coloured absorptions in fig-tree and picris—called air vessels erroneously—spiral structure of absorbent vessels—retrograde motion of them like the throats of cows. II. Pulmonary arteries in the leaves, and pulmonary veins—no general system of veins shown by experiment—experiment tending to confirm the existence of such a system—no heart—the arteries act like the vena portarum of the liver—pulmonary system in the petals of flowers—circulation owing to living irritability—vegetable absorption more powerful than animal, as in vines—not by capillary attraction.

Note XXXVII.—Vegetable Respiration.

I. Leaves not perspiratory organs, nor excretory ones—lungs of animals. 1. Great surfaces of leaves. 2. Vegetable blood changes colour in the leaves—experiment with spurge—with picris. 3. Upper surface of the leaf only acts as a respiratory organ. 4. Upper surface repels moisture—leaves laid on water. 5. Leaves killed by oil like insects—muscles at the foot stalks of leaves. 6. Use of light to vegetable leaves—experiments of Priestley, Ingenhouz, and Scheele. 7. Vegetable circulation similar to that of fish. II. Another pulmonary system belongs to flowers—colours of flowers. 1. Vascular structure of the corol. 2. Glands producing honey, wax, &c. perish with the corol. 3. Many flowers have no green leaves attending them, as colchicum. 4. Corols not for the defence of the stamens. 5. Corol of Helleborus Niger changes to a calyx. 6. Green leaves not necessary to the fruit-bud—green leaves of colchicum belong to the new bulb, not to the flower. 7. Flower-bud after the corol falls is simply an uterus—mature flowers not injured by taking off the green leaves. 8. Inosculation of vegetable vessels.

Note XXXVIII.—Vegetable Impregnation.

Seeds in broom discovered twenty days before the flower opens—progress of the seed after impregnation—seeds exist before fecundation—analogy between seeds and eggs—progress of the egg within the hen—spawn of frogs and fishes—male salamander—marine plants project a liquor not a powder—seminal fluid diluted with water, if a stimulus only? Male and female influence necessary in animals, insects, and vegetables, both in production of seeds and buds—does the embryon seed produce the surrounding fruit, like insects in gall-nuts?

Note XXXIX.—Vegetable Glandulation.

Vegetable glands cannot be injected with coloured fluids—essential oil—wax—honey—nectary, its complicate apparatus—exposes the honey to the air like the lacrymal gland—honey is nutritious—the male and female parts of flowers copulate and die like moths and butterflies, and are fed like them with honey—anthers supposed to become insects—depredation of the honey and wax injurious to plants—honey-dew—honey oxygenated by exposure to air—necessary for the production of sensibility—the provision for the embryon plant of honey, sugar, starch, &c. supplies food to numerous classes of animals—various vegetable secretions, as gum tragacanth, camphor, elemi, anime, turpentine, balsam of Mecca, aloe, myrrh, elastic resin, manna, sugar, wax, tallow, and many other concrete juices—vegetable digestion—chemical production of sugar would multiply mankind—economy of nature.

END OF PART I.

THE BOTANIC GARDEN;

PART II.

CONTAINING

THE LOVES OF THE PLANTS;

A POEM,

WITH PHILOSOPHICAL NOTES.

Vivunt in Venerem frondes; nemus omne per altum
Felix arbor amat; nutant ad mutua Palmæ
Fœdera, populeo suspirat Populus ictu,
Et Platani Platanis, Alnoque assibilat Alnus.
CLAUD. EPITH.

PREFACE.

Linnæus has divided the vegetable world into 24 Classes; these classes into about 120 Orders; these Orders contain about 2000 Families, or Genera; and these Families about 20,000 Species; besides the innumerable Varieties, which the accidents of climate or cultivation have added to these species.

The Classes are distinguished from each other in this ingenious system, by the number, situation, adhesion, or reciprocal proportion of the males in each flower. The Orders, in many of these Classes, are distinguished by the number, or other circumstances of the females. The Families, or Genera, are characterized by the analogy of all the parts of the flower or fructification. The Species are distinguished by the foliage of the plant; and the Varieties by any accidental circumstance of colour, taste, or odour; the seeds of these do not always produce plants similar to the parent; as in our numerous fruit trees and garden flowers; which are propagated by grafts or layers.

The first eleven Classes include the plants, in whose flowers both the sexes reside; and in which the Males or Stamens are neither united, nor unequal in height when at maturity; and are therefore distinguished from each other simply by the number of males in each flower, as is seen in the annexed Plate, copied from the Dictionnaire Botanique of M. Bulliard, in which the numbers of each division refer to the Botanic Classes.

CLASS I. One Male, *Monandria*; includes the plants which possess but one Stamen in each flower.
II. Two Males, *Diandria*. Two Stamens.
III. Three Males, *Triandria*. Three Stamens.
IV. Four Males, *Tetrandria*. Four Stamens.
V. Five Males, *Pentandria*. Five Stamens.
VI. Six Males, *Hexandria*. Six Stamens.
VII. Seven Males, *Heptandria*. Seven Stamens.
VIII. Eight Males, *Octandria*. Eight Stamens.
IX. Nine Males, *Enneandria*. Nine Stamens
X. Ten Males, *Decandria*. Ten Stamens.
XI. Twelve Males, *Dodecandria*. Twelve Stamens.

The next two Classes are distinguished not only by the number of equal and disunited males, as in the above eleven Classes, but require an additional circumstance to be attended to, viz. whether the males or stamens be situated on the calyx, or not.
XII. Twenty Males, *Icosandria*. Twenty Stamens inserted on the calyx or flower-cup; as is well seen in the last Figure of No. xii. in the annexed Plate.
XIII. Many Males, *Polyandria*. From 20 to 100 Stamens, which do not adhere to the calyx; as is well seen in the first Figure of No. xiii. in the annexed Plate.

In the next two Classes, not only the number of stamens are to be observed, but the reciprocal proportions in respect to height.
XIV. Two Powers, *Didynamia*. Four Stamens, of which two are lower than the other two; as is seen in the two first Figures of No. xiv.
XV. Four Powers, *Tetradynamia*. Six Stamens; of which four are taller, and the two lower ones opposite to each other; as is seen in the third Figure of the upper row in No. xv.

The five subsequent Classes are distinguished not by the number of the males, or stamens, but by their union or adhesion, either by their anthers or filaments, or to the female or pistil.
XVI. One Brotherhood, *Monadelphia*. Many Stamens united by their filaments into one company; as in the second Figure below of No. xvi.
XVII. Two Brotherhoods, *Diadelphia*. Many Stamens united by their filaments into two companies: in the uppermost Fig. No. xvii.
XVIII. Many Brotherhoods, *Polyadelphia*. Many Stamens united by their filaments into three or more companies, as in No. xviii.

XIX. CONFEDERATE MALES, *Syngenesia.*—Many Stamens united by their anthers; as in the first and second Figures, No. xix.

XX. FEMININE MALES, *Gynandria.* Many Stamens attached to the pistil.

The next three Classes consist of plants, whose flowers contain but one of the sexes; or if some of them contain both sexes, there are other flowers accompanying them of but one sex.

XXI. ONE HOUSE, *Monœcia.* Male flowers and female flowers separate, but on the same plant.

XXII. TWO HOUSES, *Diœcia.* Male flowers and female flowers separate on different plants.

XXIII. POLYGAMY, *Polygamia.* Male and female flowers on one or more plants, which have at the same time flowers of both sexes.

The last Class contains the plants whose flowers are not discernible.

XXIV. CLANDESTINE MARRIAGE, *Cryptogamia.*

The Orders of the first thirteen Classes are founded on the number of Females, or Pistils, and distinguished by the names, ONE FEMALE, *Monogynia.* Two FEMALES, *Digynia.* THREE FEMALES, *Trigynia,* &c. as is seen in No. i. which represents a plant of one male, one female; and in the first figure of No xi. which represents a flower with twelve males, and three females; (for, where the pistils have no apparent styles, the summits, or stigmas, are to be numbered) and in the first figure of No. xii. which represents a flower with twenty males and many females; and in the last Figure of the same No. which has twenty males and one female; and in No. xiii. which represents a flower with many males and many females.

The Class of TWO POWERS is divided into two natural Orders; into such as have their seeds naked at the bottom of the calyx, or flower-cup; and such as have their seeds covered; as is seen in No. xiv. Fig. 3. and 5.

The Class of FOUR POWERS is divided also into two Orders; in one of these the seeds are inclosed in a silicule, as in *Shepherd's-purse.* No. xv. Fig. 5. In the other they are inclosed in a silique, as in *Wall-flower.* Fig. 4

In all the other Classes, excepting the Classes Confederate Males, and Clandestine Marriage, as the character of each class is distinguished by the situations of the males; the character of the Orders is marked by the numbers of them. In the Class ONE BROTHERHOOD, No. xvi. Fig. 3. the Order of ten males is represented. And in the Class TWO BROTHERHOODS, No. xvii. Fig. 2. the Order ten males is represented.

In the Class CONFEDERATE MALES, the Orders are chiefly distinguished by the fertility or barrenness of the florets of the disk, or ray of the compound flower.

And in the Class of CLANDESTINE MARRIAGE the four Orders are termed FERNS, MOSSES, FLAGS, and FUNGUSSES.

The Orders are again divided into Genera, or Families, which are all natural associations, and are described from the general resemblances of the parts of fructification, in respect to their number, form, situation, and reciprocal proportion. These are the Calyx, or Flower-cup, as seen in No. iv. Fig. 1. No. x. Fig. 1. and 3. No. xiv. Fig. 1, 2, 3, 4. Second, the Corol, or Blossom, as seen in No. i, ii. &c. Third, the Males or Stamens, as in No. iv. Fig. 1. and No. viii. Fig. 1. Fourth, the Females, or Pistils, as in No. i. No. xii. Fig. 1. No. xiv. Fig. 3. No. xv. Fig. 3. Fifth, the Pericarp or Fruit-vessel, as No. xv. Fig. 4. 5. No. xvii. Fig. 2. Sixth, the Seeds.

The illustrious author of the Sexual System of Botany, in his preface to his account of the Natural Orders, ingeniously imagines, that one plant of each Natural Order was created in the beginning; and that the intermarriages of these produced one plant of every Genus, or Family: and that the intermarriages of these Generic, or Family plants, produced all the species: and lastly, that the intermarriages of the individuals of the Species produced the Varieties.

In the following POEM, the name or number of the Class or Order of each plant is printed in italics; as " *Two* brother swains": *One* House contains them:' and the word "*secret*" expresses the Class of Clandestine Marriage.

The Reader, who wishes to become further acquainted with this delightful field of science, is advised to study the works of the Great Master, and is apprized that they are exactly and literally translated into English, by a Society at Litchfield, in four Volumes Octavo.

To the System of Vegetables is prefixed a copious explanation of all the terms used in Botany, translated from a thesis of Dr. Elmagreen, with the plates and references from the Philosophia Botanica of Linneus.

To the Families of Plants is prefixed a Catalogue of the names of plants, and other Botanic terms, carefully accented, to show their proper pronunciation; a work of great labour, and which was much wanted, not only by beginners, but by proficients in Botany.

THE LOVES OF THE PLANTS.

CANTO I.

Descend, ye hovering Sylphs! aerial quires,
And sweep with little hands your silver lyres;
With fairy footsteps print your grassy rings,
Ye Gnomes! accordant to the tinkling strings:
While in soft notes I tune to oaten reed
Gay hopes, and amorous sorrows of the mead.—
From giant oaks, that wave their branches dark,
To the dwarf moss that clings upon their bark,
What beaux and beauties crowd the gaudy groves,
And woo and win their vegetable loves.   10
How snow drops cold, and blue-eyed harebells blend
Their tender tears, as o'er the stream they bend;
The love-sick violet, and the primrose pale,
Bow their sweet heads, and whisper to the gale;
With secret sighs the virgin lily droops,
And jealous cowslips hang their tawny cups.
How the young rose in beauty's damask pride
Drinks the warm blushes of his bashful bride;
With honey'd lips enamour'd woodbines meet,
Clasp with fond arms, and mix their kisses sweet.—   20

Stay thy soft murmuring waters, gentle rill;
Hush, whispering winds; ye rustling leaves, be still;
Rest, silver butterflies, your quivering wings;
Alight, ye beetles, from your airy rings;
Ye painted moths, your gold-eyed plumage furl,
Bow your wide horns, your spiral trunks uncurl;
Glitter, ye glow-worms, on your mossy beds;
Descend, ye spiders, on your lengthen'd threads;   [shells;
Slide here, ye horned snails, with varnish'd
Ye bee-nymphs, listen in your waxen cells!   30

Botanic Muse! who in this latter age
Led by your airy hand the Swedish sage,
Bade his keen eye your secret haunts explore
On dewy dell, high wood, and winding shore;
Say on each leaf how tiny graces dwell;
How laugh the pleasures in a blossom's bell;
How insect loves arise on cobweb wings,
Aim their light shafts, and point their little stings.

" First the tall Canna lifts his curled brow
Erect to heaven, and plights his nuptial vow;
The virtuous pair, in milder regions born,   41
Dread the rude blast of autumn's icy morn;
Round the chill fair he folds his crimson vest,
And clasps the timorous beauty to his breast.

Thy love, Callitriche, *two* virgins share,
Smit with thy starry eye and radiant hair;—
On the green margin sits the youth, and laves
His floating train of tresses in the waves;
Sees his fair features paint the streams that pass,
And bends for ever o'er the watery glass.   50

Two brother swains, of Collin's gentle name,
The same their features, and their forms the same,

Vegetable loves. l. 10. Linneus, the celebrated Swedish naturalist, has demonstrated, that all flowers contain families of males or females, or both; and on their marriages has constructed his invaluable system of Botany.

Canna. l. 39. Cane, or Indian reed. One male and one female inhabit each flower. It is brought from between the tropics to our hot-houses, and bears a beautiful crimson flower; the seeds are used as shot by the Indians, and are strung for prayer-beads in some Catholic countries.

Callitriche. l. 45. Fine-hair, stargrass. One male and two females inhabit each flower. The upper leaves grow in form of a star, whence it is called stellaria aquatica by Ray and others; its stems and leaves float far on the water, and are often so matted together, as to bear a person walking on them. The male sometimes lives in a separate flower.

Collinsonia, l. 51. Two males one female. I have lately observed a very singular circumstance in this flower; the two males stand widely diverging from each other, and the female bends herself into contact first with one of them, and after some time leaves this and ap-

With rival love for fair Collinia sigh,
Knit the dark brow, and roll the unsteady eye.
With sweet concern the pitying beauty mourns,
And soothes with smiles the jealous pair by turns.

Sweet blooms Genista in the myrtle shade,
And *ten* fond brothers woo the haughty maid.
Two knights before thy fragrant altar bend,
Adored Melissa! and *two* squires attend.— 60
Meadia's soft chains *five* suppliant beaux confess,
And hand in hand the laughing belle address;

Alike to all she bows with wanton air,
Rolls her dark eye, and waves her golden hair.

Woo'd with long care, Curcuma, cold and shy
Meets her fond husband with averted eye:

---

plies herself to the other. It is probable one of the anthers may be mature before the other. See note on Gloriosa, and Genista. The females in Nigella, devil in the bush, are very tall compared to the males; and bending over in a circle to them, give the flower some resemblance to a regal crown. The female of the epilobium augustifolium, rose bay willow herb, bends down amongst the males for several days, and becomes upright again when impregnated.

Genista. l. 57. Dyer's broom. Ten males and one female inhabit this flower. The males are generally united at the bottom in two sets, whence Linneus has named the class "two brotherhoods." In the genista, however, they are united in but one set. The flowers of this class are called papilionaceous, from their resemblance to a butterfly, as the pea-blossom. In the Spartium Scoparium, or common broom, I have lately observed a curious circumstance, the males or stamens are in two sets, one set rising a quarter of an inch above the other; the upper set does not arrive at their maturity so soon as the lower, and the stigma, or head of the female, is produced amongst the upper or immature set; but as soon as the pistil grows tall enough to burst open the keel-leaf, or hood of the flower, it bends itself round in an instant, like a French horn, and inserts its herd, or stigma, amongst the lower or mature set of males. The pistil, or female, continues to grow in length; and in a few days the stigma arrives again amongst the upper set, by the time they become mature. This wonderful contrivance is readily seen by opening the keel-leaf of the flowers of broom before they burst spontaneously. See note on Collinsonia, Gloriosa, Draba.

Melissa. l. 60. Balm. In each flower there are four males and one female; two of the males stand higher than the other two; whence the name of the class "two powers." I have observed in the ballota, and others of this class, that the two lower stamens, or males, become mature before the two higher. After they have shed their dust, they turn themselves away outwards, and the pistil, or female, continuing to grow a little taller, is applied to the upper stamens. See Gloriosa and Genista.

All the plants of this class, which have naked seeds, are aromatic. The Marum and Nepeta are particularly delightful to cats; no other brute animals seem delighted with any odours but those of their food or prey.

Meadia. l. 61. Dodecatheon. American cowslip. Five males and one female. The males, or anthers, touch each other. The uncommon beauty of this flower occasioned Linneus to give it a name signifying the twelve heathen gods; and Dr. Mead to affix his own name to it.

The pistil is much longer than the stamens, hence the flower-stalks have their elegant bend, that the stigma may hang downwards to receive the fecundating dust of the anthers. And the petals are so beautifully turned back to prevent the rain or dew-drops from sliding down and washing off this dust prematurely; and at the same time exposing it to the light and air. As soon as the seeds are formed, it erects all the flower-stalks to prevent them from falling out, and thus loses the beauty of its figure. Is this a mechanical effect, or does it indicate a vegetable storge to preserve its offspring? See note on Ilex, and Gloriosa.

In the meadia, the borago, cyclamen, solanum, and many others, the filaments are very short compared with the style. Hence it became necessary, first, to furnish the stamens with long anthers. 2d. To lengthen and bend the peduncle or flower-stalk, that the flower might hang downwards. 3d. To reflect the petals. 4th. To erect these peduncles when the germ was fecundated. We may reason upon this by observing, that all this apparatus might have been spared, if the filaments alone had grown longer; and that thence in these flowers that the filaments are the most unchangeable parts; and that thence their comparative length, in respect to the style, would afford a most permanent mark of their generic character.

Curcuma. l. 65. Turmeric. One male and one female inhabit this flower; but there are besides four imperfect males, or filaments without anthers upon them, called by Linneus eunuchs. The flax of our country has ten filaments, and but five of them are terminated with anthers; the Portugal flax has ten perfect males or stamens; the verbena of our country has four males; that of Sweden has but two; the genus albuca, the bignonia catalpa, gratiola, and hemlock-leaved geranium, have only half their filaments crowned with anthers. In like manner the florets, which form the rays of the flowers of the order frustraneous polygamy of the class syngenesia, or confederate males, as the sunflower, are furnished with a style only, and no stigma: and are thence barren. There is also a style without a stigma in the whole order diœcia gynandria; the male flowers of which are thence barren. The opulus is another plant which contains some unprolific flowers. In like manner some tribes of insects have males, females, and neuters among them; as bees, wasps, ants.

There is a curious circumstance belonging to the class of insects which have two wings, or diptera, analogous to the rudiments of stamens above described; viz. two little knobs are found placed each on a stalk or peduncle, generally under a little arched scale; which appear to be rudiments of hinder wings, and are called by Linneus halteres, or poisers, a term of his introduction. A. T. Bladh. Amæn. Acad. V. 7. Other animals have marks of having in a long process of time undergone changes in some parts of their bodies, which may have been effected to accommodate them to new ways of procuring

Four beardless youths the obdurate beauty move
With soft attentions of Platonic love.

With vain desires the pensive Alcea burns,
And, like sad Eloisa, loves and mourns. 70
The freckled Iris owns a fiercer flame,
And *three* unjealous husbands wed the dame.
Cupressus dark disdains his dusky bride,
One dome contains them, but *two* beds divide.

The proud Osyris flies his angry fair,
Two houses hold the fashionable pair.

With strange deformity Plantago treads,
A monster-birth! and lifts his hundred heads
Yet with soft love a gentle belle he charms,
And clasps the beauty in his hundred arms. 80
So hapless Desdemona, fair and young,
Won by Othello's captivating tongue,
Sigh'd o'er each strange and piteous tale, distress'd,
And sunk enamour'd on his sooty breast.

Two gentle shepherds and their sister-wives
With thee, Anthoxa! lead ambrosial lives;

---

their food. The existence of teats on the breasts of male animals, and which are generally replete with a thin kind of milk at their nativity, is a wonderful instance of this kind. Perhaps all the productions of nature are in their progress to greater perfection—an idea countenanced by the modern discoveries and deductions concerning the progressive formation of the solid parts of the terraqueous globe, and consonant to the dignity of the Creator of all things.

Alcea. l. 69. Flore pleno. Double hollyhock. The double flowers, so much admired by the florists, are termed by the botanist vegetable monsters; in some of these the petals are multiplied three or four times, but without excluding the stamens, hence they produce some seeds, as campanula and stramoneum; but in others the petals become so numerous as totally to exclude the stamens or males; as caltha, peonia, and alcea; these produce no seeds, and are termed eunuchs. Philos. Botan. No. 150.

These vegetable monsters are formed in many ways; 1st. By the multiplication of the petals and the exclusion of the nectaries, as in larkspur. 2d. By the multiplication of the nectaries and exclusion of the petals, as in columbine. 3d. In some flowers growing in cymes, the wheel-shape flowers in the margin are multiplied to the exclusion of the bell-shape flowers in the centre, as in gelder-rose. 4th. By the elongation of the florets in the centre. Instances of both these are found in daisy and feverfew; for other kinds of vegetable monsters, see Plantago.

The perianth is not changed in double flowers, hence the genus or family may be often discovered by the calyx, as in hepatica, ranunculus, alcea. In those flowers, which have many petals the lowest series of the petals remains unchanged in respect to number; hence the natural number of the petals is easily discovered. As in poppies, roses, and nigella, or devil in a bush. Phil. Bot. p. 128.

Iris. l. 71. Flower de luce. Three males, one female. Some of the species have a beautifully freckled flower; the large stigma or head of the female covers the three males, counterfeiting a petal with its divisions.

Cupressus. l. 78. Cypress. One house. The males live in separate flowers, but on the same plants. The males of some of these plants, which are in separate flowers from the females, have an elastic membrane; which disperses their dust to a considerable distance, when the anthers burst open. This dust, on a fine day, may often be seen like a cloud hanging round the common nettle. The males and females of all the cone bearing plants are in separate flowers, either on the same or on different plants; they produce resins, and many of them are supposed to supply the most durable timber: what is called Venice-turpentine is obtained from the larch by wounding the bark about two feet from the ground, and catching it as it exsudes; sandarach is procured from common juniper; and incense from a juniper with yellow fruit. The unperishable chests, which contain the Egyptian mummies, were of cypress; and the cedar, with which black-lead pencils are covered, is not liable to be eaten by worms. See Miln's Bot. Dict. art. Coniferæ. The gates at St. Peter's church at Rome, which had lasted from the time of Constantine to that of Pope Eugene the fourth, that is to say, eleven hundred years, were of cypress, and had in that time suffered no decay. According to Thucydides, the Athenians buried the bodies of their heroes in coffins of cypress, as being not subject to decay. A similar durability has also been ascribed to cedar. Thus Horace,

———*speramus carmina fingi*
Posse linenda cedro et lævi servanda cupresso.

Osyris. l. 75. Two houses. The males and females are on different plants. There are many instances on record, where female plants have been impregnated at very great distance from their male; the dust discharged from the anthers is very light, small, and copious, so that it may spread very wide in the atmosphere, and be carried to the distant pistils, without the supposition of any particular attraction; these plants resemble some insects, as the ants, and cochineal insects, of which the males have wings, but not the female.

Plantago. l. 77. Rosea. Rose-plantain. In this vegetable monster the bractes, or divisions of the spike, become wonderfully enlarged, and are converted into leaves. The chaffy scales of the calyx in xeranthemum, and in a species of dianthus, and the glume in some alpine grasses, and the scales of the ament in the salix rosea, rose willow, grow into leaves; and produce other kinds of monsters. The double flowers become monsters by the multiplication of their petals or nectaries. See note on Alcea.

Anthoxanthum. l. 86. Vernal grass. Two males, two females. The other grasses have three males and two females. The flowers of this grass give the fragrant scent to hay. I am informed it is frequently viviparous, that is, that it bears sometimes roots or bulbs instead of seed, which after a time drop off and strike root into the ground. This circumstance is said to obtain in many of the alpine grasses, whose seeds are perpetually devoured by small birds. The festuca dumetorum, fescue grass of the bushes, produces bulbs from the sheaths of its straw. The allium magicum, or magical onion, produces onions on its

Where the wide heath in purple pride extends,
And scatter'd furze its golden lustre blends,
Closed in a green recess, unenvy'd lot !   89
The blue smoke rises from their turf-built cot ;
Bosom'd in fragrant blush their infant train,
Eye the warm sun, or drink the silver rain.

The fair Osmúnda seeks the silent dell,
The ivy canopy, and dripping cell ;
There hid in shades *clandestine* rites approves,
Till the green progeny betrays her loves.

With charms despotic fair Chondrilla reigns
O'er the soft hearts of *five* fraternal swains ;
If sighs the changeful nymph, alike they mourn ;
And, if she smiles, with rival raptures burn.   100
So, tuned in unison, Eolian lyre !
Sounds in sweet symphony thy kindred wire ;
Now, gently swept by zephyr's vernal wings,
Sink in soft cadences the love-sick strings ;
And now with mingling chords, and voices higher,
Peal the full anthems of the aërial choir.

Five sister-nymphs to join Diana's train
With thee, fair Lychnis ! vow,—but vow in vain ;

Beneath one roof resides the virgin band,
Flies the fond swain, and scorns his offer'd hand ;   110
But when soft hours on breezy pinions move,
And smiling May attunes her lute to love,
Each wanton beauty, trick'd in all her grace,
Shakes the bright dew-drops from her blushing face ;
In gay undress displays her rival charms,
And calls her wondering lovers to her arms.

When the young Hours amid her tangled hair
Wove the fresh rose-bud, and the lily fair,
Proud Gloriosa led *three* chosen swains,
The blushing captives of her virgin chains.   120
— When Time's rude hand a bark of wrinkle spread
Round her weak limbs, and silver'd o'er her head,
Three other youths her riper years engage,
The flatter'd victims of her wily age.

So, in her wane of beauty, Ninon won
With fatal smiles her gay unconscious son.—
Clasp'd in his arms she own'd a mother's name,
—" Desist, rash youth ! restrain your impious flame,
First on that bed your infant form was press'd,
Born by my throes, and nurtured at my breast."   130

---

head instead of seeds. The polygonum viviparum viviparous bistort, rises about a foot high, with a beautiful spike of flowers, which are succeeded by buds or bulbs, which fall off and take root. There is a bush frequently seen on birch-trees, like a bird's nest, which seems to be a similar attempt of nature to produce another tree; which falling off, might take root in spongy ground.

There is an instance of this double mode of production in the animal kingdom, which is equally extraordinary, the same species of aphis is viviparous in summer, and oviparous in autumn. A. T. Bladh. Amæn. Acad. V. 7.

Osmunda. l. 93. This plant grows on moist rocks; the parts of its flower or its seeds are scarce discernible; whence Linneus has given the name of clandestine marriage to this class. The younger plants are of a beautiful vivid green.

Chondrilla. l. 97. Of the class confederate males. The numerous florets, which constitute the disk of the flowers in this class, contain in each five males surrounding one female, which are connected at top, whence the name of the class. An Italian writer, in a discourse on the irritability of flowers, asserts, that if the top of the floret be touched, all the filaments which support the cylindrical anther will contract themselves, and that by thus raising or depressing the anther the whole of the prolific dust is collected on the stigma. He adds, that if one filament be touched after it is separated from the floret, that it will contract like the muscular fibres of animal bodies; his experiments were tried on the centaurea calcitrapoides, and on artichokes, and globe-thistles. Discourse on the irritability of plants. Dodsley.

Lychnis. l. 108. Ten males and five females. The flowers which contain the five females, and those which contain the ten males, are found on different plants; and often at a great distance from each other. Five of the ten males arrive at their maturity some days before the other five, as may be seen by opening the corol before it naturally expands itself. When the females arrive at their maturity, they rise above the petals, as if looking abroad for their distant husbands; the scarlet ones contribute much to the beauty of our meadows in May and June.

Gloriosa. l. 119. Superba. Six males, one female. The petals of this beautiful flower with three of the stamens, which are first mature, stand up in apparent disorder; and the pistil bends at nearly a right angle to insert its stigma amongst them. In a few days, as these decline, the other three stamens bend over, and approach the pistil. In the fritillaria persica, the six stamens are of equal lengths, and the anthers lie at a distance from the pistil, and three alternate ones approach first; and, when these decline, the other three approach: in the lithrum salicaria, (which has twelve males and one female) a beautiful red flower, which grows on the banks of rivers, six of the males arrive at maturity, and surround the female some time before the other six; when these decline, the other six rise up, and supply their places. Several other flowers have in a similar manner two sets of stamens of different ages, as adoxa, lychnis, saxifraga. See Genista. Perhaps a difference in the time of their maturity obtains in all these flowers, which have numerous stamens. In the kalmia the ten stamens lie round the pistil like the radii of a wheel; and each anther is concealed in a nich of the corol to protect it from cold and moisture; these anthers rise separately from their niches, and approach the pistil for a time, and then recede to their former situations.

Back as from death he sprung, with wild amaze
Fierce on the fair he fix'd his ardent gaze;
Dropp'd on one knee, his frantic arms outspread,
And stole a guilty glance toward the bed;
Then breathed from quivering lips a whisper'd vow,
And bent on heaven his pale repentant brow;
" Thus, thus!" he cried, and plunged the furious dart,
And life and love gush'd mingled from his heart.

The fell Silene, and her sisters fair, 139
Skill'd in destruction, spread the viscous snare,
The harlot-band *ten* lofty bravoes screen,
And, frowning, guard the magic nets unseen.
Haste, glittering nations, tenants of the air,
Oh, steer from hence your viewless course afar!
If with soft words, sweet blushes, nods, and smiles,
The *three* dread syrens lure you to their toils,
Limed by their art, in vain you point your stings,
In vain the efforts of your whirring wings!—
Go, seek your gilded mates and infant hives, 149
Nor taste the honey purchased with your lives!

When heaven's high vault condensing clouds deform,
Fair Amaryllis flies the incumbent storm,
Seeks with unsteady step the shelter'd vale,
And turns her blushing beauties from the gale.
Six rival youths, with soft concern impress'd,
Calm all her fears, and charm her cares to rest.
—So shines at eve the sun-illumined fane,
Lifts its bright cross, and waves its golden vane;
From every breeze the polish'd axle turns,
And high in air the dancing meteor burns. 160

Four of the giant brood with Ilex stand,
Each grasps a thousand arrows in his hand;

Silene. l. 139. Catchfly. Three females and ten males inhabit each flower; the viscous material, which surrounds the stalks under the flowers of this plant, and of the cucubalus otites, is a curious contrivance to prevent various insects from plundering the honey, or devouring the seed. In the dionæa muscipula there is a still more wonderful contrivance to prevent the depredations of insects : the leaves are armed with long teeth, like the antennæ of insects, and lie spread upon the ground round the stem; and are so irritable, that when an insect creeps upon them, they fold up, and crush or pierce it to death. The last professor Linneus, in his Supplementum Plantarum, gives the following account of the arum muscivorum. The flower has the smell of carrion; by which the flies are invited to lay their eggs in the chamber of the flower, but in vain endeavour to escape, being prevented by the hairs pointing inwards; and thus perish in the flower, whence its name of flyeater. P. 411. In the dypsacus is another contrivance for this purpose, a bason of water is placed round each joint of the stem. In the drosera is another kind of fly-trap. See Dypsacus and Drosera ; the flowers of silene and cucubalus are closed all day, but are open and give an agreeable odour in the night. See Cerea. See additional notes at the end of the poem.

Amaryllis. l. 152. Formosissima. Most beautiful amarylis. Six males, one female. Some of the bell-flowers close their apertures at night, or in rainy or cold weather, as the convolvulus, and thus protect their included stamens and pistils. Other bell-flowers hang their apertures downwards, as many of the lilies; in those the pistil, when at maturity, is longer than the stamens; and by this pendant attitude of the bell, when the anthers burst, their dust falls on the stigma; and these are at the same time sheltered as with an umbrella from rain and dews. But, as a free exposure to the air is necessary for their fecundation, the style and filaments in many of these flowers continue to grow longer after the bell is open, and hang down below its rim. In others, as in the martagon, the bell is deeply divided, and the divisions are reflected upwards, that they may not prevent the access of air, and at the same time afford some shelter from perpendicular rain or dew. Other bell flowers, as the hemerocallis, and amaryllis have their bells nodding only, as it were, or hanging obliquely towards the horizon ; which, as their stems are slender, turn like a weathercock from the wind, and thus very effectually preserve their inclosed stamens and anthers from the rain and cold. Many of these flowers, both before and after their season of fecundation, erect their heads perpendicular to the horizon, like the meadia, which cannot be explained from mere mechanism.

The amaryllis formosissima is a flower of the last-mentioned kind, and affords an agreeable example of *art* in the vegetable economy. 1. The pistil is of great length compared with the stamens; and this I suppose to have been the most unchangeable part of the flower, as in Meadia, which see. 2. To counteract this circumstance, the pistil and stamens are made to decline downwards, that the prolific dust might fall from the anthers on the stigma. 3. To produce this effect, and to secure it when produced, the corol is lacerated, contrary to what occurs in other flowers of this genus, and the lowest division with the two next lowest ones are wrapped closely over the style and filaments, binding them forcibly down lower towards the horizon than the usual inclination of the bell in this genus, and thus constitutes a most elegant flower. There is another contrivance for this purpose in the hemerocallis flava: the long pistil often is bent somewhat like the capital letter N, with design to shorten it, and thus to bring the stigma amongst the anthers.

Ilex. l. 161. Holly. Four males, four females. Many plants, like many animals, are furnished with arms for their protection ; these are either aculei, prickles, as in rose and barberry, which are formed from the outer bark of the plant; or spinæ, thorns, as in hawthorn, which are an elongation of the wood, and hence more difficult to be torn off than the former ; or stimuli, stings, as in the nettles, which are armed with a venomous fluid for the annoyance of naked animals. The shrubs and trees, which have prickles or thorns, are grateful food to

A thousand steely points on every scale
Form the bright terrors of his bristly mail.—
So arm'd, immortal Moore uncharm'd the spell,
And slew the wily dragon of the well.—
Sudden with rage their *injured* bosoms burn,
Retort the insult, or the *wound* return;
Unwrong'd, as gentle as the breeze that sweeps
The unbending harvests or undimpled deeps,
They guard the kings of Needwood's wide domains, 171
Their sister-wives and fair infantine trains;
Lead the lone pilgrim through the trackless glade,
Or guide in leafy wilds the wandering maid.

So Wright's bold pencil from Vesuvio's height
Hurls his red lavas to the troubled night;
From Calpe starts the intolerable flash,
Skies burst in flames, and blazing oceans dash;
Or bids in sweet repose his shades recede,
Winds the still vale, and slopes the velvet mead;
On the pale stream expiring zephyrs sink, 181
And moonlight sleeps upon its hoary brink.

Gigantic nymph! the fair Kleinhovia reigns,
The grace and terror of Orixa's plains;
O'er her warm cheek the blush of beauty swims,
And nerves Herculean bend her sinewy limbs;
With frolic eye she views the affrighted throng,
And shakes the meadows as she towers along;
With playful violence displays her charms,
And bears her trembling lovers in her arms. 190
So fair Thalestris shook her plumy crest,
And bound in rigid mail her jutting breast;
Poised her long lance amid the walks of war,
And beauty thunder'd from Bellona's car;
Greece arm'd in vain, her captive heroes wove
The chains of conquest with the wreaths of love.

When o'er the cultured lawns and dreary wastes
Retiring Autumn flings her howling blasts,
Bends in tumultuous waves the struggling woods, 199
And showers their leafy honours on the floods,
In withering heaps collects the flowery spoil,
And each chill insect sinks beneath the soil;
Quick flies fair Tulipa the loud alarms,
And folds her infant closer in her arms;
In some lone cave, secure pavilion, lies,
And waits the courtship of serener skies.—

---

many animals, as gooseberry and gorse; and would be quickly devoured, if not thus armed; the stings seem a protection against some kinds of insects, as well as the naked mouths of quadrupeds. Many plants lose their thorns by cultivation, as wild animals lose their ferocity; and some of them their horns. A curious circumstance attends the large hollies in Needwood forest; they are armed with thorny leaves about eight feet high, and have smooth leaves above, as if they were conscious that horses and cattle could not reach their upper branches. See note on Meadia, and on Mancinella. The numerous clumps of hollies in Needwood forest serve as land-marks to direct the travellers across it in various directions; and as a shelter to the deer and cattle in winter; and in scarce seasons supply them with much food. For when the upper branches, which are without prickles, are cut down, the deer crop the leaves and peel off the bark. The bird-lime made from the bark of hollies seems to be a very similar material to the elastic gum, or Indian rubber, as it is called. There is a fossile elastic bitumen found at Matlock in Derbyshire, which much resembles these substances in its elasticity and inflammability. The thorns of the mimosa cornigera resemble cow's horns in appearance as well as in use. System of Vegetables, p. 782.

Hurls his red lavas. l. 176. Alluding to the grand paintings of the eruption of Vesuvius, and of the destruction of the Spanish vessels before Gibraltar; and to the beautiful landscapes and moonlight scenes, by Mr. Wright of Derby.

Kleinhovia. l. 183. In this class the males in each flower are supported by the female. The name of the class may be translated "viragoes," or "feminine males."

The largest tree perhaps in the world is of the same natural order as kleinhovia; it is the adansonia, or Ethiopian sourgourd, or African calabash-tree. Mr. Adanson says the diameter of the trunk frequently exceeeds 25 feet, and the horizontal branches are from 45 to 55 feet long, and so large that each branch is equal to the largest trees of Europe. The breadth of the top is from 120 to 150 feet; and one of the roots bared only in part by the washing away of the earth from the river, near which it grew, measured 110 feet long; and yet these stupendous trees never exceed 70 feet in height. Voyage to Senegal.

Tulipa. l. 203. Tulip. What is in common language called a bulbous-root, is by Linneus termed the hybernacle, or winter-lodge of the young plant. As these bulbs in every respect resemble buds, except in their being produced under ground, and include the leaves and flower in miniature, which are to be expanded in the ensuing spring. By cautiously cutting in winter through the concentric coats of a tulip-root, longitudinally from the top to the base, and taking them off successively, the whole flower of the next summer's tulip is beautifully seen by the naked eye, with its petals, pistil, and stamens; the flowers exist in other bulbs, in the same manner, as in hyacinths, but the individual flowers of these being less, they are not so easily dissected, or so conspicuous to the naked eye.

In the seeds of the nymphæa nelumbo, the leaves of the plant are seen so distinctly, that Mr. Ferber found out by them to what plant the seeds belonged. Amæn. Acad. V. vi. No. 120. He says that Mariotte first observed the future flower and foliage in the bulb of a tulip; and adds, that it is pleasant to see in the buds of the hepatica and pedicularis hirsuta, yet lying in the earth; and in the gems of daphne mezereon; and at the base of osmunda lunaria, a perfect plant of the future year complete in all its parts. Ibid.

So, six cold moons, the dormouse charm'd to rest,
Indulgent sleep! beneath thy elder breast,
In fields of fancy climbs the kernel'd groves, 209
Or shares the golden harvests with his loves.—
Then bright from earth amid the troubled sky
Ascends fair Colchica with radiant eye,
Warms the cold bosom of the hoary year,
And lights with beauty's blaze the dusky sphere.
Three blushing maids the intrepid nymph attend,
And *six* gay youths, enamour'd train! defend.
So shines with silver guards the Georgian star,
And drives on night's blue arch his glittering car;
Hangs o'er the billowy clouds his lucid form, 219
Wades through the mist, and dances in the storm.

Great Helianthus guides o'er twilight plains
In gay solemnity his dervise-trains;
Marshall'd in *fives* each gaudy band proceeds,
Each gaudy band a plumed lady leads;
With zealous step he climbs the upland lawn,
And bows in homage to the rising dawn;
Imbibes with eagle eye the golden ray,
And watches, as it moves, the orb of day. 228

Queen of the marsh imperial Drosera treads
Rush-fringed banks, and moss-embroider'd beds
Redundant folds of glossy silk surround
Her slender waist, and trail upon the ground;
Five sister-nymphs collect with graceful ease,
Or spread the floating purple to the breeze;
And *five* fair youths with duteous love comply
With each soft mandate of her moving eye.
As with sweet grace her snowy neck she bows,
A zone of diamonds trembles round her brows;
Bright shines the silver halo, as she turns;
And, as she steps, the living lustre burns. 240

Fair Lonicera prints the dewy lawn,
And decks with brighter blush the vermil dawn;

Colchicum autumnale. l. 212. Autumnal meadow-saffron. Six males, three females. The germ is buried within the root, which thus seems to constitute a part of the flower. Families of Plants, p. 242. These singular flowers appear in the autumn without any leaves, whence in some countries they are called naked ladies: in the March following the green leaves spring up, and in April the seed-vessel rises from the ground; the seeds ripen in May, contrary to the usual habits of vegetables, which flower in the spring, and ripen their seeds in the autumn. Miller's Dict. The juice of the root of this plant is so acrid as to produce violent effects on the human constitution, which also prevents it from being eaten by subterranean insects, and thus guards the seed-vessel during the winter. The defoliation of deciduous trees is announced by the flowering of the colchicum; of these the ash is the last that puts forth its leaves, and the first that loses them. Phil. Bot. p. 275.

The hamamelis, witch hazel, is another plant which flowers in autumn; when the leaves fall off, the flowers come out in clusters from the joints of the branches, and in Virginia ripen their seed in the ensuing spring; but in this country their seeds seldom ripen. Lin. Spec. Plant. Miller's Dict.

Helianthus. l. 221. Sun flower. The numerous florets which constitute the disk of this flower, contain in each five males surrounding one female, the five stamens have their anthers connected at top, whence the name of the class "confederate males;" see note on Chondrilla. The sun-flower follows the course of the sun by nutation, not by twisting its stem. (Hales veg. stat.) Other plants, when they are confined in a room, turn the shining surface of their leaves, and bend their whole branches to the light. See Mimosa.

- *A plumed lady leads.* l. 224. The seeds of many plants of this class are furnished with a plume, by which admirable mechanism they are disseminated by the winds far from their parent stem, and look like a shuttlecock, as they fly. Other seeds are disseminated by animals; of these some attach themselves to their hair or feathers by a gluten, as misletoe; others by hooks, as cleavers, burdock, hounds-tongue; and others are swallowed whole for the sake of the fruit, and voided uninjured, as the hawthorn, juniper, and some grasses. Other seeds again disperse themselves by means of an elastic seed-vessel, as oats, geranium, and impatiens; and the seeds of aquatic plants, and of those which grow on the banks of rivers, are carried many miles by the currents, into which they fall. See Impatiens. Zostera. Cassia. Carlina.

Drosera. l. 229. Sun-dew. Five males, five females. The leaves of this marsh-plant are purple, and have a fringe very unlike other vegetable productions. And, which is curious, at the point of every thread of this erect fringe stands a pellucid drop of mucilage, resembling an earl's coronet. This mucus is a secretion from certain glands, and like the viscous material round the flower stalks of silene (catchfly) prevents small insects from infesting the leaves. As the ear-wax in animals seems to be in part designed to prevent fleas and other insects from getting into their ears. See Silene. Mr. Wheatly, an eminent surgeon in Cateaton-street, London, observed these leaves to bend upwards when an insect settled on them, like the leaves of the muscipula veneris, and pointing all their globules of mucus to the centre, that they completely intangled and destroyed it. M. Broussonet, in the Mem. de l'Acad. des Sciences for the year 1784, p. 615, after having described the motion of the Dionæa, adds, that a similar appearance has been observed in the leaves of two species of drosera.

Lonicera. l. 241. Caprifolium, honeysuckle. Five males, one female. Nature has in many flowers used a wonderful apparatus to guard the nectary or honey gland from insects. In the honeysuckle the petal terminates in a long tube like a cornucopiæ, or horn of plenty; and the honey is produced at the bottom of it. In aconitum, monks-hood, the nectaries stand upright like two horns covered with a hood, which abounds with such acrid matter that no insects penetrate it. In helleborus, hellebore, the many nectaries are placed in a circle like little pitchers, and add much to the beauty of the flower. In

Winds round the shadowy rocks, and pancied vales, [gales,
And scents with sweeter breath the summer
With artless grace and native ease she charms,
And bears the horn of plenty in her arms.
Five rival swains their tender cares unfold,
And watch with eye askance the treasured gold.

Where rears huge Tenerif his azure crest,
Aspiring Draba builds her eagle nest;   250
Her pendant eyry icy caves surround,
Where erst volcanoes mined the rocky ground.

Pleased round the fair *four* rival lords ascend
The shaggy steeps, *two* menial youths attend.
High in the setting ray the beauty stands,
And her tall shadow waves on distant lands.

Oh, stay, bright habitant of air, alight,
Celestial Visca, from thy angel-flight!—
—— Scorning the sordid soil, aloft she springs,
Shakes her white plume, and claps her golden wings;   260
High o'er the fields of boundless ether roves,
And seeks amid the clouds her soaring loves!

Stretch'd on her mossy couch, in trackless deeps,
Queen of the coral groves, Zostera sleeps;
The silvery sea-weed matted round her bed,
And distant surges murmuring o'er her head.
High in the flood her azure dome ascends,
The crystal arch on crystal columns bends;

---

the columbine, aquilegia, the nectary is imagined to be like the neck and body of a bird, and the two petals standing upon each side to represent wings; whence its name of columbine, as if resembling a nest of young pigeons fluttering whilst their parent feeds them. The importance of the nectary in the economy of vegetation is explained at large in the notes on part the first.

Many insects are provided with a long and pliant proboscis for the purpose of acquiring this grateful food, as a variety of bees, moths, and butterflies: but the sphinx convolvuli, or unicorn moth, is furnished with the most remarkable proboscis in this climate. It carries it rolled up in concentric circles under its chin, and occasionally extends it above three inches in length. This trunk consists of joints and muscles, and seems to have more versatile movements than the trunk of the elephant; and near its termination is split into two capillary tubes. The excellence of this contrivance for robbing the flowers of their honey, keeps this beautiful insect fat and bulky; though it flies only in the evening, when the flowers have closed their petals, and are thence more difficult of access; and at the same time the brilliant colours of the moth contribute to its safety, by making it mistaken by the late sleeping birds for the flower it rests on.

Besides these there is a curious contrivance attending the ophrys, commonly called the bee-orchis, and the fly-orchis, with some kinds of the delphinium, called bee-larkspurs, to preserve their honey; in these the nectary and petals resemble in form and colour the insects which plunder them; and thus it may be supposed, they often escape these hourly robbers, by having the appearance of being pre-occupied. See note on Rubia, and Conferva polymorpha, and on Epidendrum.

Draba. l. 250. Alpina. Alpina whitlow-grass. One female and six males. Four of these males stand above the other two; whence the name of the class "four powers." I have observed in several plants of this class, that the two lower males arise, in a few days after the opening of the flower, to the same height as the other four, not being mature as soon as the higher ones. See note on Gloriosa. All the plants of this class possess similar virtues; they are termed acrid and antiscorbutic in their raw state, as mustard, watercress; when cultivated and boiled, they become a mild wholesome food, as cabbage, turnip.

There was formerly a volcano on the Peak of Tenerif, which became extinct about the year 1684. Philos. Trans. In many excavations of the mountain, much below the summit, there is now found abundance of ice at all seasons. Tench's Expedition to Botany Bay, p. 12. Are these congelations in consequence of the daily solution of the hoar-frost, which is produced on the summit during the night?

Viscum. l. 258. Misletoo. Two houses. This plant never grows upon the ground; the foliage is yellow, and the berries milk-white; the berries are so viscous as to serve for bird-lime; and when they fall adhere to the branches of the tree, on which the plant grows, and strike root into its bark, or are carried to distant trees by birds. The tillandsia, or wild pine, grows on other trees, like the misletoe, but takes little or no nourishment from them, having large buckets in its leaves to collect and retain the rain water. See note on Dypsacus. The mosses, which grow on the bark of trees, take much nourishment from them; hence it is observed that trees, which are annually cleared from moss by a brush, grow nearly twice as fast. (Phil Trans.) In the cyder countries the peasants brush their apple-trees annually. See Epidendrum.

Zostera. l. 264. Grass-wrack. Class, Feminine Males. Order, many males. It grows at the bottom of the sea, and rising to the surface when in flower, covers many leagues; and is driven at length to the shore. During its time of floating on the sea, numberless animals live on the under surface of it; and being specifically lighter than the sea-water, or being repelled by it, have legs placed as it were on their backs for the purpose of walking under it. As the scyllœa. See Barbut's Genera Vermium. It seems necessary that the marriages of plants thould be celebrated in the open air, either because the powder of the anther, or the mucilage on the stigma, or the reservoir of honey might receive injury from the water. Mr. Needham observed, that in the ripe dust of every flower, examined by the microscope, some vesicles are perceived, from which a fluid had escaped; and that those which still retain it, explode if they be wetted, like an eolipile suddenly exposed to a strong heat. These observations have been verified by Spallanzani and others. Hence rainy seasons make a scarcity of grain, or hinder its fecundity, by bursting the pollen before it arrives at the moist stigma of the flower. Spallanzani's Dissertations, v. II. p. 321. Thus the flowers of the male Vallisneria

Roof'd with translucent shell the turrets blaze,
And far in ocean dart their colour'd rays; 270
O'er the white floor successive shadows move,
As rise and break the ruffled waves above.—
Around the nymph her mermaid-trains repair,
And weave with orient pearl her radiant hair;
With rapid fins she cleaves the watery way,
Shoots like a silver meteor up to day;
Sounds a loud conch, convokes a scaly band,
Her sea-born lovers, and ascends the strand.

E'en round the pole the flames of love aspire,
And icy bosoms feel the *secret* fire!— 280
Cradled in snow and fann'd by arctic air
Shines, gentle Barometz! thy golden hair;

Rooted in earth each cloven hoof descends,
And round and round her flexile neck she bends;
Crops the gray coral moss, and hoary thyme,
Or laps with rosy tongue the melting rime.
Eyes with mute tenderness her distant dam,
Or seems to bleat, a *vegetable lamb*.
—So, warm and buoyant in his oily mail,
Gambols on seas of ice the unwieldy whale; 290
Wide waving fins round floating islands urge
His bulk gigantic through the troubled surge;
With hideous yawn the flying shoals he seeks,
Or clasps with fringe of horn his massy cheeks;
Lifts o'er the tossing wave his nostrils bare,
And spouts pellucid columns into air;
The silvery arches catch the setting beams,
And transient rainbows tremble o'er the streams.

Weak with nice sense the chaste Mimosa stands,
From each rude touch withdraws her timid hands; 300
Oft as light clouds o'erpass the summer-glade,
Alarm'd she trembles at the moving shade;
And feels, alive through all her tender form,
The whisper'd murmurs of the gathering storm;
Shuts her sweet eye-lids to approaching night,
And hails with freshen'd charms the rising light.

---

are produced under water, and when ripe detach themselves from the plant, and rising to the surface are wafted by the air to the female flowers. See Vallisneria.

Barometz. 1. 282. Polypodium Barometz. Tartarian lamb. Clandestine marriage. This species of fern is a native of China, with a decumbent root, thick, and every where covered with the most soft and dense wool, intensely yellow. Lin. Spec. Plant.

This curious stem is sometimes pushed out of the ground in its horizontal situation by some of the inferior branches of the root, so as to give it some resemblance to a lamb standing on four legs; and has been said to destroy all other plants in its vicinity. Sir Hans Sloane describes it under the name of Tartarian lamb, and has given a print of it. Philos. Trans. abridged, vol. ii. p. 646. but thinks some art had been used to give it an animal appearance. Dr. Hunter, in his edition of the Terra of Evelyn, has given a more curious print of it, much resembling a sheep. The down is used in India externally for stopping hemorrhages, and is called golden moss.

The thick downy clothing of some vegetables seems designed to protect them from the injuries of cold, like the wool of animals. Those bodies, which are bad conductors of electricity, are also bad conductors of heat, as glass, wax, air. Hence either of the two former of these may be melted by the flame of a blow-pipe very near the fingers which hold it without burning them; and the last, by being confined on the surface of animal bodies, in the interstices of their fur or wool, prevents the escape of their natural warmth; to which should be added, that the hairs themselves are imperfect conductors. The fat or oil of whales, and other northern animals, seems designed for the same purpose of preventing the too sudden escape of the heat of the body in cold climates. Snow protects vegetables which are covered by it from cold, both because it is a bad conductor of heat itself, and contains much air in its pores. If a piece of camphor be immersed in a snow-ball, except one extremity of it, on setting fire to this, as the snow melts, the water becomes absorbed into the surrounding snow by capillary attraction; on this account, when living animals are buried in snow, they are not moistened by it; but the cavity enlarges as the snow dissolves, affording them both a dry and warm habitation.

Mimosa. 1. 299. The sensitive plant. Of the class polygamy, one house. Naturalists have not explained the immediate cause of the collapsing of the sensitive plant; the leaves meet and close in the night during the sleep of the plant, or when exposed to much cold in the day-time, in the same manner as when they are affected by external violence, folding their upper surfaces together, and in part over each other like scales or tiles, so as to expose as little of the upper surface as may be to the air; but do not indeed collapse quite so far, since I have found, when touched in the night during their sleep, they fall still farther; especially when touched on the foot-stalks between the stems and the leaflets, which seems to be their most sensitive or irritable part. Now, as their situation after being exposed to external violence resembles their sleep, but with a greater degree of collapse, may it not be owing to a numbness or paralysis consequent to too violent irritation, like the faintings of animals from pain or fatigue? I kept a sensitive plant in a dark room till some hours after day-break; its leaves and leaf-stalks were collapsed as in its most profound sleep, and on exposing it to the light, above twenty minutes passed before the plant was thoroughly awake, and had quite expanded itself. During the night the upper or smoother surfaces of the leaves are appressed together; this would seem to show that the office of this surface of the leaf was to expose the fluids of the plant to the light as well as to the air. See note on Helianthus. Many flowers close up their petals during the night. See note on Vegetable Respiration in Part I.

T

Veil'd, with gay decency and modest pride,
Slow to the mosque she moves, an eastern
    bride;
There her soft vows unceasing love record,
Queen of the bright seraglio of her lord.— 310
So sinks or rises with the changeful hour
The liquid silver in its glassy tower.
So turns the needle to the pole it loves,
With fine librations quivering, as it moves.

All wan and shivering in the leafless glade
The sad Anemone reclined her head;
Grief on her cheeks had paled the roseate hue,
And her sweet eye-lids dropp'd with pearly
    dew.
—" See, from bright regions, born on odorous
    gales
The swallow, herald of the summer, sails; 320

Breath, gentle Air! from cherub-lips impart
Thy balmy influence to my anguish'd heart;
Thou, whose soft voice calls forth the tender
    blooms,
Whose pencil paints them, and whose breath
    perfumes;
Oh chase the fiend of frost, with leaden mace
Who seals in death-like sleep my hapless race;
Melt his hard heart, release his iron hand,
And give my ivory petals to expand.
So may each bud, that decks the brow of
    spring,   329
Shed all its incense on thy wafting wing!"—
To her fond prayer propitious Zephyr yields,
Sweeps on his sliding shell through azure fields,
O'er her fair mansion waves his whispering
    wand,
And gives her ivory petals to expand!
Gives with new life her filial train to rise,
And hail with kindling smiles the genial skies.
So shines the nymph in beauty's blushing
    pride,
When Zephyr wafts her deep calash aside,
Tears with rude kiss her bosom's gauzy veil,
And flings the fluttering kerchief to the gale. 340
So bright, the folding canopy undrawn,
Glides the gilt landau o'er the velvet lawn,
Of beaux and belles displays the glittering
    throng,
And soft airs fan them, as they roll along.

Where frowning Snowden bends his dizzy
    brow
O'er Conway, listening to the surge below;
Retiring Lichen climbs the topmost stone,
And drinks the aerial solitude alone.—

Anemone. l. 316. Many males, many females. Pliny says this flower never opens its petals but when the wind blows; whence its name: it has properly no calyx, but two or three sets of petals, three in each set, which are folded over the stamens and pistil in a singular and beautiful manner, and differs also from ranunculus in not having a melliferous pore on the claw of each petal.

The swallow. l. 320. There is a wonderful conformity between the vegetation of some plants, and the arrival of certain birds of passage. Linneus observes that the wood anemone blows in Sweden on the arrival of the swallow; and the marsh mary-gold, caltha, when the cuckoo sings. Near the same coincidence was observed in England by Stillingfleet. The word coccux in Greek signifies both a young fig and a cuckoo, which is supposed to have arisen from the coincidence of their appearance in Greece. Perhaps a similar coincidence of appearance in some part of Asia gave occasion to the story of the love of the rose and nightingale, so much celebrated by the eastern poets. See Dianthus. The times however of the appearance of vegetables in the spring seem occasionally to be influenced by their acquired habits, as well as by their sensibility to heat: for the roots of potatoes, onions, &c. will germinate with much less heat in the spring than in the autumn; as is easily observable where these roots are stored for use; and hence malt is best made in the spring. 2d. The grains and roots brought from more southern latitudes germinate here sooner than those which are brought from more northern ones, owing to their acquired habits. Fordyce on Agriculture. 3d. It was observed by one of the scholars of Linneus, that the apple trees sent from hence to New England blossomed for a few years too early for that climate, and bore no fruit; but afterwards learnt to accommodate themselves to their new situation. (Kalm's Travels.) 4th. The parts of animals become more sensible to heat after having been previously exposed to cold, as our hands glow on coming into the house after having held snow in them; this seems to happen to vegetables; for vines in grape-houses, which have been exposed to the winter's cold, will become forwarder and more vigorous than those which have been kept during the winter in the house. (Kennedy on Gardening.) This accounts for the very rapid vegetation in the northern latitudes after the solution of the snows.

The increase of the irritability of plants in respect to heat, after having been previously exposed to cold, is farther illustrated by an experiment of Dr. Walker's. He cut apertures into a birch-tree at different heights; and on the 26th of March some of these apertures bled, or oozed with the sap-juice, when the thermometer was at 39; which same apertures did not bleed on the 13th of March, when the thermometer was at 44. The reason of this I apprehend was, because on the night of the 25th the thermometer was as low as 34; whereas on the night of the 12th it was at 41; though the ingenious author ascribes it to another cause. Trans. of the Royal Soc. of Edinburgh, v. l. p. 19.

Lichen. l. 347. Calcareum. Liver-wort. Clandestine marriage. This plant is the first that vegetates on naked rocks, covering them with a kind of tapestry, and draws its nourishment perhaps chiefly from the air; after it perishes, earth enough is left for other mosses to root themselves; and after some ages a soil is produced sufficient for the growth of more succulent and large vegetables. In this manner perhaps the whole earth has been gradually covered with vegetation, after it was raised out of the primeval ocean by subterraneous fires.

Bright shine the stars unnumber'd *o'er her head*,
And the cold moon-beam gilds her flinty bed;
While round the rifted rocks hoarse whirlwinds breathe, 351
And dark with thunder sail the clouds beneath.
The steepy path her plighted swain pursues,
And tracks her light step o'er the imprinted dews;
Delighted Hymen gives his torch to blaze,
Winds round the crags, and lights the mazy ways;
Sheds o'er their *secret* vows his influence chaste,
And decks with roses the admiring waste.

High in the front of heaven when Sirius glares,
And o'er Britannia shakes his fiery hairs: 360
When no soft shower descends, no dew distils,
Her wave-worn channels dry, and mute her rills;
When droops the sickening herb, the blossom fades, [glades;
And parch'd earth gapes beneath the withering
—With languid step fair Dypsaca retreats,
" Fall, gentle dews!" the fainting nymph repeats,
Seeks the low dell, and in the sultry shade
Invokes in vain the Naiads to her aid.—
Four sylvan youths in crystal goblets bear
The untasted treasure to the grateful fair; 370
Pleased from their hands with modest grace she sips,
And the cool wave reflects her coral lips.

With nice selection modest Rubia blends
Her vermil dyes, and o'er the cauldron bends;

Warm mid the rising steam the beauty glows,
As blushes in a mist the dewy rose.
With chemic art *four* favour'd youths aloof
Stain the white fleece, or stretch the tinted woof;
O'er age's cheek the warmth of youth diffuse,
Or deck the pale-ey'd nymph in roseate hues.
So when Medea to exulting Greece 381
From plunder'd Colchis bore the golden fleece;
On the loud shore a magic pile she raised,
The cauldron bubbled, and the faggots blazed;
Pleased on the boiling wave old Æson swims,
And feels new vigour stretch his swelling limbs;

Dypsacus. 1. 365. Teasel. One female, and four males. There is a cup around every joint of the stem of this plant, which contains from a spoonful to half a pint of water; and serves both for the nutriment of the plant in dry seasons, and to prevent insects from creeping up to devour its seed. See Silene. The tillandsia, or wild pine of the West Indies, has every leaf terminated near the stalk with a hollow bucket, which contains from half a pint to a quart of water. Dampier's Voyage to Campeachy. Dr. Sloane mentions one kind of aloe furnished with leaves, which, like the wild pine and banana, hold water; and thence afford necessary refreshment to travellers in hot countries. Nepenthes has a bucket for the same purpose at the end of every leaf. Burm. Zeyl. 42. 17.

Silphium perfoliatum has a cup round every joint to reserve water after rain. It rises during the summer twelve or fourteen feet high on a slender stem, which is square, and thus is stronger to resist the winds than if it had been made round with the same quantity of materials.

The most curious plant of this kind is the sarracenia purpurea, which resembles the nymphœa, an aquatic plant, but catches so much water in its sessile cup-like leaves, as to enable it to live on land, a wonderful provision of nature! System. Plant. a Reichard. Vol. II. p. 577.

Rubia. 1. 373. Madder. Four males and one female. This plant is cultivated in very large quantities for dying red. If mixed with the food of young pigs or chickens, it colours their bones red. If they are fed alternate fortnights, with a mixture of madder, and with their usual food alone, their bones will consist of concentric circles of white and red. Belchier. Phil. Trans. 1736. Animals fed with madder for the purpose of these experiments were found upon dissection to have thinner gall. Comment. de rebus. Lipsiæ. This circumstance is worth farther attention. The colouring materials of vegetables, like those which serve the purpose of tanning, varnishing, and the various medical purposes, do not seem essential to the life of the plant; but seem given it as a defence against the depredations of insects or other animals, to whom these materials are nauseous or deleterious. The colours of insects and many smaller animals contribute to conceal them from the larger ones which prey upon them. Caterpillars which feed on leaves are generally green; and earth-worms the colour of the earth which they inhabit; butterflies which frequent flowers are coloured like them; small birds which frequent hedges have greenish backs like the leaves, and light coloured bellies like the sky, and are hence less visible to the hawk, who passes under them or over them. Those birds which are much amongst flowers, as the goldfinch, (fringilla carduelis) are furnished with vivid colours. The lark, partridge, hare, are the colour of dry vegetables, on which they rest. And frogs vary their colour with the mud of the streams which they frequent; and those which live on trees are green. Fish, which are generally suspended in water, and swallows, which are generally suspended in air, have their backs the colour of the distant ground, and their bellies of the sky. In the colder climates many of these become white during the existence of the snows. Hence there is apparent design in the colours of animals, whilst those of vegetables seem consequent to the other properties of the materials which possess them.

Pleased on the boiling wave. 1. 385. The story of Æson becoming young, from the medicated bath of Medea, seems to have been intended to teach the efficacy of warm bathing in retarding the progress of old age. The words *relaxation* and *bracing*, which are generally thought expressive of the effects of warm and cold bathing, are mechanical terms, properly applied to drums or strings; but are only metaphors when applied to the effects of cold or warm bathing on animal

Through his thrill'd nerves forgotten ardours
  dart,
And warmer eddies circle round his heart;
With softer fires his kindling eye-balls glow,
And darker tresses wanton round his brow. 390

Where Java's isle, horizon'd with the floods,
Lifts to the skies her canopy of woods;
Pleased Epidendra climbs the waving pines,
And high in heaven the intrepid beauty shines,
Gives to the tropic breeze her radiant hair,
Drinks the bright shower, and feeds upon the air.
Her brood delighted stretch their callow wings,
As poised aloft their pendent cradle swings,
Eye the warm sun, the spicy zephyr breathe,
And gaze unenvious on the world beneath. 400

As dash the waves on India's breezy strand,
Her flush'd cheek press'd upon her lily hand,
Vallisner sits; up-turns her tearful eyes,
Calls her lost lover, and upbraids the skies;
For him she breathes the silent sigh, forlorn,
Each setting day; for him each rising morn.—
" Bright orbs, that light yon high ethereal
  plain,
Or bathe your radiant tresses in the main;
Pale moon, that silver'st o'er night's sable
  brow;
For ye were witness to his parting vow! 410
Ye shelving rocks, dark waves, and sounding
  shore,—
Ye echoed sweet the tender words he swore!—
Can stars or seas the sails of love retain?
O guide my wanderer to my arms again!"

Her buoyant skiff intrepid Ulva guides,
And seeks her lord amid the trackless tides,
Her *secret* vows the Cyprian Queen approves,
And hovering halcyons guard her infant-loves;
Each in his floating cradle round they throng,
And dimpling ocean bears the fleet along.—420

---

bodies. The immediate cause of old age seems to reside in the inirritability of the finer vessels or parts of our system; hence these cease to act, and collapse, or become horny or bony. The warm bath is peculiarly adapted to prevent these circumstances by its increasing our irritability, and by moistening and softening the skin, and the extremities of the finer vessels, which terminate in it. To those who are past the meridian of life, and have dry skins, and begin to be emaciated, the warm bath, for half an hour twice a week, I believe to be eminently serviceable in retarding the advances of age.

Epidendrum flos aeris. l. 393. Of the class of gynandria, or feminine males. This parasite plant is found in Java, and is said to live on air without taking root in the trees on which it grows; and its flowers resemble spiders. Syst. Veg. a Reichard. Vol. IV. p. 35. By this curious similitude the bees and butterflies are supposed to be deterred from plundering the nectaries. See Visca.

Vallisneria. l. 403. This extraordinary plant is of the class Two Houses. It is found in the East Indies, in Norway, and various parts of Italy. Lin. Spec. Plant. They have their roots at the bottom of the Rhone; the flowers of the female plant float on the surface of the water, and are furnished with an elastic spiral stalk, which extends or contracts as the water rises and falls; this rise or fall, from the rapid descent of the river, and the mountain torrents which flow into it, often amounts to many feet in a few hours. The flowers of the male plant are produced under water, and as soon as their farina, or dust, is mature, they detach themselves from the plant, and rise to the surface, continue to flourish, and are wafted by the air, or borne by the currents to the female flowers. In this resembling those tribes of insects, where the males at certain seasons acquire wings, but not the females, as ants, coccus, lampyris, phalæna, brumata, lichanella. These male flowers are in such numbers, though very minute, as frequently to cover the surface of the river to considerable extent. See Families of Plants, translated from Linneus, p. 677.

Ulva. l. 415. Clandestine marriage. This kind of sea-weed is buoyed up by bladders of air, which are formed in the duplicatures of its leaves, and forms immense floating fields of vegetation; the young ones, branching out from the larger ones, and borne on similar little air-vessels. It is also found in the warm baths of Patavia, where the leaves are formed into curious cells or labyrinths for the purpose of floating on the water. See Ulva labyrinthi-formis, Lin. Spec. Plant. The air contained in these cells was found by Dr. Priestley to be sometimes purer than common air, and sometimes less pure; the air bladders of fish seem to be similar organs, and serve to render them buoyant in the water. In some of these, as in the cod and haddock, a red membrane, consisting of a great number of leaves or duplicatures, is found within the air-bag, which probably secretes this air from the blood of the animal. (Monro. Physiol. of Fish, p. 28.) To determine whether this air, when first separated from the blood of the animal or plant, be dephlogisticated air, is worthy inquiry. The bladder-sena (colutea) and bladder-nut (staphylæa) have their seed-vessels distended with air; and the ketmia has the upper joint of the stem immediately under the receptacle of the flower much distended with air; these seem to be analogous to the air-vessel at the broad end of the egg, and may probably become less pure as the seed ripens; some, which I tried, had the purity of the surrounding atmosphere. The air at the broad end of the egg is probably an organ serving the purpose of respiration to the young chick, some of whose vessels are spread upon it like a placenta, or permeate it. Many are of opinion that even the placenta of the human fetus, and cotyledons of quadrupeds, are respiratory organs rather than nutritious ones.

The air in the hollow stems of grasses, and of some umbelliferous plants, bears analogy to the air in the quills, and in some of the bones of birds; supplying the place of the pith, which shrivels up after it has performed its office of protruding the young stem or feather. Some of these cavities of the bones are said to communicate with the lungs in birds. Phil. Trans.

The air-bladders of fish are nicely adapted to their intended purpose; for though they render them buoyant near the surface without the la-

Thus o'er the waves, which gently bend and
    swell,
Fair Galatea steers her silver shell;
Her playful dolphins stretch the silken rein,
Hear her sweet voice, and glide along the
    main.
As round the wild meandering coast she moves
By gushing rills, rude cliffs, and nodding
    groves;   [locks,
Each by her pine the wood-nymphs wave their
And wondering Naiads peep amid the rocks!
Pleased trains of mermaids rise from coral
    cells;
Admiring tritons sound their twisted shells; 430
Charm'd o'er the car pursuing Cupids sweep,
Their snow-white pinions twinkling in the
And, as the lustre of her eye she turns, [deep;
Soft sighs the gale, and amorous Ocean burns.

    On Dove's green brink the fair Tremella
        stood,
And view'd her playful image in the flood;

To each rude rock, lone dell, and echoing
    grove
Sung the sweet sorrows of her *secret* love.   438
" Oh, stay!"—return!—along the sounding
    shore   439
Cried the sad Naiads,—she return'd no more!—
Now girt with clouds the sullen evening frown'd,
And withering Eurus swept along the ground;
The misty moon withdrew her horned light,
And sunk with hesper in the skirt of night;
No dim electric streams, (the northern dawn)
With meek effulgence quiver'd o'er the lawn;
No star benignant shot one transient ray
To guide or light the wanderer on her way.
Round the dark crags the murmuring whirl-
    winds blow,   449
Woods groan above, and waters roar below;
As o'er the steeps with pausing foot she moves,
The pitying Dryads shriek amid their groves.
She flies—she stops—she pants—she looks be-
    hind,
And hears a demon howl in every wind.
—As the bleak blast unfurls her fluttering vest,
Cold beats the snow upon her shuddering breast;
Through her numb'd limbs the chill sensations
    dart,
And the keen ice-bolt trembles at her heart.
" I sink, I fall! oh, help me, help!" she cries,
Her stiffening tongue the unfurnish'd sound
    denies;   460
Tear after tear adown her cheek succeeds,
And pearls of ice bestrew the glittering meads;
Congealing snows her lingering feet surround;
Arrest her flight, and root her to the ground;
With suppliant arms she pours the silent prayer;
Her suppliant arms hang crystal in the air;
Pellucid films her shivering neck o'erspread,
Seal her mute lips, and silver o'er her head;
Veil her pale bosom, glaze her lifted hands, 469
And shrined in ice the beauteous statue stands.
—Dove's azure nymphs on each revolving
    year
For fair Tremella shed the tender tear;
With rush-wove crowns in sad procession move,
And sound the sorrowing shell to hapless love."

---

bour of using their fins, yet, when they rest at greater depths, they are no inconvenience, as the increased pressure of the water condenses the air which they contain into less space. Thus, if a cork or bladder of air was immersed a very great depth in the ocean, it would be so much compressed, as to become specifically as heavy as the water, and would remain there. It is probable the unfortunate Mr. Day, who was drowned in a diving-ship of his own construction, miscarried from not attending to this circumstance: it is probable the quantity of air he took down with him, if he descended much lower than he expected, was condensed into so small a space as not to render the ship buoyant when he endeavoured to ascend.

Tremella. l. 435. Clandestine marriage. I have frequently observed fungusses of this genus on old rails and on the ground to become a transparent jelly, after they had been frozen in autumnal mornings; which is a curious property, and distinguishes them from some other vegetable mucilage; for I have observed that the paste, made by boiling wheat-flour in water, ceases to be adhesive after having been frozen. I suspected that the tremella nostoc, or stargelly, also had been thus produced; but have since been well informed, that the tremella nostoc is a mucilage voided by herons after they have eaten frogs; hence it has the appearance of having been pressed through a hole; and limbs of frogs are said sometimes to be found amongst it; it is always seen upon plains, or by the sides of water, places which herons generally frequent.

Some of the fungusses are so acrid, that a drop of their juice blisters the tongue; others intoxicate those who eat them. The Ostiacks in Siberia use them for the latter purpose; one fungus of the species agaricus muscarum, eaten raw, or the decoction of three of them, produces intoxication for 12 or 16 hours. History of Russia, V. I. Nichols. 1780. As all acrid plants become less so, if exposed to a boiling heat, it is probable the common mushroom may sometimes disagree from not being sufficiently stewed. The Ostiacks blister their skin by a fungus found on birch-trees; and use the agaricus officin. for soap. Ib.

There was a dispute whether the fungusses should be classed in the animal or vegetable department. Their animal taste in cookery, and their animal smell when burnt, together with their tendency to putrefaction, insomuch that the phallus impudicus has gained the name of stink-horn; and lastly, their growing and continuing healthy without light, as the licoperdon tuber or truffle, and the fungus vinosus or mucor in dark cellars, and the esculent mushrooms on beds covered thick with straw, would seem to show that they approach towards the animals, or make a kind of isthmus connecting the two mighty kingdoms of animal and of vegetable nature.

Here paused the Muse,—across the darken'd pole,
Sail the dim clouds, the echoing thunders roll;
The trembling wood-nymphs, as the tempest lowers,
Lead the gay goddess to their inmost bowers;
Hang the mute lyre the laurel shade beneath,
And round her temples bind the myrtle wreath. 480
—Now the light swallow with her airy brood
Skims the green meadow, and the dimpled flood;
Loud shrieks the lone thrush from his leafless thorn,
Th' alarmed beetle sounds his bugle horn;
Each pendent spider winds with fingers fine
His ravel'd clue, and climbs along the line;
Gay gnomes in glittering circles stand aloof
Beneath a spreading mushroom's fretted roof;
Swift bees returning seek their waxen cells, 489
And sylphs cling quivering in the lily's bells.
Through the still air descend the genial showers,
And pearly rain-drops deck the laughing flowers.

INTERLUDE.

Bookseller. Your verses, Mr. Botanist, consist of *pure description;* I hope there is *sense* in the notes.

Poet. I am only a flower-painter, or occasionally attempt a landscape; and leave the human figure, with the subjects of history, to abler artists.

B. It is well to know what subjects are within the limits of your pencil; many have failed of success from the want of this self-knowledge. But pray tell me, what is the essential difference between poetry and prose? Is it solely the melody or measure of the language?

P. I think not solely; for some prose has its melody; and even measure. And good verses, well spoken in a language unknown to the hearer, are not easily to be distinguished from good prose.

B. Is it the sublimity, beauty, or novelty of the sentiments?

P. Not so; for sublime sentiments are often better expressed in prose. Thus when Warwick, in one of the plays of Shakspeare, is left wounded on the field after the loss of the battle, and his friend says to him, " O, could you but fly!" what can be more sublime than his answer, " Why then, I would not fly." No measure of verse, I imagine, could add dignity to this sentiment. And it would be easy to select examples of the beautiful or new from prose writers, which, I suppose, no measure of verse could improve.

B. In what then consists the essential difference between poetry and prose?

P. Next to the measure of the language, the principal distinction appears to me to consist in this: that poetry admits of but few words expressive of very abstracted ideas, whereas prose abounds with them. And as our ideas derived from visible objects are more distinct than those derived from the objects of our other senses, the words expressive of these ideas belonging to vision make up the principal part of poetic language. That is, the poet writes principally to the eye; the prose-writer uses more abstracted terms. Mr. Pope has written a bad verse in the Windsor Forest:

" And Kennet swift for silver eels *renoun'd.*"

The word renown'd does not represent the idea of a visible object to the mind, and is thence prosaic. But change this line thus:

" And Kennet swift, where silver graylings *play,*"

and it becomes poetry, because the scenery is then brought before the eye.

B. This may be done in prose.

P. And when it is done in a single word, it animates the prose; so it is more agreeable to read in Mr. Gibbon's History—" Germany was at this time *over-shadowed* with extensive forests;" than " Germany was at this time *full* of extensive forests." But where this mode of expression occurs too frequently, the prose approaches to poetry; and in graver works, where we expect to be instructed rather than amused, it becomes tedious and impertinent. Some parts of Mr. Burke's eloquent orations become intricate and enervated by superfluity of poetic ornament; which quantity of ornament would have been agreeable in a poem, where much ornament is expected.

B. Is then the office of poetry only to amuse?

P. The muses are young ladies; we expect to see them dressed; though not like some modern beauties, with so much gauze and feather, that " the lady herself is the least part of her." There are, however, didactic pieces of poetry, which are much admired, as the Georgics of Virgil, Mason's English Garden, Hayley's Epistles; nevertheless science is best delivered in prose, as its mode of reasoning is from stricter analogies than metaphors or similies.

B. Do not personifications and allegories distinguish poetry?

P. These are other arts of bringing objects before the eye; or of expressing sentiments in the language of vision; and are indeed better suited to the pen than the pencil.

B. That is strange, when you have just said

they are used to bring their objects before the eye.

P In poetry the personification or allegoric figure is generally indistinct, and therefore does not strike us so forcibly as to make us attend to its improbability; but in painting, the figures being all much more distinct, their improbability becomes apparent, and seizes our attention to it. Thus the person of Concealment is very indistinct, and therefore does not compel us to attend to its improbability, in the following beautiful lines of Shakespeare:

" ——— She never told her love;
But let Concealment, like a worm i' th' bud,
Feed on her damask cheek."—

But in these lines below, the person of Reason obtrudes itself into our company, and becomes disagreeable by its distinctness, and consequent improbability:

" To Reason I flew, and intreated her aid,
Who paused on my case, and each circumstance weigh'd;
Then gravely replied in return to my prayer,
That Hebe was fairest of all that were fair.
That's a truth, replied I, I've no need to be taught,
I came to you, Reason, to find out a fault.
If that's all, says Reason, return as you came,
To find fault with Hebe would forfeit my name."

Allegoric figures are on this account in general less manageable in painting and in statuary than in poetry; and can seldom be introduced in the two former arts in company with natural figures, as is evident from the ridiculous effect of many of the paintings of Reubens in the Luxemburgh gallery; and for this reason, because their improbability becomes more striking, when there are the figures of real persons by their side to compare them with.

Mrs. Angelica Kauffman, well apprised of this circumstance, has introduced no mortal figures amongst her Cupids and her Graces. And the great Roubiliac, in his unrivalled monument of Time and Fame struggling for the trophy of General Wade, has only hung up a medallion of the head of the hero of the piece. There are, however, some allegoric figures, which we have so often heard described or seen delineated, that we almost forget that they do not exist in common life; and thence view them without astonishment; as the figures of the heathen mythology, of angels, devils, death, and time; and almost believe them to be realities, even when they are mixed with representations of the natural forms of man. Whence I conclude, that a certain degree of probability is necessary to prevent us from revolting with distaste from unnatural images; unless we are otherwise so much interested in the contemplation of them as not to perceive their improbability.

B. Is this reasoning about degrees of probability just?—When Sir Joshua Reynolds, who is unequalled both in the theory and practice of his art, and who is a great master of the pen as well as the pencil, has asserted in a discourse delivered to the Royal Academy, December 11, 1786, that " the higher styles of painting, like the higher kinds of the drama, do not aim at any thing like deception; or have any expectation that the spectators should think the events there represented are really passing before them." And he then accuses Mr. Fielding of bad judgment, when he attempts to compliment Mr. Garrick in one of his novels, by introducing an ignorant man, mistaking the representation of a scene in Hamlet for a reality; and thinks, because he was an ignorant man, he was less liable to make such a mistake.

P. It is a metaphysical question, and requires more attention than Sir Joshua has bestowed upon it.—You will allow that we are perfectly deceived in our dreams: and that even in our waking reveries, we are often so much absorbed in the contemplation of what passes in our imaginations, that for a while we do not attend to the lapse of time, or to our own locality; and thus suffer a similar kind of deception as in our dreams. That is, we believe things present before our eyes, which are not so.

There are two circumstances which contribute to this complete deception in our dreams. First, because in sleep the organs of sense are closed or inert, and hence the trains of ideas associated in our imaginations are never interrupted or dissevered by the irritations of external objects, and cannot therefore be contrasted with our sensations. On this account, though we are affected with a variety of passions in our dreams, as anger, love, joy, yet we never experience surprise.—For surprise is only produced when any external irritations suddenly obtrude themselves, and dissever our passing trains of ideas.

Secondly, because in sleep there is a total suspension of our voluntary power, both over the muscles of our bodies, and the ideas of our minds; for we neither walk about, nor reason in complete sleep. Hence, as the trains of our ideas are passing in our imaginations in dreams, we cannot compare them with our previous knowledge of things, as we do in our waking hours; for this is a voluntary exertion, and thus we cannot perceive their incongruity.

Thus we are deprived in sleep of the only two means by which we can distinguish the trains of ideas passing in our imaginations, from those excited by our sensations; and are led by their vivacity to believe them to belong to the latter. For the vivacity of these trains of ideas, passing in the imagination, is greatly increased by the causes above mentioned; that is, by their not being disturbed or dissevered, either by the appulses of external bodies, as in surprise; or by our voluntary exertions in comparing them with our previous knowledge of things, as in reasoning upon them.

B. Now to apply.

P. When by the art of the painter or poet a train of ideas is suggested to our imaginations, which interests us so much by the pain or pleasure it affords, that we cease to attend to the irritations of common external objects, and cease also to use any voluntary efforts to compare these interesting trains of ideas with our previous knowledge of things, a complete reverie is produced: during which time, however short, if it be but for a moment, the objects themselves appear to exist before us. This, I think, has been called by an ingenious critic, "the ideal presence" of such objects. (Elements of Criticism by Lord Kames.) And in respect to the compliment intended by Mr. Fielding to Mr. Garrick, it would seem that an ignorant rustic at the play of Hamlet, who has some previous belief in the appearance of ghosts, would sooner be liable to fall into a reverie, and continue in it longer, than one who possessed more knowledge of the real nature of things, and had a greater facility of exercising his reason.

B. It must require great art in the painter or poet to produce this kind of deception?

P. The matter must be interesting from its sublimity, beauty, or novelty; this is the scientific part; and the art consists in bringing these distinctly before the eye, so as to produce (as above mentioned) the ideal presence of the object, in which the great Shakspeare particularly excels.

B. Then it is not of any consequence whether the representations correspond with nature?

P. Not if they so much interest the reader or spectator as to induce the reverie above described. Nature may be seen in the market-place, or at the card table; but we expect something more than this in the play-house or picture-room. The farther the artist recedes from nature, the greater novelty he is likely to produce; if he rises above nature, he produces the sublime; and beauty is probably a selection and new combination of her most agreeable parts. Yourself will be sensible of the truth of this doctrine, by recollecting over in your mind the works of three of our celebrated artists. Sir Joshua Reynolds has introduced sublimity even into his portraits; we admire the representation of persons, whose reality we should have passed by unnoticed. Mrs. Angelica Kauffman attracts our eyes with beauty, which I suppose no where exists; certainly few Grecian faces are seen in this country. And the daring pencil of Fuseli transports us beyond the boundaries of nature, and ravishes us with the charm of the most interesting novelty. And Shakspeare, who excels in all these together, so far captivates the spectator, as to make him unmindful of every kind of violation of time, place, or existence. As at the first appearance of the ghost of Hamlet, "his ear must be dull as the fat weed which roots itself on Lethe's brink," who can attend to the improbability of the exhibition. So in many scenes of the tempest we perpetually believe the action passing before our eyes, and relapse with somewhat of distaste into common life at the intervals of the representation.

B. I suppose a poet of less ability would find such great machinery difficult and cumbersome to manage?

P. Just so, we should be shocked at the apparent improbabilities. As in the gardens of a Sicilian nobleman, described in Mr. Brydone's and in Mr. Swinburn's travels, there are said to be six hundred statues of imaginary monsters, which so disgust the spectators, that the state had once a serious design of destroying them; and yet the very improbable monsters in Ovid's metamorphoses have entertained the world for many centuries.

B. The monsters in your Botanic Garden, I hope, are of the latter kind?

P. The candid reader must determine.

THE LOVES OF THE PLANTS.

CANTO II.

Again the goddess strikes the golden lyre,
And tunes to wilder notes the warbling wire;
With soft suspended step attention moves,
And silence hovers o'er the listening groves;
Orb within orb the charmed audience throng,
And the green vault reverberates the song.

" Breathe soft, ye gales!" the fair Carlina cries,
" Bear on broad wings your votress to the skies.
How sweetly mutable yon orient hues,   9
As morn's fair hand her opening roses strews;
How bright, when iris blending many a ray,
Binds in embroider'd wreath the brow of day;
Soft, when the pendant moon with lustres pale
O'er heaven's blue arch unfurls her milky veil;
While from the north long threads of silver light
Dart on swift shuttles o'er the tissued night!

Carlina. l. 7. Carline Thistle. Of the class confederate males. The seeds of this and of many other plants of the same class are furnished with a plume, by which admirable mechanism they perform long aerial journeys, crossing lakes and deserts, and are thus disseminated far from the original plants, and have much the appearance of a shuttlecock as they fly. The wings are of different construction, some being like a divergent tuft of hairs, others are branched like feathers, some are elevated from the crown of the seed by a slender foot-stalk, which gives them a very elegant appearance, others sit immediately on the crown of the seed.

Nature has many other curious vegetable contrivances for the dispersion of seeds: see note on Helianthus. But perhaps none of them has more the appearance of design than the admirable apparatus of tillandsia for this purpose. This plant grows on the branches of trees, like the misletoe, and never on the ground; the seeds are furnished with many long threads on their crowns; which, as they are driven forwards by the winds, wrap round the arms of trees, and thus hold them fast till they vegetate. This is very analogous to the migration of spiders on the gossamer, who are said to attach themselves to the end of a long thread, and rise thus to the tops of trees or buildings, as the accidental breezes carry them.

Breathe soft, ye zephyrs! hear my fervent sighs,
Bear on broad wings your votress to the skies!"
—Plume over plume in long divergent lines
On whale-bone ribs the fair mechanic joins;   20
Inlays with eider down the silken strings,
And weaves in wide expanse Dædalian wings;
Round her bold sons the waving pennons binds,
And walks with angel-step upon the winds.

So on the shoreless air the intrepid Gaul
Launch'd the vast concave of his buoyant ball.—
Journeying on high, the silken castle glides
Bright as a meteor through the azure tides;
O'er towns, and towers, and temples, wins its way,   29
Or mounts sublime, and gilds the vault of day.
Silent with upturn'd eyes unbreathing crowds
Pursue the floating wonder to the clouds;
And, flush'd with transport or benumb'd with fear,
Watch, as it rises, the diminish'd sphere.
—Now less and less—and now a speck is seen;—
And now the fleeting rack obtrudes between!
With bended knees, raised arms, and suppliant brows,
To every shrine they breathe their mingled vows.
" Save him, ye Saints! who o'er the good preside;
Bear him ye winds! ye stars benignant! guide."
—The calm philosopher in ether sails,   41
Views broader stars, and breathes in purer gales;
Sees, like a map, in many a waving line
Round earth's blue plains her lucid waters shine;
Sees at his feet the forky lightnings glow,
And hears innocuous thunders roar below,
—Rise, great Mongolfier! urge thy venturous flight
High o'er the moon's pale ice-reflected light;
High o'er the pearly star, whose beamy horn
Hangs in the east, gay harbinger of morn;   50
Leave the red eye of Mars on rapid wing,
Jove's silver guards, and Saturn's crystal ring;

Leave the fair beams, which, issuing from afar,
Play with new lustres round the Georgian star;
Shun with strong oars the Sun's attractive throne,
The sparkling zodiac, and the milky zone;
Where headlong comets with increasing force
Through other systems bend their blazing course.—
For thee Cassiope her chair withdraws,
For thee the Bear retracts his shaggy paws; 60
High o'er the north thy golden orb shall roll,
And blaze eternal round the wondering pole.
So Argo, rising from the southern main,
Lights with new stars the blue ethereal plain;
With favouring beams the mariner protects,
And the bold course, which first it steer'd, directs.

Inventress of the woof, fair Lina flings
The flying shuttle through the dancing strings;
Inlays the broider'd weft with flowery dyes,
Quick beat the reeds, the pedals fall and rise; 70
Slow from the beam the lengths of warp unwind,
And dance and nod the massy weights behind.
Taught by her labours, from the fertile soil
Immortal Isis clothed the banks of Nile;
And fair Arachne with her rival loom
Found undeserved a melancholy doom.—
Five sister-nymphs with dewy fingers twine
The beamy flax, and stretch the fibre-line;
Quick eddying threads from rapid spindles reel,
Or whirl with beating foot the dizzy wheel. 80
—Charm'd round the busy fair *five* shepherds press,
Praise the nice texture of their snowy dress,
Admire the artists, and the art approve,
And tell with honey'd words the tale of love.

So now, where Derwent rolls his dusky floods
Through vaulted mountains, and a night of woods,
The nymph, Gossypia, treads the velvet sod,
And warms with rosy smiles the watery god;

His ponderous oars to slender spindles turns,
And pours o'er massy wheels his foamy urns;
With playful charms her hoary lover wins, 91
And wields his trident,—while the Monarch spins.
—First with nice eye emerging Naiads cull
From leathery pods the vegetable wool;
With wiry teeth *revolving cards* release
The tangled knots, and smooth the ravell'd fleece;
Next moves the *iron hand* with fingers fine,
Combs the wide card, and forms the eternal line;
Slow, with soft lips, the *whirling can* acquires
The tender skeins, and wraps in rising spires;
With quicken'd pace *successive rollers* move, 101
And these retain, and those extend the *rove;*
Then fly the spoles, the rapid axles glow,
And slowly circumvolves the labouring wheel below.

Papyra, throned upon the banks of Nile,
Spread her smooth leaf, and waved her silver style.

For thee the Bear. l. 60. Tibi jam brachia contrahit ardens Scorpius. Virg. Georg. l. i. 34. A new star appeared in Cassiope's chair in 1572. Herschel's Construction of the Heavens. Phil. Trans. V. 75. p. 266.

Linum. l. 67. Flax. Five males and five females. It was first found on the banks of the Nile. The linum lusitanicum, or Portugal flax, has ten males: see the note on Curcuma. Isis was said to invent spinning and weaving; mankind before that time were clothed with the skins of animals. The fable of Arachne was to compliment this new art of spinning and weaving, supposed to surpass in fineness the web of the spider.

Gossypia. l. 87. Gossypium. The cotton plant. On the river Derwent, near Matlock, in Derbyshire, Sir Richard Arkwright has erected his curious and magnificent machinery for spinning cotton, which had been in vain attempted by many ingenious artists before him. The cotton-wool is first picked from the pods and seeds by women. It is then carded by *cylindrical cards*, which move against each other, with different velocities. It is taken from these by an *iron hand* or comb, which has a motion similar to that of scratching, and takes the wool off the cards longitudinally in respect to the fibres or staple, producing a continued line loosely cohering, called the *rove* or *roving*. This rove, yet very loosely twisted, is then received or drawn into a *whirling cannister*, and is rolled by the centrifugal force in spiral lines within it, being yet too tender for the spindle. It is then passed between *two pairs of rollers;* the second pair moving faster than the first elongate the thread with greater equality than can be done by the hand; and it is then twisted on spoles or bobbins.

The great fertility of the cotton-plant in these fine flexile threads, while those from flax, hemp, and nettles, or from the bark of the mulberry-tree, require a previous putrefaction of the parenchymatous substance, and much mechanical labour, and afterwards bleaching, renders this plant of great importance to the world. And since Sir Richard Arkwright's ingenious machine has not only greatly abbreviated and simplified the labour and art of carding and spinning the cotton-wool, but performs both these circumstances *better* than can be done by hand, it is probable that the clothing of this small seed will become the principal clothing of mankind; though animal wool and silk may be preferable in colder climates, as they are more imperfect conductors of heat, and are thence a warmer clothing.

Emerging Naiads. l. 93.
—— Eam circum Milesia vellera nymphæ
Carpebant, hyali saturo fucata colore.
Vir. Georg. IV. 334.

Cyperus, Papyrus. l. 105. Three males, one female. The leaf of this plant was first used for

—The storied pyramid, the laurel'd bust,
The trophied arch had crumbled into dust;
The sacred symbol, and the epic song,
(Unknown the character, forgot the tongue,) 110
With each unconquer'd chief, or sainted maid,
Sunk undistinguished in oblivion's shade.
Sad o'er the scatter'd ruins Genius sigh'd,
And infant Arts but learn'd to lisp and died.
Till to astonish'd realms Papyra taught
To paint in mystic colours sound and thought,
With wisdom's voice to print the page sublime,
And mark in adamant the steps of time.
—*Three* favour'd youths her soft attention share,
The fond disciples of the studious Fair, 120
Hear her sweet voice, the golden process prove;
Gaze, as they learn; and, as they listen, love.
The first from Alpha to Omega joins
The letter'd tribes along the level lines;
Weighs with nice ear the vowel, liquid, surd,
And breaks in syllables the volant word.
Then forms *the next* upon the marshal'd plain
In deepening ranks his dexterous cypher-train;
And counts, as wheel the decimating bands,
The dews of Ægypt, or Arabia's sands. 130
And then *the third* on four concordant lines
Prints the lone crotchet, and the quaver joins;
Marks the gay trill, the solemn pause inscribes,
And parts with bars the undulating tribes.

---

paper, whence the word *paper;* and leaf, or folium, for a fold of a book. Afterwards the bark of a species of mulberry was used; whence *liber* signifies a book, and the bark of a tree. Before the invention of letters mankind may be said to have been perpetually in their infancy, as the arts of one age or country generally died with their inventors. Whence arose the policy, which still continues in Hindostan, of obliging the son to practise the profession of his father. After the discovery of letters, the facts of Astronomy and Chemistry became recorded in written language, though the ancient hieroglyphic characters for the planets and metals continue in use at this day. The antiquity of the invention of music, of astronomical observations, and the manufacture of gold and iron, are recorded in Scripture.

About twenty letters, ten cyphers, and seven crotchets, represent by their numerous combinations all our ideas and sensations! the musical characters are probably arrived at their perfection, unless emphasis, and tone, and swell, could be expressed, as well as note and time. Charles the Twelfth, of Sweden, had a design to have introduced a numeration by squares, instead of by decimation, which might have served the purposes of philosophy better than the present mode, which is said to be of Arabic invention. The alphabet is yet in a very imperfect state; perhaps seventeen letters could express all the simple sounds in the European languages. In China they have not yet learned to divide their words into syllables, and are thence necessitated to employ many thousand characters; it is said above eighty thousand. It is to be wished, in this ingenious age, that the European nations would accord to reform our alphabet.

Pleased round her cane-wove throne, the applauding crowd
Clapp'd their rude hands, their swarthy foreheads bow'd;
With loud acclaim " a present God!" they cried,
" A present God!" rebellowing shores replied.
Then peal'd at intervals with mingled swell
The echoing harp, shrill clarion, horn, and shell; 140
While Bards ecstatic, bending o'er the lyre,
Struck deeper chords, and wing'd the song with fire.
Then mark'd astronomers with keener eyes
The moon's refulgent journey through the skies;
Watch'd the swift comets urge their blazing cars,
And weigh'd the sun with his revolving stars.
High raised the chemists their hermetic wands,
(And changing forms obey'd their waving hands,)
Her treasured gold from earth's deep chambers tore,
Or fused and harden'd her chalybeate ore. 150
All with bent knee from fair Papyra claim
Wove by her hands the wreath of deathless fame.
—Exulting Genius crown'd his darling child,
The young Arts clasp'd her knees, and Virtue smiled.

So now Delany forms her mimic bowers,
Her paper foliage, and her silken flowers;
Her virgin train the tender scissars ply,
Vein the green leaf, the purple petal dye:
Round wiry stems the flaxen tendril bends,
Moss creeps below, and waxen fruit impends. 160
Cold Winter views amid his realms of snow
Delany's vegetable statues blow;
Smooths his stern brow, delays his hoary wing,
And eyes with wonder all the blooms of spring.

So now Delany. l. 155. Mrs. Delany has finished nine hundred and seventy accurate and elegant representations of different vegetables with the parts of their flowers, fructification, &c. according with the classification of Linneus, in what she terms paper mosaic. She began this work at the age of 74, when her sight would no longer serve her to paint, in which she much excelled: between her age of 74 and 82, at which time her eyes quite failed her, she executed the curious hortus siccus above mentioned, which I suppose contains a greater number of plants than were ever before drawn from the life by any one person. Her method consisted in placing the leaves of each plant with the petals, and all the other parts of the flowers on coloured paper, and cutting them with scissars accurately to the natural size and form, and then pasting them on a dark ground; the effect of which is wonderful, and their accuracy less liable to fallacy than drawings. She is at this time (1788) in her 89th year, with all the powers of a fine understanding still unimpaired. I am informed another very ingenious lady, Mrs. North, is constructing a similar hortus siccus, or paper-garden; which she executes on a ground of vellum with such elegant taste and scientific accuracy, that it cannot fail to become a work of inestimable value.

The gentle Lapsana, Nymphæa fair,
And bright Calendula with golden hair,
Watch with nice eye the earth's diurnal way,
Marking her solar and sidereal day,
Her slow mutation, and her varying clime 169
And trace with mimic art the march of Time;
Round his light foot a magic chain they fling,
And count the quick vibrations of his wing—
First in its brazen cell reluctant roll'd
Bends the dark spring in many a steely fold.
On spiral brass is stretch'd the wiry thong,
Tooth urges tooth, and wheel drives wheel along;
In diamond-eyes the polish'd axles flow,
Smooth slides the hand, the balance pants below.
Round the white circlet in relievo bold
A Serpent twines his scaly length in gold; 180
And brightly pencil'd on the enamel'd sphere
Live the fair trophies of the passing year.
—Here *Time's* huge fingers grasp his giant mace,
And dash proud Superstition from her base;
Rend her strong towers and gorgeous fanes, and shed
The crumbling fragments round her guilty head.
There the gay *Hours*, whom wreaths of roses deck,
Lead their young trains amid the cumbrous wreck,
And, slowly purpling o'er the mighty waste,
Plant the fair growths of science and of taste.
While each light *Moment*, as it dances by 191
With feathery foot and pleasure-twinkling eye,
Feeds from its baby-hand, with many a kiss,
The callow nestlings of domestic bliss.

As yon gay clouds, which canopy the skies,
Change their thin forms, and lose their lucid dyes;
So the soft bloom of beauty's vernal charms
Fades in our eyes, and withers in our arms.
—Bright as the silvery plume, or pearly shell,
The snow-white rose, or lily's virgin bell, 200
The fair Helleboras attractive shone,
Warm'd every sage, and every shepherd won.—
Round the gay sisters press the *enamour'd bands*,
And seek with soft solicitude their hands.
—Erewhile how changed!—in dim suffusion lies
The glance divine, that lighten'd in their eyes;
Cold are those lips, where smiles seductive hung,
And the weak accents linger on their tongue;
Each roseate feature fades to livid green—
—Disgust with face averted shuts the scene. 210

So from his gorgeous throne, which awed the world,
The mighty monarch of Assyria hurl'd,
Sojourn'd with brutes beneath the midnight storm,
Changed by avenging Heaven in mind and form.
—Prone to the earth he bends his brow superb,
Crops the young floret and the bladed herb;
Lolls his red tongue, and from the reedy side
Of slow Euphrates laps the muddy tide.
Long eagle plumes his arching neck invest,
Steal round his arms, and clasp his sharpen'd breast; 220
Dark brinded hairs, in bristling ranks, behind,
Rise o'er his back, and rustle in the wind;
Clothe his lank sides, his shrivel'd limbs surround,
And human hands with talons print the ground.
Silent in shining troops the courtier-throng
Pursue their monarch, as he crawls along;

Lapsana, Nymphæa alba, Calendula. l. 165. And many other flowers close and open their petals at certain hours of the day; and thus constitute what Linneus calls the Horologe, or watch of Flora. He enumerates 46 flowers, which possess this kind of sensibility. I shall mention a few of them with their respective hours of rising and setting, as Linneus terms them. He divides them into *meteoric* flowers, which less accurately observe the hour of unfolding, but are expanded sooner or later, according to the cloudiness, moisture, or pressure of the atmosphere. 2d. *Tropical* flowers open in the morning, and close before evening every day; but the hour of the expanding becomes earlier or later, as the length of the day increases or decreases. 3dly. *Æquinoctial* flowers, which open at a certain and exact hour of the day, and for the most part close at another determinate hour.

Hence the horologe or watch of Flora is formed from numerous plants, of which the following are those most common in this country. Leontodon taraxacum, dandelion, opens at 5—6, closes at 8—9. Hieracium pilosello, mouse-ear hawkweed, opens at 8, closes at 2. Sonchus lævis, smooth sowthistle, at 5 and at 11—12. Lactuca sativa, cultivated lettice, at 7 and 10. Tragopogon luteum, yellow goatsbeard, at 3—5 and at 9—10. Lapsana, nipplewort, at 5—6 and at 10—1. Nymphæa alba, white water lily, at 7 and 5. Papaver nudicaule, naked poppy, at 5 and at 7. Hemerocallis fulva, tawny daylily, at 5 and at 7—8. Convolvulus, at 5—6. Malva, mallow, at 9—10 and at I. Arenaria purpurea, purple sandwort, at 9—10 and at 2—3. Anagallis, pimpernel, at 7—8. Portulaca hortensis, garden purslain, at 9—10, and at 11—12. Dianthus prolifer, proliferous pink, at 8 and at 1. Cichoreum, succory, at 4—5. H‚pochæris, at 6—7, and at 4—5. Crepis, at 4—5, and at 10—11. Picris, at 4—5, and at 12. Calendula field, at 9, and at 3. Calendula African, at 7, and at 3—4.

As these observations were probably made in the botanic gardens at Upsal, they must require farther attention to suit them to our climate. See Stillingfleet's Calendar of Flora.

Helleborus. l. 201. Many males, many females. The helleborus niger, or Christmas rose, has a large beautiful white flower, adorned with a circle of tubular two lipped nectaries. After impregnation the flower undergoes a remarkable change, the nectaries drop off, but the white corol remains, and gradually becomes quite green. This curious metamorphose of the corol, when the nectaries fall off, seems to show that the white juices of the corol were before carried to the nectaries, for the purpose of producing honey; because when these nectaries fall off, no more of the white juice is secreted in the corol, but it becomes green, and degenerates into a calyx. See note on Lonicera. The nectary of the tropæolum, garden nasturtion, is a coloured horn growing from the calyx.

E'en beauty pleads in vain with smiles and tears,
Nor flattery's self can pierce his pendant ears.

Two sister-nymphs to Ganges' flowery brink
Bend their light steps, the lucid water drink, 230
Wind through the dewy rice, and nodding canes,
(As *eight* black eunuchs guard the sacred plains),
With playful malice watch the scaly brood,
And shower the inebriate berries on the flood.—
Stay in your crystal chambers, silver tribes!
Turn your bright eyes, and shun the dangerous bribes;
The tramell'd net with less destruction sweeps
Your curling shallows, and your azure deeps;
With less deceit, the gilded fly beneath, 239
Lurks the fell hook unseen,—to taste is death!
—Dim your slow eyes, and dull your pearly coat,
Drunk on the waves your languid forms shall float,
On useless fins in giddy circles play,
And herons and otters seize you for their prey.—

So, when the saint from Padua's graceless land
In silent anguish sought the barren strand,
High on the shatter'd beech sublime he stood,
Still'd with his waving arm the babbling flood;
"To man's dull ear," he cried, "I call in vain,
Hear me, ye scaly tenants of the main!"— 250
Misshapen seals approach in circling flocks,
In dusky mail the tortoise climbs the rocks,
Torpedoes, sharks, rays, porpus, dolphins, pour
Their twinkling squadrons round the glittering shore;
With tangled fins, behind, huge phocæ glide,
And whales and grampi swell the distant tide.
Then kneel'd the hoary seer, to Heaven address'd
His fiery eyes, and smote his sounding breast;
"Bless ye the Lord," with thundering voice he cried,
"Bless ye the Lord!" the bending shores replied; 260
The winds and waters caught the sacred word,
And mingling echoes shouted "Bless the Lord!"
The listening shoals the quick contagion feel,
Pant on the floods, inebriate with their zeal,
Ope their wide jaws, and bow their slimy heads,
And dash with frantic fins their foamy beds.

Sofa'd on silk, amid her charm-built towers,
Her meads of asphodel, and amaranth bowers,
Where sleep and silence guard the soft abodes,
In sullen apathy Papaver nods. 270
Faint o'er her couch in scintillating streams
Pass the thin forms of fancy and of dreams;
Froze by inchantment on the velvet ground,
Fair youths and beauteous ladies glitter round;
On crystal pedestals they seem to sigh,
Bend the meek knee, and lift the imploring eye.
—And now the sorceress bares her shrivel'd hand,
And circles thrice in air her ebon wand;
Flush'd with new life descending statues talk,
The pliant marble softening as they walk; 280
With deeper sobs reviving lovers breathe,
Fair bosoms rise, and soft hearts pant beneath;
With warmer lips relenting damsels speak,
And kindling blushes tinge the Parian cheek;
To viewless lutes aerial voices sing,
And hovering loves are heard on rustling wing.
—She waves her wand again!—fresh horrors seize [freeze;
Their stiffening limbs, their vital currents
By each cold nymph her marble lover lies,
And iron slumbers seal their glassy eyes. 290
So with his dread Caduceus Hermes led
From the dark regions of the imprison'd dead,
Or drove in silent shoals the lingering train
To night's dull shore, and Pluto's dreary reign.

So with her waving pencil Crewe commands
The realms of taste, and fancy's fairy lands;
Calls up with magic voice the shapes, that sleep
In earth's dark bosom or unfathom'd deep;
That shrined in air on viewless wings aspire,
Or blazing bathe in elemental fire. 300
As with nice touch her plastic hand she moves,
Rise the fine forms of beauties, graces, loves;
Kneel to the fair inchantress, smile or sigh,
And fade or flourish, as she turns her eye.

Two sister-nymphs. l. 229. Menispermum, cocculus. Indian berry. Two houses, twelve males. In the female flower there are two styles and eight filaments without anthers on their summits; which are called by Linneus eunuchs. See the note on Curcuma. The berry intoxicates fish. Saint Anthony of Padua, when the people refused to hear him, preached to the fish, and converted them. Addison's Travels in Italy.

Papaver. l. 270. Poppy. Many males, many females. The plants of this class are almost all of them poisonous; the finest opium is procured by wounding the heads of large poppies with a three-edged knife, and tying muscle-shells to them to catch the drops. In small quantities it exhilarates the mind, raises the passions, and invigorates the body: in large ones it is succeeded by intoxication, languor, stupor, and death. It is customary in India for a messenger to travel above a hundred miles without rest or food, except an appropriated bit of opium for himself, and a larger one for his horse at certain stages. The emaciated and decrepid appearance, with the ridiculous and idiotic gestures, of the opium-eaters in Constantinople is well described in the Memoirs of Baron de Tott.

So with her waving pencil. l. 295. Alluding to the many beautiful paintings by Miss Emma Crewe, to whom the author is indebted for the very elegant frontispiece, where Flora, at play with Cupid, is loading him with garden-tools.

Fair Cista, rival of the rosy dawn,
Call'd her light choir, and trod the dewy lawn;
Hail'd with rude melody the new-born May,
As cradled yet in April's lap she lay.

I.

" Born in yon blaze of orient sky,
   Sweet May! thy radiant form unfold,   310
Unclose thy blue voluptuous eye,
   And wave thy shadowy locks of gold.

II.

For thee the fragrant zephyrs blow,
   For thee descends the sunny shower;
The rills in softer murmurs flow,
   And brighter blossoms gem the bower.

III.

Light Graces dress'd in flowery wreaths,
   And tiptoe Joys their hands combine;
And Love his sweet contagion breathes,
   And laughing dances round thy shrine.   320

IV.

Warm with new life the glittering throngs
   On quivering fin and rustling wing
Delighted join their votive songs,
   And hail thee, Goddess of the Spring,"

O'er the green brinks of Severn's oozy bed,
In changeful rings, her sprightly troops she led;
Pan tripp'd before, where Eudness shades the mead,
And blew with glowing lips his sevenfold reed;
Emerging Naiads swell'd the jocund strain, 328
And aped with mimic step the dancing train.—
" I faint, I fall!"—*at noon* the beauty cried,
" Weep o'er my tomb, ye nymphs!"—and sunk and died.
—Thus, when white Winter o'er the shivering clime
Drives the still snow, or showers the silver rime;
As the lone shepherd o'er the dazzling rocks
Prints his steep step, and guides his vagrant flocks;
Views the green holly veil'd in net-work nice,
Her vermil clusters twinkling in the ice;
Admires the lucid vales, and slumbering flood,
Suspended cataracts, and crystal woods,   340
Transparent towns, with seas of milk between,
And eyes with transport the refulgent scene:
If breaks the sunshine o'er the spangled trees,
Or flits on tepid wing the western breeze,
In liquid dews descends the transient glare,
And all the glittering pageant melts in air.

Where Andes hides his cloud-wreath'd crest in snow,
And roots his base on burning sands below;
Cinchona, fairest of Peruvian maids,
To health's bright goddess in the breezy glades
On Quito's temperate plain an altar rear'd, 351
Trill'd the loud hymn, the solemn prayer preferr'd:
Each balmy bud she culled, and honey'd flower,
And hung with fragrant wreaths the sacred bower;
Each pearly sea she search'd, and sparkling mine,
And plied their treasures on the gorgeous shrine;
Her suppliant voice for sickening Loxa raised,
Sweet breathed the gale, and bright the censor blazed.
" —Divine Hygeia! on thy votaries bend
Thy angel-looks, oh, hear us, and defend! 360
While streaming o'er the night with baleful glare
The star of Autumn rays his misty hair;
Fierce from his fens the giant Ague springs,
And wrapp'd in fogs descends on vampire wings;
Before, with shuddering limbs, cold Tremor reels,
And Fever's burning nostril dogs his heels;
Loud claps the grinning fiend his iron hands,
Stamps with black hoof, and shouts along the lands;

Cistus labdaniferus. l. 305. Many males, one female. The petals of this beautiful and fragrant shrub, as well as of the Œnothera, tree-primrose, and others, continue expanded but a few hours, falling off about noon, or soon after, in hot weather. The most beautiful flowers of the Cactus grandiflorus (see Cerea) are of equally short duration, but have their existence in the night. And the flowers of the Hibiscus trionum are said to continue but a single hour. The courtship between the males and females in these flowers might be easily watched; the males are said to approach and recede from the females alternately. The flowers of the Hibiscus sinensis, mutable rose, live in the West Indies, their native climate, but one day; but have this remarkable property, they are white at their first expansion, then change to deep red, and become purple as they decay.

The gum or resin of this fragrant vegetable is collected from extensive underwoods of it in the East by a singular contrivance. Long leathern thongs are tied to poles and cords, and drawn over the tops of these shrubs about noon; which thus collect the dust of the anthers, which adheres to the leather, and is occasionally scraped off. Thus in some degree is the manner imitated, in which the bee collects on his thighs and legs the same material for the construction of his combs.

Sevenfold reed. l. 328. The sevenfold reed, with which Pan is frequently described, seems to indicate that he was the inventor of the musical gamut.

Cinchona. l. 349. Peruvian bark-tree. Five males, and one female. Several of these trees were felled for other purposes into a lake, when an epidemic fever of a very mortal kind prevailed at Loxa in Peru, and the woodmen, accidentally drinking the water, were cured; and thus were discovered the virtues of this famous drug.

Withers the damask cheek, unnerves the strong,
And drives with scorpion-lash the shrieking throng. 370
Oh, goddess! on thy kneeling votaries bend
Thy angel-looks, oh, hear us, and defend!"
—Hygeia, leaning from the bless'd abodes,
The crystal mansions of the immortal gods,
Saw the sad nymph uplift her dewy eyes,
Spread her white arms, and breathe her fervid sigh;
Call'd to her fair associates, Youth and Joy,
And shot all radiant through the glittering sky;
Loose waved behind her golden train of hair,
Her sapphire mantle swam diffused in air. 380
O'er the grey matted moss, and pansied sod,
With step sublime the glowing goddess trod,
Gilt with her beamy eye the conscious shade,
And with her smile celestial bless'd the maid.
" Come to my arms, with seraph voice she cries,
Thy vows are heard, benignant nymph! arise;
Where yon aspiring trunks fantastic wreath
Their mingled roots, and drink the rill beneath,
Yield to the biting axe thy sacred wood,
And strew the bitter foliage on the flood." 390
In silent homage bow'd the blushing maid,—
Five youths athletic hasten to her aid,
O'er the scar'd hills re-echoing strokes resound,
And headlong forests thunder on the ground.
Round the dark roots, rent bark, and shatter'd boughs,
From ocherous beds the swelling fountain flows;
With streams austere its winding margin laves,
And pours from vale to vale its dusky waves.
—As the pale squadrons, bending o'er the brink,
View with a sigh their alter'd forms, and drink;
Slow-ebbing life with refluent crimson breaks
O'er their wan lips, and paints their haggard cheeks: 403
Through each fine nerve rekindling transports dart, [heart.
Light the quick eye, and swell the exulting
—Thus Israel's heaven-taught chief o'er trackless sands
Led to the sultry rock his murmuring bands.
Bright o'er his brows the forky radiance blazed,
And high in air the rod divine he raised.—
Wide yawns the cliff!—amid the thirsty throng
Rush the redundant waves, and shine along;
With gourds, and shells, and helmets, press the bands, 411
Ope their parch'd lips, and spread their eager hands, [shower,
Snatch their pale infants to the exuberant
Kneel on the shatter'd rock, and bless the Almighty Power.

Bolster'd with down, amid a thousand wants,
Pale dropsy rears his bloated form, and pants;
" Quench me, ye cool pellucid rills!" he cries,
Wets his parch'd tongue, and rolls his hollow eyes.

So bends tormented Tantalus to drink,
While from his lips the refluent waters shrink;
Again the rising stream his bosom laves, 421
And thirst consumes him, 'mid circumfluent waves.

—Divine Hygeia, from the bending sky
Descending, listens to his piercing cry;
Assumes bright Digitalis' dress and air,
Her ruby cheek, white neck, and raven hair;
Four youths protect her from the circling throng,
And like the nymph the goddess steps along.—
O'er him she waves her serpent-wreathed wand,
Cheers with her voice, and raises with her hand,
Warms with rekindling bloom his visage wan,
And charms the shapeless monster into man. 432

So when contagion with mephitic breath
And wither'd famine urged the work of death;
Marseilles' good Bishop, London's generous Mayor, [prayer,
With food and faith, with medicine and

Digitalis. l. 425. Of the class two powers. Four males, one female. Foxglove. The effect of this plant in that kind of dropsy, which is termed anasarca, where the legs and thighs are much swelled, attended with great difficulty of breathing, is truly astonishing. In the ascites accompanied with anasarca of people past the meridian of life, it will also sometimes succeed. The method of administering it requires some caution, as it is liable, in greater doses, to induce very violent and debilitating sickness, which continues one or two days, during which time the dropsical collection, however, disappears. One large spoonful, or half an ounce, of the following decoction, given twice a day, will generally succeed in a few days. But in more robust people, one large spoonful every two hours, till four spoonfuls are taken, or till sickness occurs, will evacuate the dropsical swellings with greater certainty, but is liable to operate more violently. Boil four ounces of the fresh leaves of purple foxglove (which leaves may be had at all seasons of the year) from two pints of water to twelve ounces; add to the strained liquor, while yet warm, three ounces of rectified spirit of wine. A theory of the effects of this medicine, with many successful cases, may be seen in a pamphlet, called, " Experiments on Mucilaginous and Purulent Matter," published by Dr. Darwin, in 1780.

Marseilles' good Bishop. l. 435. In the year 1720 and 1722, the plague made dreadful havock at Marseilles; at which time the Bishop was indefatigable in the execution of his pastoral office, visiting, relieving, encouraging, and absolving the sick with extreme tenderness; and though perpetually exposed to the infection, like Sir John Lawrence, mentioned below, they both are said to have escaped the disease.

London's generous Mayor. l. 435. During the great plague at London in the year 1665, Sir John Lawrence, the then Lord Mayor, continued the whole time in the city; heard complaints and redressed them; enforced the wisest regulations then known, and saw them executed. The day after the disease was known with certainty to be the plague, above 40,000 servants were dis-

Raised the weak head, and stay'd the parting sigh,
Or with new life relumed the swimming eye.—
—And now, Philanthropy! thy rays divine
Dart round the globe from Zembla to the Line;
O'er each dark prison plays the cheering light,
Like northern lustres o'er the vault of night.—
From realm to realm, with cross or crescent crown'd, 443
Where'er mankind and misery are found,
O'er burning sands, deep waves, or wilds of snow,
Thy Howard journeying seeks the house of wo.
Down many a winding step to dungeons dank,
Where anguish wails aloud, and fetters clank;
To caves bestrew'd with many a mouldering bone,
And cells, whose echoes only learn to groan; 450
Where no kind bars a whispering friend disclose,
No sunbeam enters, and no zephyr blows,
He treads, inemulous of fame or wealth,
Profuse of toil, and prodigal of health,
With soft assuasive eloquence expands
Power's rigid heart, and opes his clenching hands;
Leads stern-eyed Justice to the dark domains,
If not to sever, to relax the chains;
Or guides awaken'd Mercy through the gloom,
And shows the prison, sister to the tomb!— 460
Gives to her babes the self-devoted wife,
To her fond husband liberty and life!—
—The spirits of the good, who bend from high
Wide o'er these earthly scenes their partial eye,
When first, array'd in Virtue's purest robe,
They saw her Howard traversing the globe,
Saw round his brows her sun-like glory blaze
In arrowy circles of unwearied rays;
Mistook a mortal for an angel-guest, 469
And ask'd what seraph-foot the earth imprest.
—Onward he moves!—Disease and Death retire,
And murmuring Demons hate him, and admire."

Here paused the Goddess—on Hygeia's shrine
Obsequious Gnomes repose the lyre divine;
Descending Sylphs relax the trembling strings,
And catch the rain-drops on their shadowy wings.
—And now her vase a modest Naiad fills
With liquid crystal from her pebbly rills;
Piles the dry cedar round her silver urn,
(Bright climbs the blaze, the crackling faggots burn,) 480
Culls the green herb of China's envy'd bowers,
In gaudy cups the streaming treasure pours;
And, sweetly smiling, on her bended knee
Presents the fragrant quintessence of Tea.

---

missed, and turned into the streets to perish, for no one would receive them into their houses; and the villages near London drove them away with pitch-forks and fire-arms. Sir John Lawrence supported them all, as well as the needy who were sick, at first by expending his own fortune, till subscriptions could be solicited and received from all parts of the nation. *Journal of the Plague-year.*

x

INTERLUDE II.

Bookseller. The monsters of your Botanic Garden are as surprising as the bulls with brazen feet, and the fire-breathing dragons, which guarded the Hesperian fruit; yet are they not disgusting, nor mischievous: and in the manner you have chained them together in your exhibition, they succeed each other amusingly enough, like prints of the London Cries, wrapped upon rollers, with a glass before them. In this at least they resemble the monsters in Ovid's Metamorphoses; but your similes, I suppose, are Homeric?

Poet. The great bard well understood how to make use of this kind of ornament in epic poetry. He brings his valiant heroes into the field with much parade, and sets them a fighting with great fury; and then, after a few thrusts and parries, he introduces a long string of similes. During this the battle is supposed to continue: and thus the time necessary for the action is gained in our imaginations; and a degree of probability produced, which contributes to the temporary deception or reverie of the reader.

But the similes of Homer have another agreeable characteristic; they do not quadrate, or go upon all fours (as it is called), like the more formal similes of some modern writers; any one resembling feature seems to be with him a sufficient excuse for the introduction of this kind of digression; he then proceeds to deliver some agreeable poetry on this new subject, and thus converts every simile into a kind of short episode.

B. Then a simile should not very accurately resemble the subject?

P. No; it would then become a philosophical analogy, it would be ratiocination instead of poetry: it need only so far resemble the subject, as poetry itself ought to resemble nature. It should have so much sublimity, beauty, or novelty, as to interest the reader; and should be expressed in picturesque language, so as to bring the scenery before his eye; and should lastly bear so much veri-similitude as not to awaken him by the violence of improbability or incongruity.

B. May not the reverie of the reader be dissipated or disturbed by disagreeable images being presented to his imagination, as well as by improbable or incongruous ones?

P. Certainly; he will endeavour to rouse himself from a disagreeable reverie, as from the night-mare. And from this may be discovered the line of boundary between the tragic and the horrid; which line, however, will veer a little this way or that, according to the prevailing manners of the age or country, and the peculiar association of ideas, or idiosyncrasy of mind, of individuals. For instance, if an artist should represent the death of an officer in battle, by showing a little blood on the bosom of his shirt, as if a bullet had there penetrated, the dying figure would affect the beholder with pity; and if fortitude was at the same time expressed in his countenance, admiration would be added to our pity. On the contrary, if the artist should choose to represent his thigh as shot away by a cannon ball, and should exhibit the bleeding flesh and shattered bone of the stump, the picture would introduce into our minds ideas from a butcher's shop, or a surgeon's operation room, and we should turn from it with disgust. So if characters were brought upon the stage with their limbs disjointed by torturing instruments, and the floor covered with clotted blood and scattered brains, our theatric reverie would be destroyed by disgust, and we should leave the playhouse with detestation.

The painters have been more guilty in this respect than the poets; the cruelty of Apollo in flaying Marsyas alive is a favourite subject with the ancient artists: and the tortures of expiring martyrs have disgraced the modern ones. It requires little genius to exhibit the muscles in convulsive action either by the pencil or the chisel, because the interstices are deep, and the lines strongly defined: but those tender gradations of muscular action, which constitute the graceful attitudes of the body, are difficult to conceive or to execute, except by a master of nice discernment and cultivated taste.

B. By what definition would you distinguish the Horrid from the Tragic?

P. I suppose the latter consists of distress attended with pity, which is said to be allied to Love, the most agreeable of all our passions; and the former in distress, accompanied with disgust, which is allied to Hate, and is one of our most disagreeable sensations. Hence, when horrid scenes of cruelty are represented in pictures, we wish to disbelieve their existence, and voluntarily exert ourselves to escape from the deception: whereas the bitter cup of true Tragedy is mingled with some sweet consolatory drops, which endear our tears, and we continue to contemplate the interesting delusion with a delight, which is not easy to explain.

B. Has not this been explained by Lucretius, where he describes a shipwreck; and says, the spectators receive pleasure from feeling themselves safe on land? and by Akenside, in his beautiful poem on the Pleasures of Imagination, who ascribes it to our finding objects for the due exertion of our passions?

P. We must not confound our sensations at the contemplation of real misery with those, which we experience at the scenical representations of tragedy. The spectators of a shipwreck may be attracted by the dignity and novelty of the object; and from these may be said to receive pleasure; but not from the distress of the sufferers. An ingenious writer who has criticised this dialogue in the English Review for August, 1789, adds, that one great source of our pleasure from scenical distress arises from our, at the same time, generally contemplating one of the noblest objects of nature, that of Virtue triumphant over difficulty and oppression, or supporting its votary under ever suffering: or where this does not occur, that our minds are relieved by the justice of some signal punishment awaiting the delinquent. But, besides this, at the exhibition of a good tragedy, we are not only amused by the dignity, and novelty, and beauty, of the objects before us; but, if any distressful circumstance occur too forcibly for our sensibility, we can voluntarily exert ourselves, and recollect, that the scenery is not real: and thus not only the pain, which we had received from the apparent distress, is lessened, but a new source of pleasure is open to us, similar to that which we frequently have felt on awaking from a distressful dream; we are glad that it is not true. We are at the same time unwilling to relinquish the pleasure which we receive from the other interesting circumstances of the drama; and on that account quickly permit ourselves to relapse into the delusion; and thus alternately believe and disbelieve, almost every moment, the existence of the objects represented before us.

B. Have those two sovereigns of poetic land, Homer and Shakspeare, kept their works entirely free from the horrid?—or even yourself in your third Canto?

P. The descriptions of the mangled carcases of the companions of Ulysses, in the cave of Polypheme, is in this respect certainly objectionable, as is well observed by Scaliger. And in the play of Titus Andronicus, if that was written by Shakspeare (which from its internal evidence I think very improbable,) there are many horrid and disgustful circumstances. The following Canto is submitted to the candour of the critical reader, to whose opinion I shall submit in silence.

THE
LOVES OF THE PLANTS.

CANTO III.

AND now the Goddess sounds her silver shell,
And shakes with deeper tones the enchanted dell;
Pale, round her grassy throne, bedew'd with tears,
Flit the thin forms of Sorrows, and of Fears;
Soft Sighs responsive whisper to the chords,
And Indignations half-unsheath their swords.

" Thrice round the grave Circæa prints her tread,
And chants the numbers, which disturb the dead;
Shakes o'er the holy earth her sable plume,
Waves her dread wand, and strikes the echoing tomb! 10
—Pale shoot the stars across the troubled night,
The tim'rous moon withholds her conscious light;
Shrill scream the famish'd bats, and shivering owls,
And loud and long the dog of midnight howls!
—Then yawns the bursting ground!—two imps obscene
Rise on broad wings, and hail the baleful queen;
Each with dire grin salutes the potent wand,
And leads the sorceress with his sooty hand; 18
Onward they glide, where sheds the sickly yew
O'er many a mouldering bone its nightly dew;
The ponderous portals of the church unbar,—
Hoarse on their hinge the ponderous portals jar;
As through the colour'd glass the moon-Beam falls,
Huge shapeless spectres quiver on the walls;
Low murmurs creep along the hollow ground,
And to each step the pealing aisles resound;
By glimmering lamps, protecting saints among,
The shrines all trembling as they pass along,
O'er the still choir with hideous laugh they move,
(Fiends yell below, and angels weep above!) 30
Their impious march to God's high altar bend,
With feet impure the sacred steps ascend;
With wine unbless'd the holy chalice stain,
Assume the mitre, and the cope profane:
To heaven their eyes in mock devotion throw
And to the cross with horrid mummery bow;
Adjure by mimic rites the powers above,
And plight alternate their Satanic love.

Circæa. l. 7. Enchanters Nightshade. Two males, one female. It was much celebrated in the mysteries of witchcraft, and for the purpose of raising the devil, as its name imports. It grows amid the mouldering bones and decayed coffins in the ruinous vaults of Sleaford church in Lincolnshire. The superstitious ceremonies or histories belonging to some vegetables have been truly ridiculous; thus the Druids are said to have cropped the misletoe with a golden axe or sickle; and the bryony, or mandrake, was said to utter a scream when its root was drawn from the ground; and that the animal which drew it up became diseased and soon died: on which account, when it was wanted for the purpose of medicine, it was usual to loosen and remove the earth about the root, and then to tie it by means of a cord to a dog's tail, who was whipped to pull it up, and was then supposed to suffer for the impiety of the action. And even at this day bits of dried root of peony are rubbed smooth, and strung, and sold under the name of Anodyne necklaces, and tied round the necks of children, to facilitate the growth of their teeth! Add to this, that in Price's History of Cornwall, a book published about ten years ago, the Virga divinatoria, or divining rod, has a degree of credit given to it. This rod is of hazel, or other light wood, and held horizontally in the hand, and is said to bow towards the ore whenever the conjuror walks over a mine. A very few years ago, in France, and even in England, another kind of divining rod has been used to discover springs of water in a similar manner, and gained some credit. And in this very year, there were many in France, and some in England, who underwent an enchantment without any divining rod at all, and believed themselves to be affected by an invisible agent, which the enchanter called Animal Magnetism!

Avaunt, ye Vulgar! from her sacred groves
With maniac step the Pythian Laura moves;
Full of the god her labouring bosom sighs, 41
Foam on her lips, and fury in her eyes,
Strong writhe her limbs, her wild dishevell'd hair
Starts from her laurel-wreath, and swims in air.
While *twenty* Priests the gorgeous shrine surround,
Cinctured with ephods, and with garlands crown'd,
Contending hosts and trembling nations wait,
The firm immutable behests of Fate;
—She speaks in thunder from her golden throne
With words *unwill'd*, and wisdom not her own.

So on his Nightmare through the evening fog
Flits the squab Fiend o'er fen, and lake, and bog; [press'd,
Seeks some love-wilder'd maid with sleep oppress'd
Alights, and grinning sits upon her breast.
—Such as of late amid the murky sky
Was mark'd by Fuseli's poetic eye;
Whose daring tints, with Shakspeare's happiest grace,
Gave to the airy phantom form and place.—
Back o'er her pillow sinks her blushing head,
Her snow-white limbs hang helpless from the bed; 60
While with quick sighs, and suffocative breath,
Her interrupted heart-pulse swims in death.
—Then shrieks of captured towns, and widows' tears, [biers,
Pale lovers stretch'd upon their blood-stain'd
The headlong precipice that thwarts her flight,
The trackless desert, the cold starless night,
And stern-eyed murderer with his knife behind,
In dread succession agonize her mind.
O'er her fair limbs convulsive tremors fleet,
Start in her hands, and struggle in her feet; 70

In vain to scream with quivering lips she tries,
And strains in palsy'd lids her tremulous eyes;
In vain she *wills* to run, fly, swim, walk, creep;
The Will presides not in the bower of Sleep.
—On her fair bosom sits the Demon-Ape
Erect, and balances his bloated shape;
Rolls in their marble orbs his Gorgon eyes,
And drinks with leathern ears her tender cries.

Arm'd with her ivory beak, and talon-hands,
Descending Fica dives into the sands; 80
Chamber'd in earth with cold oblivion lies;
Nor heeds, *ye suitor-train*, your amorous sighs;
Erewhile with renovated beauty blooms,
Mounts into air, and moves her leafy plumes.
—Where Hamps and Manifold, their cliffs among,
Each in his flinty channel winds along;
With lucid lines the dusky moor divides,
Hurrying to intermix their sister tides.

Laura. l. 40. Prunus Lauro-cerasus. Twenty males, one female. The Pythian priestess is supposed to have been made drunk with infusion of laurel-leaves when she delivered her oracles. The intoxication or inspiration is finely described by Virgil, Æn. L. vi. The distilled water from laurel-leaves is, perhaps, the most sudden poison we are acquainted with in this country. I have seen about two spoonfuls of it destroy a large pointer dog in less than ten minutes. In a smaller dose it is said to produce intoxication: on this account there is reason to believe it acts in the same manner as opium and vinous spirit; but that the dose is not so well ascertained. See note on Tremella. It is used in the ratifia of the distillers, by which some dram-drinkers have been suddenly killed. One pint of water, distilled from fourteen pounds of black cherry stones bruised, has the same deleterious effect, destroying as suddenly as laurel-water. It is probable apricot-kernels, peach-leaves, walnut-leaves, and whatever possesses the kernel-flavour, may have similar qualities.

The Will presides not. l. 74. Sleep consists in the abolition of all voluntary power, both over our muscular motions and our ideas; for we neither walk nor reason in sleep. But at the same time, many of our muscular motions, and many of our ideas continue to be excited into action in consequence of internal irritations and of internal sensations; for the heart and arteries continue to beat, and we experience variety of passions, and even hunger and thirst in our dreams. Hence I conclude, that our nerves of sense are not torpid or inert during sleep; but that they are only precluded from the perception of external objects, by their external organs being rendered unfit to transmit to them the appulses of external bodies, during the suspension of the power of volition; thus the eyelids are closed in sleep, and I suppose the tympanum of the ear is not stretched, because they are deprived of the voluntary exertions of the muscles appropriated to these purposes; and it is probable something similar happens to the external apparatus of our other organs of sense, which may render them unfit for their office of perception during sleep: for milk put into the mouths of sleeping babes occasions them to swallow and suck; and, if the eyelid is a little opened in the day-light by the exertions of disturbed sleep, the person dreams of being much dazzled. See first Interlude.

When there arises in sleep a painful desire to exert the voluntary motions, it is called the nightmare or incubus. When the sleep becomes so imperfect that some muscular motions obey this exertion of desire, people have walked about, and even performed some domestic offices in sleep; one of these sleep-walkers I have frequently seen: once she smelt of a tube-rose, and sung, and drank a dish of tea in this state; her awaking was always attended with prodigious surprise, and even fear; this disease had daily periods, and seemed to be of the epileptic kind.

Ficus Indica. l. 80. Indian Fig-tree. Of the class Polygamy. This large tree rises with opposite branches on all sides, with long egged leaves; each branch emits a slender flexile depending appendage from its summit like a cord, which roots into the earth and rises again. Sloan. Hist. of Jamaica. Lin. Spec. Plant. See Capri-ficus.

Where still their silver-bosom'd Nymphs
  abhor,   89
The blood-smear'd mansion of gigantic Thor,—
—Erst, fires volcanic in the marble womb
Of cloud-wrapp'd Wetton raised the massy
  dome;
Rocks rear'd on rocks in huge disjointed piles
Form the tall turrets, and the lengthen'd aisles;
Broad ponderous piers sustain the roof, and wide
Branch the vast rainbow ribs from side to side.
While from above descends in milky streams
One scanty pencil of illusive beams,
Suspended crags and gaping gulfs illumes,   99
And gilds the horrors of the deepen'd glooms.
—Here oft the Naiads, as they chanced to stray
Near the dread fane on Thor's returning day,
Saw from red altars streams of guiltless blood
Stain their green reed-beds, and pollute their
  flood;
Heard dying babes in wicker prisons wail,
And shrieks of matrons thrill the affrighted gale;
While from dark caves infernal echoes mock,
And fiends triumphant shout from every rock!
—So still the Nymphs emerging lift in air
Their snow-white shoulders and their azure
  hair;   110
Sail with sweet grace the dimpling streams along,
Listening the shepherd's or the miner's song;

But when afar they view the giant-cave,
On timorous fins they circle on the wave,
With streaming eyes and throbbing hearts recoil,
Plunge their fair forms, and dive beneath the
  soil.—
Closed round their heads reluctant eddies sink,
And wider rings successive dash the brink.—
Three thousand steps in sparry clefts they stray,
Or seek through sullen mines their gloomy way;
On beds of lava sleep in coral cells,   121
Or sigh o'er jasper fish, and agate shells.
Till, where famed Ilam leads his boiling floods
Through flowery meadows and impending
  woods
Pleased with light spring they leave the dreary
  night,
And 'mid circumfluent surges rise to light;
Shake their bright locks, the widening vale pur-
  sue,   [dew;
Their sea-green mantles, fringed with pearly
In playful groups by towering Thorp they move,
Bound o'er the foaming wears, and rush into
  the Dove.   130

With fierce distracted eye Impatiens stands,
Swells her pale cheeks, and brandishes her hands,

Gigantic Thor. l. 90. Near the village of Wetton, a mile or two above Dove-Dale, near Ashburn in Derbyshire, there is a spacious cavern about the middle of the ascent of the mountain, which still retains the name of Thor's house; below it is an extensive and romantic common, where the rivers Hamps and Manifold sink into the earth, and rise again in Ilam gardens, the seat of John Port, Esq. about three miles below. Where these rivers rise again there are impressions resembling fish, which appear to be of jasper bedded in limestone. Calcareous spars, shells converted into a kind of agate, corallines in marble, ores of lead, copper, and zinc, and many strata of flint, or chert, and of toadstone, or lava, abound in this part of the country. The Druids are said to have offered human sacrifices inclosed in wicker idols to Thor. Thursday had its name from this Deity.

The broken appearance of the surface of many parts of this country; with the swallows, as they are called, or basons on some of the mountains, like volcanic craters, where the rain-water sinks into the earth; and the numerous large stones, which seem to have been thrown over the land by volcanic explosions; as well as the great masses of toadstone or lava; evince the existence of violent earthquakes at some early period of the world. At this time the channels of these subterraneous rivers seem to have been formed, when a long tract of rocks were raised by the sea flowing in upon the central fires, and thus producing an irresistible explosion of steam; and when these rocks again subsided, their parts did not exactly correspond, but left a long cavity arched over in this operation of nature. The cavities at Castleton and Buxton in Derbyshire seem to have had a similar origin, as well as this cavern termed Thor's house. See Mr. Whitehurst's and Dr. Hutton's theories of the Earth.

Impatiens. l. 131. Touch me not. The seed vessel consists of one cell with five divisions; each of these, when the seed is ripe, on being touched, suddenly folds itself into a spiral form, leaps from the stalk, and disperses the seeds to a great distance by its elasticity. The capsule of the geranium and the beard of wild oats are twisted for a similar purpose, and dislodge their seeds on wet days, when the ground is best fitted to receive them. Hence one of these, with its adhering capsule or beard fixed on a stand, serves the purpose of an hygrometer, twisting itself more or less according to the moisture of the air.

The awn of barley is furnished with stiff points, which, like the teeth of a saw, are all turned towards one end of it; as this long awn lies upon the ground, it extends itself in the moist air of night, and pushes forward the barley corn, which it adheres to; in the day it shortens as it dries; and as these points prevent it from receding, it draws up its pointed end; and thus, creeping like a worm, will travel many feet from the parent stem. That very ingenious mechanic philosopher, Mr. Edgeworth, once made on this principle a wooden automaton; its back consisted of soft fir-wood, about an inch square, and four feet long, made of pieces cut the cross-way in respect to the fibres of the wood, and glued together: it had two feet before, and two behind, which supported the back horizontally; but were placed with their extremities, which were armed with sharp points of iron, bending backwards. Hence, in moist weather the back lengthened, and the two foremost feet were pushed forwards; in dry weather the hinder feet were drawn after, as the obliquity of the points of the feet prevented it from receding. And thus, in a month or two, it walked across the room which it inhabited. Might not this machine be applied as an hygrometer to some meteorological purpose?

With rage and hate the astonish'd groves alarms,
And hurls her infants from her frantic arms.
—So when Medea left her native soil,
Unaw'd by danger, unsubdued by toil;
Her weeping sire and beckoning friends withstood,
And launch'd enamour'd on the boiling flood;
One ruddy boy her gentle lips caress'd,
And one fair girl was pillow'd on her breast;
While high in air the golden treasure burns,
And Love and Glory guide the prow by turns.
But, when Thessalia's inauspicious plain
Received the matron-heroine from the main;
While horns of triumph sound, and altars burn,
And shouting nations hail their Chief's return;
Aghast, she saw new-deck'd the nuptial bed,
And proud Creusa to the temple led;
Saw her in Jason's mercenary arms
Deride her virtues, and insult her charms; 150
Saw her dear babes from fame and empire torn,
In foreign realms deserted and forlorn;
Her love rejected, and her vengeance braved,
By him her beauties won, her virtues saved.—
With stern regard she eyed the traitor-king,
And felt, Ingratitude! thy keenest sting;
" Nor Heaven," she cried, " nor Earth, nor Hell can hold
A heart abandon'd to the thirst of gold!"
Stamp'd with wild foot, and shook her horrent brow,
And call'd the furies from their dens below. 160
—Slow out of earth, before the festive crowds,
On wheels of fire, amid a night of clouds,
Drawn by fierce fiends arose a magic car,
Received the Queen, and hovering flamed in air.—   [kneel,
As with raised hands the suppliant traitors
And fear the vengeance they deserve to feel,
Thrice with parch'd lips her guiltless babes she press'd,   [breast;
And thrice she clasp'd them to her tortured
Awhile with white uplifted eyes she stood,
Then plunged her trembling poniard in their blood. 170
" Go, kiss your sire! go, share the bridal mirth!"
She cried, and hurl'd their quivering limbs on earth.
Rebellowing thunders rock the marble towers,
And red-tongued lightnings shoot their arrowy showers;   [all
Earth yawns!—the crashing ruin sinks!—o'er
Death with black hands extends his mighty pall;   [quaff,
Their mingling gore the fiends of Vengeance
And Hell receives them with convulsive laugh.

Round the vex'd isles where fierce tornadoes roar,
Or tropic breezes sooth the sultry shore; 180
What time the eve her gauze pellucid spreads
O'er the dim flowers, and veils the misty meads;

Slow o'er the twilight sands or leafy walks,
With gloomy dignity Dictamna stalks;
In sulphurous eddies round the weird dame
Plays the light gas, or kindles into flame.
If rests the traveller his weary head,
Grim Mancinella haunts the mossy bed,

Dictamnus. l. 184. Fraxinella. In the still evenings of dry seasons this plant emits an inflammable air or gas, and flashes on the approach of a candle. There are instances of human creatures who have taken fire spontaneously, and been totally consumed. Phil. Trans.

The odours of many flowers, so delightful to our sense of smell, as well as the disagreeable scents of others, are owing to the exhalation of their essential oils. These essential oils have greater or less volatility, and are all inflammable; many of them are poisons to us, as those of laurel and tobacco; others possess a narcotic quality, as is evinced by the oil of cloves instantly relieving slight tooth-achs; from oil of cinnamon relieving the hiccup; and balsam of Peru relieving the pain of some ulcers. They are all deleterious to certain insects, and hence their use in the vegetable economy, being produced in flowers or leaves to protect them from the depredations of their voracious enemies. One of the essential oils, that of turpentine, is recommended, by M. de Thosse, for the purpose of destroying insects which infect both vegetables and animals. Having observed that the trees were attacked by multitudes of small insects of different colours (pucins ou pucerons) which injured their young branches, he destroyed them all entirely in the following manner: he put into a bowl a few handfuls of earth, on which he poured a small quantity of oil of turpentine; he then beat the whole together with a spatula, pouring on it water till it became of the consistence of soup; with this mixture he moistened the ends of the branches, and both the insects and their eggs were destroyed, and other insects kept aloof by the scent of the turpentine. He adds, that he destroyed the fleas of his puppies by once bathing them in warm water impregnated with oil of turpentine. Mem. d'Agriculture, An. 1787, Tremest. Printemp. p. 109. I sprinkled some oil of turpentine, by means of a brush, on some branches of a nectarine tree, which was covered with the aphis; but it killed both the insect and the branches; a solution of arsenic much diluted did the same. The shops of medicine are supplied with resins, balsams, and essential oils; and the tar and pitch, for mechanical purposes, are produced from these vegetable secretions.

Mancinella. l. 188. Hippomane. With the milky juice of this tree the Indians poison their arrows; the dew-drops which fall from it are so caustic as to blister the skin, and produce dangerous ulcers; whence many have found their death by sleeping under its shade. Variety of noxious plants abound in all countries; in our own the deadly night-shade, henbane, houndstongue, and many others, are seen in almost every high road untouched by animals. Some have asked, what is the use of such abundance of poisons? The nauseous or pungent juices of some vegetables, like the thorns of others, are given them for their defence from the depredations of animals; hence the thorny plants are in general wholesome and agreeable food to granivorous animals. See note on Ilex. The flowers

Brews her black henbane, and, stealing near,
Pours the curst venom in his tortured ear.— 190
Wide o'er the mad'ning throng Urtica flings
Her barbed shafts, and darts her poison'd stings.
And fell Lobelia's suffocating breath
Loads the dank pinion of the gale with death.
—With fear and hate they blast the affrighted groves,
Yet own with tender care their *kindred Loves!*

So, where Palmyra 'mid her wasted plains,
Her shatter'd aqueducts, and prostrate fanes,

(As the bright orb of breezy midnight pours
Long threads of silver through her gaping towers,
O'er mouldering tombs, and tottering columns gleams, 201
And frosts her deserts with diffusive beams,)
Sad o'er the mighty wreck in silence bends,
Lifts her wet eyes, her tremulous hands extends.—
If from lone cliffs a bursting rill expands
Its transient course, and sink into the sands;
O'er the moist rock the fell hyæna prowls
The leopard hisses, and the panther growls;
On quivering wing the famish'd vulture screams,
Dips his dry beak, and sweeps the gushing streams; 210
With foaming jaws, beneath, and sanguine tongue,
Laps the lean wolf, and pants, and runs along;
Stern stalks the lion, on the rustling brinks
Hears the dread snake, and trembles as he drinks;
Quick darts the scaly monster o'er the plain,
Fold, after fold, his undulating train;
And bending o'er the lake his crested brow,
Starts at the crocodile, that gapes below.

Where seas of glass with gay reflections smile
Round the green coasts of Java's palmy isle; 220
A spacious plain extends its upland scene,
Rocks rise on rocks, and fountains gush between;
Soft zephyrs blow, eternal summers reign,
And showers prolific bless the soil,—in vain!
—No spicy nutmeg scents the vernal gales,
Nor towering plaintain shades the mid-day vales;
No grassy mantle hides the sable hills,
No flowery chaplet crowns the trickling rills;
Nor tufted moss, nor leathery lichen creeps
In russet tapestry on the crumbling steeps. 230
—No step retreating, on the sand impress'd,
Invites the visit of a second guest;
No refluent fin the unpeopled stream divides,
No revelant pinion cleaves the airy tides;
Nor handed moles, nor beaked worms return,
That mining pass the irremeable bourn.—
Fierce in dread silence on the blasted heath
Fell Upas sits, the Hydra-Tree of death.

---

or petals of plants are perhaps in general more acrid than their leaves; hence they are much seldomer eaten by insects. This seems to have been the use of the essential oil in the vegetable economy, as observed above in the notes on Dictamnus and Ilex. The fragrance of plants is thus a part of their defence. These pungent or nauseous juices of vegetables have supplied the science of medicine with its principal materials, such as purge, vomit, intoxicate, &c.

Urtica. l. 191. Nettle. The sting has a bag at its base, and a perforation near its point, exactly like the stings of wasps and the teeth of adders; Hook, Microgr. p. 142. Is the fluid contained in this bag, and pressed through the perforation into the wound, made by the point, a caustic essential oil, or a concentrated vegetable acid? The vegetable poisons, like the animal ones, produce more sudden and dangerous effects, when instilled into a wound, than when taken into the stomach; whence the families of Marsi and Psilli, in ancient Rome sucked the poison without injury out of wounds made by vipers, and were supposed to be indued with supernatural powers for this purpose. By the experiments related by Beccaria, it appears that four or five times the quantity, taken by the mouth, had about equal effects with that infused into a wound. The male flowers of the nettle are separate from the female, and the anthers are seen in fair weather to burst with force, and to discharge a dust, which hovers about the plant like a cloud.

Lobelia. l. 193. Longiflora. Grows in the West Indies, and spreads such deleterious exhalations around it, that an oppression of the breast is felt on approaching it at many feet distance when placed in the corner of a room or hothouse. Ingenhousz, Exper. on Air, p. 146. Jacquini hort. botanic. Vindeb. The exhalations from ripe fruit or withering leaves are proved much to injure the air in which they are confined; and, it is probable, all those vegetables which emit a strong scent may do this in a greater or less degree, from the rose to the lobelia; whence the unwholesomeness in living perpetually in such an atmosphere of perfume as some people wear about their hair, or carry in their handkerchiefs. Either Boerhave or Dr. Mead have affirmed they were acquainted with a poisonous fluid whose vapour would presently destroy the person who sat near it. And it is well known, that the gas from fermenting liquors, or obtained from lime-stone, will destroy animals immersed in it, as well as the vapour of the Grotto del Cani near Naples.

So, where Palmyra. l. 197. Among the ruins of Palmyra, which are dispersed not only over the plains but even in the deserts, there is one single colonade above 2600 yards long, the bases of the Corinthian columns of which exceed the height of a man: and yet this row is only a small part of the remains of that one edifice! Volney's Travels.

Upas. l. 238. There is a poison-tree in the island of Java, which is said by its effluvia to have depopulated the country for 12 or 14 miles round the place of its growth. It is called, in the Malayan language, Bohun-Upas; with the juice of it the most poisonous arrows are prepared; and, to gain this, the condemned criminals are sent to the tree with proper directions both to get the juice and to secure themselves from the malignant exhalations of the tree; and are pardoned if they bring back a certain quantity

Lo; from one root, the envenom'd soil below,
A thousand vegetative serpents grow; 240
In shining rays the scaly monster spreads
O'er ten square leagues his far-diverging heads;
Or in one trunk entwists his tangled form,
Looks o'er the clouds, and hisses in the storm.
Steep'd in fell poison, as his sharp teeth part,
A thousand tongues in quick vibration dart;
Snatch the proud eagle towering o'er the heath,
Or pounce the lion, as he stalks beneath;
Or strew, as marshall'd hosts contend in vain
With human skeletons the whiten'd plain. 250
—Chain'd at his root two scion-demons dwell,
Breathe the faint hiss, or try the shriller yell;
Rise, fluttering in the air on callow wings,
And aim at insect-prey their little stings.
So time's strong arms with sweeping sithe erase
Art's cumbrous works, and empires, from their base:
While each young Hour its sickle fine employs,
And crops the sweet buds of domestic joys!

With blushes bright as morn fair Orchis charms,
And lulls her infant in her fondling arms; 260

Soft plays *Affection* round her bosom's throne,
And guards his life, forgetful of her own.
So wings the wounded deer her headlong flight,
Pierced by some ambush'd archer of the night,
Shoots to the woodlands with her bounding fawn,
And drops of blood bedew the conscious lawn;
There hid in shades she shuns the cheerful day,
Hangs o'er her young, and weeps her life away.

So stood Eliza on the wood-crown'd height
O'er Minden's plain, spectatress of the fight,
Sought with bold eye amid the bloody strife 271
Her dearer self, the partner of her life;
From hill to hill the rushing host pursued,
And view'd his banner, or believed she view'd.
Pleased with the distant roar, with quicker tread
Fast by his hand one lisping boy she led;
And one fair girl amid the loud alarm
Slept on her kerchief, cradled by her arm;
While round her brows bright beams of honour dart, 279
And loves warm eddies circle round her heart.
—Near and more near the intrepid beauty press'd,   [crest;
Saw through the driving smoke his dancing

---

of the poison. But by the registers there kept, not one in four are said to return. Not only animals of all kinds, both quadrupeds, fish, and birds, but all kinds of vegetables also are destroyed by the effluvia of the noxious tree; so that, in a district of 12 or 14 miles round it, the face of the earth is quite barren and rocky, intermixed only with the skeletons of men and animals, affording a scene of melancholy beyond what poets have described or painters delineated. Two younger trees of its own species are said to grow near it. See London Magazine for 1784 or 1783. Translated from a description of the poison-tree of the island of Java, written in Dutch by N. P. Foersch. For a further account of it, see a note at the end of the work.

Orchis. 1. 259. The Orchis morio in the circumstance of the parent-root shrivelling up and dying, as the young one increases, is not only analogous to other tuberous or knobby roots, but also to some bulbous roots, as the tulip. The manner of the production of herbaceous plants from their various perennial roots, seems to want further investigation, as their analogy is not yet clearly established. The caudex, or true root, in the orchis lies above the knob; and from this part the fibrous roots and the new knob are produced. In the tulip the caudex lies below the bulb; from whence proceed the fibrous roots and the new bulbs; the root after it has flowered dies like the orchis-root; for the stem of the last year's tulip lies on the outside, and not in the centre of the bulb; which I am informed does not happen in the three or four first years when raised from seed, when it only produces a stem, and slender leaves without flowering. In the tulip root, dissected in the early spring, just before it begins to shoot, a perfect flower is seen in its centre; and between the first and second coat the large next year's bulb is, I believe, produced; between the second and third coat, and between this and the fourth coat, and perhaps further, other less and less bulbs are visible, all adjoining to the caudex at the bottom of the mother bulb; and which I am told, require as many years before they will flower, as the number of the coats with which they are covered. This annual reproduction of the tulip-root induces some florists to believe that tulip-roots never die naturally, as they lose so few of them; whereas the hyacinth-roots, I am informed, will not last above five or seven years after they have flowered.

The hyacinth-root differs from the tulip-root, as the stem of the last year's flower is always found in the centre of the root, and the new off-sets arise from the caudex below the bulb, but not beneath any of the concentric coats of the root, except the external one: hence Mr. Eaton, an ingenious florist of Derby, to whom I am indebted for most of the observations in this note, concludes, that the hyacinth-root does not perish annually after it has flowered like the tulip. Mr. Eaton gave me a tulip-root which had been set too deep in the earth, and the caudex had elongated itself near an inch, and the new bulb was formed above the old one, and detached from it, instead of adhering to its side. See Additional Notes to Part I. No. XIV.

The caudex of the ranunculus, cultivated by the florists, lies above the claw-like root; in this the old root or claws die annually, like the tulip and orchis, and the new claws, which are seen above the old ones, draw down the caudex lower into the earth. The same is said to happen to scabiosa, or Devil's bit, and some other plants, as valerian and greater plantain; the new fibrous roots rising round the caudex above the old ones, the inferior end of the root becomes stumped, as if cut off, after the old fibres are decayed, and the caudex is drawn down into the earth by these new roots. See Arum and Tulipa.

Saw on his helm, her virgin-hands inwove,
Bright stars of gold, and mystic knots of love;
Heard the exulting shout, " They run! they run!"
" Great God!" she cried, " he's safe; the battle's won!"
—A ball now hisses through the airy tides,
(Some Fury wing'd it, and some Demon guides!)
Parts the fine locks, her graceful head that deck, 289
Wounds her fair ear, and sinks into her neck;
The red stream, issuing from her azure veins,
Dyes her white veil, her ivory bosom stains.—
—" Ah me;" she cried, and sinking on the ground,
Kiss'd her dear babes, regardless of the wound;
" Oh, cease not yet to beat, thou vital urn!
Wait, gushing life, oh, wait my love's return!
Hoarse barks the wolf, the vulture screams from far!—
The angel, Pity, shuns the walks of war!—
Oh, spare, ye war-hounds, spare their tender age!— 299
On me, on me," she cried, "exhaust your rage!"
Then with weak arms her weeping babes caress'd,
And, sighing, hid them in her blood-stain'd vest.

From tent to tent the impatient warrior flies,
Fear in his heart, and frenzy in his eyes;
Eliza's name along the camp he calls,
Eliza echoes through the canvas walls;
Quick through the murmuring gloom his footsteps tread,
O'er groaning heaps, the dying and the dead,
Vault o'er the plain, and in the tangled wood,
Lo! dead Eliza weltering in her blood!— 310
—Soon hears his listening son the welcome sounds,
With open arms and sparkling eyes he bounds;—
" Speak low," he cries, and gives his little hand,
" Eliza sleeps upon the dew-cold sand;
Poor weeping babe with bloody fingers press'd,
And tried with pouting lips her milkless breast;
Alas! we both with cold and hunger quake—
Why do you weep!—Mamma will soon awake."
—" She'll wake no more!" the hopeless mourner cried,
Upturn'd his eyes, and clasp'd his hands, and sigh'd: [lay, 320
Stretch'd on the ground awhile entranced he
And press'd warm kisses on the lifeless clay;
And then upsprung with wild convulsive start,
And all the father kindled in his heart;
" Oh, Heavens!" he cried, " my first rash vow forgive;
These bind to earth, for these I pray to live!"—

Round his chill babes he wrapp'd his crimson vest,
And clasp'd them sobbing to his aching breast.

Two harlot-nymphs, the fair Cuscutas, please
With labour'd negligence, and studied ease; 330
In the meek garb of modest worth disguised,
The eye averted, and the smile chastised,
With sly approach they spread their dangerous charms,
And round their victim wind their wiry arms.
So by Scamander when Laocoon stood,
Where Troy's proud turrets glitter'd in the flood,

Cuscuta. l. 329. Dodder. Four males, two females. This parasite plant (the seed splitting without cotyledons) protrudes a spiral body, and not endeavouring to root itself in the earth, ascends the vegetables in its vicinity, spirally W. S. E. or contrary to the movement of the sun; and absorbs its nourishment by vessels apparently inserted into its supporters. It bears no leaves, except here and there a scale, very small, membraneous, and close under the branch. Lin. Spec. Plant. edit. a Reichard. Vol. I. p. 352. The Rev. T. Martyn, in his elegant letters on botany, adds, that, not content with support, where it lays hold, there it draws its nourishment; and, at length, in gratitude for all this, strangles its entertainer. Letter xv. A contest for air and light obtains throughout the whole vegetable world; shrubs rise above herbs, and, by precluding the air and light from them, injure or destroy them; trees suffocate or incommode shrubs; the parasite climbing plants, as ivy, clematis, incommode the taller trees; and other parasites, which exist without having roots on the ground, as misletoe, tillandsia, epidendrum, and the mosses and fungusses, incommode them all.

Some of the plants with voluble stems ascend other plants spirally east-south-west, as humulus, hop, lonicera, honey-suckle, tamus, black bryony, helxine. Others turn their spiral stems west-south-east, as convolvulus, corn bind, phaseolus, kidney-bean, basella, cynanche, euphorbia, eupatorium. The proximate or final causes of this difference have not been investigated. Other plants are furnished with tendrils for the purpose of climbing: if the tendril meets with nothing to lay hold of in its first revolution, it makes another revolution; and so on till it wraps itself quite up like a cork-screw; hence, to a careless observer, it appears to move gradually backwards and forwards, being seen sometimes pointing eastward and sometimes westward. One of the Indian grasses, panicum arborescens, whose stem is no thicker than a goose-quill, rises as high as the tallest trees in this contest for light and air. Spec. Plant. a Reichard, Vol. I. p. 161. The tops of many climbing plants are tender from their quick growth; and, when deprived of their acrimony by boiling, are an agreeable article of food. The hop-tops are in common use. I have eaten the tops of white bryony, bryonia alba, and found them nearly as grateful as asparagus, and think this plant might be profitably cultivated as an early garden vegetable. The tamus (called black bryony) was less agreeable to the taste when boiled. See Galanthus.

Raised high his arm, and with prophetic call
To shrinking realms announced her fated fall;
Whirl'd his fierce spear with more than mortal
        force,   339
And pierced the thick ribs of the echoing horse;
Two serpent-forms incumbent on the main,
Lashing the white waves with redundant train,
Arch'd their blue necks, and shook their towering crests,
And plough'd their foamy way with speckled
        breasts;
Then, darting fierce amid the affrighted throngs,
Roll'd their red eyes, and shot their forked
        tongues.—
—Two daring youths to guard the hoary sire,
Thwart their dread progress, and provoke their
        ire.
Round sire and sons the scaly monsters roll'd,
Ring above ring, in many a tangled fold,   350
Close and more close their writhing limbs surround,
And fix with foamy teeth the envenom'd wound.
—With brow upturn'd to heaven the holy Sage
In silent agony sustains their rage;
While each fond youth, in vain, with piercing
        cries
Bends on the tortured Sire his dying eyes.

" Drink deep, sweet youths," seductive Vitis
        cries,
The maudlin tear-drop glittering in her eyes;
Green leaves and purple clusters crown her head,
And the tall Thyrsus stays her tottering tread.
—Five hapless swains with soft assuasive smiles
The harlot meshes in her deathful toils;   362
" Drink deep," she carols, as she waves in air
The mantling goblet, " and forget your care."
O'er the dread feast malignant Chemia scowls,
And mingles poison in the nectar'd bowls;
Fell Gout peeps grinning through the flimsy
        scene,
And bloated Dropsy pants behind unseen;
Wrapp'd in his robe white Lepra hides his
        stains,
And silent Frenzy writhing bites his chains. 370

Vitis. l. 357. Vine. Five males, one female. The juice of the ripe grape is a nutritive and agreeable food, consisting chiefly of sugar and mucilage. The chemical process of fermentation converts this sugar into spirit; converts food into poison! And it has thus become the curse of the Christian world, producing more than half of our chronical diseases; which Mahomet observed, and forbade the use of it to his disciples. The Arabians invented distillation; and thus by obtaining the spirit of fermented liquors in a less diluted state, added to its destructive quality A theory of the diabetes and dropsy, produced by drinking fermented or spirituous liquors, is explained in a treatise on the inverted motions of the lymphatic system, published by Dr. Darwin.

So when Prometheus braved the Thunderer's
        ire,
Stole from his blazing throne ethereal fire,
And lantern'd in his breast, from realms of day
Bore the bright treasure to his Man of clay;—
High on cold Caucasus by Vulcan bound,
The lean impatient vulture fluttering round,
His writhing limbs in vain he twists and strains
To break or loose the adamantine chains.
The gluttonous bird, exulting in his pangs,
Tears his swoln liver with remorseless fangs.

The gentle Cyclamen with dewy eye   381
Breaths o'er her lifeless babe the parting sigh;
And, bending low to earth, with pious hands
Inhumes her dear departed in the sands.
" Sweet Nursling! withering in thy tender
        hour,
Oh, sleep," she cries, " and rise a fairer flower!"
—So when the plague o'er London's gasping
        crowds   [clouds;
Shook her dank wing, and steer'd her murky
When o'er the friendless bier no rites were read,
No dirge slow-chanted, and no pall out-spread;

Prometheus. l. 371. The ancient story of Prometheus, who concealed in his bosom the fire he had stolen, and afterwards had a vulture perpetually gnawing his liver, affords so apt an allegory for the effects of drinking spirituous liquors, that one should be induced to think the art of distillation, as well as some other chemical processes (such as calcining gold,) had been known in times of great antiquity, and lost again. The swallowing drams cannot be better represented in hieroglyphic language than by taking fire into one's bosom; and certain it is, that the general effect of drinking fermented or spirituous liquors is an inflamed, scirrhous, or paralytic liver, with its various critical or consequential diseases, as leprous eruptions on the face, gout, dropsy, epilepsy, insanity. It is remarkable, that all the diseases from drinking spirituous or fermented liquors are liable to become hereditary, even to the third generation, gradually increasing, if the cause be continued, till the family becomes extinct.

Cyclamen. l. 381. Shew-bread, or showbread. When the seeds are ripe, the stalk of the flower gradually twists itself spirally downwards, till it touches the ground, and forcibly penetrating the earth lodges its seeds, which are thought to receive nourishment from the parent root, as they are said not to be made to grow in any other situation.

The trifolium subterraneum, subterraneous trefoil, is another plant which buries its seeds, the globular head of the seed penetrating the earth; which, however, in this plant may be only an attempt to conceal its seeds from the ravages of birds; for there is another trefoil, the trifolium globosum, or globular woolly-headed trefoil, which has a curious manner of concealing its seeds; the lower florets only have corols, and are fertile; the upper ones wither into a kind of wool, and, forming a head, completely conceal the fertile calyxes. Lin. Spec. Plant. Reichard.

While death and night piled up the naked throng, 391
And silence drove their ebon cars along;
Six lovely daughters, and their father, swept
To the throng'd grave Cleone saw, and wept;
Her tender mind, with meek Religion fraught,
Drank all-resign'd Affliction's bitter draught;
Alive and listening to the whisper'd groan
Of others' woes, unconscious of her own!—
One smiling boy, her last sweet hope, she warms
Hush'd on her bosom, circled in her arms.— 400
Daughter of wo! ere morn, in vain caress'd,
Clung the cold babe, upon thy milkless breast,
With feeble cries thy last sad aid required,
Stretch'd its stiff limbs, and on thy lap expired!
—Long with wide eyelids on her child she gazed, [raised;
And long to heaven their tearless orbs she
Then with quick foot and throbbing heart she found
Where Chartreuse open'd deep his holy ground;
Bore her last treasure through the midnight gloom,
And kneeling dropp'd it in the mighty tomb;
"I follow next!" the frantic mourner said, 411
And living plunged amid the festering dead.

Where vast Ontario rolls his brineless tides,
And feeds the trackless forests on his sides,
Fair Cassia trembling hears the howling woods,
And trusts her tawny children to the floods.—

Cinctured with gold while *ten* fond brothers stand,
And guard the beauty on her native land,

Where Chartreuse. l. 408. During the plague in London, 1665, one pit to receive the dead was dug in the Charter-house, 40 feet long, 16 feet wide, and about 20 feet deep; and in two weeks received 1114 bodies. During this dreadful calamity there were instances of mothers carrying their own children to those public graves, and of people delirious, or in despair from the loss of their friends, who threw themselves alive into these pits. Journal of the Plague-year in 1665.

Rolls his brineless tide. l. 413. Some philosophers have believed that the continent of America was not raised out of the great ocean at so early a period of time as the other continents. One reason for this opinion was, because the great lakes, perhaps nearly as large as the Mediterranean Sea, consist of fresh water. And as the sea-salt seems to have its origin from the destruction of vegetable and animal bodies, washed down by rains, and carried by rivers into lakes or seas; it would seem that this source of sea-salt had not so long existed in that country. There is, however, a more satisfactory way of explaining this circumstance; which is, that the American lakes lie above the level of the ocean, and are hence perpetually desalited by the rivers which run through them; which is not the case with the Mediterranean, into which a current from the main ocean perpetually passes.

Cassia. l. 415. Ten males, one female. The seeds are black, the stamens gold-colour. This is one of the American fruits, which are annually thrown on the coasts of Norway; and are frequently in so recent a state as to vegetate, when properly taken care of. The fruit of the anacardium, cashew-nut; of cucurbita legenaria, bottle-gourd; of the mimosa scandens, cocoons; of the piscidia erythrina, log-wood-tree; and cocoa-nuts are enumerated by Dr. Tonning, (Amæn. Acad. 149.) amongst these emigrant seeds. The fact is truly wonderful, and cannot be accounted for but by the existence of under currents in the depth of the ocean; or from vortexes of water passing from one country to another through caverns of the earth.

Sir Hans Sloane has given an account of four kinds of seeds which are frequently thrown by the sea upon the coasts of the islands of the northern parts of Scotland. Phil. Trans. abridged, Vol. III. p. 540, which seeds are natives of the West Indies, and seem to be brought thither by the Gulf-stream described below. One of these is called, by Sir H. Sloane, Phaseolus maximus perennis, which is often thrown also on the coasts of Kerry in Ireland; another is called in Jamaica Horse-eye-bean; and a third is called Niker in Jamaica. He adds, that the Lenticula marina, or Sargosso, grows on the rocks about Jamaica, is carried by the winds and current towards the coasts of Florida, and thence into the North-America ocean, where it lies very thick on the surface of the sea.

Thus a rapid current passes from the gulf of Florida to the N. E. along the coast of North-America, known to seamen by the name of the Gulf-stream. A chart of this was published by Dr. Franklin in 1768, from the information principally of Capt. Folger. This was confirmed by the ingenious experiments of Dr. Blagden published in 1781, who found that the water of the Gulf-stream was from six to eleven degrees warmer than the water of the sea through which it ran; which must have been occasioned by its being brought from a hotter climate. He ascribes the origin of this current to the power of the trade-winds, which, blowing always in the same direction, carry the waters of the Atlantic ocean to the westward, till they are stopped by the opposing continent on the west of the Gulf of Mexico, and are thus accumulated there, and run down the Gulf of Florida. Philos. Trans. V. 71, p. 335. Governor Pownal has given an elegant map of this Gulf-stream, tracing it from the Gulf of Florida northward as far as Cape Sable in Nova Scotia, and then across the Atlantic Ocean to the coast of Africa, between the Canary Islands and Senegal, increasing in breadth, as it runs, till it occupies five or six degrees of latitude. The Governor likewise ascribes this current to the force of the trade-winds *protruding* the waters westward, till they are opposed by the continent, and accumulated in the Gulf of Mexico. He very ingeniously observes, that a great eddy must be produced in the Atlantic ocean between this Gulf-stream and the westerly current protruded by the tropical winds, and in this eddy are found the immense fields of floating vegetables, called Saragosa weeds, and Gulf-weeds, and some light woods, which circulate in these vast eddies, or are occasionally driven out of them by the winds. Hydraulic and Nautical Observations by Governor Pownal, 1787. Other currents are mentioned by the Governor in this in-

Soft breathes the gale, the current gently moves,
And bears to Norway's coasts her infant loves.
—So the sad mother at the noon of night 421
From bloody Memphis stole her silent flight;
Wrapp'd her dear babe beneath her folded vest,
And clasp'd the treasure to her throbbing breast,
With soothing whispers hush'd its feeble cry,
Press'd the soft kiss, and breathed the secret sigh.— [shore,
—With dauntless step she seeks the winding
Hears unappal'd the glimmering torrents roar;
With paper-flags a floating cradle weaves,
And hides the smiling boy in Lotus-leaves; 430
Gives her white bosom to his eager lips,
The salt-tears mingling with the milk he sips;
Waits on the reed-crown'd brink with pious guile,
And trusts the scaly monster of the Nile.—
—Erewhile majestic from his lone abode,
Ambassador of Heaven, the Prophet trod;
Wrench'd the red scourge from proud Oppression's hands,
And broke, curst Slavery! thy iron bands.

Hark! heard ye not that piercing cry, 439
Which shook the waves and rent the sky?—

E'en now, e'en now, on yonder Western shores
Weeps pale Despair, and writhing Anguish roars:
E'en now in Afric's groves with hideous yell
Fierce Slavery stalks, and slips the dogs of hell;
From vale to vale the gathering cries rebound,
And sable nations tremble at the sound!
—Ye bands of Senators! whose suffrage sways
Britannia's realms, whom either Ind obeys;
Who right the injured, and reward the brave,
Stretch your strong arm, for ye have power to save! 450
Throned in the vaulted heart, his dread resort,
Inexorable Conscience holds his court;
With still small voice the plots of Guilt alarms,
Bares his mask'd brow, his lifted hand disarms;
But, wrapp'd in night with terrors all his own,
He speaks in thunder, when the deed is done.
Hear him, ye Senates! hear this truth sublime,
" He, who allows oppression, shares the crime."

No radiant pearl, which crested Fortune wears, [ears,
No gem, that twinkling hangs from Beauty's
Not the bright stars, which night's blue arch adorn, 461
Nor rising suns that gild the vernal morn,
Shine with such lustre as the tear, that flows
Down Virtue's manly cheek for others' woes."

Here ceased the Muse, and dropp'd her tuneful shell,
Tumultuous woes her panting bosom swell,
O'er her flush'd cheek her gauzy veil she throws,
Folds her white arms, and bends her laurel'd brows;
For human guilt awhile the Goddess sighs,
And human sorrows dim celestial eyes. 470

---

genious work, as those in the Indian Sea, northward of the line, which are ascribed to the influence of the monsoons. It is probable, that in process of time the narrow tract of land on the west of the Gulf of Mexico, may be worn away by this elevation of water dashing against it, by which this immense current would cease to exist, and a wonderful change take place in the Gulf of Mexico and West-Indian Islands, by the subsiding of the sea, which might probably lay all those islands into one, or join them to the continent.

INTERLUDE III.

Bookseller. Poetry has been called a sister-art both to Painting and to Music; I wish to know what are the particulars of their relationship?

Poet. It has been already observed, that the principal part of the language of poetry consists of those words, which are expressive of the ideas, which we originally receive by the organ of sight; and in this it nearly indeed resembles painting; which can express itself in no other way, but by exciting the ideas or sensations belonging to the sense of vision. But besides this essential similitude in the language of the poetic pen and pencil, these two sisters resemble each other, if I may so say, in many of their habits and manners. The painter, to produce a strong effect, makes a few parts of his picture large, distinct, and luminous, and keeps the remainder in shadow, or even beneath its natural size and colour, to give eminence to the pricipal figure. This is similar to the common manner of poetic composition, where the subordinate characters are kept down, to elevate and give consequence to the hero or heroine of the piece.

In the south aisle of the cathedral church at Lichfield, there is an ancient monument of a recumbent figure; the head and neck of which lie on a roll of matting in a kind of niche or cavern in the wall; and about five feet distant horizontally in another opening or cavern in the wall are seen the feet and ankles, with some folds of garment, lying also on a matt; and though the intermediate space is a solid stone-wall, yet the imagination supplies the deficiency, and the whole figure seems to exist before our eyes. Does not this resemble one of the arts both of the painter and the poet? The former often shows a muscular arm amidst a group of figures, or an impassioned face; and, hiding the remainder of the body behind other objects, leaves the imagination to complete it. The latter, describing a single feature or attitude in picturesque words, produces before the mind an image of the whole.

I remember seeing a print, in which was represented a shrivelled hand stretched through an iron grate, in the stone-floor of a prison-yard, to reach at a mess of porrage; which affected me with more horrid ideas of the distress of the prisoner in the dungeon below, than could have been perhaps produced by an exhibition of the whole person. And in the following beautiful scenery from the Midsummer-night's Dream, (in which I have taken the liberty to alter the place of a comma,) the description of the swimming step and prominent belly brings the whole figure before our eyes with the distinctness of reality.

When we have laugh'd to see the sails conceive,
And grow big-bellied with the wanton wind;
Which she with pretty and with swimming gait,
Following her womb, (then rich with my young
    squire,)
Would imitate, and sail upon the land.

There is a third sister-feature, which belongs both to the pictorial and poetic art; and that is the making sentiments and passions visible, as it were, to the spectator; this is done in both arts by describing or pourtraying the effects or changes which those sentiments or passions produce upon the body. At the end of the unaltered play of Lear, there is a beautiful example of poetic painting; the old King is introduced as dying from grief for the loss of Cordelia; at this crisis, Shakspeare, conceiving the robe of the king to be held together by a clasp, represents him as only saying to an attendant courtier in a faint voice, " Pray, Sir, undo this button,—thank you, Sir," and dies. Thus by the art of the poet, the oppression at the bosom of the dying King is made visible, not described in words.

B. What are the features, in which these sister-arts do not resemble each other?

P. The ingenious Bishop Berkeley, in his treatise on Vision, a work of great ability, has evinced, that the colours which we see, are only a language suggesting to our minds the ideas of solidity and extension, which we had before received by the sense of touch. Thus when we view the trunk of a tree, our eye can only acquaint us with the colours or shades; and from the previous experience of the sense of touch, these suggest to us the cylindrical form, with the prominent or depressed wrinkles on it. From hence it appears, that there is the strictest analogy between colours and sounds; as they are both but languages, which do not represent their corresponding ideas, but only suggest them to the mind from the habits or associations of previous experience. It is therefore reasonable to conclude, that the more artificial arrangements of these two languages by the poet and the painter bear a similar analogy.

But in one circumstance the pen and the pencil differ widely from each other, and that is the quantity of time which they can include in their respective representations. The former can unravel a long series of events, which may constitute the history of days or years; while the latter can exhibit only the actions of a moment. The poet is happier in describing successive scenes; the painter in representing stationary ones: both have their advantages.

Where the passions are introduced, as the poet, on one hand, has the power gradually to prepare the mind of his reader by previous climacteric circumstances; the painter, on the other hand, can throw stronger illumination and distinctness on the principal moment or catastrophe of the action; besides the advantage he has in using a universal language which can be *read* in an instant of time. Thus when a great number of figures are all seen together, supporting or contrasting each other, and contributing to explain or aggrandize the principal effect, we view a picture with agreeable surprise, and contemplate it with unceasing admiration. In the representation of the sacrifice of Jephtha's Daughter, a print done from a painting of Ant. Coypel, at one glance of the eye we read all the interesting passages of the last act of a well-written tragedy; so much poetry is there condensed into a moment of time.

B. Will you now oblige me with an account of the relationship between Poetry, and her other sister, Music?

P. In the poetry of our language I don't think we are to look for any thing analogous to the notes of the gamut: for, except perhaps in a few exclamations or interrogations, we are at liberty to raise or sink our voice an octave or two at pleasure, without altering the sense of the words. Hence, if either poetry or prose be read in melodious tones of voice, as is done in recitativo, or in chanting, it must depend on the speaker, not on the writer: for though words may be selected which are less harsh than others, that is, which have fewer sudden stops or abrupt consonants amongst the vowels, or with fewer sibilant letters, yet this does not constitute melody, which consists of agreeable successions of notes referable to the gamut; or harmony, which consists of agreeable combinations of them. If the Chinese language has many words of similar articulation, which yet signify different ideas, when spoken in a higher or lower musical note, as some travellers affirm, it must be capable of much finer effect, in respect to the audible part of poetry, than any language we are acquainted with.

There is however another affinity, in which poetry and music more nearly resemble each other than has generally been understood, and that is in their measure or time. There are but two kinds of time acknowledged in modern music, which are called *triple time* and *common time*. The former of these is divided by bars, each bar containing three crotchets, or a proportional number of their subdivisions into quavers and semiquavers. This kind of time is analogous to the measure of our heroic or iambic verse. Thus the two following couplets are each of them divided into five bars of *triple time*, each bar consisting of two crotchets and two quavers; nor can they be divided into bars analogous to *common time* without the bars interfering with some of the crotchets, so as to divide them.

3 Soft-warbling beaks | in each bright blos | som rove,
4 And vo | cal rosebuds thrill | the inchanted grove.

In these lines there is a quaver and a crotchet alternately in every bar, except in the last, in which *the in* make two semiquavers; the *e* is supposed by Grammarians to be cut off, which any one's ear will readily determine not to be true.

3 Life buds or breathes | from Indus to | the poles,
4 And the | vast surface kin | dles, as it rolls.

In these lines there is a quaver and a crotchet alternately in the first bar; a quaver, two crotchets, and a quaver make the second bar. In the third bar there is a quaver, a crotchet, and a rest after the crotchet, that is after the word *poles*, and two quavers begin the next line. The fourth bar consists of quavers and crotchets alternately. In the last bar there is a quaver, and a rest after it, *viz*. after the word *kindles*; and then two quavers and a crotchet. You will clearly perceive the truth of this, if you prick the musical characters above mentioned under the verses.

The *common time* of musicians is divided into bars, each of which contains four crotchets, or a proportional number of their subdivision into quavers and semiquavers. This kind of musical time is analogous to the dactyle verses of our language, the most popular instances of which are in Mr. Anstie's Bath-Guide. In this kind of verse the bar does not begin till after the first or second syllable; and where the verse is quite complete, and written by a good ear, these first syllables added to the last complete the bar, exactly in this also corresponding with many pieces of music;

$\frac{2}{4}$ Yet | if one may guess by the | size of his calf, Sir, He | weighs above twenty-three | stone and a half, Sir.

$\frac{2}{4}$ Master | Mamozet's head was not | finished so soon, For it | took up the barber a | whole afternoon.

In these lines each bar consists of a crotchet, two quavers, another crotchet, and two more quavers: which are equal to four crotchets, and, like many bars of *common time* in music, may be subdivided into two in beating time without disturbing the measure.

The following verses from Shenstone belong likewise to common time:

$\frac{2}{4}$ A | river or a sea | —— Was to him a dish | of tea, And a king | dom bread and butter.

The first and second bars consist each of a crotchet, a quaver, a crotchet, a quaver, a crotchet. The third bar consists of a quaver, two crotchets, a quaver, a crotchet. The last bar is not complete without adding the letter A which begins the first line, and then it consists of a quaver, a crotchet, a quaver, a crotchet, two quavers.

It must be observed, that the crotchets in triple time are in general played by musicians slower than those of common time, and hence minuets are generally pricked in triple time, and country dances generally in common time. So the verses above related, which are analogous to *triple time*, are generally read slower than those analogous to *common time*; and are thence generally used for graver compositions. I suppose all the different kinds of verses to be found in our odes, which have any measure at all, might be arranged under one or other of these two musical times; allowing a note or two sometimes to precede the commencement of the bar, and occasional rests, as in musical compositions: if this was attended to by those who set poetry to music, it is probable the sound and sense would oftener coincide. Whether these musical times can be applied to the lyric and heroic verses of the Greek and Latin poets, I do not pretend to determine; certain it is, that the dactyle verse of our language, when it is ended with a double rhyme, much resembles the measure of Homer and Virgil, except in the length of the lines.

B. Then there is no relationship between the other two of these sister-ladies, Painting and Music?

P. There is at least a mathematical relationship, or perhaps I ought rather to have said a metaphysical relationship between them. Sir Isaac Newton has observed, that the breadths of the seven primary colours in the sun's image refracted by a prism, are proportional to the seven musical notes of the gamut, or to the intervals of the eight sounds contained in an octave, that is, proportional to the following numbers:

Sol.	La.	Fa.	Sol.	La.	Mi.	Fa.	Sol.
Red.	Orange.	Yel.	Green.	Blue.	Indig.	Violet.	
$\frac{1}{9}$	$\frac{1}{16}$	$\frac{1}{10}$	$\frac{1}{9}$	$\frac{1}{16}$	$\frac{1}{16}$	$\frac{1}{9}$	

Newton's Optics, Book I. part 2. prop. 3. and 6. Dr. Smith in his Harmonics, has an explanatory note upon this happy discovery, as he terms it, of Newton. Sect. 4. Art. 7.

From this curious coincidence, it has been proposed to produce a luminous music, consisting of successions or combinations of colours, analogous to a tune in respect to the proportions above mentioned. This might be performed by a strong light, made by means of Mr. Argand's lamps, passing through coloured glasses, and falling on a defined part of a wall, with moveable blinds before them, which might communicate with the keys of a harpsichord, and thus produce at the same time visible and audible music in unison with each other.

The execution of this idea is said by Mr Guyot to have been attempted by Father Caffel, without much success.

If this should be again attempted, there is another curious coincidence between sounds and colours, discovered by Dr. Darwin, of Shrewsbury, and explained in a paper on what he calls *Ocular Spectra*, in the *Philosophical Transactions*, Vol. LXXVI. which might much facilitate the execution of it. In this treatise the Doctor has demonstrated, that we see certain colours, not only with greater ease and distinctness, but with relief and pleasure, after having for some time contemplated other certain colours; as green after red, or red after green; orange after blue, or blue after orange; yellow after violet, or violet after yellow. This, he shows, arises from the ocular spectrum of the colour last viewed coinciding with the irritation of the colour now under contemplation. Now as the pleasure we receive from the sensation of melodious notes, independent of the previous associations of agreeable ideas with them, must arise from our hearing some proportions of sounds after others more easily, distinctly, or agreeably; and as there is a coincidence between the proportions of the primary colours, and the primary sounds, if they may be so called; he argues, that the same laws must govern the sensations of both. In this circumstance, therefore, consists the sisterhood of Music and Painting; and hence they claim a right to borrow metaphors from each other; musicians to speak of the brilliancy of sounds, and the light and shade of a concerto; and painters of the harmony of colours, and the tone of a picture. Thus it is not quite so absurd, as was imagined, when the blind man asked if the colour scarlet was like the sound of a trumpet. As the coincidence or opposition of these *ocular spectra*, (or colours which remain in the eye after we have for some time contemplated a luminous object) are more easily and more accurately ascertained, now their laws have been investigated by Dr. Darwin, than the *relicts* of evanescent sounds upon the ear; it is to be wished that some ingenious musician would further cultivate this curious field of science: for if visible music can be agreeably produced, it would be more easy to add sentiment to it by representations of groves and Cupids, and sleeping nymphs amid the changing colours, than is commonly done by the words of audible music?

B. You mentioned the greater length of the verses of Homer and Virgil. Had not these poets great advantage in the superiority of their languages compared to our own?

P. It is probable, that the introduction of philosophy into a country must gradually affect the language of it; as philosophy converses in more appropriated and abstracted terms; and thus by degrees eradicates the abundance of metaphor, which is used in the more early ages of society. Otherwise, though the Greek compound words have more vowels in proportion to their consonants than the English ones, yet the modes of compounding them are less general; as may be seen by variety of instances given in the Preface of the translators, prefixed to the System of Vegetables by the Lichfield Society; which happy property of our own language rendered that translation of Linneus as expressive and as concise, perhaps more so than the original.

And in one respect, I believe, the English language serves the purpose of poetry better than the ancient ones, I mean in the greater ease of producing personifications; for as our nouns have in general no genders affixed to them in prose-compositions, and in the habits of conversation, they become easily personified only by the addition of a masculine or feminine pronoun, as,

Pale Melancholy sits, and round *her* throws
A death-like silence, and a dread repose.
Pope's Abelard.

And secondly, as most of our nouns have the article *a* or *the* prefixed to them in prose-writing and in conversation, they in general become personified even by the omission of these articles; as in the bold figure of Shipwreck in Miss Seward's Elegy on Capt. Cook:

But round the steepy rocks and dangerous strand
Rolls the white surf, and Shipwreck guards the land.

Add to this, that if the verses in our heroic poetry be shorter than those of the ancients, our words likewise are shorter; and in respect to their measure or time, which has erroneously been called melody and harmony, I doubt, from what has been said above, whether we are so much inferior as is generally believed; since many passages, which have been stolen from ancient poets, have been translated into our language without losing any thing of the beauty of the versification. The following line translated from Juvenal by Dr. Johnson, is much superior to the original:

Slow rises Worth by Poverty depress'd.

The original is as follows:

Difficile emergunt, quorum virtutibus obstat
Res angusta domi.

B. I am glad to hear you acknowledge the thefts of the modern poets from the ancient ones, whose works I suppose have been reckoned lawful plunder in all ages. But have not you borrowed epithets, phrases, and even half a line occasionally from modern poets?

P. It may be difficult to mark the exact boundary of what should be termed plagiarism: where the sentiment and expression are both borrowed without due acknowledgment, there can be no doubt;—single words, on the contrary, taken from other authors, cannot convict a writer of plagiarism: they are lawful game, wild by nature, the property of all who can capture them; —and perhaps a few common flowers of speech may be gathered, as we pass over our neighbour's inclosure, without stigmatising us with the title of thieves; but we must not therefore plunder his cultivated fruit.

The four lines at the end of the plant Upas are imitated from Dr. Young's Night Thoughts. The line in the episode adjoined to Cassia, " The salt tear mingling with the milk he sips," is from an interesting and humane passage in Langhorne's Justice of Peace. There are probably many others, which, if I could recollect them, should here be acknowledged. As it is, like exotic plants, their mixture with the native ones, I hope, adds beauty to my Botanic Garden: and such as it is, *Mr. Bookseller*, I now leave it to you to desire the Ladies and Gentlemen to walk in; but please to apprize them, that, like the spectators at an unskilful exhibition in some village-barn, I hope they will make Good-humour one of their party; and thus themselves supply the defects of the representation.

THE LOVES OF THE PLANTS.

CANTO IV.

Now the broad Sun his golden orb unshrouds,
Flames in the west, and paints the parted clouds;
O'er heaven's wide arch refracted lustres flow,
And bend in air the many-colour'd bow.—
—The tuneful Goddess on the glowing sky
Fix'd in mute ecstacy her glistening eye;
And then her lute to sweeter tones she strung,
And swell'd with softer chords the Paphian song;
Long aisles of oaks return'd the silver sound,
And amorous echoes talk'd along the ground;
Pleased Lichfield listen'd from her sacred bowers, 11
Bow'd her tall groves, and shook her stately towers.

"Nymph! not for thee the radiant day returns,
Nymph! not for thee the golden solstice burns,
Refulgent Cerea!—at the dusky hour
She seeks with pensive step the mountain-bower,
Bright as the blush of rising morn, and warms
The dull cold eye of Midnight with her charms:
There to the skies she lifts her pencill'd brows,
Opes her fair lips, and breathes her virgin vows; 20
Eyes the white zenith; counts the suns that roll
Their distant fires, and blaze around the pole;
Or marks where Jove directs his glittering car
O'er heaven's blue vault,—herself a brighter star.
—There as soft zephyrs sweep with pausing airs
Thy snowy neck, and part thy shadowy hairs,
Sweet Maid of Night! to Cynthia's sober beams
Glows thy warm cheek, thy polish'd bosom gleams.
In crowds around thee gaze the admiring swains,
And guard in silence the enchanted plains; 30
Drop the still tear, or breathe the impassion'd sigh,
And drink inebriate rapture from thine eye.

Pleased Lichfield. l. 11. The scenery described at the beginning of the first part, or Economy of Vegetation, is taken from a botanic garden about a mile from Lichfield.

Cerea. l. 15. Cactus grandiflorus, or Cereus. Twenty males, one female. This flower is a native of Jamaica and Veracrux. It expands a most exquisitely beautiful corol, and emits a most fragrant odour for a few hours in the night, and then closes to open no more. The flower is nearly a foot in diameter; the inside of the calyx of a splendid yellow, and the numerous petals of a pure white: it begins to open about seven or eight o'clock in the evening, and closes before sun-rise in the morning. Martyn's Letters, p. 294. The Cistus labdaniferus, and many other flowers, lose their petals after having been a few hours expanded in the day-time; for in these plants the stigma is soon impregnated by the numerous anthers: in many flowers of the Cistus labdaniferus I observed two or three of the stamens were perpetually bent into contact with the pistil.

The Nyctanthes, called Arabian Jasmine, is another flower, which expands a beautiful corol, and gives out a most delicate perfume during the night, and not in the day, in its native country, whence its name; botanical philosophers have not yet explained this wonderful property; perhaps the plant sleeps during the day as some animals do; and its odoriferous glands only emit their fragrance during the expansion of the petals; that is, during its waking hours; the Geranium triste has the same property of giving up its fragrance only in the night. The flowers of the Cucurbita lagenaria are said to close when the sun shines upon them. In our climate many flowers, as tragopogon, and hibiscus, close their flowers before the hottest part of the day comes on; and the flowers of some species of cucubalus, and Silene, viscous campion, are closed all day; but when the sun leaves them they expand, and emit a very agreeable scent; whence such plants are termed noctiflora.

Thus when old Needwood's hoary scenes the night
Paints with blue shadow, and with milky light;
Where Mundy pour'd, the listening nymphs among,
Loud to the echoing vales his parting song;
With measured step the Fairy Sovereign treads,
Shakes her high plume, and glitters o'er the meads; [train,
Round each green holly leads her sportive
And little footsteps mark the circled plain; 40
Each haunted rill with silver voices rings,
And night's sweet bird in livelier accents sings.

Ere the bright star, which leads the morning sky,
Hangs o'er the blushing east his diamond eye,
The chaste Tropæo leaves her secret bed;
A saint-like glory trembles round her head:
Eight watchful swains along the lawns of night
With amorous steps pursue the virgin light;

O'er her fair form the electric lustre plays,
And cold she moves amid the lambent blaze 50
So shines the glow-fly, when the sun retires,
And gems the night-air with phosphoric fires;
Thus o'er the marsh aerial lights betray,
And charm the unwary wanderer from his way.
So when thy King, Assyria, fierce and proud,
Three human victims to his idol vow'd;
Rear'd a vast pyre before the golden shrine
Of sulphurous coal, and pitch-exsuding pine;—
—Loud roar the flames, the iron nostrils breathe, 59
And the huge bellows pant and heave beneath;
Bright and more bright the blazing deluge flows, [glows.
And white with seven-fold heat the furnace
And now the Monarch fix'd with dread surprise
Deep in the burning vault his dazzled eyes.
"Lo! Three unbound amid the frightful glare,
Unscorch'd their sandals, and unsing'd their hair!
And now a fourth with seraph-beauty bright
Descends, accosts them, and outshines the light!
Fierce flames innocuous, as they step, retire!
And slow they move amid a world of fire!" 70
He spoke,—to Heaven his arms repentant spread,
And kneeling bow'd his gem-encircled head.

Two Sister-Nymphs, the fair Avenas, lead
Their fleecy squadrons on the lawns of Tweed;

Where Mundy. l. 35. Alluding to an unpublished poem by F. N. C. Mundy, Esq. on his leaving Needwood-Forest. See the passage in the notes at the end.

Tropæolum. l. 45. Majus. Garden Nasturtion, or greater Indian cress. Eight males, one female. Miss E. C. Linneus first observed the Tropæolum Majus to emit sparks or flashes in the mornings before sun-rise, during the months of June or July, and also during the twilight in the evening, but not after total darkness came on; these singular scintillations were shown to her father and other philosophers; and Mr. Wilcke, a celebrated electrician, believed them to be electric. Lin. Spec. Plantar. p. 490. Swedish Acts for the year 1762. Pulteney's View of Linneus, p. 220. Nor is this more wonderful than that the electric eel and torpedo should give voluntary shocks of electricity; and in this plant perhaps, as in those animals, it may be a mode of defence, by which it harasses or destroys the night flying insects which infest it; and probably it may emit the same sparks during the day, which must be then invisible. This curious subject deserves further investigation. See Dictamnus. The ceasing to shine of this plant after twilight might induce one to conceive, that it absorbed and emitted light, like the Bolognian Phosphorus, or calcined oyster-shells, so well explained by Mr. B. Wilson, and by T. B. Beccari. Experiments on Phosphori, by B. Wilson. The light of the evening, at the same distance from noon, is much greater, as I have repeatedly observed, than the light of the morning; this is owing, I suppose, to the phosphorescent quality of almost all bodies in a greater or less degree, which thus absorb light during the sun-shine, and continue to emit it again for some time afterwards, though not in such quantity as to produce apparent scintillations. The nectary of this plant grows from what is supposed to be the calyx; but this supposed calyx is coloured, and perhaps, from this circumstance of its bearing the nectary, should rather be esteemed a part of the corol. See an additional note at the end of the poem.

So shines the glow-fly. l. 51. In Jamaica, in some seasons of the year, the fire flies are seen in the evenings in great abundance. When they settle on the ground, the bull-frog greedily devours them; which seems to have given origin to a curious, though cruel, method of destroying these animals: if red-hot pieces of charcoal be thrown towards them in the dusk of the evening, they leap at them, and, hastily swallowing them, are burnt to death.

Avena. l. 73. Oat. The numerous families of grasses have all three males, and two females, except Anthoxanthum, which gives the grateful smell to hay, and has but two males. The herbs of this order of vegetables support the countless tribes of graminivorous animals. The seeds of the smaller kinds of grasses, as of aira, poa, briza, stipa, &c. are the sustenance of many sorts of birds. The seeds of the large grasses, as of wheat, barley, rye, oats, supply food to the human species.

It seems to have required more ingenuity to think of feeding nations of mankind with so small a seed, than with the potato of Mexico, or the bread-fruit of the southern islands; hence Ceres in Egypt, which was the birth-place of our European arts, was deservedly celebrated amongst their divinities, as well as Osyris, who invented the Plough.

Mr. Wahlborn observes, that as wheat, rye,

Pass with light step his wave-worn banks along,
And wake his Echoes with their silver tongue;
Or touch the reed, as gentle Love inspires,
In notes accordant to their chaste desires.

I.

"Sweet Echo! sleeps thy vocal shell,
Where this high arch o'erhangs the dell; 80
While Tweed with sun-reflecting streams
Chequers thy rocks with dancing beams?—

II.

Here may no clamours harsh intrude,
No brawling hound or clarion rude;
Here no fell beast of midnight prowl,
And teach thy tortured cliffs to howl!

III.

Be thine to pour these vales along
Some artless shepherd's evening song;
While night's sweet bird, from yon high spray
Responsive, listen to his lay. 90

IV.

And if, like me, some love-lorn maid
Should sing her sorrows to thy shade,
Oh, sooth her breast, ye rocks around!
With softest sympathy of sound."

From ozier bowers the brooding halcyons peep,
The swans pursuing cleave the glassy deep,
On hovering wings the wondering reed-larks play,
And silent bitterns listen to the lay.—
Three shepherd-swains beneath the beechen shades
Twine rival garlands for the tuneful maids;
On each smooth bark the mystic love-knot frame, 101
Or on white sands inscribe the favour'd name.
Green swells the beech, the widening knots improve,
So spread the tender growths of living love;
Wave follows wave, the letter'd lines decay,
So love's soft forms uncultured melt away.

From time's remotest dawn where China brings
In proud succession all her patriot-kings;
O'er desert-sands, deep gulfs, and hills sublime,
Extends her massy wall from clime to clime;
With bells and dragons crests her pagod-bowers,
Her silken palaces, and porcelain towers; 112
With long canals a thousand nations laves;
Plants all her wilds, and peoples all her waves;
Slow treads fair Cannabis the breezy strand,
The distaff streams dishevell'd in her hand;
Now to the left her ivory neck inclines,
And leads in Paphian curves its azure lines;
Dark waves the fringed lid, the warm cheek glows,
And the fair ear the parting locks disclose; 120
Now to the right with airy sweep she bends,
Quick join the threads, the dancing spole depends.
—*Five* swains attracted guard the Nymph, by turns
Her grace inchants them, and her beauty burns;
To each she bows with sweet assuasive smile,
Hears his soft vows, and turns her spole the while.

So when with light and shade, concordant strife!
Stern Clotho weaves the chequer'd thread of life;
Hour after hour the growing line extends,
The cradle and the coffin bound its ends; 130
Soft cords of silk the whirling spoles reveal,
If smiling Fortune turn the giddy wheel;
But if sweet Love with baby-fingers twines,
And wets with dewy lips the lengthening lines,
Skein after skein celestial tints unfold,
And all the silken tissue shines with gold.

Warm with sweet blushes bright Galantha glows,
And prints with frolic step the melting snows:

---

and many of the grasses, and plantain, lift up their anthers on long filaments, and thus expose the enclosed fecundating dust to be washed away by the rains, a scarcity of corn is produced by wet summers; hence the necessity of a careful choice of seed-wheat, as that, which had not received the dust of the anthers, will not grow, though it may appear well to the eye. The straw of the oat seems to have been the first musical instrument, invented during the pastoral ages of the world, before the discovery of metals. See note on Cistus.

Cannabis. l. 115. Chinese hemp. Two houses. Five males. A new species of hemp, of which an account is given by K. Fitzgerald, Esq. in a letter to Sir Joseph Banks, and which is believed to be much superior to the hemp of other countries. A few seeds of this plant were sown in England on the 4th of June, and grew to fourteen feet seven inches in height by the middle of October; they were nearly seven inches in circumference, and bore many lateral branches, and produced very white and tough fibres. At some parts of the time these plants grew nearly eleven inches in a week.—Philos. Trans. Vol. LXXII. p. 46.

Paphian curves. l. 118. In his ingenious work, entitled, The Analysis of Beauty, Mr. Hogarth believes that the triangular glass, which was dedicated to Venus in her temple at Paphos, contained in it a line bending spirally round a cone with a certain degree of curvature; and that this pyramidal outline and serpentine curve constitute the principles of Grace and Beauty.

Galanthus. l. 137. Nivalis. Snowdrop. Six

O'er silent floods, white hills, and glittering meads,
Six rival swains the playful beauty leads, 140
Chides with her dulcet voice the tardy Spring,
Bids slumbering Zephyr stretch his folded wing,
Wakes the hoarse cuckoo in his gloomy cave,
And calls the wondering dormouse from his grave,
Bids the mute redbreast cheer the budding grove,
And plaintive ringdove tune her notes to love.

Spring! with thy own sweet smile and tuneful tongue,
Delighted Bellis calls her infant throng.
Each on his reed astride, the cherub-train 149
Watch her kind looks, and circle o'er the plain;
Now with young Wonder touch the sliding snail,
Admire his eye-tipp'd horns, and painted mail;
Chase with quick step, and eager arms outspread,
The pausing butterfly from mead to mead;
Or twine green oziers with the fragrant gale,
The azure harebel, and the primrose pale,
Join hand in hand, and in procession gay
Adorn with votive wreaths the shrine of May.
—So moves the Goddess to the Idalian groves,
And leads her gold-hair'd family of Loves. 160
These, from the flaming furnace, strong and bold
Pour the red steel in many a sandy mould;
On tinkling anvils (with Vulcanian art,)
Turn with hot tongs, and forge the dreadful dart;
The barbed head on whirling jaspers grind,
And dip the point in poison for the mind;
Each polish'd shaft with snow-white plumage wing,
Or strain the bow reluctant to its string.
Those on light pinion twine with busy hands,
Or stretch from bough to bough the flowery bands; 170
Scare the dark beetle, as he wheels on high,
Or catch in silken nets the gilded fly;

---

males, one female. The first flower that appears after the winter solstice. See Stillingfleet's Calendar of Flora.

Some snowdrop-roots taken up in winter, and boiled, had the insipid mucilaginous taste of the orchis, and, if cured in the same manner, would probably make as good salep. The roots of the hyacinth, I am informed, are equally insipid, and might be used as an article of food. Gmelin, in his history of Siberia, says the Martagon Lily makes a part of the food of that country, which is of the same natural order as the snowdrop. Some roots of crocus, which I boiled, had a disagreeable flavour.

The difficulty of raising the orchis from seed, has, perhaps, been a principal reason of its not being cultivated in this country as an article of food. It is affirmed, by one of the Linnean school, in the Amœnit. Academ. that the seeds of orchis will ripen, if you destroy the new bulb; and that lily of the valley, convallaria, will produce many more seeds, and ripen them, if the roots be crowded in a garden-pot, so as to prevent them from producing many bulbs, Vol. VI. p. 120. It is probable either of these methods may succeed with these and other bulbous-rooted plants, as snowdrops, and might render their cultivation profitable in this climate. The root of the asphodelus ramosus, branchy asphodel, is used to feed swine in France; the starch is obtained from the alstromeria licta. Mém. d'Agricult.

Bellis prolifera. l. 148. Hen and chicken daisy. In this beautiful monster not only the impletion or doubling of the petals takes place, as described in the note on Alcea; but a numerous circlet of less flowers on peduncles, or footstalks, rise from the sides of the calyx, and surround the proliferous parent. The same occurs in calendula, marigold; in heracium, hawkweed; and in scabiosa, scabious. Phil. Botan. p. 82.

The fragrant gale. l. 155. The buds of the myrica gale possess an agreeable aromatic fragrance, and might be worth attending to as an article of the materia medica. Mr. Sparman suspects, that the green wax-like substance, with which at certain times of the year the berries of the myrica cerifera, or candle-berry myrtle, are covered, are deposited there by insects. It is used by the inhabitants for making candles, which he says burn rather better than those made of tallow. Voyage to the Cape, V. I. p. 345. Du Valde gives an account of a white wax made by small insects round the branches of a tree in China in great quantity, which is there collected for medical and economical purposes. The tree is called tong-tsin. Descript. of China. Vol. I. p. 230.

Deep in wide caves. l. 179. The arguments which tend to show that the warm springs of this country are produced from steam raised by deep subterraneous fires, and afterwards condensed between the strata of the mountains, appear to me much more conclusive than the idea of their being warmed by chemical combinations near the surface of the earth; for, 1st, their heat has kept accurately the same perhaps for many centuries, certainly as long as we have been possessed of good thermometers; which cannot be well explained, without supposing that they are first in a boiling state. For as the heat of boiling water is 212, and that of the internal parts of the earth 48, it is easy to understand that the steam raised from boiling water, after being condensed in some mountain, and passing from thence through a certain space of the cold earth, must be cooled always to a given degree; and it is probable the distance from the exit of the spring to the place where the steam is condensed, might be guessed by the degree of its warmth.

2. In the dry summer of 1780, when all other springs were either dry or much diminished, those of Buxton and Matlock (as I was well informed on the spot) had suffered no diminution; which proves that the sources of these warm springs are at great depths below the surface of the earth.

3. There are numerous perpendicular fissures in the rocks of Derbyshire, in which the ores of lead and copper are found, and which pass to unknown depths, and might thence afford a passage to steam from great subterraneous fires.

Call the young Zephyrs to their fragrant bowers,
And stay with kisses sweet the vernal Hours.
Where, as proud Masson rises rude and bleak,
And with misshapen turrets crests the Peak,
Old Matlock gapes with marble jaws, beneath,
And o'er scared Derwent bends his flinty teeth;
Deep in wide caves below the dangerous soil
Blue sulphurs flame, imprison'd waters boil. 180
Impetuous streams in spiral columns rise
Through rifted rocks, impatient for the skies;
Or o'er bright seas of bubbling lavas blow;
As heave and toss the billowy fires below;
Condensed on high, in wandering rills they glide
From Masson's dome, and burst his sparry side;
Round his grey towers, and down his fringed walls,
From cliff to cliff, the liquid treasure falls;
In beds of stalactite, bright ores among, 189
O'er corals, shells, and crystals, winds along;
Crusts the green mosses, and the tangled wood,
And sparkling plunges to its parent flood.
—O'er the warm wave a smiling youth presides,
Attunes its murmurs, its meanders guides,
(The blooming Fucus) in her sparry coves
To amorous Echo sings his *secret* loves,
Bathes his fair forehead in the misty stream,
And with sweet breath perfumes the rising steam.
—So, erst, an Angel o'er Bethesda's springs,
Each morn descending, shook his dewy wings;
And as his bright translucent form he laves,
Salubrious powers enrich the troubled waves.

Amphibious nymph, from Nile's prolific bed
Emerging Trapa lifts her pearly head;
Fair glows her virgin cheek and modest breast,
A panoply of scales deforms the rest;
Her quivering fins and panting gills she hides,
But spreads her silver arms upon the tides;

Trapa. l. 204. Four males, one female. The lower leaves of this plant grow under water, and are divided into minute capillary ramifications; while the upper leaves are broad and round, and have air-bladders in their footstalks to support them above the surface of the water. As the aerial leaves of vegetables do the office of lungs, by exposing a large surface of vessels with their contained fluids to the influence of the air; so these aquatic leaves answer a similar purpose like the gills of fish; and perhaps gain from water or give to it a similar material. As the material thus necessary to life seems to abound more in air than in water, the subaquatic leaves of this plant, and of sisymbrium, oenanthe, ranunculus aquatilis, water crowfoot, and some others, are cut into fine divisions to increase the surface; whilst those above water are undivided. So the plants on high mountains have their upper leaves more divided, as pimpinella, petroselinum, and others, because here the air is thinner, and thence a larger surface of contact is required. The stream of water also passes but once along the gills of fish, as it is sooner deprived of its virtue; whereas the air is both received and ejected by the action of the lungs of land-animals. The whale seems to be an exception to the above, as he receives water and spouts it out again from an organ, which I suppose to be a respiratory one; and probably the lamprey, so frequent in the month of April both in the Severn and Derwent, inspires and expires water on the seven holes on each side of the neck, which thus perform the office of the gills of other fish. As spring-water is nearly of the same degree of heat in all climates, the aquatic plants, which grow in rills or fountains, are found equally in the torrid, temperate, and frigid zones, as water-cress, water-parsnip, ranunculus, and many others.

In warmer climates the watery grounds are usefully cultivated, as with rice; and the roots of some aquatic plants are said to have supplied food, as the ancient lotus in Egypt, which some have supposed to be the nymphæa.—In Siberia the roots of the butomus, or flowering rush, are eaten, which is well worth further inquiry, as they grow spontaneously in our ditches and rivers, which at present produce no esculent vegetables; and might thence become an article of useful cultivation. Herodotus affirms that the Egyptian lotus grows in the Nile, and resembles a lily. That the natives dry it in the sun, and take the pulp out of it, which grows like the head of a poppy, and bake it for bread. Euterpe. Many grit-stones and coals, which I have seen, seem to bear an impression of the roots of the nymphæa, which are often three or four inches thick, especially the white-flowered one.

---

4. If these waters were heated by the decomposition of pyrites, there would be some chalybeate taste or sulphureous smell in them. See note in part I. on the existence of central fires.

Fucus. l. 195. Clandestine marriage. A species of fucus, or of conferva, soon appears in all basons which contain water. Dr. Priestley found that great quantities of pure dephlogisticated air were given up in water at the points of this vegetable, particularly in the sunshine, and that hence it contributed to preserve the water in reservoirs from becoming putrid. The minute divisions of the leaves of subaquatic plants as mentioned in the note on Trapa, and of the gills of fish, seem to serve another purpose besides that of increasing their surface, which has not, I believe, been attended to, and that is to facilitate the separation of the air, which is mechanically mixed or chemically dissolved in water by their points or edges: this appears on immersing a dry hairy leaf in water fresh from a pump; innumerable globules like quicksilver appear on almost every point; for the extremities of these points attract the particles of water less forcibly than those particles attract each other; hence the contained air, whose elasticity was but just balanced by the attractive power of the surrounding particles of water to each other, find at the point of each fibre a place where the resistance to its expansion is less; and in consequence it there expands, and becomes a bubble of air. It is easy to foresee that the rays of the sunshine, by being refracted and in part reflected by the two surfaces of these minute air-bubbles, must impart to them much more heat than to the transparent water; and thus facilitate their ascent by further expanding them; and that the points of vegetables attract the particles of water less than they attract each other, is seen by the spherical form of dew-drops on the points of grass. See note on Vegetable Respiration in Part I.

Slow as she sails, her ivory neck she laves,
And shakes her golden tresses o'er the waves.
Charm'd round the Nymph, in circling gambols glide 211
Four Nereid-forms, or shoot along the tide;
Now all as one they rise with frolic spring,
And beat the wondering air on humid wing;
Now all descending plunge beneath the main,
And lash the foam with undulating train;
Above, below, they wheel, retreat, advance
In air and ocean weave the mazy dance;
Bow their quick heads, and point their diamond eyes, 219
And twinkle to the sun with ever-changing dyes.

Where Andes, crested with volcanic beams,
Sheds a long line of light on Plata's streams;
Opes all his springs, unlocks his golden caves,
And feeds and freights the immeasurable waves;
Delighted Ocyma at twilight hours
Calls her light car, and leaves the sultry bowers;
Love's rising ray, and youth's seductive dye,
Bloom'd on her cheek, and brighten'd in her eye;

Ocymum salinum. l. 225. Saline basil. Class Two Powers. The Abbe Molina, in his History of Chili, translated from the Italian by the Abbe Grewvel, mentions a species of basil, which he calls ocymum salinum : he says it resembles the common basil, except that the stalk is round and jointed; and that though it grows sixty miles from the sea, yet every morning it is covered with saline globules, which are hard and splendid, appearing at a distance like dew; and that each plant furnishes about half an ounce of fine salt every day, which the peasants collect, and use as common salt, but esteem it superior in flavour.

As an article of diet, salt seems to act simply as a stimulus, not containing any nourishment, and is the only fossil substance which the caprice of mankind has yet taken into their stomachs along with their food; and, like all other unnatural stimuli, is not necessary to people in health, and contributes to weaken our system; though it may be useful as a medicine. It seems to be the immediate cause of the sea-scurvy, as those patients quickly recover by the use of fresh provisions; and is probably a remote cause of scrofula (which consists in the want of irritability in the absorbent vessels) and is therefore serviceable to these patients; as wine is necessary to those whose stomachs have been weakened by its use. The universality of the use of salt with our food, and in our cookery, has rendered it difficult to prove the truth of these observations. I suspect that flesh-meat cut into thin slices, either raw or boiled, might be preserved in coarse sugar or treacle; and thus a very nourishing and salutary diet might be presented to our seamen. See note on salt-rocks, in Part I. Canto II. If a person unaccustomed to much salt should eat a couple of red herrings, his insensible perspiration will be so much increased by the stimulus of the salt, that he will find it necessary in about two hours to drink a quart of water : the effects of a continued use of salt in weakening the action of the lymphatic system may hence be deduced.

Chaste, pure, and white, a zone of silver graß
Her tender breast, as white, as pure, as chaste
—By *four* fond swains in playful circles drawn,
On glowing wheels she tracks the moon-bright lawn, 232
Mounts the rude cliff, unveils her blushing charms,
And calls the panting zephyrs to her arms.
Emerged from ocean springs the vaporous air,
Bathes her light limbs, uncurls her amber hair,
Incrusts her beamy form with films saline,
And beauty blazes through the crystal shrine.—
So with pellucid studs the ice-flower gems
Her rimy foliage and her candied stems. 240
So from his glassy horns, and pearly eyes,
The diamond-beetle darts a thousand dyes;
Mounts with enamel'd wings the vesper gale,
And wheeling shines in adamantine mail.

Thus when loud thunders o'er Gomorrah burst, [curst,
And heaving earthquakes shook his realms accurst,
An Angel-guest led forth the trembling fair
With shadowy hand, and warn'd the guiltless pair; [fly,
" Haste from these lands of sin, ye righteous!
Speed the quick step, nor turn the lingering eye!"— 250
—Such the command, as fabling bards recite,
When Orpheus charm'd the grisly king of night;
Sooth'd the pale phantoms with his plaintive lay,
And led the fair assurgent into day.—
Wide yawn'd the earth, the fiery tempest flash'd,
And towns and towers in one vast ruin crash'd;
Onward they move,—loud horror roars behind,
And shrieks of anguish bellow in the wind.
With many a sob, amid a thousand fears,
The beauteous wanderer pours her gushing tears; 260
Each soft connection rends her troubled breast,
—She turns, unconscious of the stern behest!—
" I faint!—I fall!—ah, me!—sensations chill
Shoot through my bones, my shuddering bosom thrill! [fault,
I freeze! I freeze! just Heaven regards my
Numbs my cold limbs, and hardens into salt!—
Not yet, not yet, your dying love resign!
This last, last kiss receive!—no longer thine!"—
She said, and ceased,—her stiffen'd form he press'd, 269
And strain'd the briny column to his breast;
Printed with quivering lips the lifeless snow,
And wept, and gazed the monument of wo.—
So when Æneas through the flames of Troy
Bore his pale sire, and led his lovely boy;
With loitering step the fair Creusa stay'd,
And death involved her in eternal shade.—

Ice-flower. l. 239. Mysembryanthemum crystallinum.

—Oft the lone Pilgrim, that his road forsakes,
Marks the wide ruins, and the sulphur'd lakes;
On mouldering piles amid asphaltic mud
Hears the hoarse bittern, where Gomorrah
   stood; 280
Recalls the unhappy Pair with lifted eye,
Leans on the crystal tomb, and breathes the
   silent sigh.

With net-wove sash and glittering gorget
   dress'd,
And scarlet robe lapell'd upon her breast,
Stern Ara frowns, the measured march as-
   sumes, [plumes;
Trails her long lance, and nods her shadowy
While Love's soft beams illume her treacherous
   eyes,
And Beauty lightens through the thin disguise.
So erst, when Hercules, untamed by toil,
Own'd the soft power of Dejanira's smile:— 290
His lion-spoils the laughing Fair demands,
And gives the distaff to his awkward hands;
O'er her white neck the bristly mane she
   throws,
And binds the gaping whiskers on her brows;
Plaits round her slender waist the shaggy vest,
And clasps the velvet paws across her breast.

Arum. l. 285. Cuckow-pint, of the class Gynandria, or masculine ladies. The pistil or female part of the flower, rises like a club, is covered above or clothed, as it were, by the anthers or males; and some of the species have a large scarlet blotch in the middle of every leaf.
The singular and wonderful structure of this flower has occasioned many disputes amongst botanists. See Tournef. Malpig. Dillen. Riven. &c. The receptacle is enlarged into a naked club, with the germs at its base; the stamens are affixed to the receptacle amidst the germs (a natural prodigy,) and thus do not need the assistance of elevating filaments: hence the flower may be said to be inverted. *Families of Plants* translated from Linneus, p. 618.
The spadix of this plant is frequently quite white, or coloured, and the leaves liable to be streaked with white, and to have black or scarlet blotches on them. As the plant has no corol or blossom, it is probable the coloured juices in these parts of the sheath or leaves may serve the same purpose as the coloured juices in the petals of other flowers; from which I suppose the honey to be prepared. See note on Helleborus. I am informed that those tulip-roots which have a red cuticle produce red flowers. See Rubia.
When the petals of the tulip become striped with many colours, the plant loses almost half of its height; and the method of making them thus break into colours is by transplanting them into a meagre or sandy soil, *after they have previously enjoyed a richer soil:* hence it appears, that the plant is weakened when the flower becomes variegated. See note on Anemone. For the acquired habits of vegetables, see Tulipa, Orchis.
The roots of the Arum are scratched up and eaten by thrushes in severe snowy seasons. White's Hist. of Selbourn, p. 43.

Next with soft hands the knotted club she rears,
Heaves up from earth, and on her shoulder
   bears.
Onward with loftier step the Beauty treads,
And trails the brinded ermine o'er the meads;
Wolves, bears, and pards, forsake the affrighted
   groves, 301
And grinning Satyrs tremble, as she moves.

Caryo's sweet smile Dianthus proud admires,
And gazing burns with unallow'd desires;
With sighs and sorrows her compassion moves,
And wins the damsel to illicit loves.
The Monster-offspring heirs the father's pride,
Mask'd in the damask beauties of the bride.
So, when the Nightingale in eastern bowers 309
On quivering pinion woos the Queen of flowers;
Inhales her fragrance, as he hangs in air,
And melts with melody the blushing fair;

Dianthus. l. 303. Superbus. Proud Pink. There is a kind of pink called Fairchild's mule, which is here supposed to be produced between a Dianthus superbus, and the Caryophyllus, Clove. The Dianthus superbus emits a most fragrant odour, particularly at night. Vegetable mules supply an irrefragable argument in favour of the sexual system of botany. They are said to be numerous; and, like the mules of the animal kingdom, not always to continue their species by seed. There is an account of a curious mule from the Antirrhinum linaria, Toadflax, in the Amœnit. Acadam. V. I. No. 3. and many hybrid plants described in No. 32. The urtica alienta is an evergreen plant, which appears to be a nettle from the male flowers, and a Pellitory (Parietaria) from the female ones and the fruit; and is hence between both. Murray, Syst. Veg. Amongst the English indigenous plants, the veronica hybrida, mule speedwell, is supposed to have originated from the officinal one, and the spiked one. And the Sibthorpia Europœa to have for its parents the golden saxifrage and marsh pennywort. Pulteney's View of Linneus, p. 253. Mr. Graberg, Mr. Schreber, and Mr. Ramstrom, seem of opinion, that the internal structure or parts of fructification in mule-plants resemble the female parent; but that the habit or external structure resembles the male parent. See treatises under the above names in V. VI. Amœnit. Academic. The mule produced from a horse and the ass resembles the horse externally with his ears, mane, and tail; but with the nature or manners of an ass: but the Hinnus, or creature produced from a male ass, and a mare, resembles the father externally in stature, ash-colour, and the black cross, but with the nature or manners of a horse. The breed from Spanish rams and Swedish ewes resembled the Spanish sheep in wool, stature, and external form; but was as hardy as the Swedish sheep; and the contrary of those which were produced from Swedish rams and Spanish ewes. The offspring from the male goat of Angora and the Swedish female goat had long soft camel's hair; but that from the male Swedish goat, and the female one of Angora, had no improvement of their wool. An English ram without horns, and a Swedish horned ewe, produced sheep without horns. Amœn. Acad. Vol. VI. p. 13.

Half-rose, half-bird, a beauteous Monster springs,
Waves his thin leaves, and claps his glossy [wings;
Long horrent thorns his mossy legs surround,
And tendril-talons root him to the ground;
Green films of rind his wrinkled neck o'erspread,
And crimson petals crest his curled head;
Soft warbling beaks in each bright blossom move,
And vocal Rosebuds thrill the enchanted grove!
Admiring Evening stays her beamy star, 321
And still Night listens from his ebon car;
While on white wings descending Houries throng,
And drink the floods of odour and of song.

When from his golden urn the Solstice pours,
O'er Afric's sable sons the sultry hours;
When not a gale flits o'er her tawny hills,
Save where the dry Harmattan breathes and kills;

When stretch'd in dust her gasping panthers lie,
And writh'd in foamy folds her serpents die: 330
Indignant Atlas mourns his leafless woods,
And Gambia trembles for his sinking floods;
Contagion stalks along the briny sand,
And Ocean rolls his sick'ning shoals to land.
—Fair Chunda smiles amid the burning waste,
Her brow unturban'd, and her zone unbraced;
Ten brother-youths with light umbrellas shade,
Or fan with busy hands the panting maid;
Loose wave her locks, disclosing, as they break,
The rising bosom and averted cheek; 340
Clasp'd round her ivory neck with studs of gold
Flows her thin vest in many a gauzy fold;
O'er her light limbs the dim transparence plays,
And the fair form, it seems to hide, betrays.

Cold from a thousand rocks, where Ganges leads
The gushing waters to his sultry meads;

The dry harmattan. l. 328. The harmattan is a singular wind blowing from the interior parts of Africa to the Atlantic ocean, sometimes for a few hours, sometimes for several days without regular periods. It is always attended with a fog or haze, so dense as to render those objects invisible which are at the distance of a quarter of a mile; the sun appears through it only about noon, and then of a dilute red, and very minute particles subside from the misty air so as to make the grass, and the skins of negroes appear whitish. The extreme dryness which attends this wind or fog, without dews, withers and quite dries the leaves of vegetables; and is said by Dr. Lind at some seasons to be fatal and malignant to mankind; probably after much preceding wet, when it may become loaded with the exhalations from putrid marshes; at other seasons it is said to check epidemic diseases, to cure fluxes, and to heal ulcers and cutaneous eruptions; which is probably effected by its yielding no moisture to the mouths of the external absorbent vessels, by which the actions of the other branches of the absorbent system is increased to supply the deficiency. *Account of the Harmattan, Phil. Trans.* Vol. LXXI.

The Rev. Mr. Sterling gives an account of a darkness for six or eight hours at Detroit in America, on the 19th of October, 1762, in which the sun appeared as red as blood, and thrice its usual size: some rain falling, covered white paper with dark drops, like sulphur or dirt, which burnt like wet gun-powder, and the air had a very sulphureous smell. He supposes this to have been emitted from some distant earthquake or volcano. *Philos. Trans.* Vol. LIII. p. 63.

In many circumstances this wind seems much to resemble the dry fog which covered most parts of Europe for many weeks in the summer of 1780, which has been supposed to have had a volcanic origin, as it succeeded the violent eruption of Mount Hecla, and its neighbourhood. From the subsidence of a white powder, it seems probable that the harmattan has a similar origin, from the unexplored mountains of Africa. Nor is it improbable, that the epidemic coughs, which occasionally traverse immense tracts of country, may be the products of volcanic eruptions; nor impossible, that at some future time contagious miasmata may be thus emitted from subterraneous furnaces, in such abundance as to contaminate the whole atmosphere, and depopulate the earth!

His sickening shoals. l. 334. Mr. Marsden relates, that in the island of Sumatra, during the November of 1775, the dry monsoons, or S. E. winds, continued so much longer than usual, that the large rivers became dry; and prodigious quantities of sea-fish, dead and dying, were seen floating for leagues on the sea, and driven on the beach by the tides. This was supposed to have been caused by the great evaporation, and the deficiency of fresh-water rivers having rendered the sea too salt for its inhabitants. The season then became so sickly as to destroy great numbers of people, both foreigners and natives. *Phil. Trans.* Vol. LXXI. p. 384.

Chunda. l. 335. Chundali borrum is the name which the natives give to this plant; it is the hedysarum gyrans, or moving plant; its class is two brotherhoods, ten males. Its leaves are continually in spontaneous motion; some rising and others falling; and others whirling circularly by twisting their stems; this spontaneous movement of the leaves, when the air is quite still and very warm, seems to be necessary to the plant, as perpetual respiration is to animal life. A more particular account, with a good print of the hedysarum gyrans is given by M. Broussonet, in a paper on vegetable motions in the Histoire de l'Académie des Sciences. Ann. 1784, p. 609.

There are many other instances of spontaneous movements of the parts of vegetables. In the marchantia polymorpha some yellow wool proceeds from the flower-bearing anthers, which moves spontaneously in the anther, while it drops its dust like atoms, Murray, Syst. Veg. See note on Collinsonia for other instances of vegetable spontanety. Add to this, that as the sleep of animals consists in a suspension of voluntary motion, and as vegetables are likewise subject to sleep, there is reason to conclude, that the various actions of opening and closing their petals and foliage may be justly ascribed to a voluntary power: for without the faculty of volition, sleep would not have been necessary to them.

By moon-crown'd mosques with gay reflections
    glides,
And vast pagodas trembling on his sides;
With sweet loquacity Nelumbo sails,
Shouts to his shores, and parleys with his gales;
Invokes his echoes, as she moves along,   351
And thrills his rippling surges with her song.
—As round the Nymph her listening lovers
    play,
And guard the Beauty on her watery way;
Charm'd on the brink relenting tygers gaze,
And pausing buffaloes forget to graze;
Admiring elephants forsake their woods,
Stretch their wide ears, and wade into the floods;
In silent herds the wondering sea-calves lave,
Or nod their slimy foreheads o'er the wave;   360
Poised on still wing attentive vultures sweep,
And winking crocodiles are lull'd to sleep.

Where leads the northern Star his lucid train
High o'er the snow-clad earth, and icy main,
With milky light the white horizon streams,
And to the moon each sparkling mountain
    gleams.
Slow o'er the printed snows with silent walk
Huge shaggy forms across the twilight stalk;
And ever and anon with hideous sound   369
Burst the thick ribs of ice, and thunder round.
There, as old Winter flaps his hoary wing,
And lingering leaves his empire to the Spring,
Pierced with quick shafts of silver-shooting
    light
Fly in dark troops the dazzled imps of night.—
"Awake, my Love!" enamour'd Muschus
    cries,
"Stretch thy fair limbs, refulgent maid arise;
Ope thy sweet eye-lids to the rising ray,
And hail with ruby lips returning day.
Down the white hills dissolving torrents pour,
Green springs the turf, and purple blows the
    flower;   380
His torpid wing the Rail exulting tries,
Mounts the soft gale, and wantons in the skies;
Rise, let us mark how bloom the awaken'd
    groves,
And 'mid the banks of roses *hide* our loves."

Night's tinsel beams on smooth Loch-lomond
    dance,
Impatient Æga views the bright expanse;
In vain her eyes the passing floods explore,
Wave after wave rolls freightless to the shore.
—Now dim amid the distant foam she spies
A rising speck,—"'tis he!'tis he!" she cries; 390
As with firm arms he beats the streams aside,
And cleaves with rising chest the tossing tide,
With bended knee she prints the humid sands,
Up-turns her glistening eyes, and spreads her
    hands;
—"'Tis he, 'tis he!—my lord, my life, my
    love!
Slumber, ye winds; ye billows, cease to move!
Beneath his arms your buoyant plumage spread,
Ye Swans! ye Halcyons! hover round his
    head!"
—With eager step the boiling surf she braves,
And meets her refluent lover in the waves;   400
Loose o'er the flood her azure mantle swims,
And the clear stream betrays her snowy limbs.

Nelumbo. l. 349. Nymphæa Nelumbo. A beautiful rose-red flower on a receptacle as large as an artichoke. The capsule is perforated with holes at the top, and the seeds rattle in it. Perfect leaves are seen in the seeds before they germinate. Linneus, who has enlisted all our senses into the service of botany, has observed this rattling of the Nelumbo; and mentions what he calls an electric murmur, like distant thunder, in hop-yards, when the wind blows; and asks the cause of it. We have one kind of pedicularis, in our meadows, which has obtained the name of rattle-grass, from the rattling of its dry seed vessels under our feet.

Burst the thick ribs of ice. l. 370. The violent cracks of ice heard from the Glaciers seem to be caused by some of the snow being melted in the middle of the day; and the water thus produced running down into valleys of ice, and congealing again in a few hours, forces off by its expansion large precipices from the ice-mountains.

Muschus. l. 375. Corallinus, or lichen rangiferinus. Coral-moss. Clandestine-marriage. This moss vegetates beneath the snow, where the degree of heat is always about 40; that is, in the middle between the freezing point, and the common heat of the earth; and is for many months of the winter the sole food of the reindeer, who digs furrows in the snow to find it; and as the milk and flesh of this animal is almost the only sustenance which can be procured during the long winters of the higher latitudes, this moss may be said to support some millions of mankind.

The quick vegetation that occurs on the solution of the snows in high latitudes appears very astonishing; it seems to arise from two causes, 1. the long continuance of the approaching sun above the horizon; 2. the increased irritability of plants which have been long exposed to the cold. See note on Anemone.

All the water-fowl on the lakes of Siberia are said by Professor Gmelin to retreat southwards on the commencement of the frost, except the Rail, which sleeps buried in the snow. Account of Siberia.

Æga. l. 386. Conferva ægagropila. It is found loose in many lakes in a globular form, from the size of a walnut to that of a melon, much resembling the balls of hair found in the stomachs of cows; it adheres to nothing, but rolls from one part of the lake to another. The conferva vagabunda dwells on the European seas, travelling along in the midst of the waves; (Spec. Plant.) These may not improperly be called itinerant vegetables. In a similar manner the fucus natans (swimming) strikes no roots into the earth, but floats on the sea in very extensive masses, and may be said to be a plant of passage, as it is wafted by the winds from one shore to another.

So on her sea-girt tower fair Hero stood
At parting day, and mark'd the dashing flood;
While high in air, the glimmering rocks above,
Shone the bright lamp, the pilot-star of love.
—With robe outspread the wavering flame behind
She kneels, and guards it from the shifting wind;
Breathes to her goddess all her vows, and guides
Her bold Leander o'er the dusky tides;   410
Wrings his wet hair, his briny bosom warms,
And clasps her panting lover in her arms.

Deep, in wide caverns and their shadowy ailes,
Daughter of Earth, the chaste Truffelia smiles;
On silvery beds, of soft asbestus wove,
Meets her Gnome-husband, and avows her love.
—*High* o'er her couch impending diamonds blaze,
And branching gold the crystal roof inlays;
With verdant light the modest emeralds glow,
Blue sapphires glare, and rubies blush, *below*;
Light piers of lazuli the dome surround,   421
And pictured mochoes tesselate the ground:
In glittering threads along reflective walls
The warm rill murmuring twinkles, as it falls;
Now sink the Eolian strings, and now they swell,
And Echoes woo in every vaulted cell;
While on white wings delighted Cupids play,
Shake their bright lamps, and shed celestial day.

Closed in an azure fig by fairy spells,
Bosom'd in down, fair Capri-fica dwells;— 430

So sleeps in silence the Curculio, shut
In the dark chambers of the cavern'd nut,
Erodes with ivory beak the vaulted shell,
And quits on filmy wings its narrow cell.
So the pleased Linnet in the moss-wove nest,
Waked into life beneath its parent's breast,
Chirps in the gaping shell, bursts forth erelong,
Shakes its new plumes, and tries its tender song.—
—And now the talisman she strikes, that charms
Her husband-Sylph,—and calls him to her arms.—   440
Quick, the light Gnat her airy lord bestrides,
With cobweb reins the flying courser guides,
From crystal steeps of viewless ether springs,
Cleaves the soft air on still expanded wings;
Darts like a sunbeam o'er the boundless wave,
And seeks the beauty in her *secret* cave.
So with quick impulse through all nature's frame
Shoots the electric air its subtle flame.
So turns the impatient needle to the pole,   449
Tho' mountains rise between, and oceans roll.

Where round the Orcades white torrents roar,
Scooping with ceaseless rage the incumbent shore,

Truffelia. l. 414. (Lycoperdon Tuber) Truffle. Clandestine marriage. This fungus never appears above ground, requiring little air, and perhaps no light. It is found by dogs or swine, who hunt it by the smell. Other plants, which have no buds or branches on their stems, as the grasses, shoot out numerous stoles or scions under ground: and this the more, as their tops or herbs are eaten by cattle, and thus preserve themselves.

Caprificus. l. 430. Wild fig. The fruit of the fig is not a seed-vessel, but a receptacle inclosing the flower within it. As these trees bear some male and others female flowers, immured on all sides by the fruit, the manner of their fecundation was very unintelligible, till Tournefort and Pontedera discovered, that a kind of gnat produced in the male figs carried the fecundating dust on its wings, (Cynips Psenes Syst. Nat. 919.) and penetrating the female fig, thus impregnated the flowers; for the evidence of this wonderful fact, see the word Caprification, in Milne's Botanical Dictionary. The figs of this country are all female, and their seeds not prolific; and therefore they can only be propagated layers and suckers.

Monsieur de la Hire has shown in the Mémoir. de l'Acadèm. des Sciences, that the summer figs of Paris, in Provence, Italy, and Malta, have all perfect stamina, and ripen not only their fruits, but their seed; from which seed other fig trees are raised; but that the stamina of the autumnal figs are abortive, perhaps owing to the want of due warmth. Mr. Milne, in his Botanical Dictionary, (art. Caprification) says, that the cultivated fig-trees have a few male flowers placed above the female within the same covering or receptacle; which in warmer climates perform their proper office, but in colder ones become abortive. And Linneus observes, that some figs have the navel of the receptacle open; which was one reason that induced him to remove this plant from the class Clandestine Marriage to the class Polygamy. Lin. Spec. Plant.

From all these circumstances I should conjecture, that those female fig flowers, which are closed on all sides in the fruit or receptacle without any male ones, are monsters, which have been propagated for their fruit, like barberries, and grapes without seeds in them; and that the Caprification is either an ancient process of imaginary use, and blindly followed in some countries, or that it may contribute to ripen the fig by decreasing its vigour, like cutting off a circle of the bark from the branch of a pear-tree. Tournefort seems inclined to this opinion; who says, that the figs in Provence and at Paris ripen sooner, if their buds be pricked with a straw dipped in olive oil. Plums and pears punctured by some insects ripen sooner, and the part round the puncture is sweeter. Is not the honey-dew produced by the puncture of insects? will not wounding the branch of a pear-tree, which is too vigorous, prevent the blossoms from falling off; as from some fig-trees the fruit is said to fall off unless they are wounded by caprification? I had last spring six young trees of the Ischia fig with fruit on them in pots in a stove; on removing them into larger boxes, they protruded very vigorous shoots, and the figs all fell off; which I ascribed to the increased vigour of the plants.

Wide o'er the deep a dusky cavern bends
Its marble arms, and high in air impends;
Basaltic piers the ponderous roof sustain,
And steep their massy sandals in the main;
Round the dim walls, and through the whispering aisles
Hoarse breathes the wind, the glittering water boils.
Here the charm'd Byssus with his blooming [bride
Spreads his green sails, and braves the foaming tide; 460
The star of Venus gilds the twilight wave,
And lights her votaries to the *secret* cave;
Light Cupids flutter round the nuptial bed,
And each coy Sea-maid hides her blushing head.

Where cool'd by rills, and curtain'd round by woods,
Slopes the green dell to meet the briny floods,
The sparkling noon-beams trembling on the tide,
The Proteus-lover woos his playful bride,
To win the fair he tries a thousand forms,
Basks on the sands, or gambols in the storms.

A Dolphin now, his scaly sides he laves, 471
And bears the sportive Damsel on the waves;
She strikes the cymbal as he moves along,
And wondering Ocean listens to the song.
—And now a spotted Pard the lover stalks,
Plays round her steps, and guards her favour'd walks;
As with white teeth he prints her hand, caress'd,
And lays his velvet paw upon her breast,
O'er his round face her snowy fingers strain
The silken knots, and fit the ribbon-rein. 480
—And now a Swan, he spreads his plumy sails,
And proudly glides before the fanning gales;
Pleased on the flowery brink with graceful hand
She waves her floating lover to the land;
Bright shines his sinuous neck, with crimson beak
He prints fond kisses on her glowing cheek,
Spreads his broad wings, elates his ebon crest,
And clasps the beauty to his downy breast.

A *hundred* virgins join a *hundred* swains,
And fond Adonis leads the sprightly trains;
Pair after pair, along his sacred groves 491
To Hymen's fane the bright procession moves;
Each smiling youth a myrtle garland shades,
And wreaths of roses veil the blushing maids;
Light Joys on twinkling feet attend the throng,
Weave the gay dance, or raise the frolic song;
—Thick, as they pass, exulting Cupids fling
Promiscuous arrows from the sounding string;
On wings of gossamer soft Whispers fly,
And the sly Glance steals side-long from the eye. 500
—As round his shrine the gaudy circles bow,
And seal with muttering lips the faithless vow,
Licentious Hymen joins their mingled hands,
And loosely twines the meretricious bands.—

Basaltic piers. l. 455. This description alludes to the cave of Fingal in the island of Staffa. The basaltic columns, which compose the Giants Causeway on the coast of Ireland, as well as those which support the cave of Fingal, are evidently of volcanic origin, as is well illustrated in an ingenious paper of Mr. Keir, in the Philos. Trans. who observed in the glass, which had been long in a fusing heat at the bottom of the pots in the glass-houses at Stourbridge, that crystals were produced of a form similar to the parts of the basaltic columns of the Giants Causeway.

Byssus. l. 459. Clandestine Marriage. It floats on the sea in the day, and sinks a little during the night; it is found in caverns on the northern shores, of a pale green colour, and as thin as paper.

The Proteus-lover. l. 468. Conferva polymorpha. This vegetable is put amongst the cryptogamia, or clandestine marriages, by Linneus; but, according to Mr. Ellis, the males and females are on different plants. Philos. Trans. Vol. LVII. It twice changes its colour, from red to brown, and then to black; and changes its form by losing its lower leaves, and elongating some of the upper ones, so as to be mistaken by the unskilful for different plants. It grows on the shores of this country.

There is another plant, Medicago polymorpha, which may be said to assume a great variety of shapes; as the seed-vessels resemble sometimes snail-horns, at other times caterpillars with or without long hair upon them, by which means it is probable they sometimes elude the depredations of those insects. The seeds of Calendula, Marygold, bend up like a hairy caterpillar, with their prickles bristling outwards, and may thus deter some birds or insects from preying upon them. Salicornia also assumes an animal similitude. Phil. Bot. p. 87. See note on Iris in additional notes; and Cypripedia in Part I.

Adonis. l. 490. Many males and many females live together in the same flower. It may seem a solecism in language to call a flower, which contains many of both sexes, an individual; and the more so to call a tree or shrub an individual, which consists of so many flowers. Every tree, indeed, ought to be considered as a family or swarm of its respective buds; but the buds themselves seem to be individual plants; because each has leaves or lungs appropriated to it; and the bark of the tree is only a congeries of the roots of all these individual buds. Thus hollow oak-trees and willows are often seen with the whole wood decayed and gone; and yet the few remaining branches flourish with vigour; but in respect to the male and female parts of a flower, they do not destroy its individuality any more than the number of paps of a sow, or the number of her cotyledons, each of which includes one of her young.

The society, called the Areoi, in the island of Otaheite, consists of about 100 males and 100 females, who form one promiscuous marriage.

Thus where pleased Venus, in the southern main,
Sheds all her smiles on Otaheite's plain,
Wide o'er the isle her silken net she draws,
And the loves laugh at all but Nature's laws."

Here ceased the Goddess,—o'er the silent strings
Applauding zephyrs swept their fluttering wings; 510
Enraptured Sylphs arose in murmuring crowds
To air-wove canopies and pillowy clouds;
Each Gnome reluctant sought his earthy cell,
And each chill Floret closed her velvet bell.
Then, on soft tiptoe, Night approaching near
Hung o'er the tuneless lyre his sable ear;
Gem'd with bright stars the still ethereal plain,
And bade his Nightingales repeat the strain.

ADDITIONAL NOTES.

CURCUMA.—Canto I. l. 65.

These antherless filaments seem to be an endeavour of the plant to produce more stamens, as would appear from some experiments of Mr. Reynier, instituted for another purpose: he cut away the stamens of many flowers, with design to prevent their fecundity, and in many instances the flower threw out new filaments from the wounded part of different lengths, but did not produce new anthers. The experiments were made on the geum rivale, different kinds of mallows, and the æchinops citro. Critical Review for March, 1788.

IRIS.—Canto I. l. 71.

In the Persian Iris the end of the lower petal is purple, with white edges and orange streaks, creeping, as it were, into the mouth of the flower like an insect; by which deception in its native climate it probably prevents a similar insect from plundering it of its honey: the edges of the lower petal lap over those of the upper one, which prevents it from opening too wide on fine days, and facilitates its return at night; whence the rain is excluded, and the air admitted. See Polymorpha, Rubia, and Cypripedia, in Part I.

CHONDRILLA.—Canto I. l. 97.

In the natural state of the expanded flower of the barberry, the stamens lie on the petals; under the concave summits of which the anthers shelter themselves, and in this situation remain perfectly rigid; but on touching the inside of the filament near its base with a fine bristle, or blunt needle, the stamen instantly bends upwards, and the anther, embracing the stigma, sheds its dust. Observations on the Irritation of Vegetables, by T. E. Smith, M. D.

SILENE.—Canto I. l. 139.

I saw a plant of the dionæa muscipula, flytrap of Venus, this day, in the collection of Sir B. Boothby, at Ashburn-Hall, Derbyshire, Aug. 20th, 1788; and on drawing a straw along the middle of the rib of the leaves as they lay upon the ground round the stem, each of them, in about a second of time, closed and doubled itself up, crossing the thorns over the opposite edge of the leaf, like the teeth of a spring rat-trap: of this plant I was favoured with an elegant coloured drawing, by Miss Maria Jackson, of Tarporly, in Cheshire, a lady who adds much botanical knowledge to many other elegant acquirements.

In the apocynum androsæmifolium, one kind of dog's-bane, the anthers converge over the nectaries, which consist of five glandular oval corpuscles surrounding the germ; and at the same time admit air to the nectaries at the interstice between each anther. But when a fly inserts its proboscis between these anthers to plunder the honey, they converge closer, and with such violence as to detain the fly, which thus generally perishes. This account was related to me by R. W. Darwin, Esq. of Elston, in Nottinghamshire, who showed me the plant in flower, July 2d, 1788, with a fly thus held fast by the end of its proboscis, and was well seen by a magnifying lens, and which in vain repeatedly struggled to disengage itself, till the converging anthers were separated by means of a pin: on some days he had observed that almost every flower of this elegant plant had a fly in it thus entangled; and a few weeks afterwards favoured me with his further observations on this subject.

"My apocynum is not yet out of flower. I have often visited it, and have frequently found four or five flies, some alive, and some dead, in its flowers; they are generally caught by the trunk or proboscis, sometimes by the trunk and a leg; there is one at present only caught by a leg: I don't know that this plant sleeps, as the flowers remain open in the night; yet the flies frequently make their escape. In a plant of Mr. Ordoyno's, an ingenious gardener at Newark, who is possessed of a great collection of plants, I saw many flowers of an apocynum with three dead flies in each; they are a thin-bodied fly, and rather less than the common house-fly; but I have seen two or three other sorts of flies thus arrested by the plant. Aug. 12, 1788."

ILEX.—Canto I. l. 161.

The efficient cause, which renders the hollies prickly in Needwood Forest only as high as the animals can reach them, may arise from the lower branches being constantly cropped by them, and thus shoot forth more luxuriant foliage: it is probable the shears in garden-hollies may produce the same effect, which is equally curious, as prickles are not thus produced on other plants

ULVA.—Canto. I. l. 415.

M. Hubert made some observations on the air contained in the cavities of the bambou. The stems of these canes were from 40 to 50 feet in height, and 4 or 5 inches in diameter, and might contain about 30 pints of elastic air. He cut a bambou, and introduced a lighted candle into the cavity, which was extinguished immediately on its entrance. He tried this about 60 times in a cavity of the bambou, containing about two pints. He introduced mice at different times into these cavities, which seemed to be somewhat affected, but soon recovered their agility. The stem of the bambou is not hollow till it rises more than one foot from the earth; the divisions between the cavities are convex downwards. Observ. sur la Physique, par M. Rozier, l. 33. p. 130.

TROPÆOLUM.—Canto IV. l. 45.

In Sweden a very curious phenomenon has been observed on certain flowers, by M. Haggren, Lecturer in Natural History. One evening he perceived a faint flash of light repeatedly dart from a Marigold; surprised at such an uncommon appearance, he resolved to examine it with attention; and, to be assured that it was no deception of the eye, he placed a man near him, with orders to make a signal at the moment when he observed the light. They both saw it constantly at the same moment.

The light was most brilliant on Marigolds of an orange or flame colour, but scarcely visible on pale ones.

The flash was frequently seen on the same flower two or three times in quick succession, but more commonly at intervals of several minutes; and when several flowers in the same place emitted their light together, it could be observed at a considerable distance.

This phenomenon was remarked in the months of July and August, at sun-set, and for half an hour after, when the atmosphere was clear; but after a rainy day, or when the air was loaded with vapours, nothing of it was seen.

The following flowers emitted flashes, more or less vivid, in this order:
1. The Marigold, *(Calendula officinalis.)*
2. Garden Nasturtion, *(Tropæolum majus.)*
3. Orange Lily, *(Lilium bulbiferum.)*
4. African Marigold, *(Tagetes patula et erecta.)*

Sometimes it was also observed on the Sunflowers, *(Helianthus annuus.)* But bright yellow, or flame-colour, seemed in general necessary for the production of this light; for it was never seen on the flowers of any other colour.

To discover whether some little insects, or phosphoric worms, might not be the cause of it, the flowers were carefully examined even with a microscope, without any such being found.

From the rapidity of the flash, and other circumstances, it might be conjectured, that there is something of electricity in this phenomenon. It is well known, that when the *pistil* of a flower is impregnated, the *pollen* bursts away by its elasticity, with which electricity may be combined. But M. Haggren, after having observed the flash from the Orange-lily, the *anthers* of which are a considerable space distant from the *petals*, found that the light proceeded from the *petals* only; whence he concludes, that this electric light is caused by the *pollen*, which in flying off is scattered upon the *petals*. Obser. Physique par M. Rozier, Vol. XXXIII. p. 111.

UPAS.—Canto III. l. 238.

Description of the Poison-Tree in the Island of Java. Translated from the Original Dutch of N. P. Foersch.

This destructive tree is called in the Malayan language *Bohun-Upas*, and has been described by naturalists; but their accounts have been so tinctured with the *marvellous*, that the whole narration has been supposed to be an ingenious fiction by the generality of readers. Nor is this in the least degree surprising when the circumstances which we shall faithfully relate in this description are considered.

I must acknowledge, that I long doubted the existence of this tree, until a stricter inquiry convinced me of my error. I shall now only relate simple unadorned facts, of which I have been an eye-witness. My readers may depend upon the fidelity of this account. In the year 1774, I was stationed at Batavia, as a surgeon, in the service of the Duch East-India Company. During my residence there I received several different accounts of the Bohun-Upas, and the violent effects of its poison. They all then seemed incredible to me, but raised my curiosity in so high a degree, that I resolved to investigate this subject thoroughly, and to trust only to *my own observations*. In consequence of this resolution, I applied to the Governor-general, Mr. Petrus Albertus van der Parra, for a pass to travel through the country: my request was granted; and, having procured every information, I set out on my expedition. I had procured a recommendation from an old Malayan priest, to another priest, who lives on the nearest inhabitable spot to the tree which is about fifteen or sixteen miles distant. The letter proved of great service to me in my undertaking, as that priest is appointed by the Emperor to reside there, in order to prepare for eternity the souls of those who for different crimes are sentenced to approach the tree, and to procure the poison.

The *Bohun-Upas* is situated in the island of *Java*, about twenty-seven leagues from *Batavia*, fourteen from *Soura-Charta*, the seat of the Emperor, and between eighteen and twenty leagues from *Tinkjoe*, the present residence of the Sultan of Java. It is surrounded on all sides by a circle of high hills and mountains; and the country round it, to the distance of ten or twelve miles from the tree, is entirely barren. Not a tree nor a shrub, nor even the least plant or grass is to be seen. I have made the tour all around this dangerous spot, at about eighteen miles distant from the centre, and I found the aspect of the country on all sides equally dreary. The easiest ascent of the hills is from that part where the old ecclesiastic dwells. From his house the criminals are sent for the poison, into which the points of all warlike instruments are dipped. It is of high value, and produces a considerable revenue to the Emperor.

Account of the manner in which the Poison is procured.

The poison which is procured from this tree is a gum that issues out between the bark and the tree itself, like the *camphor*. Malefactors, who for their crimes are sentenced to die, are the only persons who fetch the poison; and this is the only chance they have of saving their lives. After sentence is pronounced upon them by the judge, they are asked in court, whether they will die by the hands of the executioner, or whether they will go to the Upas tree for a box of poison? They commonly prefer the latter proposal, as there is not only some chance of preserving their lives, but also a certainty, in case of their safe return, that a provision will be made for them in future by the Emperor. They are also permitted to ask a favour from the Emperor, which is generally of a trifling nature, and commonly granted. They are then provided with a silver or tortoise-shell box, in which they are to put the poisonous gum, and are properly instructed how to proceed while they are upon their dangerous expedition. Among other particulars, they are always told to attend to the direction of the winds; as they are to go towards the tree before the wind, so that the effluvia from the tree is always blown from them. They are told likewise, to travel with the utmost despatch, as that is the only method of insuring a safe return. They are afterwards sent to the house of the old priest, to which place they are commonly attended by their friends and relations. Here they generally remain some days, in expectation of a favourable breeze. During that time the ecclesiastic prepares them for their future fate by prayers and admonitions.

When the hour of their departure arrives, the priest puts on them a long leather cap, with two glasses before their eyes, which comes down as far as their breast; and also provides them with a pair of leather-gloves. They are then conducted by the priest, and their friends and relations, about two miles on their journey. Here the priest repeats his instructions, and tells them where they are to look for the tree. He shows them a hill, which they are told to ascend, and that on the other side they will find a rivulet, which they are to follow, and which will conduct them directly to the Upas. They now take leave of each other; and, amidst prayers for their success, the delinquents hasten away.

The worthy old ecclesiastic has assured me, that during his residence there, for upwards of thirty years, he had dismissed above seven hundred criminals in the manner which I have described; and that scarcely two out of twenty have returned. He showed me a catalogue of all the unhappy sufferers, with the date of their departure from his house annexed; and a list of the offences for which they had been condemned: to which was added, a list of those who had returned in safety. I afterwards saw another list of these culprits, at the jail-keeper's at *Soura-Charta*, and found that they perfectly corresponded with each other, and with the different informations which I afterwards obtained.

I was present at some of these melancholy ceremonies, and desired different delinquents to bring with them some pieces of the wood, or a small branch, or some leaves of this wonderful tree. I have also given them silk cords, desiring them to measure its thickness. I never could procure more than two dry leaves that were picked up by one of them on his return; and all I could learn from him, concerning the tree itself, was, that it stood on the border of a rivulet, as described by the old Priest; that it was of a middling size; that five or six young trees of the same kind stood close by it; but that no other shrub or plant could be seen near it; and that the ground was of a brownish sand, full of stones, almost impracticable for travelling, and covered with dead bodies. After many conversations with the old Malayan priest, I questioned him about the first discovery, and asked his opinion of this dangerous tree; upon which he gave me the following answer:

"We are told in our new alcoran, that above a hundred years ago, the country around the tree was inhabited by a people strongly addicted to the sins of Sodom and Gomorrah; when the great prophet Mahomet determined not to suffer them to lead such detestable lives any longer, he applied to God to punish them: upon which God caused this tree to grow out of the earth, which destroyed them all, and rendered the country for ever uninhabitable."

Such was the Malayan opinion. I shall not attempt a comment; but must observe, that all the Malayans consider this tree as an holy instrument of the great prophet to punish the sins of mankind; and, therefore, to die of the poison of the Upas is generally considered among them as an honourable death. For that reason I also observed, that the delinquents, who were going to the tree, were generally dressed in their best apparel.

This however is certain, though it may appear incredible, that from fifteen to eighteen miles round this tree, not only no human creature can exist, but that, in that space of ground, no living animal of any kind has ever been discovered. I have also been assured by several persons of veracity, that there are no fish in the waters, nor has any rat, mouse, or any other vermin, been seen there; and when any birds fly so near this tree that the effluvia reaches them, they fall a sacrifice to the effects of the poison. This circumstance has been ascertained by different delinquents, who, in their return, have seen the birds drop down, and have picked them up *dead*, and brought them to the old ecclesiastic.

I will here mention an instance, which proves the fact beyond all doubt, and which happened during my stay at Java.

In 1775 a rebellion broke out among the subjects of the Massay, a sovereign prince, whose dignity is nearly equal to that of the Emperor. They refused to pay a duty imposed upon them by their sovereign, whom they openly opposed. The Massay sent a body of a thousand troops to disperse the rebels, and to drive them, with their families, out of his dominions. Thus four hundred families, consisting of above sixteen hundred souls, were obliged to leave their native country. Neither the Emperor nor the Sultan would give them protection, not only because they were rebels, but also through fear of displeasing their neighbour, the Massay. In this distressful situation, they had no other resource than to repair to the uncultivated parts round the Upas, and requested permission of the Emperor to settle there. Their request was granted, on condition of their fixing their abode not more than twelve or fourteen miles from the tree, in order not to deprive the inhabitants already settled there at a greater distance of their cultivated lands. With this they were obliged to comply; but the consequence was, that in less than two months their number was reduced to about three hundred. The chiefs of those who remained returned to the Masseey, informed him of their losses, and intreated his pardon, which induced him to receive them again as subjects, thinking them sufficiently punished for their misconduct. I have seen and conversed with several of those who survived, soon after their return. They all had the appearance of persons tainted with an infectious disorder; they looked pale and weak, and from the account which they gave of the loss of their comrades, and of the symptoms and circumstances which attended their dissolution, such as convulsions, and other signs of a violent death, I was fully convinced that they fell victims to the poison.

This violent effect of the poison at so great a distance from the tree, certainly appears surprising, and almost incredible: and especially, when we consider that it is possible for delinquents who approach the tree to return alive. My wonder, however, in a great measure, ceased, after I had made the following observations:

I have said before, that malefactors are instructed to go to the tree with the wind, and to return against the wind. When the wind continues to blow from the same quarter while the delinquent travels thirty, or six and thirty miles, if he be of a good constitution, he certainly survives. But what proves the most destructive is, that there is no dependence on the wind in that part of the world for any length of time.— There are no regular land-winds; and the sea wind is not perceived there at all, the situation of the tree being at too great a distance, and surrounded by high mountains and uncultivated forests. Besides, the wind there never blows a fresh regular gale, but is commonly merely a current of light, soft breezes, which pass through the different openings of the adjoining mountains. It is also frequently difficult to determine from what part of the globe the wind really comes, as it is divided by various obstructions in its passage, which easily change the direction of the wind, and often totally destroy its effects.

I therefore impute the distant effects of the poison, in a great measure, to the constant gentle winds in these parts, which have not power enough to disperse the poisonous particles. If high winds were more frequent and durable there, they would certainly weaken very much, and even destroy the obnoxious effluvia of the poison; but without them the air remains infected and pregnant with these poisonous vapours.

I am the more convinced of this, as the worthy ecclesiastic assured me, that a dead calm is always attended with the greatest danger, as there is a continual perspiration issuing from the tree, which is seen to rise and spread in the air, like the putrid steam of a marshy cavern.

Experiments made with the Gum of the Upas-Tree.

In the year 1776, in the month of February, I was present at the execution of thirteen of the Emperor's concubines, at *Soura-Charta*, who were convicted of infidelity to the Emperor's bed. It was in the forenoon, about eleven o'clock, when the fair criminals were led into an open space within the walls of the emperor's palace. There the judge passed sentence upon them, by which they were doomed to suffer death by a lancet poisoned with Upas. After this the Alcoran was presented to them, and they were, according to the law of their great prophet Mahomet, to acknowledge and to affirm by oath, that the charges brought against them, together with the sentence and their punishment, were fair and equitable. This they did, by laying their right hands upon the Alcoran, their left hands upon their breast, and their eyes lifted towards heaven; the judge then held the Alcoran to their lips, and they kissed it.

These ceremonies over, the executioner proceeded on his business in the following manner: —Thirteen posts, each about five feet high, had been previously erected. To these the delinquents were fastened, and their breasts stripped naked. In this situation they remained a short time in continual prayers, attended by several priests, until a signal was given by the judge to the executioner; on which the latter produced an instrument, much like the spring lancet used by farriers for bleeding horses. With this instrument, it being poisoned with the gum of the Upas, the unhappy wretches were lanced in the middle of their breasts, and the operation was performed upon them all in less than two minutes.

My astonishment was raised to the highest degree, when I beheld the sudden effects of that poison, for in about five minutes after they were lanced they were taken with a *tremor* attended with a *subsultus tendinum*, after which they died in the greatest agonies, crying out to God and Mahomet for mercy. In sixteen minutes by my watch, which I held in my hand, all the criminals were no more. Some hours after their death, I observed their bodies full of livid spots, much like those of the *Petechiæ*, their faces swolled, their colour changed to a kind of blue, their eyes looked yellow, &c. &c.

About a fortnight after this, I had an opportunity of seeing such another execution at Samarang. Seven Malayans were executed there with the same instrument, and in the same manner; and I found the operation in the poison, and the spots in their bodies, exactly the same.

These circumstances made me desirous to try an experiment with some animals, in order to be convinced of the real effects of this poison; and as I had then two young puppies, I thought them the fittest objects for my purpose. I accordingly procured with great difficulty some grains of Upas. I dissolved half a grain of that gum in a small quantity of arrack, and dipped a lancet into it. With this poisoned instrument I made an incision in the lower muscular part of the belly in one of the puppies. Three minutes after it received the wound the animal began to cry out most piteously, and ran as fast as possible from one corner of the room to the other. So it continued during six minutes, when all its strength being exhausted, it fell upon the ground, was taken with convulsions, and died in the eleventh minute. I repeated this experiment with two other puppies, with a cat and a fowl, and found the operation of the poison in all of them the same: none of these animals survived above thirteen minutes.

I thought it necessary to try also the effect of the poison given inwardly, which I did in the following manner. I dissolved a quarter of a grain of the gum in half an ounce of arrack, and made a dog of seven months old drink it. In seven minutes, a retching ensued, and I observed, at the same time, that the animal was delirious, as it ran up and down the room, fell on the ground, and tumbled about; then it rose again, cried out very loud, and in about half an hour after was seized with convulsions, and died. I opened the body, and found the stomach very much inflamed, as the intestines were in some parts, but not so much as the stomach. There was a small quantity of coagulated blood in the stomach; but I could discover no orifice from which it could have issued; and therefore supposed it to have been squeezed out of the lungs, by the animal's straining while it was vomiting.

From these experiments I have been convinced that the gum of the Upas is the most dangerous and most violent of all vegetable poisons; and I am apt to believe that it greatly contributes to the unhealthiness of that island. Nor is this the only evil attending it: hundreds of the natives of Java, as well as Europeans, are yearly destroyed and treacherously murdered by that poison, either internally or externally. Every man of quality or fashion has his dagger or other arms poisoned with it; and in times of war the Malayans poison the springs and other waters with it; by this treacherous practice the Dutch suffered greatly during the last war, as it occasioned the loss of half their army. For this reason, they have ever since kept fish in the springs of which they drink the water, and sentinels are placed near them, who inspect the waters every hour, to see whether the fish are alive. If they march with an army or body of troops into an enemy's country, they always carry live fish with them, which they throw into the water some hours before they venture to drink it; by which means they have been able to prevent their total destruction.

This account, I flatter myself, will satisfy the curiosity of my readers, and the few facts which I have related will be considered as a certain proof of the existence of this pernicious tree, and its penetrating effects.

If it be asked why we have not yet any more satisfactory accounts of this tree, I can only answer, that the object of most travellers to that part of the world consists more in commercial pursuits than in the study of Natural History and the advancement of the Sciences. Besides, Java is so universally reputed an unhealthy island, that rich travellers seldom make any long stay in it; and others want money, and generally are too ignorant of the language to travel, in order to make inquiries. In future, those who visit this island will now probably be induced to make it an object of their researches, and will furnish us with a fuller description of this tree.

I will therefore only add, that there exists also a sort of Cajoe-Upas on the coast of Macasser, the poison of which operates nearly in the same manner, but is not half so violent or malignant as that of Java, and of which I shall likewise give a more circumstantial account in a description of that island.—*London Magazine.*

Another account of the Boa Upas, or Poison-Tree of Macasser, from an inaugural Dissertation published by Christ. Aejmelæus, and approved by Professor Thunberg, at Upsal.

DOCTOR AEJMELÆUS first speaks of poisons in general, enumerating many virulent ones from the mineral and animal, as well as from the vegetable kingdoms of Nature. Of the first he mentions arsenical, mercurial, and antimonial preparations; amongst the second he mentions the poisons of several serpents, fishes, and insects; and amongst the last the Curara on the bank of the Oroonoko, and the Woorara on the banks of the Amazons, and many others. But he thinks the strongest is that of a tree hitherto undescribed, known by the name of Boa Upas, which grows in many of the warmer parts of India, principally in the islands of Java, Sumatra, Borneo, Bali, Macasser, and Celebes.

Rumphius testifies concerning this Indian poison, that it was more terrible to the Dutch than any warlike instrument; it is by him styled Arbor toxicaria, and mentions two species of it, which he terms male and female; and describes the tree as having a thick trunk, with spreading branches, covered with a rough dark bark. The wood, he adds, is very solid, of a pale yellow, and variegated with black spots, but the fructification is yet unknown.

Professor Thunberg supposes the Boa Upas to be a Cestrum, or a tree of the same natural family; and describes a Cestrum of the Cape of Good Hope, the juice of which the Hottentots mix with the venom of a certain serpent, which is said to increase the deleterious quality of them both.

The Boa Upas tree is easily recognised at a distance, being always solitary, the soil around it being barren, and as it were burnt up; the dried juice is dark brown, liquifying by heat, like other resins. It is collected with the greatest caution, the person having his head, hands, and feet carefully covered with linen, that his whole body may be protected from the vapour as well as from the droppings of the tree. No one can approach so near as to gather the juice, hence they supply bamboos, pointed like a spear, which they thrust obliquely, with great force, into the trunk; the juice oozing out gradually fills the upper joint; and the nearer the root the wound is made, the more virulent the poison is supposed to be. Sometimes upwards of twenty reeds are left fixed in the tree for three or four days, that the juice may collect and harden in the cavities; the upper joint of the reed is then cut off from the remaining part, the concreted juice is formed into globules or sticks, and is kept in hollow reeds, carefully closed, and wrapped in tenfold linen. It is every week taken out to prevent its becoming mouldy, which spoils it. The deleterious quality appears to be volatile, since it loses much of its power in the time of one year, and in a few years becomes totally effete.

The vapour of the tree produces numbness and spasms of the limbs, and if any one stands under it bare-headed, he loses his hair; and if a drop falls on him, violent inflammation ensues. Birds which sit on its branches a short time, drop down dead, and can even with difficulty fly over it; and not only no vegetables grow under it, but the ground is barren a stone cast around it.

A person wounded by a dart poisoned with this juice feels immediately a sense of heat over his whole body, with great vertigo, to which death soon succeeds. A person wounded with the Java poison was affected with tremor of the limbs, and starting of the tendons of five minutes, and died in less than sixteen minutes, with marks of great anxiety; the corpse, in a few hours, was covered with petechial spots, the face became tumid and lead-coloured, and the white part of the eye became yellow.

The natives try the strength of their poison by a singular test; some of the expressed juice of the root of Amomum Zerumbet is mixed with a little water, and a bit of the poisonous gum or resin is dropped into it; an effervescence instantly takes place, by the violence of which they judge of the strength of the poison.—What air can be extricated during this effervescence?—This experiment is said to be dangerous to the operator.

As the juice is capable of being dissolved in arrack, and is thence supposed to be principally of a resinous nature, the Professor does not credit that fountains have been poisoned with it.

This poison has been employed as a punishment for capital crimes in Macasser and other islands; in those cases some experiments have been made, and when a finger only had been wounded with a dart, the immediate amputation of it did not save the criminal from death.

The poison from what has been termed the female tree, is less deleterious than the other, and has been used chiefly in hunting; the carcases of animals thus destroyed are eaten with impunity. The poison-juice is said to be used externally as a remedy against other poisons, in the form of a plaster; also to be used internally for the same purpose; and is believed to alleviate the pain and extract the poison of venomous insects sooner than any other application.

The author concludes that these accounts have been exaggerated by Mahomedan priests, who have persuaded their followers that the Prophet Mahomet planted this obnoxious tree as a punishment for the sins of mankind.

An abstract of this Dissertation of C. Aejmelæus is given in Dr. Duncan's Medical Commentaries for the Year 1790, Decad. 2d. Vol. V

AN ADDITION

To be inserted near the end of the Additional Note XXXIII. p. 116, of the first Part, immediately before the last sentence.

THE following circumstance, which I observed this week, is sufficiently curious to be here inserted.

On the fifth of April 1799 the wind, which has blown for several days from the N. E. and a great part of that time was very violent, became due E. The barometer sunk nearly an inch, clouds were produced, and much snow fell during the whole day; and on the next day the wind became again N. E. and the barometer rose again. The same circumstances exactly recurred on the eighth of April; the wind again changed from N. E. to due E. The barometer sunk, and snow and afterwards rain were the consequence.

Which is thus to be explained. On April the fifth the atmosphere became lighter, I suppose, because no more air was supplied from the arctic circle, and the snow was produced from some of the southern air over this country falling down, I suppose, on the lowered current of northern air. But why did the N. E. wind on both these days change to due E.? To this it may be answered, that as no new air was now brought from the N. and in consequence the barometer sunk; and as air from the S. evidently became mixed with that from the N. whence the clouds and consequent snow; the further progress of the N. E. air towards the S. was stopped by the opposing air from the S. but its easterly direction was not stopped; and as this remained, it became due E. This idea was further countenanced, because the wind on both days became a few points on the southerly side of the E. for an hour or two before the snow ceased.

FAIRY-SCENE

FROM

MR. MUNDY'S "NEEDWOOD FOREST,"

REFERRED TO IN CANTO IV. l. 35.

HERE, seen of old, the *elfin* race
With sprightly vigils mark'd the place;
Their gay processions charm'd the sight,
Gilding the lucid noon of night;
Or, when obscure the midnight hour
With glow-worm lanterns hung the bower
—Hark!—the soft lute!—along the green
Moves with majestic step the Queen!
Attendant Fays around her throng,
And trace the dance or raise the song;
Or touch the shrill reed, as they trip,
With finger light and ruby lip.
   High, on her brow sublime, is borne
One scarlet woodbine's tremulous horn;
A gaudy Bee-bird's* triple plume
Sheds on her neck its waving gloom;
With silvery gossamer entwined
Stream the luxuriant locks behind.
Thin folds of tangled network break
In airy waves adown her neck;—
Warp'd in his loom, the spider spread
The far-diverging rays of thread,
Then round and round with shuttle fine
Inwrought the undulating line;—
Scarce hides the woof her bosom's snow,
One pearly nipple peeps below.

---

* The *humming-bird.*

One rose-leaf-forms her crimson vest,
The loose edge crosses o'er her breast;
And one translucent fold, that fell
From the tall lily's ample bell,
Forms with sweet grace her snow-white train,
Flows, as she steps, and sweeps the plain.
Silence and Night enchanted gaze,
And Hesper hides his vanquish'd rays!—
   Now the waked reed-finch swells his throat,
And night-larks trill their mingled note:
Yet hush'd in moss with writhed neck
The blackbird hides his golden beak;
Charm'd from his dream of love, he wakes,
Opes his gay eye, his plumage shakes,
And, stretching wide each ebon wing,
First in low whispers tries to sing;
Then sounds his clarion loud, and thrills
The moon-bright lawns, and shadowy hills.
Silent the choral Fays attend,
And then their silver voices blend,
Each shining thread of sound prolong,
And weave the magic woof of song.
Pleased Philomela takes her stand
On high, and leads the Fairy band,
Pours sweet at intervals her strain,
And guides with beating wing the train.
Whilst interrupted Zephyrs bear
Hoarse murmurs from the distant wear;
And at each pause is heard the swell
Of Echo's soft symphonious shell.

CATALOGUE

OF THE

POETIC EXHIBITION.

CANTO I.

	LINE		LINE
Group of insects	21	Dervise procession	221
Tender husband	39	Lady in full dress	229
Self-admirer	45	Lady on a precipice	249
Rival lovers	51	Palace in the sea	263
Coquette	61	Vegetable lamb	281
Platonic wife	65	Whale	289
Monster-husband	77	Sensibility	299
Rural happiness	85	Mountain-scene by night	345
Clandestine marriage	93	Lady drinking water	359
Sympathetic lovers	97	Lady and cauldron	373
Ninon d'Enclos	125	Medea and Æson	361
Harlots	139	Aerial lady	391
Giants	161	Forlorn nymph	401
Mr. Wright's paintings	175	Galatea on the sea	421
Thalestris	191	Lady frozen to a statue	435
Autumnal scene	197		

CANTO II.

	LINE		LINE
Air-balloon of Montgolfier	25	St. Anthony preaching to fish	245
Arts of weaving and spinning	67	Sorceress	267
Arkwright's cotton mills	85	Miss Crew's drawings	295
Invention of letters, figures, and crotchets	105	Song to May	309
Mrs. Delany's paper-garden	155	Frost scene	333
Mechanism of a watch, and design for its case	165	Discovery of the bark	347
		Moses striking the rock	405
Time, hours, moments	183	Dropsy	415
Transformation of Nebuchadnezzar	211	Mr. Howard and prisons	459

CANTO III.

	LINE		LINE
Witch and imps in a church	7	Lady shot in battle	269
Inspired Priestess	39	Harlots	329
Fuseli's night mare	51	Laocoon and his sons	335
Cave of Thor and subterranean Naiads	85	Drunkards and diseases	357
Medea and children	135	Prometheus and the vulture	371
Palmyra weeping	197	Lady burying her child in the plague	387
Group of wild creatures drinking	205	Moses concealed on the Nile	421
Poison-tree of Java	219	Slavery of the Africans	439
Time and hours	255	Weeping Muse	465
Wounded deer	263		

CANTO IV.

	LINE		LINE
Maid of night	13	Dejanira in a lion's skin	289
Fairies	33	Offspring from the marriage of the Rose and Nightingale	309
Electric lady	43	Parched deserts in Africa	325
Shadrec, Meshec, and Abednego, in the fiery furnace	55	Turkish lady in an undress	335
Shepherdesses	73	Ice-scene in Lapland	363
Song to Echo	79	Loch-lomond by moon-light	385
Kingdom of China	107	Hero and Leander	403
Lady and distaff	115	Gnome-husband and palace under ground	413
Cupid spinning	133	Lady inclosed in a fig	429
Lady walking in snow	137	Sylph-husband	439
Children at play	147	Marine cave	451
Venus and Loves	159	Proteus-lover	465
Matlock Bath	175	Lady on a Dolphin	471
Angel bathing	199	Lady bridling a Pard	475
Mermaid and Nereids	203	Lady saluted by a Swan	481
Lady in salt	221	Hymeneal procession	489
Lot's wife	245	Night	515
Lady in regimentals	283		

CONTENTS

OF THE

NOTES TO PART II.

CANTO I.

	LINE
SEEDS of Canna used for prayer-beads	39
Stems and leaves of Callitriche so matted together, as they float on the water, as to bear a person walking on them	45
The female in Collinsonia approaches first to one of the males, and then to the other. Females in nigella and epilobium bend towards the males for some days, and then leave them	51
The stigma or head of the female in spartium (common broom) is produced amongst the higher set of males; but when the keel-leaf opens, the pistil suddenly twists round like a French horn, and places the stigma amidst the lower set of males	57
The two lower males in ballota become mature before the two higher; and when their dust is shed, turn outwards from the female. The plants of the class two powers with naked seeds are all aromatic. Of these marum and nepeta are delightful to cats	60
The filaments in meadia, borago, cyclamen, solanum, &c. shown *by reasoning* to be the most unchangeable parts of those flowers,	61
Rudiments of two hinder wings are seen in the class diptera, or two-winged insects. Teats of male animals. Filaments without anthers in curcuma, linum, &c. and styles without stigmas in many plants, show the advance of the works of nature towards greater perfection	65
Double flowers, or vegetable monsters, how produced	69, 77
The calyx and lower series of petals not changed in double flowers	69
Dispersion of the dust in nettles and other plants	73, 75
Cedar and cyprus unperishable	73
Anthoxanthum gives the fragrant scent to hay	86
Viviparous plants: the aphis is viviparous in summer, and oviparous in autumn	ib.
Irritability of the stamen of the plants of the syngenesia, or confederate males	97
Some of the males in lychnis, and other flowers, arrive sooner at their maturity,	108, 119
Males approach the female in gloriosa, Fritillaria, and kalmia	119
Contrivances to destroy insects in silene, dionæa muscipula, arum muscivorum, dypsacus, &c.	139
Some bell-flowers close at night; others hang the mouths downwards; others nod and turn from the wind; stamens bound down to the pistil in amaryllis formosissima; pistil is crooked in hemerocallis flava, yellow day-lily	152
Thorns and prickles designed for the defence of the plant; tall hollies have no prickles above the reach of cattle	161
Bird-lime from the bark of hollies like elastic gum	ib.
Adansonia the largest tree known, its dimensions	183
Bulbous roots contain the embryon flower, seen by dissecting a tulip root	204
Flowers of colchicum and hamamelis appear in autumn, and ripen their seed in the spring following	219
Sunflower turns to the sun by nutation, not by gyration	221
Dispersion of seeds	224
Drosera catches flies	229
Of the nectary, its structure to preserve the honey from insects	241
Curious proboscis of the sphinx convolvuli,	ib.
Final cause of the resemblance of some flowers to insects, as the bee-orchis	ib.

CONTENTS.

	LINE
In some plants of the class Tetradynamia, or Four Powers, the two shorter stamens, when at maturity, rise as high as the others	250
Ice in the caves on Teneriff, which were formerly hollowed by volcanic fires	ib.
Some parasites do not injure trees, as Tillandsia and Epidendrum	258
Mosses growing on trees injure them	ib.
Marriages of plants necessary to be celebrated in the air	264
Insects with legs on their backs	ib.
Scarcity of grain in wet seasons	ib.
Tartarian lamb; use of down on vegetables; air, glass, wax, and fat, are bad conductors of heat; snow does not moisten the living animals buried in it, illustrated by burning camphor in snow	282
Of the collapse of the sensitive plant	299
Birds of passage	320
The acquired habits of plants	ib.
Irritability of plants increased by previous exposure to cold	ib.
Lichen produces the first vegetation on rocks	347
Plants holding water	365
Madder colours the bones of young animals	373
Colours of animals serve to conceal them	ib.
Warm bathing retards old age	385
Plant living on air without taking root	393
Male flowers of Vallisneria detach themselves from the plant, and float to the female ones	403
Air in the cells of plants, its various uses	415
Air-bladders of fish	ib.
How Mr. Day probably lost his life in his diving ship	ib.
Star-gelly is voided by Herons	435
Intoxicating mushrooms	ib.
Mushrooms grow without light, and approach to animal nature	ib.

CANTO II.

Seeds of Tillandsia fly on long threads, like spiders on the gossamer	7
Account of cotton mills	87
Invention of letters, figures, crotchets	105
Mrs. Delany's and Mrs. North's paper-gardens	155
The horologe of Flora	165
The white petals of Helleborus niger become first red, and then change into a green calyx	201
Berries of Menispermum intoxicate fish	229
Effects of opium	270
Frontispiece by Miss Crewe	295
Petals of Cistus and Oenothera continue but a few hours	305

	LINE
Method of collecting the gum from Cistus by leathern thongs	305
Discovery of the bark	349
Foxglove how used in dropsies	425
Bishop of Marseilles and Lord Mayor of London	432

CANTO III.

Superstitious uses of plants, the divining rod, animal magnetism	7
Intoxication of the Pythian Priestess, poison from Laurel leaves, and from Cherry kernels	40
Sleep consists in the abolition of voluntary power; nightmare explained	74
Indian fig emits slender cords from its summit	80
Cave of Thor in Derbyshire; and subterraneous rivers explained	90
The capsule of the Geranium makes an hygrometer; Barley creeps out of a barn	131
Mr. Edgeworth's creeping hygrometer	ib.
Flower of Fraxinella flashes on the approach of a candle	184
Essential oils narcotic, poisonous, deleterious to insects	ib.
Dew-drops from Mancinella blister the skin	188
Uses of poisonous juices in the vegetable economy	ib.
The fragrance of plants a part of their defence	ib.
The sting and poison of a nettle	191
Vapour from Lobelia suffocative; unwholesomeness of perfumed hair-powder	193
Ruins of Palmyra	197
The poison-tree of Java	238
Tulip-roots die annually	259
Hyacinth and Ranunculus roots	ib.
Vegetable contest for air and light	329
Some voluble stems turn E. S. W. and others W. S. E.	ib.
Tops of white bryony as grateful as asparagus	ib.
Fermentation converts sugar into spirit, food into poison	357
Fable of Prometheus applied to dram-drinkers	371
Cyclamen buries its seeds and trifolium subterraneum	381
Pits dug to receive the dead in the plague	406
Lakes of America consist of fresh water	413
The seeds of Cassia and some others are carried from America, and thrown on the coasts of Norway and Scotland	415
Of the Gulf-stream	ib.
Wonderful change predicted in the Gulf of Mexico	ib.

CANTO IV.

	LINE
In the flowers of Cactus grandiflorus and Cistus some of the stamens are perpetually bent to the pistil	15
Nyctanthes and others are only fragrant in the night; Cucurbita lagenaria closes when the sun shines on it	ib.
Tropeolum, nasturtion, emits sparks in the twilight: Nectary on its calyx	45
Phosphorescent lights in the evening	51
Hot embers eaten by bull frogs	ib.
Long filaments of grasses, the cause of bad seed wheat	73
Chinese hemp grew in England above fourteen feet in five months	115
Roots of snow-drop and hyacinth insipid like orchis	137
Orchis will ripen its seeds if the new bulb be cut off	ib.
Proliferous flowers	148
The wax on the candle-berry myrtle said to be made by insects	155
The warm springs of Matlock produced by the condensation of steam raised from great depths by subterranean fires	179
Air separated from water by the attraction of points to water being less than that of the particles of water to each other	195
Minute division of sub-aquatic leaves	204
Water-cress and other aquatic plants inhabit all climates	ib.
Butomus esculent; Lotus of Egypt; Nymphæ	ib.
Ocymum covered with salt every night	225
Salt a remote cause of scrofula, and immediate cause of sea-scurvy	ib.
Coloured spatha of Arum, and blotched leaves, if they serve the purpose of a coloured petal	285
Tulip roots with a red cuticle produce red flowers	ib.
Of vegetable mules the internal parts, as those of fructification, resemble the female parent; and the external parts the male one	303
The same occurs in animal mules, as the common mule and the hinnus, and in sheep	ib.
The wind called Harmattan from volcanic eruptions; some epidemic coughs or influenza have the same origin	328
Fish killed in the sea by dry summers in Asia	334
Hedysarum gyrans perpetually moves its leaves like the respiration of animals	335
Plants possess a voluntary power of motion	ib.
Loud cracks from ice-mountains explained	370
Muschus corallinus vegetates below the snow, where the heat is always about 40	375
Quick growth of vegetables in northern latitudes after the solution of the snows explained	ib.
The Rail sleeps in the snow	ib.
Conferva ægagropila rolls about the bottom of lakes	386
Lycoperdon tuber, truffle, requires no light	414
Account of caprification	430
Figs wounded with a straw, and pears and plumbs wounded by insects, ripen sooner, and become sweeter	ib.
Female figs closed on all sides, supposed to be monsters	ib.
Basaltic columns produced by volcanoes shown by their form	455
Byssus floats on the sea in the day, and sinks in the night	459
Conferva polymorpha twice changes its colour and its form	468
Some seed-vessels and seeds resemble insects	ib.
Individuality of flowers not destroyed by the number of males or females which they contain	490
Trees are swarms of buds, which are individuals	ib.

INDEX

OF THE

NAMES OF THE PLANTS.

	Page		Page
Adonis	188	Drósera	143
Aegagrópila	186	Dy'psacus	147
A'lcea	139		
Amary'llis	141	Epidendrum	148
Anemone	146		
Anthoxánthum	139	Ficus	165
Arum	184	Fúcus	182
Avéna	179	Fraxinélla	167
Bárometz	145	Galánthus	180
Béllis	181	Genísta	138
Byssus	188	Gloriósa	140
		Gossy'pium	155
Cáctus	178		
Caléndula	157	Hedy'sarum	186
Callítriche	137	Heliánthus	143
Cánna	ib.	Helléborus	157
Cánnabis	180	Hippómane	167
Cápri-ficus	187		
Carlína	154	Ilex	141
Caryophy'llus	184	Impátiens	166
Cássia	172	Iris	139
Céreus	178		
Crondrílla	140	Kleinhóvia	142
Chunda	185		
Cinchóna	159	Lápsana	157
Circæa	164	Láuro-cérasus	165
Cístus	159	Líchen	146
Cócculus	158	Línum	155
Cólchicum	143	Lobélia	168
Collinsónia	137	Lonicéra	143
Confèrva	186, 188	Lychnis	140
Cupréssus	139	Lycopérdon	187
Curcúma	138		
Cuscúta	170	Mancinélla	167
Cy'clamen	171	Méadia	138
Cypérus	155	Melíssa	ib.
		Menispérmum	158
Diánthus	184	Mimósa	145
Dictámnus	167	Múschus	186
Digitális	160		
Dodecáthèon	138	Nymphæa	157
Drába	144	Nelumbo	186

INDEX.

	Page		Page
Ocymum	183	Trápa	182
Orchis	169	Tremélla	149
Osmúnda	140	Tropæ'olum	179
Osy'ris	139	Truffélia	187
		Túlipa	142
Papáver	153		
Papy'rus	155	Ulva	148
Plantágo	139	Upas	168
Polymórpha	188	Urtica	ib.
Polypódium	145		
Prúnus	165	Vallisnéria	148
		Víscum	144
Rúbia	147	Vítis	171
Siléne	141	Zostéra	144

THE END.

GLASGOW:
ANDREW & JOHN M. DUNCAN,
Printers to the University.

DIRECTIONS TO THE BINDER.

The Binder will please observe that the Plates to Darwin's Botanic Garden are to be put at the end of the Volume.

SECTION OF THE STRATA TO THE LOW MAIN COAL AT ST. ANTHON'S COLLIERY.

RESTORATION PIT 135¼ FATHOMS

Stratum	Fath.	Feet	Inch.
Soil and Clay	5		
Brown Post	12		
Coal			6
Blue Metal Stone	2	5	
White Girdles	2	1	
Coal			8
White and Grey Post	6		
Soft Blue Metal Stone	5		
Coal			6
White Post Girdles	3		
Whin	1	4	6
Strong White Post	3	1	
Coal			1
Soft Blue Thill	1	5	
Soft Girdles mixed with Whin	5	5	
Coal			6
Blue and Black Stone	3	4	
Coal			8
Strong White Post	1	3	
Grey Metal Stone	1	4	
Coal			8
Grey Post mixed with Whin	4	1	
Grey Girdles	3	1	
Blue and Black Stone	2	2	

SCALE OF FATHOMS

RESTORATION PIT 135¼ FATHOMS

Stratum	Fath.	Feet	Inch.
Brought up	66	0	0
Strong White Post	6		
Black Metal Stone with hard Girdles	3		
HIGH MAIN COAL	1 / 76		
Grey Metal	4	3	
Post Girdles		2	
Blue Metal	4	1	2
Girdles			
Blue Metal Stone	5		
Post		1	
Blue Metal Stone	3		
Whin and Blue Metal	1	6	
Strong White Post	3	3	
Brown Post with Water			7
Blue Metal Stone with Grey Girdles	2	2	
COAL		3	
Blue Metal Stone	3		3
White Post	4		
Coal			6
Strong Grey Metal with Post Girdles	2		6
Strong White Post	1	1	
Whin		1	
Blue Metal Stone	1	2	7
Grey Metal Stone with Post Girdles	2	4	5
Blue Metal Stone with Whin Girdles	1	4	3
Coal		4	6
Blue Grey Metal	3		8
White Post	2		7
White Post mixed with Whin	2		
White Post	1	2	
Dark Blue Metal and Coal		2	2
Grey Metal Stone and Girdles	2	2	
White Post mixed with Whin	3		7
Whin		1	
White Post mixed with Whin	1		6
Coal		3	3
Dark Grey Metal Stone	3	3	6
Grey Metal and Whin Girdles	1	4	10
Grey Metal and Girdles	1		
White Post		3	
		4	2
Total	135		6

5379A

Lightning Source UK Ltd
Milton Keynes UK
UKOW03f1908020616

275502UK00011B/307/P